VOLUME ONE

The American Nation

A History of the United States to 1877

SEVENTH EDITION

JOHN A. GARRATY
Gouverneur Morris Professor of History
Columbia University

with

ROBERT A. McCAUGHEY
Professor and Dean of the Faculty
Barnard College, Columbia University

HarperCollins*Publishers*

For Kathy, Jack, and Sarah

Sponsoring Editors: Lauren Silverman/Bruce Borland
Development Editor: Kathleen Dolan
Project Editor: Karen Trost
Design Supervisor: Dorothy Bungert
Text and Cover Design: Delgado Design, Inc.
Cover Illustration: *Fort Snelling* (1844), by John Casper Wild. Minnesota Historical Society.
Photo Research: Cheryl Mannes and Suzanne Volkman Skloot
Production: Willie Lane
Compositor: Arcata Graphics/Kingsport
Printer and Binder: Arcata Graphics/Hawkins
Cover Printer: New England Book Components

The American Nation: A History of the United States to 1877, Volume One, Seventh Edition

Library of Congress Cataloging-in-Publication Data

Garraty, John Arthur, 1920–
    The American nation : a history of the United States / John A.
  Garraty with Robert A. McCaughey.
      p.   cm.
    Includes bibliographical references and index.
    ISBN 0-06-042243-2   (v. 1) (student edition). ISBN 0-06-500036-6 (v. 1) (teacher edition).—ISBN
0-06-042244-0 (v. 2) (student edition). ISBN 0-06-500037-4 (v. 2) (teacher edition)
    1. United States—History.   I. McCaughey, Robert A.   II. Title.
  E178.1.G24   1991
  973—dc20   90–48476
                                                                                CIP

  91 92 93   9 8 7 6 5 4 3 2

Contents

VI Jeffersonian Democracy   166

VII America Escapes from Europe   196

VIII   The Cords of Union   216

IX   Toward a National Economy   232

X   Jacksonian Democracy   254

XI The Making of Middle-Class America 280

XII A Democratic Culture 312

XIII Expansion and Slavery 334

XIV   The Sections Go Their Ways   358

XV   The Coming of the Civil War   386

XVI   The War to Save the Union   414

Maps and Graphs

Maps

Graphs

Preface

This is the seventh edition of *The American Nation,* the sixth time I have revised it, and the process remains for me both challenging and endlessly fascinating. Historians try to explain what happened in the past and of course "what happened" does not change. But what is important to point out about the past is that it changes constantly as more information about past events comes to light and as current events raise new questions about the events and people of earlier times. Year by year hundreds of new books and articles are published about various aspects of American history; when those dealing with any particular subject have been digested and synthesized and combined with already existing knowledge, a new, "up-to-date" description of that topic results. This process keeps authors like me who write American history textbooks very busy.

Goals of This Revision

The work of revising a survey of all American history takes many forms. First there are the small alterations involved in incorporating new details and examples, and in clarifying obscurities that have previously escaped notice. Then there is the matter of bringing the narrative as close to the present as possible, something that is relatively easy to do, but difficult to do well. Nearly always revision also involves changes in emphasis—some subjects need to be condensed or eliminated; others require more space either because more has been discovered about them or because recent developments make them seem more significant. Finally, and most important, are the larger changes made necessary because historians, responding to contemporary interests, to noteworthy work being done by colleagues and other specialists, and to the questions and interests of their students, have produced persuasive new interpretations and even opened up entirely new subjects. Dealing with this work, in turn, requires more of the simpler kinds of revisions just mentioned.

This revision of *The American Nation* contains many examples of all these types of change; in sum, I believe it is the most thorough and broad-ranging restructuring and re-thinking of the six such revisions that I have made.

Organizational Changes

To improve the flow of topics, I have shifted many sections to different chapters, for example, moving the discussion of the Great Awakening and the colonial Enlightenment to the chapter on the events leading to the Revolution, where these inter-colonial, "national" topics seem more properly to belong. I have also consolidated the material on the Federalist era and on the Jefferson administrations into separate chapters, and I have divided the previously combined account of the political and economic events of the Monroe and John Quincy Adams period.

Similarly, several chapters covering the period 1877–1896 have been completely reorganized, and the chapter on World War I has been expanded to include an account of the Red Scare and other events of the immediate postwar period. The three chapters dealing with the 1920s and 1930s in the sixth edition have been drastically restructured; that period now is covered in four chapters. I have also made changes only slightly less extensive in the chapters on the post–World War II period.

New Coverage and Features

As to new topics and significantly expanded coverage of old ones, readers will notice that there is much more information about society in the colonial south and about southern political and religious institutions; on the activities of women during the American Revolution and other social changes of the period; on the Whiskey Rebellion and the opening of the Ohio country after the Revolution; on changes in early 19th-century family life; on the westward movement, the Second Great Awakening, the Know-Nothing movement; and on plantation life, particularly the lives of southern women, slave and free.

In Chapter XX, "American Society in the Industrial Age," there is much new information about middle-class life, about the daily activities of farmers, about the family lives and social attitudes of wage earners of both sexes, about social and economic mobility in the 1870s and 1880s, and about the development of spectator sports and other leisure activities. Chapter XXVI treats these and other aspects of social history before and after World War I in much greater detail than in earlier editions. There is also expanded and more up-to-date coverage of radicalism, the effects of the Great Depression on the unemployed, the treatment of minorities during World War II and the contributions of women in that conflict, the "Baby Boom" generation that followed the war, the counterculture of the 1960s, the modern women's movement, and many other subjects.

I have paid a good deal of attention also to the "Suggestions for Further Reading" that follow each chapter. I have eliminated many older titles that, although valuable, are out of print, and I have substituted more recent and in most instances equally worthwhile volumes that are readily available, often in paperback. This edition also contains a new feature, American Lives, designed to give students a better understanding of how ordinary people lived and thought in various times and places. It consists of accounts of the life-styles of "ordinary" people whom we know a great deal about only because they had children who became famous, and of the childhoods and youths of men and women who were later to become important figures. Most of the material comes from biographies, autobiographies, and other personal writings. There are seven of these features, some treating more than one person in a comparative manner.

Approach

In making all these changes and others less important, I have not, I trust, altered my basic approach to American history, which is to deal with the subject in narrative fashion and to use the political history of the nation as the frame or skeleton on which social, economic, and cultural developments depend. The American nation (the United States) is, after all, a political institution.

The people of the United States, in their infinite variety, also remain central to my account. The theory that a few great individuals, cut from larger cloth than the general run of human beings, have shaped the course of past events oversimplifies history. But the past becomes more comprehensible when attention is paid to how the major figures on the historical stage have reacted to events and to one another. Since generalizations require concrete illustration if they are to be grasped fully, readers will find many anecdotes and quotations on the following pages, along with the facts and dates and statistics every good history must contain. This illustrative material is interesting, and most of it is entertaining, but I believe it is instructive as well.

I also believe that one need not be an uncritical admirer of the American nation and its people to recognize that the history of the United States deserves to be treated with dignity and respect. Individually and as a society, we have rarely lived up perfectly to the principles enunciated in the Declaration of Independence and the Constitution, but recent events in Eastern Europe demonstrate how cherished these "American" values are by people who have been deprived of them. American values are not well served by patriotic hoopla or by slighting or excusing dark and discreditable aspects of the American past. The English radical Oliver Cromwell is said to have told an artist who was painting his picture to portray him "warts and all." Cromwell wanted to be remembered as he was, confident that, on balance, history would judge him fairly. This is another principle on which *The American Nation* continues to be based.

Acknowledgments

I wish to thank the many friends, colleagues, and students who, over the years, have given me the benefit of their advice and encouragement in keeping this book up to date. In particular I am grateful to the following reviewers for their comments and suggestions regarding the revision: Robert M. Barrow, Georgia Southern University; Sidney R. Bland, James Madison University; Paul C. Bowers, The Ohio State University; Dean R. Esslinger, Towson State University; George E. Frakes, Santa Barbara City College; David A. Johnson, Portland State University; George M. Lubick, Northern Arizona University; Thomas C. Mackey, Kansas State University; Michael S. Mayer, University of Montana; Howard N. Rabinowitz, University of New Mexico; G. S. Rowe, University of Northern Colorado; Herbert Shapiro, University of Cincinnati; Harry F. Snapp, University of North Texas; Ken L. Weath-

erbie, Del Mar College; and Herbert H. Wubben, Oregon State University.

John A. Garraty
Gouverneur Morris Professor of History
Columbia University

SUPPLEMENTS

An extensive package of supplements has been developed to accompany the seventh edition of *The American Nation*. To order supplements, contact your HarperCollins representative.

■ The *Instructor's Resource Manual*, written by Michael Mayer of the University of Montana, has been designed to aid both the novice and the experienced instructor in teaching the American History course. Each chapter of the *Instructor's Resource Manual* includes a concise chapter overview, a list of points for student mastery, lecture supplements, and questions for class discussion. A special feature of each chapter is a set of excerpted documents with accompanying questions for student analysis. The *Instructor's Resource Manual* also includes essays on teaching American History through films and maps, and a full-length class activity on teaching essay writing using the rhetoric of the Declaration of Independence.

■ The *Test Bank*, prepared by Larry Peterson of North Dakota State University, contains over 2000 test items, including multiple-choice, true/false, and essay questions, and map exercises. The questions are referenced by topic, cognitive type (factual, applied, or interpretive), difficulty level, and relevant text page.

   In addition to the printed format, the *Test Bank* is available on *TestMaster*, HarperCollins's computerized testing system. Available for IBM, Apple, and Macintosh computers, this powerful software allows the instructor to scramble and edit questions from the *Test Bank* and add original questions.

■ The two-volume *Student Study Guide*, co-authored by Kenneth Weatherbie of Del Mar College and Billy Hathorn of Laredo State University, is designed to provide students

with a comprehensive review of text material, and to encourage application and critical analysis of the material. Each chapter contains a chapter overview, learning objectives, important glossary terms, identification, map, and critical thinking exercises, and multiple-choice and essay questions. In addition, an essay on writing about history is provided.

■ *SuperShell*, HarperCollins's computerized tutorial, is an interactive program that provides sophisticated diagnostic feedback including an end-of-session reading assignment based on the student's performance, and tracking of the student's performance from session to session. In addition to review questions in a variety of formats, *SuperShell* contains comprehensive chapter outlines keyed to the headings and subheadings in the text. A "Flash Card" program helps students learn important terms and concepts. *SuperShell* is available for IBM computers only.

■ *Mapping American History*, created by Gerald Danzer of the University of Illinois at Chicago, features numerous varied map exercises and activities for students. In addition to increasing basic locational literacy, these exercises provide students with opportunities for map interpretation and analysis, as well as an appreciation of cartographic materials as historical documents. Each copy of *The American Nation* purchased from HarperCollins entitles the instructor to a free copy of this student map workbook.

■ *Discovering American History Through Maps and Views*, also prepared by Gerald Danzer, provides 140 four-color transparencies of images selected from key primary sources. Assembled in a three-ring binder, the collection begins with an essay on teaching history using maps, and contains detailed commentary on each transparency. The program consists of cartographic materials, various photos and views including urban plans, building diagrams, and works of art, and is free to adopters of the text.

■ *American Historical Geography: A Computerized Atlas*, prepared by William Hambin of Brigham Young University, offers map exercises pertaining to the rise of the Americas, the Revolutionary War, the Civil War, transportation systems, and elections. Free upon adoption of the textbook, the program is available for Macintosh computers only.

■ *Historical Viewpoints: Notable Articles from* American Heritage, *Sixth Edition*, edited by John Garraty, is a collection of interesting and substantive articles that have appeared in *American Heritage.* Available in a two-volume format, the sixth edition contains many new selections.

■ *Visual Archives of American History*, a new laser disk, provides over 500 photos and 29 minutes of film coverage of major events in American history. Each photo or film clip may be instantly accessed, making this collection ideal for classroom use.

■ *The Winner's Circle* is a collection of recent prize-winning films and videos relating to American History. Available for loan at no charge to adopters of the text.

■ *Grades,* HarperCollins's easy-to-use classroom management software, records quiz and exam scores for up to 200 students.

To help instructors make effective use of this comprehensive supplement package, HarperCollins offers *The Integrator,* a cross-reference and index to all print, software, and media supplements available with *The American Nation. The Integrator* also includes teaching techniques for multimedia presentations.

I

Europe Discovers America

In the beginning, all the world was America.

JOHN LOCKE

T he first human beings to set foot on the continents of North and South America were the ancestors of the modern Indians. These people entered the North American continent tens of thousands of years ago during the Ice Age, when a land bridge connected their home in northeastern Asia with Alaska. Hunters and herders, they were simply moving from camp to camp in search of game and green grass. No doubt the first humans in other parts of the world found their way in the same manner and at about the same time to what are now Egypt, Iran, India, China, Australia, and for that matter England, France, and the rest of Europe. Almost certainly the settlers of the Americas were unaware that they were entering "new" territory. So we must look elsewhere (and much later in time) for the "discoverer" of America as we use that word.

Probably the first European to reach America was a Norseman, Leif Eriksson. He ventured before the day of the compass into the void of the North Atlantic and, around the year 1000, reached the shores of Labrador. Yet Eriksson's discovery passed practically unnoticed for centuries, and to most modern inhabitants of the New World he lives only in legend.

Amerigo Vespucci, a clever Italian with an eye for publicity, visited the northern coast of South America in 1499. He wrote an account of his experiences that was widely circulated. In 1507, after reading a distorted copy of Vespucci's tale, a German geographer, Martin Waldseemüller, concluded that the author was the discoverer of the New World and suggested that it be named America in his honor. Today millions call themselves Americans, but few know much about Amerigo Vespucci.

Another Italian mariner, Cristoforo Colombo, brave, persistent, an inspired sailor but a fumbling administrator, spent a decade cruising in the Caribbean Sea under the mistaken impression that he was next door to China. He killed some of the people he encountered, established a few rickety settlements, ventured no nearer to North America than Cuba, and died poor, embittered, and frustrated, hotly denying that he had found anything more than a new route to the Orient. Today, whether he be known as Colombo, Colón, or Columbus, he is honored in the Old World and the New as the discoverer of the Western Hemisphere.

Why Columbus rather than Eriksson, the real European pioneer, or Vespucci, whose name has become immortal? The answer is that Eriksson came on the scene too soon and Vespucci too late. Europe in the year 1000 was not yet ready to find a new world, and by 1499 it had already found one. Amerigo Vespucci gave his name to the region, but the adventures of Christopher Columbus inspired the European invasion and development of the whole area between Hudson Bay and the Strait of Magellan.

Columbus and the Discovery of America

About two o'clock on the morning of October 12, 1492, a sailor named Roderigo de Triana, clinging in a gale to the mast of the ship *Pinta*, saw a gleam of white on the moonlit horizon and shouted: *"Tierra! Tierra!"* The land he had spied was an island in the West Indies called Guanahaní by its inhab-

In this engraving by Theodore de Bry, Columbus is about to depart from Palos; Ferdinand and Isabella, at right, bid him farewell.

itants, a place distinguished by neither beauty nor size. Nevertheless, when Triana's master, Christopher Columbus, went ashore bearing the flag of Spanish Castile, he named it San Salvador, or Holy Savior. Columbus selected this imposing name for the island out of gratitude and wonder at having found it—he had sailed with three frail vessels more than 3,000 miles for 33 days without sight of land. The name was appropriate, too, from history's far larger viewpoint. Neither Columbus nor any of his men suspected it, but the discovery of San Salvador was probably the most important event in the history of western civilization since the birth of Christ.

San Salvador was the gateway to two continents. Columbus did not know it, and he refused to learn the truth, but his voyage threw open to exploitation by the peoples of western Europe more than a quarter of all the land in the world, a region of more than 16 million square miles, an area lushly endowed with every imaginable resource. He made possible a mass movement from Europe (and later from Africa and to a lesser extent from other regions) into the New World. Gathering force rapidly, this movement did not slacken until the 20th century, and it still has not ceased; something on the order of 70 million persons have been involved in the migration.

Columbus was an intelligent as well as dedicated and skillful mariner. He failed to grasp the significance of his accomplishment because he had no idea that he was on the edge of two huge continents previously unknown to Europeans. He was seeking a way to China and Japan and the Indies, the amazing countries described by the Venetian Marco Polo in the late 13th century.

Having read carefully Marco Polo's account of his adventures in the service of Kublai Khan, Columbus had decided that these rich lands could be reached by sailing directly west from Europe. The idea was not original, but while others merely talked about it (in the jawbreaking phrase of one scholar, experts had been slow to consider "the cosmographical implications of the earth's sphericity"), Columbus pursued it with brilliant persistence.

If one could sail to Asia directly, the trading possibilities and the resulting profits would be limitless. Oriental products were highly valued all over Europe. Spices such as pepper, cinnamon, ginger, nutmeg, and cloves were of first importance, their role being not so much to titillate the palate as to disguise the taste of spoiled meats in regions that had little ice. Europeans also prized such tropical foods as rice, figs, and oranges, as well as perfumes (often used as a substitute for soap), silk and cotton, rugs, textiles such as muslin and damask, dyestuffs, fine steel products, precious stones, and various drugs.

These products flowed into western Europe by way of the Italian city-states. By the 11th century, Venice had established a thriving trade with Constantinople, shipping large quantities of European foodstuffs to the metropolis on the Bosporus. The Venetians also supplied young Slavs, captured or purchased along the nearby Dalmatian coast, to the markets of Egypt and Syria (the word *slave* originally meant "Slav").

The Venetians brought back oriental products from these voyages, and the effect was like that of tossing a stone into a pond. Europeans bestirred themselves, searching for more goods to offer in exchange. They possessed surpluses of grain and food, but these bulky products were expensive to transport over long distances. However, in Flanders, in the Low Countries, woolen cloth of high quality was being manufactured. Other areas were producing furs and lumber. Demand led to increased output; thus the flow of commerce stimulated manufacturing, which in turn spurred the growth of towns. As towns became larger and more numerous, the market for food expanded, and surrounding rural areas increased their agricultural output.

Urban growth also created a demand for more clothmakers. The resulting labor shortage in both town and country produced important changes in the structure of medieval society. The manorial system, based on serfdom, soon began to change. As their labor became more valuable, serfs won the right to pay off their traditional obligations in money rather than in service and to leave the manors and move to the towns or to newly opened farmland. The lords themselves often instituted this change, for they wished to increase agricultural output by draining swamps and clearing forests, and they willingly granted freedom to serfs who would move to the new lands. They also needed money rather than the services of serfs to buy the expensive oriental luxuries being dangled before their eyes by traders.

The Crusades further accelerated the tempo of this new activity. Genuine religious motives seem to have inspired these mighty efforts, protracted over two centuries from 1095 to about 1290, to drive the Muslims from the Holy Land. Once the cru-

sading armies had won a foothold in Asia Minor, the commerce of Venice and of other Italian cities increased still more, and their merchant fleets expanded. The business of transporting and supplying the European armies was itself profitable and when Crusaders returned home, they brought with them more oriental products and a taste for these things that persisted after the goods themselves had been consumed.

The volume of this trade kept the fleets of the thriving Italian cities busy, but it was not impressive by modern standards. In the 1920s the Belgian historian Henri Pirenne estimated that the entire tonnage of the 13th-century Venetian fleet would scarcely fill a single freighter, the cargo of which, in turn, would scarcely serve as ballast for a modern supertanker. Nor did the increase in trade cause universal prosperity or even a steady economic expansion in western Europe. In fact, the period of the 14th and early 15th centuries seems to have been marked by depression and economic decline in the West.

This decline resulted principally from the terrible losses occasioned by the plague known as the Black Death, which ravaged Europe in the mid-14th century. Part of the difficulty, however, stemmed from the steady drain of precious metals to the Orient (because of the unfavorable balance of East-West trade) and the high cost of oriental goods. It was easy to blame this on the greed of the Italians, who monopolized East-West trade. Certainly the Venetians have never possessed a reputation for altruism nor the Pisans for being poor businessmen. However, even if the Italians had labored only for the joy of serving their fellow human beings or if other merchants had been able to break the Italian monopoly, the cost of Eastern products would have remained high. To transport spices from the Indies, silk from China, or rugs, cloth, and steel from the Middle East was extremely costly. The combined sea-land routes were long and complicated—across strange seas, through deserts, over high mountain passes—with pirates or highwaymen a constant threat. Every petty tyrant through whose domain the caravans passed levied taxes, a quasi-legal form of robbery. Few merchants operated on a continental scale; typically, goods passed from hand to hand and were loaded and unloaded many times between Eastern producer and Western consumer, with each middleman exacting as large a profit as

Europeans of the 15th century hungered for goods from abroad. In the north, their wants were often supplied by ships of the Hanseatic League, an association of over 70 cities along the Baltic and North seas. These vessels exchanged northern products—wool, furs, fish, and metallic ores—for luxuries imported into southern Europe from Asia. In this miniature painting, Hanseatic merchants prepare shipments for their branch offices.

he could. In the end the western European consumer had to pay for all this.

But during the 15th century, Europe recovered from the human and economic losses of the plague years. By the 1450s strong rulers were consolidating countless small fiefs into what were to become the nations of today. They established uniform laws, maintained internal order, and, in effect, focused the resources and energies of their subjects in ways that led to the exploration of the world and the founding of European settlements in distant lands.

Merchants profited from this concentration of political and economic power, but overland trade with the East remained expensive and arduous. If

oriental produce could be carried to Europe by water, the trip would be both cheaper and more comfortable. The goods would have to be loaded and unloaded only once. A small number of sailors could provide all the necessary labor, and the free wind would supply the power to move the cargo to its destination. By the 15th century, this idea was beginning to be transformed into action.

The great figure in the transformation was Prince Henry the Navigator, third son of John I, king of Portugal. After distinguishing himself in 1415 in the capture of Ceuta, on the African side of the Strait of Gibraltar, the prince became interested in navigation and exploration. Sailing a vessel out of sight of land was still, in Henry's day, more an art than a science and was extremely hazardous. Ships were small and clumsy. Primitive compasses and instruments for reckoning latitude existed, but under shipboard conditions they were inaccurate. Navigators could determine longitude only by keeping track of direction and estimating speed; even the most skilled could place little faith in their estimates.

Henry attempted to improve and codify navigational knowledge. To his court at Sagres, hard by Cape St. Vincent, the extreme southwestern point of Europe, he brought geographers, astronomers, and mapmakers, along with Arab and Jewish mathematicians. He built an observatory and supervised the preparation of tables measuring the declination of the sun and other navigational data. Searching for a new route to the Orient, Henry's captains sailed westward to the Madeiras and the Canaries and south along the coast of Africa, seeking a way around that continent. In 1445 Dinis Dias reached Cape Verde, site of present-day Dakar.

Henry was interested in trade, but he cared more for the advancement of knowledge, for the glory of Portugal, and for spreading Christianity. When his explorers developed a profitable business in slaves, he tried to stop it. Nevertheless, the movement he began had, like the Crusades, important commercial overtones. Probably half of the Portuguese voyages were undertaken by private merchants. Without the gold, ivory, and other African goods, which brought great prosperity to Portugal, the explorers would probably not have been so bold or persistent. Yet, like Henry, they were idealists, by and large. The Age of Discovery was in a sense the last Crusade; its leaders displayed mixed religious and material motives along with a love of adventure. In any case,

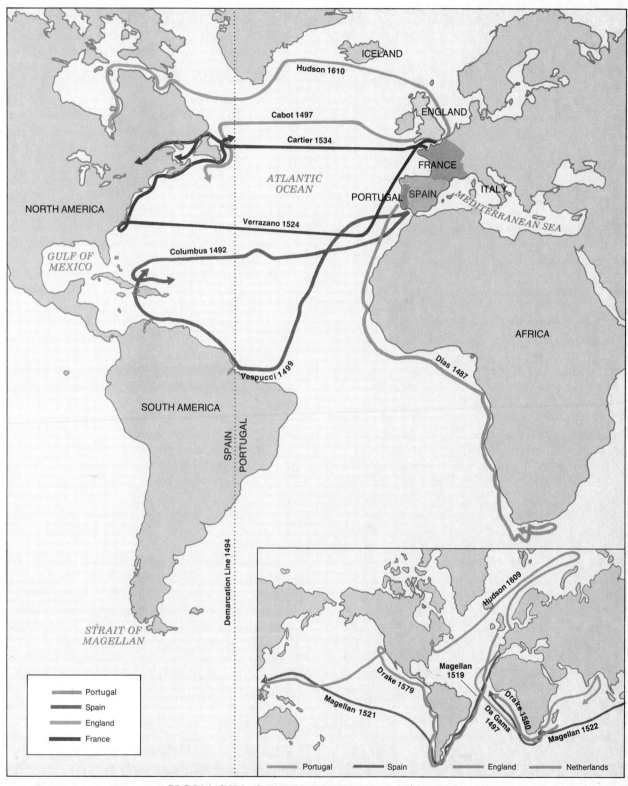

ICELAND

Hudson 1610

Cabot 1497

ENGLAND

Cartier 1534

FRANCE

ATLANTIC OCEAN

PORTUGAL SPAIN

ITALY

MEDITERRANEAN SEA

NORTH AMERICA

Verrazano 1524

GULF OF MEXICO

Columbus 1492

AFRICA

Dias 1487

Vespucci 1499

SOUTH AMERICA

SPAIN

PORTUGAL

STRAIT OF MAGELLAN

Demarcation Line 1494

Portugal
Spain
England
France

Hudson 1609

Drake 1579

Magellan 1519

Magellan 1521

Drake 1580

Da Gama 1497

Magellan 1522

Portugal   Spain   England   Netherlands

VOYAGES OF DISCOVERY, 1487–1610

the Portuguese realized that if they could find a way around Africa, they might well sail directly to India and the Spice Islands.* The profits from such a voyage would surely be spectacular.

For 20 years after Henry's death in 1460, the Portuguese concentrated on exploiting his discoveries. In the 1480s King John II undertook systematic new explorations focused on reaching India. Gradually his caravels probed southward along the sweltering coast—to the equator, to the region of Angola, and beyond.

Into this bustling, expectant little country in the corner of Europe came Christopher Columbus in 1476. Columbus was a weaver's son from Genoa, born in 1451. He had taken to the sea early, ranging widely in the Mediterranean. His arrival in Portugal was unplanned, since it resulted from the loss of his ship in a battle off the coast. For a time he became a chartmaker in Lisbon. He married a local woman. Then he was again at sea. He cruised northward, perhaps as far as Iceland, south to the equator, westward in the Atlantic to the Azores. Had his interest lain in that direction, he might well have been the first person to reach Asia by way of Africa, for in 1488, in Lisbon, he met and talked with Bartholomeu Dias, just returned from his voyage around the southern tip of Africa, which had demonstrated that the way lay clear for a voyage to the Indies. But by this time Columbus had committed himself to the westward route. When King John II refused to finance him, he turned to the Spanish court, where, after many disappointments, he finally persuaded Queen Isabella to equip his expedition. In August 1492 he set out from the port of Palos with his tiny fleet, the *Santa Maria,* the *Pinta,* and the *Niña.* A little more than two months later, after a stopover in the Canary Islands to repair the *Pinta*'s rudder, his lookout sighted land.

Columbus's success was due in large part to his single-minded conviction that the Indies could be reached by sailing westward for a relatively short distance and that a profitable trade would develop over this route. He had persuaded Isabella to grant him, in addition to the title Admiral of the Ocean Sea, political control over all the lands he might discover and 10 percent of the profits of the trade that would follow in the wake of his expedition. Now

the combination of zeal and tenacity that had got him across the Atlantic cost him dearly. He refused to accept the plain evidence that this was an entirely new world. All about were strange plants, known neither to Europe nor to Asia. The copper-colored people who paddled out to inspect his fleet could no more follow the Arabic widely understood in the East than they could Spanish. Yet Columbus, consulting his charts, convinced himself that he had reached the Indies. That is why he called the natives Indians.

Searching for treasure, he pushed on to Cuba. When he heard the native word *Cubanocan,* meaning "middle of Cuba," he mistook it for *El Gran Can* (Marco Polo's "Grand Khan") and sent emissaries on a fruitless search through the jungle for the khan's palace. He finally returned to Spain relatively empty-handed but certain that he had explored the edge of Asia. Three later voyages failed to shake his conviction.

Columbus died in 1506. By that time other captains had taken up the work, most of them more willing than he to accept the New World on its own terms. As early as 1493, Pope Alexander VI had divided the non-Christian world between Spain and Portugal. The next year, in the Treaty of Tordesillas, these powers negotiated an agreement about exploiting the new discoveries. In effect, Portugal continued to concentrate on Africa, leaving the New World, except for what eventually became Brazil, to the Spanish. Thereafter, from their base on Hispaniola (Santo Domingo), founded by Columbus, the Spaniards quickly fanned out through the Caribbean and then over large parts of the two continents that bordered it.

In 1513 Juan Ponce de León made the first Spanish landing on the mainland of North America, exploring the east coast of Florida. In the same year Vasco Núñez de Balboa crossed the isthmus of Panama and discovered the Pacific Ocean. In 1519 Hernán Cortés landed an army in Mexico and overran the empire of the Aztecs, rich in gold and silver. That same year Ferdinand Magellan set out on an epic three-year voyage around the world. By discovering the strait that bears his name, at the southern tip of South America, he gave the Spanish a clear idea of the size of the continent. In the 1530s Francisco Pizarro subdued the Inca empire in Peru, providing the Spaniards with still more treasure, drawn chiefly from the silver mines of Potosí. In 1536 Buenos Aires was founded by Pedro de Men-

---

* In the geography of the 15th century, the Spice Islands were part of "the Indies," a vague region that encompassed the southeastern rim of Asia from India to what is now Indonesia.

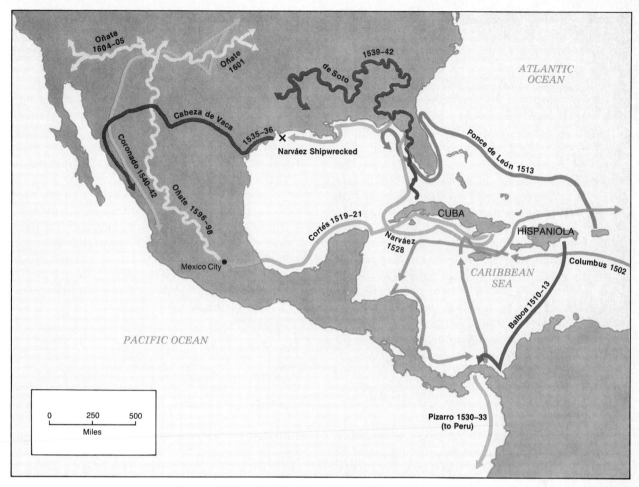

SPANISH EXPLORATIONS, 1502–1605

doza. Within another decade Francisco Vásquez de Coronado had marched as far north as Kansas and west to the Grand Canyon, and Hernando de Soto had discovered the Mississippi River. Fifty years after Columbus's first landfall, Spain was master of a huge American empire.

What explains this mighty surge of exploration and conquest? Greed for gold and power, a sense of adventure, the desire to Christianize the Indians—mixed motives propelled the conquistadores onward. Some saw the New World as a reincarnation of the Garden of Eden, a land of infinite promise. Ponce de León and many others actually expected to find the Fountain of Youth in America. Their vision, at once so selfish and so exalted, reveals the central paradox of New World history. This immense land brought out both the best and the worst in human beings. Virgin America—like all virgins—

inspired conflicting feelings in men's hearts. They worshiped it for its purity and promise, yet they could not resist the opportunity to take advantage of its innocence.

The Indian and the European

The conquistadores were brave and imaginative men, well worthy of their fame. It must not, however, be forgotten that they wrenched their empire from innocent hands; in an important sense, the settlement of the New World, which the historian Francis Jennings has called "the invasion of America," ranks among the most flagrant examples of unprovoked aggression in human history. When Columbus landed on San Salvador, he planted a cross, "as a sign," he explained to Ferdinand and

Isabella, "that your Highnesses held this land as your own." Of the Lucayans, the native inhabitants of San Salvador, Columbus wrote:

> The people of this island . . . are artless and generous with what they have, to such a degree as no one would believe. . . . If it be asked for, they never say no, but rather invite the person to accept it, and show as much lovingness as though they would give their hearts.

The Indians of San Salvador behaved this way because the Spaniards seemed the very gods. "All believe that power and goodness dwell in the sky," Columbus reported, "and they are firmly convinced that I have come from the sky." The products of Europe fascinated them. For a bit of sheet copper an inch square, they would part with a bushel of corn, while knives, hatchets, and even fishhooks made of metal were beyond price to a people whose own technology was still in the Stone Age.

But the Spaniards would not settle for the better of the bargain. Columbus also remarked of the Lucayans: "These people are very unskilled in arms . . . with fifty men they could all be subjected and made to do all that one wished." He and his compatriots tricked and cheated the Indians at every turn. Before entering a new area, Spanish generals customarily read a *Requerimiento* (requirement) to the inhabitants. This long-winded document recited a Spanish version of the history of the human race from the Creation to the division of the non-Christian world by Pope Alexander VI and then called upon the Indians to recognize the sovereignty of the reigning Spanish monarch. ("If you do so . . . we shall receive you in all love and charity.") If this demand was rejected, the Spanish promised: "We shall powerfully enter into your country, and . . . shall take you, your wives, and your children, and shall make slaves of them. . . . The death and losses which shall accrue from this are your fault." This arrogant harangue was read in Spanish and often out of earshot of the Indians. When they responded by fighting, the Spaniards decimated them, drove them from their lands, and held the broken survivors in contempt. As Bartolomé de las Casas, a priest among them, said, the conquistadores behaved "like the most cruel Tygres, Wolves, and Lions, enrag'd with a sharp and tedious hunger."

Wherever they went, the Europeans mistreated the people they encountered. When the Portuguese reached Africa, they carried off thousands into slavery. The Dutch behaved shamefully in the East Indies, as did the French in their colonial posessions—although in North America, at least, the French record was better than most.

English settlers described the Indians as being "of a tractable, free, and loving nature, without guile or treachery," yet in most instances they exploited and all but exterminated them. "Why should you take by force from us that which you can obtain by love?" one puzzled chief asked an early Virginia colonist, according to the latter's own account. The first settlers of New England dealt fairly with the local inhabitants. They made honest, if somewhat misguided, efforts to Christianize and educate them and to respect their rights. But within a few years their relations with the Indians deteriorated, and in King Philip's War (1675–1676), proportionately the bloodiest in American history, they destroyed the tribes as independent powers.

Native American Civilizations

Of course, the victims of the Europeans' cruelty were not innocent "noble savages." Being human, Indians suffered from all the human failings in one form or another. During thousands of years they had occupied the hemisphere from Alaska to Tierra del Fuego. By 1500 there were somewhere between 50 and 60 million of them, 1 or 2 million living in what is now the United States. (Exactly how many is impossible to discover. As the anthropologist Bruce Trigger has written, "It is notoriously difficult to determine the size of aboriginal American populations.")

In the course of many centuries the Indians' cultures had evolved in different ways. Climate, soil conditions, wars, and other factors, including pure chance, shaped their ways of life profoundly, just as these forces shaped the civilizations that had developed over the ages in Asia, Africa, and Europe. More than 1,000 languages were spoken in North and South America at the time of Columbus, some as different from one another as English is from Russian or Chinese.

Even in the relatively limited area that the first Spanish explorers visited, the native cultures displayed an extraordinary variety. If the Lucayans who greeted Columbus were a naive people, their institutions relatively primitive, the civilizations of

tecpatepec

xochinilco

Hacopā

coyouacā

A page from a codex (illustrated manuscript) shows Cortés's troops with their native allies advancing on Tenochtitlán, now Mexico City. The four major attacking divisions surround Montezuma's capital as dismembered Aztecs are trampled underfoot.

the Incas of Peru and the Aztecs of Mexico were in many respects as highly developed as any in Europe or Asia. The Incas built roads as enduring as those of the Romans. Montezuma, the Aztec emperor, lived in a great palace surrounded by courtiers and servants in a city as large as Madrid, the home of Cortés's master, Charles V, and far more impressive architecturally.

In the immense land north of Mexico no such imposing civilizations existed, but there, too, the number of different patterns of life was enormous. About 200 languages were spoken. Some groups were nomads who traveled in small bands and lived by hunting and fishing. Others lived settled lives based on a combination of hunting and agriculture. It is therefore difficult to generalize, and the problem of describing the lives and attitudes of these original Americans is made more difficult still by the absence of written records before the arrival of the Europeans and the fact that most of the accounts written by European explorers and settlers are biased and incomplete.

Certain traits the Indians had in common, and many of these the Europeans shared. Cruelty and

war, slavery and plunder existed in the New World long before Columbus. When the good Father Las Casas wrote that Indians were "without evil and without guile," he was as far off the mark as the Spaniard who claimed that they indulged in "every kind of intemperance and wicked lust." Indian men were by current standards chauvinists, as indeed were most Europeans of that day. Hunting and fishing—which, again like many Europeans, the Indians regarded as sports as well as sources of food—were usually male occupations, as was warfare. In agricultural communities, men and women shared other tasks; in general, the men did the heavy work of clearing land and building shelters; the women did the planting, cultivating, and harvesting. When Indians observed European men planting seeds and weeding their fields, they scoffed at them for being effeminate.

Most of the terrible decimation that was everywhere the Indians' fate was caused by European diseases such as smallpox and measles. The population of Mexico was at least 20 million when Cortés invaded the country and only 2 million a century later. European germs killed far more of the in-

The watercolor paintings of John White, one of the earliest English settlers, provide a glimpse of the Indians through European eyes. Here White depicts "their sitting at meat"—"deer's flesh, or of some other beast, and fish."

habitants than European gunpowder and steel. The Arawak population of Hispaniola fell from perhaps 8 million when Columbus first touched there to a few hundred 50 years later.

The Europeans could not be blamed for these deaths. They did not understand the diseases any better than the Indians did. The fact remains that in conflicts between Indians and whites, far more often than not, the whites were the main cause of the trouble.

Most Europeans had what the historian David B. Quinn described as "almost complete confidence in the rectitude of whatever they did." They simply assumed that non-Europeans were inferior beings. This was their fundamental misconception. Apparently their prejudices were not always of racial origin; some early colonists seemed to have considered Indians members of the white race whose skin had been darkened by exposure to the elements. The term *red man* did not become current until the 18th century.

The relativity of cultural values escaped all but a handful of the Europeans. If some of the natives were naive in thinking that the invaders, with their huge ships and their potent fire sticks, were gods, these "gods" were equally naive in their thinking. Since the Indians did not worship the Christian God and indeed worshiped a large number of other gods, the Europeans dismissed them as contemptible heathens. Some insisted that the Indians were servants of Satan. "Probably the devil decoyed these miserable savages hither," one English colonist explained.

In fact, most Indians were deeply religious people. But their religious values were so different from those of the Europeans that many of the latter believed that even if the Indians were not minions of Satan, they were unworthy of becoming Christians. Others, such as the Spanish friars, did try to convert the Indians, and with considerable success; but as late as 1569, when Spain introduced the Inquisition into its colonies, the natives were exempted from its control on the ground that they were incapable of rational judgment and thus not responsible for their "heretical" religious beliefs.

Most Indians lived in close harmony with their surroundings. They adjusted to and took advantage of existing ecologies (for example, by trapping fur-bearing animals in winter and netting fish during spring spawning runs), whereas the Europeans sought to change ecologies to their advantage (as by plowing fields and building fences). Indians who depended on hunting and fishing lived nomadic lives and therefore had small use for personal property that was not easily portable. They had little interest in amassing wealth, as individuals or as tribes. Even the Aztecs, with their treasures of gold and silver, valued the metals for their durability and the beautiful things that could be made with them rather than as objects of commerce.

This lack of concern for material things led Europeans to conclude that the native people of America were childlike creatures, not to be treated as equals. Indians "do but run over the grass, as do also foxes and wild beasts," an Englishman wrote in 1622, "so it is lawful now to take a land, which none useth, and make use of it." The first part of this statement contained a grain of truth, though of course the second did not follow from it logically.

Other troubles grew out of similar misunderstandings. English colonists assumed that Indian chiefs ruled with the same authority as their own kings. When Indians, whose loyalties were shaped by complex kinship relations more than by identification with any one leader, sometimes failed to honor commitments made by their chiefs, the English accused them of treachery.

The Europeans' inability to grasp the communal nature of land tenure among Indians also led to innumerable quarrels. Traditional tribal boundaries were neither spelled out in deeds or treaties nor marked by fences or any other sign of occupation. Often corn grown by a number of families was stored in a common bin and drawn upon by all as needed. Such practices were alien to the European mind. Indians put more emphasis on who was using land than on who first obtained or "owned" it. Among some agricultural tribes, if a farmer failed to cultivate a plot of land, another could take over no matter how long the first had previously used it.

The Indians, writes William Cronon in his fascinating book *Changes in the Land: Indians, Colonists, and the Ecology of New England*, "moved from habitat to habitat to find maximum abundance through minimal work, and so reduce their impact on the land." English colonists, Cronon goes on to say, "believed in and required permanent settlements." And he concludes: "English fixity sought to replace Indian mobility; here was the central conflict in the ways Indians and colonists interacted with their environments."

The Spanish Decline

While Spain waxed fat on the wealth of the Americas, the other nations of western Europe did little. In 1497 and 1498 King Henry VII of England sent

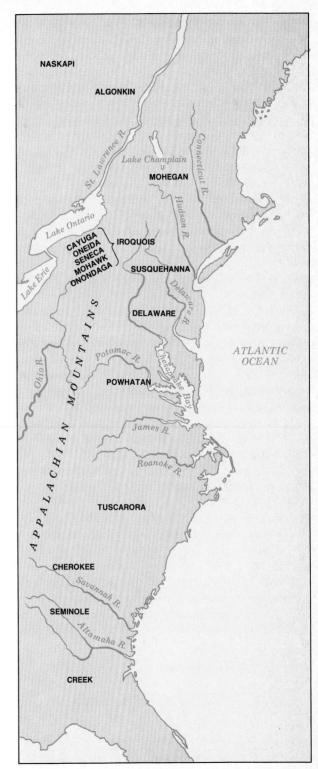

PRIMARY EAST COAST INDIAN TRIBES IN THE 1600s

John Cabot to the New World. Cabot visited New-foundland and the northeastern coast of the continent. His explorations formed the basis for later British claims in North America, but they were not followed up for many decades. In 1524 Giovanni da Verrazano made a similar voyage for France, coasting the continent from Carolina to Nova Scotia. Some ten years later the Frenchman Jacques Cartier explored the St. Lawrence River as far inland as present-day Montreal. During the 16th century, fishermen from France, Spain, Portugal, and England began harvesting the limitless supplies of cod and other fish in the cold waters off Newfoundland. They landed at many points along the mainland coast from Nova Scotia to Labrador to collect water and wood and to dry their catches, but they made no permanent settlements until the next century.

There were many reasons for this delay, the most important probably the fact that Spain had achieved a large measure of internal tranquillity by the 16th century, while France and England were still torn by serious religious and political conflicts. The Spanish also profited from having seized areas in America best suited to producing quick returns. Reinforced by the treasure of the Aztecs and the Incas, Spain seemed too mighty to be challenged in either the New World or the Old.

Under King Philip II Spanish strength seemed at its peak, especially after Philip added Portugal to his domain in 1580. But beneath the pomp and splendor (so well captured by such painters as Velázquez and El Greco), the great empire was in trouble. The corruption of the Spanish court had much to do with this. So did the ever-increasing dependence of Spain on the gold and silver of its colonies, which tended to undermine the local Spanish economy. Even more important was the disruption of the Catholic church throughout Europe by the Protestant Reformation.

The Protestant Reformation

The spiritual lethargy and bureaucratic corruption besetting the Roman Catholic church in the early 16th century made it a fit target for reform. A thriving business in the sale of indulgences, payments that were supposed to win for departed loved ones forgiveness for their earthly sins, was a public scandal. The luxurious life-style of the popes and the papal court in Rome was another. Probably more important were the political possibilities let loose by the challenge of Martin Luther, John Calvin, and other reformers to Rome's spiritual authority. German princes seized upon Luther's campaign against the sale of indulgences to stop all payments to Rome and to confiscate church property within their domains. Swiss cities like Geneva, where Calvin took up residence in 1536, joined the Protestant revolt for spiritual reasons but also to establish their political independence from Catholic kings. Francis I of France remained a Catholic, but he took advantage of Rome's troubles to secure control over the clergy of his kingdom.

The decision of Henry VIII of England to break with Rome was at bottom a political one. The refusal of Pope Clement VII to agree to an annulment of Henry's marriage of 20 years to Catherine of Aragon, the daughter of Ferdinand and Isabella, provided the occasion. Catherine had given birth to six children, but all were girls, and only Mary survived childhood; Henry was without a male heir. By repudiating the pope's spiritual authority and (with the support of Parliament) declaring himself head of the English church in 1533, Henry freed himself to divorce Catherine and to marry whomever—and however often—he saw fit. By the time of his death, five wives and 13 years later, England had become a Protestant nation and the dominant character of the future English colonies in America had also been determined.

The growing political and religious conflict had economic overtones. In some lands the business classes tended to support Protestant leaders, in part because the new sects, stressing simplicity, made fewer financial demands on the faithful than the Catholics did. And as the commercial classes rose to positions of influence, England, France, and the United Provinces of the Netherlands experienced a flowering of trade and industry. The Dutch built the largest merchant fleet in the world. Dutch traders captured most of the Far Eastern business once monopolized by the Portuguese, and they infiltrated Spain's Caribbean stronghold. A number of English merchant companies, soon to play a vital role as colonizers, sprang up in the second half of the 16th century. These joint-stock companies, ancestors of the modern corporation, enabled groups of investors to pool their capital and limit their individual responsibilities to the sums actually invested—a very important protection in such risky enterprises. The Muscovy Company, the Levant Company, and the East India Company were the most important of these ventures.

English Beginnings in America

English merchants took part in many kinds of international activity. The Muscovy Company spent large sums searching for a passage to China around Scandinavia and dispatched six overland expeditions in an effort to reach the Orient by way of Russia and Persia. In the 1570s Martin Frobisher made three voyages across the Atlantic, hoping to discover a northwest passage to the Orient or new gold-bearing lands.

Such projects, particularly in North America, received concealed support from Queen Elizabeth I, who invested heavily in Frobisher's expeditions. England was still too weak to challenge Spain openly, but Elizabeth hoped to break the Spanish overseas monopoly just the same. She encouraged her boldest sea dogs to plunder Spanish merchant ships on the high seas. When Captain Francis Drake was about to set sail on his fabulous round-the-world voyage in 1577, the queen said to him: "Drake . . . I would gladly be revenged on the King of Spain for divers injuries that I have received." Drake, who hated the Spaniards because of a treacherous attack they had once made on the fleet of his kinsman and former chief, Sir John Hawkins, took her at her word. He sailed through the Strait of Magellan and terrorized the west coast of South America, capturing the Spanish treasure ship *Cacafuego*, heavily laden with Peruvian silver. After exploring the coast of California, which he claimed for England, Drake crossed the Pacific and went on to circumnavigate the globe, returning home in triumph in 1580. Although Elizabeth took pains to deny it to the Spanish ambassador, Drake's voyage was officially sponsored. Elizabeth being the principal shareholder in the venture, most of the ill-gotten Spanish bullion went into the Royal Treasury rather than Drake's pocket. He had to settle for a knighthood.

When schemes to place settlers in the New World began to mature at about this time, the queen again became involved. The first English effort was led by Sir Humphrey Gilbert, an Oxford-educated sol-

Sir Francis Drake, one of the boldest sea captains to serve Queen Elizabeth I, sailed around the world from 1577 to 1580 and gratified his sovereign by plundering the Spanish-held west coast of South America.

dier and courtier with a lifelong interest in far-off places. Gilbert owned a share of the Muscovy Company; as early as 1566 he was trying to get a royal grant for an expedition in search of a northeast passage to the Orient. But soon his interests concentrated on the northwest route. He read widely in navigational and geographic lore and in 1576 wrote the persuasive *Discourse . . . to Prove a Passage by the North West to Cathaia.*

Little is known about Gilbert's first attempt except that it occurred in 1578 and 1579; in 1583 he set sail again with five ships and more than 200 settlers. He landed them on Newfoundland, then evidently decided to seek a more congenial site farther south. However, no colony was established, and on his way back to England, his ship went down in a storm off the Azores.

Gilbert's half brother, Sir Walter Raleigh, took up the work. Handsome, ambitious, and impulsive, Raleigh was a great favorite of Elizabeth. He sent a number of expeditions to explore the east coast of North America, a land he named Virginia in honor of his unmarried sovereign. In 1585 he settled about 100 men on Roanoke Island, off the North Carolina coast, but these settlers returned home the next year. In 1587 Raleigh sent another group to Roanoke, including a number of women and children. Unfortunately, the supply ships sent to the colony in 1588 failed to arrive; when help did get there in 1590, not a soul could be found. The fate of this "lost colony" has never been determined.

One reason for the delay in getting aid to the Roanoke colonists was the attack of the Spanish Armada on England in 1588. Angered by English raids on his shipping and by the assistance Elizabeth was giving to the rebels in the Spanish Netherlands, King Philip II had decided to invade England. His great fleet of some 130 ships bore huge crosses on the sails as if on another crusade. The Armada carried 30,000 men and 2,400 guns, the largest naval force ever assembled up to that time. However, the English fleet badly mauled this Armada, and a series of storms completed its destruction. Thereafter, although the war continued and Spanish sea power remained formidable, Spain could no longer block English penetration of the New World.

Experience had shown that the cost of planting settlements in a wilderness 3,000 miles from England was more than any individual purse could bear. (Raleigh lost about £40,000 in his overseas ventures; early in the game he began to advocate government support of colonization.) As early as 1584 Richard Hakluyt, England's foremost authority on the Americas and a talented propagandist for colonization, made a convincing case for royal aid. In his *Discourse on Western Planting*, Hakluyt stressed the military advantages of building "two or three strong fortes" along the Atlantic coast of North America. Ships operating from such bases would make life uncomfortable for "King Phillipe" by intercepting his treasure fleets—a matter, Hakluyt added coolly, "that toucheth him indeede to the quicke." Colonies in America would also enrich the mother country by expanding the market for English woolens, bringing in valuable tax revenues, and by providing employment for the swarms of "lustie youthes that be turned to no profitable use" at home. From the great American forests would come the timber and naval stores needed to build

a bigger navy and merchant marine.

Queen Elizabeth read Hakluyt's essay, but she was too cautious and too devious to act boldly on his suggestions. Only after her death in 1603 did full-scale efforts to found English colonies in America begin, and even then the organizing force came from merchant capitalists, not from the Crown. This was unfortunate, because the search for quick profits dominated the thinking of these enterprisers. Larger national ends (while not neglected, because the Crown was always involved) were subordinated. Yet if private investors had not taken the lead, no colony would have been established at this time.

The Settlement of Virginia

In September 1605 two groups of English merchants petitioned the new king, James I, for a license to colonize Virginia, as the whole area claimed by England was then named. This was granted the following April, and two joint-stock companies were organized, one controlled by London merchants, the other by a group from the area around Plymouth and Bristol.* Both were under the control of the Royal Council for Virginia.

This first charter revealed the commercial motivation of both king and company in the plainest terms. Although it spoke of spreading Christianity and bringing "the Infidels and Savages, living in those Parts, to human Civility," it stressed the right "to dig, mine, and search for all Manner of Mines of Gold, Silver, and Copper."

The London Company dispatched about 100 settlers aboard the *Susan Constant*, the *Discovery*, and the *Godspeed*. This little band reached the Chesapeake Bay area in May 1607 and founded Jamestown. From the start everything seemed to go wrong. The immigrants established themselves in what was practically a malarial swamp simply because it appeared easily defensible against Indian attack. They failed to get a crop in the ground because of the lateness of the season and were soon almost without food. The settlers lacked the skills

---

* The London Company was to colonize south Virginia, while the Plymouth Company, the Plymouth-Bristol group of merchants, was granted northern Virginia.

A 16th-century engraving by John White shows English ships off the coast of Virginia. Wrecked vessels lie along the barrier islands near Hatteras ("Hatorasck"). On Roanoke Island and the mainland beyond it are palisaded Indian villages and warriors armed with bows and arrows.

that pioneers need. More than a third were "gentlemen" unused to manual labor, and the gentlemen's servants, almost equally unequipped for the task of colony building. The rest were hired laborers obliged to work for the company for seven years. During the first winter more than half the settlers died.

All the land belonged to the company, and aside from the gentlemen and their retainers, most of the settlers were only hired laborers who had contracted to work for it for seven years. This was unfortunate. The situation demanded people skilled in agriculture, and such a labor force was available. In England times were bad. The growth of the textile industry had led to an increased demand for wool, and great landowners were dismissing laborers and tenant farmers and shifting from labor-intensive agriculture to sheep raising. Inflation, caused by a shortage of goods to supply the needs of a growing population and by the influx of large amounts of American silver into Europe, worsened the plight of the dispossessed. Many landless farmers were eager to migrate if offered a decent opportunity to obtain land and make new lives for themselves.

The merchant directors of the London Company, knowing little or nothing about Virginia, failed to provide the colony with effective guidance. They set up a council of settlers, but they kept all

real power in their own hands. Instead of stressing farming and public improvements, they directed the energies of the colonists into such futile labors as searching for gold (the first supply ship devoted precious space to two goldsmiths and two "refiners"), glassblowing, silk raising, winemaking, and exploring the local rivers in hopes of finding a water route to the Pacific and the riches of China.

One colonist, Captain John Smith, tried to stop some of this foolishness. Smith had come to Virginia after a fantastic career as a soldier of fortune in eastern Europe, where he had fought many battles, been enslaved by a Turkish pasha, and triumphed in a variety of adventures, military and amorous. He quickly realized that building houses and raising food were essential to survival, and he soon became an expert forager and Indian trader. Smith was as eager as any 17th-century European to take advantage of the Indians, and he had few compunctions about the methods employed in doing so. But he recognized both the limits of the colonists' power and the vast differences between Indian customs and values and his own. It was necessary, he insisted, to dominate the "proud Savages" yet to avoid bloodshed.

Smith pleaded with company officials in London to send over more people accustomed to working with their hands, such as farmers, fishermen, carpenters, masons, and "diggers up of trees," and fewer gentlemen and "Tuftaffety humorists."* "A plaine soldier who can use a pickaxe and a spade is better than five knights," he said.

Whether Smith was actually rescued from death at the hands of the Indians by the princess Pocahontas is not certain, but there is little doubt that without his direction, the colony would have perished in the early days.

Lacking intelligent leaders—Smith only stayed in Virginia two years—and facing appalling hardships, the Jamestown colonists failed to develop a sufficient sense of common purpose. Each year they died in wholesale lots. The causes of death were disease, starvation (there was even a case of cannibalism among the desperate survivors), Indian attack, and, above all, ignorance and folly. Between 1606 and 1622 the London Company invested more than £160,000 in Virginia and sent over about 6,000 settlers. Yet no dividends were ever earned, and of the 6,000, fewer than 2,000 were still alive in 1622. In 1625 the population was down to about 1,300. The only profits were those taken by certain shrewd investors who had organized a joint-stock company to transport women to Virginia "to be made wives" by the colonists.

One major problem, the mishandling of the local Indians, was largely the colonists' doing. It is likely that the settlement would not have survived if the Powhatan Indians had not given the colonists food in the first hard winters, taught them the ways of the forest, introduced them to valuable new crops such as corn and yams, and showed them how to clear dense timber by girdling the trees and burning them down after they were dead. The settlers accepted Indian aid, then took whatever else they wanted by force. They "conciliated the Powhatan people while they were of use," one historian has written, "and pressed them remorselessly, facelessly, mechanically, as innocent of conscious ill will as a turning wheel, when they became of less value than their land."

The Indians did not submit meekly to such treatment. They proved brave, skillful, and ferocious fighters, once they understood that their very existence was at stake. The burden of Indian fighting might easily have been more than the frail settlement could bear.

What saved the Virginians was not the brushing aside of the Indians but the gradual realization that they must produce their own food—cattle raising was especially important—and cultivate tobacco, which flourished there and could be sold profitably in England. Once the settlers discovered tobacco, no amount of company pressure could keep them at wasteful tasks like looking for gold. The "restraint of plantinge Tobacco," one company official commented, "is a thinge so distastefull to them that they will with no patience indure to heare of it."

John Rolfe, who is also famous for marrying Pocahontas, introduced West Indian tobacco—much milder than the local "weed" and thus more valuable—in 1612. With money earned from the sale of tobacco, the colonists could buy the manufactured articles they could not produce in a raw new country; this freed them from dependence on outside subsidies. It did not mean profit for the London Company, however, for by the time tobacco caught on, the surviving original colonists had served their seven years and were no longer hired hands. To attract more settlers, the company had permitted first tenancy and then outright ownership of farms. Thus the profits of tobacco went largely to the planters, not to the "adventurers" who had organized the colony.

A revised charter in 1612 extended the London Company's control over its affairs in Virginia. Despite serious intracompany rivalry between groups headed by Sir Thomas Smythe and Sir Edwin Sandys, a somewhat more intelligent direction of Virginia's affairs resulted. First the merchants appointed a single resident governor and gave him sufficient authority to control the settlers. Then they made it much easier for settlers to obtain land of their own. In 1619 a rudimentary form of self-government was instituted: A House of Burgesses, consisting of delegates chosen in each district, met at Jamestown to advise the governor. The company was not bound by the actions of the burgesses, but from this seed sprang the system of representative government that became the American pattern.

These reforms, however, came too late to save the fortunes of the London Company. In 1619 the Sandys faction won control and started an extensive development program, but in 1622 a bloody Indian attack took the lives of 347 colonists. Morale sank,

---

* Smith was referring to the gold tassels worn by titled students at Oxford and Cambridge at that time.

and James I, who disliked Sandys, decided that the colony was being badly managed. In 1624 the charter was revoked and Virginia became a royal colony, subject to direct control by the government in London. As a financial proposition the company was a fiasco; the shareholders lost every penny they had invested. Nonetheless, by 1624 Virginia was firmly established and beginning to prosper.

The sociologist Sigmund Diamond has offered an interesting theoretical explanation of how and why the Virginia colony changed from a mere commercial organization to a real society. In the beginning, he asserts, there was no cement binding the colonists into a community; either employees or bosses, they were all oriented toward company headquarters in London. To attract more settlers and motivate them to work, the company had to grant them special privileges and status, such as political power and the right to own land, which had the effect of making them more dependent on one another. By destroying the reliance of the colonists on the company, these actions undermined company control over the colonists. "It was the company's fate to have created a country and to have destroyed itself in the process," Diamond explains.

A 1641 English cartoon comments on the religious turmoil of the period. The Roman Catholic, "The Papist," at lower right joins in a game of "abusing" the Bible along with three Protestant sects opposed to the Church of England.

The English Puritans

Although the prospect of a better material life brought most English settlers to America, for some, economic opportunity was not the only reason they abandoned what their contemporary, William Shakespeare, called "dear mother England." A profound unease with England's spiritual state—and therefore with their own while they remained there—explains why many colonists embarked on their "errand into the wilderness."

The Church of England became once and for all the official Church during the long reign of Elizabeth I (1558–1603). Like her father, Elizabeth took more interest in politics than in religion. She took her religion seriously, but so long as England had its own church, with her at its head, she was content.

This middle way satisfied most, but not all, of Elizabeth's subjects. Steadfast Catholics could not accept it. Some left England; the rest practiced their faith in private. At the other extreme, more radical Protestants, including a large percentage of England's university-trained clergy, insisted that Elizabeth had not gone far enough. Her church was still too much like the Church of Rome, they claimed. They objected to the richly decorated vestments worn by the clergy and to the use of candles, incense, and music in church services. They insisted that emphasis should be put on reading the Bible and analyzing the meaning of the Scriptures in order to encourage ordinary worshipers to understand their faith. Since they wanted to "purify" the Church of England, these critics were called Puritans. At first the name was a pejorative assigned to them by their opponents. Later it became a badge of honor.

Puritans objected to the way Elizabeth's bishops interpreted the Protestant doctrine of predestination. Their reading of the Book of Genesis convinced them that all human beings had been damned by Adam's original sin and that what one did on earth had no effect on a person's fate after death. To believe otherwise was to limit God's power, which was precisely what the Catholic church did in stressing its ability to forgive sins by granting indulgences. The bishops agreed that God had already decided whether or not a person was saved, but they implied that an individual's efforts to lead a good life might somehow cause God to change His mind. They did not insist that good works and faith in God could win a person admission to Heaven—that doctrine was called Arminianism. But they encouraged people to hope that good works were something more than ends in themselves.

Some Puritans—later called Congregationalists—favored a completely decentralized arrangement, with the members of each church and their chosen minister beholden only to one another. Others, called Presbyterians, favored some organization above the local level, but one with power moving up from the local churches, not down from the top as in the Church of England.

Puritans were also of two minds as to whether reform could be accomplished within the Church of England. During Elizabeth's reign most hoped that it could. After King James I succeeded her in 1603, however, their fears that the royal court might be backsliding into its old "popish" ways mounted. James was married to a Catholic, and the fact that he favored toleration for Catholics gave further substance to the rumor that he was himself a secret member of that church. This rumor proved to be false, but in his 22-year reign (1603–1625) James did little to advance the Protestant cause. His one contribution—which had a significance far beyond what he or anyone else anticipated—was to authorize a new translation of the Bible. The King James Version (1611) was both a monumental scholarly achievement and a literary masterpiece of the first order.

"Of Plymouth Plantation"

In 1606, worried about the future of their faith, members of the church in Scrooby, Nottinghamshire, "separated" from the Church of England, declaring it corrupt beyond salvage. In 17th-century England, Separatists had to go either underground or into exile. Since only the latter option would permit them to practice their religious faith openly, exile it was. In 1608 some 125 of the group left England for the Low Countries. They settled in the town of Leyden. In 1619, however, disheartened by the difficulties they had encountered in making a living, disappointed by the failure of others in England to join them, and distressed because their children were being "subjected to the great licentiousness" of the Dutch, these "Pilgrims" decided to move again—to seek "a place where they might have liberty and live comfortably."

Negotiations with Sir Edwin Sandys of the Virginia Company raised the possibility of America. Although unsympathetic to their religious views, Sandys appreciated the Pilgrims' inherent worth and supported their request to establish a settlement near the mouth of the Hudson River, on the northern boundary of the Virginia Company's grant. Since the Pilgrims were short of money, they formed a joint-stock company with other prospective emigrants and some optimistic investors who agreed to pay the expenses of the group in return for half the profits of the venture. In September 1620, about 100 strong—only 35 of them Pilgrims from Leyden—they set out from Plymouth, England, on the ship *Mayflower*.

Had the *Mayflower* reached its intended destination, the Pilgrims might have been soon forgotten. Instead their ship touched America slightly to the north, on Cape Cod Bay. Unwilling to remain longer at the mercy of storm-tossed December seas, they decided to settle where they were. Since they were outside the jurisdiction of the London Company, some members of the group claimed to be free of all governmental control. Therefore, before going ashore, the Pilgrims drew up the Mayflower Compact. "We whose names are underwritten," the Compact ran,

> do by these Presents, solemnly and mutually in the presence of God and one another covenant and combine ourselves under into a civil Body Politick . . . and by Virtue hereof do enact . . . such just and equal laws . . . as shall be thought most meet and convenient for the general Good of the Colony.

This early in American history, the idea was advanced that a society should be based on a set of rules chosen by its members, an idea carried further in the Declaration of Indpendence. The Pilgrims chose William Bradford as their first governor. In this simple manner, ordinary people created a government that they hoped would enable them to cope with the unknown wilderness before them.

The story of the first 30 years of the Pilgrims' colony has been preserved in *Of Plymouth Plantation*, written by Bradford. Having landed on the bleak Massachusetts shore at a place they named Plymouth, the Pilgrims had to endure a winter of desperate hunger. About half of them died. But by great good luck there was an Indian in the area, named Squanto, who spoke English! Squanto had been kidnapped in 1615 by an English sea captain, Thomas Hunt, who took him to Spain and sold him as a slave. Squanto soon escaped, however, and somehow made his way to England, where he fell in with people involved in colonization and exploring. He spent some time in Newfoundland in 1617 and 1618, returned to England, and in 1619 made another voyage to America as a pilot. This time he remained. It is easy to understand why the Pilgrims believed that Squanto was "a special instrument sent of God for their good." In addition to serving as an interpreter, he showed them the best places to fish, as well as what to plant and how to cultivate it. In general, he provided them with all kinds of advice and support in an unfamiliar world. They, in turn, worked hard, got their crops in the ground in good time, and after a bountiful harvest the following November, treated themselves and their Indian neighbors to a Thanksgiving feast.

But if the Pilgrims had quickly secured themselves a safe place in the wilderness, what followed was hardly all cranberries and drumsticks. Bradford's flock grew neither rich nor numerous on the thin New England soil. In 1650 there were still fewer than 1,000 settlers, most of them living beyond the reach of the original church. Among these were a few who tried to take advantage of the freedom from social control afforded by the wilderness. In 1628 a group led by one Thomas Morton, "Lord of Misrule" of the outlying community of Mount Wollaston, which he renamed Merrymount, declared its liberation from all restraints by setting up a maypole. They then invited neighboring Indian women to join them, provided drinks all around, and began (as the disapproving Bradford described the doings) "dancing and frisking together like so many fairies." Troops were dispatched to break up the carousing and take Morton into custody, after which he was packed off to England.

Morton was not a Pilgrim; his antics do not jeopardize the Pilgrims' place in American history. That place is one of honor. Theirs were victories won not with sword and gunpowder like those of Cortés or with bulldozer and dynamite like those of modern pioneers, but with simple courage and practical piety.

A Puritan Commonwealth

The Pilgrims were not the first English colonists to inhabit the northern regions. The Plymouth Company had settled a group on the Kennebec River in 1607. These colonists gave up after a few months, but fishermen and traders continued to visit the area, which was christened New England by Captain John Smith after an expedition there in 1614.

In 1620 the Plymouth Company was reorganized as the Council for New England, which had among its principal stockholders Sir Ferdinando Gorges and his friend John Mason, former governor of an English settlement on Newfoundland. Their particular domain included a considerable part of what is now Maine and New Hampshire. More interested in real estate deals than in colonizing, the council disposed of a number of tracts in the area north of Cape Cod. The most significant of these grants was a small one made to a group of Puritans from Dorchester, who in 1629 founded the Massachusetts Bay Company and obtained a royal grant to the area between the Charles and Merrimack rivers. The Massachusetts Bay Company was organized like any other commercial venture, but the Puritans, acting with single-minded determination, made it a way of obtaining religious refuge in America.

Unlike the Separatists in Plymouth, most Puritans had managed to satisfy both Crown and conscience while James I was king. The England of his son Charles I, who succeeded to the throne in 1625, posed a more serious challenge. Whereas James had been content to keep Puritans at bay, Charles and his favorite Anglican cleric, William Laud, intended to bring them to heel. With the king's support, Laud proceeded to embellish even further the already elaborate Anglican ritual and to tighten the central control that the Puritans found so distasteful. He removed ministers with Puritan leanings from their pulpits and threatened church elders who harbored such ministers with imprisonment.

No longer able to remain within the Anglican fold in good conscience and now facing prison if they tried to worship in the way they thought right, the Puritans decided to migrate to America in force.

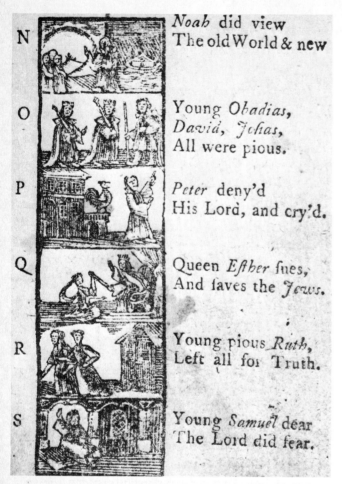

N — *Noah* did view
The old World & new

O — Young *Obadias,*
David, Jofias,
All were pious.

P — *Peter* deny'd
His Lord, and cry'd.

Q — Queen *Efther* fues,
And faves the *Jews.*

R — Young pious *Ruth,*
Left all for Truth.

S — Young *Samuel* dear
The Lord did fear.

A page from this New England primer reflects the pervasive influence of religion on every aspect of Puritan life, from politics to the education of the young.

In the summer of 1630 nearly 1,000 of them set out from England, carrying the charter of the Massachusetts Bay Company with them. By the fall they had founded Boston and several other towns. The Puritan commonwealth was under way.

Massachusetts settlers suffered fewer hardships in the early years than had the early Jamestown and Plymouth colonists. Luck played a part in this, but so did the careful planning that went into the transplantation. They also benefited from a constant influx of new recruits, who came with families and worldly possessions in tow. Continuing bad times and the persecution of Puritans at home led to the Great Migration of the 1630s. Many thousands more poured into new English colonies in the West Indies, but by 1640 well over 10,000 had arrived in Massachusetts. These industrious, well-educated, and fairly prosperous colonists swiftly created a complex and distinct civilization on the edge of what one of the pessimists among them called "a hideous and desolate wilderness, full of wild beasts and wild men."

The directors of the Massachusetts Bay Company believed their enterprise to be divinely inspired. Before leaving England, they elected John Winthrop, a 29-year-old attorney, as governor of the colony. Throughout his 20 years of almost continuous service as governor, Winthrop spoke for the solid and sensible core of the Puritans and their high-minded experiment. His lay sermon, "A Modelle of Christian Charity," delivered in mid-Atlantic on the deck of the ship *Arbella* in 1630, made clear his sense of the momentousness of that experiment:

> Wee must Consider that wee shall be as a Citty upon a Hill, the eies of all people are upon us; soe that if wee shall deale falsely with our god in this worke wee have undertaken and soe cause him to withdrawe his present help from us, wee shall be made a story and a by-word through the world, wee shall open the mouthes of enemies to speake evill of the wayes of god and all professours for Gods sake.

The founders also established an elected legislature, the General Court. Their system was not democratic in the modern sense because the right to vote and hold office was limited to church members, but this did not mean that the government was run by clergymen or that it did not reflect the popular will. Clergymen were influential, but since they were not allowed to hold public office, their authority was indirect and based on the respect of the parishioners, not on law or force. At least until the mid-1640s, most families contained at least one adult male church member. Since these "freemen" soon secured the right to choose the governor and elect the representatives ("deputies") to the General Court, a kind of practical democracy existed.

The Puritans had a clear sense of what their churches should be like. After getting permission from the General Court, a group of colonists who wished to form a new church could select a minister and conduct their spiritual affairs as they saw fit.

Membership, however, was restricted to those who could present satisfactory evidence of their having experienced "saving grace," such as by a compelling recounting of some extraordinary emotional experience or some mystical sign of intimate contact with God. This meant that full membership in the churches of early Massachusetts was reserved for "visible saints." During the 1630s, however, the need for harmony in the community was so important that few applicants were denied membership. Having removed oneself from England was considered in most cases sufficient proof of spiritual purity.

Troublemakers

As Winthrop had more than one occasion to lament, most of the colony's early troublemakers came not from those of doubtful spiritual condition but from its certified saints. The "godly and zealous" Roger Williams was a prime example. The Pilgrim leader William Bradford described Williams as possessed of "many precious parts, but very unsettled in judgment." Even by Plymouth's standards, Williams was an extreme separatist. He was ready to bring down upon New England the wrath of Charles I rather than accept the charters signed by him or his father, even if these documents provided the only legal basis for the governments of the Plymouth and Massachusetts Bay colonies.

Williams had arrived in Massachusetts in 1631. Following a short stay in Plymouth, he joined the church in Salem, which elected him minister in 1635. Well before then, however, his opposition to the alliance of church and civil government turned both ministers and magistrates against him. Part of his contrariness stemmed from his religious libertarianism. Magistrates should have no voice in spiritual matters, he insisted—"forced religion stinks in God's nostrils." He also offended property owners (which meant nearly everyone) by advancing the radical idea that it was "a Nationale sinne" for anyone, including the king, to take possession of any American land without buying it from the Indians.

As long as Williams enjoyed the support of his Salem church, there was little the magistrates could do to silence him. But his refusal to heed those who counseled moderation—"all truths are not seasonable at all times," Governor Winthrop reminded him—swiftly eroded that support. In the fall of 1635, economic pressure put on Salem by the General Court turned his congregation against him. The General Court then ordered him to quit the colony.

Williams left Massachusetts in January 1636, traveling south to the head of Narragansett Bay. There he worked out mutually acceptable arrangements with the local Indians and founded the town of Providence. In 1644, after obtaining a charter from Parliament, he established the colony of Rhode Island and Providence Plantations. All religions were tolerated, and church and state were rigidly separated. Whatever Williams's temperamental excesses, he was more than ready to practice what he preached when given the opportunity.

Anne Hutchinson, who arrived in Boston in 1631, was another "visible saint" who, in the judgment of the Puritan establishment, went too far. Hutchinson was not to be taken lightly. According to Governor Winthrop, her husband William was "a man of mild temper and weak parts, wholly guided by his wife." (He was not too weak to father Anne's 15 children.) Duties as a midwife brought her into the homes of other Boston women, with whom she discussed and more than occasionally criticized the sermons of their minister, John Wilson. Where Wilson and virtually all the ministers in the Bay Colony except her favorite, John Cotton, went wrong, she contended, was in emphasizing the obligation of the saved to lead morally pure lives in order to be models for the unregenerate. By taking the Puritan view that there was no necessary relationship between moral conduct and salvation to its extreme limits, she concluded that those possessed of saving grace were exempt from the rules of good behavior and even from the laws of the commonwealth. As her detractors pointed out, this was the conclusion some of the earliest German Protestants had reached, for which they were judged guilty of the heresy of antinomianism ("belief against the law") and burned at the stake.

In 1636 the General Court charged Hutchinson with defaming the clergy and brought her to trial. When her accusers quoted the Bible ("Honor thy father and thy mother") to make their case, she coolly announced that even the Ten Commandments must yield to one's own insights if these were directly inspired by God. When pressed for details, she acknowledged that she was a regular recipient of divine insights, communicated, as they were to Abraham, "by the voice of His own spirit in my soul." The General Court, upon hearing this claim, banished her.

Hutchinson, together with her large family and a group of supporters, left Massachusetts in the spring of 1637 for Rhode Island, thereby adding to the reputation of that colony as the "sink" of New England. After her husband died in 1642, she and six of her children moved to the Dutch colony of New Netherland, where, the following year, she and all but her youngest daughter were killed by Indians.

The banishments of Roger Williams, whom some historians have called the first American democrat, and Anne Hutchinson, who, if not a feminist in the modern sense, refused to defer to her male "betters," did not endear the Massachusetts Puritans to posterity. In both cases, outspoken individualists seem to have been done in by frightened politicians and self-serving ministers. Yet Williams and Hutchinson posed genuine threats to the Puritan community. Massachusetts was truly a social experiment. Could it accommodate such uncooperative spirits and remain intact? When forced to choose between the peace of the commonwealth and sending dissenters packing, Winthrop, the magistrates, and the ministers did not hesitate.

Other New England Colonies

From the successful Massachusetts Bay Colony, settlement radiated outward, propelled by an expanding population and Puritan intolerance. In 1629 Sir Ferdinando Gorges and John Mason divided their holdings, Gorges taking the Maine section (enlarged in 1639) and Mason getting New Hampshire, but neither succeeded in making much of his claim. Massachusetts bought title to Maine for a pittance (£1,250) in 1677 and New Hampshire became a royal colony in 1680.

Meanwhile, beginning in 1635, a number of Massachusetts congregations had pushed southwestward into the fertile valley of the Connecticut River. A group headed by the Reverend Thomas Hooker founded Hartford in 1636. Hooker was influential in the drafting of the Fundamental Orders, a sort of constitution creating a government for the valley towns, in 1639. The Fundamental Orders resembled the Massachusetts system, except that they did not limit voting to church members. Other groups of Puritans came directly from England to settle towns in and around New Haven in the 1630s. These were incorporated into Connecticut shortly after the Hooker colony obtained a royal charter in 1662.

French and Dutch Settlements

While the English were settling Virginia and New England, other Europeans were challenging Spain's monopoly in the New World. French explorers had pushed up the St. Lawrence River as far as the site of Montreal in the 1530s, and beginning in 1603, Samuel de Champlain made several voyages to the region. In 1608 he founded Quebec, and he had penetrated as far inland as Lake Huron before the Pilgrims left Leyden. The French also planted colonies on Guadeloupe, Martinique, and other islands in the West Indies after 1625.

Through their West India Company, the Dutch also established themselves in the Caribbean. On the mainland they founded New Netherland in the Hudson Valley, basing their claim to the region on the explorations of Henry Hudson in 1609. As early as 1624 there was a Dutch outpost, Fort Orange, on the site of present-day Albany. Two year later New Amsterdam was located at the mouth of the Hudson River, and Manhattan Island was purchased from the Indians by Peter Minuit, the director general of the West India Company, for trading goods worth about 60 guilders. The Dutch traded with the Indians for furs and plundered Spanish colonial commerce enthusiastically. Through the Charter of Privileges of Patroons, which authorized large grants of land to individuals who would bring more than 50 settlers, they tried to encourage large-scale agriculture. Only one such estate—Rensselaerswyck, on the Hudson south of Fort Orange, owned by the rich Amsterdam merchant Kiliaen Van Rensselaer—was successful. Peter Minuit was removed from his post in New Amsterdam in 1631, but he organized a group of Swedish settlers several years later and founded the colony of New Sweden on the lower reaches of the Delaware River. New Sweden was in constant conflict with the Dutch, who finally overran it in 1655.

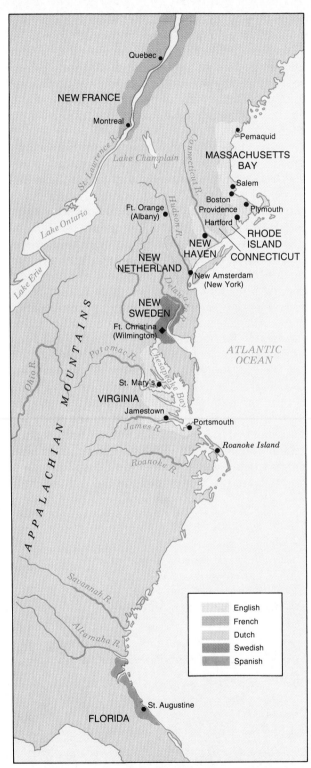

NORTH AMERICAN COLONIES
TO 1650

Maryland and the Carolinas

The Virginia and New England colonies were essentially corporate ventures. Most of the other English colonies in America were founded by individuals or by a handful of partners who obtained charters from the ruling sovereign. It was becoming easier to establish settlements because experience had taught the English a great deal about the colonization process. Settlers knew better what to bring with them and what to do after they arrived. Moreover, the psychological barrier was much less formidable. Like a modern athlete seeking to run a mile in less than four minutes, colonizers knew after about 1630 that what they were attempting could be accomplished. And conditions in Europe in the mid-17th century encouraged thousands to migrate. Both in England and on the Continent the economic future seemed unpromising, and political and religious persecution erupted in one country after another, each time supplying America with waves of refugees.

Numbers of influential Englishmen were eager to try their luck as colonizers. The grants they received made them "proprietors" of great estates which were, at least in theory, their personal property. By granting land to settlers in return for a small annual rent, they hoped to obtain a steadily increasing income while holding a valuable speculative interest in all undeveloped land. At the same time, their political power, guaranteed by charter, would become increasingly important as their colonies expanded. In practice, however, the realities of life in America limited their freedom of action and their profits.

One of the first of the proprietary colonies was Maryland, granted by Charles I to George Calvert, Lord Baltimore. Calvert had a deep interest in America, being a member of both the London Company and the Council for New England. He hoped to profit financially from Maryland, but since he was a Catholic, he also intended the colony to be a haven for his coreligionists.

Calvert died shortly before Charles approved his charter, so the grant went to his son Cecilius. The first settlers arrived in 1634, founding St. Mary's, just north of the Potomac. The presence of the now well established Virginia colony nearby greatly aided the Marylanders; they had little difficulty in getting started and in developing an economy based, like Virginia's, on tobacco. However, an acrimonious dispute raged for some years between the two colonies over their common boundary. Despite the emptiness of the American wilderness, settlers could squabble over a few acres as bitterly as any European peasants.

The Maryland charter was similar to that of the old county palatine of Durham in the north of England, whose bishop-overlords had held almost regal authority. Lord Baltimore had the right to establish feudal manors, hold people in serfdom, make laws, and set up his own courts. He soon discovered, however, that to attract settlers he had to allow them to own their farms and that to maintain any political influence at all he had to give the settlers considerable say in local affairs. Other wise concessions marked his handling of the religious question. He would have preferred an exclusively Catholic colony, but there existed from the beginning a large Protestant majority. Baltimore dealt with this problem by agreeing to the Toleration Act (1649), which guaranteed freedom of religion to anyone "professing to believe in Jesus Christ." Even so, religious conflicts occurred repeatedly in the early years. However, because the Calverts adjusted their pretensions to American realities, they made a fortune out of Maryland and maintained an influence in the colony until the Revolution.

During the period of the English Civil War and Oliver Cromwell's Protectorate, no important new colonial enterprises were undertaken. With the restoration of the monarchy in 1660 came a new wave of settlement, for the government wished to expand and strengthen its hold on North America. To do so, it granted generous terms to settlers: easy access to land, religious toleration, and political rights—all far more extensive than those available in England.

Most of the earlier colonies were organized by groups of merchants; those of the Restoration period reflected the concerns of great English landowners. The first new venture involved a huge grant south of Virginia to eight proprietors with large interests in colonial affairs. The proprietors did not intend to recruit large numbers of European settlers. Instead they depended on the "excess" population of New England, Virginia, and the West Indies. They (and the Crown) hoped for a diversified economy, the charter granting tax concessions to exporters of wine, silk, oil, olives, and other exotic products. The region was called Carolina in honor of Charles I.

The Carolina charter, like that of Maryland, accorded the proprietors wide authority. With the help of the political philosopher John Locke, they drafted a grandiose plan of government called the Fundamental Constitutions, which authorized a hereditary nobility and provided for huge paper land grants to a hierarchy headed by the proprietors and lesser "landgraves" and "caciques." The human ef-

The earliest known painting of Charles Town, South Carolina (Charleston after 1783), shows the harbor in the 1730s. As the most important seaport in the southern colonies, the city carried on a busy export trade in rice, indigo, and deerskins.

fort to support the feudal society was to be supplied by peasants (whom the Fundamental Constitutions called "leet-men").

This pretentious system proved unworkable. The landgraves and caciques got grants, but they could not find leet-men willing to toil on their domains. Probably the purpose of all this feudal nonsense was promotional; the proprietor hoped to convince investors that they could make fortunes in Carolina rivaling those of English lords. Life actually followed a more mundane pattern similar to what was going on in Virginia and Maryland, with property relatively easy to obtain.

The first settlers arrived in 1670, most of them from the sugar plantations of Barbados, where slave labor was driving out small independent farmers. Charles Town (now Charleston) was founded in 1680. Another center of population sprang up in the Albemarle district, just south of Virginia, settled largely by individuals from that colony. Two quite different societies evolved. The Charleston colony, with an economy based on a thriving trade in furs and on the export of foodstuffs to the West Indies, was prosperous and cosmopolitan. The Albemarle settlement, where the soil was less fertile, was poorer and more primitive. Eventually, in 1712, the two were formally separated, becoming North and South Carolina.

The Middle Colonies

Gradually it became clear that the English would dominate the entire coast between the St. Lawrence Valley and Florida. After 1660 only the Dutch challenged their monopoly. The two nations, once allies against Spain, had fallen out because of the fierce competition of their textile manufacturers and merchants. England's efforts to bar Dutch merchant vessels from its colonial trade also brought the two countries into conflict in America. Charles II precipitated a showdown by granting his brother James, duke of York, the entire area between Connecticut and Maryland. This was tantamount to declaring war. In 1664 English forces captured New Amsterdam without a fight—there were only 1,500 people in the town—and soon the rest of the Dutch settlements capitulated. New Amsterdam became New York. The duke did not interfere much with the way of life of the Dutch settlers, and they were quickly reconciled to English rule.

In 1664, even before the capture of New Amsterdam, the duke of York gave New Jersey, the region between the Hudson and Delaware rivers, to John Lord Berkeley and Sir George Carteret. To attract settlers, these proprietors offered land on easy terms and established freedom of religion and a democratic local government. A considerable number of Puritans from New England and Long Island moved to the new province.

In 1674 Berkeley sold his interest in New Jersey to two Quakers. Originally a sect emotional to the point of fanaticism, by the 1670s the Quakers had come to stress the doctrine of the Inner Light—the direct, mystical experience of religious truth, which they believed possible for all persons. They were at once humble and fiercely proud, pacifistic yet unwilling to bow before any person or to surrender their right to worship as they pleased. They distrusted the intellect in religious matters, and though ardent proselytizers of their own beliefs, they tolerated those of others cheerfully. When faced with opposition, they resorted to passive resistance, a tactic that embroiled them in grave difficulties in England and in most of the American colonies.

The acquisition of New Jersey (when Sir George Carteret died in 1680, they purchased the rest of the colony) gave the Quakers a place where they could practice their religion in peace. The proprietors, in keeping with their principles, drafted an extremely liberal constitution for the colony, the Concessions and Agreements of 1677, which created an autonomous legislature and guaranteed settlers freedom of conscience, the right of trial by jury, and other civil rights. The main Quaker effort at colonization came in the region immediately west of New Jersey, a fertile area belonging to William Penn, the son of a wealthy English admiral. Penn had early rejected a life of ease and had become a Quaker missionary. As a result, he was twice jailed. Yet he possessed qualities that enabled him to hold the respect and friendship of people who found his religious ideas abhorrent. From his father, Penn had inherited a claim to £16,000 that the admiral had lent Charles II. The king, reluctant to part with that much cash, paid off the debt in 1681 by giving Penn the region north of Maryland and west of the Delaware River, insisting only that it be named Pennsylvania, in honor of the admiral. The duke of York then added Delaware, the region between Maryland and Delaware Bay, to Penn's holdings.

William Penn considered his colony a "Holy Experiment." He treated the Indians fairly, buying title to their lands and trying to protect them in their dealings with settlers and traders. Anyone who believed in "one Almighty and Eternal God" was entitled to freedom of worship. Penn's political ideas were paternalistic rather than democratic; the assembly he established could only approve or reject laws proposed by the governor and council. But individual rights were as well protected in Pennsylvania as in New Jersey.

Altruism, however, did not prevent Penn from taking excellent care of his own interests. He sold land to settlers large and small on easy terms but reserved huge tracts for himself and attached quitrents (see page 34) to the land he disposed of. He promoted Pennsylvania tirelessly, writing glowing, although perfectly honest, descriptions of the colony that were circulated widely in England and, in translation, on the Continent. These attracted many settlers, including large numbers of Germans—the Pennsylvania "Dutch" (a corruption of *Deutsch*, meaning "German").

William Penn was neither a doctrinaire nor an ivory-tower philosopher. He came to Pennsylvania himself when trouble developed between settlers and his representatives and agreed to adjustments in his first Frame of Government when he realized that local conditions demonstrated the need for change. His combination of toughness, liberality, and good salesmanship helped the colony to prosper. Of course, the presence of well-settled colonies on all sides and the richness of the soil had much to do with this happy state of affairs. By 1685 there were almost 9,000 settlers in Pennsylvania, and by 1700 twice that number, a heartening contrast to the early history of Virginia and Plymouth. Pennsylvania produced wheat, corn, rye, and other crops in abundance and found a ready market for its surpluses on the sugar plantations of the West Indies.

William Penn met with a group of Delaware Indians in the fall of 1683 to arrange the terms of a land transfer in eastern Pennsylvania. Good will between Indians and settlers lasted for about 50 years, until the latter began forcing the Indians westward. This re-creation of Penn's famous treaty is an engraving based on a painting by Benjamin West.

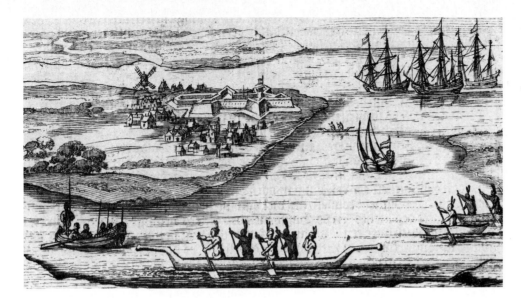

This 1651 engraving, the first known view of Manhattan Island, shows the new fort of New Amsterdam in the 1620s. Indians bring beaver pelts in their canoes to sell to the Dutch.

Indians and Europeans as "Americanizers"

Interaction with the native peoples was characteristic of life in all the English colonies. *Interaction* is the key word. The so-called Columbian Exchange between Indian and European was a two-way street. The Indians taught the colonists a great deal about how to live in the American forest: the names of plants and animals (hickory, pecan, raccoon, skunk, moose); what to eat in their new home and how to catch or grow it; what to wear (leather leggings and especially moccasins); how best to get from one place to another; how to fight; and in some respects how to think.

The colonists learned from the Indians how best to use many wild plants and animals for food and clothing, but they would probably have discovered most of these if the continent had been devoid of human life when they arrived. Corn, however, the staple of the diet of agricultural tribes, was something the Indians had domesticated. Its contribution to the success of English colonization was enormous.

The colonists also took advantage of that marvel of Indian technology, the birchbark canoe. An early explorer, Martin Pring, brought one back to England in 1603; it was 17 feet long and 4 feet wide and capable, according to Pring, of carrying nine full-grown men. Yet it weighed "not at the most above sixtie pounds," a thing, Pring added, "almost incredible in regard to the largenesse and capacitie thereof."

For their part, the Indians adopted European technology eagerly. All metal objects were indeed of great usefulness to them, though the products and tools that metals replaced were neither crude nor inefficient in most cases. (To say that a gun is a more deadly weapon than a bow and arrow is a more accurate statement about modern guns than about a 17th-century firelock. A bowman could get off six times as many shots in a given time as a soldier armed with a firelock and would probably hit the target more frequently.)

Indians took on many of the colonists' attitudes along with their tools, clothing, weapons, alcohol, and ornaments. Some tribes used the products of European technology to tyrannize tribes in more remote areas. During wars Indians fought almost as often with colonists against other Indians as with other Indians against colonists.

The fur trade illustrates the pervasiveness of Indian-colonist interaction. It was in some ways a perfect business arrangement. Both groups profited greatly. The colonists got "valuable" furs for "cheap" European products, while the Indians got "priceless" tools, knives, and other trade goods in exchange for "cheap" beaver pelts and deerskins. The market for furs caused the Indians to become more efficient hunters and trappers and even to absorb some of the colonists' ideas about private property and capitalist accumulation. Hunting parties became larger. Farming tribes shifted their villages in order to be nearer trade routes and waterways. In some cases, tribal organization was altered:

Small groups combined into confederations in order to control more territory when their hunting reduced the supplies of furs nearer home. Early in the 17th century, Huron Indians in the Great Lakes region, who had probably never seen a Frenchman, owned French products obtained from eastern tribes in exchange for Huron corn. All in all, as one historian puts it, "the fur trade set off a chain reaction . . . within the Indian world." In *The European and the Indian,* James Axtell makes an important point about the relative impact of the two cultures on each other. Although the colonists learned much from the Indians and adopted certain elements of Indian culture and technology eagerly, their objective was not to be like the Indians, whom they considered the epitome of savagery and barbarism. That they feared they might become "Indianized," Axtell notes, is clear from the adage "It is very easy to make an Indian out of a white man,

but you cannot make a white man out of an Indian." Yet this very fear, the colonial rejection of Indian ways, caused what Axtell calls "reactive changes" that are at the heart of what made them Americans rather than transplanted Europeans. The constant conflicts with Indians forced the colonists to band together and in time gave them a sense of having shared a common history. And later, when they broke away from Great Britain, they used the image of the Indian to symbolize the freedom and independence they sought for themselves.

In sum, during the 200-odd years that followed Columbus's first landfall in the Caribbean, a complex development had taken place in the Americas, one that profoundly affected the civilizations of the people who preceded Columbus and those who followed him. We shall now turn to a more detailed look at how this happened in the part of that vast region on which our own civilization has evolved.

Milestones

Exploration

c. 1000	Leif Eriksson reaches Newfoundland
1445–1488	Portuguese captains explore the west coast of Africa
1492	First voyage of Christopher Columbus
1497	John Cabot explores the east coast of North America
1498	Vasco da Gama sails around Africa to India
1513	Ponce de León explores Florida
1519–1521	Hernán Cortés conquers Mexico
1519–1522	Ferdinand Magellan's crew circumnaviagates the globe
1539–1542	Hernando de Soto explores the lower Mississippi River valley
1540–1542	Francisco Vásquez de Coronado explores the Southwest
1579	Francis Drake explores the coast of California
1609	Henry Hudson discovers the Hudson River

Settlement

c. 50,000 B.C.	First humans reach North America from Asia
1493	La Navidad, Hispaniola, founded by Columbus
1494	Treaty of Tordesillas divides the New World between Spain and Portugal
1576	St. Augustine, Florida, settled
1587	"Lost colony" of Roanoke Island founded
1607	Jamestown settled
1620	Plymouth settled; Mayflower Compact signed
1624	New Amsterdam settled
1630	Massachusetts Bay Colony established
1634	Maryland settled
1636	Rhode Island founded
1639	Connecticut founded
1664	New Amsterdam conquered by the English
1670	Charles Town (Charleston) settled
1681	Philadelphia settled

SUPPLEMENTARY READING

Titles marked with an asterisk have been published in paperback.

On the explorers and the world they opened up, see D. B. Quinn, **North America from Earliest Discovery to First Settlements*** (1977), S. E. Morison, **The European Discovery of America** (1971–1974), and C. O. Sauer, **Sixteenth-Century North America*** (1971). Morison's biography of Columbus, **Admiral of the Ocean Sea** (1942), is a model of sound scholarship and good writing.

Accounts of the English background of colonization can be found in A. L. Rowse, **The Elizabethans and America*** (1959), and Carl Bridenbaugh, **Vexed and Troubled Englishmen*** (1968). J. H. Elliott, **The Old World and the New*** (1970), analyzes the impact of the discovery of America on Europe.

On French and Spanish colonization, see W. J. Eccles, **France in America*** (1972), and Charles Gibson, **Spain in America*** (1966). On the interactions of European and Indian civilizations, consult James Axtell, **The European and the Indian** (1981), Karen Kupperman, **Settling with the Indian** (1980), and William Cronon, **Changes in the Land** (1981). W. E. Washburn, **The Indian in America** (1975), contains a good discussion of the culture and history of North American Indian groups. Francis Jennings, **The Invasion of America*** (1975), is extremely critical of white dealings with the Indians. A. T. Vaughan, **New England Frontier*** (1965), argues that New Englanders treated the Indians fairly.

W. F. Craven, **The Colonies in Transition*** (1968), is a first-rate study of late 17th- and early 18th-century English colonization. On the southern colonies, W. F. Craven, **The Southern Colonies in the Seventeenth Century*** (1949), is also excellent, as is, on Virginia, E. S. Morgan, **American Slavery, American Freedom** (1975). For Maryland, consult G. T. Main, **Tobacco Colony** (1982), and A. C. Land, **Colonial Maryland** (1981).

D. R. Rutman, **Winthrop's Boston** (1965), is good on Massachusetts Bay. For the middle colonies, see Michael Kammen, **Colonial New York** (1975), and G. B. Nash, **Quakers and Politics** (1968). For Carolina, consult A. R. Ekirch, **Poor Carolina** (1981).

No student should miss at least dipping into the works of Francis Parkman on the French in America. His **Pioneers of France in the New World** (1855) covers the early period. William Bradford's classic **Of Plymouth Plantation** is also well worth sampling.

Biographies worth noting include A. T. Vaughan, **American Genesis: Captain John Smith*** (1975), and E. S. Morgan, **The Puritan Dilemma: The Story of John Winthrop*** (1958).

II

American Society in the Making

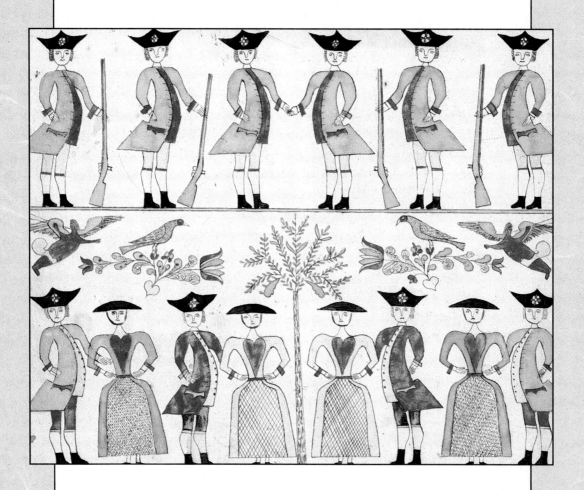

The great Increase of Offspring in particular Families is not always owing to greater Fecundity of Nature, but sometimes to Examples of Industry in the Heads, and industrious Education; by which the Children are enabled to provide better for themselves, and their marrying earlier is encouraged from the Prospect of good Subsistence.

BENJAMIN FRANKLIN, *1751*

T he colonies were settled chiefly by English people at first, with a leavening of Germans, Scots, Scotch-Irish, Dutch, French, Swedes, Finns, a scattering of other nationalities, a handful of Sephardic Jews, and a gradually increasing number of black African slaves. The cultures these people brought with them varied according to the nationality, social status, intelligence, and taste of the individual. The newcomers never lost this heritage entirely, but they—and certainly their descendants—became quite different from their relatives who remained in the Old World. They became what we call Americans.

But not right away.

What Is an American?

The subtle but profound changes that occurred when Europeans moved to the New World were hardly self-willed. Most of the settlers came, it is true, hoping for a more bountiful existence, and sometimes also for nonmaterialistic reasons, such as the opportunity to practice their religions in ways barred to them at home. For some whose alternative was prison or execution, there was really no choice. Still, even the most rebellious or alienated seldom intended to develop an entirely new civilization; rather, they wished to reconstruct the old on terms more favorable to themselves. Nor did a single "American" type result from the careful selection of particular kinds of Europeans as colonizers. Settlers came from every walk of life and in rough proportion to their numbers in Europe (if we exclude the very highest social strata). Certainly there was no systematic selection of the finest grain to provide seed for cultivating the wilderness.

Why then did America become something more than another Europe? Why was New England not merely a new England, Virginia not simply an English province west of Ireland? If not just another "poor European immigrant" away from home, a French settler, Hector St. John de Crèvecoeur, wondered in 1762, "What then is the American, this new man?" And how did this American come to be?

The fact of physical separation provides an important part of the answer. America was isolated from Europe by 3,000 miles of ocean. The Atlantic served as an umbilical cord but also as a barrier. The crossing took anywhere from a few weeks to several months, depending on wind and weather. No one undertook an ocean voyage lightly in colonial times, and few who made the westward crossing ever thought seriously of returning. The modern mind can scarcely grasp the awful isolation that enveloped the settler. One had to face forward (westward) and construct a new life or perish—if not of hunger, then of loneliness.

More than physical separation went into the process by which the people Crèvecoeur called this "promiscuous breed" fashioned for themselves a new national identity and the outlines of a distinctive civilization. Unlike separation from Europe, some factors affected some settlers differently than others. Factors as material as the landscape encountered, as quantifiable as population patterns, as elusive as chance and calculation all shaped colonial social arrangements. Their cumulative impact did not at first produce anything like a uniform society throughout the 2,000-mile-long and 50-mile-wide corridor that contained England's American colonies. Two quite different societies developed, one at each end of the corridor. A third society in the middle shared elements of both. The Americans who evolved in these regional societies were in many ways as different from each other as all were from their European cousins. The process by which these identities merged into an American nation remained incomplete. It was—and is—ongoing.

The Southern Colonies: A Hustling People

The southern parts of English North America comprised three regions: the Chesapeake Bay, consisting of "tidewater" Virginia and Maryland; the "low country" of the Carolinas (and eventually Georgia); and the "back country," a vast territory that extended from the fall line in the foothills of the Appalachians where falls and rapids put an end to navigation on the tidal rivers to the farthest point of western settlement. Not until well into the 18th century would the emergence of common features—export-oriented agricultural economies, a labor force in which black slaves figured prominently, the absence of towns of any size—prompt people to think of "the South" as a single region.

The Chesapeake: "Seasoning Time"

When the English philosopher Thomas Hobbes wrote in 1651 that human life tended to be "nasty, brutish, and short," he might well have had in mind the royal colony of Virginia. Although the colony grew from about 1,300 to nearly 5,000 in the decade after the Crown took it over in 1624, the death rate remained appalling. Since more than 9,000 immi-

grants had entered the colony, nearly half the population died during that decade.

The climate helped make the Chesapeake area a death trap. "Hot and moist" is how Robert Beverly described the weather in *The History and Present State of Virginia* (1705), the dampness "occasioned by the abundance of low grounds, marshes, creeks, and rivers." Europeans found that these conditions took getting used to. Almost without exception, newcomers underwent "seasoning," a period of illness that in its mildest form consisted of "two or three fits of a fever and ague." If they survived this period, and a great many did not, settlers still ran the seasonal risk of contracting a particularly virulent strain of malaria, which, though seldom fatal in itself, could so debilitate its victims that they often died of dysentery and other ailments.

Long after food shortages and Indian warfare had ceased to be serious problems, life in the Chesapeake remained precarious. Well into the 1700s a white male of 20 in Middlesex County could look forward to about 25 more years of life. Across Chesapeake Bay, in Charles County, Maryland, the average life expectancy was even lower. "Grandparents," writes David Freeman Hawke in this connection, "were all but nonexistent."

Because of the persistent shortage of women in the Chesapeake region (men outnumbered women by three to two even in the early 1700s), widows easily found new husbands. Many men spent their entire lives alone or in the company of other men. Others married Indian women and became part of Indian society.

All Cheasapeake settlers felt the psychological effects of their precarious and frustrating existence. Random mayhem and calculated violence posed a continuous threat to life and limb. Social arrangements were rude at best and often as "brutish" as Hobbes had claimed, even allowing for the difficulties involved in carving out a community in the wilderness. "Success," writes Gloria T. Main in *Tobacco Colony: Life in Early Maryland*, "was primarily the product of good timing and good health." If a white man got started when tobacco prices were high and survived the seasoning period, he could "begin to amass the necessary capital with which to acquire land, a wife, and then a servant. . . . By rigorously saving and reinvesting his cash income, he could secure his own enterprise and help his children launch theirs."

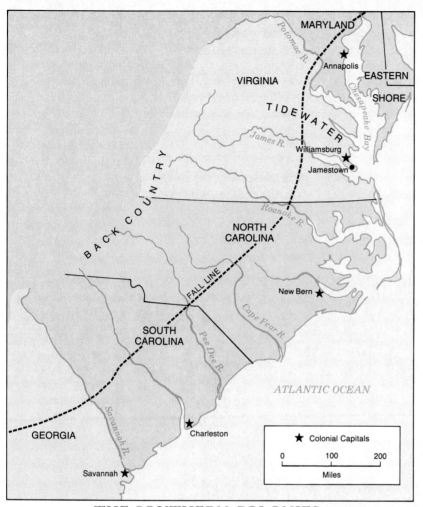

THE SOUTHERN COLONIES

The Lure of Land

Agriculture was the bulwark of life for the Chesapeake settlers and the rest of the colonial south; the tragic experiences of the Jamestown settlement revealed this quickly enough. Jamestown also suggested that a colony could not succeed unless its inhabitants were allowed to own their own land. The first colonists, it will be recalled, were employees of the London Company who had agreed to work for seven years in return for a share of the profits. When their contracts expired, there were few profits. To satisfy these settlers and to attract new capital, the company declared a "dividend" of land, its only asset. The surviving colonists each received 100 acres. Thereafter, as prospects continued poor, the company relied more and more on grants of land to attract both capital and labor. A number of wealthy Englishmen were given immense tracts, some running to several hundred thousand acres. Lesser persons willing to settle in Virginia received more modest grants. Whether dangled before a great tycoon, a country squire, or a poor farmer, the offer of land had the effect of encouraging immigration to the colony. This was a much-desired end, for without the labor to develop it, the land was worthless.

Soon what was known as the headright system

became entrenched in both Virginia and Maryland. Behind the system lay the eminently sound principle that land should be parceled out according to the availability of labor to cultivate it. For each "head" entering the colony, the government issued a "right" to take any 50 acres of unoccupied land. To "seat" a claim and receive title to the property, the holder of the headright had to mark out its boundaries, plant a crop, and construct some sort of habitation. This system was adopted in all the southern colonies and in Pennsylvania and New Jersey.

The first headrights were issued with no strings attached, but generally the grantor demanded a small annual payment called a quitrent. A quitrent was actually a tax, perhaps a shilling for 50 acres, which provided a way for the proprietors to derive incomes from their colonies. However, quitrents were usually resented and difficult to collect.

The headright system encouraged landless Europeans to migrate to America. More often than not, however, those most eager to come could not afford passage across the Atlantic. In order to bring together those with money who sought land and labor and those without funds who wanted to go to America, the indentured servant system was developed. Indenture resembled apprenticeship. In return for transportation, the indentured servants agreed to

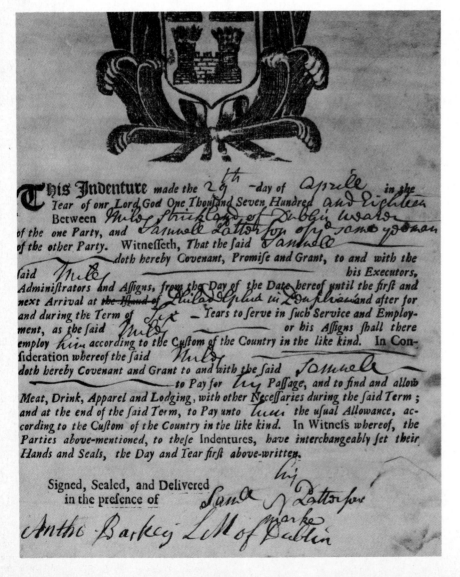

The indentured servant system allowed those with little money to emigrate to America, sometimes on the same ship as their new master. In this 1718 indenture, Samuel Patterson agrees to serve Miles Strickland for six years in return for his passage to Pennsylvania as well as food, clothing, and other necessary effects.

work for a stated period, usually about five years. During that time they were subject to strict control by the master and received no compensation beyond their keep. Indentured women were forbidden to marry, and if they became pregnant (as many did in a land where men outnumbered women by seven to one), the time lost from work that resulted was added to their terms of service. Servants lacked any incentive to work hard, whereas masters tended to "abuse their servantes . . . with intollerable oppression." In this clash of wills the advantage lay with the master; servants lacked full political and civil rights, and masters could administer physical punishment and otherwise abuse them. An indenture, however, was a contract binding on both parties; servants could and did sue when planters failed to fulfill their parts of the bargain, and surviving court records suggest that they fared reasonably well when they did so.

Servants who completed their years of labor became free. Usually the ex-servant was entitled to an "outfit" (a suit of clothes, some farm tools, seed, and perhaps a gun). Custom varied from colony to colony and according to the bargain struck by the two parties when the indenture was signed. In the Carolinas and in Pennsylvania, for example, servants received small grants of land from the colony when their service was completed.

The headrights issued when indentured servants entered the colonies went to whoever paid their passage, not to the servants. Thus the system gave a double reward to capital—land and labor for the price of the labor alone. Since well over half of the white settlers of the southern colonies came as indentured servants, the effect on the structure of southern society was enormous.

Most servants eventually became landowners, but with the passage of time their lot became harder. The best land belonged to the large planters, and low tobacco prices and high local taxes combined to keep many ex-servants in dire poverty. Some were forced to become "squatters" on land along the fringes of settlement that no one had yet claimed. Squatting often led to trouble; eventually someone was sure to turn up with a legal title to the squatter's homestead. Squatters then demanded what they called squatters' rights, the privilege of buying the land from the legal owner without paying for the improvements they had made on it. This led to arguments and lawsuits and sometimes to violence.

By the 1670s conflicts between Virginians who owned choice land and ex-servants on the outer edge of settlement brought the colony to the brink of class warfare. The costs of meeting the region's ever-growing need for labor with indentured servants were becoming prohibitive. Some other solution was needed.

The Resort to Slavery

The first African blacks brought to English North America arrived on a Dutch ship and were sold at Jamestown in 1619. Early records are vague and incomplete, so it is not possible to say whether these Africans were treated as slaves or freed after a period of years like indentured servants. What is certain is that by about 1640 *some* blacks were slaves (a few, with equal certainty, were free) and that by the 1660s local statutes had firmly established the institution in Virginia and Maryland.

Whether slavery produced race prejudice in America or prejudice slavery is a hotly debated, important, and difficult-to-answer question. Most 17th-century Europeans were prejudiced against Africans; the usual reasons that led them to look down on "heathens" with customs other than their own were in the case of Africans greatly reinforced by their blackness, which the English equated with dirt, the devil, danger, and death. "Black is the Colour of Night, Frightful, Dark and Horrid," a popular disquisition of 1704 proclaimed.

Yet the English knew that the Portuguese and Spaniards had enslaved blacks—*negro* is Spanish for "black." Since the English adopted the word as a name for Africans, their treatment of Africans in the New World may also have derived from the Spanish, which suggests that they treated the first blacks in their colonies as slaves from the start.

Probably the Africans' blackness lay at the root of the tragedy. Winthrop D. Jordan, whose research has added enormously to our understanding of the question, has stressed the process by which prejudice and existing enslavement interacted as both cause and effect, bringing about the total debasement of the African. With specific reference to the Chesapeake region, Jordan writes

> The concept of Negro slavery was neither borrowed from foreigners, nor extracted from books, nor invented out of whole cloth, nor extrapolated for servitude, nor generated by English reaction to Negroes

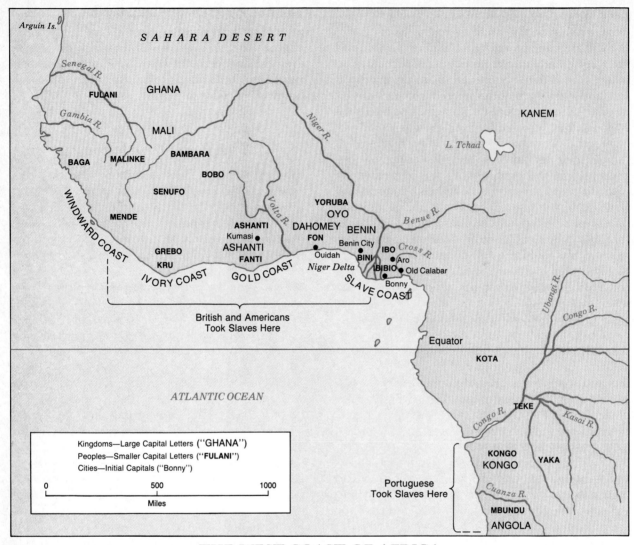

THE WEST COAST OF AFRICA

as such, nor necessitated by the exigencies of the New World. Not any one of these made the Negro a slave, *but all.*

Slavery soon spread throughout the colonies. As early as 1626 there were 11 slaves in New Netherland, and when the English conquered that colony in 1664 there were 700 slaves in a population of about 8,000. The Massachusetts Body of Liberties of 1641—strange title—provided that "there shall never be any bond-slavery . . . amongst us; unlesse it be lawful captives taken in just warrs [i.e., Indians]

and such strangers as willingly sell themselves, or *are solde* to us." However, relatively few blacks were imported until late in the 17th century, even in the southern colonies. In 1650 there were only 300 blacks in Virginia and as late as 1670 no more than 2,000.

White servants were much more highly prized. The African, after all, was utterly alien to both the European and the American ways of life. In a country starved for capital, the cost of slaves—roughly five times that of servants—was another disadvantage. In 1664 the governor of Maryland informed

TO BE SOLD on board the Ship *Bance-Island*, on tuesday the 6th of *May* next, at *Asbley-Ferry*; a choice cargo of about 250 fine healthy

NEGROES,

just arrived from the Windward & Rice Coast. —The utmost care has already been taken, and shall be continued, to keep them free from the least danger of being infected with the SMALL-POX, no boat having been on board, and all other communication with people from *Charles-Town* prevented.

Austin, Laurens, & Appleby.

N. B. Full one Half of the above Negroes have had the SMALL-POX in their own Country.

Announcements for the sale of newly imported slaves were plentiful in colonial newspapers—notice the claim that these captives are free from smallpox, an important selling point.

Lord Baltimore that local planters would use more "neigros" "if our purses would endure it."

For these reasons, so long as white servants could be had in sufficient numbers, there were few slaves in the Chesapeake and those that were there generally worked alongside white servants and shared roughly the same food, clothing, and quarters.

In the 1670s the flow of new servants slackened, the result of improving economic conditions in England and the competition of other colonies for servants. At the same time, the formation of the Royal African Company (1672) made slaves more readily available. Then in 1689 a war in Europe cut off a principal market for tobacco, causing the price to fall and thus making migration to the colonies less attractive. The indenture system began to give way to slavery as the "permanent" solution to the region's chronic need for labor. An additional inducement causing planters and politicians to switch was the recognition that, unlike white servants, black slaves (and their offspring) would be forever barred from competing with whites for land or political power.

"Their Darling Tobacco"

Labor and land made agriculture possible, but it was necessary to find a market for American crops in the Old World if the colonists were to enjoy anything but the crudest sort of existence. They could not begin to manufacture all the articles they required; to obtain from England such items as plows and muskets and books and chinaware, they had to have cash crops, what their English creditors called "merchantable commodities." Here, at least, fortune favored the Chesapeake.

The founders of Virginia tried to produce all sorts of things that were needed in the old country: grapes and silk in particular, indigo, cotton, oranges, olives, sugar, and many other plants. But it was tobacco, unwanted, even strongly opposed at first, that became for farmers on both sides of Chesapeake Bay "their darling."

Tobacco was unknown in Europe until Spanish explorers brought it back from the West Indies. It was not common in England until the time of Sir Walter Raleigh. Then it quickly proved irresistible to thousands of devotees.

At first the London Company discouraged its colonists from growing tobacco. Since it clearly contained some habit-forming drug, many people opposed its use. King James I wrote a pamphlet attacking the weed, in which, among other things, he anticipated the findings of modern cancer researchers by saying that smoking was a "vile and stinking" habit "dangerous to the Lungs." But English smokers and partakers of snuff ignored their king, and the Virginians ignored their company. By 1617 a pound of tobacco was worth more than 5 shillings in London. Company and Crown then changed their tune, granting the colonists a monopoly and encouraging them in every way.

Unlike wheat, which required expensive plows and oxen to clear the land and prepare the soil, tobacco plants could be set on semicleared land and cultivated with a simple hoe. Tobacco required lots of human labor, but a single laborer working 2 or 3 acres could produce as much as 1,200 pounds of cured tobacco, which, in a good year, yielded a profit of more than 200 percent. This being the case, production in America leaped from 2,500 pounds in 1616 to nearly 30 million pounds in the late 17th century, or roughly 400 pounds of tobacco for every man, woman, and child in the Chesapeake colonies.

The tidewater region was blessed with many navigable rivers, and the planters spread along their banks, giving the Chesapeake a shabby, helter-skelter character of rough habitations and growing tobacco, mostly planted in stump-littered fields, surrounded by fallow land and thickets interspersed with dense forest. There were no towns and almost no roads. English ships made their way up the rivers from farm to farm, gathering the tobacco at each planter's wharf. The vessels also served as general stores of a sort where planters could exchange tobacco for everything from cloth, shoes, tools, salt, and nails to such exotic items as tea, coffee, chocolate, and spices.

However, the tremendous expansion of the supply of tobacco caused the price to plummet in the last decades of the 17th century. This did not stop the expansion of the tobacco colonies, but it did alter the structure of their society. Small farmers found it more difficult to make a decent living. At the same time, men with capital and individuals with political influence were engrossing large tracts of land. If well managed, a big plantation gave its owner important competitive advantages over the small farmer. Tobacco was notorious for the speed with which it exhausted the fertility of the soil. Growers with a lot of land could shift frequently to new fields within their holdings, allowing the old fields to lie fallow and thus maintain high yields, but the only option that small farmers had when their land gave out was to sell it for whatever it would bring, pack up, and move to unsettled land on the frontier. To do that in the 1670s was to risk trouble with properly indignant Indians. It might also violate colonial laws designed to slow westward migration and limit tobacco production—not that either was about to stop settlement.

Bacon's Rebellion

Chesapeake settlers showed little respect for constituted authority, partly because most people lived on isolated plantations and partly because the government in London was usually ignorant of their needs and relatively powerless to control them. The first Virginians often ignored directives of the London Company, and early Marylanders regularly disputed the right of the Calverts' agents to direct the affairs of the proprietorship. The most serious challenge took place in Virginia in 1676. Planters in the outlying counties had many reasons for disliking the officials in Jamestown who ran the colony. The royal governor, Sir William Berkeley, and his "Green Spring" faction (the organization took its name from the governor's plantation, where the leaders customarily met) had ruled Virginia for more than 30 years. Outsiders resented the way Berkeley and his henchmen used their offices to line their pockets. They also resented their social pretensions, for Green Springers made no effort to conceal their opinion, which had considerable basis in fact, that western planters were a crude and vulgar lot.

Early in 1676 planters on the western edge of settlement, always looking for excuses to grab land by doing away with the Indians who owned it, asked Berkeley to authorize an expedition against Indians who had been attacking nearby plantations. Berkeley refused. The planters then took matters into their own hands. Their leader, Nathaniel Bacon, was (and remains today) a controversial figure. His foes described him as extremely ambitious and possessed "of a most imperious and dangerous hidden Pride of heart." But even his sharpest critics conceded that he was "of an inviting aspect and powerful elocution" and well qualified "to lead a giddy and unthinking multitude."

When Berkeley refused to authorize him to attack the Indians, Bacon promptly showed himself only too willing to lead that multitude not only against Indians but even against the governor. Without permission, he raised an army of 500 men, described by the Berkeley faction as "rabble of the basest sort." Berkeley then declared him a traitor.

Several months of monumental confusion followed. Bacon murdered some peaceful Indians, marched on Jamestown and forced Berkeley to legitimize his authority, then headed west again to kill more Indians. In September he returned to Jamestown and burned it to the ground. Berkeley fled across Chesapeake Bay to the Eastern Shore. The Baconites plundered the estates of some of the Green Spring faction. But a few weeks after the destruction of Jamestown, Bacon came down with a "violent flux"—probably a bad case of dysentery—and he died. Soon thereafter an English naval squadron arrived with enough soldiers to restore order. Bacon's Rebellion was over.

On the surface, the uprising changed nothing. No sudden shift in political power occurred. Indeed, Bacon had not sought to change either the political

Sir William Berkeley looks every inch the autocrat in this portrait, a copy of one painted by Sir Peter Lely. After Bacon's death, the governor took his revenge and had 23 rebels hanged. Said King Charles II: "The old fool has killed more people in that naked country than I have done for the murder of my father."

system or the social and economic structure of the colony. But if the rebellion did not change anything specifically, nothing was ever again quite the same after it ended. With seeming impartiality, the Baconites had warred against Indians and against other planters. In retrospect, we might wonder which was the real enemy of anyone interested in growing tobacco. Surely Baconite and Green Springer had no differences that could not be compromised. And their common interest extended beyond the question of how to deal with Indians. "For men bent on the maximum exploitation of labor," the historian Edmund S. Morgan has written, "the implication should have been clear."

There is every reason to think that it was clear. In the quarter century following Bacon's Rebellion, the Chesapeake region, for the reasons just explained, became committed to black slavery. Large differences in the wealth and life-styles of growers

of tobacco resulted. The few who succeeded in accumulating 20 or more slaves and enough land to keep them occupied grew richer. The majority either grew poorer or at best had to struggle to hold their own.

More important, Bacon's Rebellion sealed an implicit contract between the inhabitants of the "great houses" and those who lived in more modest lodgings: Southern whites might differ greatly in wealth and influence, but they stood as one and forever behind the principle that blacks must have neither. This was the basis—the price—of the harmony and prosperity achieved by those who survived "seasoning" in the Chesapeake colonies.

The Carolinas: "More Like a Negro Country"

The English and, in increasing proportions after 1700, the Scotch-Irish settlers of the tidewater parts of the Carolinas turned to agriculture as enthusiastically as their Chesapeake neighbors had. In substantial sections of what became North Carolina, tobacco flourished. In South Carolina, after two decades in which furs and cereals were the chief products, Madagascar rice was introduced in the low-lying coastal areas in 1696. It quickly proved its worth as a cash crop. By 1700 almost 100,000 pounds were being exported annually; by the eve of the Revolution, rice exports from South Carolina and Georgia exceeded 65 million pounds a year.

Rice culture required water for flooding the fields. At first freshwater swamps were adapted to the crop, but by the middle of the 18th century the chief rice fields lay along the tidal rivers and inlets. Dikes and floodgates allowed fresh water to flow across the fields with the rising tide; when the tide fell, the gates closed automatically to keep the water in. The process was reversed when it was necessary to drain the land. Then the water ran out as the tide ebbed, and the pressure of the next flood pushed the gates shut.

In the 1740s another cash crop, indigo, was introduced in South Carolina by Eliza Lucas. Indigo did not compete with rice for either land or labor. It prospered on high ground and needed care in seasons when the slaves were not busy in the rice paddies. The British were delighted to have a new source of indigo because the blue dye was important in their woolens industry. Parliament quickly placed a bounty on it to stimulate production.

The production of tobacco, rice, and indigo, along with furs and forest products such as tar and resin, meant that the southern colonies had no difficulty in obtaining manufactured articles from abroad. Planters dealt with agents in England and Scotland, called factors, who managed the sale of their crops, filled their orders for manufactures, and supplied them with credit. This was a great convenience but not necessarily an advantage, for it prevented the development of a diversified economy. Throughout the colonial era, while small-scale manufacturing developed rapidly in the north, it was stillborn in the south.

Reliance on European middlemen also retarded the development of urban life. Until the rise of Baltimore in the 1750s, Charleston was the only city of importance in the south, but it never rivaled Boston, New York, or Philadelphia, despite its rich export trade and fine harbor.

On the South Carolina rice plantations, slave labor predominated from the beginning, for free workers would not submit to the backbreaking and unhealthy regimen. The first quarter of the 18th century saw an enormous influx of Africans into all the southern colonies. By 1730 roughly three out of every ten people south of Pennsylvania were black, and in South Carolina the blacks were in the majority. "Carolina," remarked a newcomer in 1737, "looks more like a negro country than like a country settled by white people."

Given the existing race prejudice and the degrading impact of slavery, this demographic change had an enormous impact on life wherever blacks were concentrated. In each colony, regulations governing the behavior of blacks, both free and slave, increased in severity as the density of the black population increased. The South Carolina Negro Act of 1740 denied slaves "freedom of movement, freedom of assembly, freedom to raise (their own) food, to earn money, to learn to read English." The blacks had no civil rights under any of these codes, and punishments were sickeningly severe. Whipping was common for minor offenses, death by hanging or by being burned alive for serious crimes. Blacks were sometimes castrated for sexual offenses—even for lewd talk about white women—or for repeated attempts to escape.

That blacks resented slavery goes without saying, but since slavery did not mean the same thing to all of them, their reactions to it varied. Throughout the 18th century a constant stream of new slaves was arriving from Africa. These "outlandish" blacks tended to respond differently than American-born slaves. Among the latter, field hands experienced a different kind of slavery than household servants, and slave artisans faced still another set of circumstances. In short, the slaves' places in society influenced their behavior.

The master race sought to acculturate the slaves in order to make them more efficient workers. A slave who could understand English was easier to order about; one who could handle farm tools or wait on table was more useful than one who could not; a carpenter or a mason was more valuable still. But acculturation increased the slave's independence and mobility, and this posed problems. Field hands seldom tried to escape; they expressed their dissatisfactions by pilferage and petty sabotage, by laziness, or by feigning stupidity. Most runaways were artisans who hoped to "pass" as free in a nearby town. It was one of the many paradoxes of slavery that the more valuable a slave became, the harder that slave was to control.

Yet few runaway slaves became rebels. Indeed, organized slave rebellions were rare, and though individual assaults by blacks on whites were common enough, personal violence was also common among whites, then and throughout American history. But the masters had sound reasons for fearing their slaves; the particular viciousness of the system lay in the fact that oppression bred resentment, which in turn produced still greater oppression.

What is superficially astonishing is that the whites—absolute masters of their human property—grossly exaggerated the danger of slave revolts. They pictured the black as a kind of malevolent ogre, powerful, bestial, and lascivious, a caldron of animal emotions that had to be restrained at any cost. Probably the characteristics they attributed to the blacks were really projections of their own passions. The most striking illustration of this process was the universal white fear of the "mongrelization" of the race: If blacks were free, they would breed with whites. Yet in practice the interbreeding, which indeed took place, was almost exclusively the result of white men using their power as masters to have sexual relations with female slaves.

Thus the "peculiar institution" was fastened upon America with economic, social, and psychic

An idealized view of slave life shows the black family when work for the master is finished, catching their own fish, harvesting fruits from their own garden plot. In reality most slaves had time to pursue such tasks only at the end of an exhausting day in the master's fields.

barbs. Ignorance and self-interest, lust for gold and for the flesh, primitive prejudices and complex social and legal ties all combined to convince the whites that black slavery was not so much a good thing as a fact of life. A few isolated reformers, mostly Quakers, attacked the institution on the religious ground that all human beings are equal before God: "Christ dyed for all, both *Turks, Barbarians, Tartarians,* and *Ethyopians.*" Yet a few Quakers owned slaves, and even the majority who did not usually succumbed to color prejudice. Blackness was a defect, but it was no justification for enslavement, they argued. And they attracted little attention anywhere—none in areas where slavery was important.

Home and Family in the Colonial South

Life for all but the most affluent planters was by modern standards crude and uncomfortable. Houses were mostly one- and two-room affairs. Professor Gloria L. Main describes them as "small, dark, crowded . . . crudely built of green wood, unpainted and unadorned," and another colonial historian, David Freeman Hawke, employs the word *hovel.* Furniture and utensils were sparse and crudely made. Chairs were rare; if a family possessed one it was reserved for the head of the house (hence *chairman,* the man in the chair). People sat, slept, and ate on benches and planks. The typical dining table (the term itself was not in use) was made of two boards nailed together and covered, if at all, with a "board cloth." Toilets and plumbing of any kind were unknown; even chamber pots were beyond the reach of poorer families.

Work clothes—and few ordinary people possessed anything else—were equally crude, and since soap was expensive, they were rarely washed and therefore foul-smelling and often infested with vermin. Food was plentiful but nearly always prepared without art. Corn, served as bread, hominy, pancakes, and in various other forms, was the chief staple. But there was plenty of beef and pork (as well as a profusion of game), usually boiled in a pot along with various vegetables over an open fire.

Women (even indentured ones) rarely worked in the fields, but every aspect of household maintenance was their responsibility, including tending to farm animals, making butter and cheese, pickling and preserving, spinning and sewing, and, of course, caring for the children, which often involved orphans and stepchildren because of the fragility of life in the region. For exceptional women, the labor shortage created opportunities to develop their talents. Some managed large plantations; Eliza Lucas ran three in South Carolina for her absent father while still in her teens, and after the death of her husband, Charles Pinckney, she successfully managed his large properties.

Because of the high death rate, second and third marriages were common. Despite the likelihood that a widow would soon remarry, studies of wills reveal that most southern men took special pains to provide for their wives and expressed confidence in their ability to manage the inheritance effectively. The effects of the deaths of so many parents on children are hard to gauge but apparently were not often psychologically damaging, no doubt because they were so common and because someone could always be found to take in and care for an orphan.

Southern children were not usually subjected to the strict discipline that children in New England were (see page 48), but the difference was relative. Formal schooling for ordinary youngsters was nonexistent; the isolated rural character of society made the maintenance of schools prohibitively expensive. Whatever most children learned, they got from their parents or other relatives. A large percentage of

A southern plantation of the "middling" sort was this Virginia property, Rippon Lodge. The steeply pitched roofs and tall chimneys show English influence. Like almost all colonial homes, no matter how grand, this one lacked screens or nets to keep out the numerous flies and mosquitoes.

southerners were illiterate. As in other regions, children were put to some kind of useful work at an early age.

More well-to-do, "middling" planters had different, more comfortable life-styles, but they still lived in relatively crowded quarters, having perhaps three rooms to house a family of four or five and a couple of servants. To sleep between sheets in a soft bed under blankets and quilts was luxury indeed in that world. Food in greater variety and abundance was another indication of a higher standard of living, but cooking methods remained for such families rudimentary.

Until the early 18th century only a handful achieved real affluence. (The richest by far was Robert "King" Carter of Lancaster County, Virginia, who at the time of his death in 1732 owned 1,000 slaves and 300,000 acres.) That fortunate few, masters of several plantations and many slaves, lived in solid, two-story houses of six or more rooms, fur-

nished with English and other imported carpets, chairs, tables, wardrobes, chests, china, and silver. When the occasion warranted, the men wore fine broadcloth, the women the latest (or more likely the next-to-latest, for this was a provincial society) fashions. Some even sent their children abroad for schooling. The founding of the College of William and Mary in Williamsburg, Virginia, in 1696 was an effort to provide the region with its own institution of higher learning. However, staffing problems and insufficient funding kept William and Mary from offering much more than a grammar school education for decades.

These large planters also controlled politics; they held the commissions in the militia, the county judgeships, and the seats in the colonial legislatures. The control that these "leading families" exercised over their neighbors was not entirely unearned, and it was not, of course, total. They were, in general, responsible leaders, and ordinary planters deferred to them in most instances as a matter of course. Custom required that they throw open their houses and serve copious amounts of punch and rum to ordinary voters when election time rolled around. Such gatherings served to acknowledge the representative nature of the system.

Their scattered existence meant that no matter what their station, southern families led relatively isolated lives. Churches, which might be expected to serve as centers of community life, were few and far between. By the middle of the 18th century, the Anglican church was the official religion, its ministers supported by public funds. The Virginia assembly had made attendance at Anglican services compulsory in 1619. In Maryland, Lord Baltimore's Toleration Act did not survive the invasion of the colony by militant Puritans. It was repealed in 1654, reenacted in 1657, then repealed again in 1692 when the Anglican church was established. But for all its legal standing, the Anglican church was not a very powerful force in the south. Most of the ministers the bishop of London sent to America were second-rate men unable to obtain a decent living at home. If they had intellectual or spiritual ambitions when they arrived, their rural circumstances provided little opportunity to develop them. Most people, regardless of their particular faith, had few opportunities to attend formal services. One result was that marriages tended to become civil rather than religious ceremonies.

Social events of any kind, such as the aforementioned politicking, were great occasions. Births, marriages, and especially funerals called for much feasting; if there were neither heirs nor debts to satisfy, which was not unusual in the early days, it was possible to consume the entire contents of a modest estate in celebrating the deceased's passing. (At one Maryland funeral the guests were provided with 55 gallons of an alcoholic concoction composed of brandy, cider, and sugar.)

Other forms of entertainment and relaxation included hunting and fishing, cockfights, and horse racing. Horses were widely owned, used for getting from place to place rather than as draft animals, since tobacco was transported by water and cultivated with hoes, not plows.

However, southern planters, even the most successful, were hardworking, conserving types, not idle grandees concerned chiefly with conspicuous display. The vast, undeveloped country encouraged them to produce and then invest their savings in more production. William Byrd II (1674–1744), one of the richest men in Virginia, habitually rose before dawn. Besides his tobacco fields, he operated a sawmill and a gristmill, prospected for iron and coal, and engaged in the Indian trade. Of another wealthy planter, Robert Beverly, a visitor wrote: "Though rich, he has nothing in or about his house but what is necessary. . . . He lives upon the product of his land."

Georgia and the Back Country

West of the fall line of the rivers that irrigated tidewater Chesapeake and Carolina lay the back country, or "back parts." This region included the Great Valley of Virginia, the Piedmont, and what became the final English colony to be founded in North America, Georgia.

The circumstances of the founding of Georgia were most unusual. A group of London philanthropists concerned over the plight of honest persons imprisoned for debt conceived of settling these unfortunates in the New World, where they might make a fresh start. (Here is striking evidence that Europeans were still beguiled by the prospect of regenerating their society in the New World. All told, about 50,000 British convicts were "transported" to America in the colonial period, partly to get rid of "undesirables" but partly for humane reasons.) They petitioned for a grant south of the Carolinas, and the government, eager to create a buffer between South Carolina and the hostile Spanish in Florida, readily granted a charter (1732) to a group of "trustees" who were to manage the colony without profit to themselves for a period of 21 years.

In 1733 the leader of the trustees, James Oglethorpe, founded Savannah. Oglethorpe was a complicated person, vain, high-handed, and straitlaced, yet hardworking and idealistic. He hoped to people the colony with sober and industrious yeoman farmers. Land grants were limited to 50 acres and made nontransferable. To ensure sobriety, rum and other "Spirits and Strong Waters" were banned. To guarantee that the colonists would have to work hard, the entry of "any Black . . . Negroe" was prohibited. The Indian trade was to be strictly regulated in the interest of fair dealing.

Oglethorpe intended that silk, wine, and olive oil be the main products—none of which, unfortunately, could be profitably produced in Georgia.

His noble intentions came to naught. The settlers swiftly found ways to circumvent all restrictions. Rum flowed, slaves were imported, and large land-holdings were amassed. Georgia developed an economy much like South Carolina's. In 1752 the trustees, disillusioned, abandoned their responsibilities. Georgia then became a royal colony.

It was only about this time that settlers in any numbers penetrated the rest of the southern back country. So long as cheap land remained available closer to the coast and Indians along the frontier remained a threat, only the most daring and foot-loose hunters or fur traders lived far inland. But once settlement began, it began with a rush. Chief among those making the trek were Scotch-Irish and German immigrants. By 1770 the back country contained about 250,000 settlers, 10 percent of the population of the colonies.

This internal migration did not proceed altogether peacefully. In 1771 a pitched battle was fought in North Carolina between frontiersmen calling themselves Regulators and 1,200 troops dispatched by the Carolina assembly, which was dominated by low-country interests. The Regulators were protesting their lack of representation in the assembly. They were crushed and their leaders executed. This was neither the last nor the bloodiest sectional conflict in American history.

Salem was an early settlement in the Piedmont region of North Carolina, founded in the 1760s by Moravians. It boasted brick dwellings more substantial than the usual frontier cabins. Early in the 20th century Salem was united with nearby Winston to form the city of Winston-Salem.

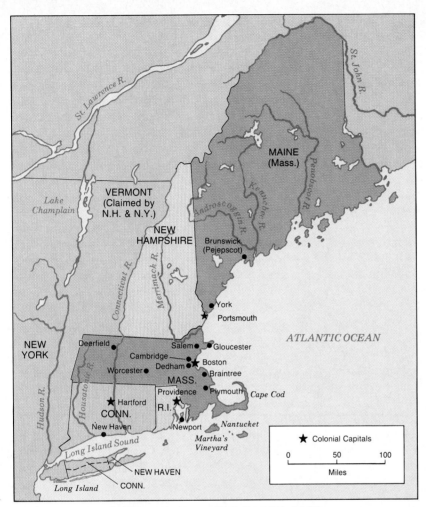

COLONIAL NEW ENGLAND

Colonial New England: A Covenanted People

If survival in the Chesapeake required junking many European notions about social arrangements and submitting to the dictates of the wilderness, was this also true in Massachusetts and Connecticut? Ultimately it probably was, but in the early going, Puritan ideas certainly fought the New England reality to a draw.

Boston is located slightly more than 5° latitude north of Jamestown and almost 10° north of Charleston. Like other early New England towns and unlike these southern ones, Boston had a dependable water supply. The surrounding patchwork of forest, pond, dunes, and tide marsh was much more open than the malaria-infested terrain of the tidewater and low-country south. These differences alone made New England a much healthier habitat for settlers. "Seasoning" proceeded so imperceptibly as almost to escape notice. One consequence was that New Englanders escaped the "agues and fevers" that beset settlers to the south, leaving them free to attend to their spiritual, economic, and social well-being.

The Stamp of Puritanism: Family Bonds

New England's Puritans were set apart from other English settlers by how much—and how long—they lived out of their baggage. The supplies the first arrivals brought with them eased their adjustment, as did the wherewithal of later, equally heavily laden arrivals. The Puritans' baggage, however, included besides pots and pans, saws and shovels, a plan for the proper ordering of society.

At the center of the plan was a covenant, or agreement, to ensure the upright behavior of all who took up residence. They sought to provide what John Winthrop described to the passengers on the *Arbella* as the two imperatives of human existence: "that every man might have need of other, and from hence they might be all knitt more nearly together in the Bond of brotherly affection."

The first and most important covenant governing Puritan behavior was that binding family members. The family's authority was backed by the Fifth Commandment: "Honor thy father and thy mother, that thy days may be long upon the land." In a properly ordered Puritan family, as elsewhere in the colonies, authority flowed downward. Sociologists describe such a family as nuclear and patriarchal; each household contained one family, and in it, the father was boss. His principal responsibilities consisted of providing for the physical welfare of all members of the household, including any servants, and making sure that they behaved properly, in private and in public. Economic dealings between the family and other parties were also transacted by him, even when the property involved had been owned by his wife prior to their marriage.

The Reverend John Cotton's outline of a woman's responsibilities clearly establishes her subordinate position: She should keep house, educate the children, and improve "what is got by the industry of the man." Cotton, please recall, had been Anne Hutchinson's favorite minister! The poet Anne Bradstreet reduced the functions of a Puritan woman to two: "loving Mother and obedient Wife." Colonial New England, and the southern colonies as well, did have their female blacksmiths, silversmiths, shipwrights, gunsmiths, and butchers as well as shopkeepers and teachers. Such early examples of domestic "liberation," however, were mostly widows and the wives of incapacitated husbands. Even so, most widows, especially young ones, quickly remarried. According to the historian Laurel Thatcher Ulrich, colonial women generally, and New England women in particular, "were by definition basically domestic."

Women and Children

Dealings with neighbors and relatives and involvement in church activities marked the outer limits of the social range of most Puritan women. Care of the children was a full-time occupation when broods of 12 or 14 were more common than those of 1 or 2. Fewer children died in New England than in the Chesapeake or in Europe, though few families escaped a miscarriage or a child's death along the way. Childbearing and motherhood, therefore, likely extended over two decades of a woman's life. Meanwhile, she also functioned as the chief operating officer of the household. Cooking, baking, sewing, and supervising servants, as well as mastering such arcane knowledge as the chemistry needed to make cheese from milk, bacon from pork, and beer from malt, all fell to her. These jobs were physically demanding, though not so debilitating as to prevent large numbers of New England wives from seeing one or more husbands off to the hereafter.

As Puritan social standards required husbands to rule over wives, so parents ruled over children. As in the South, the virtue most insistently impressed upon New England children was obedience. Refusal to submit to parental direction was disturbing in itself and for what it implied about the child's eternal condition. Cotton Mather's advice, "Better whipt, than damned," graced many a New England rod taken up by a parent in anger, from there to be rapidly transferred to the afterparts of misbehaving offspring.

Besides the generous use of corporal punishment, chores kept children out of mischief. By age 6 or 7, girls were set to sewing and helping with housework and boys put to work outdoors. When a few years older, a child might be sent to live with another family to take up the duties of a servant or apprentice. Discussing a later period, the historian Mary P. Ryan writes: "Parents conceived of their children as their own flesh, blood, and labor supply." Only when well into adulthood would children emerge from under parental control.

Such practices, particularly when set beside portraits of early New England families, which depict toddlers as somber-faced miniature adults wearing clothes indistinguishable from those of their parents, convey the impression that Puritans hustled their young through childhood with as little love as possible. New Englanders harbored no illusions.

New England children like David, Joanna, and Abigail Mason (painted by an unknown artist about 1670) were expected to emulate adults in their chores and their appearance. Nevertheless, indications are that they were cherished by their parents in a way closer to modern family love than what their European contemporaries experienced.

"Innocent vipers" is how one minister described children, having 14 of his own to submit as evidence. Anne Bradstreet, mother of eight, characterized one as harboring "a perverse will, a love of what's forbid / a serpent's sting in pleasing face lay hid."

Yet for all their acceptance of the Calvinist doctrine of infant damnation, Puritan parents were not indifferent to the fate of their children. "I do hope," Cotton Mather confessed at the burial of one of the eight children he lost before the age of 2, "that when my children are gone they are not lost; but carried unto the Heavenly Feast with Abraham." Even the dour Michael Wigglesworth assigned children who died in infancy "the easiest room in hell."

Population growth reinforced Puritan ideas about the family. With the end of the Great Migration in the early 1640s, immigration virtually ceased. Thereafter growth was entirely due to the region's extraordinarily high birthrate (50 births for every 1,000 population, more than three times the

rate today) and strikingly low mortality rate (about 20 per 1,000). This resulted in a population much more evenly distributed by age and sex than that in the south. The fact that most New England women married in their early twenties rather than their late teens suggests that the demand for women matched the supply. Demographic realities joined with Puritan expectations to create a society of nuclear families distinct to the region.

Visible Saints and Others

When it came to religion, Puritans believed that church membership ought not to be a presumptive right, as in Catholic countries or in Anglican England, but the joint decision of a would-be member and those already in the church.

Obvious sinners and people ignorant of Christian doctrine were rejected out of hand. But what of "outwardly just" applicants who lacked compelling evidence that they had experienced God's saving grace? In the late 1630s, with the Great Migration in full swing and new arrivals clamoring for admission to the churches, such "merit-mongers" were excluded, thereby limiting church membership to the community's "visible saints." A decade later, the Great Migration over and applications down, some of the saints began to have second thoughts.

By the early 1650s fewer than half of all New England adults were church members, and so exacting had the examination for membership become, particularly in churches where the minister and elders outdid each other in the ferocity of their questioning, that most young people refused to submit themselves to such scrutiny. How these growing numbers of nonmembers could be compelled to attend church services was a problem ministers could not long defer. Meanwhile, the magistrates found it harder to defend the policy of not letting taxpayers vote because they were not church members. But what really forced reconsideration of the membership policy was the concerns of nonmember parents about the souls of their children, who could not be baptized.

At first the churches permitted baptism of the children of church members. Later, some biblical purists (including a Harvard president fired for insisting as much) came out against infant baptism altogether. But most early Puritans approved of the practice, which allowed them the hope that a child who died after receiving baptism might at least be spared Hell's hottest precincts. Since most of the first generation were church members, nearly all the second-generation New Englanders were baptized, whether they became church members or not. The problem began with the third generation, the offspring of parents who had been baptized but who did not become church members. By the mid-1650s it was clear that if nothing were done, soon a majority of the people would be living in a state of original sin. If that happened, how could Puritan values, and for that matter the churches themselves, remain the dominant force in New England life?

Fortunately, a way out was at hand. In 1657 an assembly of Massachusetts and Connecticut ministers recommended a form of intermediate church membership that would permit the baptism of people who were not visible saints. Five years later, some 80 ministers and laymen met at Boston's First Church to hammer out what came to be called the Half-Way Covenant. It provided limited (halfway) membership for any applicant not known to be a sinner who was willing to accept the provisions of the church covenant. They and their children could be baptized, but the sacrament of communion and a voice in church decision making were reserved for full members.

The General Court of Massachusetts promptly endorsed the recommendations of the Half-Way Synod and urged all the churches of the commonwealth to adopt them. Two years later it quietly extended the right to vote to halfway church members.

Opponents of the Half-Way Covenant argued that it reflected a slackening of religious fervor. Michael Wigglesworth gave poetic voice to these views in "God's Controversy with New England" and "The Day of Doom," both written in 1662.

Perry Miller, an authority on Puritan New England, argued that the early 1660s marked the beginning of the decline, or "declension," of the Puritan experiment. Some loss of religious intensity there may have been, but the rise in church memberships, the continuing prestige accorded ministers, and the lessening of intrachurch squabbling in the decades after the Half-Way Covenant was adopted suggest that the secularization of New England society had a long way to go.

Democracies Without Democrats

Like the southern colonies, the governments of Massachusetts, Connecticut, Rhode Island, and New Hampshire derived their authority from charters granted by the Crown or Parliament. Except for rare fits of meddling London bureaucrats, they were largely left to their own devices where purely local interests were concerned. This typically involved maintaining order by regulating how people behaved.

According to Puritan theory, government was both a civil covenant, entered into by all who came within its jurisdiction, and the principal mechanism for policing the institutions on which the maintenance of the social order depended. When the Massachusetts and Connecticut general courts passed laws requiring church attendance, levying taxes for the support of the clergy, and banning Quakers from practicing their faith, they were acting as a "shield of the churches." When they provided the death penalty both for adultery and for blaspheming a parent, they were defending the integrity of families, the "nurseries of the commonwealth." When they set the price a laborer might charge for his services or even the amount of gold braid that servants might wear on their jackets, they believed they were enforcing the Puritan principle that people must accept their assigned stations in life.

Most of these laws went unnoticed in England. Those upholding the privileged position of the Congregational church, however, came under sharp attack from English Anglicans, Presbyterians, and Quakers. When the Massachusetts General Court condemned to death four stubborn Quakers who returned after being expelled from the colony, a royal order of 1662 forbade further executions.

Laws like these have prompted historians and Americans generally to characterize New England colonial legislation as socially repressive and personally invasive. Yet many of the laws remained in force through the colonial period without arousing much local opposition. Others, particularly those upholding religious discrimination or restricting economic activity, were repealed at the insistence of Parliament.

A healthy respect for the backsliding ways of humanity obliged New Englanders not to depend too much on provincial governments, whose jurisdiction extended over several thousand square miles. Almost of necessity, the primary responsibility for maintaining "Good Order and Peace" fell to the more than 500 towns of the region. These differed greatly in size and development. By the early 18th century the largest—Boston, Newport, and Portsmouth—were well along toward becoming urban centers. This was before "frontier" towns like Amherst, Kent, and Hanover had even been founded. Nonetheless, town life gave New England the distinctiveness it has still not wholly lost.

Dedham: A Typical Town

Dedham, Massachusetts, whose early history has been meticulously reconstructed by Kenneth Lockridge, illustrates how this worked. In 1634 the heads of 30 households in Watertown, already feeling crowded in that then two-year-old village, petitioned the General Court for a grant of land to establish a new town. A year later they became the proprietors of a 200-square-mile tract west of Watertown on the condition that they all move there, "gather" a church, and organize a town government. These "proprietors" then drew up a town covenant, which committed all who signed it to conduct themselves "according to that most perfect rule, the foundation wherof is everlasting love." Other clauses bound them to keep out the "contrary minded," to submit personal differences to the judgment of the town, and to conduct their business so as to create a "loving and comfortable society in our said town."

The covenant provided that town business be decided at semiannual town meetings, at which all male adults who had subscribed to the covenant could vote. At these meetings a representative to the General Court was to be elected and seven selectmen chosen to run the town between town meetings. In addition, matters relating to town lands were to be decided, taxes to pay the minister's salary set, and provisions for poor and incompetent people made.

The next century brought many changes to Dedham. Yet when the town's 1,200 residents celebrated its centenary in 1736, they were governing themselves much as their great-grandparents had. Looking back, they could only be struck by the continuities that shaped their lives.

But was colonial New England democratic? To be democratic, a government must at least offer those subject to its authority a voice in its operations. With the possible exception of the 1670s and 1680s, when a stiff property-holding requirement (£80 of taxable estate) was in effect in Massachusetts and Connecticut, most adult male New Englanders could vote. Compared with England or with the southern colonies, where blacks had no political rights, the New England governments were democratic.

Relatively few voters, however, bothered to participate in elections because most offices went uncontested. Furthermore, the men elected to office consistently came from the wealthiest and most established levels of the community. In Dedham, 5 percent of the adult males filled 60 percent of the town's positions. Even in Rhode Island, widely regarded as almost too democratic, Providence and Newport voters usually elected their wealthiest and longest-settled townsmen. Important families, such as the Otises of Barnstable, the Quincys of Braintree, and the Wolcotts of Windsor, had members serving as moderator of the town meeting or deputy to the General Court so often as to make these offices almost hereditary.

Ordinary voters tended to choose their "betters," and those they selected took the responsibilities of public office seriously. Together they created what one voter called "a speaking aristocracy in the face of a silent democracy."

The Dominion of New England

The most serious threat to these arrangements occurred in the 1680s. Following the execution of Charles I in 1649, England was ruled by one man, the Lord Protector, Oliver Cromwell. Cromwell's death in 1658 led to the restoration of the Stuart monarchy in the person of Charles II (1660–1685). During his reign and the abbreviated one of his brother, James II (1685–1688), the government sought to bring the colonies under effective royal control.

Massachusetts seemed in particular need of supervision. Accordingly, in 1684 its charter was annulled, and the colony, along with all those north of Pennsylvania, became part of the Dominion of New England, governed by Edmund Andros.

Andros arrived in Boston in late 1686 with orders to make the northern colonies, Massachusetts most of all, behave in ways consistent with their status as colonies. Specifically, he set out to abolish popular assemblies, to change the land-grant system so as to provide the king with quitrents, and to enforce religious toleration, particularly of Anglicans. The historian Stephen Saunders Webb has characterized the Dominion as designed to bring about the political and cultural "Anglicization" of New England. Andros, a professional soldier and administrator, scoffed at people who resisted his authority. "Knoweing no other government then their owne," he said, they "think it best, and are wedded to . . . it."

Fortunately for New Englanders so wedded, the Dominion fell victim two years later to yet another political turnabout in England, the Glorious Revolution. In 1688 Parliament decided it had had enough of the Catholic-leaning Stuarts and sent James II packing. In his place it installed a more resolutely Protestant Dutchman, William of Orange, and his wife, James's daughter Mary. When news of these events reached Boston in the spring of 1689, a force of more than 1,000 colonists led by a contingent of ministers seized Andros and lodged him in jail. Two years later Massachusetts was made a royal colony that also included Plymouth and Maine. As in all such colonies, the governor was appointed by the king. The new General Court was elected by property owners; church membership was no longer required for voting.

Crisis in Salem Village

Many New England towns resembled "peaceable kingdoms." But in some, tensions developed between generations when they ran out of land sufficient to support the grandchildren of the founders. Others allowed petty disputes to divide townspeople into rival camps. Still others seemed doomed to serious discord. Among these, Salem Village provides a singular example.

In 1666, families living in the rural outback of the thriving town of Salem petitioned the General Court for the right to establish their own church. Politically and economically, this was a questionable move and the Salem selectmen, fearing the loss of taxes, vigorously objected. But in 1672 the General Court authorized the establishment of a separate parish. In so doing the court put the 600-odd inhabitants of the village politically on their own as well.

Over the next 15 years three preachers came and went before, in 1689, one Samuel Parris became minister. He had spent 20 years in the Caribbean as a merchant and had taken up preaching only three years before coming to Salem Village. Accompanying him were his wife; a daughter, Betty; a niece, Abigail; and the family's West Indian slave, Tituba, who told fortunes and practiced magic on the side.

Parris proved as incapable of bringing peace to the feuding factions of Salem Village as his predecessors had. In January 1692 the church voted to dismiss him.

At this point Betty and Abigail, now 9 and 11, along with Ann Putnam, the 12-year-old daughter of their father's principal supporter, started "uttering foolish, ridiculous speeches which neither they themselves nor any others could make sense of." A doctor diagnosed the girls' ravings as the work of the "Evil Hand" and declared them bewitched.

But who had done the bewitching? The first persons accused were three women whose unsavory reputations and frightening appearances made them likely candidates. Sarah Good, a pauper with a nasty tongue, Sarah Osborne, a bedridden widow, and the slave Tituba, who had brought suspicion on herself by volunteering to bake a "witch cake," made of rye meal and the girls' urine. The cake should be fed to a dog, Tituba said. If the girls were truly afflicted, the dog would show signs of bewitchment!

The three women were brought before the local deputies to the General Court to determine whether they should be formally charged. As each was questioned, the girls went into contortions; "their arms, necks and backs turned this way and that way . . . their mouths stopped, their throats choaked, their limbs wracked and tormented." Tituba, likely impressed by the powers ascribed to her, promptly confessed to being a witch. Sarah Good and Sarah Osborne each claimed to be innocent, although Sarah Good expressed doubts about Sarah Osborne. All three were sent to jail on suspicion of witchcraft.

These proceedings triggered new accusations. By the end of April, 24 more people had been charged with practicing witchcraft, among them several prominent residents of the town of Salem.

These scenes from an English treatise on witches, devils, and other supernatural beings reflect common beliefs about what such creatures might do. Belief in witchcraft was widespread in Europe and America in the 17th century, but no other episode in the colonies matched the Salem crisis in severity. All convictions were eventually reversed—the last ones in 1957.

Officials in neighboring Andover, lacking their own "bewitched," called in the girls to help with their investigations. By May the hunt had extended to Maine and Boston and up the social ladder to some of the colony's most prominent citizens, including Lady Mary Phips, whose husband, William, had just been appointed governor.

By June, when Governor Phips convened a spe-

cial court consisting of members of his council, more than 150 persons (Lady Phips no longer among them) stood formally charged with practicing witchcraft. In the next four months the court found grounds for convicting 28 persons, most of them women. Five "confessed" and were spared; the rest were condemned to death. One woman won a reprieve because she was pregnant. Two others escaped. But 19 persons were hanged. The husband of a convicted witch refused to enter a plea when charged with being a "wizard." He was executed by having stones piled on him until he suffocated.

Because anyone who spoke in defense of the accused was in danger of being charged with witchcraft, hostile testimony dominated the proceedings. Even so, some brave souls did challenge both the procedures and the findings of the court. Finally, at the urging of the leading ministers of the commonwealth, Governor Phips adjourned the court and forbade any further executions.

No one involved in these gruesome proceedings escaped with reputation intact, but those whose reputations suffered most were the ministers. Among the clergy, only Increase Mather deserves any credit. He persuaded Phips to halt the executions, arguing that "it were better that ten witches should escape, than that one innocent person should be condemned."

The behavior of his son Cotton defies apology. It was not that Cotton Mather accepted the existence of witches—at the time everyone did, which suggests that Tituba was not the only person in Salem who practiced witchcraft—or even that Mather took such pride in being the resident expert on demonology. It was rather his vindictiveness. He insisted repeatedly that only the most "vigorous prosecution" could rid the commonwealth of its demonic afflictions. He even stood at the foot of the gallows bullying hesitant hangmen into doing "their duty."

"To Advance Learning"

Along with the farmers and artisans who settled in New England with their families during the Great Migration came nearly 150 university-trained colonists. Nearly all had studied divinity. Most of the older ones had started out as Anglican ministers. The younger ones despaired of securing pulpits in the England of King Charles and Bishop Laud. For both generations, New England held the promise of religious freedom and professional fulfillment.

These men became the first ministers in Massachusetts and Connecticut. In the late 1630s, churches were being founded at a rate of more than 15 a year. A brisk "seller's market" existed for would-be ministers. Larger churches began stockpiling candidates by hiring newly arrived Cambridge and Oxford graduates as assistants or teachers in anticipation of the retirement of their senior ministers. But what to do when as a 1643 promotional pamphlet, *New Englands First Fruits*, put it, "our present ministers shall lie in the dust"? More than any other factor, fear of leaving "an illiterate Ministry to the Churches" turned New Englanders early and resolutely to finding a way to "advance learning and perpetuate it to Posterity."

In 1636 the Massachusetts General Court appropriated £400 to found "a schoole or colledge." Two years later, just as the first freshmen gathered in Cambridge, John Harvard left the college £800 and his library. After a shaky start, during which students conducted a hunger strike against a sadistic and larcenous headmaster, Harvard settled into an annual pattern of admitting a dozen or so 14-year-old boys, stuffing their heads with four years of theology, logic, and mathematics, and then sending them out into the wider world of New England.

Immediately below Harvard on the educational ladder came the grammar schools, where boys spent seven years learning Latin and Greek "so far as they may be fitted for the Universitie." Boston founded the first, the Boston Latin School, in 1636. Massachusetts and Connecticut soon passed education acts that required all towns of any size to establish such schools. New Englanders hoped, as the preamble to the Massachusetts law of 1647 stated, to thwart "that old deluder, Satan," whose "chief object was to keep men from the knowledge of the Scriptures."

Not every New England town required to maintain a school actually did so. Towns that did often paid their teachers poorly. Only the most dedicated or otherwise unemployable Harvard graduates took up teaching as a career. Some parents kept their children at their chores rather than at school. Yet the cumulative effect of the Puritan community's educational institutions, the family and the church as well as the school, was impressive. Historians estimate that a majority of men in 17th-century New England could read and write and by the middle of the 18th century, the region was approaching universal male literacy. In Europe only Scotland and Sweden had achieved this happy state so early. Literacy among women also improved steadily, despite the almost total neglect of formal education for girls.

Spreading literacy created a thriving market for the printed word. Many of the first settlers brought impressive libraries with them, and large numbers of English books were imported throughout the colonial period. The first printing press in the English colonies was founded in Cambridge in 1638, and by 1700 Boston's many presses were producing a veritable avalanche of printed matter.

Most of these publications were reprints of sermons. Ministers required only the smallest encouragement from their congregations to send off last Sunday's remarks to the local printer. But if ministers exercised a near-monopoly of the printed word, they did not limit their output entirely to religious topics. They also produced modest amounts of history, poetry, reports of scientific investigations, and treatises on political theory.

By the early 18th century the intellectual life of New England had taken on a character different from and potentially at odds with the ideas of the first Puritans. In the 1690s Harvard acquired a reputation for encouraging religious toleration. According to orthodox Puritans, its graduates were unfit for the ministry and its professors were no longer interested in training young men for the clergy. In 1701 several Connecticut ministers, most of them Harvard graduates, founded a new "collegiate school" designed to uphold the Puritan values that Harvard seemed ready to abandon. The new college was named after its first English benefactor, Elihu Yale. It fulfilled its founders' hopes by sending more than half of its early graduates into the ministry. Nonetheless, as became all too clear at commencement ceremonies in 1722 when its president and six tutors announced themselves Anglicans, Yale quickly acquired purposes well beyond those assigned it by its creators.

The assumption that the clergy had the last word on learned matters, still operative at the time of the witchcraft episode, came under direct challenge in 1721. When a smallpox epidemic swept through Boston that summer, Cotton Mather, at the time the most prestigious clergyman in New England, recommended that the citizenry be inoculated. He

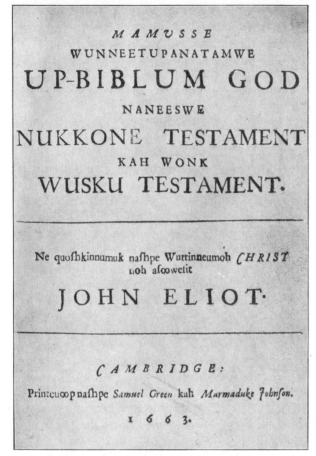

MAMUSSE
WUNNEETUPANATAMWE
UP-BIBLUM GOD
NANEESWE
NUKKONE TESTAMENT
KAH WONK
WUSKU TESTAMENT.

Ne quoſhkinnumuk naſhpe Wuttinneumoh CHRIST
noh aſooweſit

JOHN ELIOT·

CAMBRIDGE:
Printcuoopnaſhpe Samuel Green kah Marmaduke Johnſon.
1 6 6 3.

The Bible, translated into the Algonkian language of the Massachuset Indians, was the first book printed in the English colonies. Its translator, John Eliot, was known as the "Apostle to the Indians" for his missionary labors.

nalistic satire. He was soon joined in the enterprise by his 16-year-old brother, Benjamin. The younger Franklin's "Silence Dogood" essays were particularly infuriating to members of the Boston intellectual establishment. Franklin described Harvard as an institution where rich and lazy "blockheads . . . learn little more than how to carry themselves handsomely . . . and from whence they return, after Abundance of Trouble, as Blockheads as ever, only more proud and conceited."

James Franklin was jailed in 1722 for criticizing the General Court, and shortly thereafter the *New England Courant* went out of business. Meanwhile, Ben had left Boston for Philadelphia, where, as everyone knows, fame and fortune awaited him.

The Serpent Prosperity

Prior experience (and the need to eat) turned the first New Englanders to farming. They grew barley (used to make beer), rye, oats, green vegetables, and native crops such as potatoes, pumpkins, and, most important, Indian corn, or maize. Corn was easy to cultivate, and its yield per acre under rough frontier conditions exceeded that of other grains. It proved versatile and tasty when prepared in a variety of ways and also made excellent fodder for livestock. In the form of corn liquor, it was easy to store, to transport, and, in a pinch, to imbibe.

The colonists also had plenty of meat. They grazed cattle, sheep, and hogs on the common pastures or in the surrounding woodlands. Deer, along with turkey and other game birds, abounded. The Atlantic provided fish, especially cod, which was easily preserved by salting. In short, New Englanders ate an extremely nutritious diet. Abundant surpluses of firewood kept the winter cold from their doors. The combination contributed significantly to their good health and longevity.

The trouble was that virtually everything that New England farmers grew could be grown in Europe. The shortness of the growing season, the rocky and often hilly terrain, and careless methods of cultivation, which exhausted the soil, meant that farmers did not produce large surpluses. Thus while New Englanders could feed themselves without difficulty, they had relatively little to spare and no place to sell it.

The earliest Puritans accepted this economic

favored a method described in the *Transactions of the Royal Society* in England, of which, he informed the community, he was a member. But instead of accepting Mather's authority, his heretofore silent critics seized on his support of the then radical idea of inoculation to challenge both his motives and his professional credentials. They filled the unsigned contributor columns of New England's first newspaper, the *Boston Gazette,* and the *New England Courant,* which opened in the midst of the inoculation controversy, with their views.

The *Courant* was published by James Franklin, a printer just back from London, where he had been impressed by the commercial possibilities of jour-

marginality. The more pious positively welcomed it as insurance against "the serpent prosperity," which might otherwise deflect their spiritual mission into commercial opportunism. No prominent English merchants joined the Great Migration, though many were devoted Puritans and some had invested in the Massachusetts Bay Company. Settlers who turned to business upon arrival attracted suspicion, if not open hostility. Laws against usury (lending money at excessive rates) and profiteering in scarce commodities were in effect from the first days of settlement. In 1639 and again in 1643, Robert Keayne, a prosperous Boston merchant, was fined £200 by the General Court and admonished by his church for "taking above six-pence in the shilling profit; in some above eight-pence; and in some small things, above two for one." Keayne paid the fines and made "penitential acknowledgment" to his church, all the while convinced that "my goods and prices were cheap pennyworths."

Winthrop and the other early leaders resisted the argument of people like Keayne that business was a calling no less socially useful than the ministry or public office. Differences in wealth should be modest and should favor those to whom the community looked for leadership. In the Puritan scheme of things, since Governor Winthrop was a far more valuable member of the community than Robert Keayne, he should stand higher than Keayne in all rankings, wealth included. But Winthrop died in 1649 broke and in debt, whereas Keayne died three years later in sufficient prosperity (despite those stiff fines) to leave the town of Boston and Harvard College impressive benefactions. The gap between the Puritan ideal and the emerging reality was becoming embarrassingly clear.

A Merchant's World

Winthrop's generation had tried to minimize dependence on European-manufactured goods such as iron tools, glass, and cloth by producing their own. When their efforts failed, they next pinned their hopes on establishing direct trade links with European suppliers by offering the skins of beaver and such other fur-bearing animals as otter, muskrat, and mink. Several towns in the Connecticut Valley and New Hampshire became collection centers for these furs. Unfortunately, the beavers soon caught wind of what was going on and took off for points west and north. By the end of the 1650s the New Englanders were back where they had started. As one English merchant wrote, as trading partners "they have noe returns."

The colonists then turned to indirect trading schemes, in which merchants like Robert Keayne played a central role and from which they ultimately derived stature as well as wealth. The anticommercial bias of the early Puritans did not, however, vanish as quickly as the elusive beaver had. At the beginning of the 18th century a Boston minister could still tell his congregation this story with every confidence that they shared his belief that his colleague got the better of the Maine fisherman: Once, some years after Keayne's death, a minister in Maine was reminding his flock that "the main end of planting this wilderness" was religion. A prominent member of the congregation could not contain his disagreement. "Sir," he cried out, "you are mistaken. You think you are preaching to the people of the Bay; our main end was to catch fish."

Actually, fish, caught offshore on grounds that extended from Cape Cod to Newfoundland, provided merchants with their opening into the world of transatlantic commerce. In 1643 five New England vessels set out with their holds packed with fish, which they sold in Spain and the Canary Islands; they took payment in sherry and madeira, for which a market existed in England. One of these ships also had the dubious distinction of initiating New England into the business of trafficking in human beings when her captain took payment in African slaves, whom he subsequently sold in the West Indies.

This was the start of the famous "triangular trade," for once New England merchants discovered that access to English markets was no less feasible or less profitable for being indirect, they were in business for keeps. Only occasionally was the pattern truly triangular; more often, intermediate legs gave it a polygonal character. So long as their ships ended up with something that could be exchanged for English goods needed at home, it did not matter what they started out with or how many things they bought and sold along the way.

So maritime trade and the people who engaged in it became the driving force of the New England economy, important all out of proportion to the number of persons directly involved. Because those engaged congregated in Portsmouth, Salem, Boston, Newport, and New Haven, these towns soon differed greatly from towns in the interior. They were larger and growing faster, and fewer of their inhabitants were engaged in farming.

The largest and most thriving town was Boston, which by 1720 had become the commercial hub of the region. It had a population of more than 10,000; in the entire British Empire, only London and Bristol were larger. More than one-quarter of Boston's male adults either had invested in shipbuilding or were directly employed in maritime commerce. Ship captains and merchants held most of the public offices.

Beneath this emergent mercantile elite lived a stratum of artisans and small shopkeepers, and be-

neath these a substantial population of mariners, laborers, and "unattached" people with little or no property and still less political voice. By 1720 street crime had become a serious problem, as had prostitution (of which the town fathers first took public notice in the 1670s, when at least a dozen women plied the trade in Boston). The public relief rolls during this period frequently exceeded 200 souls, while dozens of criminals languished in the town jail.

All in all, as Boston approached the centennial of its founding, it bore little resemblance to what the first Puritans had in mind when they planted their "Citty upon a Hill." But neither was it like any

This map summarizes the chief routes of colonial trade in the 1700s. An instance of the so-called triangular slave trade is shown in black for clarity. Most southern exports went to England, but a lack of suitable English markets led the northern and middle colonies to seek outlets for their products in the West Indies and southern Europe.

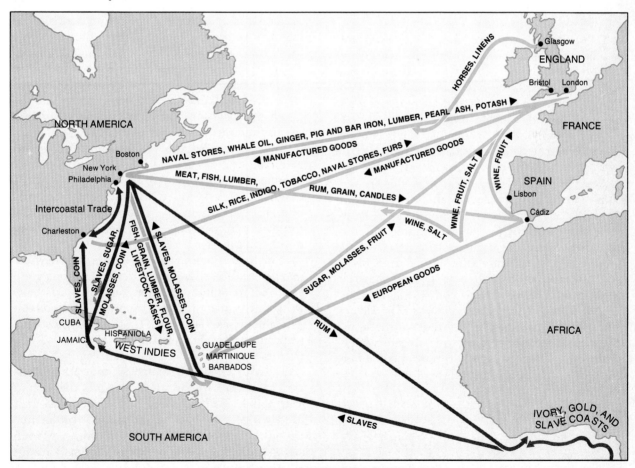

COLONIAL OVERSEAS TRADE

European city of the time. It stood there on Massachusetts Bay, midway between its Puritan origins and its American future.

The Middle Colonies: A Rising People

New York, New Jersey, Pennsylvania, and Delaware owe their collective name, the Middle Colonies, to geography. Sandwiched between New England and the Chesapeake region, they often receive only passing notice in accounts of colonial America. The lack of a distinctive institution, such as slavery or the town meeting, explains part of this neglect.

Actually, both institutions existed there. Black slaves made up about 10 percent of the population; indeed, one New York county in the 1740s had proportionally more blacks than large sections of Virginia. And eastern Long Island was settled by people from Connecticut who brought the town meeting system with them.

Like colonists elsewhere, most of the inhabitants became farmers. But where northern farmers concentrated on producing crops for local consumption and southerners for export, they did both. In addition to raising foodstuffs and keeping livestock, they grew wheat, which the thin soil and shorter growing season of New England did not permit but for which there existed an expanding market in the densely settled Caribbean sugar islands.

Unlike New England settlers, who clustered together in agricultural villages, families in the Hudson Valley of New York and in southeastern Pennsylvania lived on the land they cultivated, often as spatially dispersed as the tobacco planters of the Chesapeake. In contrast with Virginia and Maryland, however, substantial numbers congregated in the seaport centers of New York City and Philadelphia. They also settled interior towns like Albany, an important center of the fur trade on the upper Hudson, and Germantown, an "urban village" northwest of Philadelphia where many people were engaged in trades like weaving and tailoring and flour milling.

"This Promiscuous Breed"

The New Yorkers and Pennsylvanians also possessed traits that later would be seen as distinctly "American." Their ethnic and religious heterogeneity is a case in point. Traveling through Pennsylvania in 1744, the Swedish botanist Peter Kalm encountered "a very mixed company of different nations and religions." In addition to "Scots, English, Dutch, Germans, and Irish," he reported, "there were Roman Catholics, Presbyterians, Quakers, Methodists, Seventh day men, Moravians, Anabaptists, and one Jew."

The English population of New York City was smaller than the Dutch for decades. Scandinavian and Dutch settlers outnumbered the English in New Jersey and Delaware even after the English took over these colonies. William Penn's first success in attracting colonists was with German Quakers and other persecuted religious sects, among them Mennonites and Moravians from the Rhine Valley. The first substantial influx of immigrants into New York after it became a royal colony consisted of French Huguenots.

Early in the 18th century, hordes of Scotch-Irish settlers from Northern Ireland and Scotland descended on Pennsylvania. These colonists spoke English but felt little loyalty to the English government, which had treated them badly back home, and less to the Anglican church, since most of them were Presbyterians. Large numbers of them followed the valleys of the Appalachians south into the back country of Virginia and the Carolinas.

Why so few English? Here again, timing provides the best answer. The English economy was booming. There seemed to be work for all. Migration from England to the North American colonies, though never drying up, slowed to a trickle. The result was colonies in which English settlers were in the minority.

The intermingling of ethnic groups gave rise to many prejudices. Benjamin Franklin, although generally complimentary toward Pennsylvania's hardworking Germans, thought them clannish to a fault. The already cited Hector St. John de Crèvecoeur, while marveling at the adaptive qualities of "this promiscuous breed," complained that "the Irish . . . love to drink and to quarrel; they are litigious, and soon take to the gun, which is the ruin of everything." Yet by and large the various types managed to get along with each other successfully enough. Crèvecoeur attended a wedding in Pennsylvania where the groom's grandparents were English and Dutch and one of his uncles had married a Frenchwoman. The groom and his three brothers,

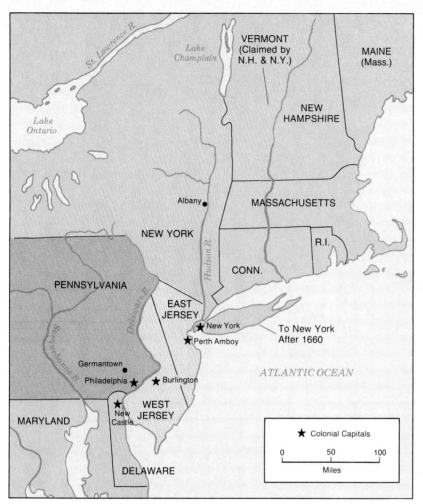

THE MIDDLE COLONIES

Crèvecoeur added with some amazement, "now have four wives of different nations."

"The Best Poor Man's Country"

Ethnic differences seldom caused conflict in the Middle Colonies because they seldom limited opportunity. The promise of prosperity (promotional pamphlets proclaimed Pennsylvania "the best poor man's country in the world") had attracted all in the first place, and achieving prosperity was relatively easy, even for those who came with only a willingness to work. From its founding, Pennsylvania granted upward of 500 acres of land to families upon arrival, provided that they would pay the pro-prietor an annual quitrent. Similar arrangements existed in New Jersey and Delaware. Soon travelers were being struck by the "pleasing uniformity of decent competence."

New York was something of an exception to this favorable economic situation. When the English took over New York, they extended the Dutch patroon system by creating 30 manorial estates covering 2 million–odd acres. But ordinary New Yorkers never lacked ways of becoming landowners. A hundred acres along the Hudson River could be bought in 1730 for what an unskilled laborer could earn in three months. Even tenants on the manorial estates could obtain long-term leases that had most of the advantages of ownership but did not require the investment of any capital. "One may think one-

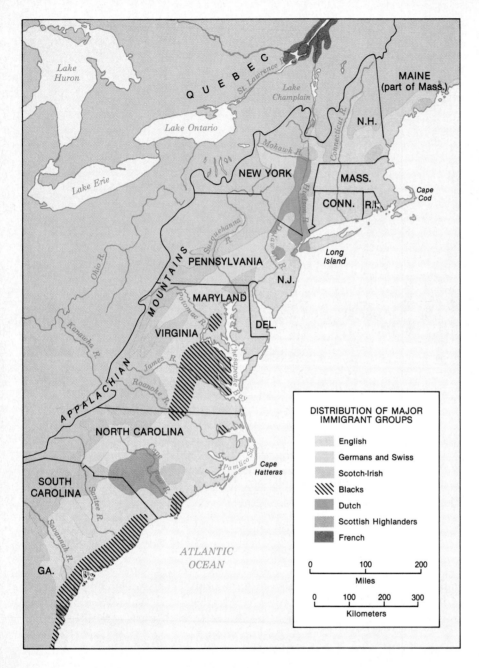

ETHNIC GROUPS IN EASTERN NORTH AMERICA, 1750

From early settlement, the future United States was a multiethnic society. For the first time, national and religious groups were mixed. In a frontier environment there was no room for intergroup bickering; the different groups had to learn to get along and work together.

DISTRIBUTION OF MAJOR IMMIGRANT GROUPS

English
Germans and Swiss
Scotch-Irish
Blacks
Dutch
Scottish Highlanders
French

0   100   200
Miles

0   100   200   300
Kilometers

self to be a great lord," one frustrated "lord" of a New York manor wrote a colleague, "but it does not amount to much, as you well know."

Mixed farming offered the most commonly trod path to prosperity, but not the only one. Inland communities offered comfortable livelihoods for artisans. Farmers always needed barrels, candles, rope, horseshoes and nails, and dozens of other articles in everyday use. Countless opportunities awaited the ambitious settler in the shops, yards,

and offices of New York and Philadelphia. Unlike Boston, New York and Philadelphia profited from navigable rivers that penetrated deep into the back country. Although founded half a century after New York and Boston, Philadelphia grew more rapidly than either. In the 1750s, when its population reached 15,000, it passed Boston to become the largest city in English America.

Most Philadelphians who stuck to their business, particularly if it happened to be maritime commerce, did well for themselves. John Bringhurst, a merchant, began his career as a clerk. At his death in 1751 he left an estate of several thousand pounds. According to the historian Gary Nash, the city's "leather-apron" artisans often accumulated estates of more than £400, a substantial sum at the time. By contrast, in Boston after 1710, economic stagnation made it much more difficult for a skilled artisan to rise in the world.

The Politics of Diversity

"Cannot more friendly and private courses be taken to set matters right in an infant province?" an exasperated William Penn asked the people of Pennsylvania in 1704. "For the love of God, me, and the poor country, be not so governmentish." However well intentioned Penn's advice, however justified his annoyance, the Pennsylvanians ignored him. Instead, they and their fellows throughout the region constructed a political culture that diverged sharply from the patterns of New England and the south both in contentiousness and in the sophistication required of local politicians.

Superficially, the governments of these colonies closely resembled those of earlier settlements. All had popularly elected representative assemblies and most male adults could vote. In Pennsylvania, where Penn had insisted that there be no religious test and where 50 acres constituted a freehold, something close to universal manhood suffrage existed. In New York even non-property-holding white male residents voted in local elections, and rural tenants with lifetime leases enjoyed full voting rights.

In Pennsylvania and most of New York, representatives were elected by counties. In this they resembled Virginia and Maryland. But unlike the southerners, voters did not tend to defer in politics to the landed gentry. In New York in 1689, during the political vacuum following the abdication of King James II, Jacob Leisler, a disgruntled merchant and militia captain, seized control of the government. "Leisler's Rebellion" did not amount to much. He held power for less than two years before he was overthrown and sent to the gallows. Yet for two decades New York politics continued to be a struggle between the Leislerians, and other self-conscious "outs" who shared Leisler's dislike of English rule, and anti-Leislerians, who had in common only that they had opposed his takeover. Each group sought the support of a succession of ineffective governors, and the one that failed to get it invariably proceeded to make that poor man's tenure as miserable as possible. (Governor Edward Cornbury [1702–1708] had an especially difficult time asserting the royal authority after being spotted on the streets of New York wearing a dress.)

In the early 1730s conflict broke out over a claim for back salary by Governor William Cosby. When Lewis Morris, who was also chief justice of the supreme court, opposed Cosby's claim, the governor replaced him. Morris and his assembly allies responded by establishing the *New York Weekly Journal*. To edit the paper they hired an itinerant German printer, John Peter Zenger.

Governor Cosby might have tolerated the *Weekly Journal*'s front-page lectures on the right of the people to criticize their rulers had the back pages not contained advertisements referring to his supporters as spaniels and to him as a monkey. After submitting to two months of "open and implacable malice against me," he shut down the paper, arrested Zenger, and charged him with seditious libel.

What began as a squalid salary dispute became one of the most celebrated tests of freedom of the press in the history of journalism. At the trial, Zenger's attorney, James Hamilton, argued that the truth of his client's criticisms of Cosby constituted a proper defense against seditious libel. This reasoning (though contrary to English law at the time) persuaded the jury to acquit Zenger.

Politics in Pennsylvania turned on conflict between two interest groups. One clustered around the proprietor, the other around the assembly, which was controlled by a coalition of Quaker representatives from Philadelphia and the German-speaking Pennsylvania Dutch.

Neither the proprietary party nor the Quaker party qualifies as a political party in the modern sense of being organized and maintained for the purpose of winning elections. Nor can either be categorized as standing for "democratic" or "aristocratic" interests. But their existence guaranteed that the political leaders had to take popular opinion into account. Moreover, having once appealed to public opinion, they had to be prepared to defer to it. Success turned as much on knowing how to follow as on knowing how to lead.

The 1763 uprising of the "Paxton Boys" of western Pennsylvania put this policy to a full test. The uprising was triggered by eastern indifference to Indian attacks on the frontier—an indifference

Pennsylvania welcomed newcomers of ethnically diverse backgrounds, most of whom prospered. This view of Philadelphia dates from the 1730s, when the city was a half-century old. Engraved "prospects" like this one were widely circulated to attract new settlers.

made possible by the fact that the east outnumbered the west in the assembly, 26 to 10. Fuming because they could obtain no help from Philadelphia against the Indians, a group of Scotch-Irish from Lancaster County fell upon a village of peaceful Conestoga Indians and murdered them in cold blood. Then these Paxton Boys marched on the capital, several hundred strong.

Fortunately, a delegation of burghers, headed by Benjamin Franklin, talked them out of attacking the town by acknowledging the legitimacy of their grievances about representation and by promising to vote a bounty on Indian scalps! It was just such fancy footwork that established Franklin, the leader of the assembly party, as Pennsylvania's consummate politician. "Tell me, Mr. Franklin," a testy member of the proprietary party asked, "how is it that you are always with the majority?" Soon thereafter, the assembly sent Franklin to London to defend local interests against the British authorities, a situation in which he would definitely not be "with the majority."

Milestones

1609–1611	"Seasoning time" in Jamestown
1612	Tobacco cultivation introduced in Virginia
1619	First Africans sold in Virginia
1630–1640	"Great Migration" of Puritans to America
1636	Boston Latin School and Harvard College founded
1657	Half-Way Covenant
1676	Bacon's Rebellion
1684–1688	Dominion of New England
1689	Leisler's Rebellion
1692	Salem witchcraft trials
1693	College of William and Mary founded
1696	Rice cultivation introduced in South Carolina
1733	Georgia settled

SUPPLEMENTARY READING

Titles marked with an asterisk have been published in paperback.

Among general interpretations of colonial society, D. J. Boorstin, **The Americans: The Colonial Experience*** (1958), and H. M. Jones, **O Strange New World*** (1964), remain stimulating. D. F. Hawke, **The Colonial Experience** (1966), provides a good survey of colonial history generally, while Richard Hofstadter, **America at 1750*** (1971), offers a compelling social portrait of the colonies at mid-century. S. S. Webb, **1676: The End of American Independence** (1984), is similarly pointed in time and comprehensive in regional coverage.

J. A. Henretta, **The Evolution of American Society*** (1973), R. V. Wells, **The Population of the British Colonies in America Before 1776** (1975), and G. B. Nash, **The Urban Crucible*** (1979), present the results of recent demographic research on the period. Among older interpretations, David Potter's **People of Plenty*** (1954), which stresses economic abundance as a shaping influence on American development, remains illuminating.

On economic conditions, E. J. Perkins, **The Economy of Colonial America** (1980), is an up-to-date survey, while Stuart Bruchey, **The Roots of American Economic Growth** (1965), explores the dynamics of American economic development. On the institution of slavery generally, see Herbert Klein, **The Middle Passage** (1978), D. B. Davis, **The Problem of Slavery in Western Culture** (1966), and W. D. Jordan, **White over Black: American Attitudes Toward the Negro*** (1968). A. E. Smith, **Colonists in Bondage*** (1971), is a good study of indentured servitude, but see also W. D. Galenson, **White Servitude in Colonial America** (1981); A. B. Ekirch, **Bound for America** (1987), which deals with convict labor; and R. B. Morris, **Government and Labor in Early America** (1946).

On life in the colonial south, see T. W. Tate and David Ammerman (eds.), **The Chesapeake in the Seventeenth Century** (1979), D. B. and A. H. Rutman, **A Place in Time** (1984), P. H. Wood, **Black Majority: Negroes in Colonial South Carolina** (1974), and T. H. Breen and Stephen Innes, **"Myne Owne Ground": Race and Freedom on Virginia's Eastern Shore*** (1980).

Family and community life are surveyed in D. F. Hawke, **Everyday Life in Early America** (1988), C. N. Degler, **At Odds** (1980), and E. S. Morgan, **The Puritan Family*** (1966). See also John Demos, **A Little Commonwealth*** (1970), R. L. Bushman, **From Puritan to Yankee*** (1967), K. A. Lockridge, **A New England Town*** (1970), and Philip Greven, **Four Generations*** (1970). The places of women and children are effectively presented in L. T. Ulrich, **Good Wives: Image and Reality in the Lives of Women in Northern New England** (1982), and Philip Greven, **The Protestant Temperament: Patterns of Child-rearing, Religious Experience, and the Self in Early America** (1980).

For the evolution of the New England landscape and ideas about it, see William Cronon, **Changes in the Land*** (1983).

The works of Perry Miller remain the starting point for any serious study of the cultural life of colonial New England. Among them, **Errand into the Wilderness*** (1956) provides a good introduction. More recent studies, most of which seek to modify Miller's judgments, include E. S. Morgan, **Visible Saints*** (1963), and R. G. Pope, **The Half-Way Covenant** (1969).

On the interplay of religion and social thought, see Stephen Foster, **Their Solitary Way** (1971), T. H. Breen, **The Character of the Good Ruler** (1970), and E. S. Morgan's biography of John Winthrop, **The Puritan Dilemma*** (1958). The disturbances in Salem Village are discussed in Paul Boyer and Stephen Nissenbaum, **Salem Possessed*** (1974), while the subject is considered generally in John Demos, **Entertaining Satan: Witchcraft and the Culture of Early New England*** (1982).

Educational and intellectual developments are treated in Bernard Bailyn, **Education in the Forming of American Society*** (1960), and L. A. Cremin, **American Education: The Colonial Experience*** (1970).

On the Middle Colonies, see R. C. Ritchie, **The Duke's Province** (1977), Patricia Bonomi, **A Factious People: Politics and Society in Colonial New York** (1971), and G. B. Nash, **Quakers and Politics** (1968). The best brief biographical account of the region's leading citizen is V. W. Crane, **Benjamin Franklin and a Rising People*** (1954).

Patterns of Development

Before Europeans like the Van Bergens settled on the land, the Indians had their own types of dwellings, all attuned to the climate of the area in which they lived. John White's watercolor shows the houses of Pomeiock, in the Virginia tidewater region; they are made of poles covered with bark and woven mats. Shade and fresh air could be controlled by adjusting these coverings.

This panorama of the Van Bergen farm in New York's Catskill Mountains was painted by an unknown artist about 1735. The picture graced the farm's living-room mantel. It gives a clear sense of the family's self-sufficiency, with their house, outbuildings, servants, and domestic animals, and of their general prosperity.

Climate, wealth, family size, and many other influences shaped the patterns of life that developed in the colonies. The three sections—north, middle, south—were distinct entities throughout the period, and this was true despite the fact that in each region the people came from diverse social and economic backgrounds and encountered widely different experiences after they arrived.

At the same time, the colonists became increasingly American (as distinct from European or African) as the generations passed. By the middle of the 18th century they were beginning to notice the uniqueness of some aspects of their civilization, and this was certainly a stage in their transition from dependence on Great Britain (psychological as well as material) to independence.

But if the sectional differences were ultimately less significant than the trends common to all the colonies, they were nonetheless important. In all three sections farming was the principal occupation, but in New England and the Middle Colonies the growing towns were exerting political and cultural influence out of proportion to their populations. In most families, fathers ruled the roost; children, while cherished, were expected to obey orders and work hard. However, growing up on a New England farm was a far different experience from growing up on a southern plantation. Foreigners were always struck by the general prosperity of the people compared to conditions in Europe, but the gap between the circumstances of a well-to-do eastern merchant and a frontier farmer was large, and widening.

The Virginia plantation "Greenway," later owned by President John Tyler, is typical of southern plantations, with its large but unostentatious main house and its numerous outbuildings. Far different were the slave cabins of a South Carolina plantation, which provided only the minimum shelter needed in a warm climate.

New England houses—this parsonage in Newington, New Hampshire, is typical—tended to be built as a single "salt-box" in order to conserve heat during the long, hard winters. As families grew and prospered, rooms were added, hugging the original structure.

BY THE HONORABLE
RICHARD PENN, Esq;

Lieutenant Governor and Commander in Chief of the Province of PENNSYLVANIA, *and Counties of* NEW-CASTLE, KENT, *and* SUSSEX, *on* DELAWARE.

To any PROTESTANT MINISTER.

Rich.ᵈ Penn

WHEREAS Application hath been made unto me by

to be joined together in HOLY MATRIMONY, and there appearing no lawful Let or Impediment, by Reason of *Pre-Contract, Confanguinity, Affinity*, or any juft Caufe whatfoever, to hinder the faid Marriage; Thefe are therefore to licence and authorife you to join the faid

in the HOLY BANDS OF MATRIMONY, and them to pronounce MAN and WIFE.

GIVEN *under my Hand and Seal at Arms, at* Philaᵈelphia, *the* ____ *Day of* ____ *in the Year of our* LORD *One Thoufand Seven Hundred and Seventy*

Then, as now, couples had to obtain a marriage certificate from the civil authorities before having a religious ceremony. This pre-printed version issued in the name of Richard Penn (William Penn's son) is addressed to any Protestant minister, and is good for the province of Pennsylvania and the counties of Delaware.

A charming primitive painting of a toddler napping in a red high chair gives an idyllic picture of colonial childhood.

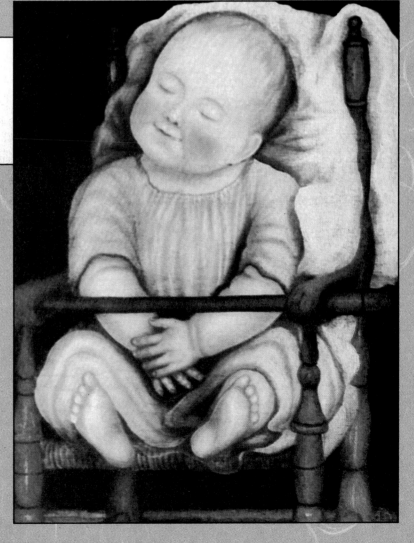

This group portrait of the New England Cheneys shows what is apparently three generations of the family. Genealogies indicate that Dr. Samuel Cheney's first wife had seven children. Since his second wife (in the white cap) had none, the youngest children are presumably her stepgrandchildren.

Two contrasting views of prosperous families of the late 1700s, one from New England and one from the South.

This handsome painting of Alexander Spotswood Payne and his younger brother John Robert Dandridge Payne, with their black nurse and their dog, provides a glimpse of youth in an upper-class Virginia family.

American Lives:
Benjamin Franklin and John Adams

Benjamin Franklin was born in Boston in 1706, the next-to-last of the 13 children of Josiah Franklin, a candle and soap maker, and Abiah Franklin. Although early on he exhibited a "Thirst for Knowledge" and a "Bookish Inclination," he was taken out of school when he was ten in order to help his father. He disliked that trade, and after two years he was apprenticed to his half-brother, James, a printer. Besides learning to be a compositor and type maker, Ben was soon writing articles for his brother's newspaper, the *New England Courant*, at first anonymously, since being so young, he did not think his brother would consider anything he produced worth printing.

To improve his style, Ben practiced writing by the hour. He would read over a passage he admired in a book or article, making notes (he called them "short hints") on its contents. He would put the notes aside for a few days and then use them to try to reconstruct the passage. By comparing the result with the original, he learned to correct awkward phrases and imprecise passages in his work. Another somewhat more difficult technique was to turn the passages into verse, and later turn the verse back into prose in the same manner.

Ben's articles in the *Courant* attracted much notice, but his brother resented his success. The two were constantly at odds. Finally, without telling his parents, Ben left Boston by ship for New York. Not finding work there he moved on to Philadelphia, where he arrived in October 1723, knowing not a soul and with only "a Dutch Dollar and about a shilling in Copper" in his pocket.

Being an exceptionally skilled printer, he soon found work in the shop of Samuel Kleimer. Through the trade he met many "Lovers of Reading" and other people with intellectual interests like his own, including some of what he called "the leading men of the Province." One of these was the governor, Sir William Keith, who offered to set him up in his own business; Keith sent him off to England to buy the necessary press, type, and other equipment, and promised to provide a letter of credit to cover the cost.

However, when Ben arrived in England, there was no letter of credit, for Sir William was better at making promises than at keeping them. Undismayed, he practiced his trade in London for two years before returning to Philadelphia in 1726. Four years later he was sole owner of the *Pennsylvania Gazette*. In 1732 he began publishing his *Poor Richard's Almanack*, the instant success of which assured his prosperity.

John Adams of Braintree, Massachusetts, was of old Puritan stock; the first Adams came to Massachusetts in 1638. John was a bright boy and his parents were determined that he get a good education, but while the family was eminently respectable (his father was a selectman and a deacon of the church) the Adamses were farmers, comfortably off but by no means wealthy. They sent John to the local public school. He did not do well there, however, primarily because the teacher, one Joseph Cleverly, was "the most indolent Man I ever knew." Bored, John spent much time sailing toy boats, flying kites, swimming, skating, and playing marbles and other games with his friends. Finally he persuaded his father to send him to a private school run by a neighbor, whereupon his work improved spectacularly—within a year he was ready to apply to Harvard College.

Doing so was far less complicated, although not necessarily easier, than getting into any college today. After a brief interview with President Edward Holyoke, he was taken by one of Harvard's four tutors, Joseph Mayhew, into another room, given a Latin dictionary, paper and pen, and a passage of English prose, and was told to translate the passage into Latin. After Mayhew read the translation and found it satisfactory, he admitted John to Harvard on the spot.

The Harvard curriculum consisted chiefly of Latin, Greek, logic, mathematics, and theology; the teaching, which involved an enormous amount of memorization, was uninspiring. But John enjoyed his college years. He was what can best be described as a stern self-disciplinarian. "I was of an amorous disposition," he wrote in a famous passage in his *Autobiography*, "and very early from ten or eleven Years of Age, was very fond of the Society of females. . . . This disposition . . . engaged me too much until I was married." But he added, "my natural temperament was always overawed by my Principles and Sense of decorum."

After graduating Adams decided to study law and, not wanting to be a further financial drain on his parents, he took a job teaching in the town of Worcester. Once established there, he approached James Putnam, Worcester's lone lawyer, who agreed to take him into his home; for the sum allowed by the town for his room and board and "an hundred dollars when I should find it convenient," Putnam supervised his legal training. This took two years, and consisted of reading "all the most essential Law Books" and discussing them with Putnam.

When he finished his studies he was invited to practice in Worcester, but he decided to return to Braintree. "I panted for want of Breezes from the Sea," he explained. Back home he presented himself to Jeremiah Gridley, a leader of the Boston bar, who asked him a few questions about his reading and pronounced him qualified to practice law in Massachusetts.

Franklin and Adams were exceptional people, intelligent, energetic, and ambitious. But their early lives throw light on much that was typical of colonial society. That both were omnivorous readers might be explained by their high intelligence, but their experiences suggest that love of books and learning was characteristic of the times. Franklin tells of visiting New York while traveling from Boston to Philadelphia by ship and being invited to the residence of William Burnet, the governor of the province. Burnet had heard from the captain of the ship that a young man on his vessel had a great many books. "The Governor treated me with great Civility, show'd me his Library, which was a very large one, and we had a good deal of conversation about Books and Authors," Franklin recalled in his autobiography.

Adams's account of his life in Worcester is full of the titles of books and his conversations about them with James Putnam, which ranged over history, philosophy, and theology. Jeremiah Gridley also owned a substantial library, access to which he generously provided the young lawyer.

Their lives also illustrate the openness of 18th-century society. Franklin was an exceptionally outgoing person, and he excelled, as the historian Carl Becker once wrote, "in the fine art of inducing others to appropriate as their own the ideas or the projects which he wished to have prevail." He was open-minded and tolerant, of himself as well as others. Adams was quite different. He tended to take a dim view of most people. He noted, for example, that Jeremiah Gridley was more a buyer of books than a reader. He was also extremely straitlaced. Unlike Franklin, who had two illegitimate children, he was able to assure his descendants that he had never wandered from the straight and narrow, before or after his marriage to Abigail Smith. But he too entered easily into the upper ranks of New England society. While an obscure young schoolmaster in Worcester, he was invited to meet General Jeffrey Amherst, who spent a few days there in 1758 while en route from Boston to Albany at the head of 4,000 Redcoats during the French and Indian war. On another occasion Adams volunteered to deliver an urgent call for militiamen to the governor of Rhode Island. He found the governor riding with a single aide on the road between Providence and Newport, handed him the dispatch, and watched him open and read it and then dash off to Providence to raise the troops.

The American colonies were large geographically; however, their inhabitants lived in small, but remarkably open and interesting, worlds.

Harvard College, by Paul Revere

America in the British Empire

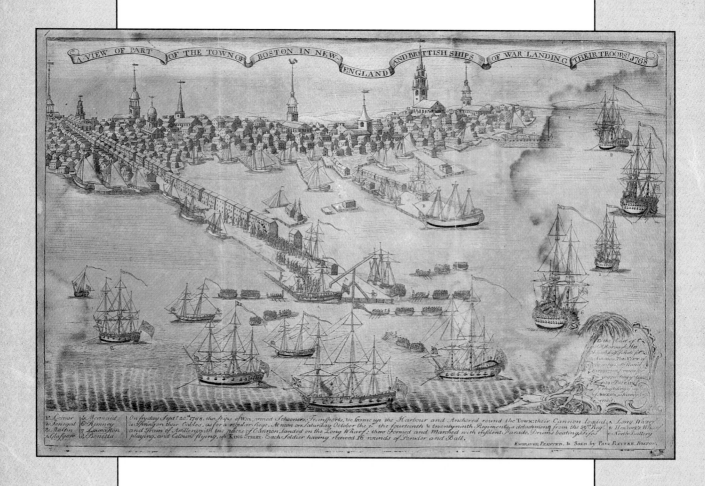

> North America was once indeed a great strength to this nation. . . .
> We found her a sound, an active, a vigorous member of the empire. I
> hope, by wise management, she will again be so. But one of our
> capital present misfortunes is her discontent and disobedience.
>
> EDMUND BURKE, *1769*

Since the colonies were founded piecemeal by persons with varying motives and backgrounds, common traditions and loyalties developed slowly. For the same reason, the British government was slow to think of its American possessions as a unit or to deal with them in any centralized way. They were the king's possessions. No authority challenged his right to dispose of one section of his American domain to this group of merchants under such-and-such terms and another to that personal friend or creditor under a different arrangement. The specific form of each colony's government and the degree of local independence permitted depended on how this was done.

The British Colonial System

There was a pattern basic to all colonial governments and a general framework of imperial control for all the king's overseas plantations. English political and legal institutions (the common law, private property, more or less representative legislative assemblies, systems of local administration) took hold everywhere in British America. While the colonists and the home authorities often had different motives in establishing new settlements, they were seldom conflicting motives. Colonists might leave home with grievances, bent on securing certain rights denied them in England, but prosperity, political and economic expansion, and the reproduction of Old World civilization were aims common to ruler and ruled.

In the earliest days of any settlement, the need to rely on home authorities was so obvious that few questioned England's sovereignty. Thereafter, as the fledglings grew strong enough to think of using their own wings, distance and British political inefficiency combined to allow them a great deal of freedom. Although royal representatives in America tried to direct policy, the Crown generally yielded the initiative in local matters to the colonies while reserving the right to veto actions it deemed to be against the national interest. External affairs were controlled entirely in London.

Each colony had a governor. By the 18th century he was an appointed official, except in Rhode Island and Connecticut. Governors were chosen by the king in the case of the royal colonies and by the proprietors of Maryland, Delaware, and Pennsylvania. The governors' powers were much like those of the king in Great Britain. They executed the local laws, appointed many minor officials, summoned and dismissed the colonial assemblies, and proposed legislation to them. They possessed the right to veto colonial laws, but in most colonies, again like the king, they were financially dependent on their "subjects."

Each colony also had a legislature. Except in Pennsylvania, these assemblies consisted of two houses. The lower house, chosen by qualified voters, had general legislative powers, including control of the purse. In the royal colonies, members of the upper house, or council, were appointed by the king except in Massachusetts, where they were elected by the General Court. The councils served primarily

Typical of colonial governors was Lewis Morris, a wealthy landowner with extensive holdings in the Middle Colonies. He was named New Jersey's first governor when the colony became politically independent from New York in 1738. Honest but overbearing, Morris quarreled constantly with the state assembly over taxation, the militia, and land titles.

as advisers to the governors, but they also had some judicial and legislative powers. Judges were appointed by the king and served at his pleasure. Yet both councilors and judges were normally selected from among the leaders of the local communities; London had neither the time nor the will to investigate their political beliefs. The system therefore tended to strengthen the influence of the entrenched colonials.

Although the power of the lower houses was severely restricted in theory, they dominated the government in nearly every colony. Financial power (including the right to set the governor's salary) gave them some importance, and the fact that the assemblies usually had the backing of public opinion was significant.

Most colonial legislators were practical men. Knowing their own interests, they pursued them steadily, without much regard for political theories or the desires of the royal authorities. In the words of one Virginia governor, they were "Expedient Mongers in the highest Degree." They extended their influence by slow accretion. Governors came and went, but the lawmakers remained, accumulating experience, building on precedent, widening decade by decade their control over colonial affairs.

The official representatives of the Crown, whatever their powers, whatever their intentions, were prisoners of their surroundings. A royal governor lived thousands of miles fromh London, alone in a colonial world. To defend the British position at every turn when one had to make one's life amid a vigorous and strong-willed people who usually had solid practical arguments to buttress their side if it clashed with the Crown's was no easy task. In their dealings with the assemblies they were often bound by rigid and impractical royal instructions that restricted their ability to maneuver. They had few jobs and favors to offer in their efforts to influence the legislators. Judges might interpret the law according to English precedents, but in local matters colonial juries had the final say. And juries were seldom awed by precedents that clashed with their own conceptions of justice.

Within the British government, the king's Privy Council had the responsibility for formulating colonial policy. It did so on an ad hoc basis, treating each situation as it arose and seldom generalizing. Everything was decentralized, managed by departments that had been created long before the colonies were founded: The Treasury had charge of financial matters, the Army and the Admiralty of military and naval affairs, and so on. The Privy Council could and did disallow (annul) specific colonial laws, but it did not proclaim constitutional principles to which all colonial legislatures must conform. It acted as a court of last appeal in colonial disputes and handled each case individually. One day the council might issue a set of instructions to the governor of Virginia, the next a different set to the governor of South Carolina. No one person or committee thought broadly about the administration of the overseas empire.

Parliamentary legislation applied to the colonies, yet there was little distinctively *American* legislation. For example, Parliament passed laws regulating the trade of the entire British Empire, and until late in the colonial period it directed its attention specifically to North American conditions only on rare occasions.

At times the British authorities, uneasy about their lack of control over the colonies, attempted to create a more effective system. Whenever possible, the original, broadly worded charters were revoked. To transform proprietary and corporate colonies into royal colonies (whose chief officials were appointed by the king) seems to have been London's official policy by the late 17th century. The Privy Council appointed a number of subcommittees to advise it on colonial affairs at this time. The most important was the Lords of Trade. In the 1680s when James II brought New York, New Jersey, and all of New England under one administration, the Dominion of New England, he apparently planned to unify the southern colonies in a similar manner. The colonists deeply resented James's actions, and after the Glorious Revolution and the collapse of the Dominion of New England, no further important efforts at unification were attempted. Instead, the tendency was in the other direction. Delaware partially separated from Pennsylvania in 1704, and the two Carolinas formally split in 1712.

In 1696 the new Board of Trade took over the functions of the Lords of Trade and expanded them considerably. It nominated colonial governors and other high officials. It reviewed all the laws passed by the colonial legislatures, recommending the disallowance of those that seemed to conflict with imperial policy. The efficiency, assiduousness, and wisdom of the Board of Trade fluctuated over the years, but the Privy Council and the Crown nearly always accepted its recommendations.

Colonists naturally disliked having their laws disallowed, but London exercised this power with considerable restraint; only about 5 percent of the laws reviewed were rejected. Furthermore, the board served as an important intermediary for colonists seeking to influence king and Parliament. All the colonies in the 18th century maintained agents in London to present the colonial point of view before board members. The most famous colonial agent was Benjamin Franklin, who represented Pennsylvania, Georgia, New Jersey, and Massachusetts at various times during his long career. In general, however, colonial agents were seldom able to exert much influence on British policy.

The British never developed an effective centralized government for the American colonies. By and large, their American "subjects" ran their own affairs. This fact more than any other explains our present federal system and the wide areas in which the state governments are sovereign and independent.

Mercantilism

The Board of Trade, as its name implies, was concerned with commerce as well as colonial administration. According to prevailing European opinion, colonies were important chiefly for economic reasons. The 17th century being a period of hard times and considerable unemployment, some authorities saw the colonies as excellent dumping grounds for surplus people. If only two idlers in each parish were shipped overseas, one clergyman calculated in 1624, England would be rid of 16,000 undesirables. But most 17th-century economic thinkers envisaged colonies more as potential sources of raw materials. To obtain these, they developed a number of loosely related policies that later economists called mercantilism. The most important raw materials in the eyes of mercantilists were gold and silver, since these metals, being universally valued and relatively rare, could be exchanged at any time for anything the owner desired or, being durable and compact, stored indefinitely for future use. For these reasons, how much gold and silver ("treasure," according to mercantilists) a nation possessed was considered the best barometer of its prosperity and power.

Since gold and silver could not be mined in significant amounts in western Europe, every early colonist dreamed of finding "El Dorado." The Spanish were the winners in this search; from the mines of Mexico and South America a treasure in gold and silver poured into the Iberian peninsula. Failing to control the precious metals at the source, the other powers tried to obtain them by guile and warfare (witness the exploits of Francis Drake).

In the mid-17th century another method, less hazardous and in the long run far more profitable, called itself to the attention of the statesmen of western Europe. If a country could make itself as nearly self-sufficient as possible and at the same time keep all its citizens busy producing items marketable in other lands, it could sell more abroad than it imported. This state of affairs was known as "having

The value of sugar from the West Indies far outweighed the value of imports to Britain from the mainland American colonies. Refining the sugar before shipping, as shown in the engraving, resulted in far higher import duties.

a favorable balance of trade." The expression is misleading; in reality, trade, which involves an exchange, *always* balances unless some party simply gives its goods away, a practice not recommended by mercantilists. A country with a favorable balance in effect made up the difference by "importing" money in the form of gold and silver. Nevertheless, mercantilism came to mean concentrating on producing for export and limiting imports of ordinary goods and services in every way possible. Colonies that did not have deposits of precious metals were well worth having if they supplied raw materials that would otherwise have to be purchased from foreign sources or if their people bought substantial amounts of the manufactured goods produced in the mother country.

Of the English colonies in the New World, those in tropical and subtropical climes were valued for their raw materials. The more northerly ones were important as markets, but because they were small in the 17th century, in English eyes they took second place. In 1680 the sugar imported from the single West Indian island of Barbados was worth more than the goods sent to England by all the mainland colonies.

If the possession of gold and silver signified wealth, trade was the route that led to riches, and merchants were the captains who would pilot the ship of state to prosperity. "Trade is the Wealth of the World," Daniel Defoe wrote in 1728. One must, of course, have something to sell, so internal production must be stimulated. Parliament encouraged the British people to concentrate on manufacturing by placing tariffs on foreign manufactured goods and subsidizing British-made textiles, iron, and other products.

The Navigation Acts

The nurture of commerce was fundamental. Toward this end Parliament enacted the Navigation Acts. These laws, put into effect over a period of more than half a century, were designed to bring money into the Royal Treasury, to develop the imperial merchant fleet, to channel the flow of colonial raw materials into England, and to keep foreign goods and vessels out of colonial ports (since the employment of foreign ships in the carrying trade was as much an import as the consumption of foreign wheat or wool).

The system originated in the 1650s in response to the stiff commercial competition offered by the Dutch, whose sailors roamed the world's oceans in search of business. Before 1650 a large share of the produce of the English colonies in America reached Europe in Dutch vessels; the first slaves in Virginia, it will be recalled, arrived on a Dutch ship and were doubtless paid for in tobacco that was later burned in the clay pipes of the burghers of Amsterdam and Rotterdam.

Dismayed by this trend, Parliament in 1650 and 1651 barred foreign ships from the English colonies (except when specially licensed) and prohibited the importation into England of goods that were not carried in English ships or those of the country where the goods had been originally produced. All foreign vessels were excluded from the English coastal trade. Although phrased in general terms, this legislation struck primarily at the Dutch, and in 1652 the English provoked the first of three wars with the Dutch Republic that were only extensions of the policy laid down in the first Navigation Acts.

The laws of 1650 and 1651 were not rigidly enforced because England did not have enough ships to supply its overseas possessions. The colonies protested vigorously and then ignored the regulations. Nevertheless, the English persisted. New laws were passed, and as the merchant marine expanded (tonnage doubled between 1660 and 1688) and the Royal Navy gradually reduced Dutch power in the New World, enforcement became fairly effective.

The Navigation Act of 1660 reserved the entire trade of the colonies to English ships and required that the captain and three-quarters of his crew be English. (Colonists, of course, were English, and their ships were treated on the same terms as those sailing out of London or Liverpool.) The act also provided that certain colonial "enumerated articles"—sugar, tobacco, cotton, ginger, and dyes like indigo and fustic—could not be "shipped, carried, conveyed or transported" outside the empire. Three years later Parliament required that with trifling exceptions, all European products destined for the colonies be brought to England before being shipped across the Atlantic. Since trade between England and the colonies was reserved to English vessels, this meant that the goods would have to be unloaded and reloaded in England.

Legislation in 1673 and 1696 was concerned with enforcing these laws: It dealt with the posting of bonds, the registration of vessels, and the appointment of customs officials. Early in the 18th century the list of enumerated articles was expanded to include rice, molasses, naval stores, furs, and copper.

The English looked on the empire broadly; they envisioned the colonies as part of an economic unit, not as servile dependencies to be exploited for England's selfish benefit. The growing of tobacco in England was prohibited, and valuable bounties were paid to colonial producers of indigo and naval stores. A planned economy, England specializing in manufacturing and the colonies in the production of raw materials, was the grand design. By and large the system suited the realities of life in an underdeveloped country that was rich in raw materials and suffering from a chronic labor shortage.

Much has been made by some historians of the restrictions that the British placed on colonial manufacturing. The Wool Act of 1699 prohibited the export (but not the manufacture for local sale) of colonial woolen cloth. A similar law regarding hats was passed in 1732, and in 1750 the Iron Act outlawed the construction of new rolling and slitting mills in America. No other restrictions on manufacturing were imposed.

At most the Wool Act stifled a potential American industry; the law was directed chiefly at Irish woolens rather than American. The hat industry cannot be considered a major one. Iron, however, was important; by 1775 the industry was thriving in Virginia, Maryland, New Jersey, and Pennsylvania, and America was turning out one-seventh of the world supply. Yet the Iron Act was designed to steer the American iron industry in a certain direction, not to destroy it. Eager for iron to feed English mills, Parliament eliminated all duties on colonial pig and bar iron entering England, a great stimulus to the basic industry.

The Effects of Mercantilism

All this legislation reflected, more than it molded, the imperial economy. It made England the colonies' main customer and chief supplier of manufactures, but that would have happened in any case, and it remained the case after the Revolution, when the Navigation Acts no longer applied to America. The chronic colonial shortage of hard money was superficially caused by the flow of specie to England to meet the "unfavorable" balance that resulted from this trade, and this, too, reflected natural conditions. The rapidly growing colonial economy consumed far more manufactured products than it could pay for out of current production. To be "in debt" to England really meant that the English were investing capital in America, a state of affairs that benefited borrower and lender alike.

Important colonial products for which no market existed in England (such as fish, wheat, and corn) were never enumerated and moved freely and directly to foreign ports. Most colonial manufacturing was untouched by English law. Shipbuilding benefited from the Navigation Acts, since many English merchants bought vessels built in the colonies. Between 1769 and 1771, Massachusetts, New Hampshire, and Rhode Island yards constructed perhaps 250 ships of 100 to 400 tons for transatlantic commerce and twice that many sloops and schooners for fishermen and coastal traders. The manufacture of rum for local consumption and for the slave trade

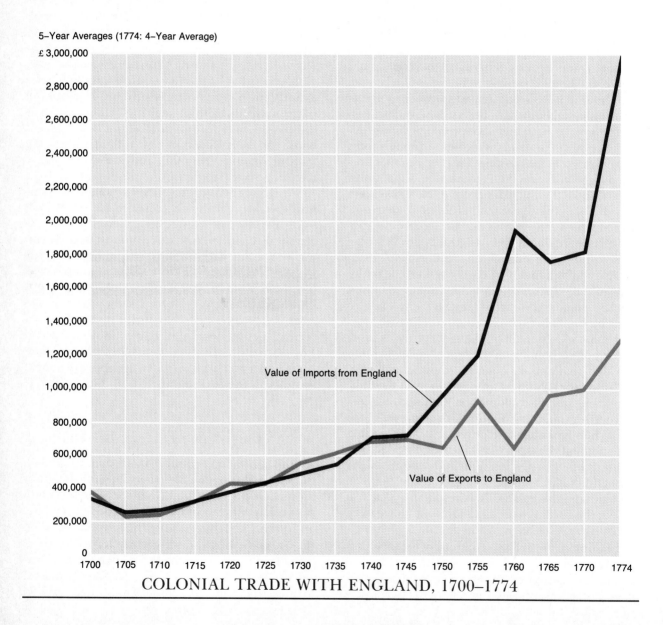

5–Year Averages (1774: 4–Year Average)

Value of Imports from England

Value of Exports to England

COLONIAL TRADE WITH ENGLAND, 1700–1774

was significant; so were barrelmaking, flour milling, shoemaking, and dozens of other crafts that operated without restriction.

Two forces that worked in opposite directions must be considered before arriving at any judgment about English mercantilism. Although the theory presupposed a general imperial interest above that of both colony and mother country, when conflicts of interest arose, the latter nearly always predominated. Whenever Parliament or the Board of Trade resolved an Anglo-American disagreement, the colonists tended to lose out.

The requirement that foreign goods destined for the colonies must first be unloaded in England increased the cost of certain goods to Americans for the benefit of English merchants and dockworkers. The enumeration of tobacco and other colonial products meant that English merchants could profit by reexporting surpluses to the Continent; by 1700 this reexport trade amounted to 30 percent of the value of all England's exports.

Complementary interests conspired to keep conflicts at a minimum, but in the long run, as the American economy became more complex, the colonies would have been seriously hampered and much more trouble would have occurred had the system continued to operate.

However, the restrictions of English mercantilism were greatly lessened by inefficiency. The king and his ministers handed out government posts to win political favor or to repay political debts, regardless of the recipient's ability to perform the duties of the office.

Transported to remote America, this bumbling and cynical system scarcely functioned at all when local opinion resisted it. Smuggling became a respected profession, bribery of English officials standard practice. Despite a supposedly prohibitive duty of sixpence a gallon imposed by the Molasses Act of 1733, molasses from the French West Indies continued to be imported. The duty was seldom collected. A customs officer in Salem offered to pass French molasses for 10 percent of the legal tax, and in New Jersey the collectors "entered into a composition with the Merchants and took a Dollar a Hogshead or some such small matter."

Mercantilistic policies hurt some colonists such as the tobacco planters, who grew far more than British consumers could smoke. But the policies helped others, and most people proved adept at getting around the aspects of the system that threatened them. In any case, the colonies enjoyed almost continuous prosperity, as even so dedicated a foe of mercantilistic restrictions as Adam Smith admitted.

By the same token, England profited greatly from its overseas possessions. With all its inefficiencies, mercantilism worked. Prime Minister Sir Robert Walpole's famous policy of "salutary neglect," which involved looking the other way when Americans violated the Navigation Acts, was partly a bowing to the inevitable, partly the result of complacency. English manufactures were better and cheaper than those of other nations. This fact, together with ties of language and a common heritage, predisposed Americans toward doing business in England. All else followed naturally; the mercantilistic laws merely steered the American economy in a direction it had already taken.

The Great Awakening

Although a majority of the settlers were of English, Scottish, or Scotch-Irish descent, and their interests generally coincided with those of their cousins in the mother country, people in the colonies were beginning to recognize their common interests and character. Their interests and loyalties were still predominantly local, but by 1750 the word *American*, used to describe something characteristic of all the British possessions in North America, had entered the language. Events in one part of America were beginning to have direct effects on other regions. One of the first of these developments was the so-called Great Awakening.

By the early 18th century, religious fervor had slackened in all the colonies. Prosperity turned many colonists away from their forebears' preoccupation with the rewards of the next world to the more tangible ones of this world. John Winthrop invested his faith in God and his own efforts in the task of creating a spiritual community; his grandsons invested in Connecticut real estate.

The proliferation of religious denominations made it impracticable to enforce laws requiring regular religious observances. Even in South Carolina, the colony that came closest to having an "Anglican establishment," only a minority of persons were churchgoers. Settlers in frontier districts lived beyond the reach of church or clergy. The result was a large and growing number of "persons careless of all religion."

This state of affairs came to an abrupt end with the Great Awakening of the 1740s. The Awakening began in the Middle Colonies as the result of religious developments that originated in Europe. In the late 1720s two newly arrived ministers, Theodore Frelinghuysen, a Calvinist from Westphalia, and William Tennent, an Irish-born Presbyterian, sought to instill in their sleepy Pennsylvania and New Jersey congregations the evangelical zeal and spiritual enthusiasm they had witnessed among the Pietists in Germany and the Methodist followers of John Wesley in England. Their example inspired other clergymen, including Tennent's two sons.

A more significant surge of religious enthusiasm followed the arrival in 1738 in Georgia of the Reverend George Whitefield, a young Oxford-trained Anglican minister. Whitefield was a marvelous pulpit orator and no mean actor. He played on the feelings of his audience the way a conductor directs a symphony orchestra.

He undertook a series of fund-raising tours throughout the colonies. The most successful began in Philadelphia in 1739. Benjamin Franklin, not a very religious person and not easily moved by emotional appeals, heard one of these sermons. "I silently resolved he should get nothing from me," he later recalled.

> I had in my Pocket a Handful of Copper Money, three or four silver Dollars, and five Pistoles in Gold. As he proceeded I began to soften and concluded to give the Coppers. Another Stroke of his Oratory . . . determin'd me to give the Silver; and he finish'd so admirably that I empty'd my Pocket wholly into the Collector's Dish.

Whitefield's visit changed the "manners of our inhabitants,' Franklin added.

Wherever Whitefield went he filled the churches. If no local clergyman offered his pulpit, he attracted thousands to meetings out-of-doors. During a three-day visit to Boston, 19,000 people (more than the population of the town) thronged to hear him.

His oratorical brilliance aside, Whitefield succeeded in releasing an epidemic of religious emotionalism because his message was so well suited to American ears. By preaching a theology that one critic said was "scaled down to the comprehension of twelve-year-olds," he spared his audiences the rigors of hard thought. Though he usually began by chastising his listeners as sinners, "half animals and half devils," he invariably took care to leave them with the hope that eternal salvation could be theirs. While not denying the doctrine of predestination, he preached a God responsive to good intentions. He disregarded sectarian differences and encouraged his listeners to do the same. "God help us to forget party names and become Christians in deed and truth," he prayed.

Whitefield attracted some supporters among ministers with established congregations, but many more from among younger "itinerants," as preachers who lacked permanent pulpits were called. A visit from him or one of his followers inevitably prompted comparisons between this new, emotionally charged style and the more restrained "plaine style" favored by the typical settled minister. Parishioners who had heard a revivalist preacher listened the next Sunday to the droning of their regular minister with what one of Whitefield's imitators claimed was the fear that their souls were at risk because they had been "living under the ministry of dead men."

Of course, not everyone found the Whitefield style edifying. When those who did not spoke up, churches sometimes split into factions. Those who supported the incumbent minister were called, among Congregationalists, "Old Lights," and among Presbyterians, "Old Sides," while those who favored revivalism were known as "New Lights" and "New Sides."

These splits often ran along class lines. The richer, better-educated, and more influential members of the church tended to stay with the traditional arrangements.

The strains these divisions put on communities already struggling to maintain a sense of civic unity produced what the historian Richard Bushman has called a "psychological earthquake." Persons chafing under the restraints of Puritan authoritarianism and made guilt-ridden by their rebellious feelings now found release. For some the release was more than spiritual; Timothy Cutler, a conservative Anglican clergyman, complained that as a result of the

An ELEGIAC

POEM,

On the DEATH of that celebrated Divine, and eminent Servant of JESUS CHRIST, the late Reverend, and pious

GEORGE WHITEFIELD,

Chaplain to the Right Honourable the Countess of Huntingdon, &c. &c.

Who made his Exit from this transitory State, to dwell in the celestial Realms of Bliss, on LORD's-Day, 30th of September, 1770, when he was seiz'd with a Fit of the Asthma, at Newbury-Port, near Boston, in New-England.   In which is a Condolatory Address to His truly noble Benefactress the worthy and pious Lady Huntingdon,---and the Orphan-Children in Georgia ; who, with many Thousands, are left, by the Death of this great Man, to lament the Loss of a Father, Friend, and Benefactor.

By Phillis, a Servant Girl of 17 Years of Age, belonging to Mr. J. Wheatley, of Boston :---And has been but 9 Years in this Country from Africa.

Phyllis Wheatley, one of America's first black poets, was a 17-year-old slave when she wrote this testimony to George Whitefield: "Thou didst, in strains of eloquence refin'd, / Inflame the soul, and captivate the mind."

Awakening, "our presses are forever teeming with books and our women with bastards." Whether or not Cutler was correct, the Great Awakening helped some people to rid themselves of the idea that disobedience to authority guaranteed damnation. Anything that God justified, human law could not condemn.

Other institutions besides the churches were affected by the Great Awakening. In 1741 the president of Yale College criticized the theology of itinerant ministers. One of these promptly retorted that a Yale faculty member had no more divine grace than a chair! Other revivalists called on the New Light churches of Connecticut to withdraw their support from Yale and endow a college of their own. The result was the College of New Jersey (now Princeton), founded in 1746 by New Side Presbyterians. Three other educational by-products of the Great Awakening followed: the College of Rhode Island (Brown), founded by Baptists in 1765; Queen's College (Rutgers), founded by Dutch Reformers in 1766; and Dartmouth, founded by New Light Congregationalists in 1769. These institutions promptly set about to refute the charge that the evangelical temperament was hostile to learning.

The Rise and Fall of Jonathan Edwards

Jonathan Edwards, the most famous native-born revivalist of the Great Awakening, was living proof that it need not be. Edwards, though deeply pious, was passionately devoted to intellectual pursuits. But in 1725, four years after graduating from Yale, he was offered the position of assistant at his grandfather Solomon Stoddard's church in Northampton, Massachusetts. He accepted, and when Stoddard died two years later, Edwards became pastor.

During his six decades in Northampton, Stoddard had so dominated the ministers of the Connecticut Valley that some referred to him as "pope." His prominence came in part from the "open enrollment" admission policy he adopted for his own church. Evidence of saving grace was neither required nor expected of members; mere good behavior sufficed. As a result, the grandson inherited a congregation whose members were possessed of an "inordinate engagedness after this world." How ready they were to meet their Maker in the next was another question.

Edwards set out to change this. When a 5-year-old girl begged her mother to take her to church so that she could "hear Mr. Edwards preach," he knew he was on the right track.

For all his learning and intellectual brilliance, Edwards did not stick at dramatizing what unconverted listeners had to look forward to. The heat of Hell's consuming fires and the stench of brimstone became palpable at his rendering. In his most famous sermon, "Sinners in the Hands of an Angry God," delivered at Enfield, Connecticut, in 1741, he pulled out all the stops, depicting a "dreadfully provoked" God holding the unconverted over the pit of Hell, "much as one holds a spider, or some loathsome insect." Later, on the off chance that his listeners did not recognize themselves among the "insects" in God's hand, he declared that "this is the dismal case of every soul in this congregation that has not been born again, however moral and strict, sober and religious, they may otherwise be." A great moaning reverberated through the church. People cried out, "What must I do to be saved?"

Unfortunately for some church members, Edwards's warnings about the state of their souls caused much anxiety. One disconsolate member, Joseph Hawley, slit his throat. Edwards took the suicide calmly. "Satan seems to be in a great rage," he declared. But for some of Edwards's most prominent parishioners, Hawley's death aroused doubts. They began to miss the easy, Arminian ways of Solomon Stoddard.

Rather than soften his message, Edwards persisted, and in 1749 his parishioners voted unanimously to dismiss him. He became a missionary to some Indians in Stockbridge, Massachusetts. In 1759 he was appointed president of Princeton, but he died of smallpox before he could take office.

By the early 1750s, a reaction had set in against religious "enthusiasm" in all its forms. Except in the religion-starved south, where traveling New Side Presbyterians and Baptists continued their evangelizing efforts, the Great Awakening had run its course. Whitefield's last tour of the colonies in 1754 attracted little notice.

Although it caused divisions, the Great Awakening also fostered religious toleration. If one group claimed the right to worship in its own way, how could it deny to other Protestant churches equal freedom? The Awakening was also the first truly national event in American history. It marks the time when the previously distinct histories of the colonies began to intersect. Powerful links were being forged. As early as 1691 there was a rudimentary intercolonial postal system. In 1754, not long after the Awakening, the farsighted Benjamin Franklin advanced his Albany Plan for a colonial union to deal with common problems, such as defense against Indian attacks on the frontier. Thirteen once-isolated colonies, expanding to the north and south as well as westward, were merging.

The Enlightenment in America

The Great Awakening pointed ahead to an America marked by religious pluralism; by the 1740s many colonists were rejecting not only the stern Calvinism of Edwards but even the easy Arminianism of Samuel Stoddard in favor of a far less forbidding theology, one more in keeping with the ideas of the European Enlightenment.

The Enlightenment had an enormous impact in America. The founders of the colonies were contemporaries of the astronomer Galileo Galilei (1564–1642), the philosopher-mathematician René Descartes (1596–1650), and Sir Isaac Newton (1642–1727), the genius who revealed to the world the workings of gravity and other laws of motion. American society developed amid the excitement generated by these great discoverers, who provided both a new understanding of the natural world and a mode of thought that implied that impersonal, scientific laws governed the behavior of all matter, animate and inanimate. Earth and the heavens, human beings and the lower animals—all seemed parts of an immense, intricate machine. God had set it all in motion and remained the master technician (the divine watchmaker) overseeing it but had fewer and fewer occasions to interfere with its immutable operation.

If human reasoning powers and direct observation of natural phenomena, rather than God's revelations, provided the key to knowledge, it followed that knowledge of the laws of nature, by enabling people to understand the workings of the universe, would enable them to control their earthly destinies and to have at least a voice in their eternal destinies.

Most creative thinkers of the European Enlightenment realized that human beings were not entirely rational and that a complete understanding of the physical world was beyond their grasp. They

Benjamin Franklin is most often depicted as he looked in later life, with his own thinning hair rather than the wig which was de rigueur for an 18th-century man of good family. In this 1767 portrait, a younger Franklin follows the fashion.

did, however, believe that human beings were becoming more rational and would be able, by using their rational powers, to discover the laws governing the physical world. Their faith in these ideas produced the so-called Age of Reason. And while their confidence in human rationality now seems naive and the "laws" they formulated no longer appear so mechanically perfect (the universe is far less orderly than they imagined), they added immensely to knowledge.

Many churchgoing colonists, especially better-educated ones, accepted the assumptions of the Age of Reason wholeheartedly. Some repudiated the doctrine of original sin and asserted the benevolence of God. Others came to doubt the divinity of Christ and eventually declared themselves Unitarians. Still others, among them Benjamin Franklin, embraced Deism, a faith that revered God for the marvels of His universe rather than for His power over humankind.

The impact of Enlightenment ideas went far beyond religion. The writings of John Locke and other political theorists found a receptive audience. So did the work of the Scottish philosophers Francis

Hutcheson and David Hume and the French *philosophes* Montesquieu and Voltaire. Ideas generated in Europe often reached America with startling speed. *Cato's Letters,* a series of essays attacking political and religious corruption, written in the 1720s by the Englishmen John Trenchard and Thomas Gordon, appeared only months later in America, where they were quoted in newspapers from Massachusetts to Georgia. No colonial political controversy really heated up in America until all involved had published pamphlets citing a half dozen European authorities. Radical ideas that in Europe were discussed only by an intellectual elite became almost commonplace in the colonies.

As the topics of learned discourse expanded, ministers lost their monopoly on intellectual life. By the 1750s only a minority of Harvard and Yale graduates were becoming ministers. The College of Philadelphia (later the University of Pennsylvania), founded in 1751, and King's College (later Columbia), founded in New York in 1754, were two of the growing ranks of American colleges that were never primarily training grounds for clergymen.

Lawyers, who first appeared in any number in colonial towns in the 1740s, swiftly asserted their intellectual authority in public affairs. Physicians and the handful of professors of natural history declared themselves better able to make sense of the new scientific discoveries than clergymen. Yet because fields of knowledge were far less specialized than in modern times, self-educated amateurs could also make useful contributions.

The most famous instances of popular participation occurred in Philadelphia. It was there, in 1727, that 21-year-old Benjamin Franklin founded the Junto, a club at which he and other young artisans gathered on Friday evenings to discuss "any point of morals, politics, or natural philosophy." In 1743 Franklin established an expanded version of the Junto, the American Philosophical Society, which he hoped would "cultivate the finer arts and improve the common stock of knowledge."

Colonial Scientific Achievements

America produced no Galileo or Newton, but colonists contributed significantly to the collection of scientific knowledge. The unexplored continent provided a laboratory for the study of natural phenomena. The Philadelphia Quaker, John Bartram, a "down right plain Country Man," ranged from Florida to the Great Lakes during the middle years of the 18th century, gathering and classifying hundreds of plants. Bartram also studied Indians closely, speculating about their origins and collecting information about their culture. Cadwallader Colden, lieutenant governor of New York from 1761 to 1776, made important contributions to the systematic study of American flora and fauna.

Astronomy was another science to which 18th-century Americans were able to contribute by virtue of their distance from Europe. In 1761 Professor John Winthrop of Harvard, a descendant of the first governor of the Massachusetts Bay Colony, led a scientific expedition to Newfoundland, the only place in British North America from which the transit of the planet Venus could be observed. Winthrop's observations enabled him to calculate the distance of the sun from the earth with an error of only 2 percent. Another transit of Venus passed directly over several colonies in 1769. It attracted the attention of amateur astronomers from Massachusetts to Maryland. The most accurate observations were made by David Rittenhouse of Phil-

The first orrery (model of the solar system) constructed in America was built by David Rittenhouse in 1767 as a teaching tool. This is a modern restoration.

adelphia. Thomas Jefferson later described Rittenhouse somewhat hyperbolically as "second to no astronomer living." Rittenhouse's other claim to scientific eminence was his construction of the first orrery (a mechanical model of the solar system) in America.

Jefferson was on firmer ground when he said of Benjamin Franklin that "no one of the present age has made more important discoveries." One of Franklin's biographers called him a "harmonious human multitude." His studies of electricity, which he capped in 1752 with his famous kite experiment, established him as a scientist of international stature. He also invented the lightning rod, the iron Franklin stove (a far more efficient way to heat a room than an open fireplace), bifocal spectacles, and several other ingenious devices. In addition, he served 14 years (1751–1764) in the Pennsylvania assembly. He founded a circulating library, helped get the first hospital in Philadelphia built, and was an organizer of a volunteer fire company. In his spare time he taught himself Latin, French, Spanish, and Italian.

Franklin wrote so much about the virtues of hard work and thrift that some historians have described him as stuffy and straitlaced. Nothing could be further from the truth. He recognized the social value of conventional behavior, but he was no slave to convention. He fathered two illegitimate children and wrote satirical essays on such subjects as the advantage of having affairs with older and plain-looking women (who were, he claimed, more likely to appreciate the attention). And he had the perfect temperament, being open-minded and imaginative as well as shrewd and judicious—an unbeatable combination.

Franklin's international fame notwithstanding, the theoretical contributions of American thinkers and scientists were modest. No colony produced a Voltaire, a Gibbon, a Rousseau. Most were practical rather than speculative types, tinkerers rather than constructors of grand designs. As one observer noted, they were easily diverted "by Business or Inclination from profound Study, and prying into the Depth of Things." Thomas Jefferson, for example, made no theoretical discovery of importance, but his range was almost without limit: linguist, bibliophile, political scientist, architect, inventor, scientific farmer, and, above all, apostle of reason. "Fix reason firmly in her seat," he wrote, "and call to her tribunal every fact, every opinion."

Involvement at even the most marginal level in

the intellectual affairs of Europe gave influential New Englanders, middle colonists, and southerners a chance to get to know one another. Although their role in what Jefferson called "the Republic of Letters" was still minor, by mid-century their influence on the intellectual climate of the colonies was growing. That climate was one of eager curiosity, flexibility of outlook, and confidence.

Other People's Wars

The British colonies were part of a great empire that was part of a still larger world. Seemingly isolated in their remote communities, scattered like a broken string of beads between the wide Atlantic and the trackless Appalachian forests, Americans were constantly affected by outside events both in the Old World and in the New. Under the spell of mercantilistic logic, the western European nations competed fiercely for markets and colonial raw materials. War—hot and cold, declared and undeclared—was almost a permanent condition of 17th- and 18th-century life, and when the powers clashed, they fought wherever they could get at one another, in America, in Europe, and elsewhere.

Although the American colonies were minor pieces in the game and were sometimes casually exchanged or sacrificed by the masterminds in London, Paris, and Madrid in pursuit of some supposedly more important objective, the colonists quickly generated their own international animosities. North America, a huge and, compared to densely populated Europe, almost empty stage, evidently did not provide enough room for French, Dutch, Spanish, and English companies to perform. Frenchmen and Spaniards clashed savagely in Florida in the 16th century. Before the landing of the Pilgrims, Samuel Argall of Virginia was sacking French settlements in Maine and carrying off Jesuit priests into captivity at Jamestown. Instead of fostering tranquillity and generosity, the abundance of America seemed to make the settlers belligerent and greedy.

The North Atlantic fisheries quickly became a source of trouble between Canadian and New England colonists, despite the fact that the waters of the Grand Banks teemed with cod and other fish. To dry and salt their catch, the fishermen needed land bases, and French and English Americans struggled constantly over the harbors of Maine, Nova Scotia, and Newfoundland.

Even more troublesome was the fur trade. The yield of the forest was easily exhausted by indiscriminate slaughter, and traders contended bitterly to control valuable hunting grounds. The French in Canada conducted their fur trading through tribes such as the Algonquins and the Hurons. This brought them into conflict with the Five Nations, the powerful Iroquois confederation of central New York.

As early as 1609 the Five Nations were at war with the French and their Indian allies. For decades this struggle flared sporadically, the Iroquois more than holding their own both as fighters and as traders. They combined, according to one terrified Frenchman, the stealth and craftiness of the fox, the ferocity and courage of the lion, and the speed of a bird in flight. The Iroquois brought quantities of beaver pelts to the Dutch at Albany, some obtained by their own trappers, others taken by ambushing the fur-laden canoes of their enemies. They preyed on and ultimately destroyed the Hurons in the land north of Lake Ontario and dickered with Indian trappers in far-off Michigan. When the English took over the New Amsterdam colony, they eagerly adopted the Iroquois as allies, buying their furs and supplying them with trading goods and guns.

By the last decade of the 17th century it had become clear that the Dutch lacked the strength to maintain a big empire and that Spain was declining fast. The future, especially in North America, belonged to England and France. In the wars of the next 125 years, European alliances shifted dramatically, yet the English and what the Boston lawyer John Adams called "the turbulent Gallicks" were always on opposite sides.

In the first three of these conflicts, colonists played only minor parts. The fighting in America consisted chiefly of sneak attacks on isolated outposts. In King William's War (1689–1697), the American phase of the War of the League of Augsburg, French forces raided Schenectady in New York and frontier settlements in New England. English colonists retaliated by capturing Port Royal, Nova Scotia, only to lose that outpost in a counterattack in 1691. The Peace of Ryswick in 1697 restored all captured territory in America to the original owners.

The next struggle was the War of the Spanish

English ties with the Iroquois aided the colonists both economically and politically. Here, Sir William Johnson supervises a treaty session with tribal leaders. Johnson, a rich fur trader, was sympathetic to the Indians (he married a Mohawk woman) but drove a hard bargain when negotiating with them to add to his own vast estates.

Succession (1702–1713), fought to prevent the union of Spain and France under the Bourbons. The Americans named this conflict Queen Anne's War. French-inspired Abenaki Indians razed Deerfield, Massachusetts. A party of Carolinians burned St. Augustine in Spanish Florida. The New Englanders retook Port Royal. However, in Europe the forces of England, Holland, and Austria, led by the duke of Marlborough, won a series of decisive victories. In the Treaty of Utrecht in 1713, France yielded Nova Scotia, Newfoundland, and the Hudson Bay region to Great Britain.

If the colonies were mere pawns in these wars, the people of New England (and of Canada) paid heavily in them. Many frontier settlers were killed in the raids. Hundreds of townspeople died during the campaigns in Nova Scotia. Massachusetts taxes went up sharply, and the colony issued large amounts of paper currency to pay its bills, causing an inflation that ate into the living standards of wage earners.

The American phase of the third Anglo-French conflict, the War of the Austrian Succession (1740–1748), was called King George's War. The usual Indian raids were launched in both directions across the lonely forests that separated the St. Lawrence settlements from the New York and New England frontier. A New England force captured the strategic fortress of Louisbourg on Cape Breton Island, guarding the entrance to the Gulf of St. Lawrence.

The Treaty of Aix-la-Chapelle in 1748, however, required the return of Louisbourg, much to the chagrin of the New Englanders.

As this incident suggests, the colonial wars generated a certain amount of trouble between England and the colonies; matters that seemed unimportant in London might loom large in American eyes, and vice versa. But the conflicts were seldom serious. The wars did, however, increase the bad feelings between settlers north and south of the St. Lawrence. Every Indian raid was attributed to French provocateurs, although more often than not the English colonists themselves were responsible for the Indian troubles. Conflicting land claims further aggravated the situation. Massachusetts, Connecticut, and Virginia possessed overlapping claims to the Ohio Valley, and Pennsylvania and New York also had pretensions in the region. Yet the French, ranging broadly across the midcontinent, insisted that the Ohio country was exclusively theirs.

The Great War for the Empire

In this beautiful, almost untouched land, a handful of individuals determined the future of the continent. Over the years the French had established a chain of forts and trading posts running from Mackinac Island in northern Michigan to Kaskaskia on the Mississippi and Vincennes on the Wabash and from Niagara in the east to the Bourbon River, near Lake Winnipeg, in the west. By the 1740s, however, Pennsylvania fur traders, led by George Croghan, a rugged Irishman, were setting up posts north of the Ohio River and dickering with Miami and Huron Indians who ordinarily sold their furs to the French. In 1748 Croghan built a fort at Pickawillany, deep in the Miami country, in what is now western Ohio. That same year agents of a group of Virginia land speculators who had recently organized what they called the Ohio Company reached this area.

With trifling exceptions, an insulating band of wilderness had always separated the French and English in America. Now the two powers came into contact. The immediate result was a showdown battle for control of North America, the "great war for the empire." Thoroughly alarmed by the presence of the English on land they had long considered their own, the French struck hard. Attacking suddenly in 1752, they wiped out Croghan's post at Pickawillany and drove his traders back into Pennsylvania. Then they built a string of barrier forts south from Lake Erie along the Pennsylvania line: Fort Presque Isle, Fort Le Boeuf, Fort Venango.

The Pennsylvania authorities chose to ignore this action, but Lieutenant Governor Robert Dinwiddie of Virginia (who was an investor in the Ohio Company) dispatched a 21-year-old surveyor named George Washington to warn the French that they were trespassing on Virginia territory.

Washington, a gangling, inarticulate, and intensely ambitious young planter, made his way northwest in the fall of 1753 and delivered Dinwiddie's message to the commandant at Fort Le Boeuf. It made no impression. "[The French] told me," Washington reported, "that it was their absolute Design to take Possession of the Ohio, and by G—— they would do it." Governor Dinwiddie thereupon promoted Washington to lieutenant colonel and sent him back in the spring of 1754 with 150 men to seize a strategic junction south of the new French forts, where the Allegheny and Monongahela rivers join to form the Ohio.

Eager but inexperienced in battle, young Washington botched his assignment. As his force labored painfully through the tangled mountain country southeast of the fork of the Ohio, he received word that the French had already occupied the position and were constructing a powerful post, Fort Duquesne. Outnumbered by perhaps four to one, Washington foolishly pushed on. He surprised and routed a French reconnaissance party, but this brought upon him the main body of enemy troops.

Hastily he threw up a defensive position, aptly named Fort Necessity, but the ground was ill chosen; the French easily surrounded the fort, and Washington had to surrender. After tricking the young officer, who could not read French, into signing an admission that he had "assassinated" the leader of the reconnaissance party, his captors, with the gateway to the Ohio country firmly in their hands, permitted him and his men to march off. Nevertheless, Washington returned to Virginia a hero, for although still undeclared, this was war, and he had struck the first blow against the hated French.

In the resulting conflict, which they called the French and Indian War, the English colonists outnumbered the French by about l.5 million to 90,000. But the English were divided and disorganized, the

French disciplined and united. The French controlled the disputed territory, and most of the Indians took their side. As a colonial official wrote, together they made formidable forest fighters, "sometimes in our Front, sometimes in our Rear, and often on all sides of us, Hussar Fashion, taking the Advantage of every Tree and Bush." With the ignorance and arrogance typical of 18th-century colonial administration, the British mismanaged the war and failed to make effective use of local resources. For several years they stumbled from one defeat to another.

General Edward Braddock, a competent but uninspired soldier, was dispatched to Virginia to take command. In June 1755 he marched against Fort Duquesne with 1,400 Redcoats and a smaller number of colonials, only to be ambushed and decisively defeated by a much smaller force of French and Indians. Braddock died bravely in battle, and only 500 of his men, led by Colonel Washington, who was serving as his aide-de-camp, made their way back to Virginia.

Elsewhere Anglo-American arms fared little better in the early years of the war. Expeditions against

A key phase of Pitt's American strategy involved capturing the French strong-points guarding the approaches to Canada: Louisbourg, protecting the St. Lawrence; Fort Ticonderoga and Crown Point, on Lake Champlain; and Fort Duquesne, in the Ohio country. Colonial forces played a significant role in this strategy, with John Forbes seizing Fort Duquesne, John Bradstreet winning control of Lake Ontario, and William Johnson taking Fort Niagara.

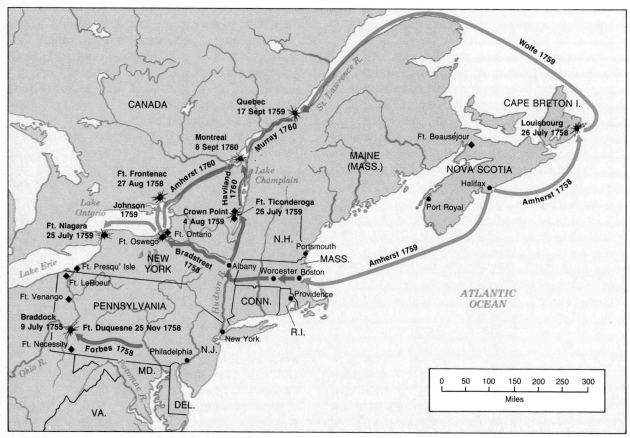

PITT'S STRATEGY, FRENCH AND INDIAN WAR, 1758–1760

Wolfe and Amherst recaptured the French fortress of Louisbourg in July 1758. This watercolor is the work of Thomas Davies, an English artillery officer. Louisbourg is at center, under attack from Amherst's siege lines at right and Admiral Boscawen's British fleet lying offshore. French ships are aflame in the harbor.

Fort Niagara, key to all French defenses in the west, and Crown Point, gateway to Montreal, bogged down. Meanwhile Indians, armed by the French, bathed the frontier in blood. Venting the frustration caused by 150 years of white advance, they attacked defenseless outposts with unrestrained brutality. They poured molten lead into their victims' wounds, ripped off the fingernails of captives, even drank the blood of those who endured their tortures stoically.* The most feared of the "French" Indians were the Delawares, a once-peaceful Pennsylvania tribe that had been harried from their homelands by the English and the Iroquois. General Braddock paid his Indian allies only £5 each for French scalps but offered £200 for the hair of Shinngass, the Delaware chieftain.

In 1756 the conflict spread to Europe to become the Seven Years' War. Prussia sided with Great Britain, Austria with the French. On the world stage, too, things went badly for the British. Finally, in 1757, as defeat succeeded defeat, King George II was forced to allow William Pitt, whom he detested, to take over leadership of the war effort. Pitt, grandson of "Diamond" Pitt, a *nouveau riche* East India merchant, was an unstable man who spent much of his life on the verge of madness, but he was a brilliant strategist and capable of inspiring the nation in its hour of trial.

Pitt recognized, as few contemporaries did, the potential value of North America. Instead of relying on the tightfisted and shortsighted colonial assemblies for men and money, he poured regiment after regiment of British regulars and the full resources of the British treasury into the contest, mortgaging the future recklessly to secure the prize. Grasping the importance of sea power in fighting a war on the other side of the Atlantic, he used the British navy to bottle up the enemy fleet and hamper French communications with Canada. He possessed a keen eye for military genius, and when he discovered it, he ignored seniority and the outraged

---

* The anthropologist Bruce Trigger writes: "If the prisoner had been a brave man, his heart was cooked and eaten by the young [Huron] warriors, who believed that they would acquire his courage in this manner. . . . It was an act of religious significance."

feelings of mediocre generals and promoted talented young officers to top commands. (His greatest find was James Wolfe, whom he made a brigadier at 31.)

In the winter of 1758, as Pitt's grand strategy matured, Fort Duquesne fell. It was appropriately renamed Fort Pitt, the present Pittsburgh. The following summer Fort Niagara was overrun. General Jeffrey Amherst took Crown Point, and Wolfe sailed up the St. Lawrence to Quebec. There General Louis Joseph de Montcalm had prepared formidable defenses, but after months of probing and planning, Wolfe found and exploited a chink in the city's armor and captured it. Both he and Montcalm died in the battle. In 1760 Montreal fell and the French abandoned all Canada to the British.

Spain attempted to stem the British advance but failed utterly. A Far Eastern fleet captured Manila in 1762, and another British force took Cuba. The French sugar islands in the West Indies were also captured, while in India, British troops reduced the French posts one by one.

The Peace of Paris

Peace was restored in 1763 by the Treaty of Paris. Its terms were moderate considering the extent of the British triumph. France abandoned all claim to North America except for two small islands near Newfoundland; Great Britain took over Canada and the eastern half of the Mississippi Valley. Although the British considered the French sugar islands, Guadeloupe and Martinique, more economically valuable than the cold Canadian wilderness, they kept Canada for military and strategic reasons and returned the islands to France, along with some of the captured French bases in India and Africa. Spain got back both the Philippine Islands and Cuba but in exchange ceded East and West Florida to Great Britain. In a separate treaty, Spain also got New Orleans and the huge area of North America west of the Mississippi River. France and Spain thus remained important colonial powers.

"Half the continent," the historian Francis Parkman wrote, "had changed hands at the scratch of a pen." From the point of view of the English colonists in America, the victory was overwhelming. All threat to their frontiers seemed to have been swept away. Surely, they believed in the first happy

moments of victory, their peaceful and prosperous expansion was assured for countless generations.

No honest American could deny that the victory had been won chiefly by British troops and with British gold. Colonial militiamen fought well in defense of their homes or when some highly prized objective seemed ripe for the plucking; they lacked discipline and determination when required to fight far from home and under commanders they did not know. As one American official admitted, it was difficult to get New Englanders to enlist "unless assurances can be given that they shall not march to the southward of certain limits."

Colonials were delighted that scarlet-clad British regulars had borne the brunt of the fighting and happier still that the Crown had shouldered most of the financial burden of the long struggle. The local assemblies contributed to the cost, but except for Massachusetts and Virginia, their outlays were trivial compared with the £82 million poured into the worldwide conflict by the British.

Little wonder that the great victory produced a burst of praise for king and mother country throughout America. Parades, cannonading, fireworks, banquets, the pealing of church bells—these were the order of the day in every colonial town. Ezra Stiles, later president of Yale, extolled "the illustrious House of Hanover," whose new head, the young George III, had inherited the throne in 1760. "Nothing," said Thomas Pownall, wartime governor of Massachusetts and a student of colonial administration, "can eradicate from [the colonists'] hearts their natural, almost mechanical affection to Great Britain."

Putting the Empire Right

In London peace proved a time for reassessment; that the empire of 1763 was not the same as the empire of 1754 was obvious. The new, far larger dominion would be much more expensive to maintain. Pitt had spent a huge sum winning and securing it, much of it borrowed money. Great Britain's national debt had doubled between 1754 and 1763. Now this debt must be serviced and repaid, and the strain that this would place on the economy was clear to all. Furthermore, the day-to-day cost of administering an empire that extended from Hudson Bay to India was far larger than what the already burdened British taxpayer could be expected to bear. Before the great war for the empire, Britain's North American possessions were administered for about £70,000 a year; after 1763 the cost was five times as much.

The American empire had also grown far more complex. A system of administration that treated it as a string of separate plantations struggling to exist on the edge of the forest would no longer suffice. The war had been fought for control of the Ohio Valley. Now that the prize had been secured, ten thousand hands were eager to make off with it. The urge to expand was, despite the continent's enormous empty spaces, an old American drive. As early as the 1670s, eastern stay-at-homes were lamenting the "insatiable desire after Land" that made people willing to "live like Heathen, only that so they might have Elbow-room enough in the world." Frontier warfare had frustrated this urge for seven long years. How best could it be satisfied now that peace had come?

Conflicting colonial claims, based on charters drafted by men who thought the Pacific lay over the next hill, threatened to make the great valley a battleground once more. The Indians remained unpacified. Rival land companies contested for charters, while fur traders strove to hold back the wave of settlement that must inevitably destroy the world of the beaver and the deer. One Englishman who traveled through America at this time predicted that if the colonists were left to their own devices, "there would soon be civil war from one end of the continent to the other."

Apparently only Great Britain could deal with these problems and rivalries, for when Franklin had proposed a rudimentary form of colonial union—the Albany Plan of 1754—it was rejected by almost everyone. Unfortunately, the British government did not rise to the challenge. Perhaps this was to be expected. A handful of aristocrats (fewer than 150 peers were active in government affairs) dominated British politics, and they were more concerned with local offices and personal advantage than with large questions of policy. An American who spent some time in London in 1764 trying to obtain approval for a plan for the development of the west reported: "The people hear Spend thire time in Nothing but abuseing one Another and Striveing who shall be in power with a view to Serve themselves and Thire friends." King George III was not a tyrant, as once

was commonly believed, but he was an inept politician and the victim of frequent bouts of illness.

Even the best-educated English leaders were nearly all monumentally ignorant of American conditions. The British imperial system lacked effective channels of communication. Information about American attitudes came from royal officials in the colonies and others with special interests to protect or advance, or from the colonial agents and merchants in London, whose information was often out-of-date.

Serene in their ignorance, most English leaders insisted that colonials were uncouth and generally inferior beings. During the French and Indian War, General Wolfe characterized colonial troops as "the dirtiest, most contemptible cowardly dogs you can conceive," and another English officer compared the ordinary run to "broken innkeepers, horse jockeys and Indian traders."

Any officer with a royal commission outranked all officers of the colonial militia, regardless of title. Young Colonel Washington, for example, had to travel all the way from Virginia to the headquarters of the commander in chief in Boston to establish his precedence over one Captain John Dagworthy, a Maryland officer who had formerly held a royal commission and who did not propose to let a mere colonial colonel outrank him.

Many English people resented the colonists because they were rapidly becoming rich and powerful. Shortly after the war, John Adams predicted that within a century America would be wealthier and more populous than Great Britain.* If the English did not say much about this possibility, they too considered it from time to time—without Adams's relish.

Tightening Imperial Controls

The attempt of the inefficient British government to deal with the intricate colonial problems that resulted from the great war for the empire led to the American Revolution—a rebellion that was costly but produced excellent results for the colonists, for Great Britain, for the rest of the empire, and eventually for the entire world. Trouble began when the

---

* As early as 1751, Franklin predicted that in a century "the greatest number of Englishmen will be on this Side of the Water."

British decided after the war to intervene more actively in American affairs. Theoretically, the colonies were entirely subordinate to Crown and Parliament, yet except for the disastrous attempt to centralize control of the colonies in the 1680s, they had been allowed a remarkable degree of freedom to manage their own affairs. Of course, they had come to expect this as their right.

Parliament had never attempted to raise a revenue in America. "Compelling the colonies to pay money without their consent would be rather like raising contributions in an enemy's country than taxing Englishmen for their own benefit," Benjamin Franklin wrote. Sir Robert Walpole, initiator of the policy of salutary neglect, recognized the colonial viewpoint. He responded to a suggestion that Parliament tax the colonies by saying: "I will leave that for some of my successors, who may have more courage than I have." Nevertheless, the *legality* of parliamentary taxation, or of other parliamentary

intervention in colonial affairs, had not been seriously contested. During King George's War and again during the French and Indian War, many British officials in America suggested that Parliament tax the colonies.

Nothing was done until 1759, when British victories had made ultimate triumph sure. Then a general tightening of imperial regulations began. Royal control over colonial courts was strengthened. In Massachusetts the use of general search warrants (writs of assistance) was authorized in 1761. These writs enabled customs officers searching for smuggled goods to enter homes and warehouses without evidence or specific court orders. Nearly all Americans resented the invasions of privacy that the writs caused. A Boston lawyer, James Otis, argued in a case involving 63 merchants that the writs were "against the Constitution" and therefore void. Otis lost the case but by boldly suggesting that Parliament's authority over the colonies was not absolute, he became a colonial hero.

After the signing of the peace treaty in 1763, events pushed the British authorities to still more vigorous activity in America. Freed of the restraint posed by French competition, Englishman and colonist increased their pressure on the Indians. Fur traders now cheated them outrageously, while callous military men hoped to exterminate them like vermin. One British officer expressed the wish that they could be hunted down with dogs.

Led by an Ottawa chief named Pontiac, the tribes made one last effort to drive the whites back across the mountains. What the whites called Pontiac's "rebellion" caused much havoc, but it failed. By 1764 most of the western tribes had accepted the peace terms offered by a royal commissioner, Sir William Johnson, one of the few whites who understood and sympathized with them. The British government then placed 15 regiments, some 6,000 soldiers, in posts along the entire arc of the frontier, as much to protect the Indians from the settlers as the settlers from the Indians. It proclaimed a new western policy: No settlers were to cross the Appalachian divide. Only licensed traders might do business with the Indians beyond that line. The purchase of Indian land was forbidden. In compensation, three new colonies—Quebec, East Florida, and West Florida—were created, but they were not permitted to set up local assemblies.

EUROPEAN CLAIMS IN ALL OF NORTH AMERICA, 1763

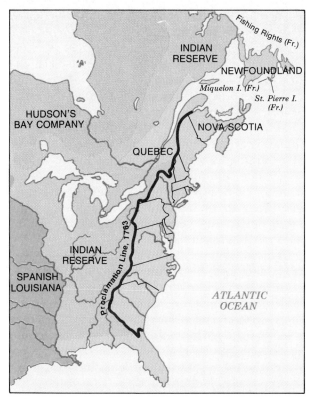

EASTERN NORTH AMERICA, 1763

George III's Proclamation of 1763 in effect reserved for the Indians the vast area across the Appalachians (except for the new royal colonies of Quebec, East Florida, and West Florida) as far west as Spanish Louisiana and as far north as the Hudson's Bay Company preserve.

This Proclamation of 1763 excited much indignation in America. The frustration of dozens of schemes for land development in the Ohio Valley angered many influential colonists. Colonel Washington referred to the proclamation contemptuously as "a temporary expedient to quiet the minds of Indians," and he continued to stake out claims to western lands.

Originally the British had intended the proclamation to be temporary. With the passage of time, however, checking westward expansion seemed a good way to save money, prevent trouble with the Indians, and keep the colonies tied closely to the mother country. The proclamation line, the Board of Trade declared, was "necessary for the preser-

vation of the colonies in due subordination."* Naturally, this attitude caused resentment in America. To close off the west temporarily in order to pacify the Indians made some sense; to keep it closed was like trying to contain a tidal wave.

The Sugar Act

Americans disliked the new western policy but realized that the problems were knotty and that no simple solution existed. Their protests were somewhat muted. Great Britain's effort to raise money in America to help support the increased cost of colonial administration caused far more vehement complaints. George Grenville, who became prime minister in 1763, was a fairly able man, although long-winded and rather narrow in outlook. His reputation as a financial expert was based chiefly on his eagerness to reduce government spending. Under his leadership Parliament passed, in April 1764, the so-called Sugar Act. This law placed tariffs on sugar, coffee, wines, and other things imported into America in substantial amounts. Taxes on European products imported by way of Great Britain were doubled, and the enumerated articles list was extended to include iron, raw silk, and potash. The sixpence-per-gallon tax on foreign molasses, imposed in 1733 and designed to be prohibitively high, was reduced to threepence, at which level the foreign product could compete with molasses from the British West Indies.

At the same time, measures aimed at enforcing all the trade laws were put into effect. (A threepenny molasses duty would not produce much revenue if it were as easy to avoid as the old levy had been.) Anyone accused of violating the Sugar Act was to be tried before British naval officers in vice-admiralty courts. Grenville was determined to end smuggling, corruption, and inefficiency. Soon the customs service was collecting each year 15 times as much in duties as it had before the war.

The Sugar Act and the decision of the government in London to restrict the printing of paper

---

* The British were particularly concerned about preserving the colonies as markets for their manufactures. They feared that the spread of population beyond the mountains would stimulate local manufacturing because the high cost of land transportation would make British goods prohibitively expensive.

money in the colonies disturbed Americans deeply. Throughout the 18th century, local assemblies had issued paper currency in anticipation of tax payments to finance emergencies such as wars. The act of 1764 did not entirely ban the use of colonial paper money. But the colonists saw the law as an attack on the power of their assemblies. The law also came at a bad time. During the war the seaports prospered and shipbuilding boomed. Merchants earned fat profits supplying the British forces with food and other goods. British soldiers and sailors, 40,000 of them, spent most of their wages in the colonies.

When the fighting shifted to the Caribbean after the fall of Canada, most of this spending stopped. The soldiers "are gone to drink [rum] in a warmer Region, the place of its production," a New York merchant mourned. A depression increased the impact of the new laws. Hard-hit merchants and artisans found British policy alarming.

Far more alarming was the nature of the Sugar Act and the manner of its passage. The Navigation Act duties had been intended to regulate commerce, and the sums collected had not cut deeply into profits. Indeed, the Navigation Acts might well be considered an instrument of imperial foreign policy, an area of government that everyone willingly conceded to London. Yet few Americans were willing to concede that Parliament had the right to tax them. As *Englishmen* they believed that no one should be deprived arbitrarily of property and that, as James Otis put it in his stirring pamphlet *The Rights of the British Colonies Asserted and Proved,* written during the controversy over writs of assistance, everyone should be "free from all taxes but what he consents to in person, or by his representative." John Locke had made clear in his *Second Treatise on Government* (1690) that property ought never be taken from people without their consent, not because material values transcend all others but because human liberty can never be secure when arbitrary power of any kind exists. "If our Trade may be taxed why not our Lands?" the Boston town meeting asked when news of the Sugar Act reached America. "Why not the produce of our Lands and every Thing we possess or make use of?"

"Essential Rights and Liberties"

To most people in Great Britain, the colonial protest against taxation without representation seemed a hypocritical quibble, and it is probably true that in 1764 many of the protesters had not thought the argument through. The distinction between tax laws and other types of legislation was artificial, the British reasoned. Either Parliament was sovereign in America or it was not, and only a fool or a traitor would argue that it was not. If the colonists were loyal subjects of George III, as they claimed, they should bear cheerfully their fair share of the cost of governing his widespread dominions. As to representation, the colonies *were* represented in Parliament; every member of that body stood for the interests of the entire empire. If Americans had no say in the election of members of Commons, neither did most English subjects.

This concept of "virtual" representation accurately described the British system. But it made no sense in America, where from the time of the first settlements members of the colonial assemblies had represented the people of the districts in which they stood for office. The confusion between virtual and actual (geographically based) representation revealed the extent to which colonial and British political practices had diverged over the years.

The British were correct in concluding that selfish motives influenced colonial objections to the Sugar Act. The colonists denounced taxation without representation, but an offer of a reasonable number of seats in Parliament would not have satisfied them. They would probably have complained about paying taxes to support imperial administration even if imposed by their own assemblies. American abundance and the simplicity of colonial life had enabled them to prosper without assuming any considerable tax burden. Now their maturing society was beginning to require communal rather than individual solutions to the problems of existence. Not many of them were prepared to face up to this hard truth.

Over the course of colonial history, Americans had taken a narrow view of imperial concerns. They had avoided complying with the Navigation Acts whenever they could profit by doing so. Colonial militiamen had compiled a sorry record when asked to fight for Britain or even for the inhabitants of colonies other than their own. True, most Americans professed loyalty to the Crown, but not many would voluntarily open their purses except to benefit themselves. In short, they were provincials, in attitude and in fact.

But the colonists were opposed in principle to

taxation without representation. They failed, however, to agree on a common plan of resistance. Many of the assemblies drafted protests, but these varied in force as well as in form. Merchant groups that tried to organize boycotts of products subject to the new taxes met with indifferent success. Then in 1765 Parliament provided the flux necessary for welding colonial opinion by passing the Stamp Act.

The Stamp Act: The Pot Set to Boiling

The Stamp Act placed stiff excise taxes on all kinds of printed matter—newspapers, legal documents, licenses, even playing cards. Stamp duties were intended to be relatively painless to pay and cheap to collect; in England similar taxes brought in about £100,000 annually. Grenville hoped that the Stamp Act would produce £60,000 a year in America, and the law provided that all revenue should be applied to "defraying the necessary expenses of defending, protecting, and securing" the colonies.

Hardly a farthing was collected. As the Boston clergyman Jonathan Mayhew explained, "Almost every British American . . . considered it as an infraction of their rights, or their dearly purchased privileges." The Sugar Act had been related to Parliament's uncontested power to control colonial trade, but the Stamp Act was a direct tax. When Parliament ignored the politely phrased petitions of the colonial assemblies, more vigorous protests quickly followed.

Virginia took the lead. In late May 1765 Patrick Henry, fresh from his triumph in the "Parson's Cause" controversy, in which he had opposed the right of the British Privy Council to void a law passed by the House of Burgesses, introduced resolutions asserting redundantly that the Burgesses possessed "the only and sole and exclusive right and power to lay taxes" on Virginians and suggesting that Parliament had no legal authority to tax the colonies at all. Henry spoke for what the royal governor called the "Young, hot and Giddy Members" of the legislature (most of whom, incidentally, had absented themselves from the meeting). The more extreme of Henry's resolutions failed of enactment, but the debate they occasioned attracted wide and favorable attention. On June 6 the Massachusetts assembly proposed an intercolonial Stamp Act Con-

gress, which, when it met in New York City in October, passed another series of resolutions of protest. The Stamp Act and other recent acts of Parliament were "burthensome and grievous," the delegates declared. "It is unquestionably essential to the freedom of a people . . . that no taxes be imposed on them but with their own consent."

During the summer, irregular organizations known as the Sons of Liberty began to agitate against the act. Far more than anyone realized, this marked the start of the revolution. For the first time, extralegal organized resistance was taking place, distinct from protest and argument conducted by constituted organs of government like the House of Burgesses and the Massachusetts General Court.

Although led by men of character and position, the "Liberty Boys" frequently resorted to violence to achieve their aims. In Boston they staged vicious riots, looting and vandalizing the houses of the stamp master and his brother-in-law, Lieutenant Governor Thomas Hutchinson. In Connecticut stamp master Jared Ingersoll, a man of great courage and dignity, faced an angry mob demanding his resignation. When threatened with death if he refused, he coolly replied that he was prepared to die "perhaps as well now as another Time." Probably his life was not really in danger, but the size and determination of the crowd convinced him that resistance was useless, and he capitulated.

The stamps were printed in England and shipped to stamp masters (all Americans) in the colonies well in advance of November 1, 1765, the date the law was to go into effect. The New York stamp master had resigned, but the stamps were stored in the city under military guard. Radicals distributed placards reading, "The first Man that either distributes or makes use of Stampt Paper let him take care of his House, Person, and Effects. We dare." When Major Thomas James, the British officer who had charge of the stamps, promised that "the stamps would be crammed down New Yorkers' throats," a mob responded by breaking into his house, drinking all his wine, and smashing his furniture and china, reducing the place to a shambles.

In some colonies the stamps were snatched by mobs and put to the torch amid rejoicing. Elsewhere they were locked up in secret by British officials or held on shipboard. For a time no business requiring stamped paper was transacted; then, gradually, people began to defy the law by issuing and accepting unstamped documents. Threatened by mob action

Outrage at the Stamp Act was demonstrated all over the colonies in incidents like this, where the effigy of a New Hampshire stamp master is ridiculed by the towns-people.

should they resist, British officials stood by help-lessly. The law was a dead letter.

The looting associated with this crisis alarmed many colonists, including some prominent opponents of the Stamp Act. "When the pot is set to boil," the lawyer John Adams remarked sadly, "the scum rises to the top." Another Bostonian called the vandalizing of Thomas Hutchinson's house a "flagrant instance of to what a pitch of infatuation an incensed populace can rise." Such people worried that the protests might be aimed at the wealthy and powerful in America as well as at British tyranny. This does not mean that they disapproved of crowd protests, or even the destruction of property during such protests, as distinct from stealing. Many such people took part in the rioting. "State-quakes," John Adams also said, this time complacently, were comparable to earthquakes and other kinds of natural violence.

Rioters or Rebels?

That many of the poor resented the colonial elite goes without saying, as does the fact that in many instances the rioting got out of hand and took on a social as well as a political character. Times were hard, and the colonial elite, including most of the leading critics of British policy, had little compassion for the poor, who they feared could be corrupted

by anyone who offered them a square meal or a glass of rum. Once aroused, laborers and artisans may well have directed their energies toward righting what they considered local wrongs.

Yet the mass of the people, being owners of property and capable of influencing political decisions, were not social revolutionaries. They might envy and resent the wealth and power of the great landowners and merchants, but there is no evidence that they wished to overthrow the established order.

The British were not surprised that Americans disliked the Stamp Act. They had not anticipated, however, that Americans would react so violently and so unanimously. Americans did so for many reasons. Business continued poor in 1765, and at a time when 3 shillings was a day's wage for an urban laborer, the stamp tax was 2 shillings for an advertisement in a newspaper, 5 shillings for a will, and 20 shillings for a license to sell liquor. The taxes would hurt the business of lawyers, merchants, newspaper editors, and tavernkeepers. Even clergymen dealt with papers requiring stamps. The protests of such influential and articulate people had a powerful impact on public opinion.

The greatest cause of concern to the colonists was Great Britain's flat rejection of the principle of no taxation without representation. This alarmed them for two closely related reasons. First of all, as *Americans* they objected to being taxed by a legislative body they had not been involved in choosing. To buy a stamp was to surrender all claim to self-government. Second, as *British subjects* they valued what they called "the rights of Englishmen." They saw the Stamp Act as only the worst in a series of arbitrary invasions of these rights.

Already Parliament had passed yet another measure, the Quartering Act, requiring local legislatures to house and feed new British troops sent to the colonies. A standing army was universally deemed to be a threat to liberty. Why were Redcoats necessary in Boston and New York where there was no foreign enemy for thousands of miles in any direction? Soldiers were particularly unwelcome in hard times because, being miserably underpaid, they took any odd jobs they could get in their off hours, thus competing with unemployed colonists.

Reluctantly, many Americans were beginning to fear that the London authorities had organized a conspiracy to subvert the liberties of all British subjects.

Taxation or Tyranny?

In the 18th century the English were universally recognized as the freest people in the world. In Mozart's opera *The Abduction from the Seraglio* (1782), when the Turk Osmin tells the kidnapped Blonde that she is his slave, a "gift" from his master, she replies contemptuously: "A slave! I am an English-woman, born to freedom." Americans, like their English cousins, attributed their freedom to what they called their balanced government. In Britain power appeared to be shared by the Crown, the House of Lords (representing the aristocracy), and the House of Commons (representing the rest of the realm). The governors, councils, and assemblies seemed to play analogous roles in the colonies.

In reality this balance of separate forces never existed, either in Britain or in America. The apparent harmony of society was in both instances the product of a lack of seriously divisive issues, not of dynamic tension between rival forces. But the new laws seemed to Americans to threaten the balance, and this idea was reinforced by their observations of the corruption of English elections. Benjamin Franklin, being at the time a colonial agent in London, knew British politics well. He complained that the entire country was "at market" and "might be bought . . . by the Devil himself" for about £12

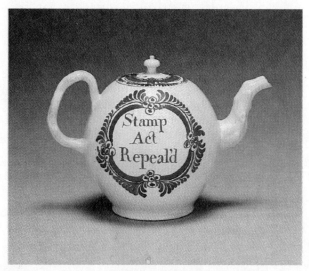

A decorated teapot—made in England!—symbolizes both American rejoicing over repeal of the Stamp Act and the resumption of colonial trade with the mother country.

million. A clique seeking unlimited power was trying to destroy balanced government in Britain and in America, or so many colonists thought.

There was no such conspiracy; yet to the question. "Were American rights actually in danger?" no certain answer can be given. Grenville and his successors were English politicians, not tyrants. They looked down on bumptious colonials but surely had no wish to destroy either them or their prosperity. The British attitude was like that of a parent making a recalcitrant youngster swallow a bitter medicine: Protests were understandable, but in the patient's own interest they must be ignored.

At the same time, British leaders believed that the time had come to assert royal authority and centralize imperial power at the expense of colonial autonomy. The need to maintain a substantial British army in America to control the western Indians tempted the government to use some of the troops to control white Americans as well. This attitude probably had as much to do with the coming of the revolution as any specific act of Parliament because it flew in the face of the reality that the colonies had progressed beyond the childhood stage. They were no longer entirely dependent on the mother country. Indeed, an increasing number of important colonists believed that America would soon become what Franklin called "a great country, populous and mighty . . . able to shake off any shackles that may be imposed on her."

This view of America's future place in the world did not necessarily mean breaking away from the British Empire. However, it surely meant dealing with Great Britain on terms approaching equality. But psychologically British leaders were not ready to deal with Americans as equals or to consider American interests on a par with their own. In the long run, American liberty would be destroyed if this attitude was not changed.

Besides refusing to use stamps, Americans responded to the Stamp Act by boycotting British goods. Nearly 1,000 merchants signed nonimportation agreements. These struck British merchants hard in their pocketbooks, and they in turn began to bring pressure on Parliament for repeal. After a hot debate—Grenville, whose ministry had fallen over another issue, advocated using the army to enforce the act—the hated law was repealed in March 1766. In America there was jubilation at the news. The ban on British goods was lifted, and the colonists congratulated themselves on having stood fast in defense of principle.

The Declaratory Act

The great controversy over the constitutional relationship of colony to mother country was only beginning. The same day that it repealed the Stamp Act, Parliament passed the Declaratory Act, which stated that the colonies were "subordinate" and that Parliament could enact any law it wished "to bind the colonies and people of America."

To most Americans this bald statement of parliamentary authority seemed unconstitutional, a flagrant violation of their understanding of how the British imperial system was supposed to work. Actually, the Declaratory Act highlighted the degree to which British and American views of the system had drifted apart. The English and the colonials were using the same words but giving them different meanings. Their conflicting definitions of the word *representation* was a case in point. Another involved the word *constitution*, the term that James Otis had used in his attack on writs of assistance. To the British the constitution was the totality of laws, customs, and institutions that had developed over time and under which the nation functioned. In America, partly because governments were based on specific charters, the word meant a written document or contract spelling out, and thus limiting, the powers of government. If in England Parliament passed an "unconstitutional" law, the result might be rebellion, but that the law existed none would deny. "If the parliament will positively enact a thing to be done which is unreasonable," the great 18th-century English legal authority Sir William Blackstone wrote, "I know of no power that can control it." In America people were beginning to think that an unconstitutional law simply had no force.

Even more basic were the differing meanings that English and Americans were giving to the word *sovereignty*. As Bernard Bailyn has explained in *The Ideological Origins of the American Revolution*, 18th-century English political thinkers believed that sovereignty (ultimate political power) could not be divided. Government and law being based ultimately on force, some "final, unqualified, indivisible" authority had to exist if social order was to be preserved. The Glorious Revolution in England had settled the question of where sovereignty resided: in Parliament. The Declaratory Act, so obnoxious to Americans, seemed to the English the mere explication of the obvious. That colonial governments had passed local laws the English did not deny, but they had done so at the sufferance of the sovereign legislative power, Parliament.

Given these ideas and the long tradition out of which they had sprung, one can sympathize with the British failure to follow the colonists' reasoning (which had not yet evolved into a specific proposal for constitutional reform). But most responsible British officials refused even to listen to the American argument.

The Townshend Duties

Despite the repeal of the Stamp Act, the British did not abandon the policy of taxing the colonies. If direct taxes were inexpedient, indirect ones like the Sugar Act certainly were not. To persuade Parliament to repeal the Stamp Act, some Americans (most notably Benjamin Franklin) had claimed that the colonists objected only to direct taxes. To draw such a distinction as a matter of principle was absurd, and in fact few colonists had done so. British leaders saw the absurdity but easily convinced themselves that Americans were making the distinction.

Therefore, in June 1767, the chancellor of the exchequer, Charles Townshend, introduced a series of levies on glass, lead, paints, paper, and tea imported into the colonies. Townshend was a charming man experienced in colonial administration, but he was something of a playboy (his nickname was Champagne Charlie), and he lacked both integrity and common sense. He liked to think of Americans as ungrateful children; he once said he would rather see the colonies turned into "Primitive Desarts" than treat them as equals. Townshend thought it "perfect nonsense" to draw a distinction between direct and indirect taxation, yet in his arrogance he believed that the colonists were stupid enough to do so.

By this time the colonists were thoroughly on guard, and they responded quickly to the Townshend levies with a new boycott of British goods. In addition, they made elaborate efforts to stimulate colonial manufacturing. By the end of 1769, imports from the mother country had been almost halved. Meanwhile, administrative measures enacted along with the Townshend duties were creating more ill will. The Board of Customs Commissioners, with headquarters in Boston, took charge of enforcing the trade laws, and new vice-admiralty courts were set up at Halifax, Boston, Philadelphia, and Charleston to handle violations. These courts operated without juries, and the new commissioners proved to be a gang of rapacious racketeers who systematically attempted to obtain judgments against honest merchants in order to collect the huge forfeitures—one-third of the value of ship and cargo—that were their share of all seizures.

The struggle forced Americans to do some deep thinking about both American and imperial political affairs. The colonies' common interests and growing economic and social interrelationships probably made some kind of union inevitable. Trouble with England speeded the process. In 1765 the Stamp Act Congress (another extralegal organization and thus a further step in the direction of revolution) had brought the delegates of nine colonies to New York. Now, in 1768, the Massachusetts General Court took the next step. It sent the legislatures of the other colonies a "circular letter" expressing the "humble opinion" that the Townshend Acts "imposing Duties on the People . . . with the sole & express purpose of raising a Revenue are Infringements of their natural & constitutional Rights."

The question of the limits of British power in America was much debated, and this too was no doubt inevitable, again because of change and growth. Even in the late 17th century the assumptions that led Parliament to pass the Declaratory Act would have been unrealistic. In 1766 they were absurd.

After the passage of the Townshend Acts, John Dickinson, a Philadelphia lawyer, published "Letters from a Farmer in Pennsylvania to the Inhabitants of the British Colonies." Dickinson considered himself a loyal British subject trying to find a solution to colonial troubles. "Let us behave like dutiful children, who have received unmerited blows from a beloved parent," he wrote. Nevertheless, he stated plainly that Parliament had no right to tax the colonies, though it might collect incidental revenues in the process of regulating commerce.

Some Americans were much more radical than Dickinson. Samuel Adams of Boston, a genuine revolutionary agitator, believed by 1768 that Parliament had no right at all to legislate for the colonies.

If few were ready to go that far, fewer still accepted the reasoning behind the Declaratory Act.

The British ignored American thinking. The Massachusetts Circular Letter had been framed in moderate language and clearly reflected the convictions of most of the people in the Bay Colony, yet when news of it reached England, the secretary of state for the colonies, Lord Hillsborough, ordered the governor to dissolve the legislature. Two regiments of British troops were transferred from the frontier to Boston, part of the aforementioned policy of bringing the army closer to the centers of colonial unrest.

In Copley's flattering portrait painted in 1771, Samuel Adams points to the Massachusetts charter as if reminding Great Britain of the colonists' rights.

The Boston Massacre

These acts convinced more Americans that the British were conspiring to destroy their liberties. Resentment was particularly strong in Boston, where the postwar depression had come on top of two decades of economic stagnation. Crowding 4,000 tough British soldiers into a town of 16,000 people, many of them as capable of taking care of themselves when challenged as any Redcoat, was a formula for disorder.

How many scuffles and minor riots took place in waterfront taverns and darkened alleys that winter is lost to history. But on March 5, 1770, real trouble erupted. Late that afternoon a crowd of idlers began tossing snowballs at a company of Redcoats guarding the Custom House. Some of these missiles had been carefully wrapped around suitably sized rocks. Gradually the crowd increased in size and its mood grew meaner. The soldiers panicked and began firing their muskets. When the smoke cleared, five Bostonians lay dead and dying on the bloody ground.

This so-called Boston Massacre infuriated the populace. The violence played into the hands of radicals like Samuel Adams. But just as at the time of the Stamp Act riots, cooler heads prevailed. Announcing that he was "defending the rights of man and unconquerable truth," John Adams volunteered his services to make sure that the soldiers got a fair trial. Most were acquitted; the rest were treated leniently by the standards of the day. In Great Britain confrontation also gave way to adjustment. In April 1770 all the Townshend duties except the threepenny tax on tea were repealed. The tea tax was maintained as a matter of principle. "A peppercorn in acknowledgment of the right was of more value than millions without it," one British peer declared smugly—a glib fallacy.

At this point the nonimportation movement collapsed; although the boycott on tea was continued, many merchants imported British tea and paid the tax too. "Drank green tea," one patriot wrote in describing an afternoon at the merchant John Hancock's. "From Holland, I hope, but don't know."

A kind of postmassacre truce settled over Boston and the rest of British America. During the next two years no serious crisis erupted. Imports of British goods were nearly 50 percent higher than before the nonimportation agreement. So long as the Brit-

Paul Revere's engraving of the Boston Massacre was potent propaganda fully exploited by the Boston radicals. Many copies were made. His view of a deliberately ordered, concerted volley fired into a group of innocent citizens bore slight resemblance to fact. At the trial of the British soldiers, the jury was warned against "the prints exhibited in our houses" that added "wings to fancy." Two soldiers were punished mildly, the rest acquitted.

ish continued to be conciliatory, the colonists seemed satisfied with their place in the empire.

The Pot Spills Over

In 1772 this informal truce ended and new troubles broke out. The first was plainly the fault of the colonists involved. Early in June the British patrol boat *Gaspee* ran aground in Narragansett Bay, south of Providence, while pursuing a suspected smuggler. The *Gaspee*'s commander, Lieutenant Dudingston, had antagonized everyone in the area by his officiousness and zeal; that night a gang of local people boarded the helpless *Gaspee* and put it to the torch. This action was clearly criminal, but when the British attempted to bring the culprits to justice, no one would testify against them. The British, frustrated and angry, were strengthened in their conviction that the colonists were utterly lawless.

Then Thomas Hutchinson, now governor of Massachusetts, announced that henceforth the Crown rather than the local legislature would pay his salary. Since control over the salaries of royal officials gave the legislature a powerful hold on them, this development was disturbing. Groups of radicals formed "committees of correspondence" and stepped up communications with one another, planning joint action in case of trouble. This was another monumental step along the road to revolution; an organized colonywide resistance movement, lacking in any "legitimate" authority but ready to consult and act in the name of the public interest, was taking shape.

The Tea Act Crisis

In the spring of 1773 an entirely unrelated event precipitated the final crisis. The British East India Company held a monopoly of all trade between India and the rest of the empire. This monopoly had yielded fabulous returns, but decades of corruption and inefficiency together with heavy military expenses in recent years had weakened the company until it was almost bankrupt.

Among the assets of this venerable institution were some 17 million pounds of tea stored in English warehouses. The decline of the American market, a result first of the boycott and then of the smuggling of cheaper Dutch tea, partly accounted for the glut. Normally, East India Company tea was sold to English wholesalers. They in turn sold it to American wholesalers, who distributed it to local merchants for sale to the consumer. A substantial British tax was levied on the tea as well as the threepenny Townshend duty. Now Lord North, the new prime minister, decided to remit the British tax and to allow the company to sell directly in America through its own agents. The savings would permit a sharp reduction of the retail price and at the same time yield a nice profit to the company. The Townshend tax was retained, however, to preserve (as Lord North said when the East India Company directors suggested its repeal) the principle of Parliament's right to tax the colonies.

The company then shipped 1,700 chests of tea to colonial ports. Though the idea of high-quality tea offered at bargain prices was tempting, after a little thought nearly everyone in America appreciated the dangers involved in buying it. If Parliament could grant the East India Company a monopoly of the tea trade, it could parcel out all or any part of American commerce to whomever it pleased. More important, the act appeared utterly diabolical, a dastardly trick to trap them into paying the tea tax. The plot seemed obvious: The real price of Lord North's tea was American submission to parliamentary taxation.

Public indignation was so great in New York and Philadelphia that when the tea ships arrived, the authorities ordered them back to England without attempting to unload. The tea could only be landed "under the Protection of the Point of the Bayonet and Muzzle of the Cannon," the governor of New York reported. "Even then," he added, "I do not see how the Sales or Consumption could be effected."

The situation in Boston was different. The tea ship *Dartmouth* arrived on November 27. The radicals, marshaled by Sam Adams, were determined to prevent it from landing its cargo; Governor Hutchinson (who had managed to have two of his sons appointed to receive and sell the tea) was equally determined to collect the tax and enforce the law. For days the town seethed. Crowds milled in the streets, harangued by Adams and his friends, while the *Dartmouth* and two later arrivals swung with the tides on their moorings. Then, on the night of December 16, as Hutchinson was preparing to seize the tea for nonpayment of the duty, a band of colonists disguised as Indians rowed out to the ships and dumped the hated tea chests in the harbor.

The destruction of the tea was a serious crime, and it was obvious that a solid majority of the people of Boston approved of it. The painted "Patriots" who jettisoned the chests were a veritable cross section of society, and a huge crowd gathered at wharfside and cheered them on. The British burned with indignation when news of the "Tea Party" reached London. People talked (fortunately it was only talk) of flattening Boston with heavy artillery. Nearly everyone, even such a self-described British friend of the colonists as Edmund Burke, agreed that the colonists must be taught a lesson. George III himself said, "We must master them or totally leave them to themselves." What particularly infuriated the

This English caricature of 1775 mocks the protest of the "Patriotic Ladies at Edenton in North Carolina." While women in the background empty their tea canisters, others (amidst some distractions) sign a pledge "not to Conform to that Pernicious Custom of Drinking Tea."

British was the certain knowledge that no American jury would render a judgment against the criminals; the memory of the *Gaspee* affair was fresh in everyone's mind in England, as undoubtedly it was in the minds of those Bostonians who, wearing the thinnest of disguises, brazenly destroyed the tea.

From Resistance to Revolution

Parliament responded in the spring of 1774 by passing the Coercive Acts. The Boston Port Act closed the harbor of Boston to all commerce until its citizens paid for the tea. The Administration of Justice Act provided for the transfer of cases to courts outside Massachusetts when the governor felt that an impartial trial could not be had within the colony. The Massachusetts Government Act revised the colony's charter drastically, strengthening the power of the governor, weakening that of the local town meetings, making the council appointive rather than elective, and changing the method by which juries were selected. These were unwise laws—they cost Great Britain an empire. All of them, and especially the Port Act, were unjust laws as well. Parliament was punishing the entire community for the crimes of individuals. Even more significant, they marked a drastic change in British policy, from legislation and strict administration to treating colonial protesters as criminals, from attempts at persuasion and conciliation to coercion and punishment.

The Americans renamed the Coercive Acts (together with a new, more extensive Quartering Act and the Quebec Act, an unrelated measure that attached the area north of the Ohio River to Canada and gave the region an authoritarian centralized government) the Intolerable Acts. That the British answer to the crisis was coercion the Americans found unendurable. Although neither the British nor the colonists yet realized it, the American Revolution had begun.

Step by step, in the course of a single decade, a group of separate political bodies, inhabited by people who (if we put aside the slaves, who were outside the political system) were loyal subjects of Great Britain, had been forced by the logic of events—by new British policies and by a growing awareness of their common interests—to take political power into their own hands and to band together to exercise that power effectively. This did not yet mean that their purpose was independence. Nearly every colonist was willing to see Great Britain continue to control, or at least regulate, such things as foreign relations, commercial policy, and other matters of general American interest. Parliament, however—and in the last analysis George III and most Britons—insisted that their authority over the colonies was unlimited. Behind their stubbornness lay the arrogant psychology of the European: "Colonists are inferior. . . . We own you."

Lord North directed the Coercive Acts at Massachusetts alone because he assumed that the other colonies, profiting from the discomfiture of Massachusetts, would not intervene and because of the British tendency to think of the colonies as separate units connected only through London. His strategy failed because his assumption was incorrect: The colonies began at once to act in concert.

Extralegal political acts now became a matter of course. In June 1774 Massachusetts called for a meeting of delegates from all the colonies to consider common action. This First Continental Congress met at Philadelphia in September; only Geor-

As the colonists saw it, the flames of rebellion in America, here portrayed as a helpless woman, were fanned by the so-called Intolerable Acts. In this colonial cartoon, well-meaning colonists struggle unsuccessfully to quench the fire.

gia failed to send delegates. Many points of view were represented, but even the so-called conservative proposal, introduced by Joseph Galloway of Pennsylvania, called for a thorough overhaul of the empire. Galloway suggested an *American* government, consisting of a president general appointed by the king and a grand council chosen by the colonial assemblies, that would manage intercolonial affairs and possess a veto over parliamentary acts affecting the colonies.

This was not what the majority wanted. If taxation without representation was tyranny, so was all legislation. Therefore, Parliament had no right to legislate in any way for the colonies. John Adams, while prepared to *allow* Parliament to regulate colonial trade, now believed that Parliament had no inherent right to control it. "The foundation . . . of all free government," he declared, "is a right in the people to participate in their legislative council." Americans "are entitled to a free and exclusive power of legislation in their several provincial legislatures."

Propelled by the reasoning of Adams and others, the Congress passed a declaration of grievances and resolves that amounted to a complete condemnation of Britain's actions since 1763. A Massachusetts proposal that the people take up arms to defend their rights was endorsed. The delegates also organized a "continental association" to boycott British goods and to stop all exports to the empire. To enforce this boycott, committees were appointed locally "to observe the conduct of all persons touching this association" and to expose violators to public scorn.

If the Continental Congress reflected the views of the majority—there is no reason to suspect that it did not—it is clear that the Americans had decided that drastic changes must be made. It was not merely a question of mutual defense against the threat of British power, not only (in Franklin's aphorism) a matter of hanging together lest they hang separately. A nation was being born.

Looking back many years later, one of the delegates to the First Continental Congress made just these points. He was John Adams, and he said: "The revolution was complete, in the minds of the people, and the Union of the colonies, before the war commenced."

The First Continental Congress met for almost two months in the fall of 1774. The man in the raised chair at left is probably Peyton Randolph of Virginia, president of the assembly and much admired for his calm and moderation.

Milestones

1650–1696	Navigation Acts enacted by Parliament	**1760**	George III becomes king of England
1689–1697	King William's War (War of the League of Augsburg)	**1763**	Proclamation of 1763
1699–1750	Parliament enacts laws regulating colonial manufacturing	**1764**	Sugar Act
		1765	Stamp Act, leading to the Stamp Act Congress
1702–1713	Queen Anne's War (War of the Spanish Succession)	**1766**	Repeal of the Stamp Act and passage of the Declaratory Act
1733	Molasses Act		
1738–1742	Height of the Great Awakening	**1767**	Townshend Duties, leading to the Massachusetts Circular Letter
1740–1748	King George's War (War of the Austrian Succession)		
1743	Franklin founds the American Philosophical Society	**1770**	Boston Massacre
		1772	Burning of the *Gaspee*
1752	Franklin discovers the nature of lightning	**1773**	Tea Act, leading to the Boston Tea Party
1754	Albany Congress		
1754–1763	French and Indian War (Seven Years' War)	**1774**	Coercive Acts, leading to the First Continental Congress

SUPPLEMENTARY READING

Titles marked with an asterisk have been published in paperback.

The fullest analysis of the British imperial system can be found in the early volumes of L. H. Gipson, **The British Empire Before the American Revolution** (1936–1968). See also J. A. Henretta, **The Evolution of American Society** (1973), and Michael Kammen, **Empire and Interest** (1974). J. P. Greene, **The Quest for Power*** (1963), describes how the colonists extended their control of political affairs.

The best study of mercantilism is still Eli Heckscher, **Mercantilism** (1935). The colonial wars are described in H. H. Peckham, **The Colonial Wars*** (1963), but see also Fred Anderson, **A People's Army: Massachusetts Soldiers and Society in the Seven Years' War** (1984). Francis Jennings, **Empire of Fortune** (1988), is a revisionist's interpretation of the war, critical of all the whites involved in the conflict. On the problems posed for the British by the acquisition of French Canada, see J. M. Sosin, **Whitehall and the Wilderness** (1961).

On the causes of the Revolution, see Pauline Maier, **From Resistance to Revolution** (1972), E. S. Morgan, **The Birth of the Republic*** (1956), and Edward Countryman, **The American Revolution** (1985). Two works by Bernard Bailyn, **The Ideological Origins of the American Revolution*** (1967) and **The Origins of American Politics*** (1968), brilliantly analyze the political thinking and political structure of 18th-century America. G. B. Nash, **The Urban Crucible*** (1979), contains valuable data on political, social, and economic conditions in the largest towns, which Nash calls "crucibles of revolutionary agitation." See also Pauline Maier, **The Old Revolutionaries** (1980), and A. F. Young (ed.), **The American Revolution*** (1976).

American Lives:

George Washington

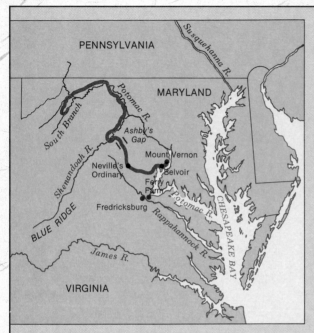

The northern neck of Virginia. The [color] line shows the route taken by sixteen-year-old Washington on the surveying expedition to Lord Fairfax's western holdings.

George Washington was born in 1732 on the tobacco plantation of his parents, Augustine and Mary Ball Washington, in the region between the Potomac and Rappahannock rivers known as the Northern Neck of Virginia. The Washingtons were members of the gentry, but not one of the great landed families. They owned some 10,000 acres and about 50 slaves. George was the first child, but Augustine Washington had three others by his first wife, who had died a few years earlier.

When George was six the family moved to Ferry Farm, a plantation further upstream on high land bordering the Rappahannock. The house was substantial but far from luxurious. It consisted of a central hall that served as a dining room, a master bedroom with its own fireplace, four other bedrooms, a kitchen, and a combination dairy and laundry room. Twenty of the Washingtons' slaves lived and worked at Ferry Farm, the rest at various other properties. A lane ran down to the Rappahannock ferry, which gave the place its name. On the other bank of the river was Fredericksburg, a town not much older than George, where there were some tobacco warehouses, the county courthouse, a prison, and St. George's Anglican church. Round about were other plantations owned by people with names like Spotswood, Taliaferro, and Mercer.

Little is known about George Washington's education except that it was supervised by tutors, perhaps fortified by some time at a school in Fredericksburg. He displayed small interest in literature (certainly nothing comparable to Franklin's and Adams's avid pursuit of reading matter). But early on he developed skill in mathematics and through that in surveying, a valuable tool in a country populated by well-to-do planters eager to engross new lands on the frontier.

In 1743 Augustine Washington died of what was diagnosed as "gout of the stomach." The bulk of his estate went to George's half-brother Lawrence, who had recently returned to Virginia after serving under Admiral Edward Vernon in the Caribbean during a conflict with Spain known as the War of Jenkins' Ear. George inherited Ferry Farm, ten slaves, and some house lots in Fredericksburg. Over the next few years, however, he lived with various relatives, including Lawrence, who had recently married Anne Fairfax; Anne was a relative of Lord Thomas Fairfax, an Englishman who had claims to more than 5 million acres in the wild upper reaches of the Northern Neck.

Growing up at Lawrence's plantation, Mount Vernon (named after the Admiral), set the course that determined George's future. He became a familiar at the Fairfax seat, Belvoir, and there got a taste of the life of the colonial elite. He grew tall and powerful; like his father he eventually topped six feet and weighed close to 200 pounds. He sedulously strove to develop the social graces, which did not come naturally to him—when he was 13 a tutor made him copy out one hundred "Rules of Civility" from an etiquette book of the period. They covered such gaffes as picking one's teeth with a fork and killing fleas in public. But he learned to dance, play cards and billiards, and ride with the hounds; above all, he mastered self-discipline and devotion to duty. Like so many others of his generation he admired the heroes of the Roman Republic, in his case particularly Cato the Younger, famous for his honesty and commitment to public service.

When George was 16 the great Lord Fairfax allowed him and his own young kinsman, George William Fairfax, to accompany a surveying party sent to locate some of the vast Fairfax holdings west of the Shenandoah valley. It was an unforgettable month-long adventure on horseback, over the "worst road ever trod by man or beast," fording rivers, and sleeping under "one threadbare blanket with double its weight of vermin, such as lice, fleas, etc." Sometimes they camped in the woods, pitching tents and cooking on an open fire. "Our spits were forked sticks," George recorded, "our plate was a large chip; and for dishes we had none." At one point they came upon a party of 30 Indians, returning from a conflict of some sort, chagrined at having taken only a single scalp. As they proceeded, pioneers emerged from the woods to gape at the mysterious activities of the surveyors. One day the party came upon a group of German settlers. "They seemed to be as ignorant a set of people as the Indians," George wrote in his diary. "When spoken to they speak all Dutch."

He returned to Mount Vernon a seasoned frontiersman and an experienced surveyor, eager to invest in western lands. The next year he was again surveying for Lord Fairfax, this time on his own and for a doubloon a day, which he saved in order to buy land for himself. Then, in 1752, Lawrence Washington died. George, at age 20, inherited Mount Vernon.

Young Washington's experiences and his reactions to them have much to tell us about southern life in the 18th century. More than a century and a quarter after the settlement of Jamestown, life remained extremely precarious. George's great-grandfather had died at age 46, his grandfather at 38. His aunt Mildred Washington buried two husbands and married a third well before her 40th birthday. In a hot and humid region plagued by clouds of mosquitoes and the various "vermin" George experienced on the frontier, where sanitary facilities were often rudimentary and medical knowledge abysmal, malaria, typhoid, smallpox, and such unfathomable lethal mysteries as the "gout of the stomach" that carried off Augustine Washington were of epidemic proportions. The Virginians appear to have lived uncomplainingly with the constant threat of extinction, certainly without doing anything about it.

Washington's youth coincided with the influx of more than 30,000 slaves into Virginia, the greatest in all history, between his birth and his 30th birthday; nearly all came directly from Africa. Neither he nor most of the whites he knew had much to say about them or the institution, although their prosperity depended entirely upon both. In later life Washington treated his slaves decently by the standards of his time and place. But in his youth (and probably always) he did not question his right to own them.

In one way Washington's early experiences resembled those of Franklin and Adams. All three, ardent revolutionaries in the 1770s, expressed not the slightest resentment of British rule as late as the early 1760s.

A View of Mount Vernon

The American Revolution

*By referring the matter from argument to arms, a new era for politics
is struck; a new method of thinking hath arisen.*

THOMAS PAINE, Common Sense, *1776*

The actions of the First Continental Congress led the British authorities to force a showdown with their bumptious colonial offspring. "The New England governments are in a state of rebellion," George III announced. "Blows must decide whether they are to be subject to this country or independent." Already General Thomas Gage, veteran of Braddock's ill-fated expedition against Fort Duquesne and now commander in chief of all British forces in North America, had been appointed governor of Massachusetts. Some 4,000 Redcoats were concentrated in Boston, camped on the town common once peacefully reserved for the citizens' cows. Parliament echoed with demands for a show of strength in America. General James Grant announced that with 1,000 men he "would undertake to go from one end of America to the other, and geld all the males, partly by force and partly by a little coaxing." Some opposed the idea of crushing the colonists, and others believed that it could not be easily managed, but they were a small minority. The House of Commons listened to Edmund Burke's magnificent speech on conciliating the colonies and then voted 270 to 78 against him.

"The Shot Heard Round the World"

The London government decided to use troops against Massachusetts in January 1775, but the order did not reach General Gage until April. In the interim both sides were active. Parliament voted new troop levies and declared Massachusetts to be in a state of rebellion. The Massachusetts Patriots, as they were now calling themselves, formed an extralegal provincial assembly, reorganized the militia, and began training "Minute Men" and other fighters. Soon companies armed with anything that would shoot were drilling on town commons throughout Massachusetts and in other colonies too.

When Gage received his orders on April 14, he acted swiftly. The Patriots had been accumulating arms at Concord, some 20 miles west of Boston. On the night of April 18, Gage dispatched 700 crack troops to seize these supplies. The Patriots were forewarned. Paul Revere set out on his famous ride to alert the countryside and warn John Hancock and Sam Adams, leaders of the provincial assembly, whose arrests had been ordered.

When the Redcoats reached Lexington early the next morning, they found the common occupied by about 70 Minute Men. After an argument, the Americans began to withdraw. Then someone fired a shot. There was a flurry of gunfire and the Minute Men fled, leaving eight of their number dead. The British then marched on to Concord, where they destroyed whatever supplies the Patriots had been unable to carry off.

But militiamen were pouring into the area from all sides. A hot skirmish at Concord's North Bridge forced the Redcoats to yield that position. Becoming alarmed, they began to march back to Boston. Soon they were being subjected to a withering fire from American irregulars along their line of march. A strange battle developed on a "field" 16 miles long and only a few hundred yards wide. Gage was obliged to send out an additional 1,500 soldiers, and total disaster was avoided only by deploying skirmishers to root out snipers hiding in barns and farmhouses along the road to Boston. When the first day of the Revolutionary War ended, the British had sustained 273 casualties, the Americans fewer than 100.

For a brief moment of history tiny Massachusetts stood alone at arms against an empire that had humbled France and Spain. Yet Massachusetts assumed the offensive! The provincial government organized an expedition that captured Fort Ticonderoga and Crown Point, on Lake Champlain. The other colonies rallied quickly to the cause, sending reinforcements to Cambridge.

The Second Continental Congress

On May 10, the day Ticonderoga fell, the Second Continental Congress met in Philadelphia. It was a distinguished group, more radical than the First Congress. Besides John and Sam Adams, Patrick Henry and Richard Henry Lee of Virginia, and Christopher Gadsden of South Carolina, all holdovers from the First Congress, there was Thomas Jefferson, a lanky, sandy-haired young planter from Virginia. Jefferson had recently published "A Summary View of the Rights of British America," an essay criticizing the institution of monarchy and warning George III that "kings are the servants, not the proprietors of the people." The Virginia convention had also sent George Washington, who knew more than any other colonist about commanding men and who wore his buff-and-blue colonel's uniform, a not-too-subtle indication of his willingness to place this knowledge at the disposal of the Congress. The renowned Benjamin Franklin was a delegate, moving rapidly to the radical position.

In this engraving by Amos Doolittle, made from a sketch by Ralph Earle, British forces at the North Bridge in Concord fight a rear-guard action. A line of riflemen holds off the Massachusetts militia on the left, while the mass of the Redcoats retreats toward Boston.

The Boston merchant John Hancock was chosen president of the Congress, which, like the first, had no legal authority. Yet the delegates had to make agonizing decisions under the pressure of rapidly unfolding military events, with the future of every American depending on their actions. Delicate negotiations and honeyed words might yet persuade king and Parliament to change their ways, but precipitate, bold effort was essential to save Massachusetts.

In this predicament the Congress naturally dealt first with the military crisis. It organized the forces gathering around Boston into the so-called Continental Army and appointed George Washington commander in chief. After Washington and his staff left for Massachusetts on June 23, the Congress turned to the task of requisitioning men and supplies.

The Battle of Bunker Hill

Meanwhile, in Massachusetts, the first major battle of the war had been fought. The British position on the peninsula of Boston was impregnable to direct assault, but high ground north and south, at Charlestown and Dorchester Heights, could be used to pound the city with artillery. When the Patriots seized Bunker Hill and Breed's Hill at Charlestown and set up defenses on the latter, Gage determined at once to drive them off. This was accomplished on June 17. Twice the Redcoats marched in close ranks, bayonets fixed, up Breed's Hill, each time being driven back after suffering heavy losses. Stubbornly they came again, and this time they carried the redoubt, for the defenders had run out of ammunition.

The British then cleared the Charlestown peninsula, but the victory was really the Americans', for they had proved themselves against professional soldiers and had exacted a terrible toll. More than 1,000 Redcoats had fallen in a couple of hours, out of a force of some 2,500, while the Patriots had lost only 400 men, most of them cut down by British bayonets after the hill was taken. "The day ended in glory," a British officer wrote, "but the loss was uncommon in officers for the number engaged."

The Battle of Bunker Hill, as it was called for no good reason, greatly reduced whatever hope remained for a negotiated settlement. The spilling of so much blood left each side determined to force

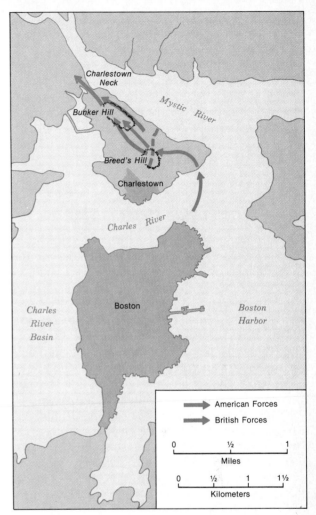

THE BATTLE OF BUNKER HILL, 1775

Most of the so-called Battle of Bunker Hill actually took place on Breed's Hill nearby. This area today is all part of the city of Boston.

the other's submission. The British recalled General Gage, replacing him with General Sir William Howe, a respected veteran of the French and Indian War, and George III formally proclaimed the colonies to be "in open rebellion." The Continental Congress dispatched one last plea to the king (the Olive Branch Petition), but this was a sop to the moderates. Immediately thereafter it adopted the

Declaration of the Causes and Necessity of Taking Up Arms, which condemned everything the British had done since 1763. Americans were "a people attacked by unprovoked enemies"; the time had come to choose between "submission" to "tyranny" and "resistance by force." The Congress then ordered an attack on Canada and created committees to seek foreign aid and to buy munitions abroad. It authorized the outfitting of a navy under Commodore Esek Hopkins of Rhode Island.

The Great Declaration

The Congress (and the bulk of the people) still hung back from a break with the Crown. To declare for independence would be to burn the last bridge, to become traitors in the eyes of the mother country. Aside from the word's ugly associations, everyone knew what happened to traitors when their efforts failed. It was sobering to think of casting off everything that being English meant: love of king, the traditions of a great nation, pride in the power of a mighty empire. "Where shall we find another Britain?" John Dickinson had asked at the time of the Townshend Acts crisis. "Torn from the body to which we are united by religion, liberty, laws, affections, relation, language and commerce, we must bleed at every vein."

Then, too, rebellion might end in horrors worse than submission to British tyranny. The disturbances following the Stamp Act and the Tea Act had revealed an alarming fact about American society. The organizers of the protests, mostly persons of wealth and status, had thought in terms of "ordered resistance." They countenanced violence only as a means of forcing the British authorities to pay attention to their complaints. But protest meetings and mob actions had brought thousands of ordinary citizens into the struggle for local self-government. Some of the upper-class leaders among the Patriots, while eager to have their support, were concerned about what they would make of actual independence. In addition, not all the property that had been destroyed belonged to Loyalists and British officials. Too much exalted talk about "rights" and "liberties" might well give the poor (to say nothing of the slaves) an exaggerated impression of their importance. Finally, in a world where every country had some kind of monarch, could common people

really govern themselves? The most ardent defender of American rights might well hesitate after considering all the implications of independence.

Yet independence was probably inevitable by the end of 1775. The belief that George III had been misled by evil or stupid advisers on both sides of the Atlantic became progressively more difficult to sustain. Mistrust of Parliament—indeed, of the whole of British society—grew apace.

Two events in January 1776 pushed the colonies a long step toward a final break. First came the news that the British were sending hired Hessian soldiers to fight against them. Colonists associated mercenaries with looting and rape and feared that the German-speaking Hessians would run amok among them. Such callousness on the part of Britain made reconciliation seem out of the question.

The second decisive event was the publication of *Common Sense*. This tract was written by Thomas Paine, a onetime English corsetmaker and civil servant turned pamphleteer, a man who had been in America scarcely a year. *Common Sense* called boldly for complete independence. It attacked not only George III but the idea of monarchy itself. Paine applied the uncomplicated logic of the zealot to the recent history of America. Where the colonists had been humbly petitioning George III and swallowing their resentment when he ignored them, Paine called George a "Royal Brute" and "the hardened sullen-tempered Pharaoh of England." Many Americans had wanted to control their own affairs but feared the instability of untried republican government. To them Paine said: "We have it in our power to begin the world again." "A government of our own is our natural right," he insisted. "O! ye that love mankind! Ye that dare oppose not only tyranny but the tyrant, stand forth!"

Virtually everyone in the colonies must have read *Common Sense* or heard it explained and discussed. About 150,000 copies were sold in the critical period between January and July. Not every Patriot was impressed by Paine's arguments. John Adams dismissed *Common Sense* as "a tolerable summary of arguments which I had been repeating again and again in Congress for nine months." But no one disputed the impact of Paine's pamphlet on public opinion.

The tone of the debate changed sharply as Paine's slashing attack took effect. In March the Congress unleashed privateers against British commerce; in April it opened American ports to foreign shipping; in May it urged the extralegal provincial conventions that had been set up by the Patriots to frame constitutions and establish state governments.

On June 7 Richard Henry Lee of Virginia introduced a resolution of the Virginia Convention:

> RESOLVED: That these United Colonies are, and of right ought to be, free and independent States, that they are absolved from all allegiance to the British Crown, and that all political connection between them and the State of Great Britain is, and ought to be, totally dissolved.

This momentous resolution was not passed until July 2; the Congress first appointed a committee consisting of Thomas Jefferson, Benjamin Franklin, John Adams, Roger Sherman, and Robert Livingston to frame a suitable justification of independence. Livingston, a member of one of the great New York landowning families, was put on the committee in an effort to push New York toward independence. Sherman, a self-educated Connecticut lawyer and merchant, was a conservative who opposed parliamentary control over colonial affairs. Franklin, the best known of all Americans and an experienced writer, was a natural choice; so was John Adams, whose devotion to the cause of independence combined with his solid conservative qualities made him perhaps the typical man of the Revolution.

Thomas Jefferson was probably placed on the committee because politics required that a Virginian be included and because of his literary skill and

A detail from John Trumbull's Declaration of Independence *portrays the five-man drafting committee presenting its handiwork to the Congress: from left, Massachusetts's John Adams, Connecticut's Roger Sherman, New York's Robert Livingston, Virginia's Thomas Jefferson, and Pennsylvania's Benjamin Franklin. Trumbull's skillful composition "ranks" the contributors, with Jefferson dominating.*

general intelligence. Aside from writing "A Summary View of the Rights of British America," he had done little to attract notice. At 33 he was the youngest member of the Continental Congress and was only marginally interested in its deliberations. He had been slow to take his seat in the fall of 1775, and he had gone home to Virginia before Christmas. He put off returning several times and arrived in Philadelphia only on May 14. Had he delayed another month, someone else would have written the Declaration of Independence.

The committee asked Jefferson to prepare a draft. The result, with a few amendments made by Franklin and Adams and somewhat toned down by the whole Congress, was officially adopted by the delegates on July 4, 1776, two days after the decisive break with Great Britain had been voted.

Jefferson's Declaration of Independence consisted of two parts. The first was by way of introduction: It justified the abstract right of any people to revolt and described the theory on which the Americans based their creation of a new, republican government. The second, much longer section was a list of the "injuries and usurpations" of George III, a bill of indictment explaining why the colonists felt driven to exercise the rights outlined in the first part of the document. Here Jefferson stressed the monarch's interference with the functioning of representative government in America, his harsh administration of colonial affairs, his restrictions on civil rights, and his maintenance of troops in the colonies without their consent.

Jefferson sought to marshal every possible evidence of British perfidy and he made George III, rather than Parliament, the villain because the king was the personification of the nation against which the Americans were rebelling. He held George responsible for Parliament's efforts to tax the colonies and restrict their trade, for many actions by subordinates that George had never deliberately authorized, and for some things that never happened. He even blamed the king for the existence of slavery in the colonies, a charge the Congress cut from the document not entirely because of its concern for accuracy. The long bill of particulars reads more like a lawyer's brief than a careful analysis, but it was intended to convince the world that the Americans had good reasons for exercising their right to form a government of their own.

Jefferson's general statement of the right of revolution has inspired oppressed peoples all over the world for more than 200 years:

> We hold these truths to be self-evident, that all men are created equal, that they are endowed by their Creator with certain unalienable Rights, that among these are Life, Liberty and the pursuit of Happiness. That to secure these rights, Governments are instituted among Men, deriving their just powers from the consent of the governed, That whenever any Form of Government becomes destructive of these ends, it is the Right of the People to alter or to abolish it, and to institute new Government. . . .

The Declaration was intended to influence foreign opinion, but it had little immediate effect outside Great Britain, and there it only made people angry and determined to subdue the rebels. A substantial number of European military men offered their services to the new nation, and a few of these might be called idealists, but most were adventurers and soldiers of fortune, thinking mostly of their own advantage. Why, then, has the Declaration had so much influence on modern history? Not because the thought was original with Jefferson. As John Adams later pointed out—Adams viewed his great contemporary with a mixture of affection, respect, and jealousy—the basic idea was commonplace among 18th-century liberals. "I did not consider it any part of my charge to invent new ideas," Jefferson explained, "but to place before mankind the common sense of the subject, in terms so plain and firm as to command their assent. . . . It was intended to be an expression of the American mind."

Revolution was not new, but the spectacle of a people solemnly explaining and justifying their right, in an orderly manner, to throw off their oppressors and establish a new system on their own authority was almost without precedent. Soon the French would be drawing on this example in their revolution, and rebels everywhere have since done likewise. And if Jefferson did not create the concept, he gave it a nearly perfect form.

1776: The Balance of Forces

A formal declaration of independence merely cleared the way for tackling the problems of founding a new nation. Lacking both traditions and authority based in law, the Congress had to create political institutions and a new national spirit, all in the midst of war.

Always the military situation took precedence, for a single disastrous setback might make everything else meaningless. At the start the Americans had what we might call the home-court advantage. They already possessed their lands (except for the few square miles occupied by British troops). Although thousands of colonists fought for George III, the British soon learned that to put down the American rebellion they would have to bring in men and supplies from bases on the other side of the Atlantic. This was a most formidable task.

Certain long-run factors also operated in America's favor. Whereas nearly everyone in Great Britain wanted to crack down on Boston after the Tea Party, many boggled at engaging in a full-scale war against all the colonies. Aside from a reluctance to spill so much blood, there was the question of expense. Finally, the idea of dispatching the cream of the British army to America while powerful enemies on the Continent still smarted from past defeats seemed risky. For all these reasons the British ap-

proached gingerly the task of subduing the rebellion. When Washington fortified Dorchester Heights overlooking Boston, General Howe withdrew his troops to Halifax rather than risk another Bunker Hill.

For a time the initiative remained with the Americans. An expedition under General Richard Montgomery had captured Montreal in November 1775, and another small force under Benedict Arnold advanced to the gates of Quebec after a grueling march across the wilderness from Maine. Montgomery and Arnold attempted to storm the Quebec defenses on December 31, 1775, but were repulsed with heavy losses. Even so, the British troops in Canada could not drive the remnants of the American army— perhaps 500 men in all—out of the province until reinforcements arrived in the spring.

Awareness of Britain's problems undoubtedly spurred the Continental Congress to the bold actions of the spring of 1776. However, on July 2, 1776, the same day that Congress voted for independence, General Howe was back on American soil, landing in force on Staten Island in New York harbor in preparation for an assault on the city.

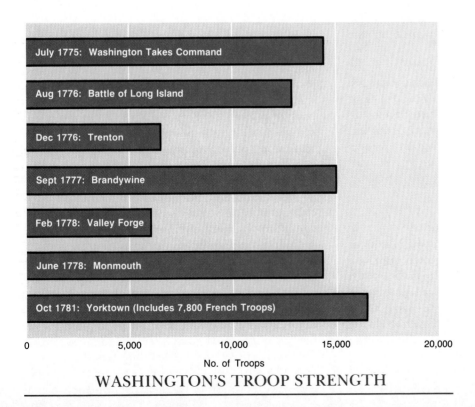

July 1775: Washington Takes Command

Aug 1776: Battle of Long Island

Dec 1776: Trenton

Sept 1777: Brandywine

Feb 1778: Valley Forge

June 1778: Monmouth

Oct 1781: Yorktown (Includes 7,800 French Troops)

0   5,000   10,000   15,000   20,000

No. of Troops

WASHINGTON'S TROOP STRENGTH

The troop count shown here includes militias as well as regular Continental Army forces. Washington's troop strength varied greatly from month to month and year to year, and at times militias accounted for more than one-third of the total.

Soon Howe had at hand 32,000 well-equipped troops and a powerful fleet commanded by his brother, Richard, Lord Howe. If the British controlled New York City and the Hudson River, they could, as Washington realized, "stop intercourse between the northern and southern Colonies, upon which depends the Safety of America."

Suddenly the full strength of the empire seemed to have descended on the Americans. Superior British resources (a population of 9 million to the colonies' 2.5 million, large stocks of war materials and the industrial capacity to boost them further, mastery of the seas, a well-trained and experienced army, a highly centralized and, when necessary, ruthless government) were now all too evident.

The demonstration of British might in New York harbor accentuated American military and economic weaknesses: Both money and the tools of war were continually in short supply in a predominantly agricultural country. Many of Washington's soldiers were armed with weapons no more lethal than spears and tomahawks. Few had proper uniforms. Even the most patriotic resisted conforming to the conventions of military discipline; the men hated drilling and all parade-ground formality. And all these problems were complicated by the fact that Washington had literally to create an army organization out of whole cloth at the same time that he was fighting a war.

Supply problems were handled inefficiently and often corruptly. Few officers knew much about such mundane but vital matters as how to construct and maintain proper sanitary facilities when large numbers of soldiers were camped at one place for extended periods of time. What was inelegantly known as "the itch" afflicted soldiers throughout the war.

Loyalists

Behind the lines, the country was far from united. Whereas nearly all colonists had objected to British policies, many still hesitated to take up arms against the mother country. Even Massachusetts harbored many Loyalists, or Tories, as they were called; about 1,000 Americans left Boston with General Howe, abandoning their homes rather than submit to the rebel army.

No one knows exactly how the colonists divided on the question of independence. John Adams's off-the-cuff estimate was that a third of the people were ardent Patriots, another third loyal to Great Britain, and the rest neutral or tending to favor whichever side seemed to be winning. This guess is probably as useful as any, though in keeping with Adams's character he may have understated the number who agreed with him and overstated those opposed to his position. Most historians think that about a fifth of the people were Loyalists and about two-fifths Patriots, but there are few hard figures to go by. What is certain is that large elements, perhaps a majority of the people, were more or less indifferent to the conflict or, in Tom Paine's famous phrase, were summer soldiers and sunshine patriots—they supported the Revolution when all was going well and lost their enthusiasm in difficult hours.

The divisions cut across geographic, social, and economic lines. Edward Countryman makes this clear in *A People in Revolution:*

> The positions that people took grew out of the lives they had led and out of what people who counted in those lives were doing. . . . They became rebels or Tories or they tried to stay out of it by reference to the whole set of material, cultural, geographical, economic, and political complexities that had been their world.

A high proportion of those holding royal appointments and many Anglican clergymen remained loyal to King George, as did numbers of merchants with close connections in Britain. There were important pockets of Tory strength in rural sections of New York, in the North Carolina back country, and among persons of non-English origin and other minority groups who tended to count on London for protection against the local majority.

Many became Tories simply out of distaste for change or because they were pessimistic about the condition of society and the possibility of improving it. "What is the whole history of human life," wrote the Tory clergyman and schoolmaster Jonathan Boucher of Virginia, "but a series of disappointments?" Still others believed that the actions of the British, however unfair and misguided, did not justify rebellion. Knowing that they possessed a remarkably free and equitable system of government, they could not stomach shedding blood merely to avoid paying more taxes or to escape from what they considered minor restrictions on their activities. "The Annals of no Country can produce an Instance of so virulent a Rebellion . . . originating from such trivial Causes," one Loyalist complained.

The Tories lacked organization. While Patriot leaders worked closely together, many of the Tory "leaders" did not even know one another. They had no central committee to lay plans or coordinate their efforts. When the revolutionaries took over a colony, some Tories fled; others sought the protection of the British army; others took up arms; others

accommodated themselves silently to the new regime.

If the differences separating Patriot from Loyalist are unclear, feelings were nonetheless bitter. Individual Loyalists were often set upon by mobs, tarred and feathered, and otherwise abused. Some were thrown into jail for no legitimate reason; others were exiled, their property confiscated. Battles between Tory units and the Continental Army were often exceptionally bloody. "Neighbor was against

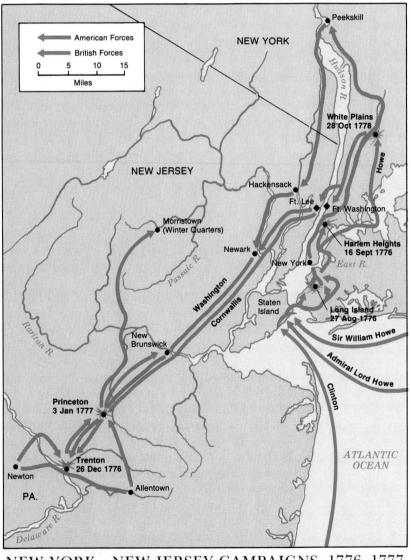

NEW YORK—NEW JERSEY CAMPAIGNS, 1776–1777

The events in and around New York, so nearly disastrous to Washington and his army, are detailed in this map.

neighbor, father against son and son against father," one Connecticut Tory reported. "He that would not thrust his own blade through his brother's heart was called an infamous villain."

Early Defeats

General Howe's campaign against New York brought to light another American weakness: the lack of military experience. Washington, expecting Howe to attack New York, had moved south to meet the threat immediately after Howe had abandoned Boston. But both he and his men failed badly in this first major test. Late in August, Howe crossed from Staten Island to Brooklyn. In the Battle of Long Island he easily outflanked and defeated Washington's army. Had he acted decisively, he could probably have ended the war on the spot, but Howe could not make up his mind whether to be a peacemaker or a conqueror. This hesitation in consolidating his gains permitted Washington to withdraw his troops to Manhattan Island.

Howe could still have trapped Washington simply by using his fleet to land troops on the northern end of Manhattan; instead he attacked New York City directly, leaving the Americans an escape route to the north. Again Patriot troops proved no match for British regulars. Though Washington threw his hat to the ground in a rage and threatened to shoot cowardly Connecticut soldiers as they fled the battlefield, he could not stop the rout and had to fall back on Harlem Heights in upper Manhattan. Yet once more Howe failed to pursue his advantage promptly.

Still Washington refused to see the peril in remaining on an island while the enemy commanded the surrounding waters. Only when Howe shifted a powerful force to Westchester, directly threatening his rear, did Washington move north to the mainland. Finally, after several narrow escapes, he crossed the Hudson River and marched south to New Jersey, where the British could not use their naval superiority against him.

The battles in and around New York City seemed to presage an easy British triumph. Yet somehow Washington salvaged a moral victory from these ignominious defeats. He learned rapidly; seldom thereafter did he place his troops in such vulnerable positions. And his men, in spite of repeated failure, had become an army. In November and December 1776 they retreated across New Jersey and into Pennsylvania. General Howe then abandoned the campaign, going into winter quarters in New York but posting garrisons at Trenton, Princeton, and other strategic points.

The troops at Trenton were hated Hessian mercenaries, and Washington decided to attack them. He crossed the ice-clogged Delaware River with 2,400 men on Christmas night during a wild storm. The little army then marched 9 miles to Trenton, arriving at daybreak in the midst of a sleet storm. The Hessians were taken completely by surprise. Those who could fled in disorder; the rest—900 of them—surrendered.

The Hessians were first-class professional soldiers, probably the most competent troops in Europe at that time. The victory gave a boost to American morale. A few days later Washington outmaneuvered General Cornwallis, who had rushed to Trenton with reinforcements, and won another battle at Princeton. These engagements had little strategic importance, since both armies then went into winter quarters. Without them, however, there might not have been an army to resume the war in the spring.

Saratoga and the French Alliance

When spring reached New Jersey in April 1777, Washington had fewer than 5,000 men under arms. Great plans—far too many and too complicated, as it turned out—were afoot in the British camp. The strategy called for General John Burgoyne to lead a large army from Canada down Lake Champlain toward Albany while a smaller force under Lieutenant Colonel Barry St. Leger pushed eastward toward Albany from Fort Oswego on Lake Ontario. General Howe was to lead a third force north up the Hudson. Patriot resistance would be smashed between these three armies and the New England states isolated from the rest.

As a venture in coordinated military tactics, the British campaign of 1777 was a fiasco. General Howe had spent the winter in New York wining and dining his officers and prominent local Loyalists and having a torrid affair with the wife of the officer

Britain's difficulties in the Revolutionary War are derided in an etching entitled "Poor old England endeavoring to reclaim his wicked American Children." In spite of their leashes, the colonists shoot pellets, shout, and otherwise show their disrespect for their peg-legged master in this English cartoon of 1777.

in charge of prisoners of war. Now he managed, in the words of his biographer, Ira Gruber, "to ignore his responsibilities toward the British army advancing south from Canada." (Sir William, Gruber notes, "had never inspired subordinates with a single-minded devotion to business.")

General "Gentleman Johnny" Burgoyne, a charming if somewhat bombastic character, part politician, part poet, part gambler, part ladies' man, yet also a brave soldier, had begun his march from Canada in mid-June. By early July his army, which consisted of 500 Indians, 650 Loyalists, and 6,000 regulars, had captured Fort Ticonderoga, at the southern end of Lake Champlain. He quickly pushed beyond Lake George but then bogged down. Burdened by a huge baggage train that included 138 pieces of generally useless artillery, more than 30 carts laden with his personal wardrobe and supply of champagne, and his mistress, he could advance at but a snail's pace through the dense woods north of Saratoga.* Patriot militia

---

* Many soldiers, enlisted men as well as officers, were accompanied by their wives or other women on campaigns. More than 2,000 accompanied the Burgoyne expedition. At one point Washington complained of "the multitude of women . . . especially those who are pregnant, or have children [that] clog upon every movement." Actually, women in 18th-century armies worked hard, doing most of the cooking, washing, and other housekeeping tasks.

impeded his way by felling trees across the forest trails.

St. Leger was also slow in carrying out his part of the grand design. He did not leave Fort Oswego until July 26, and when he stopped to besiege a Patriot force at Fort Stanwix, General Benedict Arnold had time to march west with 1,000 men from the army resisting Burgoyne and drive him back to Oswego.

Meanwhile, with magnificent disregard for the agreed-on plan, Howe wasted time trying to trap Washington into exposing his army in New Jersey. This enabled Washington to send some of his best troops to buttress the militia units opposing Burgoyne. Then, just when St. Leger was setting out for Albany, Howe took the bulk of his army off by sea to attack Philadelphia, leaving only a small force commanded by General Sir Henry Clinton to aid Burgoyne.

When Washington moved south to oppose Howe, the Britisher taught him a series of lessons in tactics, defeating him at the Battle of Brandywine, then feinting him out of position and moving unopposed into Philadelphia. But by that time it was late September, and disaster was about to befall General Burgoyne.

The American forces under Philip Schuyler and later under Horatio Gates and Benedict Arnold had erected formidable defenses immediately south of Saratoga near the town of Stillwater. Burgoyne struck at this position twice and was thrown back both times with heavy losses. Each day more local militia swelled the American forces. Soon Burgoyne was under siege, his troops pinned down by withering fire from every direction, unable even to bury their dead. The only hope was General Clinton, who had finally started up the Hudson from New York. Clinton got as far as Kingston, about 80 miles below Saratoga, but on October 16 he decided to return to New York for reinforcements. The next day, at Saratoga, Burgoyne surrendered. Some 5,700 British prisoners were marched off to Virginia.

This overwhelming triumph changed the course and character of the war. France would probably have entered the war in any case; the country had never reconciled itself to its losses in the Seven Years' War and had been building a navy capable of taking on the British for years. Helping the Americans was simply another way of weakening their British enemy. As early as May 1776 the Comte de Vergennes,

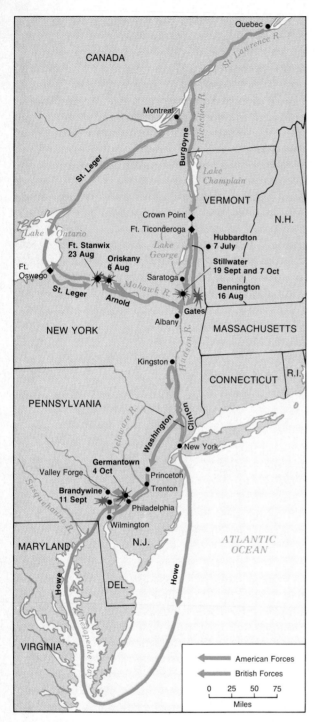

SARATOGA AND PHILADELPHIA
CAMPAIGNS, 1777

France's foreign minister, had persuaded Louis XVI to authorize the expenditure of 1 million livres for munitions for America, and more was added the next year. Spain also contributed to the cause. Soon vital supplies were being funneled secretly to the rebels. When news of the victory at Saratoga reached Paris, the time seemed ripe, and Louis XVI recognized the United States. Then Vergennes and three American commissioners in Paris, Benjamin Franklin, Arthur Lee, and Silas Deane, drafted a commercial treaty and a formal treaty of alliance. The two nations agreed to make "common cause and aid each other mutually" should war "break out" between France and Great Britain. Meanwhile, France guaranteed "the sovereignty and independence absolute and unlimited" of the United States.

When the news of Saratoga reached England, Lord North realized that a Franco-American alliance was almost inevitable. To forestall it, he was ready to give in on all the issues that had agitated the colonies before 1775. Both the Coercive Acts and the Tea Act would be repealed; Parliament would pledge never to tax the colonies.

Instead of implementing this proposal promptly, Parliament delayed until March 1778. Royal peace commissioners did not reach Philadelphia until June, a month after Congress had ratified the French treaty. The British proposals were icily rejected, and while the peace commissioners were still in Philadelphia, war broke out between France and Great Britain.

The American Revolution, however, if no longer being lost, had yet to be won. After the loss of Philadelphia, Washington had settled his army for the winter at Valley Forge, 20 miles to the northwest. The army's supply system collapsed. Often the men had nothing to eat but "fire cake," a mixture of ground grain and water molded on a stick or in a pan and baked in a campfire. According to the Marquis de Lafayette, one of many Europeans who volunteered to fight on the American side, "the unfortunate soldiers . . . had neither coats, nor hats, nor shirts, nor shoes; their feet and legs froze till they grew black, and it was often necessary to amputate them."

To make matters worse, there was grumbling in Congress over Washington's failure to win victories and talk of replacing him as commander in chief with Horatio Gates, the "hero" of Saratoga. (In fact, Gates was an indifferent soldier, lacking in decisiveness and unable to instill confidence in his subordinates. "Historical accounts of the Saratoga campaign have given abundant reasons for the American victory other than the military skill of Horatio Gates," one of his biographers has confessed.)

As the winter dragged on, the Continental Army melted away. So many officers resigned that Washington was heard to say that he was afraid of "being left Alone with the Soldiers only." Since enlisted men could not legally resign, they deserted by the hundreds. Yet the army survived. Gradually the soldiers who remained became a tough, professional fighting force. Their spirit has been described by the historian Charles Royster as a "mixture of patriotism, resentment, and fatalism."

The War Moves South

Spring brought a revival of American hopes in the form of more supplies, new recruits, and, above all, word of the French alliance. In May the British replaced General Howe as commander with General Clinton, who decided to transfer his base back to New York. While Clinton was moving across New Jersey, Washington attacked him at Monmouth Court House. The fight was inconclusive, but the Americans held the field when the day ended and were able to claim a victory.

Thereafter British strategy changed. Fighting in the northern states degenerated into skirmishes and other small-unit clashes. Instead, relying on sea power and the supposed presence of many Tories in the south, the British concentrated their efforts in South Carolina and Georgia. Savannah fell to them late in 1778, and most of the settled parts of Georgia were overrun during 1779. In 1780 Clinton led a massive expedition against Charleston. When the city surrendered in May, more than 3,000 soldiers were captured, the most overwhelming American defeat of the war. Leaving General Cornwallis and some 8,000 men to carry on the campaign, Clinton then sailed back to New York.

The Tories in South Carolina and Georgia came closer to meeting British expectations than in any other region, but the callous behavior of the British troops persuaded large numbers of hesitating citizens to join the Patriot cause. Guerrilla bands led by men like Francis Marion, the "Swamp Fox," and

Thomas Sumter—after whom Fort Sumter, famous in the Civil War, was named—provided a nucleus of resistance in areas that had supposedly been subdued.

In June 1780 Congress placed the highly regarded Horatio Gates in charge of a southern army

In an era when communications were slow and erratic at best, the coordination between the American and French land and naval forces that sealed up Cornwallis in Yorktown was nothing short of remarkable.

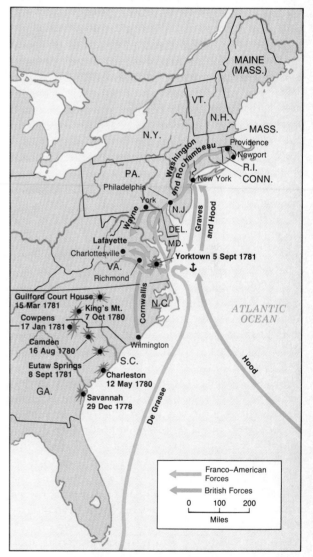

YORKTOWN AND THE WAR IN THE SOUTH, 1778–1781

consisting of the irregular militia units and a hard core of Continentals transferred from Washington's command. Gates encountered Cornwallis at Camden, South Carolina. Foolishly, he entrusted a key sector of his line to untrained militiamen, who panicked when the British charged with fixed bayonets. Gates suffered heavy losses and had to fall back. Congress then recalled him, sensibly permitting Washington to replace him with General Nathanael Greene, a first-rate officer.

A band of militiamen had trapped a contingent of Tories at King's Mountain and forced its surrender. Greene, avoiding a major engagement with Cornwallis's superior numbers, divided his troops and staged a series of raids on scattered points. In January 1781, at the Battle of Cowpens in northwestern South Carolina, General Daniel Morgan inflicted a costly defeat on Colonel Banastre Tarleton, one of Cornwallis's best officers. Cornwallis pursued Morgan hotly, but the American rejoined Greene and at Guilford Court House they again inflicted heavy losses on the British. Then Cornwallis withdrew to Wilmington, North Carolina, where he could rely on the fleet for support and reinforcements. Greene's Patriots quickly regained control of the Carolina back country.

Victory at Yorktown

Seeing no future in the Carolinas and unwilling to vegetate at Wilmington, Cornwallis marched north into Virginia, where he joined forces with troops under Benedict Arnold. (Disaffected by what he considered unjust criticism of his generalship, Arnold had sold out to the British in 1780. He intended to betray the bastion of West Point on the Hudson River. The scheme was foiled when incriminating papers were found on the person of a British spy, Major John André. Arnold fled to the British, and André was hanged.) As in the Carolina campaign, the British had numerical superiority at first but lost it rapidly when local militia and Continental forces concentrated against them. Cornwallis soon discovered that Virginia Tories were of little help in such a situation. "When a Storm threatens, our friends disappear," he grumbled.

General Clinton ordered Cornwallis to take up a defensive position at Yorktown, where he could be supplied by sea. Cornwallis objected; Yorktown, he said, was "an unhealthy swamp" where his army would be "liable to become a prey to a Foreign enemy with a temporary superiority at sea." But Clinton insisted.

It was a terrible mistake. The British navy in American waters far outnumbered American and French vessels, but the Atlantic is wide, and in those days communication was slow. The French had a fleet in the West Indies under Admiral François De Grasse and another squadron at Newport, Rhode Island, where a French army was stationed. In the summer of 1781 Washington, De Grasse, and the Comte de Rochambeau, commander of French land forces, designed and carried out with an efficiency unparalleled in 18th-century warfare a complex plan to bottle up Cornwallis.

The British navy in the West Indies and at New York might have forestalled this scheme had it moved promptly and in force. But Admiral Sir George Rodney sent only part of his Indies fleet. As a result, De Grasse, after a battle with a British fleet commanded by Admiral Thomas Graves, won control of the Chesapeake and cut Cornwallis off from the sea.

The next move was up to Washington, and this was his finest hour as a commander. He desperately wanted to attack the British base at New York, but at the urging of Rochambeau he agreed instead to strike at Yorktown. After tricking Clinton into thinking he was heading for New York, he pushed boldly south. In early September he reached Yorktown and joined up with an army commanded by Lafayette and troops from De Grasse's fleet. He soon had nearly 17,000 French and American veterans in position.

Cornwallis was helpless. He held out until October 17 and then asked for terms. Two days later more than 7,000 British soldiers marched out of their lines and laid down their arms. Then the jubilant Lafayette ordered his military band to play "Yankee Doodle."

The Peace of Paris

The British gave up trying to suppress the rebellion after Yorktown, but the event that confirmed the existence of the United States as an independent

Major John André was caught by American militiamen while trying to make his way south to New York City after a meeting with Benedict Arnold. If, as instructed by General Clinton, he had worn his uniform instead of changing into civilian clothes, he would have been treated as an officer. But as a spy, he could not escape the spy's fate of death by hanging.

nation was the signing of a peace treaty with Great Britain. Yorktown had been only one of a string of defeats suffered by British armies in the Mediterranean, the West Indies, Africa, and Asia. The national debt had doubled again since 1775. In March 1782 Lord North resigned after Parliament renounced all further efforts to coerce the colonies. At once the new ministry of Lord Rockingham prepared to negotiate a peace settlement with America.

The problem of peacemaking was complicated. The United States and France had pledged not to make a separate peace. Spain, at war with Great Britain since 1779, was allied with France but not with America. Although eager to profit at British expense, the Spanish hoped to limit American expansion beyond the Appalachians, for they had ambitions of their own in the eastern half of the Mississippi Valley. France, while ready enough to see America independent, did not want the new country to become *too* powerful; in a conflict of interest between America and Spain, France tended to support Spain.

The Continental Congress appointed John Adams, Benjamin Franklin, John Jay, Thomas Jefferson, and Henry Laurens as a commission to conduct peace talks. Franklin and Jay did most of the actual negotiating. Congress, grateful for French aid during the Revolution, had instructed the commissioners to rely on the advice of the Comte de Vergennes. In Paris, however, the commissioners soon discovered that Vergennes was not the perfect friend of America that Congress believed him to be. He was, after all, a French official, and France had other interests far more important than concern for its American ally. Vergennes "means to keep his hand under our chin to prevent us from drowning," Adams complained, "but not to lift our head out of the water."

Franklin, perhaps because as a famous scientist and sage he was wined and dined by the cream of Paris and petted and fussed over by some of the city's most beautiful women, did not press the American point of view as forcefully as he might have. But this was because he took the long view, which was to achieve a true reconciliation with the British, not simply to drive the hardest bargain possible. John Jay was somewhat more tough-minded. But on basic issues all the Americans were in agreement. They hinted to the British representative, Richard Oswald, that they would consider a separate peace if it were a generous one and suggested that Great Britain would be far better off with America, a nation that favored free trade, in control of the trans-Appalachian region than with a mercantilist power like Spain.

The British government reacted favorably, authorizing Oswald "to treat with the Commissioners appointed by the Colonys, under the title of Thirteen United States." Soon the Americans were deep in negotiations with Oswald. They told Vergennes what they were doing but did not discuss details.

Oswald was cooperative, and the Americans drove a hard bargain. One scrap of conversation reveals the tenor of the talks.

OSWALD: We can never be such damned sots as to disturb you.
ADAMS: Thank you. . . . But nations don't feel as you and I do, and your nation, when it gets a little refreshed from the fatigues of the war, and when men and money become plentiful, and allies at hand, will not feel as it does now.
OSWALD: We can never be such damned sots as to think of differing again with you.
ADAMS: Why, in truth I have never been able to comprehend the reason why you ever thought of differing with us.

By the end of November 1782, a preliminary treaty had been signed. "His Britannic Majesty," Article 1 began, "acknowledges the said United States . . . to be free, sovereign and independent States." Other terms were equally in line with American hopes and objectives. The boundaries of the nation were set at the Great Lakes, the Mississippi River, and 31° north latitude (roughly the northern boundary of Florida). Britain recognized the right of Americans to take fish on the Grand Banks off Newfoundland and, far more important, to dry and cure their catch on unsettled beaches in Labrador and Nova Scotia. The British agreed to withdraw their troops from American soil "with all convenient speed." Where the touchy problem of Tory property seized during the Revolution was concerned, the Americans agreed only that the Congress would "earnestly recommend" that the states "provide for the restitution of all estates, rights and properties which have been confiscated." They promised to prevent further property confiscation and prosecutions of Tories—certainly a wise as well as a humane policy—and they agreed not to impede the collection of debts owed to British subjects. Vergennes was flabbergasted by the success of the Americans. "The English buy the peace more than they make it," he wrote. "Their concessions . . . exceed all that I should have thought possible."

" 'Tis lost!" cries John Bull as America flies away in the hands of the devil. Spain, France, and Holland chide the Briton for his negligence.

The American commissioners obtained these favorable terms because they were shrewd diplomats and because of the rivalries that existed among the great European powers. In the last analysis, Britain preferred to have a weak nation of English-speaking people in command of the Mississippi Valley rather than France or Spain.

From their experience at the peace talks, the American leaders learned the importance of playing one power against another without committing themselves completely to any. This policy demanded constant contact with European affairs and skill at adjusting policies to changes in the European balance of power. It enabled the United States, a young and relatively feeble country, to grow and prosper.

Forming a National Government

Independence was won on the battlefield and at the Paris Peace Conference, but it could not have been achieved without the work of the Continental Congress and the new state governments. The delegates recognized that the Congress was essentially a legislative body rather than a complete government and from the start they struggled to create a workable central authority. But their effort was handicapped by much confusion and bickering, and early military defeats sapped their energy and morale. In July 1776 John Dickinson prepared a draft national constitution, but it could not command much support. The larger states objected to equal representation of all the states, and the states with large western land claims refused to cede them to the central government. It was not until November 1777 that the Articles of Confederation were submitted to the states for ratification.

It was necessary to obtain the approval of all the states before the Articles could go into effect. All but Maryland acted fairly promptly, but that state did not ratify the document until 1781. Maryland held out in order to force a change that would authorize Congress to determine the western limits of states with land claims beyond the Appalachians. There were many good reasons why this should be done. The state claims to the west were overlapping, vaguely defined, and in some instances preposter-

ous. To have permitted a few states to monopolize the west would have unbalanced the Union from the start.

Many people in the "landed" states recognized the justice of Maryland's suggestion, yet Maryland had a more selfish motive. Land speculators in the state had obtained from the Indians rights to large tracts in the Ohio Valley claimed by Virginia. Under Virginia, the Maryland titles would be worthless, but under a national administration they might be made to stand up.

Virginia resented its neighbor's efforts to grasp these valuable lands by indirection, but with the British about to advance into the state, Virginia agreed to surrender its claim to all land west and north of the Ohio River. It thwarted the Maryland speculators by insisting that all titles based on Indian purchases be declared void. Maryland then had no recourse but to ratify the Articles.

The Articles merely provided a legal basis for authority that the Continental Congress had already been exercising. Each state, regardless of size, was to have but one vote; the union it created was only a "league of friendship." Article 2 defined the limit of national power: "Each state retains its sovereignty, freedom, and independence, and every Power, jurisdiction, and right, which is not by this confederation expressly delegated to the United States, in Congress assembled." Time would prove this an inadequate arrangement, chiefly because the central government lacked the authority to impose taxes and had no way of enforcing the powers it did have. As the historian David Ramsay explained in 1789, "No coercive power was given to the general government, nor was it invested with any legislative power over individuals."

Financing the War

In practice, Congress and the states carried on the war cooperatively. General officers were appointed by Congress, lesser ones locally. The Continental Army, the backbone of Washington's force, was supported by Congress. The states raised militia chiefly for short-term service. Militiamen fought well at times but often proved unreliable, especially when asked to fight at any great distance from their homes. Washington continually fretted about their "dirty mercenary spirit" and their "intractable" na-

The Continental Army's lack of financial support is demonstrated in requisitions like this one, issued by General Washington the day after his troops limped into Valley Forge.

ture, yet he could not have won the war without them.

The fact that Congress's requisitions of money often went unhonored by the states does not mean that the states failed to contribute heavily to the war effort. Altogether they spent about $5.8 million in hard money, and they met Congress's demands for beef, corn, rum, fodder, and other military supplies. In addition, Congress raised large sums by borrowing. Americans bought bonds worth between $7 and $8 million during the war. Foreign governments lent another $8 million, most of this furnished by France. Congress also issued more than $240 million in paper money, the states over $200 million more. This currency fell rapidly in value, resulting in an inflation that caused hardship and grumbling. The people, in effect, paid much of the cost of the war through the depreciation of their savings, but it is hard to see how else the war could have been financed, given the prejudice of the populace against paying taxes to fight a war against British taxation.

At about the time the Articles of Confederation were ratified, Congress established Departments of Foreign Affairs, War, and Finance, with individual heads responsible to it. The most important of the new department heads was the superintendent of finance, Robert Morris, a Philadelphia merchant. When Morris took office, the Continental dollar was worthless, the system of supplying the army chaotic, the credit of the government exhausted. He set up an efficient method of obtaining food and uniforms for the army, persuaded Congress to charter a national Bank of North America, and aided by the slackening of military activity after Yorktown got the country back on a hard money basis. New foreign loans were obtained, partly because Morris's efficiency and industry inspired confidence.

State Governments

However crucial the role of Congress, in an important sense the real revolution occurred when the individual colonies broke their ties with Great Britain. Using their colonial charters as a basis, the states began framing new constitutions even before the Declaration of Independence. By early 1777 all but Connecticut and Rhode Island, which continued under their colonial charters well into the 19th century, had taken this decisive step.

On the surface the new governments were not drastically different from those they replaced. The most significant change was the removal of outside control, which had the effect of making the governments more responsive to public opinion. Gone were the times when a governor could be appointed and maintained in office by orders from London. The new constitutions varied in detail, but all provided for an elected legislature, an executive, and a system of courts. In general the powers of the governor and of judges were limited, the theory being that elected rulers no less than those appointed by kings were subject to the temptations of authority, that, as one Patriot put it, all men are "tyrants enough at heart." The typical governor had no voice in legislation and little in appointments. Pennsylvania went so far as to eliminate the office of governor, replacing it with an elected council of 12.

Power was concentrated in the legislature, which the people had come to count on to defend their interests. In addition to the lawmaking authority exercised by the colonial assemblies, the state constitutions gave the legislatures the power to declare war, conduct foreign relations, control the courts, and perform many other essentially executive functions. While continuing to require that voters be property owners or taxpayers, the constitution makers remained suspicious even of the legislature.

The British concept of virtual representation they rejected out of hand. They saw legislators as representatives, that is, agents reflecting the interests of the voters of a particular district rather than superior persons chosen to decide public issues according to their own best judgment. Gordon S. Wood, whose book *The Creation of the American Republic* throws much light on the political thinking of the period, describes the concept as "acutely actual representation." Where political power was involved, the common American principle was every man for himself. The constitutions contained bills of rights (such as the one George Mason wrote for Virginia) protecting the people's civil liberties against all branches of the government. In Britain such guarantees checked only the Crown; the Americans invoked them against their elected representatives as well.

The state governments combined the best of the British system, including its respect for status, fairness, and due process, with the uniquely American stress on individualism and a healthy dislike of too much authority. The idea of drafting written frames of government—contracts between the people and their representatives that carefully spelled out the powers and duties of the latter—grew out of the experience of the colonists after 1763, when the vagueness of the unwritten British constitution had caused so much controversy, and from the compact principle described in the Declaration of Independence. It represented one of the most important innovations of the Revolutionary era: a peaceful method for altering the political system. In the midst of violence, the states changed their frames of government in an orderly, legal manner—a truly remarkable achievement that became a beacon of hope to reformers all over the world. The states' example, the Reverend Simeon Howard of Massachusetts predicted, "will encourage the friends and rouse a spirit of liberty through other nations."

Social Reform

Back in 1909 the historian Carl Becker wrote that the American Revolution was not merely a fight for "home rule," that is, for independence from Great Britain. It was also, Becker insisted, a fight to determine "who should rule at home." It is certainly true that there were many riots and numerous other indications of social conflict in America during the Revolutionary era, especially in the cities. The destruction of property by mobs during the Stamp Act crisis is only the best-known case where well-to-do people had cause to fear that popular resentment was not entirely directed at the British.

Many states seized the occasion of constitution making to introduce important political and social reforms. In Pennsylvania, Virginia, North Carolina, and other states the seats in the legislature were reapportioned in order to give the western districts their fair share. Primogeniture, entail (the right of an owner of property to prevent heirs from ever disposing of it), and quitrents were abolished wherever they had existed. Steps toward greater freedom of religion were taken, especially in states where the Anglican church had enjoyed a privileged position. In Virginia the movement to separate church and state was given the force of law by Jefferson's Statute of Religious Liberty, enacted in 1786. "Our civil rights have no dependence on our religious opinions, any more than our opinions in physics or geometry," the statute declared. "Truth is great and will prevail if left to herself." Therefore, "No man shall be compelled to frequent or support any religious worship, place, or ministry . . . nor shall otherwise suffer on account of his religious opinions or belief."

Most states continued to support religion; Massachusetts did not end public support of Congregational churches until the 1830s. But after the Revolution the states usually distributed the money roughly in accordance with the numerical strength of the various Protestant denominations.

Many states moved tentatively against slavery. In attacking British policy after 1763, colonists had frequently claimed that Parliament was trying to make slaves of them. No less a personage than George Washington wrote in 1774: "We must assert our rights, or submit to every imposition, that can be heaped upon us, till custom and use shall make us tame and abject slaves." However exaggerated

The Continental Army brought together men from all over the colonies and from a wide range of backgrounds. Their variety is suggested in this watercolor by a French officer who served in America during the Revolution. From left to right are a black infantryman with a light rifle, a musketman, a soldier carrying a heavy rifle, and an artilleryman.

the language, such reasoning led to denunciations of slavery, often vague but significant in their effects on public opinion. The fact that practically every important thinker of the European Enlightenment had criticized slavery on moral and economic grounds (Montesquieu, Voltaire, Diderot, and Rousseau in France, David Hume, Samuel Johnson, and Adam Smith in England, to name the most important) also had an impact on educated opinion. Then, too, the forthright statements in the Declaration of Independence about liberty and equality seemed impossible to reconcile with slaveholding. "How is it," asked Dr. Johnson, who opposed independence vehemently, "that we hear the loudest yelps for liberty among the drivers of negroes?"

The war opened direct paths to freedom for some slaves. In November 1775 Lord Dunmore, the royal governor of Virginia, proclaimed that all slaves "able and willing to bear arms" for the British would be liberated. In fact, the British treated slaves as captured property, seizing them by the thousands in their campaigns in the south. The fate of these blacks is obscure. Some ended up in the West Indies, still slaves. Others were evacuated to Canada and liberated, and some of them settled the British colony of Sierra Leone in West Africa, founded in 1787. Probably many more escaped from bondage

by running away during the confusion accompanying the British campaigns in the south.

About 5,000 blacks served in the Patriot army and navy. Most black soldiers were assigned noncombat duties, but there were some black soldiers in every major battle from Lexington to Yorktown.

Beginning with Pennsylvania in 1780, the northern states all did away with slavery. In most cases slaves born after a certain date were to become free upon reaching maturity. Since New York did not pass a gradual emancipation law until 1799 and New Jersey not until 1804, there were numbers of slaves in the so-called free states well into the 19th century—more than 3,500 as late as 1830. But the institution was on its way toward extinction. All the states prohibited the importation of slaves from abroad, and except for Georgia and South Carolina, the southern states passed laws removing restrictions on the right of individual owners to free their slaves. The greatest success of voluntary emancipation came in Virginia, where between 1782 and 1790, as many as 10,000 blacks were freed.

These advances encouraged foes of slavery to hope that the institution would soon disappear. But slavery died only where it was not economically important. Except for owners whose slaves were "carried off" by the British, only in Massachusetts, where the state supreme court ruled slavery unconstitutional in 1783, were owners deprived of existing slaves against their will.

Despite the continuing subordination of blacks, there is no question that the Revolution permanently changed the tone of American society. In the way they dressed, in their manner of speech, and in the way they dealt with one another in public places, Americans paid at least lip service to the idea of equality.

After the publication of *Common Sense* and the Declaration of Independence, with their excoriations of that "Royal Brute," King George III, it became fashionable to denounce the granting of titles of nobility, all "aristocrats," and any privilege based on birth. In 1783 a group of army officers founded a fraternal organization, the Society of Cincinnati. Although the revered George Washington was its president, many citizens found the mere existence of a club restricted to officers alarming; the fact that membership was to be hereditary, passing on the death of a member to his oldest son, caused a furor.

Nevertheless, little of the social and economic upheaval usually associated with revolutions occurred, before, during, or after 1776. At least part of the urban violence of the period (just how large a part is difficult to determine at this distance) had no social objective. America had its share of criminals, mischievous youths eager to flex their muscles, and other people unable to resist the temptation to break the law when it could be done without much risk of punishment. Certainly there was no wholesale proscription of any class, faith, or profession.

The property of Tories was frequently seized by the state governments, but almost never with the idea of redistributing wealth or providing the poor with land. While some large Tory estates were broken up and sold to small farmers, others passed intact to wealthy individuals or to groups of speculators. The war disrupted many traditional business relationships. Some merchants were unable to cope with the changes; others adapted well and grew rich. But the changes occurred without regard for the political beliefs or social values of either those who profited or those who lost.

That the new governments were liberal but moderate reflected the spirit of the times, a spirit typified by Thomas Jefferson, who had great faith in the democratic process yet owned a large estate and

many slaves and had never suggested a drastic social revolution. More individuals of middling wealth were elected to the legislatures than in colonial times because the Revolution stimulated popular interest in politics and because republican forms subtly undermined the tendency of farmers and artisans to defer automatically to great planters and merchants.

Nevertheless, relatively high property qualifications for officeholding remained the general rule. Few "ordinary" people wanted radical changes. If they were becoming more skeptical about their "betters," they continued to look down their noses at unskilled laborers, servants, and others lower on the social ladder. There were three classes in Philadelphia society, a writer in the *Pennsylvania Packet* noted in 1781:

> The first class consists of commercial projectors . . . speculators, riotous livers, and a kind of loungers. . . . The second class are a set of honest sober men, who mind their business. . . . The third class are thieves, pick-pockets, low-cheats and dirty sots.

During the war, conflicts erupted over economic issues involving land and taxation, yet no single class or interest triumphed in all the states or in the national government. In Pennsylvania, where the western radical element was strong, the constitution was extremely democratic; in Maryland and South Carolina the conservatives maintained control handily. Throughout the country, many great landowners were ardent Patriots, but others became Tories—and so did many small farmers.

In some instances the state legislatures wrote the new constitutions. In others the legislatures ordered special elections to choose delegates to conventions empowered to draft the charters. The convention method was a further important product of the Revolutionary era, an additional illustration of the idea that constitutions are contracts between the people and their leaders. Massachusetts even required that its new constitution be ratified by the people after it was drafted.

Finally, the new governments became more responsive to public opinion, no matter what the particular shape of their political institutions. This was true principally because *Common Sense*, the Declaration of Independence, and the experience of participating in a revolution had made people conscious of their rights in a republic and of their power to enforce those rights. Conservatives swiftly discovered that state constitutions designed to insulate legislators and officials from popular pressures were ineffective when the populace felt strongly about any issue.

Effects of the Revolution on Women

In the late 18th century there was a worldwide trend, barely perceptible at the time, toward increasing the legal rights of women. This movement was strengthened in America by the events leading up to the break with Great Britain and still more by the Declaration of Independence. When Americans began to think and talk about the rights of the individual and the evils of arbitrary rule, subtle effects on relations between the sexes followed. For example, it became somewhat easier for women to obtain divorces. In colonial times divorces were rel-

atively rare, but easier for men to obtain than women. After the Revolution the difference did not disappear, but it became considerably smaller. In Massachusetts, before the 1770s no woman is known to have obtained a divorce on the ground of her husband's adultery. Thereafter, successful suits by wives against errant husbands were not unusual. In 1791 a South Carolina judge went so far as to say that the law protecting "the absolute dominion" of husbands was "the offspring of a rude and barbarous age." The "progress of civilization," he continued, "has tended to ameliorate the condition of women, and to allow even to wives, something like personal identity."

As the tone of this "liberal" opinion indicates, the change in male attitudes that took place in America because of the Revolution was small. When John Adams's wife Abigail warned him in 1776 that if he and his fellow rebels did not "remember the ladies" when reforming society, the women would "foment a Rebellion" of their own, he treated her

Abigail Adams, in asking her husband John to "remember the ladies" when reforming society, was not advocating political rights for women. Rather, she wanted fairer treatment for women within the family. "Do not put such unlimited power into the hands of the husbands," she wrote him. "Remember all men would be tyrants if they could."

remarks as a joke. He believed that voting (and as he wrote on another occasion, writing history) was "not the Province of the ladies."

However, the war effort increased the influence of women in several ways. With so many men in uniform, women took over the management of countless farms, shops, and businesses, and they became involved in the handling of other day-to-day matters that men had normally conducted. Their experiences made both them and in many cases their fathers and husbands more aware of their ability to take on all sorts of chores previously considered exclusively masculine in character. At the same time, women wanted to contribute to the winning of independence, and their efforts to do so made them conscious of their importance. Furthermore, the rhetoric of the Revolution, with its stress on liberty and equality, affected women in the same way that it caused many whites of both sexes to question the morality of slavery.

Attitudes toward the education of women also changed because of the Revolution. According to the best estimates, at least half the white women in America could not read or write as late as the 1780s. But as the historian Linda K. Kerber writes, "The republican experiment demanded a well-educated citizenry." In a land of opportunity like the United States, women seemed particularly important because of their role in training the young. "You distribute 'mental nourishment' along with physical," one orator told the women of America in 1795. "The reformation of the world is in your power. . . . The solidity and stability of your country rest with you." The idea of female education began to catch on. Schools for girls were founded, and the level of female literacy gradually rose.

Growth of a National Spirit

American independence and control of a wide and rich domain were the most obvious results of the Revolution. Changes in the structure of society, as we have seen, were relatively minor. Economic developments, such as the growth of new trade connections and the expansion of manufacturing in an effort to replace British goods, were of only modest significance. By far the most important social and economic changes involved the Tories and were thus by-products of the political revolution rather

than a determined reorganization of a people's way of life.

There was another important result of the Revolution: the growth of American nationalism. Most modern revolutions have been *caused* by nationalism and have *resulted* in independence. In the case of the American Revolution, the desire to be free antedated any intense national feeling. The colonies entered into a political union not because they felt an overwhelming desire to bring all Americans under one rule but because unity offered the only hope of winning a war against Great Britain. That they remained united after throwing off British rule reflects the degree to which nationalism had developed during the conflict.

By the middle of the 18th century the colonists had begun to think of themselves as a separate society distinct from Europe and even from Britain. Benjamin Franklin described himself not as a British subject but as "an American subject of the King," and in 1750 a Boston newspaper could urge its readers to drink "American" beer in order to free themselves from being "beholden to Foreigners" for their alcoholic beverages. Little political nationalism existed before the Revolution, however. Local ties remained predominant. A few might say, with Patrick Henry in 1774, "The distinctions between Virginians, Pennsylvanians, New Yorkers, and New Englanders are no more. I am not a Virginian, but an American." But Henry was being carried away by his own oratory; he was actually of two minds on the subject of national versus local loyalty. People who really put America first were rare indeed before the final break with Great Britain.

The new nationalism arose from a number of sources and expressed itself in different ways. Common sacrifices in war certainly played a part; the soldiers of the Continental Army fought in the summer heat of the Carolinas for the same cause that had led them to brave the ice floes of the Delaware in order to surprise the Hessians. Such men lost interest in state boundary lines; they became Americans.

John Marshall of Fauquier County, Virginia, for example, was a 20-year-old militiaman in 1775. The next year he joined the Continental Army. He served in Pennsylvania, New Jersey, and New York and endured the winter of 1777–1778 at Valley Forge. "I found myself associated with brave men from different states who were risking life and everything valuable in a common cause," he later wrote. "I was confirmed in the habit of considering America as my country and Congress as my government."

Andrew Jackson, child of the Carolina frontier, was only 9 when the Revolution broke out. One brother was killed in battle; another died as a result of untreated wounds. Young Andrew took up arms and was captured by the Redcoats. A British officer ordered Jackson to black his boots and when the boy refused, struck him across the face with the flat of his sword. Jackson bore the scar to his grave—and became an ardent nationalist on the spot. He and Marshall had very different ideas and came to be bitter enemies in later life. Nevertheless, they were both American nationalists—and for the same reason.

Civilians as well as soldiers reacted in this way. A Carolina farmer whose home and barn were protected against British looters by men who spoke with the harsh nasal twang of New England adopted a broader outlook toward politics. When the news came that thousands of Redcoats had stacked their arms in defeat after Yorktown, few people cared what state or section had made the victory possible—it was an American triumph.

The war caused many people to move from place to place. Soldiers traveled as the tide of war fluctuated; so too—far more than in earlier times—did prominent leaders. Members of Congress from every state had to travel to Philadelphia; in the process they saw much of the country and the people who inhabited it. Listening to their fellows and serving with them on committees almost inevitably broadened these men, most of them highly influential in their local communities.

With its 13 stars and 13 stripes representing the states, the American flag symbolized national unity and reflected the common feeling that such a symbol was necessary. Yet the flag had separate stars and stripes; local interests and local loyalties remained extremely strong, and these could be divisive when conflicts of interest arose.

Certain practical problems that demanded common solutions also drew the states together. No one seriously considered having 13 postal systems or 13 sets of diplomatic representatives abroad. Every new diplomatic appointment, every treaty of friendship or commerce signed, committed all to a common policy and thus bound them more closely together. And economic developments had a unifying effect. Cutting off English goods encouraged manufacturing, making America more self-sufficient and stimulating both interstate trade and national pride.

The Great Land Ordinances

The western lands, which had divided the states in the beginning, became a force for unity once they had been ceded to the national government. Everyone realized what a priceless asset they were, and all now understood that no one state could determine the future of the west.

The politicians argued hotly about how these lands should be developed. Some advocated selling the land in township units in the traditional New England manner to groups or companies; others favored letting individual pioneers stake out farms in the helter-skelter manner common in the colonial south. The decision was a compromise. The Land Ordinance of 1785 provided for surveying western territories into 6-mile-square townships before sale. Every other township was to be further subdivided into 36 sections of 640 acres (1 square mile) each. The land was sold at auction at a minimum price of $1 an acre. The law favored speculative land-development companies, for even the 640-acre units were far too large and expensive for the typical frontier family. But the fact that the land was to be surveyed and sold by the central government was a nationalizing force. Congress set aside the sixteenth section of every township for the maintenance of schools, another farsighted decision.

Still more significant was the Northwest Ordinance of 1787, which established governments for the west. As early as 1775, settlers in frontier districts were petitioning Congress to allow them to enter the Union as independent states, and in 1780 Congress had resolved that all lands ceded to the nation by the existing states should be "formed into distinct republican States" with "the same rights of sovereignty, freedom and independence" as the original 13. In 1784 a committee headed by Thomas Jefferson worked out a plan for doing this, and in 1787 it was enacted into law. The area bounded by the Ohio, the Mississippi, and the Great Lakes was to be carved into not less than three or more than five

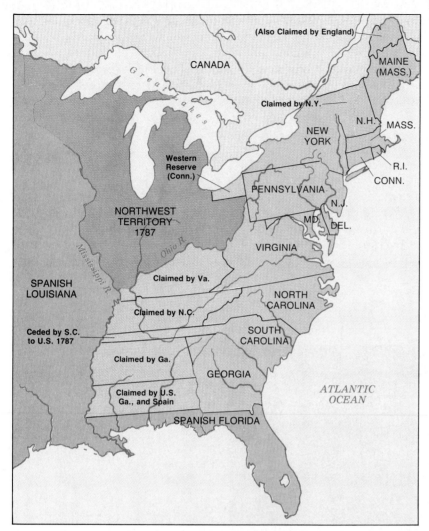

New York and Virginia gave up their claims to the vast area that became the Northwest Territory, and thus set a precedent for trans-Appalachian land policy. By 1802 the various state claims had been ceded to the national government. The original Northwest Territory (the Old Northwest) was bounded by the Ohio River, the Mississippi, and the Great Lakes.

THE UNITED STATES
UNDER THE ARTICLES OF CONFEDERATION, 1787

territories. Until the adult male population of the entire area reached 5,000, it was to be ruled by a governor and three judges, all appointed by Congress. When 5,000 men of voting age had settled in the territory, the ordinance authorized them to elect a legislature and send a nonvoting delegate to Congress. Finally, when 60,000 persons had settled in any one of the political subdivisions, it was to become a state. It could draft a constitution and operate in any way it wished, save that the government had to be "republican" and that slavery was prohibited.

Seldom has a legislative body acted more wisely. That the western districts must become states everyone conceded from the start. The people had had their fill of colonialism under British rule, and the rebellious temper of frontier settlers made it impossible even to consider maintaining the west in a dependent status. (When North Carolina ceded its trans-Appalachian lands to the United States in 1784, the settlers there, uncertain how they would fare under federal rule, hastily organized an extra-legal state of Franklin, and it was not until 1789 that the national government obtained control.) But it would have been unfair to turn the territories over to the first comers, who would have been unable to manage such large domains and would surely have taken advantage of their priority to dictate to later arrivals. A period of tutelage was necessary, a period when the "mother country" must guide and nourish its growing offspring.

Thus the intermediate territorial governments corresponded almost exactly to the governments of British royal colonies. The appointed governors could veto acts of the assemblies and could "convene, prorogue, and dissolve" them at their discretion. The territorial delegates to Congress were not unlike colonial agents. Yet it was vital that this intermediate stage end and that its end be determined in advance so that no argument could develop over when the territory was ready for statehood.

The system worked well and was applied to nearly all the regions absorbed by the nation as it advanced westward. Together with the Ordinance of 1785, which branded its checkerboard pattern on the physical shape of the west, this law gave the growing country a unity essential to the growth of a national spirit.

National Heroes

The Revolution further fostered nationalism by giving the people their first commonly revered heroes. Benjamin Franklin was widely known before the break with Great Britain through his experiments

"The chief human symbol of a common Americanism." George Washington attained heroic status perhaps as much for his modesty as for his devotion to the new nation.

with electricity, his immensely successful *Poor Richard's Almanack,* and his invention of the Franklin stove. His staunch support of the Patriot cause, his work in the Continental Congress, and his diplomatic successes in France, where he was extravagantly admired, added to his fame. Franklin demonstrated, to Europeans and to Americans themselves, that not all Americans need be ignorant rustics.

Washington, however, was "the chief human symbol of a common Americanism." Stern, cold, a man of few words, the great Virginian did not seem a likely candidate for hero worship. "My countenance never yet revealed my feelings," he himself admitted. Yet he had qualities that made people name babies after him and call him "the Father of His Country" long before the war was won: his personal sacrifices in the cause of independence, his integrity, and above all, perhaps, his obvious desire to retire to his Mount Vernon estate (for many Americans feared any powerful leader and worried lest Washington seek to become a dictator).

As a general, Washington was not a brilliant strategist like Napoleon. Neither was he a tactician of the quality of Caesar or Robert E. Lee. His lack of genius made his achievements all the more impressive. He held his forces together in adversity, avoiding both useless slaughter and catastrophic defeat. People of all sections, from every walk of life, looked on Washington as the embodiment of American virtues: a man of deeds rather than words; a man of substance accustomed to luxury yet capable of enduring great hardships stoically and as much at home in the wilderness as an Indian; a bold Patriot, quick to take arms against British tyranny, yet eminently respectable. The Revolution might have been won without Washington, but it is unlikely that the free United States would have become so easily a true nation had he not been at its call.

A National Culture

Breaking away from Great Britain accentuated certain trends toward social and intellectual independence and strengthened the national desire to create an American culture. The Anglican church in America had to form a new organization once the connection with the Crown was severed; in 1786 it became the Protestant Episcopal church. The Dutch and German Reformed churches also became independent of their European connections. Roman Catholics in America had been under the administration of the vicar apostolic of England; after the Revolution, Father John Carroll of Baltimore assumed these duties, and in 1789 he became the first American Roman Catholic bishop.

The impact of post-Revolutionary nationalism on American education was best reflected in the immense success of the textbooks of Noah Webster, later famous for his American dictionary. Webster was an ardent patriot. "We ought not to consider ourselves as inhabitants of a particular state only," he wrote in 1785, "but as *Americans.*" Webster's famous *Spelling Book* appeared in 1783 when he was a young schoolteacher in Goshen, New York. It emphasized American forms and usage and contained a patriotic preface urging Americans to pay proper respect to their own literature. Webster's *Reader,* published shortly thereafter, included selections from the speeches of Revolutionary leaders, who, according to the compiler, were the equals of Cicero and Demosthenes as orators. Some 15 million copies of the *Speller* were sold in the next five decades, several times that number by 1900. The *Reader* was also a continuing best-seller.

Webster's work was not the only sign of nationalism in education. In 1787 John M'Culloch published the first American history textbook. The colleges saw a great outburst of patriotic spirit. King's College (founded in 1754) received a new name, Columbia, in 1784. Everywhere it was recognized that the republic required educated and cultivated leaders.

Nationalism affected the arts and sciences in the years after the Revolution. Jedidiah Morse's popular *American Geography* (1789) was a paean in praise of the "astonishing" progress of the country, all the result of the "natural genius of Americans." The American Academy of Arts and Sciences, founded at Boston during the Revolution, was created "to advance the interest, honor, dignity and happiness of a free, independent and virtuous people."

American painters and writers of the period usually chose extremely patriotic themes. John Trumbull helped capture Dorchester Heights and force the evacuation of Boston, took part in the defense of northern New York against Burgoyne, and fought in Pennsylvania and Rhode Island. When he took up painting, he went to London to study, but he produced such pictures as *The Battle of Bunker's Hill*, *The Surrender of Lord Cornwallis at Yorktown*, and *The Declaration of Independence*. Trumbull referred to these and similar efforts as his "national work." Joel Barlow intended his *Vision of Columbus*, written between 1779 and 1787, to prove that America was "the noblest and most elevated part of the earth." Royall Tyler's play *The Contrast*, which was produced in New York in 1787, compared American virtue (the hero was called Colonel Manly) with British vice and contained such chauvinistic lines as these:

> *Why should our thoughts to distant countries roam*
> *When each refinement may be found at home?*

In a more subtle way, American nationalism revealed itself in the fondness of the Revolutionary generation for ancient Greek and Roman architecture, which they saw as expressing democratic and republican values. Jefferson, for example, built his home at Monticello in classical style and modeled the Virginia Capitol on the Roman *Maison Carré* in Nimes, France.

The United States in the 1780s was far from the powerful centralized nation it has since become. Probably most citizens still gave their first loyalty to their own states. In certain important respects the confederation was pitifully ineffectual. However, people were increasingly aware of their common interests and increasingly proud of their common heritage. The motto of the new nation, *E pluribus unum*—"From many, one"—perfectly describes a process that was rapidly taking place in the years after Yorktown.

Milestones

1774	Thomas Jefferson, "A Summary View of the Rights of British America"
	General Thomas Gage, commander in chief of the British army in America, named governor of Massachusetts
1775	Battles of Lexington and Concord
	Second Continental Congress names George Washington commander in chief of the Continental Army
	Battle of Bunker Hill; Gage replaced as British commander by General Sir William Howe
1776	Tom Paine, *Common Sense*
	Washington occupies Boston
	Declaration of Independence
	Battle of Long Island
	Washington evacuates New York City
	Battle of Trenton
1777	Battle of Saratoga, leading to alliance with France
	Battle of Germantown; British occupy Philadelphia
1777–1778	Continental Army winters at Valley Forge
1778	British capture Savannah
1780	British capture Charleston
1781	Articles of Confederation ratified
	General Cornwallis surrenders at Yorktown
1783	Peace of Paris; Great Britain recognizes the independence of the United States
1785	Land Ordinance of 1785

SUPPLEMENTARY READING

Titles marked with an asterisk have been published in paperback.

Good brief surveys of the Revolutionary years are Edward Countryman, **The American Revolution** (1985), and E. S. Morgan, **The Birth of the Republic*** (1956). Robert Middlekauf, **The Glorious Cause** (1982), is more detailed. Don Higgenbotham, **The War of American Independence*** (1971), provides an up-to-date account of the military aspects of the Revolution, and Charles Royster, **A Revolutionary People at War** (1979), describes the attitudes of soldiers and civilians toward the army. See also Robert A. Gross, **The Minutemen and Their World** (1976). On Washington's role, see J. R. Alden, **George Washington** (1984), and Marcus Cunliffe, **George Washington: Man and Monument*** (1958).

On the Continental Congress and the Articles of Confederation, see J. T. Main, **The Sovereign States** (1973), J. N. Rakove, **The Beginnings of National Politics** (1979), and R. B. Morris, **The Forging of the Union** (1987). Eric Foner, **Tom Paine and Revolutionary America*** (1976), is an excellent brief biography. The classic analysis of the Declaration of Independence is C. L. Becker, **The Declaration of Independence*** (1922).

The early history of the state governments is covered in Elisha P. Douglas, **Rebels and Democrats*** (1955). Edward Countryman, **A People in Revolution** (1982), deals with conditions in New York. The development of political ideas is admirably described and analyzed in G. S. Wood, **The Creation of the American Republic*** (1969), and in D. J. Boorstin, **The Genius of American Politics*** (1953). The financial problems of this period are covered in E. J. Ferguson, **The Power of the Purse*** (1968).

The classic account of the social and economic effects of the Revolution is J. F. Jameson, **The American Revolution Considered as a Social Movement*** (1926). R. E. Brown takes issue with Jameson's view in **Middle Class Democracy and the Revolution in Massachusetts** (1955), as does R. P. McCormick in **Experiment in Independence: New Jersey in the Critical Period** (1950). J. T. Main, **The Social Structure of Revolutionary America*** (1965), provides a general picture against which to evaluate the views of Jameson and his critics. On the Tories, see W. H. Nelson, **The American Tory*** (1962), M. B. Norton, **The British-Americans** (1972), and R. M. Calhoun, **The Loyalists in Revolutionary America** (1973). The effects of the Revolution on slavery are treated in W. D. Jordan, **White over Black*** (1968), Arthur Zilversmit, **The First Emancipation*** (1967), and Benjamin Quarles, **The Negro in the American Revolution*** (1961). See also Ira Berlin and Ronald Holfman (eds.), **Slavery and Freedom in the Age of the American Revolution** (1983). L. K. Kerber, **Women of the Republic** (1980), and M. B. Norton, **Liberty's Daughters** (1980), discuss the effects of the Revolution on women.

On the diplomacy of the Revolution, see J. R. Dull, **A Diplomatic History of the American Revolution** (1985). The fullest account of the peace treaty is R. B. Morris, **The Peacemakers*** (1965).

On the emergence of American nationalism and cultural history generally, see R. B. Nye, **The Cultural Life of the New Nation*** (1960). R. L. Merritt, **Symbols of American Community** (1966), concludes from a study of colonial newspapers that a sense of national identity was well developed before 1763. P. C. Nagel, **One Nation Indivisible** (1964), discusses the various views of the nature of the Union advanced in this period.

V

Nationalism Triumphant

*You and I have been sent into life at a time when the greatest
lawgivers of antiquity would have wished to live. How few of the
human race have ever enjoyed an opportunity of making an election
of government . . . for themselves or their children! When, before the
present epoch, had three millions of people full of power and a fair
opportunity to form and establish the wisest and happiest government
that human wisdom can contrive?*

JOHN ADAMS *to George Wythe*

A t first, only a relative handful of Americans resented the constraints imposed by the confederation on the power of the central government. Once the war was over, however, the need for unity seemed less pressing, and sectional conflicts reasserted themselves. Modern research has modified the thesis, advanced by John Fiske in *The Critical Period of American History* (1888), that the national government was demoralized and inadequate. If, as Washington said, it moved "on crutches . . . tottering at every step," it did move nevertheless. The negotiation of a successful peace treaty ending the Revolutionary War, the humane and farsighted federal land policies, and even the establishment of a federal bureaucracy to manage routine affairs were remarkable achievements, all carried out under the Articles of Confederation. Yet the country's evolution placed demands on the national government that its creators had not anticipated.

Border Problems

The government had to struggle to win actual control over the territory granted the United States in the treaty ending the Revolution. Both Great Britain and Spain stood in the way of this objective. The British had promised to withdraw all their troops from American soil promptly, and so they did—within the settled portions of the 13 states. Beyond the frontier, however, they had established a string of seven military posts, running from the northern end of Lake Champlain through Niagara and Detroit to the tip of the Michigan peninsula. These, despite the Treaty of Paris, they refused to surrender. Pressing against America's exposed frontier like hot coals, the posts seared national pride. They threatened to set off another Indian war, for the British intrigued constantly to stir up the tribes. The great prize was the rich fur trade of the region, which the British still controlled.

The British justified holding on to these positions by citing the failure of the Americans to live up to some terms of the peace treaty. The United States had agreed not to impede British creditors seeking to collect prewar debts and to "earnestly recommend" that the states restore confiscated Tory property. The national government complied with both requirements (which only called for words on Congress's part), but the states did not cooperate. Many passed laws making it impossible for British creditors to collect debts, and most of the property of Tory émigrés was not returned.

Yet those violations of the peace terms had little to do with the continued presence of the British. They would not have evacuated the posts at this time even if every farthing of the debt had been paid and every acre of confiscated land had been restored. Americans found the presence of British troops galling. When the French had pushed a line of forts into the Ohio country in the 1750s, it had seemed to most colonists a matter of local concern, to be dealt with by Virginia or Pennsylvania. Three decades later the inability to eject the British seemed a national disgrace.

The Mississippi teems with commerce in this watercolor, based on a sketch made about 1790 by Christophe Colomb. Two flatboats (on the right) and a keelboat are in the improbably narrow river; in the center left foreground Colomb sits on a log, sketching his father-in-law's plantation house on the other side of the river.

Then there was the question of the Spanish in the southwest. Spain had been a cobelligerent, not an ally, in the war with Great Britain. In the peace negotiations it had won back Florida and the Gulf Coast region east of New Orleans. Spanish troops had captured Natchez during the war, and although the post lay north of the boundary, Spain refused to turn it over to the United States. Far more serious, the Spaniards had closed the lower Mississippi River to American commerce. Because of the prohibitive cost of moving bulky farm produce over the mountains, settlers beyond the Appalachians depended on the Mississippi and its network of tributaries to get their corn, tobacco, and other products to eastern and European markets. If Spain closed the river, or even if it denied them the right to "deposit" goods at New Orleans while awaiting oceangoing transportation, westerners could not sell their surpluses. Frontier settlers fumed when Congress failed to win concessions from Spain.

A stronger central government might have dealt with these foreign problems more effectively, but it could not have eliminated them. United or decentralized, until the country grew more powerful, or until the Europeans began to fight among themselves, the United States was bound to suffer at their hands.

Foreign Trade

The fact that the Revolution freed American trade from the restrictions of British mercantilism proved a mixed blessing in the short run. The commercial benefits that Tom Paine had described in *Common Sense* did not materialize. Americans could now trade directly with the European powers, and commercial treaties were negotiated with a number of them. Beginning in 1784, when the 360-ton *Empress of China* reached Canton with a cargo of furs and cotton to be exchanged for silks, tea, and spices, a valuable Far Eastern trade sprang up where none had existed before. But exclusion from Britain's imperial trade union brought losses of a much larger magnitude.

Immediately after the Revolution a controversy broke out in Great Britain over fitting the former colonies into the mercantilistic system. Some people, influenced by Adam Smith's *The Wealth of Nations,* published in 1776, argued that any restriction on the buying and selling of goods was wasteful; if people could trade freely, all parties would benefit. Others, while remaining mercantilists, realized how important the American trade was for British prosperity and argued that special treatment should be afforded the former colonists. Unfortunately, a proud empire recently humbled in war could hardly be expected to exercise such forbearance. Persuaded in part by the reasoning of Lord Sheffield's pamphlet *Observations on the Commerce of the American States* that Britain could get all the American commerce it wished without making concessions, Parliament voted to try building up exports to America while holding imports to a minimum, all according to the best tenets of mercantilism.

The British attitude hurt American interests severely. In the southern states rice and tobacco growers were afflicted by a labor shortage in the 1780s because of the wartime British seizure of so many slaves, and the termination of royal bounties hit North Carolina producers of naval stores and South Carolina indigo planters hard. In addition, a new British duty on rice reduced the export of that product by almost 50 percent.

The British struck at the northern states, barring American cured meat, fish, and dairy products from the British West Indies and permitting other American products to enter the islands only in British ships. American fishermen lost the lucrative West Indian market, merchants, a host of profitable opportunities. The value of trade with the West Indies fell steeply, idling many American ships. More than 1,000 American sailors lost their jobs. Shipbuilding slumped because of these facts and because British merchants stopped ordering American-made vessels.

At the same time, British merchants, eager to regain markets closed to them during the Revolution, poured low-priced manufactured goods of all kinds into the United States. Americans, long deprived of British products, rushed to take advantage of the bargains. Soon imports of British goods were approaching the levels of the early 1770s, while exports to the empire reached no more than half their earlier volume.

The influx of British goods aggravated the situation just when the economy was suffering a certain dislocation as a result of the ending of the war. From 1784 to 1786 the country went through a period of bad times. The inability of Congress to find money to pay the nation's debts undermined public confidence. Veterans who had still not been paid, private individuals, and foreign governments that had lent the government money during the Revolution were clamoring for their due. In some regions crop failures compounded the difficulties.

Dinner plate made in China for export, painted with an American vessel named Friendship. *American trade with China, which began after the Revolution, was a profitable three-stage affair. Merchants first sailed around South America to the Northwest coast, where they exchanged manufactured products for furs. Then they voyaged to China and sold the pelts for silks and other luxury goods.*

The depression made the states stingier than ever about supplying the requisitions of Congress; at the same time, many of them levied heavy property taxes in order to pay off their own war debts. Everywhere people were hard pressed for cash. "As Money has ever been considered the root of all evils," one Massachusetts man commented sourly, "may we not presage happy times, as this source is almost done away?"

An obvious way of dealing with these problems would have been to place tariffs on British goods in order to limit imports or force the British to open the West Indies to all American goods, but the Confederation lacked the authority to do this. When individual states erected tariff barriers, British merchants easily got around them by bringing their goods in through states that did not. That the central government lacked the power to control commerce disturbed merchants, other businessmen, and the ever-increasing number of national-minded citizens in every walk of life.

Thus a movement developed to give the Confederation the power to tax imports, and in 1781 Congress sought authority to levy a 5 percent tariff duty. This would enable Congress to pay off some of its obligations and also put pressure on the British to relax their restrictions on American trade with the West Indies. Every state but Rhode Island agreed, but the measure required the unanimous consent of the states and therefore failed.

Defeat of the "impost" pointed up the need for revising the Articles of Confederation, for here was a case where nearly all of the states were ready to increase the power of the national government yet they were unable to do so. Although many individuals in every region were worried about creating a centralized monster that might gobble up the sovereignty of the states, the practical needs of the times convinced many others that this risk must be taken.

The Specter of Inflation

The depression and the unfavorable balance of trade led to increased pressures in the states for the printing of paper money and the passage of laws designed to make life easier for debtors. Before the Revolution the colonists had grappled with the chronic shortage of hard money resulting from their unfavorable balance of trade in many ways: declaring various staple products such as furs, tobacco, and even Indian wampum to be legal tender, deliberately overvaluing foreign coins to discourage their export, making it illegal to ship coins abroad, and printing paper currency. In response to wartime needs, both the Continental Congress and the states issued large amounts of paper money during the Revolution, with inflationary results (the Continental dollar became utterly worthless by 1781, and Virginia eventually called in its paper at 1,000 to 1).

After the war some states set out to restore their credit by imposing heavy taxes and severely restricting new issues of money. Combined with the postwar depression and the increase in imports, this policy had a powerful deflationary effect on prices and wages. Soon debtors, especially farmers, were crying for relief, both in the form of stay laws de-

signed to make it difficult to collect debts (these laws were popular because of the anti-British feeling of the times) and through the printing of more paper money.

More than half the states yielded to this pressure in 1785 and 1786. Issues in South Carolina, New York, and Pennsylvania were conservatively handled and succeeded, but in some states the money depreciated rapidly. The most disastrous experience was that of Rhode Island, where the government attempted to legislate public confidence in £100,000 of paper. Any landowner could borrow a share of this money from the state for 14 years, using real estate as security. Creditors feared that the loans would never be repaid, but the legislature passed a law fining persons who refused to accept it £100. When creditors fled the state to avoid being confronted, the legislature authorized debtors to discharge their obligations by turning the necessary currency over to a judge. A conservative poet described Rhode Island as a "realm of rogues, renown'd for fraud and guile" where "bankrupts their creditors with rage pursue."

Of course these measures further weakened public confidence; when the state tried to use paper money to meet its obligations to the federal government, Congress refused to accept it. Indeed, no one accepted the currency freely. The Rhode Island supreme court, in *Trevett* v. *Weeden*, declared that it was unconstitutional to fine a creditor for refusing it, and soon there was a reaction. The element of compulsion was withdrawn, and the paper depreciated rapidly.

Daniel Shays's "Little Rebellion"

Although the Rhode Island case was atypical, it alarmed conservatives. Then, close on its heels, came a disturbing outbreak of violence in Massachusetts. The Massachusetts legislature was determined to pay off the state debt and maintain a sound currency. Taxes amounting to almost £1.9 million were levied between 1780 and 1786, the burden falling most heavily on those of moderate income. The historian Merrill Jensen estimated that the average Massachusetts farmer paid about a third of every year's income in taxes. Bad times and deflation led to many foreclosures, and the prisons were crowded with honest debtors. "Our Property is torn from us," one town complained, "our Gaols filled & still our Debts are not discharged."

In the summer of 1786 mobs in the western communities began to stop foreclosures by forcibly preventing the courts from holding their sessions. Under the leadership of Daniel Shays, veteran of Bunker Hill, Ticonderoga, and Saratoga, the "rebels" marched on Springfield and prevented the state supreme court from meeting. When the state government sent troops against them, they attacked the Springfield arsenal. They were routed, and the uprising then collapsed. Shays fled to Vermont.

As Thomas Jefferson observed at safe remove from the trouble in Paris, where he was serving as minister to France, Shays's uprising was only "a *little* rebellion" and as such "a medicine necessary for the sound health of government." But Shays and his followers were genuinely exasperated by the refusal of the government even to try to provide relief for their troubles. By taking up arms they forced the authorities to heed them: At its next session the legislature made some concessions to their demands. But the Rhode Island excesses and the uprising in Massachusetts illustrated the clash between local and national interests. Newspapers in all the states followed the bizarre spectacle of debtors in Rhode Island pursuing their creditors with fistfuls of worthless paper money. The revolt of Daniel Shays worried planters in far-off Virginia and the Carolinas almost as much as it did the merchants of Boston. Most well-to-do Americans considered the uprising "liberty run mad." "What, gracious God, is man! that there should be such inconsistency and perfidiousness in his conduct?" the usually unexcitable George Washington asked when news of the riots reached Virginia. "We are fast verging to anarchy and confusion!" During the crisis, private persons had had to subscribe funds to put the rebels down, and when Massachusetts had appealed to Congress for help, there was little Congress could legally do. The lessons seemed plain: Liberty must not become an excuse for license; greater authority must be vested in the central government.

The Road to Philadelphia

If most people wanted to increase the power of Congress, they were also afraid to shift the balance too far lest they destroy the sovereignty of the states and the rights of individuals. The machinery for change established in the Articles of Confederation, which required the unanimous consent of the states for all amendments, posed a particularly delicate problem. Experience had shown it unworkable, yet to bypass it would be revolutionary and therefore dangerous.

The first fumbling step toward reform was taken in March 1785, when representatives of Virginia and Maryland, meeting at the home of George Washington to settle a dispute over the improvement of navigation on the Potomac River, suggested a conference of all the states to discuss common problems of commerce. In January 1786 the Virginia legislature sent out a formal call for such a gathering, to be held in September at Annapolis. However, the Annapolis convention disappointed advocates of reform; delegates from only five states appeared; even Maryland, supposedly the host state, did not send a representative. Being so few, the group did not feel it worthwhile to propose changes.

Among the delegates was a young New York lawyer named Alexander Hamilton, a brilliant, imaginative, and daring man who was convinced that only drastic centralization would save the nation from disintegration. Hamilton described himself as a "nationalist." While the war still raged, he contrasted the virtues of "a great Federal Republic" with the existing system of "petty states with the appearance only of union, jarring, jealous, and perverse." Instead of giving up, he proposed calling another convention to meet at Philadelphia to deal generally with constitutional reform. Delegates should be empowered to work out a broad plan for correcting "such defects as may be discovered to exist" in the Articles of Confederation.

The Annapolis group approved Hamilton's suggestion, and Congress reluctantly endorsed it. This time all the states but Rhode Island sent delegates. On May 25, 1787, the convention opened its proceedings at the State House in Philadelphia and unanimously elected George Washington its president. When it adjourned four months later, it had drafted the Constitution.

The Great Convention

As the decades have passed and the Constitution has grown more and more tradition-encrusted without losing any of its flexibility, each generation has

James Madison was a key figure at the Great Convention of 1787. He not only influenced the shaping of the Constitution but also kept the most complete record of the proceedings. "Every Person," wrote one delegate of him, "seems to acknowledge his greatness."

tried to explain how a people so young and inexperienced, so free-swinging and unruly, could have produced it. At the time of the hundredth anniversary of its signing, the British statesman William E. Gladstone called it "the most wonderful work ever struck off at a given time by the brain of man." One reason for its durability was the ability of those who drafted it. The Founding Fathers were remarkable men. Though he later had reason to quarrel with certain aspects of their handiwork, Jefferson, who was on a foreign assignment and did not attend the convention, called them "demigods." A presumably more impartial French diplomat said that "even in Europe," he had never seen "an assembly more respectable for the talents, knowledge, disinterestedness, and patriotism."

Collectively, the delegates possessed a rare combination of talents. Most of them had had considerable experience in politics and the many lawyers among them were skilled in negotiation. Furthermore, the times made them acutely aware of their opportunities. It was "a time when the greatest lawgivers of antiquity would have wished to live," an opportunity to "establish the wisest and happiest government that human wisdom can contrive," John Adams wrote. "We . . . decide for ever the fate of republican government," James Madison said during the deliberations.

If these remarks overstated the importance of their deliberations, they nonetheless represented the opinion of most of those present. They were boldly optimistic about their country. "We are laying the foundation of a great empire," Madison predicted. At the same time, the delegates recognized the difficulties they faced. The ancient Roman republic was their model, and all knew that it had been overthrown by tyrants and eventually overrun by barbarians.

Fortunately, they were nearly all of one mind on basic questions. That there should be a federal system, with both independent state governments and a national government with limited powers to handle matters of common interest, was accepted by all but one or two of them. Republican government, drawing its authority from the people and remaining responsible to them, was a universal assumption. A measure of democracy followed inevitably from this principle, for even the most aristocratic delegates agreed that ordinary citizens should share in the process of selecting those who were to make and execute the laws.

All agreed that no group within society, no matter how numerous, should have unrestricted authority. They regarded political power much as we today view nuclear energy: a force with tremendous potential value for humanity but one easily misused and therefore dangerous to unleash. People meant well and had limitless possibilities, the constitution makers believed, but they were selfish by nature and could not be counted on to respect the interests of others. The ordinary people—small farmers, artisans, taxpayers—should have a say in government in order to be able to protect themselves against those who would exploit their weakness, and the majority must somehow be prevented from plundering the rich, for property must be secure or no government could be stable. No single state or section must be allowed to predominate, nor should the legislature be supreme over the executive or the courts. Power, in short, must be divided, and the segments must be balanced one against the other.

Although the level of education among them was high and a number might fairly be described as learned, the delegates' approach was pragmatic rather than theoretical. This was perhaps their most useful asset, for their task called for reconciling clashing interests. It could never have been accomplished without compromise and an acute sense of what was possible (as distinct from what was ideally best).

At the outset the delegates decided to keep the proceedings secret. That way no one was tempted to play to the gallery or seek some personal political advantage at the expense of the common good. Next they agreed to go beyond their instructions to revise the Articles of Confederation and draft an entirely new frame of government. This was a bold decision, but it was in no way irresponsible because nothing the convention might recommend was binding on anyone, and it was absolutely essential because under the Articles a single state could have prevented the adoption of any change. Alexander Hamilton captured the mood of the gathering when he said: "We can only propose and recommend—the power of ratifying or rejecting is still in the States. . . . We ought not to sacrifice the public Good to narrow Scruples."

The Settlement

The delegates voted on May 30 that "a national Government ought to be established" and then set to work hammering out a specific plan. Two big questions had to be answered. The first, "What powers should this national government be granted?" occasioned relatively little discussion. The right to levy taxes and to regulate interstate and foreign commerce was assigned to the central government almost without debate. So was the power to raise and maintain an army and a navy and to summon the militia of the states to enforce national laws and suppress insurrections. With equal absence of argument, the states were deprived of their rights to issue money, to make treaties, and to tax either imports or exports without the permission of Congress. Thus in summary fashion was brought about

a massive shift of power, a shift made necessary by the problems that had brought the delegates to Philadelphia and made practicable by the new nationalism of the 1780s.

The second major question, "Who shall control the national government?" proved more difficult to answer in a manner satisfactory to all. Led by Virginia, the larger states pushed for representation in the national legislature based on population. The smaller states wished to maintain the existing system of equal representation for each state regardless of population. The large states rallied behind the Virginia Plan, drafted by James Madison and presented to the convention by Edmund Randolph, governor of the state. The small states supported the New Jersey Plan, prepared by William Paterson, a former attorney general of that state. The question was important; equal state representation would have been undemocratic, yet a proportional system would have effectively destroyed the influence of all the states as states. But the delegates saw it in terms of combinations of large or small states, and this was unrealistic: When the states combined, they did so on geographic, economic, or social grounds that seldom had anything to do with size. Nevertheless, the debate was long and heated, and for a time it threatened to disrupt the convention.

Day after day in the stifling heat of high summer, the weary delegates struggled to find a suitable compromise. Madison and a few others had to use every weapon in their arsenal of argument to hold the group together. (All told, during the 88 sessions of the convention, a total of 569 votes was taken.) July 2 was perhaps the most fateful day of the whole proceedings. "We are at full stop," said Roger Sherman of Connecticut, who, it will be recalled, had been one of the drafters of the Declaration of Independence. "If we do not concede on both sides," a North Carolina delegate warned, "our business must soon be at an end."

But the delegates did "concede on both sides," and the debates went on. Again on July 17 collapse threatened as the representatives of the larger states caucused to consider walking out of the convention. Fortunately, they did not walk out, and finally the delegates adopted what is known as the Great Compromise. In the lower branch of the new legislature, the House of Representatives, places were to be assigned according to population and filled by pop-

On Friday, May 25, 1787, 29 delegates from 9 of the 13 states assembled in Philadelphia to deal with constitutional reform. New Hampshire, Connecticut, and Maryland were not yet there; Rhode Island never did appear. On Monday, September 17, of that same year, 39 of the 42 delegates still in attendance signed the final document. They had met in 88 sessions and taken 569 votes in all.

What backgrounds did these men have? What do we know about them? Here are . . .

FACTS ON THE

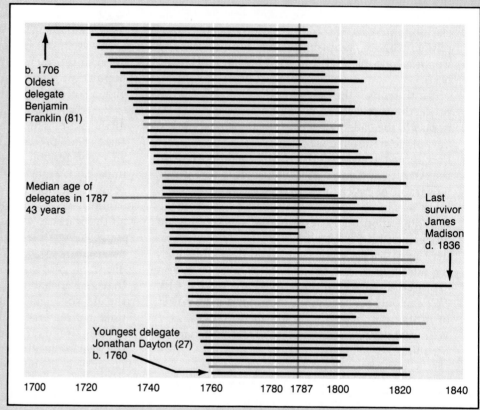

b. 1706
Oldest delegate
Benjamin Franklin (81)

Median age of delegates in 1787
43 years

Last survivor James Madison d. 1836

Youngest delegate Jonathan Dayton (27)
b. 1760

The median age of the U.S. population in 1790 was 16.

The mean age of death in 1800 was about 56.

1700   1720   1740   1760   1780 1787 1800   1820   1840

How Old Were They?

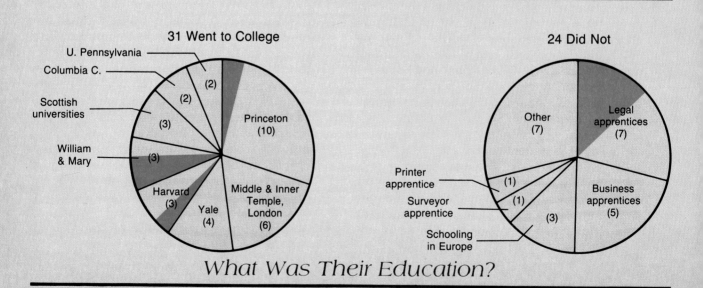

31 Went to College

U. Pennsylvania
Columbia C.
Scottish universities
William & Mary
Princeton (10)
(2)
(2)
(3)
(3)
Harvard (3)
Yale (4)
Middle & Inner Temple, London (6)

24 Did Not

Other (7)
Legal apprentices (7)
Printer apprentice (1)
Surveyor apprentice (1)
Schooling in Europe (3)
Business apprentices (5)

What Was Their Education?

The color red applies to those who opposed the Constitution.

FRAMERS

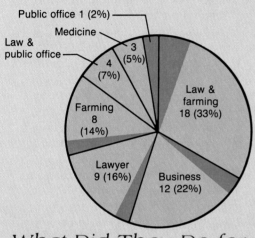

Public office 1 (2%)
Medicine 3 (5%)
Law & public office 4 (7%)
Farming 8 (14%)
Law & farming 18 (33%)
Lawyer 9 (16%)
Business 12 (22%)

What Did They Do for a Living?

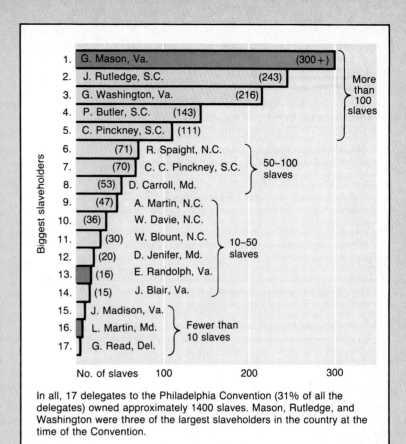

Biggest slaveholders

1. G. Mason, Va. (300+)
2. J. Rutledge, S.C. (243)
3. G. Washington, Va. (216)
4. P. Butler, S.C. (143)
5. C. Pinckney, S.C. (111)

More than 100 slaves

6. (71) R. Spaight, N.C.
7. (70) C. C. Pinckney, S.C.
8. (53) D. Carroll, Md.

50–100 slaves

9. (47) A. Martin, N.C.
10. (36) W. Davie, N.C.
11. (30) W. Blount, N.C.
12. (20) D. Jenifer, Md.
13. (16) E. Randolph, Va.
14. (15) J. Blair, Va.

10–50 slaves

15. J. Madison, Va.
16. L. Martin, Md.
17. G. Read, Del.

Fewer than 10 slaves

No. of slaves   100   200   300

In all, 17 delegates to the Philadelphia Convention (31% of all the delegates) owned approximately 1400 slaves. Mason, Rutledge, and Washington were three of the largest slaveholders in the country at the time of the Convention.

How Many Were Slaveholders?

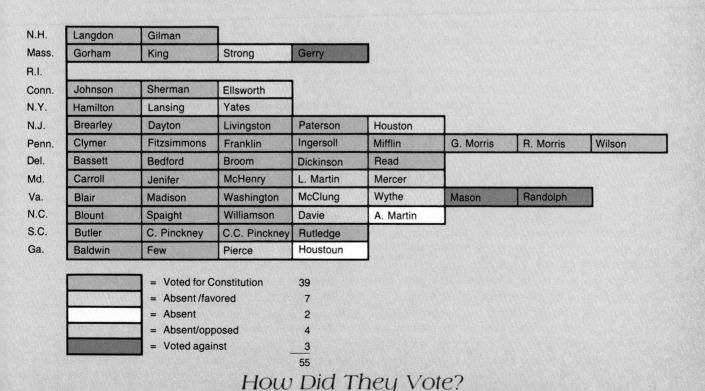

N.H.	Langdon	Gilman						
Mass.	Gorham	King	Strong	Gerry				
R.I.								
Conn.	Johnson	Sherman	Ellsworth					
N.Y.	Hamilton	Lansing	Yates					
N.J.	Brearley	Dayton	Livingston	Paterson	Houston			
Penn.	Clymer	Fitzsimmons	Franklin	Ingersoll	Mifflin	G. Morris	R. Morris	Wilson
Del.	Bassett	Bedford	Broom	Dickinson	Read			
Md.	Carroll	Jenifer	McHenry	L. Martin	Mercer			
Va.	Blair	Madison	Washington	McClung	Wythe	Mason	Randolph	
N.C.	Blount	Spaight	Williamson	Davie	A. Martin			
S.C.	Butler	C. Pinckney	C.C. Pinckney	Rutledge				
Ga.	Baldwin	Few	Pierce	Houstoun				

	= Voted for Constitution	39
	= Absent /favored	7
	= Absent	2
	= Absent/opposed	4
	= Voted against	3
		55

How Did They Vote?

ular vote. In the upper house, the Senate, each state was to have two members, elected by its legislature.

Then a complicated struggle took place between northern and southern delegates, occasioned by the institution of slavery and the differing economic interests of the regions. About one American in seven in the 1780s was a slave. Northerners contended that slaves should be counted in deciding each state's share of direct federal taxes. Southerners, of course, wanted to exclude slaves from the count. Yet southerners wished to include slaves in determining each district's representation in the House of Representatives, though they had no intention of permitting the slaves to vote. In the Three-fifths Compromise it was agreed that "three-fifths of all other Persons" should be counted for both purposes. (As it turned out, the compromise was a victory for the southerners, for no direct taxes were ever levied by Congress before the Civil War.) Settlement of the knotty issue of the African slave trade was postponed by a clause making it illegal for Congress to outlaw the trade before 1808.

Questions involving the regulation of less controversial commerce also caused sectional disagreement. Southerners disliked export taxes because their staple products were largely sold abroad. In return for a clause prohibiting such taxes, they dropped their demand that all laws regulating foreign commerce be approved by two-thirds of both houses of Congress. Many other differences of opinion were resolved by the give-and-take of practical compromise. As the historian David M. Potter once said, the Constitution was "an exchange of promises" whereby different interests gained large advantages by making large concessions.

The final document, signed on September 17, established a legislature of two houses: an executive, consisting of a president with wide powers and a vice-president whose only function was to preside over the Senate, and a national judiciary consisting of a supreme court and such "inferior courts" as Congress might decide to create. The lower, popularly elected branch of Congress was supposed to represent especially the mass of ordinary citizens. It was given the sole right to introduce bills for raising revenue. The 26-member Senate was looked on by many as a sort of advisory council similar to the upper houses of the colonial legislatures. Its consent was required before any treaty could go into effect and for major presidential appointments.

The Founding Fathers also intended the Senate to represent in Congress the interests not only of the separate states but of what Hamilton called "the rich and the well-born" as contrasted with "the great mass of the people."

The creation of a powerful president was the most drastic departure from past experience, and it is doubtful that the Founding Fathers would have gone so far had everyone not counted on Washington, a man universally esteemed for character, wisdom, and impartiality, to be the first to occupy the office. Besides giving him general responsibility for executing the laws, the Constitution made the president commander in chief of the armed forces of the nation and general supervisor of its foreign relations. He was to appoint federal judges and other officials, and he might veto any law of Congress, although his veto could be overridden by a two-thirds majority of both houses. Though not specifically ordered to submit a program of legislation to Congress, he was to deliver periodic reports on the "State of the Union" and recommend "such Measures as he shall judge necessary and expedient." Most modern presidents have interpreted this requirement as authorizing them to submit detailed legislative proposals and to use the full power and prestige of the office to get Congress to enact them.

Looking beyond Washington, whose choice was sure to come about under any system, the Constitution established a cumbersome method of electing presidents. Each state was to choose "electors" equal in number to its representation in Congress. The electors, meeting separately in their own states, were to vote for two persons for president. Supposedly the procedure would prevent anyone less universally admired than Washington from getting a majority in the "electoral college," in which case the House of Representatives would choose the president from among the leading candidates, each state having but one vote. However, the swift rise of national political parties prevented the expected fragmentation of the electors' votes, and only two elections have ever gone to the House for settlement.

The national court system was set up to adjudicate disputes under the laws and treaties of the United States. No such system had existed under the Articles, a major weakness. Although the Constitution did not specifically authorize the courts to declare laws void when they conflicted with the Constitution, the courts soon exercised this right of "ju-

The room in Independence Hall where the Constitutional Convention was held has been scrupulously restored.

dicial review" in cases involving both state and federal laws.

That the Constitution reflected the commonly held beliefs of its framers is everywhere evident in the document. It greatly expanded the powers of the central government yet did not seriously threaten the independence of the states. Foes of centralization, at the time and ever since, have predicted the imminent disappearance of the states as sovereign bodies. But despite a steady trend toward centralization, probably inevitable as American society has grown ever more complex, the states remain powerful political organizations that are sovereign in many areas of government.

The Founders believed that since the new powers of government might easily be misused, each should be held within safe limits by some countervailing force. The Constitution is full of ingenious devices ("checks and balances") whereby one power controls and limits another without reducing it to impotence. "Let Congress legislate, let others execute, let others judge," John Jay suggested. This separation of legislative, executive, and judicial functions is the fundamental example of the principle. Other examples are the president's veto; Congress's power of impeachment, cleverly divided between House and Senate; the Senate's power over treaties and appointments; judicial review; and the balance between Congress's right to declare war and the president's control of the armed forces.

Ratifying the Constitution

Influenced by the widespread approval of the decision of Massachusetts to submit its state constitution of 1780 to the voters for ratification, the framers of the Constitution provided (Article 7) that their handiwork be ratified by special state conventions. This procedure gave the Constitution what Madison called "the highest source of authority"—the endorsement of the people, expressed through representatives chosen specifically to judge it. The framers may also have been motivated by a desire to bypass the state legislatures, where many members might resent the reductions being made in state authority. This was not of central importance because the legislatures could have blocked ratification by refusing to call conventions. Only Rhode Island did so, and since the Constitution was to take effect when nine states had approved it, Rhode Island's recalcitrance did no vital harm.

Such a complex and controversial document as the Constitution naturally excited argument throughout the country. Its advocates called themselves Federalists, thereby avoiding the more accurate but politically unattractive label of Centralizers. Their opponents thus became the Antifederalists.

It is difficult to generalize about the members of these groups. The Federalists tended to be substantial individuals, members of the professions, well-to-do, active in commercial affairs, and somewhat alarmed by the changes wrought by the Revolution. They were more interested, perhaps, in orderly and efficient government than in safeguarding the maximum freedom of individual choice.

The Antifederalists were more often small farmers, debtors, and persons to whom free choice was more important than power and who resented people who sought and held power. "Lawyers and men of learning and money men . . . expect to be the managers of the Const[itution], and get all the power and all the money into their own hands," a Massachusetts Antifederalist complained. "Then they will swallow up all us little folks . . . just as the whale swallowed up *Jonah*." But many rich and worldly citizens opposed the Constitution, and many poor and obscure persons were for it. It seems likely that most did not support or oppose the new system for narrowly selfish reasons. The historian David Ramsay, who lived at the time when these groups were forming, was probably correct when he wrote that "the great body of independent men who saw the necessity of an energetic government" swung the balance in favor of the Constitution.

Whether the Antifederalists were more democratic than the Federalists is an interesting question. The loudest in support of local autonomy do not necessarily believe in equal rights for all the locals. Many Antifederalist leaders, including Richard Henry Lee, the man who had introduced the resolution that resulted in the Declaration of Independence, had reservations about democracy. Yet even Hamilton, no admirer of democracy, believed that ordinary citizens should have some say about their government. In general, practice still stood well ahead of theory when it came to popular participation in politics.

Various Antifederalists criticized many of the specific grants of authority in the new Constitution, some concocting farfetched arguments to show what disasters might ensue should it be put into effect. The routine clause (Article 1, Section 4) giving Congress the power to regulate "the times, places, and manner of holding elections" threatened to "destroy representation entirely," a North Carolina Antifederalist claimed. The chief force behind the opposition was a vague fear that the new system would destroy the independence of the states.

It is important to keep in mind that the country was large and sparsely settled, that communication was primitive, and that the central government did not influence the lives of most people to any great degree. Many persons, including some who had been in the forefront of the struggle for independence, believed that a centralized republican system would not work in a country so large and with so many varied interests as the United States. Patrick Henry considered the Constitution "horribly frightful." It "squints toward monarchy," he added. That Congress could pass all laws "necessary and proper" to carry out the functions assigned it and legislate for the "general welfare" of the country seemed alarmingly all-inclusive. The first sentence of the Constitution, beginning "We the people of the United States" rather than "We the states," convinced many that the document represented centralization run wild. Another old revolutionary who expressed doubts was Samuel Adams, who remarked: "As I enter the Building I stumble at the Threshold."

Many members of the Convention were well-to-do and stood to profit from the establishment of a sound and conservative government that would honor its obligations, foster economic development, and preserve a stable society. Since the Constitution was designed to do all these things, it has been suggested that the Founders were not true patriots but selfish men out to protect their own interests. Charles A. Beard advanced this thesis in 1913 in *An Economic Interpretation of the Constitution*, arguing that most members of the Convention owned large amounts of depreciated government securities that were bound to rise in price if the Constitution was approved. The thesis does not stand up under close examination. The Founders wanted to advance their own interests as every normal human being does. Most of them, however, had no special involvement in securities, being far more concerned with land. The closest thing to a general spirit at Philadelphia was a public spirit.

Very little of the opposition to the Constitution grew out of economic issues. Most people wanted the national debt paid off; nearly everyone opposed an unstable currency; most favored uniform trade policies; most were ready to give the new government a chance if they could be convinced that it would not destroy the states. When backers agreed to add amendments guaranteeing the civil liberties of the people against challenge by the national government and reserving all unmentioned power to the states, much of the opposition disappeared. Sam Adams ended up voting for the Constitution in the Massachusetts convention after the additions had been promised.

No one knows exactly how public opinion divided on the question of ratification. The Federalists were usually able to create an impression of strength far beyond their numbers and to overwhelm doubters with the mass of their arguments. They excelled in political organization and in persuasiveness. James Madison, for example, demolished the thesis that a centralized republican government could not function efficiently in a large country. In rule by the majority lay protection against the "cabals" of special interest groups. "Extend the sphere," Madison argued, "and you take in a greater variety of parties and interests; you make it less probable that a majority of the whole will have a common motive to invade the rights of other citizens." Moreover, the management of national affairs would surely attract leaders of greater ability and sounder character to public service than the handling of petty local concerns ever could in a decentralized system.

The Constitution met with remarkably little opposition in most of the state ratifying conventions, considering the importance of the changes it instituted. Delaware acted first, ratifying unanimously on December 7, 1787. Pennsylvania followed a few days later, voting for the document by a two-to-one majority. New Jersey approved unanimously on December 18; so did Georgia on January 2, 1788. A week later Connecticut fell in line, 128 to 40.

The Massachusetts convention provided the first close contest. Early in February, after extensive debate, the delegates ratified by a vote of 187 to 168. In April, Maryland accepted the Constitution by nearly six to one, and in May, South Carolina approved, 149 to 73. New Hampshire came along on June 21, voting 57 to 47 for the Constitution. This was the ninth state, making the Constitution legally operative.

Before the news from New Hampshire had spread throughout the country, the Virginia convention debated the issue. Virginia, the largest state and the home of so many prestigious figures, was absolutely essential if the Constitution was to succeed. With unquestioned Patriots like Richard Henry Lee and Patrick Henry opposed, the result was not easy to predict. But when the vote came on June 25, Virginia ratified, 89 to 79. Aside from Rhode Island, this left only New York and North Carolina outside the Union.

New York politics presented a complex and baffling picture. Resistance to independence had been

New York's approval of the Constitution on July 26, 1788, inspired this cartoon in the Massachusetts Centinel. *Hopes were high that North Carolina would "rise" to ratify, but prospects in Rhode Island were not as bright—and, as expected, Rhode Island did not ratify the Constitution.*

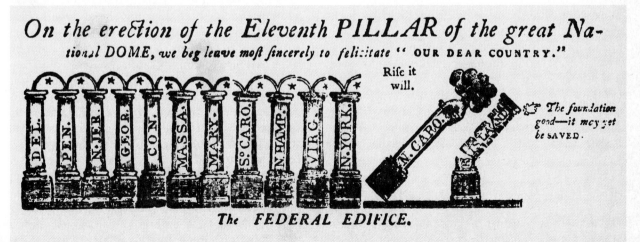

strong there in 1776 and remained a problem all through the war. Although New York was the third largest state, with a population rapidly approaching 340,000, it sided with the small states at Philadelphia, and two of its three delegates (Hamilton was the exception) walked out of the convention and took the lead in opposing ratification. A handful of great landowning and mercantile families dominated politics, but they were divided into shifting factions. In general, New York City favored ratification, and the rural areas were against it.

The Antifederalists, well organized and competently led in New York by Governor George Clinton, won 46 of the 65 seats at the ratifying convention. The New York Federalists had one great asset in the fact that so many states had already ratified and another in the person of Alexander Hamilton. Although contemptuous of the *weakness* of the Constitution, Hamilton supported it with all his energies as being incomparably stronger than the old government. Working with Madison and John Jay, he produced the *Federalist Papers,* a brilliant series of essays explaining and defending the new system. These were published in the local press and later in book form. Although generations of judges and lawyers have treated them almost as parts of the Constitution, their impact on contemporary public opinion was probably slight. Open-minded members of the convention were undoubtedly influenced, but few delegates were open-minded.

Hamilton became virtually a one-man army in defense of the Constitution, plying hesitating delegates with dinners and drinks, facing obstinate ones with the threat that New York City would secede from the state if the Constitution were rejected. Once New Hampshire and Virginia had ratified, opposition in New York became a good deal less intransigent. In the end, by promising to support a call for a second national convention to consider amendments, the Federalists carried the day, 30 to 27. With New York in the fold, the new government was free to get under way. North Carolina finally ratified in November 1789, Rhode Island the following May.

Washington as President

Elections took place in the states during January and February 1789, and by early April enough con-

gressmen had gathered in New York, the temporary national capital, to commence operation. The ballots of the presidential electors were officially counted in the Senate on April 6, Washington being the unanimous choice. John Adams, with 34 electoral votes, won the vice-presidency. On April 30 Washington took the oath of office at Federal Hall.

Washington made a firm, dignified, conscientious, but cautious president. His acute sense of responsibility led him to face the task "with feelings not unlike those of a culprit who is going to the place of his execution." Each presidential action must of necessity establish a precedent. "The eyes of Argus are upon me," he complained, "and no slip will pass unnoticed." Hoping to make the presidency appear respectable in the eyes of the world, he saw to it that his carriage was drawn by six cream-colored horses, and when he rode (he was a magnificent horseman), it was upon a great white charger, with the saddle of leopardskin and the cloth edged in gold. Twenty-one servants (seven of them slaves) attended his needs at the presidential mansion on Broadway.

Washington meticulously avoided treading on the toes of Congress, for he took seriously the principle of the separation of powers. Never would he speak for or against a candidate for Congress, nor did he think that the president should push or even propose legislation. When he knew a controversial question was to be discussed in Congress, he avoided the subject in his annual message. The veto, he believed, should be employed only when the president considered a bill unconstitutional.

Although the Constitution said nothing about a presidential cabinet, Washington established the system of calling his department heads together for general advice, a practice that was followed by his successors. In selecting these department heads and other important administrators, he favored no particular faction. He insisted only that appointees be competent and "of known attachment to the Government we have chosen." He picked Hamilton as secretary of the treasury, Jefferson as secretary of state, General Henry Knox of Massachusetts as secretary of war, and Edmund Randolph as attorney general. He called on them for advice according to the logic of his particular needs and frequently without regard for their own specialties. Thus he sometimes consulted Jefferson about financial matters and Hamilton about foreign affairs. This system

A spirited tapestry of the period depicts Washington's entry into New York City after the Revolution. When elections were held for the new government, there was little doubt in anyone's mind that he should be its first president, but Washington had little desire for the post. "My movements to the chair of government," he wrote, "will be accompanied by feelings not unlike those of a culprit who is going to the place of his execution."

caused resentment and confusion, especially when rival factions began to coalesce around Hamilton and Jefferson.

Despite his respect for the opinions of others, Washington was a strong chief executive. As Hamilton put it, he "consulted much, pondered much, resolved slowly, resolved surely." His stress on the dignity of his office suited the needs of a new country whose people tended to be perhaps too informal. It was indeed important that the first president be particularly concerned about establishing precedents. His scrupulous care lest he overstep the bounds of presidential power helped erase the prejudices of those who feared that republican government must inevitably succumb to dictatorship and tyranny. When each step is an experiment, when foreign dangers loom at the end of every errant path, it is surely wise to go slowly. And no one should forget that Washington's devotion to duty did not always come easily. Occasionally he exploded. Thomas Jefferson has left us a graphic account of

the president at a Cabinet meeting, in a rage because of some unfair criticism, swearing that "by god he had rather be on his farm than to be made emperor of the world."

Congress Under Way

By September 1789 Congress had created the State, Treasury, and War departments and passed the Judiciary Act establishing 13 federal district courts and three circuit courts of appeal. The number of Supreme Court justices was set at six, and Washington named John Jay chief justice.

True to Federalist promises—for a large majority in both houses was friendly to the Constitution—Congress prepared a list of a dozen amendments (ten were ratified) guaranteeing what Congressman James Madison, who drafted the amendments, called the "great rights of mankind." These amendments, known as the Bill of Rights, provided that

Congress should make no law infringing freedom of speech, the press, or religion. The right of trial by jury was reaffirmed, the right to bear arms guaranteed. No one was to be subject to "unreasonable" searches or seizures or compelled to testify against oneself in a criminal case. No one was to "be deprived of life, liberty, or property, without due process of law."

The Bill of Rights was unique; the English Bill of Rights of 1689 was much narrower and, as an act of Parliament, subject to parliamentary repeal at any time. The Tenth Amendment—strictly speaking not a part of the Bill of Rights—was designed to mollify those who feared that the states would be destroyed by the new government. It provided that powers not delegated to the United States or denied specifically to the states by the Constitution were to reside either in the states or in the people.

As experts pointed out, the amendments were not logically necessary because the federal government had no authority to act in such matters to begin with. But many people had wanted to be reassured. Experience has proved repeatedly that whatever the logic of the situation, the protection afforded individuals by the Bill of Rights has been anything but unnecessary.

The Bill of Rights did much to convince doubters that the new government would not become too powerful. More complex was the task of proving that it was powerful enough to deal with national problems that the Confederation had not been able to solve: the threat to the west posed by the British, Spaniards, and Indians; the disruption of the pattern of American foreign commerce resulting from independence; and the collapse of the financial structure of the country.

Hamilton and Financial Reform

One of the first acts of Congress in 1789 was to employ its new power to tax. The simplest means of raising money seemed to be that first attempted by the British after 1763, a tariff on foreign imports. Congress levied a 5 percent duty on all foreign products entering the United States, applying higher rates to certain products, such as hemp, glass, and nails, as a measure of protection for American pro-

ducers. The Tariff Act of 1789 also placed heavy tonnage duties on all foreign shipping, a mercantilistic measure designed to stimulate the American merchant marine.

Raising money for current expenses was a small and relatively simple aspect of the financial problem Washington's administration faced. The nation's debt was large, its credit shaky, its economic future uncertain. In October 1789 Congress set on the slender shoulders of Secretary of the Treasury Hamilton the task of straightening out the fiscal mess and stimulating the country's economic development.

Hamilton, at 34, had already proved himself a remarkable man. Born in the British West Indies, the illegitimate son of a shiftless Scot who was little better than a beachcomber, and raised by his mother's family, he came to New York in 1773 to attend King's College. When the Revolution broke out, he joined the army. At 22 he was a staff colonel, aide-de-camp to Washington. Later, at Yorktown, he led a line regiment, displaying a bravery approaching foolhardiness. He married the daughter of Philip Schuyler, a wealthy and influential New Yorker, and after the Revolution he practiced law in that state.

Hamilton was a bundle of contradictions. Witty, charming, possessed of a mind like a sharp knife, he was sometimes the soul of practicality, sometimes an incurable romantic. No more hardheaded realist ever lived, yet he was quick to resent any slight to his honor, even—tragically—ready to fight a duel despite his abhorrence of the custom of dueling. A self-made man, he admired aristocracy and disparaged the abilities of the common run of humankind, who, he said, "seldom judge or determine right." Although granting that Americans must be allowed to govern themselves, he was as apprehensive of the "turbulence" of the masses as a small boy passing a graveyard in the dark. "No popular government was ever without its Catilines and its Caesars," he warned—a typical example of that generation's concern about the fate of the Roman republic.

The country, Hamilton insisted, needed strong national government. "I acknowledge," he wrote in one of the *Federalist Papers*, "my aversion to every project that is calculated to disarm the government of a single weapon, which in any possible contingency might be usefully employed for the general defense and security." That government should be "a great Federal Republic," not "a number of petty

"To confess my weakness," Hamilton wrote when he was only 14, "my ambition is prevalent." This pastel drawing by James Sharples was made about 1796.

states, with the appearance only of union, jarring, jealous, perverse, without any determined direction." He wished to reduce the states to mere administrative units, like English counties.

As secretary of the treasury, Hamilton proved to be a farsighted economic planner. The United States, a "Hercules in the cradle," needed capital to develop its untapped material and human resources. To persuade investors to commit their funds in America, the country would have to convince them that it would meet every obligation in full. His *Report on the Public Credit* outlined the means for accomplishing this objective. The United States owed more than $11 million to foreigners and over $40 million to its own citizens. Hamilton suggested that this debt be funded at par, which meant calling in all outstanding securities and issuing new bonds of the same face value in their stead, and establishing an untouchable sinking fund to assure payment of interest and principal. Further, the remaining state debts should be assumed by the United States on the same terms.

While most members of Congress agreed, albeit somewhat grudgingly, that the debt should be funded at par, many believed that at least part of the new issue should go to the original holders of the old securities: the soldiers, farmers, and merchants who had been forced to accept them in lieu of cash for goods and services rendered the Confederation during the Revolution. Many of these people had sold their securities at a fraction of their face value to speculators; under Hamilton's proposal, the speculators would make a killing. To the argument for divided payment, Hamilton answered coldly: "[The speculator] paid what the commodity was worth in the market, and took the risks. . . . He . . . ought to reap the benefit of his hazard."

Hamilton was essentially correct, and in the end Congress had to go along. After all, the speculators had not caused the securities to fall in value; indeed, as a group they had favored sound money and a strong government. The best way to restore the nation's credit was to convince investors that the government would honor all obligations in full. What infuriated his contemporaries and still attracts the scorn of many historians was Hamilton's motive. He deliberately intended his plan to give a special advantage to the rich. The government would be strong, he thought, only if well-to-do Americans enthusiastically supported it. What better way to win them over than to make it worth their while financially to do so?

In part, opposition to the funding plan was sectional, for citizens of the northern states held more than four-fifths of the national debt. The scheme for assuming the state debts aggravated the controversy, since most of the southern states had already paid off much of their Revolutionary War obligations. For months Congress was deadlocked. Finally, in July 1790, Hamilton worked out a compromise with congressman James Madison and Secretary of State Jefferson. The two Virginians swung a few southern votes, and Hamilton induced some of his followers to support the southern plan for locating the permanent capital of the Union on the Potomac River.

Jefferson later claimed that Hamilton had hoodwinked him. Having only recently returned from Europe, he said, "I was really a stranger to the whole subject." Hamilton had persuaded him to "rally around" by the false tale that "our Union" was threatened with dissolution. This was nonsense; Jefferson agreed to the compromise because he expected that Virginia and the rest of the south would profit from having the capital so near at hand.

The assumption bill passed, and the entire funding plan was a great success. Soon the United States had the highest possible credit rating in the world's financial centers. Foreign capital poured into the country.

Hamilton next proposed that Congress charter a national bank. Such an institution would provide safe storage for government funds and serve as an agent for the government in the collection, movement, and expenditure of tax money. Most important, it would issue bank notes, thereby providing a vitally needed medium of exchange for the specie-starved economy. This Bank of the United States was to be partly owned by the government, but 80 percent of the $10 million stock issue was to be sold to private individuals.

The country had much to gain from such a bank, but again—Hamilton's cleverness was never more in evidence—the well-to-do commercial classes would gain still more. Government balances in the bank belonging to all the people would earn dividends for a handful of rich investors. Manufacturers and other capitalists would profit from the bank's credit facilities. Public funds would be invested in the bank, but control would remain in private hands, since the government would appoint only 5 of the 25 directors. Nevertheless, the bill creating the bank passed both houses of Congress with relative ease in February 1791.

President Washington, however, hesitated to sign it, for the bill's constitutionality had been questioned during the debate in Congress. Nowhere did the Constitution specifically authorize Congress to charter corporations or engage in the banking business. As was his wont when in doubt, Washington called on Jefferson and Hamilton for advice.

Hamilton defended the legality of the bank by enunciating the doctrine of "implied powers." If a logical connection existed between the purpose of the bill and powers clearly stated in the Constitution, he wrote, the bill was constitutional.

If the *end* be clearly comprehended within any of the specified powers, and if the measure have an obvious relation to that *end* . . . it may safely be deemed to come within the compass of the national authority. . . . A bank has a natural relation to the power of collecting taxes, to that of regulating trade, to that of providing for the common defence.

Jefferson disagreed. Congress could only do what the Constitution specifically authorized, he said. The "elastic clause" granting it the right to pass "all Laws which shall be necessary and proper" to carry out the specified powers must be interpreted literally or Congress would "take possession of a boundless field of power, no longer susceptible to any definition." Because a bank was obviously not necessary, it was not authorized.

Although not entirely convinced, Washington accepted Hamilton's reasoning and signed the bill. He could just as easily have followed Jefferson, for the Constitution is not clear. If one stresses *proper* in the "necessary and proper" clause, one ends up a Hamiltonian; if one stresses *necessary,* then Jefferson's view is correct. Historically (and this is the important point), politicians have nearly always adopted the "loose" Hamiltonian "implied powers" interpretation when they favored a measure and the "strict" Jeffersonian one when they do not. Jefferson disliked the bank; therefore, he claimed that it was unconstitutional. Had he approved, he doubtless would have taken a different tack.

In 1819 the Supreme Court officially sanctioned Hamilton's construction of the "necessary and proper" clause (see pages 250–252), and in general that interpretation has prevailed. Because the majority tends naturally toward an argument that increases its freedom of action, the pressure for this view has been continual and formidable. The Bank of the United States succeeded from the start. When its stock went on sale, investors snapped up every share in a matter of hours. People eagerly accepted its bank notes at face value. Business ventures of all kinds found it easier to raise new capital. Soon state-chartered banks entered the field. There were only three state banks in 1791; by 1801 the number was 32.

Hamilton had not finished. In December 1791 he submitted his *Report on Manufactures,* a bold call for economic planning. The pre-Revolutionary nonimportation agreements and wartime shortages had stimulated interest in manufacturing. Already a number of joint-stock companies had been founded to manufacture textiles, and an elaborate argument for economic diversification had been worked out by American economists such as Tench Coxe and Mathew Carey. Hamilton was familiar with these developments. In his *Report* he called for government tariffs, subsidies, and awards to encourage American manufacturing. He hoped to change an essentially agricultural nation into one with a complex, self-sufficient economy. Once again, business and commercial interests in particular would benefit. They would be protected against foreign competition and otherwise subsidized, whereas the general taxpayer, particularly the farmer, would pay the bill in the form of higher taxes and higher prices on manufactured goods. Hamilton argued that in the long run every interest would profit, and he was undoubtedly sincere, being too much the nationalist to favor one section at the expense of another. A majority in Congress, however, balked at so broad a scheme. Hamilton's *Report* was pigeonholed, though many of the specific tariffs he recommended were enacted into law in 1792.

Nevertheless, the secretary of the treasury had managed to transform the financial structure of the country and to prepare the ground for an economic revolution. The constitutional reforms of 1787 had made this possible, and Hamilton turned possibility into reality.

The Ohio Country: A Dark and Bloody Ground

The western issues and those related to international trade proved more difficult than the bank matter because other nations were involved. The British showed no disposition to evacuate their posts on American soil simply because the American people had decided to strengthen their central government, nor did the western Indians suddenly agree to abandon their hunting grounds to the white invaders.

Trouble came swiftly when white settlers moved onto the land north of the Ohio River in large numbers. The Indians, determined to hold this country at all costs, struck hard at the invaders. In 1790 the Miami chief Little Turtle, a gifted strategist, inflicted a double defeat on troops commanded by General Josiah Harmar. The next year Little Turtle and his men defeated the forces of General Arthur St. Clair still more convincingly. Both Harmar and St. Clair resigned from the army, their careers ruined.

By early 1792 the Indians had driven the whites

into "beachheads" at Marietta and Cincinnati on the Ohio. Resentment of the federal government in the western counties of every state from New York to the Carolinas mounted, the people feeling that it was ignoring their interests. They were convinced that the British were inciting the Indians to attack them, yet the supposedly powerful national government seemed unable to force Great Britain to surrender its forts in the west.

Still worse, the westerners believed, was the way the government was taxing them. In 1791, as part of his plan to take over the debts of the states, Hamilton had persuaded Congress to adopt an excise tax of 8 cents a gallon on American-made whiskey. Excise taxes were particularly disliked by most Americans. A duty on imported products was collected from merchants and passed on to consumers as part of the price, and it was by its nature imposed only on foreign-made products. People who did not want to pay it usually could find a domestic alternative. But the collection of excise taxes on American goods required hordes of tax collectors, armed with the power to snoop into everyone's affairs. Westerners, who were heavy drinkers and who turned much of their grain into spirits in order to cope with the high cost of transportation, were especially angered by the tax on whiskey.

Knowing that the tax would be unpopular, Hamilton promised that the distillers would "be secured from every species of injury by the misconduct of the officers to be employed" in collecting it. But he was determined to enforce the law. To western complaints, he coolly suggested that farmers drank too much to begin with. If they found the tax oppressive, they should cut down on their consumption. Of course this did nothing to reduce western opposition to the tax. Resistance was especially intense in western Pennsylvania. When treasury agents tried to collect it there, they were forcibly prevented from doing so.

The New Revolution: France

Momentous events in Europe were also affecting the situation. In 1793 war broke out between France, which was in the midst of its great revolution, and Great Britain and most of the rest of Europe.

With France fighting Great Britain and Spain, there arose the question of America's obligations under the Alliance of 1778. That treaty required the United States to defend the French West Indies "forever against all other powers." What if the British attacked Martinique; must America then go to war? Morally the United States was so obligated, but no responsible American statesman urged such a policy. With the British in Canada and Spanish forces to the west and south, the nation would be in serious danger if it entered the war. Instead, in April 1793, Washington issued a proclamation of neutrality committing the United States to be "friendly and impartial" toward both sides in the war.

Meanwhile, the French had sent a special representative, Edmond Charles Genet, to the United States to seek support. The French Revolution had excited much enthusiasm in the United States, for it seemed to indicate that American democratic ideas were already engulfing the world. The increasing radicalism in France tended to dampen some of the enthusiasm, yet when "Citizen" Genet landed at Charleston, South Carolina, the majority of Americans probably wished the revolutionaries

well. As Genet, a charming, ebullient young man, made his way northward to present his credentials, cheering crowds welcomed him in every town. Quickly concluding that the proclamation of neutrality was "a harmless little pleasantry designed to throw dust in the eyes of the British," he began, in plain violation of American law, to license American vessels to operate as privateers against British shipping and to grant French military commissions to a number of Americans in order to mount expeditions against Spanish and British possessions in North America.

Washington received Genet coolly and soon thereafter demanded that he stop his illegal activities. Genet, whose capacity for self-deception was monumental, appealed to public opinion over the president's head and continued to commission privateers. Washington then requested his recall. The incident ended on a ludicrous note. When Genet left France, he had been in the forefront of the Revolution. But events there had marched swiftly leftward, and the new leaders in Paris considered him a dangerous reactionary. His replacement arrived in America with an order for his arrest. To return might well mean the guillotine, so Genet

Frontier farmers were extremely resentful of the federal excise tax on the whiskey they made. According to this contemporary broadside, "The Distillers and Farmers pay all due deference and respect to Congress, will not refuse to contribute amply for support of Government. But resolve not to be harassed by that opprobrious character (in all free governments) Viz, an Exciseman."

asked the government that was expelling him for political asylum! Washington agreed, for he was not a vindictive man. A few months later the bold revolutionary married the daughter of the governor of New York and settled down to become a farmer on Long Island.

The Genet affair was incidental to a far graver problem. Although the European war increased the foreign demand for American products, it also led to attacks on American shipping by both France and Great Britain. Each power captured American vessels headed for the other's ports whenever it could. In 1793 and 1794 about 600 United States ships were seized.

The British attacks caused far more damage, both physically and psychologically, because the British fleet was much larger than France's, and France at least professed to be America's friend and to favor freedom of trade for neutrals. In addition, the British issued secret orders late in 1793 turning their navy loose on neutral ships headed for the French West Indies. Pouncing without warning, British warships captured about 250 American vessels and sent them off as prizes to British ports. The merchant marine, one American diplomat declared angrily, was being "kicked, cuffed, and plundered all over the Ocean."

The attacks roused a storm in America, reviving hatreds that had been smoldering since the Revolution. The continuing presence of British troops in the northwest (in 1794 the British began to build a new fort in the Ohio country) and the restrictions imposed on American trade with the British West Indies raised tempers still further. To try to avoid a war—for he wisely believed that the United States should not become embroiled in the Anglo-French conflict—Washington sent Chief Justice John Jay to London to seek a settlement with the British.

Federalists and Republicans: The Rise of Political Parties

The furor over the violations of neutral rights focused attention on a new development, the formation of political parties. Why national political parties emerged after the ratification of a Constitution that made no provision for such organizations is a question that has long intrigued historians.

Probably the main reason was the obvious one: By creating a strong central government, the Constitution produced national issues and a focus for national discussion and settlement of these issues. Furthermore, by failing to create machinery for nominating candidates for federal offices, the Constitution left a vacuum, which informal party organizations filled. That the universally admired Washington headed the government was a force limiting partisanship, but his principal advisers, Hamilton and Jefferson, were in sharp disagreement, and they soon became the leaders around which parties coalesced.

In the spring of 1791 Jefferson and James Madison began to sound out other politicians about forming an organization. Jefferson also appointed the poet Philip Freneau to a minor State Department post, and Freneau then began publishing a newspaper, the *National Gazette*, to disseminate the views of what became known as the Republican party. The *Gazette* was soon describing Jefferson as a "Colossus of Liberty" and flailing away editorially at Hamilton's policies. Hamilton hit back promptly, organizing his own followers in the Federalist party, the organ of which was John Fenno's *Gazette of the United States*.

The personal nature of early American political controversies goes far toward explaining why the party battles of the era were so bitter. So does the continuing anxiety that plagued partisans of both persuasions about the supposed frailty of a republican government. The United States was still very much an experiment; leaders who sincerely proclaimed their own devotion to its welfare suspected that their opponents wanted to undermine its institutions. Federalists feared that the Jeffersonians sought a dictatorship based on mob rule, Republicans that the Hamiltonians hid "under the mask of Federalism hearts devoted to monarchy."

At the start, Hamilton had the ear of the president, and his allies controlled a majority in Congress. Jefferson, who disliked controversy, avoided a direct confrontation as long as he could. He went along with Hamilton's funding plan and traded the assumption of state debts for a capital on the Potomac. However, when Hamilton proposed the Bank of the United States, he dug in his heels. It seemed designed to benefit the northeastern commercial classes at the expense of southern and western farmers. He sensed a dastardly plot to milk the

The Federalists often attacked Jefferson for his pro-French attitudes. A dog-eared cartoon, ca. 1790, shows Washington in the national chariot leading troops against an invasion of bloodthirsty French "Cannibals" at the left. The figures trying to halt the chariot are, from left, Albert Gallatin, Citizen Genet (holding the spoke of the wheel), and Jefferson.

producing masses for the benefit of a few capitalists.

The growing controversy over the French Revolution and the resulting war between France and Great Britain widened the split between the parties. After the radicals in France executed Louis XVI and instituted the Reign of Terror, American conservatives were horrified. The Jeffersonians, however, continued to defend the Revolution. Slave owners could be heard singing the praises of *liberté, égalité, fraternité,* and great southern landlords, whose French counterparts were losing their estates—some their heads—were extolling "the glorious successes of our Gallic brethren." In the same way the Federalists began to idealize the British, whom they considered the embodiment of the forces that were resisting French radicalism.

This created an explosive situation. Enthusiasm for a foreign country might tempt Americans, all unwittingly, to betray their own. Hamilton came to believe that Jefferson was so prejudiced in favor of France as to be unable to conduct foreign affairs rationally, and Jefferson could say contemptuously: "Hamilton is panick struck, if we refuse our breech to every kick which Great Britain may choose to give it."

In fact, Jefferson never lost his sense of perspective. When the Anglo-French war erupted, he recommended neutrality. In the Genet affair, although originally sympathetic to the young envoy,

Jefferson ended by characterizing him as "hotheaded, all imagination, no judgment, passionate, disrespectful and even indecent." He cordially approved Washington's decision to send Genet packing. Hamilton perhaps went a little too far in his friendliness to Great Britain, but the real danger was that some of Hamilton's and Jefferson's excitable followers might become so committed as to forget the true interests of the United States.

1794: Crisis and Resolution

During the summer of 1794 several superficially unrelated events brought the partisan conflicts of the period to a peak. For the better part of two years the government had been unable to collect Hamilton's whiskey tax in the west. In Pennsylvania, mobs had burned the homes of revenue agents, and several men had been killed. Late in July, 7,000 "rebels" converged on Pittsburgh, threatening to burn the town to the ground. They were turned away by the sight of federal artillery and the liberal dispensation of whiskey by the frightened inhabitants, but as the historian Thomas P. Slaughter has pointed out, this was "the largest example of armed resistance to a law between the ratification of the Constitution and the Civil War."

Early in August, President Washington determined "to go to every length that the Constitution and laws would permit" to enforce the law. He mustered an enormous army of nearly 13,000 militiamen and marched westward. This had the desired effect; when the troops arrived, rebels were nowhere to be seen; the expected Whiskey Rebellion simply did not happen. Good sense had triumphed. Moderates in the region (not everyone, after all, was a distiller) agreed that even unpopular laws should be obeyed.

More important, perhaps, than President Washington's army in pacifying the Pennsylvania frontier was another event that occurred while that army was being mobilized. This was the Battle of Fallen Timbers in Ohio near present-day Toledo, where the troops of Major General Anthony Wayne decisively defeated the Indians. Wayne's victory opened the way for the settlement of the region. (After the effort to avoid the excise collapsed, some 2,000 of the whiskey rebels simply pulled up stakes and headed for Ohio.)

Jay's Treaty

More important still was the outcome of President Washington's decision to send John Jay to England to seek a treaty settling the conflicts that were vexing the relations of the two nations. On the one hand, the British genuinely wanted to reach an accommodation with the United States—as one minister quipped, the Americans "are so much in debt to this country that we scarcely dare to quarrel with them." They also feared that the two new republics, France and the United States, would draw together in a battle against Europe's monarchies. On the other hand, they were riding the crest of a wave of important victories in the war in Europe and were not disposed to make concessions to the Americans simply to avoid trouble.

The treaty that Jay brought home contained one major concession: The British agreed to evacuate the posts in the west. They also promised to compensate American shipowners for seizures in the West Indies and to open up their colonies in Asia to American ships. They conceded nothing, however, to American demands that the rights of neutrals on the high seas be respected; in effect, Jay submitted to the so-called Rule of 1756, a British

regulation stating that neutrals could not trade in wartime with ports normally closed to them by mercantilistic restrictions in time of peace. A provision opening the British West Indies to American commerce was so hedged with qualifications limiting the size of American vessels and the type of goods allowed that the United States refused to accept it.

Jay also assented to an arrangement that prevented the United States from imposing discriminatory duties on British goods, an idea that a number of congressmen had proposed as a means of forcing Great Britain to treat American commerce more gently. He committed the United States government to paying pre-Revolutionary debts still owed to British merchants, a slap in the face to many states whose courts had been impeding their collection. Yet nothing was said about the British paying for the slaves they had abducted during the fighting in the south.

Although Jay might have driven a harder bargain, this was a valuable treaty for the United States. But it was also a humiliating one. Most of what the United States gained already legally belonged to it and the treaty sacrificed principles of tremendous importance to a nation dependent on foreign trade. When the terms became known, they raised a storm of popular protest. It seemed possible that President Washington would repudiate the treaty or, if he did not, that the Senate would refuse to ratify it.

1795: All's Well That Ends Well

Washington did not repudiate the Jay Treaty, and his decision was one of the wisest—and luckiest—of his career. The treaty marked a long step toward the regularization of Anglo-American relations, which in the long run was essential for both the economic and political security of the nation. And the evacuation of the British forts in the northwest was of enormous immediate benefit.

Still another benefit was totally unplanned. Unexpectedly, the Jay treaty enabled the United States to solve its problems in the southwest. Spain, desiring to withdraw from the European war against France and fearing a subsequent British attack on its American possessions, interpreted the Jay Treaty as a prelude to a wider Anglo-American entente. The king's chief minister, Manuel de Godoy, known as "the Prince of Peace," offered the American envoy, Thomas Pinckney, a treaty that granted the United States the free navigation of the Mississippi River and the right of deposit at New Orleans that western Americans so urgently needed. This Treaty of San Lorenzo, popularly known as Pinckney's Treaty, also settled the disputed boundary between Spanish Florida and the United States on terms favorable to the Americans.

The Senate ratified the Jay Treaty in June. Pinckney signed the Treaty of San Lorenzo in October. These agreements put an end, at least

temporarily, to European pressures in the trans-Appalachian region. Between the signings, in August 1795, as an aftermath of the Battle of Fallen Timbers, 12 tribes signed the Treaty of Greenville. The Indians surrendered huge sections of their lands, thus ending a struggle that had consumed a major portion of the government's revenues for years.

After the events of 1794 and 1795, settlers poured into the west as water bursts through a broken dike. Kentucky had become a state in 1792; in 1796 Tennessee was admitted. Two years later, Mis-

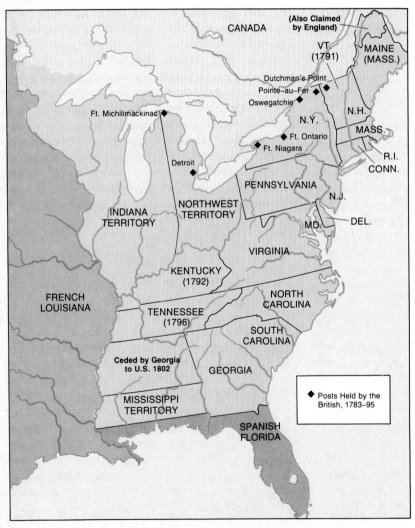

The United States on the eve of the Louisiana Purchase. In 1804 Georgia's cession became part of the Mississippi Territory. The seven British western forts were evacuated as a result of Jay's Treaty (1795).

THE UNITED STATES, 1787–1802

sissippi Territory was organized, and at the end of the century, Indiana Territory. The great westward flood reached full tide.

Washington's Farewell

However, settlement of western problems did not put an end to partisan strife. Even the sainted Washington was neither immune to attack nor entirely above the battle. On questions of finance and foreign policy he usually sided with Hamilton and thus increasingly incurred the anger of the Jeffersonians. But he was, after all, a Virginian. Only the most rabid partisan could think him a tool of northern commercial interests. He remained as he intended himself to be, a symbol of national unity. But he was determined to put away the cares of office at the end of his second term. In September 1796 he announced his retirement in a "farewell address" to the nation.

Washington found the acrimonious rivalry between Federalists and Republicans most disturbing. Hamilton advocated national unity, yet he seemed prepared to smash any individual or faction that disagreed with his vision of the country's future. Jefferson had risked his neck for independence, but he opposed the economic development needed to make America strong enough to defend that independence. Washington was less brilliant than either Hamilton or Jefferson but wiser. He appreciated how important it was that the new nation remain at peace—with the rest of the world and with itself. In his farewell he deplored the "baneful effects of the spirit of party" that led honest people to use unscrupulous means to win a mean advantage over fellow Americans. He tried to show how the north benefited from the prosperity of the south, the south from that of the north, and the east and west also, in reciprocal fashion.

Washington urged the people to avoid both "inveterate antipathies" and "passionate attachments" to any foreign nation. Nothing had alarmed him more than the sight of Americans dividing into "French" and "English" factions. Furthermore, France had repeatedly interfered in American domestic affairs. "Against the insidious wiles of foreign influence," Washington now warned, "the jealousy of a free people ought to be constantly awake." America should develop its foreign trade but steer clear of foreign political connections as far as possible. "Permanent alliances" should be avoided, although "temporary alliances for extraordinary purposes" might sometimes be useful.

The Election of 1796

Washington's farewell address was destined to have a long and important influence on American thinking, but its immediate impact was small. He had intended it to cool political passions. Instead, in the words of one Federalist congressman, people took it as "a signal, like dropping a hat, for the party racers to start." By the time the 1796 presidential campaign had ended, many Federalists and Republicans were refusing to speak to one another.

Jefferson was the only Republican candidate seriously considered in 1796. The logical Federalist was Hamilton, but, as was to happen so often in American history with powerful leaders, he was not considered "available" because his controversial policies had made him many enemies. Gathering in caucus, the Federalists in Congress nominated Vice-President John Adams for the top office and Thomas Pinckney of South Carolina, negotiator of the popular Spanish treaty, for vice-president. In the election the Federalists were victorious.

Hamilton, hoping to run the new administration from the wings, preferred Pinckney, a relatively weak character, to the tough-minded Adams. He arranged for some of the Federalist electors from South Carolina to vote only for Pinckney. Catching wind of this, a number of New England electors retaliated by cutting Pinckney. As a result, Adams won in the electoral college, 71 to 68, over Jefferson, who had the solid support of the Republican electors. Pinckney got only 59 electoral votes. Thus Jefferson became vice-president.

The unexpected result seemed to presage a decline in partisanship. Adams actually preferred the Virginian to Pinckney for the vice-presidency, while Jefferson said that if Adams would "relinquish his bias to an English constitution," he might make a fine chief executive. The two had in common a distaste for Hamilton—a powerful bond.

However, the closeness of the election indicated a trend toward the Republicans, who were making constant and effective use of the canard that the Federalists were "monocrats" (monarchists) determined to destroy American liberty. Without Washington to lead them, the Federalist politicians were already quarreling among themselves; honest, able, hardworking John Adams was too caustic and too scathingly frank to unite them. Everything seemed to indicate a Republican victory at the next election.

The XYZ Affair

At this point occurred one of the most remarkable reversals of public feeling in American history. French attacks on American shipping, begun out of irritation at the Jay Treaty and in order to influence the election, continued after Adams took office. Hoping to stop them, Adams appointed three commissioners (Charles Pinckney, United States minister to France and elder brother of Thomas*; John Marshall, a Virginia Federalist; and Elbridge Gerry of Massachusetts, who was not closely identified with either party) to try to negotiate a settlement.

Their mission was a fiasco. Talleyrand, the French foreign minister, sent three agents (later spoken of as X, Y, and Z) to demand a huge bribe as the price of making a deal. The Americans refused, more because they suspected Talleyrand's good faith than because of any distaste for bribery. "No, no, not a sixpence," Pinckney told the agents. The talks broke up, and in April 1798 President Adams released the commissioners' reports.

They caused a sensation. Americans' sense of national honor, perhaps overly tender because the country was so young and insecure, was outraged. Pinckney's laconic refusal to pay a bribe was translated into the grandiose phrase "Millions for defense, but not one cent for tribute!" and broadcast throughout the land. John Adams, never a man with mass appeal, suddenly found himself a national hero. Federalist hotheads burned for a fight. Congress unilaterally abrogated the French Alliance, created a Navy Department, and appropriated enough money to build 40-odd warships and triple the size of the army. Washington came out of retirement to lead the forces, with Hamilton, now a general, as second in command. On the seas American privateers began to attack French shipping.

---

* The Pinckney brothers were children of Eliza Pinckney, the woman responsible for the introduction of indigo cultivation in America.

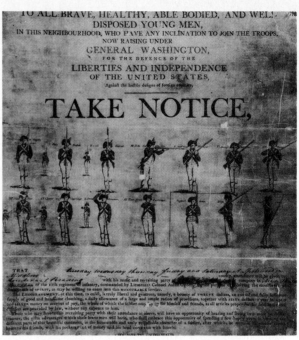

A recruiting poster of 1798 appealed for volunteers to defend the nation "against the hostile designs of foreign enemies," the "enemies" being the French.

Adams did not much like the French, and he could be extremely stubborn. A declaration of war would have been immensely popular. But perhaps—it is not an entirely illogical surmise about John Adams, who later in life described himself with some relish as "obnoxious, suspected, and unpopular"—the president did not want to be popular. He was also a realist. Instead of calling for war, he contented himself with approving the buildup of the armed forces.

The Republicans, however, committed to friendship with France, did not appreciate Adams's moderation. Though angered by the XYZ Affair, they tried, one Federalist complained, "to clog the wheels of government" by opposing the military appropriations. Their newspapers referred to Adams derisively as "His Rotundity," a term that particularly annoyed the somewhat plump president. Benjamin Bache, editor of the *Philadelphia Aurora*, described him as "blind, bald, toothless, querulous," which was three-quarters true but irrelevant. John Daly Burk of the *New York Time Piece* called him a "mock Monarch" surrounded by a "court composed of tories and speculators," which of course was a flat lie.

Many Federalists expected the Republicans to side with France if war broke out. Hysterical and near panic, they easily persuaded themselves that the danger of subversion was acute. The French Revolution and the resulting war were churning European society to the depths, stirring the hopes of liberals and striking fear in the hearts of conservatives. Refugees of both persuasions were flocking to the United States. Suddenly the presence of these foreigners seemed threatening to "native" Americans.

The Alien and Sedition Acts

Conservative Federalists saw in this situation a chance to smash the opposition. In June and July 1798 they pushed through Congress a series of repressive measures known as the Alien and Sedition Acts. The least offensive of these laws, the Naturalization Act, increased the period a foreigner had to reside in the United States before being eligible for citizenship from 5 to 14 years. The Alien Enemies Act gave the president the power to arrest or expel aliens in time of "declared war," but since the quasi-war with France was never declared, this measure had no practical importance. The Alien Act authorized the president to expel all aliens whom he thought "dangerous to the peace and safety of the United States." (Adams never invoked this law, but a number of aliens left the country out of fear that he might.)

Finally, there was the Sedition Act. Its first section, making it a crime "to impede the operation of any law" or to attempt to instigate a riot or insurrection, was reasonable enough; but the act also made it illegal to publish, or even to utter, any "false, scandalous and malicious" criticism of high government officials. Although milder than British sedition laws, this proviso rested, as James Madison said, on "the exploded doctrine" that government officials "are the masters and not the servants of the people."

As the election of 1800 approached, the Federalists made a systematic attempt to silence the leading Republican newspapers. Twenty-five persons were prosecuted and ten convicted, all in patently unfair trials. In typical cases, the editor Thomas Cooper, an English-born radical, later president of the University of South Carolina, was sentenced to six months in jail and fined $400; the

editor Charles Holt got three months and a $200 fine; and the editor James Callender got nine months and a $200 fine.

The Kentucky and Virginia Resolves

Although Thomas Jefferson did not object to state sedition laws, he believed that the Alien and Sedition Acts violated the First Amendment's guarantees of freedom of speech and the press and were an invasion of the rights of the states. He and Madison decided to draw up resolutions arguing that the laws were unconstitutional. Madison's draft was presented to the Virginia legislature and Jefferson's to the legislature of Kentucky. Jefferson argued that since the Constitution was a compact made by sovereign states, each state had "an equal right to judge for itself" when the compact had been violated. Thus a state could declare a law of Congress unconstitutional. Madison's Virginia Resolves took an only slightly less forthright position.

Neither Kentucky nor Virginia tried to implement these resolves or to prevent the enforcement of the Alien and Sedition Acts. Jefferson and Madison were protesting Federalist high-handedness and firing the opening salvo of Jefferson's campaign for the presidency, not advancing a new constitutional theory of extreme states' rights. "Keep away all show of force," Jefferson advised his supporters.

This was sound advice, for events were again playing into the hands of the Republicans. Talleyrand had never wanted war with the United States. When he discovered how vehemently the Americans had reacted to his little attempt to replenish his personal fortune, he let Adams know that new negotiators would be properly received.

President Adams quickly grasped the importance of the French change of heart. Other leading Federalists, however, had lost their heads. By shouting about the French danger, they had roused the country against radicalism, and they did not intend to surrender this advantage tamely. Hamilton in particular wanted war at almost any price—if not against France, then against Spain. He saw himself at the head of the new American army sweeping first across Louisiana and the Floridas, then on to the south. "We ought to squint at South America," he suggested. "Tempting objects will be without our grasp."

One of the most flattering likenesses of John Adams is this portrait by John Trumbull done in 1793. Public criticism of Adams ran high throughout his term of office.

But the Puritan John Adams was a specialist at resisting temptation. At this critical point his intelligence, his moderate political philosophy, and his stubborn integrity stood him in good stead. He would neither go to war merely to destroy the political opposition in America nor follow "the fools who were intriguing to plunge us into an alliance with England . . . and wild expeditions to South America." Instead he submitted to the Senate the name of a new minister plenipotentiary to France, and when the Federalists tried to block the appointment, he threatened to resign. That would have made Jefferson president! So the furious Federalists had to give in, though they forced Adams to send three men instead of one.

Napoleon had taken over France by the time the Americans arrived, and he drove a harder bargain than Talleyrand would have. But in the end he signed an agreement, the Convention of 1800, abrogating the Franco-American treaties of 1778. Nothing was said about the damage done to American shipping by the French, but the war scare was over.

Milestones

1781	States fail to approve Congress's "impost" (tariff)
1783	British order in council bans trade with the West Indies
1786	Rhode Island supreme court upholds the state legal tender act (*Trevett* v. *Weeden*)
	Shays's Rebellion in Massachusetts
	Annapolis Convention
1787	Philadelphia Constitutional Convention
1787–1788	All states but North Carolina and Rhode Island ratify the Constitution
1789	Washington inaugurated as president
	Storming of Paris Bastille begins French Revolution
1790	Alexander Hamilton, *Report on the Public Credit*
1791	Hamilton, *Report on Manufactures*
	First ten amendments (Bill of Rights) ratified
	Republican and Federalist political parties organized
	Philip Freneau's *National Gazette* and John Fenno's *Gazette of the United States* founded
1793	King Louis XVI of France executed
	Washington's Declaration of Neutrality
1794	Jay's Treaty ratified
	Battle of Fallen Timbers
1795	Whiskey Rebellion in Pennsylvania
1796	Washington's farewell address
	John Adams elected president
1798	XYZ Affair
	Congress passes the Alien and Sedition Acts
	Madison's Virginia Resolves
1798–1799	Jefferson's Kentucky Resolves

SUPPLEMENTARY READING

Titles marked with an asterisk have been published in paperback.

On the "critical period," the drafting of the Constitution, and the early history of the new nation, see R. B. Morris, **The Forging of the Union*** (1987), and J. T. Main, **Political Parties Before the Constitution** (1973). On economic development, see E. J. Ferguson, **The Power of the Purse*** (1968), R. A. East, **Business Enterprise in the American Revolutionary Era** (1938), and C. P. Nettels, **The Emergence of a National Economy*** (1962), which puts this subject in the broader perspective of the period 1775–1815. A lively treatment of Shays's Rebellion is M. L. Starkey, **A Little Rebellion** (1955); D. P. Szatmary, **Shays's Rebellion** (1980), is a more recent study.

The political thinking of the period is discussed lucidly in G. S. Wood, **The Creation of the American Republic*** (1969), and Richard Buel, Jr., **Securing the Revolution*** (1972). A good general account of the convention is Clinton Rossiter, **1787: The Grand Convention*** (1966). The best treatment of Alexander Hamilton's connection with the Constitution and of his political views generally is Clinton Rossiter, **Alexander Hamilton and the Constitution** (1964). Irving Brant, **James Madison: Father of the Constitution** (1950), provides the fullest account of Madison's role.

C. A. Beard, **An Economic Interpretation of the Constitution*** (1913), caused a veritable revolution in the thinking of historians about the motives of the Founders, but later works have caused a major reaction away from the Beardian interpretation; see especially R. E. Brown, **Charles Beard and the Constitution*** (1956), and a more detailed critique, Forrest McDonald, **We the People*** (1958). R. A. Rutland, **The Ordeal of the Constitution** (1966), and J. T. Main, **The Antifederalists*** (1961), are

helpful in understanding opposition to the Constitution, while the **Federalist Papers*** of Hamilton, Madison, and Jay, available in many editions, are essential for the arguments of the supporters of the new government. On the Bill of Rights, consult Bernard Schwartz, **The Great Rights of Mankind** (1977).

On the organization of the federal government and the history of the Washington administration, see L. D. White, **The Federalists** (1948), an administrative history, and J. C. Miller, **The Federalist Era*** (1960), a more general history of the period. Washington's presidency is treated in detail in the later volumes of D. S. Freeman, **George Washington** (1948–1957). Joseph Charles, **Origins of the American Party System*** (1961), is thought-provoking, and the early chapters of W. N. Chambers, **Political Parties in a New Nation*** (1963), are also useful.

Good biographies of Hamilton include Broadus Mitchell, **Alexander Hamilton*** (1976), J. E. Cooke, **Alexander Hamilton** (1982), and J. C. Miller, **Alexander Hamilton: A Portrait in Paradox*** (1959). On foreign affairs during the Washington administration, see Alexander De Conde, **Entangling Alliance: Politics and Diplomacy Under George Washington** (1958); Harry Ammon, **The Genet Mission** (1973); two volumes by S. F. Bemis, **Jay's Treaty*** (1923) and **Pinckney's Treaty*** (1926); Alexander De Conde, **The Quasi-War*** (1966); and William Stinchcombe, **The XYZ Affair** (1980).

On the Adams administration, consult S. G. Kurtz, **The Presidency of John Adams** (1957). On the Alien and Sedition Acts, see J. M. Smith, **Freedom's Fetters*** (1956), and L. W. Levy, **Freedom of Speech and Press in Early American History*** (1963).

VI

Jefferson Democracy

Nor is it true that Jefferson is zealot enough to do anything in pursuance of his principles, which will contravene his popularity or his interest. He is as likely as any man I know to temporize; to calculate what will be likely to promote his own reputation and advantage. . . . He is too much in earnest with his democracy.

ALEXANDER HAMILTON, *1801*

senator and a rival of Hamilton in law and politics. But Republican party solidarity had been perfect; Jefferson and Burr received 73 votes each. Because of the tie, the Constitution required that the House of Representatives (voting by states) choose between them.

In the House the Republicans could control only 8 of the 16 state delegations. On the first ballot Jefferson got these 8 votes, one short of election,

O nce the furor over war and subversion subsided, public attention focused on the presidential contest between Adams and Jefferson. Because of his stand for peace, Adams personally escaped the brunt of popular indignation against the Federalist party. His solid qualities had a strong appeal to conservatives, and fear that the Republicans would introduce radical "French" social reforms did not disappear when the danger of war with France ended. Many nationalist-minded voters worried lest the strong government established by the Federalists be weakened by the Republicans in the name of states' rights. The economic progress stimulated by Hamilton's financial reforms also seemed threatened. But when the electors' votes were counted in February 1801, the Republicans were discovered to have won narrowly, 73 to 65.

But which Republican was to be president? The Constitution did not distinguish between presidential and vice-presidential candidates; it provided only that each elector vote for two candidates, the one with the most votes becoming president and the runner-up vice-president. The development of national political parties made this system impractical. The vice-presidential candidate of the Republicans was Aaron Burr of New York, a former

The upper percentage figures show the percent of the electoral vote received by the candidate, and the lower figures the actual electoral votes for that candidate. Before the Twelfth Amendment of 1804, the Electoral College voted for two presidential candidates; the runner-up became vice-president.

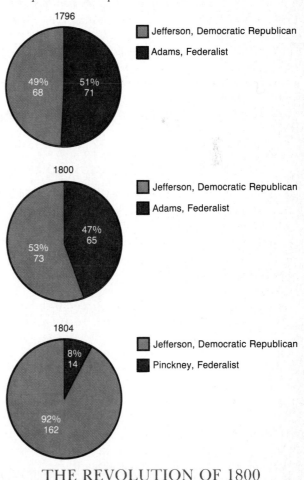

1796

Jefferson, Democratic Republican
Adams, Federalist

49% 68 | 51% 71

1800

Jefferson, Democratic Republican
Adams, Federalist

53% 73 | 47% 65

1804

Jefferson, Democratic Republican
Pinckney, Federalist

8% 14

92% 162

THE REVOLUTION OF 1800

while 6 states voted for Burr. Two state delegations, being evenly split, lost their votes. Through 35 ballots the deadlock persisted; the Federalist congressmen, fearful of Jefferson's supposed radicalism, voted solidly for Burr.

Pressures were exerted on both candidates to make deals to win additional support. Officially, at least, both refused. Burr put on a great show of remaining above the battle. (Had he been an honorable man, he would have withdrawn, since the voters had clearly intended him for the second spot.) Whether Jefferson made any promises is uncertain; there is some evidence that to break the deadlock he assured the Federalists that he would preserve Hamilton's financial system and continue the Washington-Adams foreign policy.

In the end, Alexander Hamilton decided who would be the next president. He detested Burr and threw his weight to Jefferson, exerting his considerable influence on Federalist congressmen. Finally, on February 17, 1801, Jefferson was elected. Burr became vice-president.

To make sure that this deadlock would never be repeated, the Twelfth Amendment was drafted, providing for separate balloting in the electoral college for president and vice-president. This change was ratified in 1804, shortly before the next election.

The Federalist Contribution

On March 4, 1801, in the raw new national capital on the Potomac River named in honor of the Father of His Country, Thomas Jefferson took the presidential oath and delivered his inaugural address. The new president believed that a revolution as important as that heralded by his immortal Declaration of Independence had occurred, and for once most of his political enemies agreed with him.

Certainly an era had ended. In the years between the Peace of Paris and Jay's Treaty, the Federalists had practically monopolized the political good sense of the nation. In the perspective of history they were "right" in strengthening the federal government, in establishing a sound fiscal system, in trying to diversify the economy, in seeking an accommodation with Great Britain, and in refusing to be carried away with enthusiasm for France despite the bright dreams inspired by the French Revolution.

The Federalists had displayed remarkable self-control and moderation at least until 1798. They were nationalists who did not try to destroy local patriotism, aristocrats willing to live with the spirit of democracy. The Constitution is their monument, with its wise compromises, its balance of forces, its restraints, and its practical concessions to local prejudices.

But the Federalists were unable to face up to defeat. When they saw the Republicans gathering strength by developing clever new techniques of party organization and propaganda, mouthing slogans about liberty, attacking "monocrats," glorifying both the past with its satisfying simplicity and the future with its promise of a glorious day when all men would be free, equal, and brothers, they panicked. Abandoning the sober wisdom of their great period, they fought to save themselves at any cost. The effort turned defeat into rout. The Re-

This anti-Jefferson cartoon shows the newly elected president kneeling before the altar of Gallic Despotism, whereon he is burning the writings of prominent Enlightenment philosophers. The American eagle appears to be wresting the Constitution from Jefferson's grasp.

THE PROVIDENTIAL DETECTION

publican victory, close in the electoral college, approached landslide proportions in the congressional elections, where popular feeling expressed itself directly.

Jefferson erred, however, in calling this triumph a revolution. The real upheaval had been attempted in 1798; it was Federalist-inspired, and it failed. In 1800 the voters expressed a preference for the old over the new; that is, for individual freedom and limited national power. And Jefferson, despite Federalist fears that he would destroy the Constitution and establish a radical social order, presided instead over a regime that confirmed the great achievements of the Federalist era.

What was most significant about the election of 1800 was that it was *not* a revolution. After a bitter contest, the Jeffersonians took power and proceeded to change the policy of the government. They did so peacefully. Thus American republican government passed a crucial test: Control of its machinery had changed hands in a democratic and orderly way. And only less significant, the new party system had demonstrated its usefulness. The Jeffersonians had organized popular dissatisfaction with Federalist policies, formulated a platform of reform, chosen leaders to put their plans into effect, and elected those leaders to office.

Thomas Jefferson: Political Theorist

Jefferson hardly seemed cut out for politics. Although in some ways a typical, pleasure-loving southern planter, he had in him something of the Spartan. He grew tobacco but did not smoke, and he partook only sparingly of meat and alcohol. Unlike most planters he never hunted or gambled, though he was a fine horseman and enjoyed dancing, music, and other social diversions. His practical interests ranged enormously—from architecture and geology to natural history and scientific farming—yet he displayed little interest in managing men. Controversy dismayed him, and he tended to avoid it by assigning to some thicker-skinned associate the task of attacking his enemies. Nevertheless, he wanted to have a say in shaping the future of the country, and once engaged, he fought stubbornly and at times deviously to get and hold power.

Like Hamilton, Jefferson thought human beings basically selfish. "Lions and tigers are mere lambs compared with men," he once said. Although he claimed to have some doubts about the subject, he suspected that blacks were "inferior to whites in the endowments both of body and mind." (Hamilton, who also owned slaves, stated flatly of blacks: "Their natural faculties are as good as ours.") The historian Winthrop Jordan, who has made a careful study of white attitudes during this period, claims that Jefferson's opinion, however tenuous, was "the strongest suggestion of inferiority expressed by any native American of the time."

Yet like a good child of the Enlightenment, Jefferson believed that "no definite limits can be assigned to the improvability of the human race" and that unless people were free to follow the dictates of reason, the march of civilization would grind quickly to a halt. "To preserve the freedom of the human mind," he wrote, "every spirit should be ready to devote itself to martyrdom." Democracy seemed to him not so much an ideal as a practical necessity. If people could not govern themselves, how could they be expected to govern their fellows? He had no patience with Hamilton's fondness for magnifying the virtues of the rich and the well-born. He believed that "genius" was a rare quality but one "which nature has shown as liberally among poor as rich." When a very old man he wrote: "The mass of mankind has not been born with saddles on their backs, nor a favored few booted and spurred, ready to ride them legitimately, by the grace of God."

Jefferson believed *all* government a necessary evil at best, for by its nature it restricted the freedom of the individual. For this reason, he wanted the United States to remain a society of small independent farmers.* Such a nation did not need much political organization.

Jefferson's main objection to Hamilton was that Hamilton wanted to commercialize and centralize the country. This Jefferson feared, for it would mean the growth of cities, which would complicate society and hence require more regulation. "When we get piled upon one another in large cities, as in

---

* To Jefferson, agriculture was both the most fundamental and the noblest of callings. "The greatest service which can be rendered to any country is to add a useful plant to its culture," he once said.

VENERATE THE PLOUGH

Jefferson's reverence for farming as a way of life was shared by many Americans of his time. In this etching from a periodical of the period, the plowman is followed by an allegorical figure of America, hallowed with 13 stars and carrying a sheaf of grain.

Europe," he wrote Madison in 1787, "we shall become corrupt as in Europe, and go to eating one another as they do there." Twenty years later he warned a nephew to avoid "populous cities" because, he said, in such places young men acquire "habits and partialities which do not contribute to the happiness of their afterlife." Like Hamilton, he believed that city workers were easy prey for demagogues. "I consider the class of artificers as the panderers of vice, and the instruments by which the liberties of a country are usually overturned," he said. "Those who labor in the earth," he also said, "are the chosen people of God, if ever He had a chosen people."

Jefferson objected to what he considered Hamilton's pro-British orientation. Despite his support of the Revolution, Hamilton admired English society and the orderliness of the British government, and he modeled much of his financial program on the British example. To the author of the Declaration of Independence, these attitudes passed all understanding. Jefferson thought English society immoral and decadent, the British system of gov-

ernment fundamentally corrupt. Toward France, the two took opposite positions. Jefferson was in Paris when the French Revolution broke out; he was delighted to see another blow struck at tyranny. Leading French liberals consulted him at every turn. Later, as secretary of state, he excused the excesses of the French upheaval far more than most Americans. To Hamilton, the violence and social disruption caused by the French Revolution were anathema.

Jefferson as President

The novelty of the new administration lay in its style and its moderation. Both were apparent in Jefferson's inaugural address. The new president's opening remarks showed that he was neither a demagogue nor a firebrand. "The task is above my talents," he said modestly, "and . . . I approach it with . . . anxious and awful presentiments." The people had spoken, and their voice must be heeded, but the rights of dissenters must be respected. "All . . . will bear in mind this sacred principle," he said, "that though the will of the majority is in all cases to prevail, that will to be rightful must be reasonable; that the minority possess their equal rights, which equal law must protect, and to violate would be oppression."

Jefferson spoke at some length about specific policies. He declared himself against "entangling alliances" and for economy in government, and he promised to pay off the national debt, preserve the government's credit, and stimulate both agriculture and its "handmaid," commerce. His main stress was on the cooling of partisan passions. "Every difference of opinion is not a difference of principle. We have called by different names brethren of the same principle. We are all Republicans—we are all Federalists." And he promised the country "a wise and frugal Government, which shall restrain men from injuring one another" and "leave them otherwise free to regulate their own pursuits."

Jefferson quickly demonstrated the sincerity of his remarks. He saw to it that the Whiskey Tax and other Federalist excises were repealed, and he made sharp cuts in military and naval expenditures to keep the budget in balance. The national debt was reduced from $83 million to $57 million during his eight years in office. The Naturalization Act of 1798 was repealed, and the old five-year residence requirement for citizenship restored. The Sedition Act and the Alien Act expired of their own accord in 1801 and 1802.

The changes were not drastic. Jefferson made no effort to tear down the fiscal structure that Hamilton had erected. "We can pay off his debt," the new president confessed, "but we cannot get rid of his financial system." Nor did the author of the Kentucky Resolves try to alter the balance of federal-state power.

Yet there was a different tone to the new regime. Jefferson had no desire to surround himself with pomp and ceremony; the excessive formality and punctilio of the Washington and Adams administrations had been distasteful to him. From the moment of his election, he played down the ceremonial aspects of the presidency. He asked that he be notified of his election by mail rather than by a committee, and he would have preferred to have taken the oath at Charlottesville, near Monticello, his home, rather than at Washington. After the inauguration, he returned to his boardinghouse on foot and took dinner in his usual seat at the common table.

In the White House he often wore a frayed coat and carpet slippers, even to receive the representatives of foreign powers when they arrived, resplendent with silk ribbons and a sense of their own importance, to present their credentials. At social affairs he paid little heed to the status and seniority of his guests. When dinner was announced, he offered his arm to whichever lady he was talking to at the moment and placed her at his right; other guests were free to sit wherever they found an empty chair. During business hours congressmen, friends, foreign officials, and plain citizens coming to call took their turn in the order of their arrival. "The principle of society with us," Jefferson explained, "is the equal rights of all. . . . Nobody shall be above you, nor you above anybody, *pell-mell* is our law."

"Pell-mell" was also good politics, and Jefferson turned out to be a superb politician. He gave dozens of small stag dinner parties for congressmen, serving the food personally from a dumbwaiter connected with the White House kitchen. The guests, carefully chosen to make congenial groups, were seated at a round table to encourage general conversation, and the food and wine were first-class.

Jefferson appears more relaxed and approachable in this drawing by the French expatriate Charles Saint-Mémin than he does in more formal portraits.

These were ostensibly social occasions—shoptalk was avoided—yet they paid large political dividends. Jefferson learned to know every congressman personally, Democratic Republican and Federalist alike, and not only their political views but their strengths, their quirks, their flaws as well. And he worked his personal magic on them, displaying the breadth of his knowledge, his charm and wit, his lack of pomposity. "You see, we are alone, and *our walls have no ears*," he would say, and while the wine flowed and the guests sampled delicacies prepared by Jefferson's French chef, the president manufactured political capital. "You drink as you please and converse at your ease," one guest reported.

Jefferson made effective use of his close supporters in Congress, and of Cabinet members as well, in persuading Congress to go along with his proposals. His state papers were models of sweet reason, minimizing conflicts, stressing areas where all honest people must agree. After all, as he indicated in his inaugural address, nearly all Americans did believe in having both a federal government and a republican system. No great principle divided them into irreconcilable camps. Jefferson set out to bring them all into *his* camp, and he succeeded so well in four years that when he ran for reelection against Charles Pinckney, he got 162 of the 176 electoral votes cast. Eventually even John Quincy Adams, son of the second president, became a Jeffersonian.

At the same time, Jefferson was anything but nonpartisan in the sense that Washington had been. His Cabinet consisted exclusively of men of his own party. He exerted almost continuous pressure on Congress to make sure that his legislative program was enacted into law. He did not remove many Federalist officeholders, and at one point he remarked ruefully that government officials seldom died and never resigned. But when he could, he used his power of appointment to reward his friends and punish his enemies.

Attacking the Judiciary

Although notably open-minded and tolerant, Jefferson had a few stubborn prejudices. One was against kings, another against the British system of government. A third was against judges, or rather, against entrenched judicial power. While recognizing that judges must have a degree of independence, he feared what he called their "habit of going out of the question before them, to throw an anchor ahead, and grapple further hold for future advances of power." The biased behavior of Federalist judges during the trials under the Sedition Act had enormously increased this distrust, and it burst all bounds when the Federalist majority of the dying Congress rammed through the Judiciary Act of 1801.

The Judiciary Act created six new circuit courts, presided over by 16 new federal judges and a small army of attorneys, marshals, and clerks. The expanding country needed the judges, but with the enthusiastic cooperation of President Adams, the Federalists made shameless use of the opportunity to fill all the new positions with conservative members of their own party. The new appointees were dubbed "midnight justices" because Adams had stayed up till midnight on March 3, his last day as president, feverishly signing their commissions.

The Republicans retaliated as soon as the new Congress met by repealing the Judiciary Act of 1801, but upon taking office Jefferson had discov-

ered that in the confusion of Adams's last hours, the commissions of a number of justices of the peace for the new District of Columbia had not been distributed. While these were small fry indeed, Jefferson was so angry that he ordered the commissions held up even though they had been signed by Adams.

One of the appointees, William Marbury, then petitioned the Supreme Court for a writ of mandamus (Latin for "we order") directing the new secretary of state, James Madison, to give him his commission.

The case of *Marbury* v. *Madison* placed Chief Justice John Marshall in an embarrassing position. Marbury had a strong claim: If Marshall refused to issue a mandamus, everyone would say he dared not stand up to Jefferson, and the prestige of the Court would suffer. If he issued the writ, however, he would place the Court in direct conflict with the executive. Jefferson particularly disliked Marshall. He would probably tell Madison to ignore the order, and in the prevailing state of public opinion nothing could be done about it. This would be a still more staggering blow to the judiciary. What should the chief justice do?

Marshall had studied law only briefly and had no previous judicial experience, but in this crisis he first displayed the genius that was to mark him as a great judge. By right Marbury should have his commission, he announced. However, the Court could not require Madison to give it to him. Marbury's request for a mandamus had been based on an ambiguous clause in the Judiciary Act of 1789. That clause was unconstitutional, Marshall declared, and therefore void. Congress could not legally give the Supreme Court the right to issue writs of mandamus in such circumstances.

With the skill and foresight of a chess grand master, Marshall turned what had looked like a trap into a triumph. By sacrificing the pawn, Marbury, he established the power of the Supreme Court to invalidate federal laws that conflicted with the Constitution. Jefferson could not check him because Marshall had *refused* power instead of throwing an anchor ahead, as Jefferson had feared. Yet he had certainly grappled a "further hold for future advances of power," and the president could do nothing to stop him.

The Marbury case made Jefferson more determined to strike at the Federalist-dominated courts. He decided to press for the impeachment of some of the more partisan judges. First he had the House of Representatives bring charges against District Judge John Pickering. Pickering was clearly insane—he had frequently delivered profane and drunken harangues from the bench—and the Senate quickly voted to remove him. Then Jefferson went after a much larger fish, Samuel Chase, associate justice of the Supreme Court.

Chase had been prominent for decades, an early leader of the Sons of Liberty, a signer of the Declaration of Independence, active in the affairs of the Continental Congress. Washington had named him to the Supreme Court in 1796, and he had delivered a number of important opinions. But his handling of cases under the Sedition Act had been outrageously high-handed. Defense lawyers had become so exasperated as to throw down their briefs in disgust at some of his prejudiced rulings. However, the trial demonstrated that Chase's actions had not constituted the "high crimes and misdemeanors" required by the Constitution to remove a judge. Even Jefferson became disenchanted with the efforts of some of his more extreme followers and accepted Chase's acquittal with equanimity.

The Barbary Pirates

Aside from these perhaps salutary setbacks, Jefferson's first term was a parade of triumphs. Although

Although the war against the Barbary pirates did not result in a decisive victory for the United States, its gunboats did give a good account of themselves in encounters with pirate ships. Here, in a raid on the harbor at Tripoli, an American sailor threatens a scimitar-wielding Arab.

he cut back the army and navy sharply in order to save money, he temporarily escaped the consequences of leaving the country undefended because of the lull in the European war signalized by the Treaty of Amiens between Great Britain and France in March 1802. Despite the fact that he had only seven frigates in commission, he even managed to fight a small naval war with the Barbary pirates without damage to American interests or prestige.

The North African Arab states of Morocco, Algiers, Tunis, and Tripoli had for decades made a business of piracy, seizing vessels all over the Mediterranean and holding crews and passengers for ransom. The European powers found it simpler to pay them annual protection money than to crush them. Under Washington and Adams, the United States joined in the payment of this tribute; while large, the sums were less than the increased costs of insurance for shippers when the protection was not purchased.

Such pusillanimity ran against Jefferson's grain. "When this idea comes across my mind, my faculties are absolutely suspended between indignation and impatience," he said. When the pasha of Tripoli tried to raise the charges, he balked. Tripoli then declared war in May 1801, and Jefferson dispatched a squadron to the Mediterranean.

In the words of one historian, the action was "halfhearted and ill-starred." The pirates were not overwhelmed, and a major American warship, the frigate *Philadelphia*, had to be destroyed after running aground off the Tripolitanian coast. The payment of tribute continued until 1815. Just the same, America, though far removed from the pirate bases, was the only maritime nation that tried to resist the blackmail. Although the war failed to achieve Jefferson's purpose of ending the payments, the pasha agreed to a new treaty more favorable to the United States, and American sailors, led by Commodore Edward Preble, won valuable experience and a large portion of fame. The greatest hero was Lieutenant Stephen Decatur, who captured two pirate ships, led ten men in a daring raid on another in which he took on a gigantic sailor in a wild battle of cutlass against boarding pike,* and snatched the stricken *Philadelphia* from the pirates by sneaking aboard and setting it afire.

---

* Decatur killed the pirate by drawing a small pistol from his pocket as his opponent was about to skewer him.

The Louisiana Purchase

The major achievements of Jefferson's first term had to do with the American west, and of these the greatest by far was the acquisition of the huge area between the Mississippi River and the Rocky Mountains. In a sense the purchase of this region, called Louisiana, was fortuitous, an accidental by-product of European political adjustments and the whim of Napoleon Bonaparte. Certainly Jefferson had not planned it, for in his inaugural address he had expressed the opinion that the country already had all the land it would need "for a thousand generations." It was nonetheless the perfectly logical—one might almost say inevitable—result of a long series of events in the history of the Mississippi Valley.

Along with every other American who had even a superficial interest in the west, Jefferson understood that the United States must have access to the mouth of the Mississippi and the city of New Orleans or eventually lose everything beyond the Appalachians. "There is on the globe one single spot, the possessor of which is our natural and habitual enemy," he was soon to write. "It is New Orleans." Thus when he learned shortly after his inauguration that Spain had given Louisiana back to France, he was immediately on his guard. Control of Louisiana by Spain, a "feeble" country with "pacific dispositions," could be tolerated; control by a resurgent France dominated by Napoleon, the greatest military genius of the age, was entirely different. Did Napoleon have designs on Canada? Did he perhaps mean to resume the old Spanish and British game of encouraging the Indians to harry the American frontier? And what now would be the status of Pinckney's precious treaty?

Deeply worried, the president instructed his minister to France, Robert R. Livingston, to seek assurances that American rights in New Orleans would be respected and to negotiate the purchase of West Florida in case that region had also been turned over to France.

Jefferson's concern was well founded; France was indeed planning new imperial ventures in North America. Immediately after settling its difficulties with the United States through the Convention of 1800, France signed the secret Treaty of San Ildefonso with Spain, which returned Louisiana to France. Napoleon hoped to use this region as a breadbasket for the French West Indian sugar plantations, just as colonies like Pennsylvania and Massachusetts had fed the British sugar islands before the Revolution.

However, the most important French island, Saint Domingue (Hispaniola), at the time occupied entirely by the nation of Haiti, had slipped from French control. During the French Revolution, the slaves of the island had revolted. In 1793 they were granted personal freedom, but they fought on under the leadership of the "Black Napoleon," a self-taught genius named Toussaint Louverture, and by 1801 the island was entirely in their hands. The original Napoleon, taking advantage of the slackening of war in Europe, dispatched an army of 20,000 men under General Charles Leclerc to reconquer it.

When Jefferson learned of the Leclerc expedition, he had no trouble divining its relationship to Louisiana. His uneasiness became outright alarm. In April 1802 he again urged Minister Livingston to attempt the purchase of New Orleans and Florida or, as an alternative, to buy a tract of land near the mouth of the Mississippi where a new port could be constructed. Of necessity, the mild-mannered, idealistic president now became an aggressive realist. If the right of deposit could not be preserved through negotiation, it must be purchased with gunpowder, even if that meant acting in conjuction with the despised British. "The day that France takes possession of New Orleans," he warned, "we must marry ourselves to the British fleet and nation."

In October 1802 the Spanish, who had not yet actually turned Louisiana over to France, heightened the tension by suddenly revoking the right of deposit at New Orleans. We now know that the French had no hand in this action, but it was beyond reason to expect Jefferson or the American people to believe it at the time. With the west clamoring for relief, Jefferson appointed his friend and disciple James Monroe minister plenipotentiary and sent him to Paris with instructions to offer up to $10 million for New Orleans and Florida. If France refused, he and Livingston should open negotiations for a "closer connection" with the British.

The tension broke before Monroe even reached France. General Leclerc's Saint Domingue expedition ended in disaster. Although Toussaint surrendered, Haitian resistance continued. Yellow fever raged through the French army; Leclerc himself fell before the fever, which wiped out practically his entire force.

When news of this calamity reached Napoleon early in 1803, he began to have second thoughts about reviving French imperialism in the New World. Without Saint Domingue, the wilderness of Louisiana seemed of little value. Napoleon was preparing a new campaign in Europe. He could no longer spare troops to recapture a rebellious West Indian island or to hold Louisiana against a possible British attack, and he needed money.

For some weeks the commander of the most powerful army in the world mulled the question without consulting anyone. Then, with characteristic suddenness, he made up his mind. On April 10 he ordered Foreign Minister Talleyrand to offer not merely New Orleans but all of Louisiana to the Americans. The next day Talleyrand summoned Livingston to his office on the Rue du Bac and dropped this bombshell. Livingston was almost struck speechless but quickly recovered his composure. When Talleyrand asked what the United States would give for the province, he suggested the French equivalent of about $5 million. Talleyrand pronounced the sum "too low" and urged Livingston to think about the subject for a day or two.

Livingston faced a situation that no modern diplomat would ever have to confront. His instructions said nothing about buying an area almost as large as the entire United States, and there was no time to write home for new instructions. The offer staggered the imagination. Luckily, Monroe arrived the next day to share the responsibility. The two Americans consulted, dickered with the French, and finally agreed—they could scarcely have done otherwise—to accept the proposal. Early in May they signed a treaty. For 60 million francs—about $15 million—the United States was to have all of Louisiana.

No one knew exactly how large the region was or what it contained. When Livingston asked Talleyrand about the boundaries of the purchase, he replied: "I can give you no direction. You have made a noble bargain for yourselves, and I suppose you will make the most of it." Never, as the historian Henry Adams wrote, "did the United States government get so much for so little."

Napoleon's unexpected concession caused consternation in America, though there was never real doubt that the treaty would be ratified. Jefferson

Robert Livingston was appointed Jefferson's minister to France in 1801. When he signed the treaty for the purchase of Louisiana, he commented: "From this day, the United States take their place among the powers of the first rank."

did not believe that the government had the power under the Constitution to add new territory or to grant American citizenship to the 50,000 residents of Louisiana by executive act, as the treaty required. He even drafted a constitutional amendment: "The province of Louisiana is incorporated with the United States and made part thereof," but his advisers convinced him that it would be dangerous to delay approval of the treaty until an amendment could be acted on by three-fourths of the states. Jefferson then suggested that the Senate ratify the treaty and submit an amendment afterward "confirming an act which the nation had not previously authorized." This idea was so obviously illogical that he quickly dropped it. Finally, he came to believe "that the less we say about constitutional difficulties

the better." Since what he called "the good sense of our country" clearly wanted Louisiana, he decided to "acquiesce with satisfaction" while Congress overlooked the "metaphysical subtleties" of the problem and ratified the treaty.

Some of the more partisan Federalists, who had been eager to fight Spain for New Orleans, attacked Jefferson for undermining the Constitution. One such critic described Louisiana contemptuously as a "Gallo-Hispano-Indian" collection of "savages and adventurers." Even Hamilton expressed hesitation about absorbing "this new, immense, unbounded world," though he had dreamed of seizing still larger domains himself. In the end Hamilton's nationalism reasserted itself, and he urged ratification of the treaty, as did such other important Federalists as John Adams and John Marshall. And in a way the Louisiana Purchase was as much Hamilton's doing as Jefferson's. Napoleon accepted payment in United States bonds, which he promptly sold to European investors. If Hamilton had not established the nation's credit so soundly, such a large issue could never have been so easily disposed of.

It was ironic—and a man as perceptive as Hamilton must surely have recognized the irony—that the acquisition of Louisiana assured Jefferson's reelection and further contributed to the downfall of Federalism. The purchase was popular even in the New England bastions of that party. While the negotiations were progressing in Paris, Jefferson had written of partisan political affairs: "If we can settle happily the difficulties of the Mississippi, I think we may promise ourselves smooth seas during our time." These words turned out to be no more accurate than most political predictions, but the Louisiana Purchase drove another spike into Federalism's coffin.

Federalism Discredited

The west and south were solid for Jefferson, and the north was rapidly succumbing to his charm. The addition of new western states would soon further reduce New England's power in national affairs. So complete did the Republican triumph seem that a handful of die-hard Federalists in New England began to think of secession. Led by former secretary of state Timothy Pickering, a sour, implacable conservative, a group known as the Essex Junto organized in 1804 a scheme to break away from the Union and establish a "northern confederacy."

Even within the dwindling Federalist ranks the Junto had little support. Nevertheless, Pickering and his friends pushed ahead, drafting a plan whereby, having captured political control of New York, they would take the entire northeast out of the Union. Since they could not begin to win New York for anyone in their own ranks, they hit on the idea of supporting Vice-President Aaron Burr, who was running against the "regular" Republican candidate for governor of New York. Although Burr did not promise to bring New York into their confederacy if elected, he encouraged them enough to win their backing. The foolishness of the plot was revealed in the April elections: Burr was overwhelmed by the regular Republican. The Junto's scheme collapsed.

The incident, however, had a tragic aftermath. Hamilton had campaigned against Burr, whom he considered "an embryo Caesar." When he continued after the election to cast aspersions on Burr's character (not a very difficult assignment, since Burr, despite being a grandson of the preacher Jonathan Edwards, frequently violated both the political and sexual mores of the day), Burr challenged him to a duel. It was well known that Hamilton opposed dueling in principle, his own son having been slain in such an encounter, and he certainly had no need to prove his courage. But he believed that his honor was at stake. The two met with pistols on July 11, 1804, at Weehawken, New Jersey, across the Hudson from New York City. Hamilton made no effort to hit the challenger, but Burr took careful aim. Hamilton fell, mortally wounded. Thus a great, if enigmatic, man was cut off in his prime. His work, in a sense, had been completed, and his philosophy of government was being everywhere rejected, yet the nation's loss was large.

Lewis and Clark

While the disgruntled Federalists dreamed of secession, Jefferson was planning the exploration of Louisiana and the region beyond. Early in 1803 he got $2,500 from Congress and obtained the permission of the French to send his exploring party across Louisiana. To command the expedition he appointed his private secretary, Meriwether Lewis, a young Virginian who had seen considerable service with the army in the west and who possessed, according to Jefferson, "a great mass of accurate information on all the subjects of nature." Lewis chose as his companion officer William Clark, another soldier (he had served with General Anthony Wayne at the Battle of Fallen Timbers) who had much experience in negotiating with Indians.

Jefferson, whose interest in the west was scientific as well as political, issued minute instructions to Lewis:

> Other objects worthy of notice will be, the soil and face of the country . . . the remains and accounts of any animals which may be deemed or are extinct; the mineral productions of every kind, climate, as characterized by the thermometer, by the proportion of rainy, cloudy, and clear days, by lightning, hail, snow, ice, by the access and recess of frost, by the winds prevailing at different seasons, the dates at which particular plants put forth or lose their flower or leaf, times of appearance of particular birds, reptiles or insects. . . .

Scientific matters were inextricably intertwined with practical ones, such as the fur trade, for in his nature studies Jefferson concentrated on "useful" plants and animals. He was haunted by imperialistic visions of an expanding America that were not unlike those of Hamilton. After the consummation of the Louisiana Purchase, he instructed Lewis to try to establish official relations with the Indians in the Spanish territories beyond. Lewis should assure the tribes that "they will find in us faithful friends and protectors," Jefferson said. That the expedition would be moving across Spanish territory need not concern the travelers because of "the expiring state of Spain's interests there."

Lewis and Clark gathered a group of 48 experienced men near St. Louis during the winter of 1803–1804. In the spring they set forth, pushing slowly up the Missouri River in a 55-foot keelboat and two dugout canoes called pirogues. By late fall they had reached what is now North Dakota, where they built a small station, Fort Mandan, and spent the winter. In April 1805, having shipped back to the president more than 30 boxes of plants, minerals, animal skins and bones, and Indian artifacts,

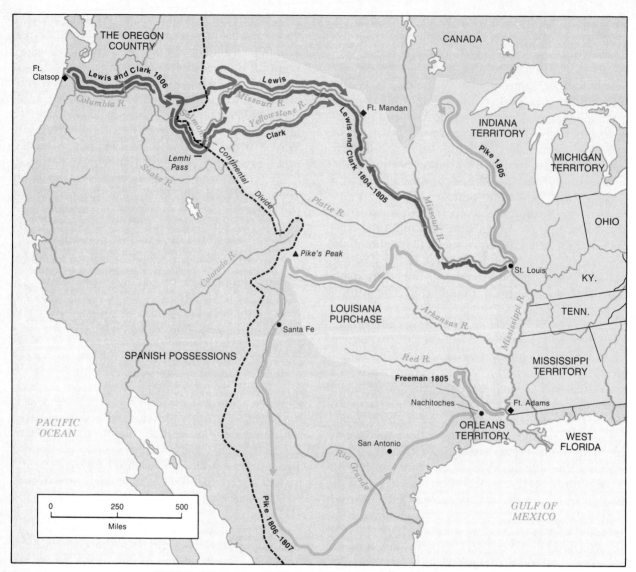

EXPLORING THE LOUISIANA PURCHASE

The explorations of Lewis and Clark, as well as those of Freeman and Pike, are traced in the map. The yellow shading shows the Louisiana Purchase as delineated by its "natural" boundaries. On their return journey, Lewis and Clark divided their party to explore more thoroughly the area around the upper Missouri and Yellowstone rivers.

they struck out again toward the mountains, accompanied by a Shoshone woman, Sacajawea, and her French-Canadian husband, Toussaint Charbonneau, who acted as interpreters and guides. They passed the Great Falls of the Missouri and then clambered over the Continental Divide at Lemhi Pass, in southwestern Montana. Soon thereafter the going became easier, and they descended to the Pacific by way of the Clearwater and Columbia rivers, reaching their destination in November.

Lewis and Clark kept careful journals, with drawings, detailing every aspect of their expedition. In the Northwest they encountered the Chinook Indians, who admired a sloping forehead. The sketch above shows such an Indian in profile. Below is an infant in a cradle especially constructed to achieve this effect.

They had hoped to return by ship, but during the long, damp winter not a single vessel appeared. In the spring of 1806 they headed back by land, reaching St. Louis on September 23.

The country greeted the news of their return with delight. Besides locating several passes across the Rockies, Lewis and Clark had established friendly relations with a great many Indian tribes to whom they presented gifts, medals, American flags, and a sales talk designed to promote peace and the fur trade. They brought back a wealth of data about the country and its resources. The journals kept by members of the group were published and, along with their accurate maps, became major sources for scientists, students, and future explorers. To Jefferson's great personal satisfaction, Lewis provided him with many specimens of the local wildlife, including two grizzly bear cubs, which he kept for a time in a stone pit in the White House lawn.

The success of Lewis and Clark did not open the gates of Louisiana very wide. Other explorers sent out by Jefferson accomplished far less. Thomas Freeman, an Irish-born surveyor, led a small party up the Red River but ran into a powerful Spanish force near the present junction of Arkansas, Oklahoma, and Texas and was forced to retreat. Between 1805 and 1807 Lieutenant Zebulon Pike explored the upper Mississippi Valley and the Colorado region. (He discovered but failed to scale the peak south of Denver that bears his name.) Pike eventually made his way to Santa Fe and the upper reaches of the Rio Grande, but he was not nearly so careful and acute an observer as Lewis and Clark were and consequently brought back much less information. By 1808 fur traders based at St. Louis were beginning to invade the Rockies, and by 1812 there were 75,000 people in the southern section of the new territory, which was admitted to the Union that year as the state of Louisiana. The northern region lay almost untouched until much later.

Jeffersonian Democracy

With the purchase of Louisiana, Jefferson completed the construction of the political institution known as the Republican party and the philosophy of government known as Jeffersonian democracy. From what sort of materials had he built his juggernaut? In part his success was a matter of personality; in the march of American democracy he stood halfway, temperamentally, between Washington and Andrew Jackson, perfectly in tune with the thinking of his times. The colonial American had practiced democracy without really believing in it; hence, for example, the maintenance of property qualifications for voting in regions where nearly everyone owned property. Stimulated by the libertarian ideas of the Revolution, Americans were rapidly adjusting their beliefs to conform with their practices. However, it took Jefferson, a man of large estates, possessed of the general prejudice in favor of the old-fashioned citizen rooted in the soil, yet deeply committed to majority rule, to oversee the transition.

Jefferson's marvelous talents as a writer help to explain his success. He expounded his ideas in language that few people could resist. He had a remarkable facility for discovering practical arguments to justify his beliefs—as when he suggested that by letting everyone vote, elections would be made more honest because with large numbers going to the polls, bribery would become prohibitively expensive.

Jefferson prepared the country for democracy by proving that a democrat could establish and maintain a stable regime. The Federalist tyranny of 1798 was compounded of selfishness and stupidity, but it was also based in part on honest fears that an egalitarian regime would not protect the fabric of society from hotheads and crackpots. The impact of the French Revolution on conservative thinking in the mid-1790s cannot be overestimated. America had fought a seven-year revolution without executing a single Tory, yet during the few months that the Terror ravaged France, nearly 17,000 persons were officially put to death for political "crimes" and many thousands more were killed in civil disturbances. Worse, in the opinion of many, the French extremists had attempted to destroy Christianity, substituting for it a "cult of reason." They confiscated property, imposed price controls, and abolished slavery in the French colonies. Little wonder that many Americans feared that the Jeffersonians, lovers of France and of *liberté, égalite, fraternité,* would try to remodel American society in a similar way.

Jefferson calmed these fears. "Pell-mell" might scandalize the British and Spanish ministers and a few other mossbacks, but it was scarcely revolutionary. The most partisan Federalist was hard put to see a Robespierre in the amiable president scratching out state papers at his desk or chatting with a Kentucky congressman at a "republican" dinner party. Furthermore, Jefferson accepted Federalist ideas on public finance, even learning to live with Hamilton's bank. As a good democrat, he drew a nice distinction between his own opinions and the wishes of the majority, which he felt must always take priority. Even in his first inaugural he admitted that manufacturing and commerce were, along with agriculture, the "pillars of our prosperity," and while believing that these activities would thrive best when "left most free to individual enterprise," he accepted the principle that the government should protect them when necessary from "casual embarrassments." Eventually he gave his backing to modest proposals for spending federal money on roads, canals, and other projects that, according to his political philosophy, ought to have been left to the states and private individuals.

During his term the country grew and prospered, the commercial classes sharing in the bounty along with the farmers so close to Jefferson's heart. Blithely he set out to win the support of all who could vote. "It is material to the safety of Republicanism," he wrote in 1803, "to detach the mercantile interests from its enemies and incorporate them into the body of its friends."

Thus Jefferson undermined the Federalists all along the line. They had said that the country must pay a stiff price for prosperity and orderly government, and they demanded prompt payment in full, both in cash (taxes) and in the form of limitations on human liberty. Under Jefferson these much-desired goals had been achieved cheaply and without sacrificing freedom. A land whose riches could only be guessed at had been obtained without firing a shot and without burdening the people with new taxes. "What farmer, what mechanic, what laborer, ever sees a tax gatherer in the United States?" the president could ask in 1805, without a single Federalist rising to challenge him. Order without discipline, security without a large military establishment, prosperity without regulatory legislation, freedom without license—truly the Sage of Monticello appeared to have led his fellow Americans into a golden age.

Flies in the President's Ointment

Republican virtue seemed to have triumphed, both at home and abroad. "With nations as with individuals," Jefferson proclaimed as he took the oath of office at the start of his second term, "our interests soundly calculated, will ever be found inseparable from our moral duties." And he added more smugly still: "Fellow citizens, you best know whether we have done well or ill." Such smugness and complacency are luxuries that politicians can seldom afford. Jefferson, beginning his second term with pride in the past and confidence in the future and with the mass support of the nation, soon found himself in trouble at home and abroad.

In part his difficulties arose from the extent of the Republican victory. In 1805 the Federalists had no useful ideas, no intelligent leadership, no effective numbers. They held only a quarter of the seats in Congress. As often happens in such situations, lack of opposition weakened party discipline and encouraged factionalism among the Republicans.

At the same time, Napoleon's renewed aggressiveness in Europe, to which the sale of Louisiana had been a prelude, produced a tangle of new problems for the neutral United States. Jefferson could not solve these problems merely by being "just" and "moral," as he had suggested in his second inaugural address. At the end of his second term he was suffering from rheumatism and recurrent headaches that were no doubt of psychosomatic origin, and he wrote feelingly to a friend: "Never did a prisoner, released from his chains, feel such relief as I shall on shaking off the shackles of power."

Jefferson's domestic troubles were not of critical importance, but they were vexing. To a considerable extent they resulted from the elements in his makeup that explain his success: his facility in ad-

John Randolph of Roanoke (as he signed his name to avoid being mistaken for his cousin "Possum" John) was painted in 1805, when he was 32, by Gilbert Stuart.

justing his principles to practical conditions, his readiness to take over the best of Federalism. Some of his disciples were less ready than he to surrender principle to expediency.

The most prominent of the Republican critics was John Randolph of Roanoke, congressman from Virginia. Randolph was unique. Although he had wit, charm, and imagination, he was also intellectually rigid, and when he thought some principle at stake, he was a vitriolic and unyielding obstructionist. Randolph made a fetish of preserving states' rights against invasion by the central government. "Asking one of the States to surrender part of her sovereignty is like asking a lady to surrender part of her chastity," he remarked in one of his typical epigrams.

Randolph first clashed with Jefferson in 1804, over an attempted settlement of the so-called Yazoo land frauds. In 1795 the Georgia legislature had sold a huge area to four land companies for less than 2 cents an acre. When it was revealed that many of the legislators had been corrupted, the next legislature canceled the grants, but not before the original grantees had unloaded large tracts on various third parties. These innocents turned to the federal government for relief when the grants were canceled. Jefferson favored a bill giving 5 million acres to these interests, but Randolph would have none of this. Rising in righteous wrath, he denounced in his shrill soprano all those who would countenance such fraud. The compromise bill was defeated. The controversy then entered the courts, and in 1810 Chief Justice Marshall held in *Fletcher* v. *Peck* that in rescinding the grant, Georgia had committed an unconstitutional breach of contract. Before Marshall's ruling, however, the federal grant was finally approved by Congress. Had it not been, *Fletcher* v. *Peck* would have provided the "victims" of the Yazoo frauds with an area considerably larger than the state of Mississippi! Randolph only rarely mustered more than a handful of supporters in Congress, but his stabbing, nerve-shattering assaults grievously disturbed the president's peace of mind.

The Burr Conspiracy

Another Republican who caused trouble for Jefferson was Aaron Burr, and again the president was partly to blame for the difficulty. After their contest for the presidency in 1801, Jefferson pursued Burr vindictively, depriving him of federal patronage in New York and replacing him as the 1804 Republican vice-presidential candidate with Governor George Clinton, Burr's chief rival in the state.

While still vice-president, Burr began to flirt with treason. He approached Anthony Merry, the British minister in Washington, and offered to "effect a separation of the Western part of the United States." His price was £110,000 and the support of a British fleet off the mouth of the Mississippi. The British did not fall in with his scheme, but he went ahead nonetheless. Exactly what he had in mind has long been in dispute. Certainly he dreamed of acquiring a western empire for himself; whether he intended to wrest it from the United States or from Spanish territories beyond Louisiana is unclear. He joined forces with General James Wilkinson, whom Jefferson had appointed governor of Louisiana Territory, and who, it will be recalled, had been involved in secessionist movements in the west and who was secretly in the pay of Spain.

The opening of the Ohio and Mississippi valleys had not totally satisfied land-hungry westerners. In 1806 Burr and Wilkinson had no difficulty raising a small force at a place called Blennerhassett Island, in the Ohio River. Some six dozen men began to move downriver toward New Orleans under Burr's command. Whether the objective was New Orleans or some part of Mexico, the scheme was clearly illegal. For some reason, however—possibly because he was incapable of loyalty to anyone*—Wilkinson betrayed Burr to Jefferson at the last moment. Burr tried to escape to Spanish Florida but was captured in February 1807, brought to Richmond, Virginia, under guard, and charged with high treason.

Any president will deal summarily with traitors, but Jefferson's attitude during Burr's trial reveals the depth of his hatred. He "made himself a party to the prosecution," personally sending evidence to the United States attorney who was handling the case and offering blanket pardons to associates of Burr who would agree to turn state's evidence. In stark contrast, Chief Justice Marshall, presiding at

Aaron Burr was sketched in 1805 by Charles Saint-Mémin, who was well-known for his profile portraits. (See the Jefferson portrait on page 171.)

the trial in his capacity as judge of the circuit court, repeatedly showed favoritism to the prisoner.

In this contest between two great men at their worst, Jefferson as a vindictive executive and Marshall as a prejudiced judge, the victory went to the judge. Organizing "a military assemblage," Marshall declared in his charge to the jury, "was not a levying of war." To "advise or procure treason" was not in itself treason. Unless two independent witnesses testified to an overt act of treason as thus defined, the accused should be declared innocent in the light of this charge. The jury, deliberating only 25 minutes, found Burr not guilty.

Throughout the trial, Burr never lost his self-possession. He seemed to view the proceedings with amiable cynicism. Then, since he was wanted either for murder or for treason in six states, he went into exile in Europe. Some years later he returned to New York, where he spent an unregenerate old age, fathering two illegitimate children in his seventies

---

* John Randolph said of him: "Wilkinson is the only man that I ever saw who was from the bark to the very core a villain."

and being divorced by his second wife on grounds of adultery at 80.

The Burr affair was a blow to Jefferson's prestige; it left him more embittered against Marshall and the federal judiciary, and it added nothing to his reputation as a statesman.

Napoleon and the British

Jefferson's difficulties with Burr may be traced at least in part to the purchase of Louisiana, which, empty and unknown, excited the cupidity of men like Burr and Wilkinson. But problems infinitely more serious were also related to Louisiana.

Napoleon had jettisoned Louisiana to clear the decks before resuming the battle for control of Europe. This war had the effect of stimulating the American economy, for the warring powers needed American goods and American vessels. Shipbuilding boomed; foreign trade, which had quintupled since 1793, nearly doubled again between 1803 and 1805. By the summer of 1807, however, the situation had changed: A most unusual stalemate had developed in the war.

In October 1805 Britain's Horatio Nelson demolished the combined Spanish and French fleets in the Battle of Trafalgar, off the coast of Spain. Napoleon, now at the summit of his powers, quickly redressed the balance, smashing army after army thrown against him by Great Britain's continental allies. By 1807 he was master of Europe, while the British controlled the seas around the Continent. Neither nation could strike directly at the other.

They therefore resorted to commercial warfare, striving to disrupt each other's economy. Napoleon struck first with his Berlin Decree (November 1806), which made "all commerce and correspondence" with Great Britain illegal. The British retaliated with a series of edicts called orders in council, blockading most continental ports and barring from them all foreign vessels unless they first stopped at a British port and paid customs duties. Napoleon then issued his Milan Decree (December 1807), declaring any vessel that submitted to the British rules "to have become English property" and thus subject to seizure.

The blockades and counterblockades seemed designed to stop commerce completely, yet this was not the case. Napoleon's "Continental System" was supposed to make Europe self-sufficient and isolate Great Britain, yet he was willing to sell European products to the British (if the price was right); his chief objective was to deprive them of their continental markets. The British were ready to sell anything on the Continent, and to allow others to do so too, provided they first paid a toll. The Continental System was, in John Quincy Adams's pithy phrase, "little more than extortion wearing the mask of prohibition," and British policy was equally immoral—a kind of piracy practiced with impunity because the Royal Navy controlled the seas.

When war first broke out between Britain and France in 1792, the colonial trade of both sides had fallen largely into American hands because the danger of capture drove many belligerent merchant vessels from the seas. This commerce had engaged Americans in some devious practices. Under the Rule of War of 1756, it will be recalled, the British denied to neutrals the right to engage in trade during time of war from which they were barred by mercantilistic regulations in time of peace. If an American ship carried sugar from the French colony of Martinique to France, for example, the British claimed the right to capture it because such traffic was normally confined to French bottoms by French law.

To avoid this risk, American merchants brought the sugar first to the United States, a legal peacetime voyage under French mercantilism. Then they reshipped it to France as American sugar. Since the United States was a neutral nation and sugar was not contraband of war, the Americans expected the British to let their ships pass with impunity. Continental products likewise reached the French West Indies by way of United States ports, and the American government encouraged the traffic in both directions by refunding customs duties on foreign products reshipped within a year. Between 1803 and 1806 the annual value of foreign products reexported from the United States jumped from $13 million to $60 million! In 1806 the United States exported 47 million pounds of coffee—none, of course, of local origin. An example of this type of trade is offered by Samuel Eliot Morison in his *Maritime History of Massachusetts:*

The brig *Eliza Hardy* of Plymouth enters her home port from Bordeaux, on May 20, 1806, with a cargo of claret wine. Part of it is immediately re-exported to Martinique in the schooner *Pilgrim,* which also carries a consignment of brandy that came from Alicante in the brig *Commerce* and another of gin that came from Rotterdam in the barque *Hannah* of Plymouth. The rest of the *Eliza Hardy*'s claret is taken to Philadelphia by coasters, and thence re-exported in seven different vessels to Havana, Santiago de Cuba, St. Thomas, and Batavia.

This underhanded commerce irritated the British. In the cases of the *Essex* and the *William* (1805–1806), a British judge, Sir William Grant, decreed that American ships could no longer rely on "mere voluntary *ceremonies*" to circumvent the Rule of 1756. Thus just when Britain and France were cracking down on direct trade by neutrals, Britain determined to halt the American reexport trade, thereby gravely threating American prosperity.

The Impressment Controversy

More dismaying were the cruel indignities being visited on American seamen by the British practice of impressment. Under British law, any able-bodied subject could be drafted for service in the Royal Navy in an emergency. Normally, when the commander of a warship found himself shorthanded, he put into a British port and sent a "press gang" ashore to round up the necessary men in harborside pubs. When far from home waters, he might hail any passing British merchant ship and commandeer the necessary men, though this practice was understandably unpopular in British maritime circles. He might also stop a *neutral* merchant vessel on the high seas and remove any British subject. Since the United States owned by far the largest merchant fleet among the neutrals, its vessels bore the brunt of this practice.

Impressment had been a cause of Anglo-American conflict for many years; American pride suffered every time a vessel carrying the flag was forced to back topsails and heave to at the command of a British man-of-war. Still more galling was the contemptuous behavior of British officers when they boarded American ships. In 1796 an American captain named Figsby was stopped twice by British war-

ships while carrying a cargo of poultry and other livestock to Guadeloupe. First a privateer, the *Sea Nymph,* impressed two of his crew, confiscated most of his chickens, "abused" him, and stole his ship's flag. Two days later H.M.S. *Unicorn* took another of Figsby's men, the rest of his poultry, four sheep, and three hogs.

Many British captains made little effort to be sure they were impressing British subjects; any likely-looking lad might be taken when the need was great. Furthermore, there were legal questions in dispute. When did an English immigrant become an American? When he was naturalized, the United States claimed. Never, the British retorted; "once an Englishman, always an Englishman."

America's lax immigration laws compounded the problem. A foreigner could become a citizen with ridiculous ease; those too impatient to wait the required five years could purchase false naturalization papers for as little as a dollar. Because working conditions in the American merchant marine were superior to those of the British, at least 10,000 British-born tars were serving on American ships. Some became American citizens legally; others obtained false papers; some admitted to being British subjects; some were deserters from the Royal Navy. From the British point of view, all were liable to impressment.

The Jefferson administration conceded the right of the British to impress their own subjects from American merchant ships. When naturalized Americans were impressed, however, the administration was irritated, and when native-born Americans were taken, it became incensed. Impressment, Secretary of State Madison said in 1807, was "anomalous in principle, . . . grievous in practice, and . . . abominable in abuse." Between 1803 and 1812 at least 5,000 sailors were snatched from the decks of United States vessels and forced to serve in the Royal Navy. Most of them—estimates run as high as three out of every four—were Americans.

The British did not claim the right to impress native-born Americans, and when it could be proved that boarding officers had done so, the men in question were released by higher authority. During the course of the controversy, the British authorities freed 3,800 impressed Americans, which suggests that many more were seized. However, the British refused to abandon impressment. "The Pretension advanced by Mr. Madison that the American Flag

THE IMPRESSMENT OF AN

American Sailor Boy,

SUNG ON BOARD THE BRITISH PRISON SHIP CROWN PRINCE, THE FOURTH OF JULY, 1814
BY A NUMBER OF THE AMERICAN PRISONERS.

THE youthful sailor mounts the bark,
  And bids each weeping friend adieu ;
Fair blows the gale, the canvass swells ;
  Slow sinks the uplands from his view.

Three mornings, from his ocean bed,
  Resplendent beams the God of day :
The fourth, high looming in the mist,
  A war-ship's floating banners play.

Her yawl is launch'd ; light o'er the deep,
  Too kind, she wafts a ruffian band :
Her blue track lengthens to the bark,
  And soon on deck the miscreants stand.

Around they throw the baleful glance :
  Suspense holds mute the anxious crew—
Who is their prey ? poor sailor boy !
  The baleful glance is fix'd on you.

Nay, why that useless scrip unfold ?
  They damn'd the " lying yankee scrawl,"
Torn from thine hand, it strews the wave—
  They force thee trembling to the yawl.

Sick was thine heart as from the deck,
  The hand of friendship wav'd farewell ;
Mad was thy brain, as far behind,
  In the grey mist thy vessel fell.

One hope, yet, to thy bosom clung,
  The captain mercy might impart ;

Vain was that hope, which bade thee look,
  For mercy in a Pirate's heart.

What woes can man on man inflict,
  When malice joins with uncheck'd power ;
Such woes, unpitied and unknown,
  For many a month the sailor bore !

Oft gem'd his eye the bursting tear,
  As mem'ry linger'd on past joy ;
As oft they flung the cruel jeer,
  And damn'd the " chicken liver'd boy."

When sick at heart, with " hope defer'd,"
  Kind sleep his wasting form embrac'd,
Some ready minion ply'd the lash,
  And the lov'd dream of freedom chas'd.

Fast to an end his miseries drew :
  The deadly hectic flush'd his cheek :
On his pale brow the cold dew hung,
  He sigh'd, and sunk upon the deck !

The sailor's woes drew forth no sigh :
  No hand would close the sailor's eye :
Remorseless, his pale corse they gave,
  Unshrouded to the friendly wave.

And as he sunk beneath the tide,
  A hellish shout arose ;
Exultingly the demons cried,
  " So fare all Albion's Rebel Foes !"

should protect every Individual sailing under it," one British foreign secretary explained, "is too extravagant to require any serious Refutation."

The combination of impressment, British interference with the reexport trade, and the general harassment of neutral commerce instituted by both Great Britain and France would have perplexed the most informed and hardheaded of leaders, and in dealing with these problems Jefferson was neither informed nor hardheaded. He believed it much wiser to stand up for one's rights than to compro-

mise, yet he hated the very thought of war. Perhaps, being a southerner, he was less sensitive than he might have been to the needs of New England commercial interests. While the American merchant fleet passed 600,000 tons and continued to grow at an annual rate of over 10 percent, Jefferson kept only a skeleton navy on active service, despite the fact that the great powers were fighting a worldwide, no-holds-barred war. Instead of building a navy that other nations would have to respect, he relied on a tiny fleet of frigates and a swarm of gunboats that

The Ograbme ("embargo" spelled backwards), a unique snapping turtle created by cartoonist Alexander Anderson, effectively frustrates an American tobacco smuggler.

were useless against the Royal Navy—"a macabre monument," in the words of one historian, "to his hasty, ill-digested ideas" about defense.*

The Embargo Act

The frailty of Jefferson's policy became obvious once the warring powers began to attack neutral shipping in earnest. Between 1803 and 1807 the British seized over 500 American ships, Napoleon over 200 more. The United States could do nothing.

The ultimate in frustration came on June 22, 1807, off Norfolk, Virginia. The American 46-gun frigate *Chesapeake* had just left port for patrol duty in the Mediterranean. Among its crew were a British sailor who had deserted from H.M.S. *Halifax* and three Americans who had been illegally impressed by the captain of H.M.S. *Melampus* and had later escaped. The *Chesapeake* was barely out of sight of land when H.M.S. *Leopard* (56 guns) approached and signaled it to heave to. Thinking that *Leopard* wanted to make some routine communication, Cap-

tain James Barron did so. A British officer came aboard and demanded that the four "deserters" be handed over to him. Barron refused, whereupon as soon as the officer was back on board, *Leopard* opened fire on the unsuspecting American ship, killing three sailors. Barron had to surrender. The "deserters" were seized, and then the crippled *Chesapeake* was allowed to limp back to port.

The attack was in violation of international law, for no nation claimed the right to impress sailors from warships. The British government admitted this, though it delayed making restitution for years. The American press clamored for war, but the country had nothing to fight with. Jefferson contented himself with ordering British warships out of American territorial waters. However, he was determined to put a stop to the indignities being heaped on the flag by Great Britain and France. The result was the Embargo Act.

The Embargo Act prohibited all exports. American vessels could not clear for any foreign port, and foreign vessels could do so only if empty. Importing was not forbidden, but few foreign ships would come to the United States if they had to return without a cargo. Although the law was sure to injure the American economy, Jefferson hoped that it would work in two ways to benefit the nation. By keeping U.S. merchant ships off the seas, it would

---

* The gunboats had performed effectively against the Barbary pirates, but Jefferson was enamored of them mainly because they were cheap. A gunboat cost about $10,000 to build, a frigate well over $300,000.

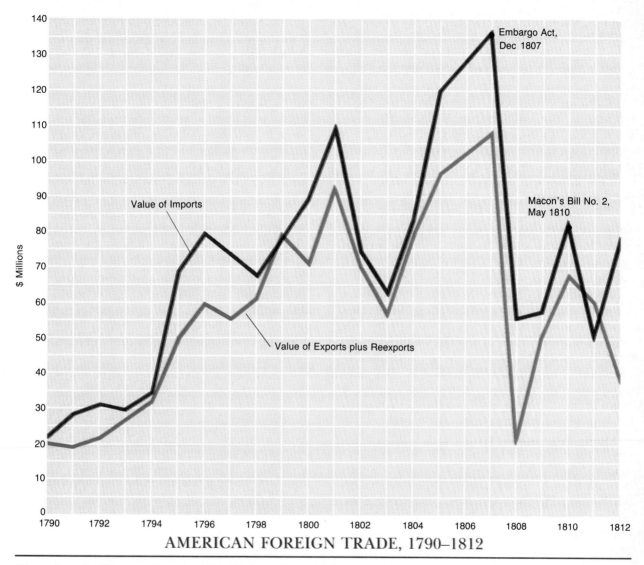

AMERICAN FOREIGN TRADE, 1790–1812

The embargo's effects are shown graphically here. The brief foreign trade spurt in 1810 was due to congressional passage of Macon's Bill No. 2. The space between the upper (import) line and the lower (export) line indicates a persistent foreign-trade deficit.

end all chance of injury to them and to the national honor. By cutting off American goods and markets, it would put great economic pressure on Britain and France to moderate policies toward American shipping. The fact that boycotts had repeatedly wrested concessions from the British during the crises preceding the Revolution was certainly in Jefferson's mind when he devised the embargo.

Seldom has a law been so bitterly resented and resisted by a large segment of the public. It de-

manded of the maritime interests far greater sacrifices than they could reasonably be expected to make. Massachusetts-owned ships alone were earning over $15 million a year in freight charges by 1807, and Bay State merchants were making far larger gains from the buying and selling of goods. Foreign commerce was the most expansive force in the economy, the chief reason for the nation's prosperity.

Losses through seizure were exasperating, but

they could be insured against. Impressment excited universal indignation, but it hit chiefly at the defenseless, the disreputable, and the obscure and never caused a labor shortage in the merchant marine. The profits of commerce were still tremendous. A Massachusetts senator estimated that if only one vessel in three escaped the blockade, the owner came out ahead. As John Randolph remarked in a typical sally, the administration was trying "to cure the corns by cutting off the toes."

The Embargo Act had catastrophic effects. Exports fell from $108 million in 1807 to $22 million in 1808, imports from $138 million to less than $57 million. Prices of farm products and manufactured goods reacted violently; seamen were thrown out of work; merchants found their businesses disrupted.

How many Americans violated the law is difficult to determine, but they were ingenious at discovering ways to do so. The most obvious way was to smuggle goods back and forth between Canada and the northeastern states. As James Madison recalled in later years, the political boundary lost all significance. People on both sides made the region "a world of itself," treating the Embargo Act as though the laws of Congress did not apply to them.

As for ocean commerce, American ships made hastily for blue water before the machinery of enforcement could be put into operation, not to return until the law was repealed. Shipping between American ports had not been outlawed, and coasting vessels were allowed to put into foreign ports when in distress. Suddenly, mysterious storms began to drive experienced skippers leagues off their courses, some as far as Europe. The brig *Commerce,* en route from Massachusetts to New Orleans, was "forced" by a shortage of water to make for Havana. Having replenished its casks, the brig exchanged its cargo for sugar.

The law permitted merchants with property abroad to send ships to fetch it. About 800 ships went off on such errands. Lawbreakers were difficult to punish. In the seaport towns, juries were no more willing to convict anyone of violating the Embargo Act than their fathers had been to convict those charged with violating the Townshend Acts. A mob at Gloucester, Massachusetts, destroyed a revenue cutter in the same spirit that Rhode Islanders exhibited in 1772 when they burned the *Gaspee.* Surely the embargo was a mistake. The United States ought either to have suffered the indignities heaped on its vessels for the sake of profits or, by constructing a powerful navy, made it dangerous for the belligerents to treat its merchant ships so roughly. Jefferson was too proud to choose the former alternative, too parsimonious to choose the latter. Instead he applied harsher and harsher regulations in a futile effort to accomplish his purpose. Militiamen patrolled the Canadian border; revenuers searched out smuggled goods without proper warrants. The illegal trade continued, and in his last months as president Jefferson simply gave up. Even then he would not admit that the embargo was a fiasco and urge its repeal. Only in Jefferson's last week in office did a leaderless Congress finally abolish it, substituting the Nonintercourse Act, which forbade trade only with Great Britain and France and authorized the president to end the boycott against either power by proclamation when and if it stopped violating the rights of Americans.

Milestones

1800	Jefferson elected president (the "Revolution of 1800")
1801	Judiciary Act of 1801 allows President Adams to appoint many Federalist judges before leaving office
1801–1805	War with the Barbary pirates
1803	Supreme Court declares part of Judiciary Act of 1793 unconstitutional (*Marbury* v. *Madison*)
	Louisiana Territory purchased from France
1804	Alexander Hamilton killed by Aaron Burr in a duel
1804–1806	Lewis and Clark expedition
1806	Burr conspiracy
1806–1807	Napoleon's Berlin and Milan decrees
1807	H.M.S *Leopard* attacks U.S.S *Chesapeake*
	Embargo Act

SUPPLEMENTARY READING

Titles marked with an asterisk have been published in paperback.

No student interested in Jefferson's political and social philosophy should miss sampling his writings. A useful compilation is Adrienne Koch and William Peden, **The Life and Selected Writings of Thomas Jefferson** (1944). Lance Banning, **The Jeffersonian Persuasion** (1978), is valuable, as are Joyce Appleby, **Capitalism and a New Social Order** (1984), and M. D. Peterson, **Thomas Jefferson and the New Nation*** (1970).

For a general treatment of the Jeffersonian era, consult Marshall Smelser, **The Democratic Republic*** (1968). On the parties of the era, see N. E. Cunningham, Jr., **The Jeffersonian Republicans in Power*** (1963), and D. H. Fischer, **The Revolution of American Conservatism: The Federalist Party in the Era of Jeffersonian Democracy*** (1965); on the structure of Jefferson's administration, see L. D. White, **The Jeffersonians*** (1951); and on Jefferson's management of the administration and of Congress, read J. S. Young, **The Washington Community*** (1966), a fascinating book.

Jefferson's battle with the judges can be followed in R. E. Ellis, **The Jeffersonian Crisis*** (1971). On *Marbury v. Madison*, see J. A. Garraty (ed.), **Quarrels That Have Shaped the Constitution*** (1964), and D. O. Dewey's more detailed **Marshall Versus Jefferson*** (1970).

On the Louisiana Purchase, see Alexander De Conde, **The Affair of Louisiana** (1976), Harry Ammon, **James Monroe** (1971), and George Dangerfield, **Chancellor Robert R. Livingston** (1960).

Jefferson's interest in the west is discussed in E. T. Martin, **Thomas Jefferson: Scientist*** (1952). An excellent general treatment of western exploration is contained in R. A. Billington, **Westward Expansion** (1967). On Lewis and Clark, see P. R. Cutright, **Lewis and Clark: Pioneering Naturalists** (1976), Richard Dillon, **Meriwether Lewis** (1965), and J. O. Steffen, **William Clark** (1977).

On the Burr Conspiracy, see T. P. Abernethy, **The Burr Conspiracy** (1954), and F. F. Bierbe, **Shout Treason: The Trial of Aaron Burr** (1959).

The best account of the neutral rights question is Bradford Perkins, **Prologue to War*** (1961).

The magnificent portrait of Jefferson at left, painted by Gilbert Stuart in 1805, is the official image of Jefferson that is currently reproduced on postage stamps. It is known as the Edgehill portrait, and it hung at Monticello for many years. The bust at right was made by the French sculptor Houdon when Jefferson was in France in 1789. It deliberately copies the look of the portrait busts so popular during the republican era of ancient Rome.

Monticello, designed in nearly every detail by Jefferson himself, was his home from 1772, the year he married the young widow Martha Skelton Wales, until his death in 1826.

Jefferson, a musician as well as a statesman and scientist, owned a number of instruments, including a harpsichord. The music stand to the right of the harpsichord allows four players to sit in a circle around it, while two more can stand and read their music from the upper tier.

Jefferson's bed was conveniently set in an alcove, so that he could get in and out of it on either side. A clock is handy on the wall at the foot of the bed. In the background, his surveying equipment stands beside the glass door, and his telescope is aimed out the window. The table has a revolving surface, like a lazy Susan.

The cluttered entry hall at Monticello greeted visitors in the years after the Lewis and Clark expedition with western mementos: the antlers of a deer and a stuffed bison's head, as well as a tableful of bones, rocks, and other natural history objects. One visitor commented, "There is no private gentleman in the world in possession of so complete a scientific, useful and ornamental collection."

Supremely practical, Jefferson devised a way to make more than one copy of a letter or document at a time. This apparatus, called a polygraph, holds a second pen, which moves over a second piece of paper as the writer composes on the first piece. Jefferson had three polygraphs.

Isaac Jefferson was born in 1775; this daguerreotype was taken about 1845. He was a Monticello slave who worked as a blacksmith and made nails for the plantation. His stories are the source of many details of Jefferson's domestic life.

A Roll of the proper slaves of Thomas Jefferson. Jan. 14. 1774.

Monticello.	Monticello.
* ⎧ Goliah.	+ ⎧ George
* ⎨ Hercules.	+ ⎨ Ursula.
+ ⎩ Jupiter. 1743.	⎧ George.
* ⎧ Gill.	⎨ Bagwell.
* ⎨ Fanny	⎩ Archy. 1773
+ ⎨ Ned. 1760	+ Frank 1757
⎨ Suckey 1765.	+ Bett. 1759
⎨ Frankey. 1767.	+ Scilla. 1762.
⎩ Gill. 1769.	
* ⎧ Quash	
* ⎨ Nell.	
* ⎨ Bella. 1757.	
* ⎨ Charles. 1760.	
⎩ Jenny. 1768.	
* Betty	
− ⎧ Juno	
* ⎨ Toby junr. 1753.	
− ⎩ Luna. 1758.	
* ⎧ Cate. about 1747.	
⎨ Hannah 1770.	
⎩ Rachael. 1773.	

* denotes a labourer in the ground.
+ denotes a titheable person following some o-
    ther occupation
− denotes a person discharged from labor on acct of age or infirmity.

A household as large as Monticello could not have been maintained without the help of many servants, and like other wealthy southerners Jefferson was a slave owner. Twenty-nine slaves are listed on the roll at right dated January 14, 1774. The persons not otherwise designated by a footnote were children under 10.

VII

America Escapes from Europe

WE OWE ALLEGIANCE TO NO CROWN.

*Our policy in regard to Europe . . . remains the same, which is, not
to interfere in the internal concerns of any of its powers, . . . to leave
the parties to themselves, in the hope that other powers will insure the
same course.*

MONROE DOCTRINE, *1823*

I t is a measure of Jefferson's popularity and of the political ineptitude of the Federalists that the Republicans won the election of 1808 handily despite the embargo. James Madison got 122 of the 173 electoral votes for the presidency, and the party carried both houses of Congress, although by reduced majorities.

Madison in Power

Madison was a small, neat, rather precise person, narrower in his interests than Jefferson but in many ways a deeper thinker. He was more conscientious in the performance of his duties and more consistent in adhering to his principles. Ideologically, however, they were as close as two active and intelligent people could be. Madison had no better solution to offer for the problem of the hour than Jefferson had had. The Nonintercourse Act proved difficult to enforce—once an American ship left port, there was no way to prevent the skipper from steering for England or France—and it exerted little economic pressure on the British, who continued to seize American vessels.

Late in 1809, at the urging of Secretary of the Treasury Albert Gallatin, who was concerned because the government was operating at a deficit, Representative Nathaniel Macon of North Carolina introduced a bill permitting American ships to go anywhere but closing United States ports to the ships of Britain and France. After protracted bickering in Congress, this measure was replaced by another, known as Macon's Bill No. 2, which removed all restrictions on commerce with France and Britain, though French and British warships were still barred from American waters. It authorized the president to reapply the principle of nonintercourse to either of the major powers if the other should "cease to violate the neutral commerce of the United States." This bill became law in May 1810.

The volume of United States commerce with the British Isles swiftly zoomed to preembargo levels. Trade with France remained much more limited because of the British fleet. Napoleon therefore announced that the Berlin and Milan decrees would be revoked in November on the understanding that Great Britain would abandon its own restrictive policies. Treating this ambiguous proposal as a statement of French policy (which it decidedly was not), Madison reapplied the nonintercourse policy to Great Britain. Napoleon, having thus tricked Madison into closing American ports to British ships and goods, continued to seize American ships and cargoes whenever it suited him to do so.

The British grimly refused to modify the orders in council unless it could be shown that the French had actually repealed the Berlin and Milan decrees—and this despite mounting complaints from their own businessmen that the new American nonimportation policy was cutting off a major market for their manufactures. Yet Madison could not afford either to admit that Napoleon had deceived him or to reverse American policy still another time. Reluctantly he came to the conclusion that unless Britain repealed the orders, the United States must declare war.

Tecumseh and the Prophet

There were other reasons for fighting besides British violations of neutral rights. The Indians were again making trouble, and western farmers believed that the British in Canada were egging them on. This had been true in the past but was no longer the case in 1811 and 1812. American domination of the southern Great Lakes region was no longer in question. Canadian officials had no desire to force a showdown between the Indians and the Americans, for that could have but one result. Aware of their own vulnerability, the Canadians wanted to preserve Indian strength in case war should break out between Great Britain and the United States.

American political leaders tended to believe that Indians should be encouraged to become farmers and to copy the "civilized" ways of whites. However, no government had been able to control the frontiersmen, who by bribery, trickery, and force were driving the tribes back year after year from the rich lands of the Ohio Valley. General William Henry Harrison, governor of Indiana Territory, a tough, relentless soldier, kept constant pressure on them. He wrested land from one tribe by promising it aid against a traditional enemy, from another as a penalty for having murdered a white man, from others by corrupting a few chiefs. Harrison justified his sordid behavior by citing the end in view—that "one of the fairest portions of the globe" be secured as "the seat of civilization, of science, and of true religion." The "wretched savages" should not be allowed to stand in the path of this worthy objective. As early as 1805 it was clear that unless something drastic was done, Harrison's aggressiveness, together with the corroding effects of white civilization, would soon obliterate the tribes.

At this point the Shawnee chief Tecumseh made a bold and imaginative effort to reverse the trend by binding all the tribes east of the Mississippi into a great confederation. Traveling from the Wisconsin country to the Floridas, he persuaded tribe after tribe to join him. "Let the white race perish," Tecumseh declared. "They seize your land; they corrupt your women. . . . Back whence they came, upon a trail of blood, they must be driven!"

To Tecumseh's political movement his brother Tenskwatawa, known as the Prophet, added the force of a moral crusade. Instead of aping white customs, the Prophet said, Indians must give up white ways, white clothes, and white liquor and reinvigorate their own culture. Ceding lands to the whites must stop because the Great Spirit intended that the land be used in common by all.

The Prophet, also called "The Open Door," lent religious fervor to his brother Tecumseh's antiwhite doctrine.

The Prophet was a fanatic who saw visions and claimed to be able to control the movement of heavenly bodies. Tecumseh, however, possessed true genius. A powerful orator and a great organizer, he had deep insight into the needs of his people. Harrison himself said of Tecumseh: "He is one of those uncommon geniuses which spring up occasionally to produce revolutions and overturn the established order of things." The two brothers made a formidable team. By 1811 thousands of Indians were organizing to drive the whites off their lands. Alarms swept through the west.

With about 1,000 soldiers, General Harrison marched boldly against the brothers' camp at Prophetstown, where Tippecanoe Creek joins the Wabash, in Indiana. Tecumseh was away recruiting men, and the Prophet recklessly ordered an assault on Harrison's camp outside the village on November 7, 1811. When the white soldiers held their ground despite the Prophet's magic, the Indians lost confidence and fell back. Harrison then destroyed Prophetstown.

While the Battle of Tippecanoe was pretty much

a draw, it disillusioned the Indians and shattered their confederation. Frontier warfare continued, but in the disorganized manner of former times. Like all such fighting, it was brutal and bloody.

Unwilling as usual to admit that their own excesses were the chief cause of the trouble, the settlers directed their resentment at the British in Canada. "This combination headed by the Shawanese prophet is a British scheme," a resolution adopted by the citizens of Vincennes, Indiana, proclaimed. As a result, the cry for war with Great Britain rang out all along the frontier.

Depression and Land Hunger

Some westerners pressed for war because they were suffering an agricultural depression. The prices they received for their wheat, tobacco, and other products in the markets of New Orleans were falling, and they attributed the decline to the loss of foreign markets and the depredations of the British. American commercial restrictions had more to do with the western depression than the British, and in any case the slow and cumbersome transportation and distribution system that western farmers were saddled with was the major cause of their difficulties. But the farmers were no more inclined to accept these explanations than they were to absolve the British from responsibility for the Indian difficulties. If only the seas were free, they reasoned, costs would go down, prices would rise, and prosperity would return.

To some extent western expansionism also heightened the war fever. The west contained immense tracts of virgin land, but westerners wanted more. Canada would surely fall to American arms in the event of war, the frontiersmen believed. So, apparently, would Florida, for Spain was now Britain's ally. Florida in itself provided no cause for a war, for it was sure to fall into American hands before long. In 1810 Madison had snapped up the extreme western section without eliciting any effective response from Spain.

So it was primarily because of Canada, nearby and presumably vulnerable, that westerners wanted war. It is also likely that President Madison saw an attack on Canada as a way to force the British to respect neutral rights. If Napoleon's Continental System cut Great Britain off from trade with northern Europe, Canada would be its only source of lumber and naval stores. Between 1808 and 1812 Canadian exports of lumber to Britain soared. Still more important in Madison's mind, if the United States conquered Canada, Britain's hope of obtaining food in Canada for its West Indian sugar islands would be shattered. Then it would have to end its hateful assaults and restrictions on American merchant ships or the islands' economy would collapse.

But westerners, and many easterners too, were more patriots than imperialists or merchants in 1811 and 1812. When their leaders in Congress, known as the "War Hawks," called for war against Great Britain, they did so because they saw no other way to defend the national honor and force repeal of the orders in council. The choice seemed to lie between war and surrender of true independence. As Madison put it, to bow to British policy would be to "recolonize" American foreign commerce.

Resistance to War

There were, however, large numbers of people who thought that a war against Great Britain would be a national calamity. Some Federalists would have resisted anything the administration proposed; Congressman Josiah Quincy of Massachusetts declared that he "could not be kicked" into the war, which he considered a cowardly, futile, and unconstitutional business designed primarily to ensure Madison's reelection. (Quincy saw no inconsistency between this opinion and his conviction that Madison was a pacifist.) According to Quincy, the War Hawks were "backwoodsmen" willing to wage a "cruel, wanton, senseless and wicked" war in order to swallow up Canada.

But other people based their objections on economics and a healthy realism. Powerful interests in the eastern maritime states were dead set against fighting, for the same reasons that had led them to resist the Embargo Act. No shipowner could view with equanimity the idea of taking on the largest navy in the world. Such persons complained sincerely enough about impressment and the orders in council, but war seemed to them worse by far. Self-interest led them to urge patience.

Such a policy would have been wise, for Great

Britain did not represent a real threat to the United States. British naval officers were high-handed, officials in London complacent, British diplomats in Washington second-rate and obtuse. Yet language, culture, and strong economic ties bound the two countries. Napoleon, in contrast, represented a tremendous potential danger. He had offhandedly turned over Louisiana, but even Jefferson, the chief beneficiary of his largess, hated everything he stood for. Jefferson called Napoleon "an unprincipled tyrant who is deluging the continent of Europe with blood."

No one understood the Napoleonic danger to America more clearly than the British; part of the stubbornness and arrogance of their maritime policy grew out of their conviction that Napoleon was a threat to all free nations. The *Times* of London declared: "The Alps and the Apennines of America are the British Navy. If ever that should be removed, a short time will suffice to establish the headquarters of a [French] Duke-Marshal at Washington." Yet by going to war with Britain, the United States was aiding Napoleon.

What made the situation even more unfortunate was the fact that by 1812 conditions had changed in England in a way that made a softening of British maritime policy likely. A depression caused chiefly by the increasing effectiveness of Napoleon's Continental System was plaguing the country. Manufacturers, blaming the slump on the loss of American markets, were urging repeal of the orders in council. Gradually, though with exasperating slowness, the government prepared to yield. On June 23, after a change of ministries, the new foreign secretary, Lord Castlereagh, suspended the orders. Five days earlier, alas, the United States had declared war.

The War of 1812

The illogic of the War Hawks in pressing for a fight was exceeded only by their ineffectiveness in planning and managing the struggle. By what possible strategy could the ostensible objective of the war be achieved? To construct a navy capable of challenging the British fleet would have been the work of many years and a more expensive proposition than the War Hawks were willing to consider. So hopeless

was that prospect that Congress failed to undertake any new construction in the first year of the conflict. Several hundred merchant ships lashed a few cannon to their decks and sailed off as privateers to attack British commerce. The navy's seven modern frigates, built during the war scare after the XYZ Affair, put to sea. But these forces could make no pretense of disputing Britain's mastery of the Atlantic.

For a brief moment the American frigates held center stage, for they were faster, tougher, larger, and more powerfully armed than their British counterparts. Barely two months after the declaration of war, Captain Isaac Hull in U.S.S. *Constitution* chanced upon H.M.S. *Guerrière* in mid-Atlantic, outmaneuvered the *Guerrière* brilliantly, brought down its mizzenmast with his first volley, and then gunned it into submission, a hopeless wreck. In October U.S.S. *United States,* captained by Stephen Decatur, hero of the war against the Barbary pirates, caught H.M.S. *Macedonian* off the Madeiras, pounded it unmercifully at long range, and forced the Britisher to surrender. The *Macedonian* was taken into New London as a prize; more than a third of the 300-man crew were casualties, while American losses were but a dozen. Then, in December, the *Constitution,* now under Captain William Bainbridge, took on the British frigate *Java* off Brazil. "Old Ironsides" shot away the *Java*'s mainmast and reduced it to a hulk too battered for salvage.

These victories had little influence on the outcome of the war. The Royal Navy had 34 frigates, 7 more powerful ships of the line, and dozens of smaller vessels. As soon as these forces could concentrate against them, the American frigates were immobilized, forced to spend the war gathering barnacles at their moorings while powerful British squadrons ranged offshore. The privateering merchantmen were more effective because they were so numerous; they captured more than 1,300 British vessels during the war. The best of them—vessels like *America* and *True-Blooded Yankee*—were redesigned, given more sail to increase their speed, and formidably armed. *America* captured 26 prizes valued at more than $1 million. *True-Blooded Yankee* took 27 and destroyed 7 more in a Scottish harbor.

Great Britain's one weak spot seemed to be Canada. The colony had but half a million inhabitants to oppose 7.5 million Americans. Only 2,257 British

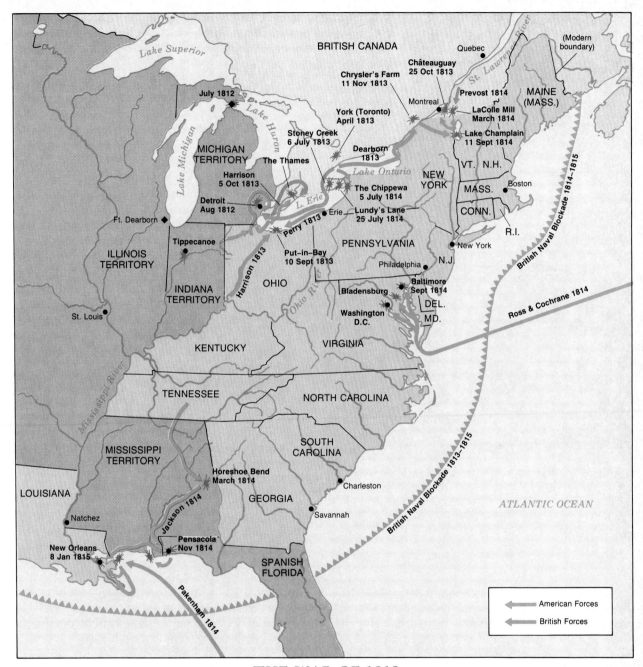

THE WAR OF 1812

regulars guarded the long border from Montreal to Detroit. The Canadian militia was feeble, and many of its members, being American-born, sympathized with the "invaders." According to the War Hawk congressman Henry Clay of Kentucky, the west was one solid horde of ferocious frontiersmen, armed to the teeth and thirsting for Canadian blood. Yet such talk was mostly brag and bluster; when Congress authorized increasing the army by 25,000 men, Kentucky produced 400 enlistments.

With a few exceptions, American forces in the War of 1812 were ill trained and led, and poor strategy resulted in several disgraceful defeats. Here, a resplendently dressed militia officer consults a map.

American military leadership proved extremely disappointing. Madison relied on officers who had served with distinction in the Revolution, but in most cases, as one biographer suggested, their abilities "appeared to have evaporated with age and long disuse." Instead of a concentrated strike against Canada's St. Lawrence River lifeline, which would have isolated Upper Canada, the generals planned a complicated three-pronged attack. It was a total failure. In July 1812 General William Hull, veteran of the battles of Trenton, Saratoga, and Monmouth and now governor of Michigan Territory, marched forth with 2,200 men against the Canadian positions facing Detroit. Hoping that the Canadian militia would desert, he delayed his assault, only to find his communications threatened by hostile Indians led by Tecumseh. Hastily he retreated to Detroit, and when the Canadians, under General Isaac Brock, pursued him, he surrendered the fort without firing a shot!

In October another force attempted to invade Canada from Fort Niagara. After an initial success, it was crushed by superior numbers, while a large contingent of New York militiamen watched from the east bank of the Niagara River, unwilling to fight outside their own state.

The third arm of the American attack was equally unsuccessful. Major General Henry Dearborn, who had fought honorably in the Revolution from Bunker Hill to Yorktown but who had grown so fat that he needed a specially designed cart to get from place to place, set out from Plattsburg, New York, at the head of an army of militiamen. Their objective was Montreal, but when they reached the border, the troops refused to cross. Dearborn meekly marched them back to Plattsburg.

Meanwhile, the British had captured Fort Michilimackinac in northern Michigan, and the Indians had taken Fort Dearborn (now Chicago), massacring 85 captives. Instead of sweeping triumphantly through Canada, the Americans found themselves trying desperately to keep the Canadians out of Ohio.

Stirred by these disasters, westerners rallied somewhat in 1813. General Harrison, the victor of Tippecanoe, headed an army of Kentuckians in a series of inconclusive battles against British troops and Indians led by Tecumseh. He found it impossible to recapture Detroit because a British squadron controlling Lake Erie threatened his communications. President Madison therefore assigned Captain Oliver Hazard Perry to the task of building a fleet to challenge this force. In September 1813, at Put-in-Bay near the western end of the lake, Perry destroyed the British vessels in a bloody battle in which 85 of the 103 men on Perry's flagship were casualties. "We have met the enemy and they are ours," he reported modestly. About a quarter of Perry's 400 men were blacks, which led him to remark that "the color of a man's skin" was no more an indication of his worth than "the cut and trimmings" of his coat.

In the midst of the battle of Lake Erie, Perry had to abandon his flagship, the Law-rence, *which had been shot to pieces by enemy fire. (Over three-fourths of the ship's crew were killed or wounded.) He was rowed to the* Niagara, *from which he directed the rest of the engagement.*

With the Americans in control of Lake Erie, Detroit became untenable for the British, and when they fell back, Harrison gave chase and defeated them at the Thames River, some 60 miles northeast of Detroit. Although little more than a skirmish, this battle had large repercussions. Tecumseh was among the dead (an eccentric American colonel, Richard Mentor Johnson, was to base a long and successful political career, culminating in his election as vice-president of the United States in 1836,* on his claim of having personally done in the great chief), and without him the Indians lost heart. But American attempts to win control of Lake Ontario and to invade Canada in the Niagara region were again thrown back. Late in 1813 the British captured Fort Niagara and burned the town of Buffalo. The conquest of Canada was as far from realization as ever.

The British fleet had intensified its blockade of American ports, extending its operations to New England waters previously spared to encourage the antiwar sentiments of local maritime interests. All along the coast, patrolling cruisers, contemptuous of Jefferson's puny gunboats, captured small craft, raided shore points to commandeer provisions, and collected ransom from port towns by threatening to bombard them. One captain even sent a detail ashore to dig potatoes for his ship's mess.

Britain on the Offensive

Until 1814 the British put relatively little effort into the American war, being concerned primarily with the struggle against Napoleon. However, in 1812 Napoleon had invaded Russia and been thrown back; thereafter, one by one, his European satellites rose against him. Gradually he relinquished his conquests; the Allies marched into France, Paris fell, and in April 1814 the emperor abdicated. Then the British, free to strike hard at the United States, dispatched some 14,000 veterans to Canada.

By the spring of 1814 British strategists had de-

---

* Of Johnson, a biographer writes: "His career as vice-president was inconspicuous. . . . As a politician, though not lacking in sagacity, he was lacking in purpose."

vised a master plan for crushing the United States. One army, 11,000 strong, was to march from Montreal, tracing the route that General Burgoyne had followed to disaster in the Revolution. A smaller amphibious force was to make a feint at the Chesapeake Bay area, destroying coastal towns and threatening Washington and Baltimore. A third army was to assemble at Jamaica and sail to attack New Orleans and bottle up the west.

It is necessary, in considering the War of 1812, to remind oneself repeatedly that in the course of the conflict many brave young men lost their lives. Without this sobering reflection, it would be easy to dismiss the conflict as a great farce compounded of stupidity, incompetence, and brag. The British, despite their years of experience against Napoleon, were scarcely more effective than the Americans when they assumed the offensive. They achieved significant success only in the diversionary attack in Chesapeake Bay.

While the main British army was assembling in Canada, 4,000 veterans under General Robert Ross sailed from Bermuda for the Chesapeake. After making a rendezvous with a fleet commanded by Vice-Admiral Sir Alexander Cochrane and Rear Admiral Sir George Cockburn, which had been terrorizing the coast, they landed in Maryland at the mouth of the Patuxent River, southeast of Washington. A squadron of gunboats "protecting" the capital promptly withdrew upstream; when the British pursued, their commander ordered them blown up to keep them from being captured.

The British troops marched rapidly toward Washington. At Bladensburg, on the outskirts of the city, they came upon an army twice their number, commanded by General William H. Winder, a Baltimore lawyer who had already been captured and released by the British in the Canadian fighting. While President Madison and other officials watched, the British charged—and Winder's army turned tail almost without firing a shot. The British swarmed into the capital and put most public buildings to the torch. Before personally setting fire to the White House, Admiral Cockburn took one of the president's hats and a cushion from Dolley Madison's chair as souvenirs and, finding the table set for dinner, derisively drank a toast to "Jemmy's health," adding, an observer coyly recalled, "pleasantries too vulgar for me to repeat."

Harrison's troops charging British artillerists and Indians at the Battle of the Thames. The death of Tecumseh in the battle was a shattering blow to the Indians of the Northwest.

"The Star-Spangled Banner"

This was the sum of the British success. When they attempted to take Baltimore, they were stopped by a formidable line of defenses devised by General Samuel Smith, a militia officer. General Ross fell in the attack. The fleet then moved up the Patapsco River and pounded Fort McHenry with its cannon, raining 1,800 shells on it in a 25-hour bombardment on September 13 and 14. While this attack was in progress, an American civilian, Francis Scott Key, who had been temporarily detained on one of the British ships, watched anxiously through the night. Key had boarded the vessel before the attack in an effort to obtain the release of an American doctor who had been taken into custody in Washington. As twilight faded, Key had seen the Stars and Stripes flying proudly over the battered fort. During the night the glare of rockets and bursting of bombs gave proof that the defenders were holding out. Then, by the first light of the new day, Key saw again the flag, still waving over Fort McHenry.

Drawing an old letter from his pocket, he dashed off the words to "The Star Spangled Banner," which, when set to music, was to become the national anthem of the United States.

To Key that dawn seemed a turning point in the war. He was roughly correct, for in those last weeks of the summer of 1814 the struggle began to move toward resolution. Unable to crack the defenses of Baltimore, the British withdrew to their ships; shortly after, they sailed to Jamaica to join the forces preparing to attack New Orleans.

The destruction of Washington had been a profound shock. Thousands came forward to enlist in the army. The new determination and spirit were strengthened by news from the northern front, where General Sir George Prevost had been leading the main British invasion force south from Montreal. At Plattsburg, on the western shore of Lake Champlain, his 1,000 Redcoats came up against a well-designed defense line manned by 3,300 Americans under General Alexander Macomb. Prevost called up his supporting fleet of four ships and a dozen gunboats. An American fleet of roughly similar strength under Captain Thomas Macdonough, a youthful officer who had served with Decatur against the Barbary pirates, came forward to oppose the British. On September 11, in a brutal battle at point-blank range, Macdonough destroyed the British ships and drove off the gunboats. With the Americans now threatening his flank, Prevost lost heart. Despite his overwhelming numerical superiority, he retreated to Canada.

The Treaty of Ghent

The war might as well have ended with the battles of Plattsburg, Washington, and Baltimore, for later military developments had no effect on the outcome. Earlier in 1814 both sides had agreed to discuss peace terms. Commissioners were appointed and negotiations begun during the summer at Ghent, in Belgium. The American delegation consisted of former secretary of the treasury Albert Gallatin; Speaker Henry Clay of the House of Representatives; James A. Bayard, a former senator; and two veteran diplomats, Jonathan Russell, minister to Sweden, and John Quincy Adams, minister to Russia. Adams was chairman. The British com-

missioners were lesser men by far, partly because they could refer important questions to the Foreign Office in nearby London for decision and partly because Britain's top-flight diplomats were engaged in settling the future of Europe at the Congress of Vienna.

The talks at Ghent were drawn out and frustrating. The British were in no hurry to sign a treaty, believing that their three-pronged offensive in 1814 would swing the balance in their favor. They demanded at first that the United States abandon practically all the Northwest Territory to the Indians and cede other points along the northern border to Canada. As to impressment and neutral rights, they would make no concessions at all. The Americans would yield no territory, for public opinion at home would have been outraged if they had. Old John Adams, for example, told President Madison at this time, "I would continue this war forever rather than surrender an acre."

Fortunately, the British came to realize that by pressing this point they would only spur the Americans to fight on. News of the defeat at Plattsburg modified their ambitions, and when the duke of Wellington advised that from a military point of view they had no case for territorial concessions so long as the United States controlled the Great Lakes, they agreed to settle for status quo antebellum, which is what the Americans sought. The other issues, everyone suddenly realized, had simply evaporated. The mighty war triggered by the French Revolution seemed finally over. The seas were free to all ships, and the Royal Navy no longer had need to snatch sailors from the vessels of the United States or of any other power. On Christmas Eve 1814 the treaty, which merely ended the state of hostilities, was signed. Although, like other members of his family, he was not noted for tact, John Quincy Adams rose to the spirit of the occasion. "I hope," he said, "it will be the last treaty of peace between Great Britain and the United States." And so it was.

The Hartford Convention

Before news of the treaty could cross the Atlantic, two events took place that had important effects yet would not have occurred had the news reached America more rapidly. The first was the Hartford

Convention, a meeting of New England Federalists held in December 1814 and January 1815 to protest the war and to plan for a convention of the states to revise the Constitution.

Sentiment in New England had opposed the war from the beginning. The governor of Massachusetts titled his annual address in 1813 "On the Present Unhappy War," and the General Court went on record calling the conflict "impolitic, improper, and unjust." The Federalist party had been quick to employ the discontent to revive its fortunes. Federalist-controlled state administrations refused to provide militia to aid in the fight and discouraged individuals and banks from lending money to the hard-pressed national government. Trade with the enemy flourished as long as the British fleet did not crack down on New England ports, and goods flowed across the Canadian line in at least as great a volume as during Jefferson's embargo.

Their attitude toward the war made the Federalists even more unpopular with the rest of the country, and this in turn encouraged extremists to talk of seceding from the Union. After Massachusetts summoned the meeting of the Hartford Convention, the fear was widespread that the delegates would propose a New England confederacy, thereby striking at the Union in a moment of great trial.

Luckily for the country, moderate Federalists controlled the convention. They approved a statement that in case of "deliberate, dangerous and palpable infractions of the Constitution" a state has the right "to interpose its authority" to protect itself. This concept, similar to that expressed in the Kentucky and Virginia resolutions by the Republicans when they were in the minority, was accompanied by a list of proposed constitutional amendments designed to make the national government conform more closely to the New England ideal. These would have (1) repealed the Three-fifths Compromise on representation and direct taxes, which favored the slaveholding states, (2) required a two-thirds vote of Congress for the admission of new states and for declaring war, (3) reduced Congress's power to restrict trade by measures such as embargoes, (4) limited presidents to a single term, and (5) made it illegal for naturalized citizens to hold national office.

Nothing formally proposed at Hartford was treasonable, but the proceedings were kept secret, and rumors of impending secession were rife. In this atmosphere came the news from Ghent of an honorable peace. The Federalists had been denouncing the war and predicting a British triumph; now they were discredited.

The Battle of New Orleans

Still more discrediting to Federalists was the second event that would not have happened had communications been more rapid: the Battle of New Orleans. During the fall of 1814 the British had gathered an army at Negril Bay in Jamaica, commanded by Major General Sir Edward Pakenham, brother-in-law of the duke of Wellington. Late in November an armada of 60 ships set out for New Orleans with 11,000 soldiers. Instead of sailing directly up from the mouth of the Mississippi as the Americans expected, Pakenham approached the city by way of Lake Borgne, to the east. Proceeding through a maze of swamps and bayous, he advanced close to the city's gates before being detected. Early on the afternoon of December 23, three mud-spattered local planters burst into the headquarters of General Andrew Jackson, commanding the defenses of New Orleans, with the news.

For once in this war of error and incompetence the United States had the right man in the right place at the right time. After his Revolutionary War experiences, Jackson had studied law, then moved west, settling in Nashville, Tennessee. He served briefly in both houses of Congress and was active in Tennessee affairs. Jackson was a hard man and fierce-tempered, frequently involved in brawls and duels, but he was an honest man and, by western standards, a good public servant. When the war broke out, he was named major general of volunteers. Almost alone among nonprofessional troops during the conflict, his men won impressive victories, crushing the Creek Indians in a series of battles in Alabama.

Jackson's success was due to his toughness and determination, a determination that his biographer Robert Remini describes as "virtually demonic," and "sheer, total, concentrated." Discipline based on fear, respect, and their awareness of his genuine concern for their well-being made his individualistic frontier militiamen into an army. His men called

Jackson Old Hickory; the Indians called him Sharp Knife.

Following these victories, Jackson was assigned the job of defending the Gulf Coast against the expected British strike. Although he had misjudged Pakenham's destination, he was ready when the news of the British arrival reached him. "By the Eternal," he vowed, "they shall not sleep on our soil." "Gentlemen," he told his staff officers, "the British are below; we must fight them tonight."

While the British rested and waited reinforcements, planning to take the city the next morning, Jackson rushed up men and guns. At 7:30 P.M. on December 23 he struck hard, taking the British by surprise. But Pakenham's veterans rallied quickly, and the battle was inconclusive. With Redcoats

Although needless militarily, the American victory at New Orleans stimulated nationalism and made Andrew Jackson a hero overnight. This imaginative view of the battle was printed on a handkerchief.

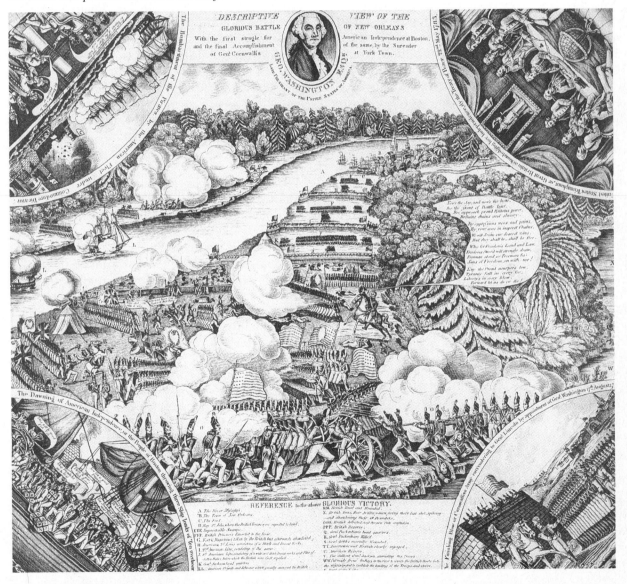

pouring in from the fleet, Jackson fell back to a point 5 miles below New Orleans and dug in.

He chose his position wisely. On his right was the Mississippi, on his left an impenetrable swamp, to the front an open field. On the day before Christmas (while the commissioners in Ghent were signing the peace treaty), Jackson's army, which included a segregated unit of free black militiamen, erected an earthen parapet about 10 yards behind a dry canal bed. Here the Americans would make their stand.

For two weeks Pakenham probed the American line. Jackson strengthened his defenses daily. At night, patrols of silent Tennesseans slipped out with knife and tomahawk to stalk British sentries. They called this grim business "going hunting." On January 8, 1815, Pakenham ordered an all-out frontal assault. The American position was formidable, but his men had defeated Napoleon. At dawn, through the lowland mists, the Redcoats moved forward with fixed bayonets. Pakenham assumed that the undisciplined Americans—about 4,500 strong—would run at the sight of bare steel.

The Americans did not run. Perhaps they feared the wrath of their commander more than enemy bayonets. Artillery raked the advancing British, and when the range closed to about 150 yards, the riflemen opened up. Jackson had formed his men in three ranks behind the parapet. One rank fired, then stepped down as another took its place. By the time the third had loosed its volley, the first had reloaded and was ready to fire again. Nothing could stand against this rain of lead. General Pakenham was wounded twice, then killed by a shell fragment while calling up his last reserves. During the battle a single brave British officer reached the top of the parapet. When retreat was finally sounded, the British had suffered almost 2,100 casualties, including nearly 300 killed. Thirteen Americans lost their lives, and 58 more were wounded or missing.

Fruits of "Victory"

Word of Jackson's magnificent triumph reached Washington almost simultaneously with the good news from Ghent. People found it easy to confuse the chronology and consider the war a victory won on the battlefield below New Orleans instead of the standoff it had been. Jackson became the "Hero of New Orleans"; his proud fellow citizens rated his military abilities superior to those of the duke of Wellington, the conqueror of Napoleon. The nation rejoiced. One sour Republican complained that the Federalists of Massachusetts had fired off more powder and wounded more men celebrating the victory than they had during the whole course of the conflict. The Senate ratified the peace treaty unanimously, and the frustrations and failures of the past few years were forgotten. Moreover, American success in holding off Great Britain despite internal frictions went a long way toward convincing European nations that both the United States and its republican form of government were here to stay. The powers might accept these truths with less pleasure than the Americans, but accept them they did.

The nation had suffered relatively few casualties and little economic loss, except to the shipping interests. The Indians were the main losers in the contest. When Jackson defeated the Creeks, for example, he forced them to cede 23 million acres to the United States.

The war completed the destruction of the Federalist party. The success of the Jeffersonians' political techniques had inspired younger Federalists in many parts of the country to adopt the rhetoric of democracy and, more important, to perfect local organizations. In 1812 the party made significant gains in the northeast, electing numbers of congressmen and winning many state and local offices. They did not run a candidate for president, but their support enabled the dissident New York Republican De Witt Clinton to obtain 89 electoral votes to Madison's 128.

Their private correspondence reveals that these Federalists were no more enchanted by the virtues of mass democracy than their elders, but by mouthing democratic slogans they revived the party in many districts. Now the results of the war undermined their efforts. They had not supported the war effort; they had argued that the British could not be defeated; they had dealt clandestinely with the enemy; they had even threatened to break up the Union. So long as the issue remained in doubt, these policies won considerable support, but New Orleans made the party an object of ridicule and scorn. It soon disappeared even in New England, swamped beneath a wave of patriotism that flooded the land.

The chief reason for the happy results of the war had little to do with American events. After 1815 Europe settled down to what was to be a century of relative peace. With peace came an end to serious foreign threats to America and a revival of commerce. European emigration to the United States, long held back by the troubled times, spurted ahead, providing the expanding country with its most valuable asset—strong, willing hands to do the work of developing the land. The mood of Jefferson's first term, when democracy had reigned amid peace and plenty, returned with a rush. And the nation, having had its fill of international complications, turned in on itself as Jefferson had wished. The politicians, ever sensitive to public attitudes, had learned what seemed at the time a valuable lesson. Foreign affairs were a potent cause of domestic conflict. The volatile character of sectional politics was thus another reason why America should escape from involvement in European affairs.

Anglo-American Rapprochement

There remained a few matters to straighten out with Great Britain, Spain, and Europe generally. Since no territory had changed hands at Ghent, neither signatory had reason to harbor a grudge. There was no sudden flowering of Anglo-American friendship. British conservatives continued, in the words of the historian George Dangerfield, to view the United States as "little more than a grimy republican thumbprint" on the pages of history, and the device of "twisting the British lion's tail" remained an important tool in the workchest of many an American politician for the rest of the century. Yet for years no serious trouble marred Anglo-American relations. The war had taught the British to respect Americans, if not to love them.

In this atmosphere the two countries worked out peaceful solutions to a number of old problems. American trade was becoming ever more important to the British, that of the sugar islands less so. In July 1815 they therefore signed a commercial convention ending discriminatory duties and making other adjustments favorable to trade. Boundary dif-

ficulties also moved toward resolution. At Ghent the diplomats had created several joint commissions to settle the disputed boundary between the United States and Canada. Many years were to pass before the line was finally drawn, but establishing the principle of defining the border by negotiation was important. In time, a line extending over 3,000 miles was agreed to without the firing of a single shot.

Immediately after the war the British reinforced their garrisons in Canada and began to rebuild their shattered Great Lakes fleet. The United States took similar steps. But both nations found the cost of rearming more than they cared to bear. When the United States suggested demilitarizing the lakes, the British agreed. The Rush-Bagot Agreement of 1817 limited each country to one 100-ton vessel armed with a single 18-pounder on Lake Champlain and another on Lake Ontario. They were to have two each for all the other Great Lakes.

Gradually, as an outgrowth of this decision, the entire border was demilitarized, a remarkable achievement. In the convention of 1818 the two countries agreed to the 49th parallel as the northern boundary of Louisiana Territory between Lake of the Woods and the Rockies and also to the joint control of the Oregon country for ten years. The question of the rights of Americans in the Labrador and Newfoundland fisheries, which had been much disputed during the Ghent negotiations, was settled amicably.

The Transcontinental Treaty

The acquisition of Spanish Florida and the settlement of the western boundary of Louisiana were also accomplished as an aftermath of the War of 1812, but in a far different spirit. Spain's control of the Floridas was feeble. West Florida had passed into American hands by 1813, and frontiersmen in Georgia were eyeing East Florida greedily. Indians struck frequently into American territory from Florida, then fled to sanctuary across the line. American slaves who escaped across the border could not be recovered. In 1818 James Monroe, who had been elected president in 1816, ordered General Andrew Jackson to clear raiding Seminole Indians from American soil and to pursue them into Florida if necessary. Seizing on these instructions, Jackson marched into Florida and easily captured two Spanish forts.

Although Jackson eventually withdrew from Florida, the impotence of the Spanish government made it obvious even in Madrid that if nothing were done, the United States would soon fill the power vacuum by seizing the territory. The Spanish also feared for the future of their tottering Latin American empire, especially the northern provinces of Mexico, which stood in the path of American westward expansion. Spain and the United States had never determined where Louisiana Territory ended and Spanish Mexico began. In return for American acceptance of a boundary as far east of the Rio Grande as possible, Spain was ready to surrender Florida.

For these reasons the Spanish minister in Washington, Luis de Onís, undertook in December 1817 to negotiate a treaty with John Quincy Adams, Monroe's secretary of state. Adams pressed the minister mercilessly on the question of the western boundary, driving a bargain that would have done credit to the most tightfisted of his Yankee ancestors. Onís opened their talks by proposing a line in the middle of what is now Louisiana, and when Adams countered by demanding a boundary running through present-day Texas, Onís professed to be shocked. Abstract right, not power, should determine the settlement, he said. "Truth is of all times, and reason and justice are founded upon immutable principles." To this Adams replied: "That truth is of all times and that reason and justice are founded upon

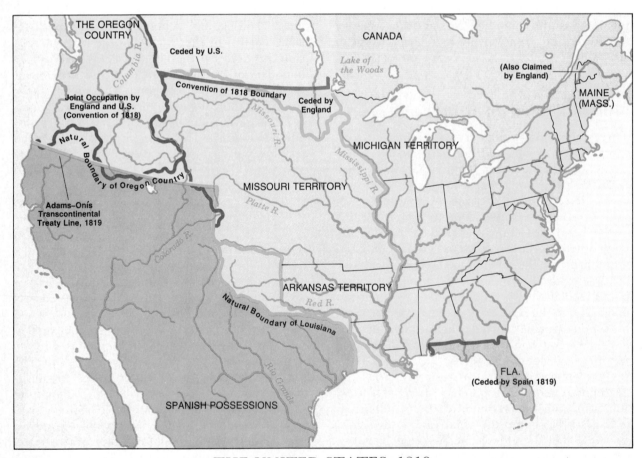

THE UNITED STATES, 1819

immutable principles has never been contested by the United States, but neither truth, reason, nor justice consists in stubbornness of assertion, nor in the multiplied repetition of error."

In the end Onís could only yield. He saved Texas for his monarch but accepted a boundary to Louisiana Territory that followed the Sabine, Red, and Arkansas rivers to the Continental Divide and the 42nd parallel to the Pacific, thus abandoning Spain's claim to a huge area beyond the Rockies that had no connection at all with the Louisiana Purchase. Adams even compelled him to agree that when the boundary followed rivers, United States territory was to extend to the farthest bank, not merely to midstream. The United States obtained Florida in return for a mere $5 million, paid not to Spain but to Americans who held claims against the Spanish government.

This "Transcontinental Treaty" was signed in 1819, though ratification was delayed until 1821. Most Americans at the time thought the acquisition of Florida the most important part of the treaty, but Adams, whose vision of America's future was truly continental, knew better. "The acquisition of a definite line of boundary to the [Pacific] forms a great epoch in our history," he recorded in his diary.

The Monroe Doctrine

Concern with defining the boundaries of the United States did not reflect a desire to limit expansion; rather, the feeling was that there should be no more quibbling and quarreling with foreign powers that might distract the people from the great task of national development. The classic enunciation of this point of view, the completion of America's withdrawal from Europe, was the Monroe Doctrine.

Two separate strands met in this pronouncement. The first led from Moscow to Alaska and down the Pacific Coast to the Oregon country. Beginning with the explorations of Vitus Bering in 1741, the Russians had maintained an interest in fishing and fur trading along the northwest coast of North America. In 1821 the czar extended his claim south to the 51st parallel and forbade the ships of other powers to enter coastal waters north of that point. This announcement was disturbing.

The second strand ran from the courts of the European monarchs to Latin America. Between 1817 and 1822 practically all of the region from the Rio Grande to the Strait of Magellan had won its independence. Spain, former master of nearly all the area except Brazil, was too weak to win it back by force, but Austria, Prussia, France, and Russia decided at the Congress of Verona in 1822 to try to regain the area for Spain in the interests of "legitimacy." There was talk of sending a large French army to South America. This possibility also caused grave concern in Washington.

To the Russian threat, Monroe and Secretary of State Adams responded with a terse warning: "The American continents are no longer subjects for any new European colonial establishments." This statement did not impress the Russians, but they had no intention of colonizing the region. In 1824 they signed a treaty with the United States abandoning all claims below the present southern limit of Alaska (54° 40′ north latitude) and removing their restrictions on foreign shipping.

The Latin American problem was more complex. The United States was not alone in its alarm at the prospect of a revival of French or Spanish power in that region. Great Britain, having profited greatly from the breakup of the mercantilistic Spanish empire by developing a thriving commerce with the new republics, had no intention of permitting a restoration of the old order. But the British monarchy preferred not to recognize the new revolutionary South American republics, for England itself was only beginning to recover from a period of social upheaval as violent as any in its history. Bad times and high food prices had combined to cause riots, conspiracies, and angry demands for parliamentary reform.

In 1823 the British foreign minister, George Canning, suggested to the American minister in London that the United States and Britain issue a joint statement opposing any French interference in South America, pledging that they themselves would never annex any part of Spain's old empire, and saying nothing about recognition of the new republics. This proposal of joint action with the British was flattering to the United States but scarcely in its best interests. The United States had already recognized the new republics, and it had no desire to help Great Britain retain its South American trade. As Secretary Adams pointed out, to agree to the proposal would be to abandon the possibility of someday adding Cuba or any other part of Latin America to the United States. America should act independently, Adams urged. "It would be more candid, as well as more dignified, to avow our principles explicitly . . . than to come in as a cockboat in the wake of the British man-of-war."

Monroe heartily endorsed Adams's argument and decided to include a statement of American policy in his annual message to Congress in December 1823. "The American continents," he wrote,

"by the free and independent condition which they have assumed and maintain, are henceforth not to be considered as subjects for future colonization by any European powers." Europe's political system was "essentially different" from that developing in the New World, and the two should not be mixed. The United States would not interfere with existing European colonies in North or South America and would avoid involvement in strictly European affairs, but any attempt to extend European control to countries in the hemisphere that had already won

The thirty years from 1790 to 1820 saw a sizable increase in population. The growth was especially great in the decade from 1810 to 1820, with a 33.1 percent increase in national population. Some of the largest increases were in what was earlier called the Old Northwest; the population of the area making up Illinois, Indiana, and Michigan territories, for example, grew from 31,000 to more than 200,000 during that decade.

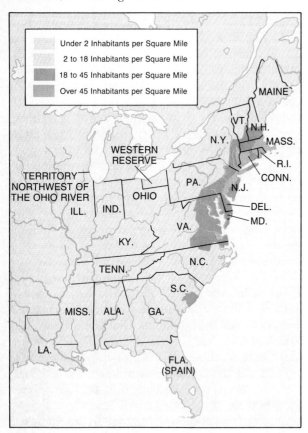

POPULATION DENSITY, 1790

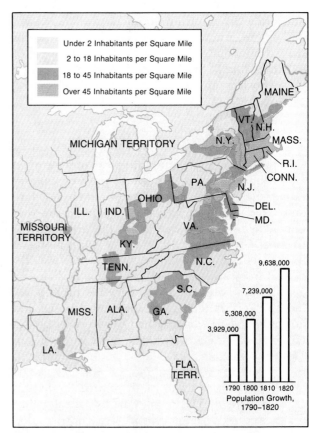

POPULATION DENSITY, 1820

their independence would be considered, Monroe warned, "the manifestation of an unfriendly disposition toward the United States" and consequently a threat to the nation's "peace and safety."

This policy statement—it was not dignified with the title Monroe Doctrine until decades later—attracted little notice in Europe or Latin America and not much more at home. Obviously, the United States, whose own capital had been overrun by a mere raiding party less than a decade before, could not police the entire Western Hemisphere. European statesmen dismissed Monroe's message as "arrogant" and "blustering," worthy only of "the most profound contempt." Latin Americans, while appreciating the intent behind it, knew better than to count on American aid in case of attack.

Nevertheless, the principles laid down by President Monroe so perfectly expressed the wishes of the people of the United States that when the country grew powerful enough to enforce them, there was little need to alter or embellish his pronouncement. However understood at the time, the doctrine may be seen as the final stage in the evolution of American independence.

From this perspective, the famous Declaration of 1776 merely began a process of separation and self-determination. The peace treaty ending the Revolutionary War was a further step, and Washington's neutrality proclamation of 1793 was another, demonstrating as it did the capacity of the United States to determine its own best interests despite the treaty of alliance with France. The removal of British troops from the northwest forts, achieved by the Jay Treaty, marked the next stage. Then the Louisiana Purchase made a further advance toward true independence by assuring that the Mississippi River could not be closed to the commerce so vital to the development of the western territories. The standoff War of 1812 ended any lingering British hope of regaining control of America, and the Transcontinental Treaty pushed the last European power from the path of westward expansion. Monroe's doctrine was a kind of public announcement that the sovereign United States had completed its independence and wanted nothing better than to be left alone to concentrate on its own development. Better yet if Europe could be made to allow the entire hemisphere to follow its own path.

The Era of Good Feelings

The person who gave his name to the so-called doctrine was an unusually lucky man. James Monroe lived a long life in good health and saw close up most of the great events in the history of the young republic. At the age of 18 he shed his blood for liberty at the glorious Battle of Trenton. He was twice governor of Virginia, a United States senator, and a Cabinet member. He was at various times the nation's representative in Paris, Madrid, and London. Elected president in 1816, his good fortune continued. The world was finally at peace, the country united and prosperous. A person of good feeling who would keep a steady hand on the helm and hold to the present course seemed called for, and Monroe possessed exactly the qualities that the times required. "He is a man whose soul might be turned wrongside outwards, without discovering a blemish," Jefferson said, and John Quincy Adams, a harsh critic of most public figures, praised Monroe's courtesy, sincerity, and sound judgment.

Courtesy and purity of soul do not always suffice to make a good president. In more troubled times Monroe might well have brought disaster, for he was neither a person of outstanding intellect nor a forceful leader. He blazed few paths, built no personal machine. Speaking of his policies and beliefs, the historian Ernest R. May concluded: "None was unique to Monroe." May added that Monroe had "less than total confidence in his opinions." The Monroe Doctrine, by far the most significant achievement of his administration, was as much the work of Secretary of State Adams as his own. No one ever claimed that Monroe was much better than second-rate, yet when his first term ended, he was reelected without organized opposition.

Monroe seemed to epitomize the resolution of the conflicts that had divided the country between the end of the Revolution and the Peace of Ghent. In his long career he was always a nationalist—his biographer Harry Ammon has subtitled the story of Monroe's life "The Quest for National Identity."

By 1817 the divisive issues of earlier days had vanished. Monroe dramatized their disappearance by beginning his first term with a goodwill tour of New England, heartland of the opposition. The tour was a triumph. Everywhere the president was greeted with tremendous enthusiasm. After he visited Boston, once the headquarters and now the graveyard of Federalism, a Federalist newspaper, the *Columbian Centinel,* gave the age its name. Pointing out that the celebrations attending Monroe's visit had brought together in friendly intercourse many persons "whom party politics had long severed," it dubbed the times the Era of Good Feelings.

It has often been said that the harmony of Monroe's administrations was superficial, that beneath the calm lay potentially disruptive issues that had not yet begun to influence national politics. The dramatic change from the unanimity of Monroe's second election to the fragmentation of four years later, when four candidates divided the vote and the House of Representatives had to choose the president, supports the point.

Nevertheless, the people of the period had good reasons for thinking it extraordinarily harmonious. Peace, prosperity, liberty, and progress—all flourished in 1817 in the United States. The heirs of Jefferson had accepted, with a mixture of resignation and enthusiasm, most of the economic policies advocated by the Hamiltonians. In 1816 Madison put his signature to a bill creating a new national bank almost exactly in the image of Hamilton's, which had expired before the War of 1812, and to a protective tariff that, if less comprehensive than the kind Hamilton had wanted, marked an important concession to rising manufacturing interests. Monroe accepted the principle of federal aid for transportation projects, approving a bill authorizing Congress to invest $300,000 in the Chesapeake and Delaware Canal Company.

The Jeffersonian balance between individual liberty and responsible government, having survived both bad management and war, had justified itself to the opposition. The new unity was symbolized by the restored friendship of Jefferson and John Adams. In 1801 Adams had slipped sulkily out of Washington without waiting to attend his successor's inauguration, but after ten years of stony silence, the two old collaborators, abetted by Dr. Benjamin Rush, effected a reconciliation. Although they continued to disagree vigorously about matters of philosophy and government, the bitterness between them disappeared entirely. By Monroe's day, Jefferson was writing long letters to "my dear friend," ranging over such subjects as theology, the proper reading of the classics, and agricultural improvements and was receiving equally warm and voluminous replies. "Whether you or I were right," Adams wrote amiably to Jefferson, "Posterity must judge."

When political divisions appeared again, as they soon did, it was not because the old balance had been shaky. Few of the new controversies challenged Republican principles or revived old issues. Instead, these controversies were children of the present and the future, products of the continuing growth of the country.

Milestones

1808	James Madison elected president		Francis Scott Key writes "The Star Spangled Banner" during the bombardment of Fort McHenry by the British
1809	Nonintercourse Act		
1810	Macon's Bill No. 2		
1811	Battle of Tippecanoe		
1812	Congress declares war on Great Britain		Hartford Convention
	Naval victories of U.S.S. *Constitution* and U.S.S. *United States*		Treaty of Ghent officially ends the War of 1812
1813	Battle of Lake Erie	1815	Battle of New Orleans
	Battle of the Thames, death of Tecumseh	1817	Rush-Bagot Agreement with Great Britain
1814	British burn Washington, D.C.	1819	Transcontinental Treaty with Spain
		1823	Monroe Doctrine

SUPPLEMENTARY READING

Titles marked with an asterisk have been published in paperback.

Madison's administration can be followed in Irving Brant, **James Madison: The President** (1956), and Ralph Ketcham, **James Madison** (1971). J. W. Pratt first played up the role of the west in triggering the War of 1812 in his **Expansionists of 1812** (1925). The best modern account of the causes and course of the war is J. C. A. Stagg, **Mr. Madison's War** (1983); a good brief treatment is H. L. Coles, **The War of 1812*** (1965). Irving Brant, **James Madison: Commander in Chief** (1961), vigorously defends Madison's handling of the war. Jackson's part in the conflict is described in R. V. Remini, **Andrew Jackson and the Course of American Empire** (1977).

On the Treaty of Ghent, see F. L. Engelman, **The Peace of Christmas Eve** (1962). Bradford Perkins, **Castlereagh and Adams** (1964), and George Dangerfield, **The Era of Good Feelings*** (1952), also discuss the settlement intelligently. On the decline of the Federalist party and the Hartford Convention, consult D. H. Fischer, **The Revolution of American Conservatism** (1965), and J. M. Banner, **To the Hartford Convention** (1981).

On the postwar diplomatic settlements and the Era of Good Feelings, see E. R. May, **The Making of the Monroe Doctrine** (1975), Perkins's **Castlereagh and Adams,** S. F. Bemis, **John Quincy Adams** (1949), Dangerfield's **Era of Good Feelings,** and Harry Ammon, **James Monroe: The Quest for National Identity** (1971).

VIII

The Cords of Union

Our confederacy comprehends within its vast limits, great diversity of interests; agricultural, planting, farming, commercial, navigating, fishing, manufacturing. . . . Some of these are peculiar to particular sections of the country. But all these great interests are confided to the protection of one government—to the fate of one ship; and a most gallant ship it is, with a noble crew.

HENRY CLAY, *1824*

N ational unity speeded national expansion, yet expansion, paradoxically, endangered national unity. For as the country grew, new differences appeared within its sections even as the ties binding the parts became stronger and more numerous. Growth in the 30 years after the ratification of the Constitution had been phenomenal even for a country that took growth for granted. The area of the United States doubled, but very little of the Louisiana Purchase had been settled by 1820. More significant, the population of the nation had more than doubled, from 4 million to 9.6 million. The pace of westward movement had also quickened; by 1820 more than 2.2 million people had settled in the Mississippi Valley, and the moving edge of the frontier ran in a long, irregular curve from Michigan to Arkansas.

Perhaps the most remarkable feature of this growth was that nearly all of it resulted from natural increase. Only about 250,000 immigrants entered the United States between 1790 and 1820, for the turbulent conditions in Europe during the wars had slowed the flow of humanity across the Atlantic to a trickle.

Sectional Issues: Tariff Policy

The War of 1812 and the depression that struck the country in 1819 shaped many of the controversies that agitated political life during the Era of Good Feelings. The tariff question was affected by both. Before the War of 1812 the level of duties averaged about 12.5 percent of the value of dutiable products, but to meet the added expenses occasioned by the conflict, Congress doubled all tariffs. In 1816, when the revenue was no longer needed, a new act kept duties close to wartime levels. Infant industries that had grown up during the years of embargo, nonintercourse, and war were able to exert considerable pressure, for they could show that imports had rocketed from $12 million in 1814 to $113 million in 1815 and were still rising. The act especially favored textiles because the British were dumping cloth in America at bargain prices in their attempt to regain lost markets. The depression added to the strength of the protectionists. Unemployed workers and many farmers became convinced that prosperity would return only if American industry were shielded against foreign competition.

There was backing for high duties in every section. Except for New England, where the shipping interests favored free trade and where the booming mills of the Boston Associates were not seriously injured by foreign competition, the North favored protection. A few southerners hoped that textile mills would spring up in their region; more supported protection on the grounds that national self-sufficiency was necessary in case of war. In the West small manufacturers in the towns added their support, and so did farmers, who were counting on workers in the new eastern factories to consume much of their wheat and corn and hogs. But with the passage of time the South rejected protection almost completely. Industry failed to develop, and since southerners exported most of their cotton and tobacco, they soon concluded that besides increasing the cost of nearly everything they bought, high duties on imports would limit the foreign market for southern staples by inhibiting international exchange. As this fact became clear, the West tended to divide on the tariff question: The Northwest and much of Kentucky, which had a special interest in protecting its considerable hemp production, fa-

217

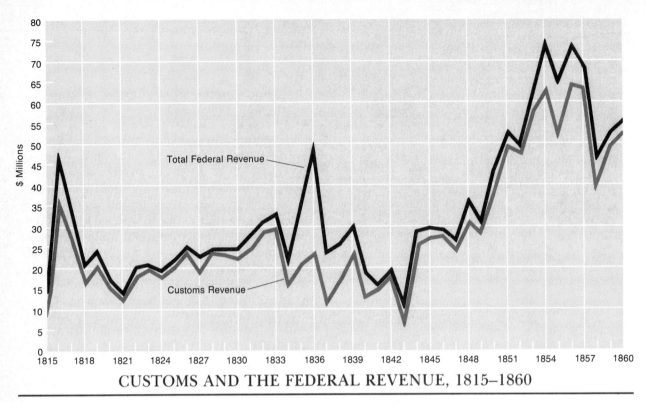

CUSTOMS AND THE FEDERAL REVENUE, 1815–1860

In some years—1841, for example—the amounts received from customs duties supplied nearly all the federal revenues, so it is no surprise that the tariff was a major political and sectional issue in the years between the War of 1812 and the Civil War. The jump in federal revenues in the mid-1830s, over and above the usual customs duties, was caused largely by increased public land sales (see chart on page 271).

vored high duties; the Southwest, where cotton was the major crop, favored low duties.

Sectional Issues: Banks

National banking policy was another important political issue affected by the war and the depression. Presidents Jefferson and Madison had managed to live with the Bank of the United States despite its dubious constitutionality, but its charter was not renewed when it expired in 1811. Aside from the constitutional question, the major opposition to recharter came from state banks eager to take over the business of the Bank for themselves. The fact

that English investors owned most of the Bank's stock (the government had sold 2,200 shares to the British banking house of Baring Brothers in 1802) was also used as an argument against recharter.

The war played havoc with American banking. Many more state banks were created after 1811, and most extended credit recklessly. When the British raid on Washington and Baltimore in 1814 sent panicky depositors scurrying to convert their deposits into gold or silver, the overextended financiers could not oblige them. All banks outside New England suspended specie payments; that is, they stopped exchanging their bank notes for hard money on demand. Paper money immediately fell in value; a paper dollar was soon worth only 85 cents in coin in Philadelphia, less in Baltimore. Government business also suffered from the absence of a national bank. In October 1814 Secretary of the Treasury Alexander J. Dallas submitted a plan for a second Bank of the United States, and after considerable wrangling over its precise form, the institution was authorized in April 1816.

The new Bank was much larger than its predecessor, being capitalized at $35 million. However, unlike Hamilton's creation, it was badly managed at the start. Its first president, William Jones, a former secretary of the treasury, was as inept as he was easygoing. He displayed, according to the historian George Dangerfield, "a kindheartedness which, in his new position, was tantamount to corruption." All kinds of chicanery went on under Jones's nose. According to the charter, no shareholder could have more than 30 votes, regardless of the number of shares owned, yet one director who owned 1,172 shares registered each in a different name, with himself as "attorney" for all, and successfully cast 1,172 votes at meetings. More important, Jones allowed his institution to join in the irresponsible creation of credit. By the summer of 1818 the Bank's 18 branches had issued notes in excess of ten times their specie reserves, far more than was prudent, considering the Bank's responsibilities. When depression struck the country in 1819, the Bank of the United States was as hard pressed as many of the state banks. Jones resigned.

The new president, Langdon Cheves of South Carolina, was as rigid as Jones had been permissive. During the bad times, when easy credit was needed, he pursued a policy of stern curtailment. The Bank thus regained a sound position at the expense of hardship to borrowers. "The Bank was saved," the contemporary economist William Gouge wrote somewhat hyperbolically, "and the people were ruined." Just at the time when John Marshall was establishing its constitutionality, it reached a low point in public favor. Irresponsible state banks resented it, as did the advocates of hard money.

Regional lines were less sharply drawn on the Bank issue than on the tariff. Northern congressmen voted against the Bank 53 to 44 in 1816—many of them because they objected to the particular proposal, not because they were against any national bank. Those from other sections favored it, 58 to 30. The collapse occasioned by the Panic of 1819 produced further opposition to the institution in the West.

Sectional Issues: Land Policy

Land policy also caused sectional controversy. No one wished to eliminate the system of survey and sale, but there was continuous pressure to reduce the price of public land and the minimum unit offered for sale. The Land Act of 1800 set $2 an acre as the minimum price and 320 acres (a half section) as the smallest unit. Buyers could pay for the land in four annual installments, which meant that one needed only $160 to take possession of a good-sized farm. In 1804 the minimum was cut to 160 acres, which could be had for about $80 down, roughly a quarter of what the average artisan could earn in a year.

Since banks were pursuing an easy-credit policy, land sales boomed. The outbreak of the War of 1812 caused a temporary slump, but by 1814 sales had reached an all-time high and were increasing rapidly. Postwar prices of agricultural products were excellent, for the seas were now free and European agriculture had not yet recovered from the ravages of the Napoleonic wars. In 1818 the government sold nearly 3.5 million acres. Thereafter, continuing expansion and the rapid shrinkage of the foreign market as European farmers resumed production led to disaster. Prices fell, the panic struck, and western debtors were forced to the wall by the hundreds.

Sectional attitudes toward the public lands were fairly straightforward. The West wanted cheap land; the North and South tended to regard the national domain as an asset that should be converted into as much cash as possible. Northern manufacturers feared that cheap land in the West would drain off surplus labor and force wages up, while southern planters were concerned about the competition that would develop when the virgin lands of the Southwest were put to the plow to make cotton. The West, however, was ready to fight to the last line of defense over land policy, while the other regions would usually compromise on the issue to gain support for their own vital interests. Sectional alignments on the question of internal improvements were almost identical, but this issue, soon to become very important, had not greatly agitated national affairs before 1820. The only significant federal internal improvement project undertaken before that date was the National Road.

Sectional Issues: Slavery

The most divisive sectional issue was slavery. After the compromises affecting the "peculiar institution" made at the Constitutional Convention, it caused remarkably little conflict in national politics before 1819. Although the importation of blacks rose in the 1790s, Congress abolished the African slave trade in 1808 without major incident. As the nation expanded, free and slave states were added to the Union in equal numbers, Ohio, Indiana, and Illinois being balanced by Louisiana, Mississippi, and Alabama. In 1819 there were 22 states, 11 slave and 11 free. The expansion of slavery occasioned by the cotton boom led southerners to support it more aggressively, which tended to irritate many northerners, but most persons considered slavery mainly a local issue. To the extent that it was a national question, the North opposed it and the South defended it ardently. The West leaned toward the southern point of view, for in addition to the southwestern slave states, the Northwest was sympathetic, partly because much of its produce was sold on southern plantations and partly because at least half of its early settlers came from Virginia, Kentucky, and other slave states.

Northern Leaders

By 1824 the giants of the Revolutionary generation had completed their work. Washington, Hamilton, Franklin, Samuel Adams, Patrick Henry, and most of their peers were dead. John Adams (88), Thomas Jefferson (81), and James Madison (73) were passing their declining years quietly on their ancestral acres, full of memories and sage advice but no longer active in national affairs. In every section new leaders had come forward, men shaped by the past but chiefly concerned with the present. Quite suddenly, between the war and the panic, they had inherited power. They would shape the future of the United States.

John Quincy Adams was the best-known political leader of the North in the early 1820s. Just completing his brilliant work as secretary of state under Monroe, he had behind him a record of public service dating to the Confederation period. At 11 he was giving English lessons to the French minister to the Continental Congress and his secretary. ("He shows us no mercy and makes us no compliments," the minister remarked.) While in his teens he served as secretary of legation in Russia and Great Britain. Later he was American minister to the Netherlands and to Prussia and a Federalist United States senator from Massachusetts. Then he gradually switched to the Republican point of view, supporting the Louisiana Purchase and even the Embargo Act. His work at Ghent on the peace commission and as Madison's secretary of state has already been mentioned.

Adams was farsighted, imaginative, hardworking, and extremely intelligent, but he was inept in personal relations. He had all the virtues and most of the defects of the Puritan, being suspicious both of others and of himself. He suffered in two ways from being his father's child: As the son of a president, he was under severe pressure to live up to the Adams name, and his father expected a great deal of him. When the boy was only 7, John Adams wrote his wife: "Train [the children] to virtue. Habituate them to industry, activity, and spirit. Make them consider vice as shameful and unmanly. Fire them with ambition to be useful. . . . Fix their ambition upon great and solid objects, and their contempt upon little, frivolous and useless ones."

Such training made John Quincy an indefatigable worker. Even in winter he normally rose at 5 A.M., and he could never convince himself that most of his associates were not lazy dolts. He was tense, compulsive, conscience-ridden. He set a standard no one could meet and consequently was continually dissatisfied with himself. As one of his grandsons remarked, "He was disappointed because he was not supernatural." Toward enemies he was merciless and overwhelming, toward friends inspiring but demanding.

Like his father, John Quincy Adams was a strong nationalist. While New England was still antiprotectionist, he was at least open-minded on the subject of high tariffs. He supported the second Bank of the United States, and unlike most easterners, he believed that the federal government should spend freely on roads and canals in the West. To slavery he was, like most New Englanders, personally opposed. As Monroe's second term drew toward its close, Adams seemed one of the most likely candidates to succeed him, and at this period his ambition to be president was his great failing. He said he would like to be elected because it would please his father, but he did not deny that being president would please him too. His ambition led him to make certain compromises with his principles, which in turn plagued his oversensitive conscience and had a corrosive effect on his peace of mind.

Daniel Webster was recognized as one of the coming leaders of New England. Born in New Hampshire in 1782, he graduated from Dartmouth College in 1801, and by the time of the War of 1812 he had made a local reputation as a lawyer and orator. After serving two terms in Congress during the conflict, he moved to Boston to concentrate on his legal practice. He soon became one of the leading constitutional lawyers of the country. In 1823 he was again elected to Congress.

Webster owed much of his reputation to his formidable presence and his oratorical skill. Dark, large-headed, craggy of brow, with deep-set, brooding eyes and a firm mouth, he projected a remarkable appearance of heroic power and moral strength. His thunderous voice, his resourceful vocabulary, his manner—all backed by the mastery of every oratorical trick—made him unique. "He . . . is never averse, whilst traversing the thorny paths of political disputation," one contemporary admirer recorded, "to scatter the flowers of rhetorical elegance around him."

Webster had a first-rate mind, powerful and logical. His faults were largely those of temperament. He was too fond of good food and fine broadcloth, of alcohol and adulation. Hard work over an extended period of time was beyond him; generally he bestirred himself only with great effort and then usually to advance his own cause. Webster could have been a lighthouse in the night, guiding his fellow citizens to safe harbor. More often he was a weather vane, shifting to accommodate the strongest breeze. The good opinion of "the best people" meant so much to him that he rarely used his gifts to shape and guide that opinion in the national interest.

Unlike the independent-minded Adams, Web-

ster nearly always reflected the beliefs of the dominant business interests of New England. His opposition to the embargo and the War of 1812 got him into Congress, where he faithfully supported the views of New England merchants. He opposed the high tariff of 1816 because the merchants favored free trade, and he voted against establishing the Bank chiefly on partisan grounds. (His view changed when the Bank hired him as its lawyer.) He was against cheap land and federal construction of internal improvements. His opposition to slavery accorded with the opinion of most of his constituents, but on this question he stood more solidly for principle. Basically he was a nationalist (as was seen in his arguments before the Supreme Court), yet he sometimes allowed political expediency and the prejudices of New England to obscure his feelings. Ahead of him lay fame and considerable construc-

Eyes like "anthracite furnaces," the English historian Thomas Carlyle remarked of Daniel Webster; this is the "Black Dan" portrait by Francis Alexander.

His ready wit and cheerful disposition made Martin Van Buren immensely likable in spite of the intensity of his political ambitions.

tive service but also bitter frustration. And one hour of greatness.

New York's man of the future was a little sandy-haired politico named Martin Van Buren. The Red Fox, as he was called, was one of the most talented politicians ever to play a part in American affairs. He was clever and hardworking, but his mind and his energy were always devoted to some political purpose. From 1812 to 1820 he served in the state legislature; in 1820 he was elected United States senator.

Van Buren had great charm and immense tact. By nature affable, he never allowed partisanship to mar his personal relationships with other leaders. The historian Richard Hofstadter once described him as the type of politician whose influence "comes in large part out of his taste for political association, his liking for people, and his sportsmanlike ability to experience political conflict without taking it as

ground for personal rancor." The members of his political machine, known as the Albany Regency, were almost fanatically loyal to him, and even his enemies could seldom dislike him as a person.

Somehow Van Buren could reconcile deviousness with honesty. He "rowed to his objective with muffled oars," as Randolph of Roanoke said, yet he was neither crooked nor venal. Politics for him was like a game or a complex puzzle: The object was victory, but one must play by the rules or lose all sense of achievement. Only a fool will cheat at solitaire, and despite his gregariousness, Van Buren was at heart a solitary operator.

His positions on the issues of the 1820s are hard to determine because he never took a position if he could avoid doing so. In part this was his politician's desire to straddle every fence; it also reflected his quixotic belief that issues were means rather than ends in the world of politics. He opposed rechartering the first Bank yet was not conspicuous among those who fought the second. He did not oppose internal improvements. No one could say with assurance what he thought about the tariff, and since slavery did not arouse much interest in New York, it is safe to suppose that at this time he had no opinion at all about the institution. Any intelligent observer in the 1820s would have predicted that "the Little Magician" would go far, for he was obviously a master of his craft. How far, and in what direction, no one could have guessed.

Southern Leaders

The most prominent southern leader was William H. Crawford, Monroe's secretary of the treasury. Born in 1772 in the shadow of Virginia's Blue Ridge, he was taken to the Deep South while still a lad, settling finally in Georgia. A giant of a man, ruddy-faced and strong jawed, he became a leader of the conservative faction in the state, speaking for the large planters against the interests of the yeomen farmers. Following service in the legislature, he was elected to the Senate in 1807. Later he put in a tour of duty as minister to France, and in 1816 he was appointed secretary of the treasury.

Crawford was direct and friendly, a marvelous storyteller, and one of the few persons in Washington who could teach the fledgling senator Martin

The striking portrait of John C. Calhoun was painted sometime between 1818 and 1825, probably by Charles Bird King. The handsome Calhoun was in his thirties.

Van Buren anything about politics. Van Buren supported him enthusiastically in the contest for the 1824 presidential nomination. (So, although not publicly, did Jefferson and Madison.) Crawford was one of the first politicians to try to build a national machine. "Crawford's Act" of 1820, limiting the term of minor federal appointees to four years, was passed, as the name suggests, largely through his efforts, for he realized before nearly anyone else that a handful of petty offices, properly distributed, could win the allegiance of thousands of voters.

Crawford had something interesting to say on most of the important issues of the times. Although predisposed toward the states' rights position, he favored recharter of the Bank and was willing to go along with a moderately protective tariff. During the depression that began in 1819 he devised an excellent relief plan for farmers who were unable to meet installment payments due on land purchased from the government. He suggested a highly original scheme for a flexible paper currency not convertible into hard money.

Crawford was controversial. Many of his contemporaries considered him no more than a cynical spoilsman, though his administration of the treasury was first-rate. Yet he had many friends. His ambition was vast, his power great. Fate, however, was about to strike Crawford a crippling blow.

John C. Calhoun, the other outstanding southern leader, was born in South Carolina in 1782 and graduated from Yale in 1804. He studied law at Tapping Reeve's remarkable law school in Litchfield, Connecticut, which in half a century turned out 15 future United States senators, 10 governors, 2 Supreme Court justices, and a number of other men prominent in public affairs. Calhoun served in the South Carolina legislature and, beginning in 1811, in Congress. A prominent War Hawk, he took a strong nationalist position on all the issues of the day. In 1817 Monroe made him secretary of war.

Although devoted to the South and its institutions, Calhoun took the broadest possible view of political affairs. "Our true system is . . . to support such measures and such men, without regard to sections, as are best calculated to advance the general interest," he said in 1820. John Quincy Adams, seldom charitable in his private opinions of colleagues (he called Crawford "a worm" and Henry Clay a "gamester" with an "undigested system of ethics"), praised Calhoun's "quick understanding" and "enlarged philosophic views" and considered him "above all sectional and factional prejudices."

Calhoun was intelligent, bookish, and given to the study of abstractions. Basically a gentle person, he was cold and restrained in most of his relationships. He had no hobbies and was utterly humorless. Legend has it that he once tried to write a poem but after putting down the word *Whereas* gave it up as beyond his powers. Some obscure failing made it impossible for him to grasp the essence of the human condition. An English observer once said that Calhoun had "an imperfect acquaintance with human nature." Yet he burned to lead his fellows. Few contemporaries could maintain themselves in debate against his powerful intelligence, yet that mind—so sharp, so penetrating—was the blind bondsman of his ambition.

This portrait of Henry Clay was completed in 1824, when he was Speaker of the House. An unidentified artist painted it after a portrait by John Neagle.

Western Leaders

The outstanding western leader of the 1820s was Henry Clay of Kentucky, one of the most charming and colorful of American statesmen. Tall, lean, gray-eyed, Clay was the kind of person who made men cheer and women swoon. On the platform he ranked with Webster; behind the political scenes he was the peer of Van Buren. In every environment he was warm and open—what a modern political scientist might call a charismatic personality. Clay loved to drink, swear, tell tales, and play poker. It was characteristic that at one sitting he won $40,000 from a friend and then cheerfully told him that a note for $500 would wipe out the obligation. He was a reasonable man, skilled at arranging political compromises, but he possessed a reckless streak: Like so many westerners, his sense of honor was

exaggerated. Twice in his career he called men out for having insulted him. Fortunately, all concerned were poor shots.

After some years in the Kentucky legislature, Clay was elected to Congress in 1810. He led the War Hawks in 1811 and 1812 and was Speaker of the House from 1811 to 1820 and from 1823 to 1825.

Clay was intellectually the inferior of Adams and Calhoun, even of Webster. But he had a perfect temperament for politics. He loved power and understood that in the United States it had to be shared to be exercised. His great gift was in seeing national needs from a broad perspective and fashioning a program that could inspire ordinary citizens with something of his vision.

In the early 1820s he was just developing his "American System." In return for eastern support of a policy of federal aid in the construction of roads and canals, the West would back the protective tariff. He justified this deal on the widest national grounds. By stimulating manufacturing, it would increase the demand for western raw materials, while western prosperity would lead to greater consumption of eastern manufactured goods.

Washington did not describe the interdependence of the sections better in his farewell address than Clay did, repeatedly, in Congress and on the stump. And like Washington, Clay was conservative. He opposed the national bank in 1811 on constitutional grounds but supported the one in 1816 and thereafter, saying, with typical candor and shrewdness, that "the force of circumstance and the lights of experience" had convinced him that he had previously misread the Constitution. His view of slavery, as his biographer Glyndon Van Deusen wrote, was "a combination of theoretical dislike and practical tolerance." He would have preferred to ignore the subject. Nevertheless, slavery repeatedly played a crucial role in Clay's career.

The West had other spokesmen in the 1820s. Thomas Hart Benton, elected to the Senate by the new state of Missouri, was an expansionist and a hard-money man of the uncompromising sort, suspicious of paper currency and therefore of all banks. He championed the small western farmer, favoring free homesteads for pioneers and an extensive federal internal improvements program. Poor workers should cast aside their tools and head west, he believed. Opposed in principle to high tariffs, he tended to vote for them "with repugance and misgiving" to obtain protection for Missouri's lead and furs.

For 30 years Benton advocated his ideas in the Senate in bluff, colorful language. "Nobody oposes Benton but a few blackjack prairie lawyers," he would roar. "Benton and democracy are one and the same, sir; synonymous terms, sir; synonymous terms, sir." A bighearted man, though vain and pompous, he remained essentially a sectional rather than a national figure.

Another western leader was General William Henry Harrison. Although he sat in the Ohio legislature and in both houses of Congress between 1816 and 1828, Harrison was primarily a soldier. During the Panic of 1819 he took an anti-Bank and pro-high-tariff stand, but he did not identify himself closely with any policy other than the extermination of the Indians. He had little to do with the newly developing political alignments of the 1820s.

Much like Harrison was Andrew Jackson, the "Hero of New Orleans," whose popularity greatly exceeded Harrison's. He had many friends, shrewd in the ways of politics, who were working devotedly, if not entirely unselfishly, to make him president. No one knew his views on most questions, but few cared. His chief assets as a presidential candidate were his military reputation and his forceful personality, but both, and especially the latter, were equally likely to get him into political hot water.

The Missouri Compromise

The sectional concerns of the 1820s repeatedly influenced politics. The depression of 1819–1822 increased tensions by making people feel more strongly about the issues of the day. For example, manufacturers who wanted high tariffs in 1816 were more vehemently in favor of protection in 1820 when their business fell off. Even when economic conditions improved, geographic alignments on key issues tended to solidify.

One of the first and most critical of the sectional questions concerned the admission of Missouri as a slave state. When Louisiana entered the Union in 1812, the rest of the Louisiana Purchase was organized as Missouri Territory. Building on a nucleus

of Spanish and French inhabitants, the region west and north of St. Louis grew rapidly, and in 1817 the Missourians petitioned for statehood. A large percentage of the settlers—the population exceeded 60,000 by 1818—were southerners who had moved into the valleys of the Arkansas and Missouri rivers. Since many of them owned slaves, Missouri would become a slave state.

The admission of new states had always been a routine matter, in keeping with the admirable pattern established by the Northwest Ordinance. But during the debate on the Missouri Enabling Act in February 1819, Congressman James Tallmadge of New York introduced an amendment prohibiting "the further introduction of slavery" and providing that all slaves born in Missouri after the territory became a state should be freed at age 25.

While Tallmadge was merely seeking to apply in the territory the pattern of race relations that had developed in the states immediately east of Missouri, his amendment represented, at least in spirit, something of a revolution. The Northwest Ordinance had prohibited slavery in the land between the Mississippi and the Ohio, but that area had only a handful of slaveowners in 1787 and little prospect of attracting more. Elsewhere, no effort to restrict the movement of slaves into new territory had been attempted. If one assumed (as whites always had) that the slaves themselves should have no say in the matter, it appeared democratic to let the settlers of Missouri decide the slavery question for themselves. Nevertheless, the Tallmadge amendment passed the House, the vote following sectional lines closely. The Senate, however, resoundingly rejected it. The less populous southern part of Missouri was then organized separately as Arkansas Territory, and an attempt to bar slavery there was stifled. The Missouri Enabling Act failed to pass before Congress adjourned.

When the next Congress met in December 1819, the Missouri issue came up at once. The vote on Tallmadge's amendment had shown that the rapidly growing North controlled the House of Representatives. It was vital, southerners felt, to preserve a balance in the Senate. Yet northerners objected to the fact that Missouri extended hundreds of miles north of the Ohio River, which they considered slavery's natural boundary. Angry debate raged in Congress for months.

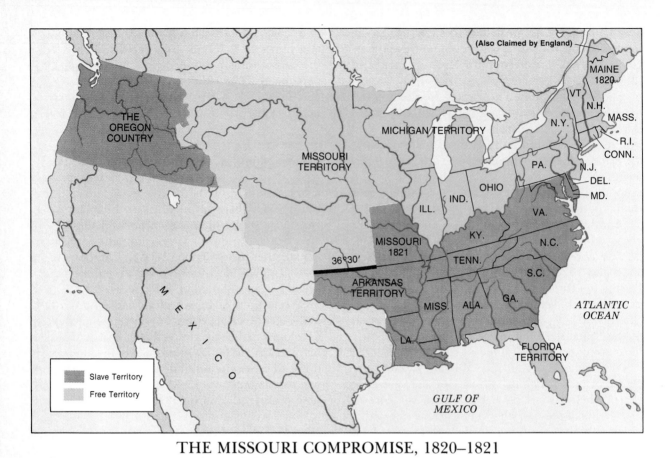

THE MISSOURI COMPROMISE, 1820–1821

This was the lineup of the slave and free states resulting from the Missouri Compromise. The Compromise was repealed by the Kansas-Nebraska Act (1854) and declared unconstitutional in the Dred Scott Case (1857).

The debate did not turn on the morality of slavery or the rights of blacks. Northerners objected to adding new slave states because under the Three-fifths Compromise these states would be over-represented in Congress (60 percent of their slaves would be counted in determining the size of the states' delegations in the House of Representatives) and because they did not relish competing with slave labor. Since the question was political influence rather than the rights and wrongs of slavery, a compromise was worked out in 1820. Missouri entered the Union as a slave state and Maine, having been separated from Massachusetts, was admitted as a free state to preserve the balance in the Senate.

To prevent further conflict, Congress adopted a proposal of Senator Jesse B. Thomas of Illinois, which "forever prohibited" slavery in all other parts of the Louisiana Purchase north of 36°30' north latitude, the westward extension of Missouri's southern boundary. Although this division would keep slavery out of most of the territory, southerners accepted it cheerfully. The land south of the line, the present states of Arkansas and Oklahoma, seemed ideally suited for the expanded plantation economy, and most persons considered the treeless northern regions little better than a desert. One northern senator, decrying the division, contemptuously described the land north and west of Missouri, today one of the world's richest agricultural regions, as "a prairie without food or water."

The Missouri Compromise did not end the crisis. When Missouri submitted its constitution for approval by Congress (the final step in the admission process), the document, besides authorizing slavery and prohibiting the emancipation of any slave without the consent of the owner, required the state legislature to pass a law barring free blacks and mulattos from entering the state "under any pretext whatever." This provision plainly violated Article 4, Section 2 of the United States Constitution: "The Citizens of each State shall be entitled to all Privileges and Immunities of Citizens in the several States." It did not, however, represent any more of a break with established racial patterns, north or south, than the Tallmadge amendment; many states east of Missouri barred free blacks without regard for the Constitution.

Nevertheless, northern congressmen hypocritically refused to accept the Missouri constitution. Once more the debate raged. Again, since few northerners cared to defend the rights of blacks, the issue was compromised. In March 1821 Henry Clay found a face-saving formula: Out of respect for the "supreme law of the land," Congress accepted the Missouri constitution with the demurrer that no law passed in conformity to it should be construed as contravening Article 4, Section 2. Of course this was pure cant.

Every thinking person recognized the political dynamite inherent in the Missouri controversy. The sectional lineup had been terrifyingly compact. What meant the Union if so trivial a matter as one new state could so divide the people? Moreover, despite the timidity and hypocrisy of the North, everyone realized that the rights and wrongs of slavery lay at the heart of the conflict. "We have the

A comment by David Claypoole Johnston on the 1824 presidential "foot-race" has Adams leading by a head, trailed by Crawford and Jackson. Clay (far right, hand on head), well behind, pulls up in dismay. The many figures and the dreadful puns ("How is Clay now?" "Oh dirt cheap" and "Hurra for our son Jack" "Hurra for our Jack-son") are typical of cartoons of the era.

wolf by the ears, and we can neither safely hold him, nor safely let him go," Jefferson wrote a month after Missouri became a state. The dispute, he said, "like a fire bell in the night, awakened and filled me with terror." Jefferson knew that the compromise had not quenched the flames ignited by the Missouri debates. "This is a reprieve only," he said. John Quincy Adams called it the "title page to a great tragic volume." Yet one could still hope that the fire bell was only a false alarm, that Adams's tragic volume would remain unread.

The Election of 1824

Other controversies that aroused strong feelings did not seem to divide the country so deeply. The question of federal internal improvements caused endless debate that split the country on geographic lines. In 1816 the nationalist-minded Calhoun had pressed a plan to set up a $1.5 million fund for roads and canals. Congress approved this despite strong opposition in New England and a divided South. In 1822 a bill providing money for the upkeep of the National Road caused another sectional split. Both measures were vetoed, but in 1824 Monroe approved a differently worded internal improvement act. Such proposals excited intense reactions. John Randolph, opposing the 1824 bill with his usual ferocity, threatened to employ "every . . . means short of actual insurrection" to defeat it. Yet no one—not even Randolph, it will be noted—threatened the Union on this issue.

The tariff continued to divide the country. When a new, still higher tariff was enacted in 1824, the slave states voted almost unanimously against it, the North and Northwest voted in favor, and New England remained of two minds. Webster (after conducting a poll of business leaders before deciding how to vote) made a powerful speech against the act, but the measure passed without creating a major storm.

These divisions were not severely disruptive, in part because the major politicians, competing for the presidency, did not dare risk alienating any section by taking too extreme a position. Calhoun, for example, had changed his mind about protective tariffs by 1824, but he avoided declaring himself because of his presidential ambitions. Another rea-

son was that the old party system had broken down; the Federalists had disappeared as a national party, and the Jeffersonians, lacking an organized opposition, had become less aggressive and more troubled by factional disputes.

The presidential fight was therefore waged on personal grounds, though the heat generated by the contest began the process of reenergizing party politics. The candidates, in addition to Calhoun, were Jackson, Crawford, Adams, and Clay. The maneuvering among them was complex, the infighting savage. In March 1824 Calhoun, who was young enough to wait for the White House, withdrew and declared for the vice-presidency, which he won easily. Crawford, who had the support of many congressional leaders, seemed the likely winner, but he suffered a series of paralytic strokes that gravely injured his chances.

Despite the bitterness of the contest, it attracted relatively little public interest; barely a quarter of those eligible took the trouble to vote. In the electoral college Jackson led with 99; Adams had 84, Crawford 41, and Clay 37. Since no one had a majority, the contest was thrown into the House of Representatives, which, under the Constitution, had to choose from among the three leaders, each state delegation having one vote. By employing his great influence in the House, Clay swung the balance. Not wishing to advance the fortunes of a rival westerner like Jackson and feeling, with reason, that Crawford's health made him unavailable, Clay gave his support to Adams, who was thereupon elected.

J. Q. Adams as President

Adams, who took a Hamiltonian view of the future of the country, hoped to use the national authority to foster all sorts of useful projects. He asked Congress for a federal program of internal improvements so vast that even Clay boggled when he realized its scope. He came out for aid to manufacturing and agriculture, for a national university, and even for a government astronomical observatory. For a nationalist of unchallengeable Jeffersonian origins like Clay or Calhoun to have pressed for so extensive a program would have been politically risky. For the son of John Adams to do so was disastrous; every doubter remembered his

Asher B. Durand's portrait of an uncompromising John Quincy Adams dates from 1835, when the former president was a congressman from Massachusetts.

Federalist background and decided that he was trying to overturn the glorious "Revolution of 1800."

Adams proved to be his own worst enemy, for he was as inept a politician as ever lived. Although capable on occasion of turning a phrase—in his first annual message to Congress he described astronomical observatories as "light-houses of the skies"—his general style of public utterance was bumbling and cumbersome. Knowing that many citizens considered things like observatories impractical extravagances, he urged Congress not to be "palsied by the will of our constituents." To persuade Americans, who were almost pathological on the subject of monarchy, to support his road-building program, he cited with approval the work being done abroad by "the nations of Europe and . . . their rulers," which revived fears that all Adamses were royalists at heart. He was insensitive

to the ebb and flow of public feeling; even when he wanted to move with the tide, he seldom managed to dramatize and publicize his stand effectively. There was wide support in the country for a federal bankruptcy law, but instead of describing himself in plain language as a friend of poor debtors, Adams called for the "amelioration" of the "often oppressive codes relating to insolvency" and buried the recommendation at the tail end of a dull state paper.

One of Adams's worst political failings was his refusal to use his power of appointment to win support. "I will not dismiss . . . able and faithful political opponents to provide for my own partisans," he said. The attitude was traditional at the time, but Adams carried it to extremes—in four years he removed only 12 men from office. Nevertheless, by appointing Henry Clay secretary of state, he laid himself open to the charge that he had won the presidency by a "corrupt bargain." Thus despite his politically suicidal attitude toward federal jobs, he was subject to the annoyance of a congressional investigation of his appointments, out of which came no less than six bills designed "to reduce the patronage of the executive."

Calhoun's "Exposition and Protest"

The tariff question added to the president's troubles. High duties, increasingly more repulsive to the export-conscious South, attracted more and more favor in the North and the West. Besides manufacturers, lead miners in Missouri, hemp raisers in Kentucky, woolgrowers in New York, and many other interests demanded protection against foreign competition. The absence of party discipline provided an ideal climate for logrolling in Congress. Legislators found themselves under pressure from their constituents to raise the duties on products of local importance; to satisfy these demands, they traded votes with other congressmen similarly situated. In this way massive support for protection was generated.

In 1828 a new tariff was hammered into shape by the House Committee on Manufactures. Northern and western agricultural interests were in command; they wrote into the bill extremely high duties on raw wool, hemp, flax, fur, and liquor. New England manufacturers protested vociferously, for although their products were protected, the proposed law would increase the cost of their raw materials. This gave southerners, now hopelessly in the minority on the tariff question, a chance to block the bill. When the New Englanders proposed amendments lowering the duties on raw materials, the southerners voted nay, hoping to force them to reject the measure on the final vote. This desperate strategy failed. New England had by this time committed its future to manufacturing, a change signalized by the somersault of Webster, who, ever responsive to local pressures, now voted for protection. After winning some minor concessions in the Senate, largely through the intervention of Van Buren, enough New Englanders accepted the so called Tariff of Abominations to assure its passage.

Vice-President Calhoun, who had watched the debate from the vantage point of his post as president of the Senate, now came to a great turning point in his career. He had thrown in his lot with Jackson, whose running mate he was to be in the coming election, and had been assured that the Jacksonians would oppose the bill. Yet northern Jacksonians had been responsible for drafting and passing it. The new tariff would impoverish the South, he believed. He warned Jackson that relief must soon be provided or the Union would be shaken to its foundations. Then he returned to his South Carolina plantation and wrote an essay, the "South Carolina Exposition and Protest," repudiating the nationalist philosophy he had previously championed.

The South Carolina legislature released this document to the country in December 1828, along with eight resolutions denouncing the protective tariff as unfair and unconstitutional. The theorist Calhoun, however, was not content with outlining the case against the tariff. His "Exposition" provided an ingenious defense of the right of the people of a state to reject a law of Congress. Starting with John Locke's revered concept of government as a contractual relationship, he argued that since the states had created the Union, logic dictated that they be the final arbiters of the meaning of the Constitution that was its framework. If a special state convention, representing the sovereignty of the people, decided that an act of Congress violated the Constitution, it could interpose its authority and "nullify" the law within its boundaries. Calhoun did not seek to implement this theory in 1828, for he hoped that the next administration would lower the tariff and make nullification unnecessary.

Milestones

1804	Size of minimum purchase reduced to 160 acres by Land Act
1808	Further importation of slaves outlawed by Congress
1816	Second Bank of the United States chartered by Congress
	Protection for manufactured goods provided by Tariff Act
1819	Beginning of Panic of 1819
1820	Federal officeholders limited to 4-year terms by Crawford's Act
1820–1821	Missouri Compromise
1820–1824	American System developed by Henry Clay
1824	J. Q. Adams elected president by House of Representatives
1828	Calhoun's "South Carolina Exposition and Protest"
	Congress passes Tariff of Abominations

SUPPLEMENTARY READING

Titles marked with an asterisk have been published in paperback.

On the economic issues of this period, see F. W. Taussig, **Tariff History of the United States*** (1923), Bray Hammond, **Banks and Politics in America from the Revolution to the Civil War*** (1957), and R. M. Robbins, **Our Landed Heritage*** (1942).

M. D. Peterson, **The Great Triumvirate** (1987), is an interesting study of Clay, Calhoun, and Webster. Other biographies of statesmen of the period include S. F. Bemis, **John Quincy Adams** (1949–1956), M. G. Baxter, **One and Indispensable: Daniel Webster and the Union** (1984), John Nivens, **Martin Van Buren** (1983), R. V. Remini, **Andrew Jackson and the Course of American Empire** (1977), and C. C. Mooney, **William H. Crawford** (1974). The fullest study of Calhoun's early career is C. M. Wiltse, **John C. Calhoun: Nationalist** (1949), but see also R. N. Current, **John C. Calhoun*** (1963). The best brief biography of Clay is **Clement Eaton, Henry Clay and the Art of American Politics*** (1957). On the Missouri Compromise, see Glover Moore, **The Missouri Controversy*** (1953).

Toward a National Economy

Nothing can exceed their activity and perseverance in all kinds of speculation, handicraft, and enterprise which promise a profitable pecuniary result.

FRANCES TROLLOPE, Domestic Manners of the Americans, *1832*

family spinning wheel or the spread of the fac-
y system to other forms of manufacturing. Most
nmercial and manufacturing businesses were still
naged by a single owner or a few partners. Meth-
s of distributing goods, keeping records, and ac-
unting remained primitive. Interchangeable fir-
; pins for rifles did not lead at once even to
tching pairs of shoes. More than 15 years were
pass after the invention of Fitch's steamboat be-
e it was widely accepted.

By the 1770s British manufacturers, especially
se in textiles, had made astonishing progress in
chanizing their operations, bringing workers to-
her in buildings called factories where water-
wer, and later steam, supplied the force to run
v spinning and weaving devices that increased
ductivity and reduced labor costs.

Since machine-spun cotton was cheaper and of
ter quality than that spun by hand, producers in
er countries were eager to adopt British meth-
. Americans had depended on Great Britain for
h products until the Revolution cut off supplies;
n the new spirit of nationalism gave impetus to
development of local industry. A number of
e legislatures offered bounties to anyone who
uld introduce the new machinery. The British,

however, guarded their secrets vigilantly. It was illegal to export any of the new machines or to send
their plans abroad. Workers skilled in their construction and use were forbidden to leave the country. These restrictions were effective for a time; the
principles on which the new machines were based
were simple enough, but to construct workable
models without plans was another matter. Although
a number of persons tried to do so, it was not until
Samuel Slater installed his machines in Pawtucket,
Rhode Island, that a successful factory was constructed.

Slater was more than a skilled mechanic. Attracted by stories of the rewards offered in the
United States, he slipped out of England in 1789.
Not daring to carry any plans, he depended on his
memory and his mechanical sense for the complicated specifications of the necessary machines.
When Moses Brown brought him to Rhode Island,
he insisted on scrapping the crude machinery Almy
& Brown had assembled. Then, working in secrecy
with a carpenter who was "under bond not to steal
the patterns nor disclose the nature of the work,"
he built and installed his machinery. In December
1790 the first American factory began production.

It was a humble beginning indeed. Slater's ma-

*nuel Slater "smuggled a textile mill out of England in his head." Two decades
r its founding, the mill and its surroundings looked like this.*

Politicians might attribute the growth of the country and the preservation of the Union to their own patriotism and ingenuity, but without the economic and technological developments of the period, neither of these much-to-be-desired objectives could have been attained. The country was still overwhelmingly agricultural in 1820, but the nation was on the brink of a major economic readjustment. Certain obscure seeds planted in the early years of the republic had taken root. Almost unnoticed, new ways of producing goods and making a living were beginning to take hold. The industrial revolution was coming to America with a rush.

America's Industrial Revolution

The growth of industry required certain technological advances and the development of a new type of business organization. Both elements existed in Europe by the time of the War for Independence, but only after the ratification of the Constitution did they cross the Atlantic. In 1790 a young English-born genius named Samuel Slater, employed by the Rhode Island merchant firm of Almy & Brown, began to spin cotton thread by machine in the first effective factory in the United States. In 1800 a youthful graduate of Yale College, Eli[?] ing contracted to make 10,000 rifle[?] ernment, succeeded in manufacturin[?] precise methods that the parts wer[?] able, a major step toward the per[?] assembly-line system of production[?] later Oliver Evans, a Philadelphia[?] come close to achieving automation i[?] A worker poured wheat down a chi[?] of the plant and a second worker hea[?] of superfine flour which emerged at[?] The intervening steps of weighing, c[?] ing, and packing were all performe[?]

Other important technological[?] cluded John Fitch's construction an[?] the world's first regularly schedule[?] 1790 and Eli Whitney's invention of[?] in 1793. The steamboat and the gin[?] ican history almost as much as the[?] and mass production. The former, [?] on western waters, cut the cost of[?] dramatically and brought the West i[?] economy. The latter made possible[?] cultivation of cotton, which transfo[?] and fed the world's cotton factories[?]

Innovations in the way busines[?] nized and financed accompanied te[?] velopments. The most spectacular st[?] den flowering of American bankin[?] tablishment of the First Bank of the[?] was of key importance. Aside from[?] ment financial operations, the Ban[?] important source of credit for priva[?] success led to the founding of many[?] banks. When the great Bank was c[?] there were only three banks in the[?] By 1800 there were 29, located i[?] towns. Bank credit, in the historia[?] mond's words, "was to Americans a[?] energy, like steam." Yet many citizen[?] this truth. "Every dollar of a bank b[?] beyond the quantity of gold and silv[?] represents nothing and is therefor[?] somebody," John Adams remarked[?]

Birth of the Fact[?]

America's industrial revolution was[?] Slater's factory did not signal the di[?]

233

chines made only cotton thread, which Almy & Brown sold in its Providence store and "put out" to individual artisans, who, working for wages, wove it into cloth in their homes. The machines were tended by a labor force of nine children, for the work was simple and the pace slow. The young operatives' pay ranged from 33 to 67 cents a week, about what a youngster could earn in other occupations.*

The factory was profitable from the start. Slater soon branched out on his own, and others trained by him opened their own establishments. By 1800 seven mills possessing 2,000 spindles were in operation; by 1815, after production had been stimulated by the War of 1812, there were 130,000 spindles turning in 213 factories. Many of the new factories were inefficient, but the well-managed ones earned large profits. Slater began with almost nothing. When he died in 1835 he owned mill properties in Rhode Island, Massachusetts, Connecticut, and New Hampshire in addition to other interests, and by the standards of the day he was a rich man.

Before long the Boston Associates, a group of merchants headed by Francis Cabot Lowell, added a new dimension to factory production. Beginning at Waltham, Massachusetts, where the Charles River provided the necessary waterpower, between 1813 and 1850 they revolutionized textile production. Some early factory owners had set up hand looms in their plants, but the weavers could not keep pace with the whirring spinning jennies. Lowell, after an extensive study of British mills, smuggled the plans for an efficient power loom into America. His Boston Manufacturing Company at Waltham, capitalized at $300,000, combined machine production, large-scale operation, efficient management, and centralized marketing procedures. It concentrated on the mass production of a standardized product.

Lowell's cloth, though plain and rather coarse, was durable and cheap. His profits averaged almost 20 percent a year during the Era of Good Feelings. In 1823 the Boston Associates began to harness the power of the Merrimack River, setting up a new

$600,000 corporation at the sleepy village of East Chelmsford, Massachusetts (population 300), where there was a fall of 32 feet in the river. Within three years the town, appropriately renamed Lowell, had 2,000 inhabitants.

The Persistence of the Household System

The efficiency of the Lowell system was obvious, yet it led to no immediate transformation of American manufacturing. While the embargo and the war with Great Britain aided the new factories by limiting foreign competition, they also stimulated nonfactory production. In Monroe's time the household-handicraft-mill complex was still dominant nearly everywhere. Except in the manufacture of textiles, factories employing as many as 50 workers did not exist. Traveling and town-based artisans produced goods ranging from hats, shoes, and other articles of clothing to barrels, clocks, pianos, ships' supplies, cigars, lead pencils, and pottery. Ironworks, brickyards, flour mills, distilleries, and lumberyards could be found even in the most rural parts

An artisan and his apprentices at work at a small pewterer's shop in New York City, pictured in a banner carried by the Society of Pewterers in a procession in New York celebrating the ratification of the Constitution.

---

* This labor pattern persisted for several decades. In 1813 a cotton manufacturer placed the following advertisement in the *Utica* (N.Y.) *Patriot:* "A few sober and industrious families of at least five children each, over the age of eight years are wanted at the Cotton Factory. Widows with large families would do well to attend this notice."

of the country. The historian George Rogers Taylor reports that in and about a single tiny Ohio town in 1815, more than 30 craftsmen of the shoemaker-baker-druggist type plied their trades.

Nearly all these "manufacturers" produced only to supply local needs, but in some instances large industries grew up without advancing to the factory stage. In the neighborhood of the Connecticut town of Danbury, hundreds of small shops turned out hats by handicraft methods. The hats were sold in all sections of the country, the trade being organized by wholesalers. The shoe industry followed a related pattern, with centers of production in Pennsylvania, New Jersey, and especially eastern Massachusetts. Merchants in these regions bought leather in wholesale lots, had it cut to patterns in central workshops, and then distributed it to craftsmen who made the shoes in their homes or shops on a piecework basis. The finished product was returned to the central shops for inspection and packaging and then shipped throughout the United States. Some strange combinations of production techniques appeared, none more peculiar than in the manufacture of stockings. Frequently the feet and legs were knit by machine in separate factories and then "put out" to handworkers who sewed the parts together in their homes.

Since technology affected American industry unevenly, contemporaries found the changes difficult to evaluate. Few people in the 1820s appreciated how profound the impact of the factory system would be. The city of Lowell seemed remarkable and important but not necessarily a herald of future trends. Yet in nearly every field apparently minor changes were being made. Beginning around 1815, small improvements in the design of waterwheels, such as the use of leather transmission belts and metal gears, made possible larger and more efficient machinery in mills and factories. The woolens industry gradually became as mechanized as the cotton. Iron production advanced beyond the stage of the blacksmith's forge and the small foundry only slowly; nevertheless, by 1810 machines were stamping out nails at a third the cost of the hand-forged type, and a few years later sheet iron, formerly hammered out laboriously

Typical of the small factories of the early American Industrial Revolution was this glass-making establishment along the Delaware River near Philadelphia.

by hand, was being produced in efficient rolling mills. At about this time the puddling process for refining pig iron made it possible to use coal for fuel instead of expensive charcoal.

Improvements were made soon after the War of 1812 in the manufacture of paper, glass, and pottery. The commercial canning of sterilized foods in airtight containers began about 1820. The invention in that year of a machine for cutting ice, which reduced the cost by over 50 percent, had equally important effects on urban eating habits.

Corporations

Besides the competition of other types of production and the inability of technology to supply instant solutions to every industrial problem, there were other reasons why the factory took hold so slowly in the United States. Mechanization required substantial capital investment, and capital was chronically in short supply. The modern method of organizing large enterprises, the corporation, was rarely used in this period. Between 1781 and 1801 only 326 corporations were chartered by the states, and only a few of them were engaged in manufacturing.

The general opinion was that only quasi-public projects, such as roads and waterworks, were entitled to the privilege of incorporation. Anyone interested in organizing a corporation had to obtain a special act of a state legislature. And even among businessmen there was a tendency to associate corporations with monopoly, corruption, and the undermining of individual enterprise. In 1820 the economist Daniel Raymond wrote:

> The very object . . . of the act of incorporation is to produce inequality, either in rights, or in the division of property. Prima facie, therefore all money corporations are detrimental to national wealth. They are always created for the benefit of the rich.

Such feelings help to explain why as late as the 1860s most manufacturing was being done by unincorporated companies.

Though the growth of industry did not suddenly revolutionize American life, it reshaped society in various ways. For many years it lessened the im-portance of foreign commerce. Some relative decline from the lush years immediately preceding Jefferson's embargo was no doubt inevitable, especially in the fabulously profitable reexport trade, but industrial growth reduced the need for foreign products and thus the business of merchants. Only in the 1850s, when the wealth and population of the United States were more than three times what they had been in the first years of the century, did the value of American exports climb back to the levels of 1807. As the country moved closer to self-sufficiency (a point it never reached), nationalistic and isolationist sentiments were subtly augmented. During the embargo and the War of 1812 a great deal of capital had been transferred from commerce to industry; afterward new capital continued to prefer industry, attracted by the high profits and growing prestige of manufacturing. The rise of manufacturing affected farmers too, for as cities grew in size and number, commercial agriculture flourished. Dairy farming, truck gardening, and fruit growing began to thrive around every manufacturing center.

Cotton Revolutionizes the South

By far the most important indirect effect of industrialization occurred in the South, which soon began to produce cotton to supply the new textile factories of Great Britain and New England. The possibility of growing large amounts of this crop in America had not been seriously considered in colonial times, but by the 1780s the demand for raw cotton to feed the voracious British mills was causing many American farmers to experiment with the crop. Most of the world's cotton at this time came from Egypt, India, and the East Indies. The plant was considered tropical, most varieties being unable to survive the slightest frost. Hamilton, who missed nothing that related to the economic growth of the country, reported: "It has been observed . . . that the nearer the place of growth to the equator, the better the quality of the cotton."

Beginning in 1786, "sea island" cotton was grown successfully in the mild, humid lowlands and offshore islands along the coasts of Georgia and South Carolina. This was a high-quality cotton, silky and long-fibered like the Egyptian. But its suscep-

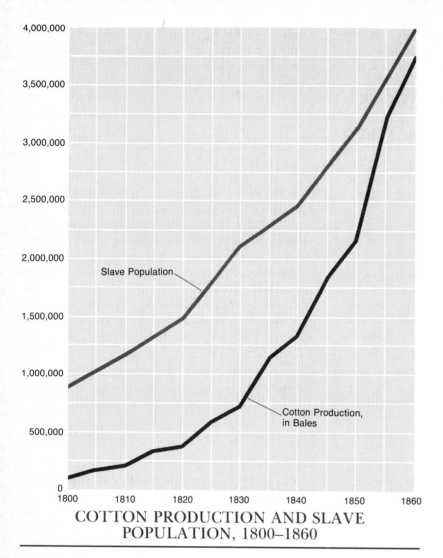

COTTON PRODUCTION AND SLAVE POPULATION, 1800–1860

tibility to frost severely limited the area of its cultivation. Elsewhere in the South, "green seed," or upland, cotton flourished, but this plant had little commercial value because the seeds could not be easily separated from the lint. When sea island cotton was passed between two rollers, its shiny black seeds simply popped out; with upland cotton, the seeds were pulled through with the lint and crushed, the oils and broken bits destroying the value of the fiber. To remove the seeds by hand was laborious; a slave working all day could clean scarcely a pound of the white fluff. This made it an uneconomical crop. In 1791 the usually sanguine Hamilton admitted in his *Report on Manufactures* that "the extensive cultivation of cotton can, perhaps, hardly be expected."

Early American cotton manufacturers used the sea island variety or imported the foreign fiber, in the latter case paying a duty of 3 cents a pound. However, the planters of South Carolina and Georgia, suffering from hard times after the Revolution, needed a new cash crop. Rice production was not expanding, and indigo, the other staple of the area, had ceased to be profitable when it was no longer possible to claim the British bounty. Cotton seemed an obvious answer. Farmers were experimenting hopefully with varieties of the plant and mulling the problem of how upland cotton could be more easily deseeded.

This was the situation in the spring of 1793, when Eli Whitney was a guest at Mulberry Grove, the plantation of Catherine Greene, widow of General Nathanael Greene, some dozen miles from Savannah.* Whitney had accepted a position as private tutor at 100 guineas a year with a nearby family and had stopped to visit a friend, Phineas Miller, who was overseer of the Greene plantation. While at Mulberry Grove, Whitney, who had never seen a cotton plant before, met a number of the local landowners. To his father he wrote:

> I heard much of the extreme difficulty of ginning Cotton, that is, separating it from its seed. There were a number of very respectable Gentlemen at Mrs. Greene's who all agreed that if a machine could be invented that would clean the Cotton with expedition, it would be a great thing both to the Country and to the inventor.

Whitney thought about the problem for a few days and then "struck out a plan of a machine." He described it to Miller, who enthusiastically offered to finance the invention. Since Whitney had just learned that his job as tutor would pay only 50 guineas, he accepted Miller's proposal.

Within ten days he had solved the problem that had baffled the planters. His "gin" (engine) consisted of a cylinder covered with rows of wire teeth rotating in a box filled with cotton. As the cylinder turned, the teeth passed through narrow slits in a metal grating. Cotton fibers were caught by the teeth and pulled through the slits. The seeds, too thick to pass through the openings, were left behind. A second cylinder, with brushes rotating in the opposite direction to sweep the cotton from the wires, prevented matting and clogging.

This "absurdly simple contrivance" almost instantly transformed southern agriculture. With a gin a slave could clean 50 times as much cotton as by hand; soon larger models driven by mules and horses were available. The machines were so easy to construct (once the basic idea was understood) that Whitney and Miller were never able to enforce their patent rights effectively. Rival manufacturers shamelessly pirated their work, and countless farmers built gins of their own. Cotton production figures tell the story: In 1790 about 3,000 bales (of an average of 500 pounds) were produced in the United States. In 1793 the total rose to 10,000 bales; two years later, to 17,000; by 1801, to 100,000. The embargo and the War of 1812 temporarily checked expansion, but in 1816 output spurted ahead by more than 25 percent, and in the early 1820s annual production averaged well over 400,000 bales.

Despite this avalanche, the price of cotton remained high. During the 1790s it ranged between 26 and 44 cents a pound, a veritable bonanza. In the next decade the price was lower (15 to 19 cents), but it still provided high profits even for inefficient planters. It was higher again after 1815 and fell below 14 cents only once before 1826. With prices at these levels, profits of $50 an acre were not unusual, and the South boomed.

Upland cotton would grow wherever there were 200 consecutive days without frost and 24 inches of rain. The crop engulfed Georgia and South Carolina and spread north into parts of Virginia. After Andrew Jackson smashed the southwestern Indians during the War of 1812, the rich "Black Belt" area of central Alabama and northern Mississippi and the delta region along the lower Mississippi River were rapidly taken over by the fluffy white staple. In 1821 Alabama alone raised 40,000 bales. Central Tennessee also became important cotton country.

Cotton stimulated the economy of the rest of the nation as well. Most of it was exported, the sale paying for much-needed European products. The transportation, insurance, and final disposition of the crop fell largely into the hands of northern merchants, who profited accordingly. And the surplus corn and hogs of western farmers helped feed the slaves of the new cotton plantations. As Douglass North explained in *The Economic Growth of the United States,* cotton was "the major expansive force" in the economy for a generation, beginning about 1815.

Revival of Slavery

Amid the national rejoicing over this prosperity, one aspect both sad and ominous was easily overlooked. Slavery, a declining or at worst stagnant institution in the decade of the Revolution, was revitalized in the following years.

Libertarian beliefs inspired by the Revolution ran into the roadblock of race prejudice as soon as some of the practical aspects of freedom for blacks

---

* The property, formerly owned by a prominent Georgia Tory, had been given to Greene by the state in gratitude for his having driven out the British during the Revolution.

became apparent. As disciples of John Locke, the Revolutionary generation had a deep respect for property rights; in the last analysis most white Americans placed these rights ahead of the personal liberty of black Americans in their constellation of values. Forced abolition of slavery therefore attracted few recruits. Moreover, the rhetoric of the Revolution had raised the aspirations of blacks. Increasing signs of rebelliousness appeared among them, especially after the slave uprising in Saint Domingue, which culminated, after a great bloodbath, in the establishment of the black Republic of Haiti in 1804. This example of a successful slave revolt filled white Americans with apprehension. Their fears were irrational (Haitian blacks outnumbered whites and mulattoes combined by seven to one) but nonetheless real. And fear led to repression; the exposure of a plot to revolt in Virginia, led by the slave Gabriel, resulted in some three dozen executions even though no actual uprising had occurred.

The mood of the Revolutionary decade had led to the manumission of many slaves; unfortunately, this led many whites to have second thoughts about ending slavery. "If the blacks see all of their color slaves, it will seem to them a disposition of Providence, and they will be content," a Virginia legislator, apparently something of an amateur psychologist, claimed. "But if they see others like themselves free . . . they will repine." As the number of free blacks rose, restrictions on them were everywhere tightened.

In the 1780s many opponents of slavery began to think of solving the "Negro problem" by colonizing freed slaves in some distant region—in the western districts or perhaps in Africa. The colonization movement had two aspects. One, a manifestation of an embryonic black nationalism, reflected the disgust of black Americans with local racial attitudes and their interest in African civilization. Paul Cuffe, a Massachusetts Quaker, managed to finance the emigration of 38 of his fellow blacks to Sierra Leone in 1815, but few others followed. Most influential northern blacks, the most conspicuous among them the Reverend Richard Allen, bishop of the African Methodist Church, opposed the idea vigorously.

The other colonization movement, led by whites, was paternalistic. Some white colonizationists genuinely abhorred slavery. Others could not stomach

living with free blacks; to them colonization was merely a polite word for deportation. Most white colonizationists were conservatives who considered themselves realists. Whether they thought blacks degenerate by nature or the victims of their surroundings, they were sure that American conditions gave them no chance to better their lot and that both races would profit from separation.

The colonization idea became popular in Virginia in the 1790s, but nothing was achieved until after the founding of the American Colonization Society in 1817. The society purchased African land and established the Republic of Liberia. However, despite the cooperation of a handful of black nationalists and the patronage of many important white southerners, including presidents Madison and Monroe and Chief Justice Marshall, it accomplished little. Although some white colonizationists expected ex-slaves to go to Africa as enthusiastic Christian missionaries who would convert and "civilize" the natives, few blacks in fact wished to migrate to a land as alien to their own experience as to their masters'. Only about 12,000 went to Liberia, and the toll taken among them by tropical diseases was large. As late as 1850 the black American population of Liberia was only 6,000.

The cotton boom of the early 19th century acted as a brake on the colonization movement. As cotton production expanded, the need for labor in the South grew apace. The price of slaves doubled between 1795 and 1804. As it rose, the inclination of even the most kindhearted masters to free their slaves began to falter. Although the importation of slaves from abroad had been outlawed by all the states, perhaps 25,000 were smuggled into the country in the 1790s. In 1804 South Carolina reopened the trade, and between that date and 1808, when the constitutional prohibition of importation became effective, some 40,000 were brought in. Thereafter, the miserable traffic in human beings continued clandestinely, though on a very small scale.

Equally obnoxious was the interstate slave trade that resulted from the cotton boom. While it had always been legal for owners to transport their own slaves to a new state if they were settling there, many states forbade, or at least severely restricted, interstate commercial transactions in human flesh. A Virginia law of 1778, for example, prohibited the importation of slaves for purposes of sale, and persons

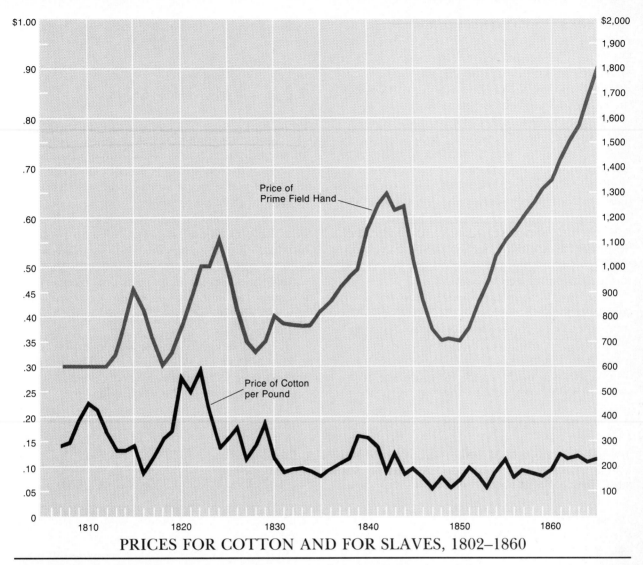

PRICES FOR COTTON AND FOR SLAVES, 1802–1860

The vertical axis on the left shows cents, and the curve for the price of cotton should be read against it; the right vertical axis shows dollars, and the price of slaves should be read against it. These prices are from New Orleans records. According to Conrad and Meyer, the rising trend of slave prices (and a growing slave population) shows the continuing profitability and viability of slavery up to 1860.

entering the state with slaves had to swear that they did not intend to sell them. Once cotton became important, these laws were systematically evaded. There was a surplus of slaves in one part of the United States and an acute shortage in another. A migration from the Upper South to the cotton lands quickly sprang up. Slaves from "free" New York and New Jersey and even from New England began to appear on the auction blocks of Savannah and

Charleston. Early in the Era of Good Feelings, newspapers in New Orleans were carrying reports such as this one: "Jersey negroes appear to be particularly adapted to this market. . . . We have the right to calculate on large importations in the future, from the success which hitherto attended the sale."

By about 1820 the letter of the law began to be changed. Soon the slave trade became an organized business, cruel and shameful, frowned on by the "best" people of the South, managed by the depraved and the greedy, yet patronized by nearly everyone who needed labor. "The native land of Washington, Jefferson, and Madison," one disgusted Virginian told a French visitor, had "become the Guinea of the United States."

The lot of blacks in the northern states was almost as bad as that of southern free blacks. Except in New England, where there were few blacks to begin with, most were denied the vote, either directly or by extralegal pressures. They could not testify in court, intermarry with whites, obtain decent jobs or housing, or get even a rudimentary education. Most states segregated blacks in theaters, hospitals, and churches and on public transportation facilities. They were barred from hotels and restaurants patronized by whites.

Northern blacks could at least protest and try to convince the white majority of the injustice of their treatment. These rights were denied their southern brethren. They could and did publish newspapers and pamphlets, organize for political action, petition legislatures and Congress for redress of grievance—in short, they applied methods of peaceful persuasion in an effort to improve their position in society.

Roads to Market

Inventions and technological improvements were extremely important in the settlement of the West. On superficial examination, this may not seem to have been the case, for the hordes of settlers who struggled across the mountains immediately after the War of 1812 were no better equipped than their ancestors who had pushed up the eastern slopes in previous generations. Many plodded on foot over hundreds of miles, dragging crude carts laden with their meager possessions. More fortunate pioneers traveled on horseback or in heavy, cumbersome wagons, the best known being the hearselike, canvas-topped Conestoga "covered wagons," pulled by horses or oxen.

In many cases the pioneers followed trails and roads no better than those of colonial days—quagmires in wet weather, rutted and pitted with potholes a good part of the year. When they settled

Much of the east-west traffic in the growing United States passed through St. Louis, a vital port on the Mississippi River and the terminus of several western trails. The city looked like this in the 1830s.

down, their way of life was no more advanced than that of the Pilgrims. At first they were creatures of the forest, feeding on its abundance, building their homes and simple furniture with its wood, clothing themselves in the furs of forest animals. They usually planted the first crop in a natural glade; thereafter, year by year, they pushed back the trees with ax and saw and fire until the land was cleared. Any source of power more complicated than an ox was beyond their ken. Until the population of the territory had grown large enough to support town life, settlers were as dependent on crude household manufactures as any earlier pioneer.

The spread of settlement into the Mississippi Valley created challenges that required technological advances if they were to be met. In the social climate of that age in the United States, these advances were not slow in coming. Most were related to transportation, the major problem for westerners. Without economical means of getting their produce to market, western settlers were condemned to lives of crude self-sufficiency. Everyone recognized that an efficient transportation network would increase land values, stimulate domestic and foreign trade, and strengthen the entire economy.

The Mississippi River and its tributaries provided a natural highway for western commerce and communication, but one that had grave disadvantages. Farm products could be floated down to New Orleans on rafts and flatboats, but the descent from Pittsburgh took at least a month. Transportation upstream was out of the question for anything but the lightest and most valuable products, and even for them it was extremely expensive. In any case, the natural flow of trade was between East and West. That is why, from early in the westward movement, much attention was given to building roads linking the Mississippi Valley to the eastern seaboard.

Constructing decent roads over the rugged Appalachians was a formidable task. The steepest grades had to be reduced by cutting through hills and filling in low places, all without modern blasting or earth-moving equipment. Streams had to be bridged. Drainage ditches were essential if the roads were not to be washed out by the first rains, and a firm foundation of stones, topped with a well-crowned gravel dressing, had to be provided if they were to stand up under the pounding of heavy wagons. The skills required for building roads of this quality had been developed in Great Britain and France, and the earliest American examples, constructed in the 1790s, were similar to good European highways. The first such road, connecting Philadelphia and Lancaster, Pennsylvania, opened to traffic in 1794.

In heavily populated areas the volume of traffic made good roads worth their cost, which ran to as much as $13,000 a mile where the terrain was difficult, though the average was perhaps half that figure. In some cases good roads ran into fairly remote areas. In New York, always a leading state in the movement for improved transportation, an excellent road had been built all the way from Albany to Lake Erie by the time of the War of 1812, and by 1821 the state had some 4,000 miles of good roads.

Transportation and the Government

Most of the improved highways and many bridges were built as business ventures by private interests. Promoters charged tolls, the rates being set by the states. Tolls were collected at gates along the way; hinged poles suspended across the road were turned back by a guard after receipt of the toll. Hence these thoroughfares were known as turnpikes, or simply pikes.

The profits earned by a few early turnpikes, such as the one between Philadelphia and Lancaster, caused the boom in private road building, but even the most fortunate of the turnpike companies did not make much money. Maintenance was expensive, traffic spotty. (Ordinary public roads paralleling turnpikes were sometimes called "shunpikes" because penny-pinching travelers used them to avoid the tolls.) Some states bought stock to bolster weak companies, and others built and operated turnpikes as public enterprises. Local governments everywhere provided considerable support, for every town was eager to develop efficient communication with its neighbors.

Despite much talk about individual self-reliance and free enterprise, local, state, and national governments contributed heavily to the development of what in the jargon of the day were called "internal improvements." They served as "primary entrepreneurs," supplying capital for risky but socially desirable enterprises, with the result that a fascinating mixture of private and public energy went into the building of these institutions. At the federal level even the parsimonious Jeffersonians became deeply involved. In 1808 Secretary of the Treasury Albert Gallatin drafted a comprehensive plan for constructing much-needed roads at a cost of $16 million. This proposal was not adopted, but the government poured money in an erratic and unending stream into turnpike companies and other organizations created to improve transportation.

Logically, the major highways, especially those over the mountains, should have been built by the national government. Strategic military requirements alone would have justified such a program. One major artery, the Old National Road, running from Cumberland, Maryland, to Wheeling, in western Virginia, was constructed by the United States between 1811 and 1818. In time it was extended as far west as Vandalia, Illinois. However, further federal road building was hampered by political squabbles in Congress, usually phrased in constitutional terms but in fact based on sectional rivalries and other economic conflicts. Thus no comprehensive highway program was undertaken in the 19th century.

While the National Road, the New York Pike, and other, rougher trails such as the Wilderness Road into the Kentucky country were adequate for the movement of settlers, they did not begin to answer the West's need for cheap and efficient transportation. Wagon freight rates averaged at least 30 cents a ton-mile around 1815. At such rates, to transport a ton of oats from Buffalo to New York would have cost 12 times the value of the oats! To put the problem another way, four horses could haul a ton and a half of oats about 18 or 20 miles a day over a good road. If they could obtain half their feed by grazing, the horses would still consume about 50 pounds of oats a day. It requires little mathematics to figure out how much oats would be left in the wagon when it reached New York City, almost 400 miles away.

Turnpikes made it possible to transport such goods as clothing, hardware, coffee, and books across the Appalachians, but the expense was considerable. It cost more to ship a ton of freight 300 miles over the mountains from Philadelphia to Pittsburgh than from Pittsburgh to Philadelphia by way of New Orleans, more than ten times as far. Until

the coming of the railroad, which was just being introduced in England in 1825, shipping bulky goods by land over the great distances common in America was uneconomical. Businessmen and inventors concentrated instead on improving water transport, first by designing better boats and then by developing artificial waterways.

"Organs of Communication"

Rafts and flatboats were adequate for downstream travel, but the only practical solution for upstream travel was the steamboat. After John Fitch's work around 1790, a number of others made important contributions to the development of steam navigation. One early enthusiast was John Stevens, a wealthy New Jerseyite, who designed an improved steam boiler for which he received one of the first patents issued by the United States. Stevens got his brother-in-law, Robert R. Livingston, interested in the problem, and the latter used his political influence to obtain an exclusive charter to operate steamboats on New York waters. In 1802, while in France trying to buy New Orleans from Napoleon, Livingston got to know Robert Fulton, a young American artist and engineer who was experimenting with steam navigation, and agreed to finance his work. In 1807, after returning to New York, Fulton constructed the *North River Steam Boat,* famous to history as the *Clermont.*

The *Clermont* measured 142 feet long and 18 feet abeam and drew 7 feet of water. With its towering stack belching black smoke, its side wheels could push it along at a steady 5 miles an hour. Nothing about it was radically new, but Fulton brought the essentials—engine, boiler, paddle wheels, and hull—into proper balance and thereby produced an efficient vessel.

No one could patent a steamboat; soon the new vessels were plying the waters of every navigable river from the Mississippi east. After 1815 steamers were making the run from New Orleans as far as Ohio. By 1820 at least 60 vessels were operating between New Orleans and Louisville, and by the end of the decade there were more than 200 steamers on the Mississippi.

The day of the steamboat had dawned, and although the following generation would experience its high noon, even in the 1820s its major effects

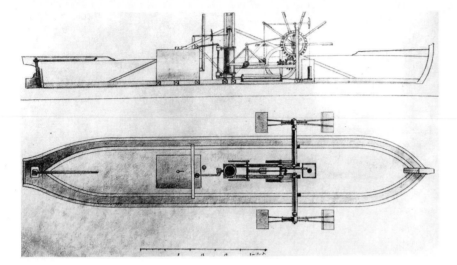

Robert Fulton spent several years in France during the Napoleonic era, trying to interest the government in his inventions. These are plans of one of his early steamboats, which was launched on the Seine in 1803.

were clear. The great Mississippi Valley, in the full tide of its development, was immensely enriched. Produce poured down to New Orleans, which soon ranked with New York and Liverpool among the world's great ports. Only 80,000 tons of freight reached New Orleans from the interior in 1816 and 1817, more than 542,000 tons in 1840 and 1841. Upriver traffic was affected even more spectacularly. Freight charges plummeted, in some cases to a tenth of what they had been after the War of 1812. Around 1818 coffee cost 16 cents a pound more in Cincinnati than in New Orleans, a decade later less than 3 cents more. The Northwest emerged from self-sufficiency with a rush and became part of the national market.

Steamboats were far more comfortable than any contemporary form of land transportation, and competition soon led builders to make them positively luxurious. The *General Pike*, launched in 1819, set the fashion. Marble columns, thick carpets, mirrors, and crimson curtains adorned its cabins and public rooms. Soon the finest steamers were floating palaces where passengers could dine, drink, dance, and gamble in luxury as they sped smoothly to their destinations. Yet raft and flatboat traffic increased. Farmers, lumbermen, and others with goods from upriver floated down in the slack winter season and returned in comfort by steamer after selling their produce—and their rafts as well, for lumber was in great demand in New Orleans. Every January and February, New Orleans teemed with westerners and Yankee sailors, their pockets jingling, bent on a fling

before going back to work. The shops displayed everything from the latest Paris fashions to teething rings made of alligator teeth mounted in silver. During the carnival season the city became one great festival, where every human pleasure could be tasted, every vice indulged. "Have you ever been in New Orleans?" one visiting bard sang in the late 1820s.

> . . . *If not you'd better go,*
> *It's a nation of a queer place; day and night a*
>   *show!*
> *Frenchmen, Spaniards, West Indians, Creoles,*
>   *Mustees,*
> *Yankees, Kentuckians, Tennesseeans, lawyers and*
>   *trustees.*
> *Clergymen, priests, friars, nuns, women of all*
>   *stains;*
> *Negroes in purple and fine linen, and slaves in*
>   *rags and chains.*
> *Ships, arks, steamboats, robbers, pirates, alligators,*
> *Assassins, gamblers, drunkards, and cotton*
>   *speculators;*
> *Sailors, soldiers, pretty girls, and ugly*
>   *fortunetellers;*
> *Pimps, imps, shrimps, and all sorts of dirty fellows;*
> *White men with black wives, et vice-versa too,*
> *A progeny of all colors—an infernal motley crew!*

The Canal Boom

While the steamboat was conquering western rivers, canals were being constructed that further improved the transportation network. Since the mid-western rivers all emptied into the Gulf of Mexico, they did not provide a direct link with the eastern seaboard. If an artificial waterway could be cut between the great central valley and some navigable stream flowing into the Atlantic, all sections would profit immensely.

Canals were more expensive than roads, but so long as the motive power used in overland transportation was the humble horse, they offered enormous economic advantages to shippers. Because there is less friction to overcome, a team plodding along a towpath could pull a canal barge with a 100-ton load and make better time over long distances than it could pulling a single ton in a wagon on the finest road.

Although canals were as old as Egypt, only about 100 miles of them existed in the United States as late as 1816. Construction costs aside, in a rough and mountainous country canals presented formidable engineering problems. To link the Mississippi Valley and the Atlantic meant somehow circumventing the Appalachian Mountains. Most people thought this impossible.

Mayor De Witt Clinton of New York believed that such a project was feasible in New York State. In 1810, while serving as state canal commissioner, he traveled across central New York and convinced himself that it would be practicable to dig a canal from Buffalo, on Lake Erie, to the Hudson River. The Mohawk Valley cuts through the Appalachian chain just north of Albany, and at no point along the route to Buffalo does the land rise more than 570 feet above the level of the Hudson. Marshaling a mass of technical, financial, and commercial information (and using his political influence cannily), Clinton placed his proposal before the New York legislature. In its defense he was eloquent and farsighted:

> As an organ of communication between the Hudson, the Mississippi, the St. Lawrence, the great lakes of the north and west, and their tributary rivers, [the canal] will create the greatest inland trade ever witnessed. The most fertile and extensive regions of

CANALS AND ROADS, 1820–1850

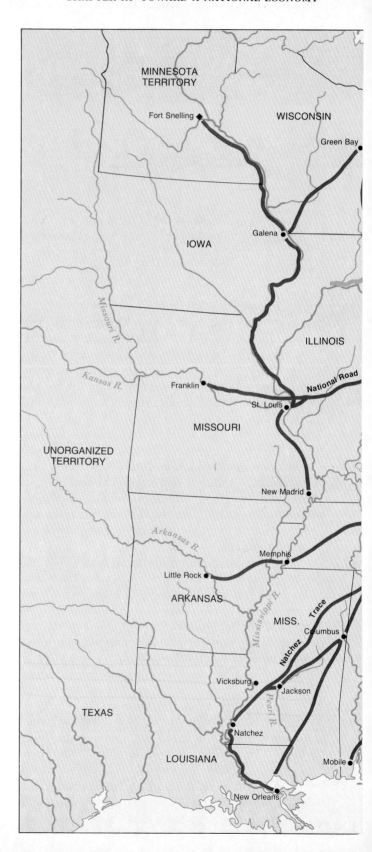

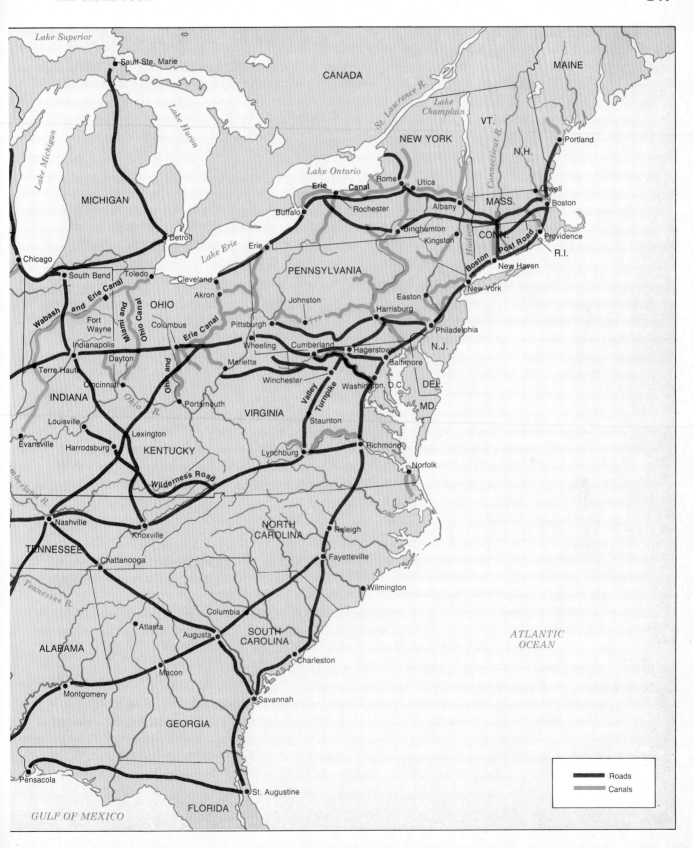

Lake Superior
Sault Ste. Marie
CANADA
MAINE
Lake Huron
Lake Michigan
St. Lawrence R.
Lake Champlain
VT.
Portland
NEW YORK
N.H.
MICHIGAN
Lake Ontario
Rome
Utica
Lowell
Detroit
Buffalo
Erie Canal
Rochester
Albany
MASS.
Boston
Chicago
Lake Erie
Erie
Binghamton
CONN.
Providence
South Bend
Toledo
Cleveland
Kingston
Hudson R.
Boston
R.I.
Wabash and Erie Canal
Akron
PENNSYLVANIA
Post Road
New Haven
Fort Wayne
Miami and Ohio Canal
Columbus
Erie Canal
Johnston
Easton
New York
Indianapolis
OHIO
Pittsburgh
Harrisburg
Philadelphia
Dayton
Ohio and
Wheeling
Cumberland
Hagerstown
N.J.
Terre Haute
Cincinnati
Ohio R.
Marietta
Baltimore
DEL.
INDIANA
Portsmouth
Winchester
Washington, D.C.
MD.
Louisville
Valley Turnpike
Lexington
VIRGINIA
Staunton
Evansville
Harrodsburg
KENTUCKY
Lynchburg
Richmond
Norfolk
Cumberland R.
Wilderness Road
Nashville
Knoxville
NORTH CAROLINA
Raleigh
TENNESSEE
Chattanooga
Fayetteville
Tennessee R.
Wilmington
Columbia
ATLANTIC OCEAN
Atlanta
Augusta
SOUTH CAROLINA
ALABAMA
Macon
Charleston
Montgomery
Savannah
GEORGIA
Pensacola
St. Augustine
FLORIDA
GULF OF MEXICO

Roads
Canals

America will avail themselves of its facilities for a market. All their surplus . . . will concentrate in the city of New York. . . . That city will, in the course of time, become the granary of the world, the emporium of commerce, the seat of manufactures, the focus of great moneyed operations. . . . And before the revolution of a century, the whole island of Manhattan, covered with habitations and replenished with a dense population, will constitute one vast city.

The legislators were convinced, and in 1817 the state began construction along a route 363 miles long, most of it across densely forested wilderness. At the time the longest canal in the United States ran less than 28 miles!

The construction of the Erie Canal, as it was called, was a remarkable accomplishment. The chief engineer, Benjamin Wright, a surveyor-politician from Rome, New York, had had almost no experience with canal building. One of his chief associates, James Geddes, possessed only an elementary school education and knew virtually nothing about surveying. Both learned rapidly by trial and error. Fortunately, Wright proved to be a good organizer and a fine judge of engineering talent. He quickly spotted young men of ability among the workers and pushed them forward. One of his finds, Canvass White, was sent to study British canals. White became an expert on the design of locks; he also discovered an American limestone that could be made into waterproof cement, a vital product in canal construction that had previously been imported at a substantial price from England. Another of Wright's proteges, John B. Jervis, began as an axman, rose in two years to resident engineer in charge of a section of the project, and went on to become perhaps the outstanding American civil engineer of his time. Workers who learned the business digging the "Big Ditch" supervised the construction of dozens of canals throughout the country in later years.

The Erie, completed in 1825, was an immediate financial success. Together with the companion Champlain Canal, which linked Lake Champlain and the Hudson, it brought in over half a million dollars in tolls in its first year. Soon its entire $7 million cost had been recovered, and it was earning profits of about $3 million a year. The effect of this prosperity on New York State was enormous. Buffalo, Rochester, Syracuse, and half a dozen lesser towns along the canal flourished.

Emporium of the Western World

New York City had already become the largest city in the nation, thanks chiefly to its merchants, who had established a reputation for their rapid and orderly way of doing business. In 1818 the Black Ball Line opened the first regularly scheduled freight and passenger service between New York and England. Previously, shipments might languish in port for weeks while a skipper waited for additional cargo. Now merchants on both sides of the Atlantic could count on the Black Ball packets to move their goods between Liverpool and New York on schedule whether or not the transporting vessel had a full cargo. This improvement brought much new business to the port. In the same year New York enacted an auction law requiring that imported goods having been placed on the block could not be withdrawn if a bid satisfactory to the seller was not forthcoming. This too was a boon to businessmen, who could be assured that if they outbid the competition, the goods would be theirs.

Now the canal cemented New York's position as the national metropolis. Most European-manufactured goods destined for the Mississippi Valley entered the country at New York and passed on to the west over the canal. The success of the Erie also sparked a nationwide canal-building boom. Most canals were constructed either by the states, as in the case of the Erie, or as "mixed enterprises" that combined public and private energies.

No state profited as much from this construction as New York, for none possessed New York's geographic advantages. In New England the terrain was so rugged as to discourage all but fanatics. Canals were built connecting Worcester and Northampton, Massachusetts, with the coast, but they were failures financially. The Delaware and Hudson Canal, running from northeastern Pennsylvania across northern New Jersey and lower New York to the Hudson, was completed by private interests in 1828. It managed to earn respectable dividends by barging coal to the eastern seaboard, but it made no attempt to compete with the Erie for the western trade. Pennsylvania, desperate to keep up with New York, engaged in an orgy of construction. In 1834 it completed a complicated system, part canal and part railroad, over the mountains to Pittsburgh. This Mainline Canal cost a staggering sum for that day. With its 177 locks and its cumbersome "in-

A view of New York's Broadway in 1835. The broad avenue was home to many of the large, modern stores that helped make New York City the commercial center of the nation.

clined-plane railroad," it was slow and expensive to operate and never competed effectively with the Erie. Efforts of Maryland to link Baltimore with the West by water failed utterly.

Beyond the mountains there was even greater zeal for canal construction in the 1820s and still more in the 1830s. Once the Erie opened the way across New York, farmers in the Ohio country demanded that links be built between the Ohio River and the Great Lakes so that they could ship their produce by water directly to the East. Local feeder canals seemed equally necessary; with corn worth 20 cents a bushel at Columbus selling for 50 cents at Marietta, on the Ohio, the value of cheap transportation became obvious to Ohio farmers.

Even before the completion of the Erie, Ohio had begun construction of the Ohio and Erie Canal running from the Ohio River to Cleveland. Another, from Toledo to Cincinnati, was begun in 1832. Meanwhile, Indiana had undertaken the 450 mile Wabash and Erie Canal. These canals were well conceived, but the western states overextended themselves building dozens of feeder lines, trying, it sometimes seemed, to supply all farmers west of the Appalachians with water connections from their barns to the New York docks. Politics made such programs almost inevitable, for in order to win support for their pet projects, legislators had to back

the schemes of their fellows. The result was frequently financial disaster. There was not enough traffic to pay for all the waterways that were dug. By 1844, some $60 million in state improvement bonds were in default. Nevertheless, the canals benefited both western farmers and the national economy.

Government Aid to Business

Throughout this period both the United States and the states were active in areas that affected the economy directly. Federal banking, tariff, and land legislation had considerable influence on economic expansion. These political activities, which also contributed to the growth of sectional conflicts in the nation, will be considered in Chapter 10; here a number of legal and judicial developments require consideration.

Though prejudice against corporations in the manufacturing field continued, incorporation was such a useful means of bringing together the substantial amounts of capital needed for building roads and canals and for organizing banks and insurance companies that a steadily increasing number of promoters applied for charters. Bills authorizing incorporations became so numerous in some eastern states that legislators found themselves devoting a disconcertingly large portion of their time to them. Soon they were tempted to issue blanket, though restricted, authorizations. In 1809 Massachusetts passed a law establishing strict rules for all manufacturing corporations in the state. One rule made shareholders individually liable for their companies' debts beyond their actual investment. While still requiring separate authorizations for each charter, the Massachusetts legislature could now dispose of applications in a more routine fashion.

Two years later New York enacted the first general incorporation law, permitting the issuance of charters without specific legislative action in each case. Although they held stockholders liable only "to the extent of their respective shares in the . . . company," which was the basic privilege sought by all incorporators, these general charters were not available to companies capitalized at more than $50,000, and they ran for only five years. This was unsatisfactory; after an initial period of enthusiasm (122 charters were issued between 1811 and 1816), the law became nearly a dead letter. Other states did not begin to permit general incorporation until 1837, and businessmen continued to seek, and obtain, special charters for decades thereafter.

Manufacturers in some states received valuable tax benefits. In Vermont no industrial concern paid local taxes. A New York law of 1817 exempted textile mills, and in 1823 Ohio extended similar privileges to textile, iron, and glass companies. Manufacturers benefited from the protection granted inventors by the United States Patent Office, created in 1790, and the attitude of most courts and juries toward labor unions and strikes in this period favored employers. Before the end of the 1820s craft unions had become numerous and active, yet judges tended to consider strikes unlawful conspiracies and to find against unions that tried to establish the closed shop. Though the public's attitude toward organized labor was beginning to change, the legal right of unions to exist was not fully established until the 1840s.

The Marshall Court

The most important legal advantages bestowed on businessmen in the period were the gift of Chief Justice John Marshall. Historians have tended to forget that he had six colleagues on the Supreme Court, and that is easy to understand. Marshall's particular combination of charm, logic, and forcefulness made the Court during his long reign, if not a rubber stamp, remarkably submissive to his view of the Constitution. Marshall's belief in a powerful central government explains his tendency to hand down decisions favorable to manufacturing and business interests. He also thought that "the business community was the agent of order and progress" and tended to interpret the Constitution in a way that would advance its interests.

Many important cases came before the Court between 1819 and 1824, and in each one Marshall's decision was applauded by most of the business community. The cases involved two major principles: the "sanctity" of contracts and the supremacy of federal legislation over the laws of the states. Marshall shared the conviction of the Revolutionary generation that property had to be protected against arbitrary seizure if liberty was to be preserved. Contracts between private individuals and between individuals and the government must be strictly enforced, he believed, or chaos will result. He therefore gave the widest possible application to the constitutional provision that no state could pass any law "impairing the Obligation of Contracts."

Two controversies settled in February 1819 illustrate Marshall's views on the subject of contracts. In *Sturges* v. *Crowninshield* he found a New York bankruptcy law unconstitutional. States could pass such laws, he conceded, but they could not make them applicable to debts incurred before the laws were passed, for debts were contracts. In *Dartmouth College* v. *Woodward* he held that a charter granted by a state was a contract and might not be canceled or altered without the consent of both parties. Contracts could scarcely be more sacred than Marshall made them in the Dartmouth College case, which involved an attempt by New Hampshire to alter the charter granted to Dartmouth by King George III in 1769. The state had sought not to destroy the college but to change it from a private to a public institution, yet Marshall held that to do so would violate the contract clause. In the light of this decision, corporations licensed by the states seemed immune against later attempts to regulate their activities, although, of course, restrictions imposed at the time of the chartering were not affected. As a result, states began to spell out the limitations of corporate charters in greater detail.

The artist Chester Harding painted John Marshall in 1828, during the chief justice's twenty-seventh year on the Supreme Court. "The unpretentious dignity [and] the sober factualism" of Harding's style (as art historian Oliver Larkin describes it) was well suited to capturing Marshall's character.

Marshall's decisions concerning the division of power between the federal government and the states were even more important. The question of the constitutionality of a national bank, first debated by Hamilton and Jefferson, had not been submitted to the courts during the life of the first Bank of the United States. By the time of the second Bank there were many state banks, and some of them felt that their interests were threatened by the national institution. Responding to pressure from local banks, the Maryland legislature placed an annual tax of $15,000 on "foreign" banks. The Maryland branch of the Bank of the United States refused to pay, whereupon the state brought suit against its cashier, John W. McCulloch. *McCulloch* v. *Maryland* was crucial to the Bank, for five other states had levied taxes on its branches, and others would surely follow suit if the Maryland law were upheld.

Marshall extinguished the threat. The Bank was constitutional, he announced in phrases taken almost verbatim from Hamilton's 1791 memorandum to Washington on the subject; its legality was implied in many of the powers specifically granted to Congress. Full "discretion" must be allowed Congress in deciding exactly how its powers "are to be carried into execution." Since the Bank was legal, the Maryland tax was unconstitutional. Marshall found a "plain repugnance" in the thought of "conferring on one government a power to control the constitutional measures of another." He put this idea in the simplest possible language: "The power to tax involves the power to destroy . . . the power to destroy may defeat and render useless the power to create." The long-range significance of the decision lay in its strengthening of the implied powers of Congress and its confirmation of the Hamiltonian or "loose" interpretation of the Constitution. By establishing the legality of the Bank, it also aided the growth of the economy.

In 1824 Marshall handed down an important decision involving the regulation of interstate commerce. This was the "steamboat case," *Gibbons* v. *Ogden.* In 1815 Aaron Ogden, former United States senator and governor of New Jersey, had purchased the right to operate a ferry between Elizabeth Point, New Jersey, and New York City from Robert Fulton's backer, Robert R. Livingston, who held a New York monopoly of steamboat navigation on the Hudson. When Thomas Gibbons, who held a federal coasting license, set up a competing line, Ogden sued him. Ogden argued in effect that Gibbons could operate his boat (whose captain was Cornelius Vanderbilt, later a famous railroad magnate) on the New Jersey side of the Hudson but had no right to cross into New York waters. After complicated litigation in the lower courts, the case reached the Supreme Court on appeal. Marshall decided in favor of Gibbons, effectively destroying the New York monopoly. A state can regulate commerce that begins and ends in its own territory but not when the transaction involves crossing a state line; then the national authority takes precedence. "The act of Congress," he said, "is supreme; and the law of the state . . . must yield to it."

This decision threw open the interstate steamboat business to all comers, and since an adequate 100-ton vessel could be built for as little as $7,000, dozens of small operators were soon engaged in it. Their competition tended to keep rates low and service efficient, to the great advantage of the country. More important in the long run was the fact that in order to include the ferry business within the federal government's power to regulate inter-

state commerce, Marshall had given the word the widest possible meaning. "Commerce, undoubtedly, is traffic, but it is something more—it is intercourse." By construing the "commerce" clause so broadly, he made it easy for future generations of judges to extend its coverage to include the control of interstate electric power lines and even radio and television transmission.

Many of Marshall's decisions aided the economic development of the country in specific ways, but his chief contribution lay in his broadly national view of economic affairs. When he tried consciously to favor business by making contracts inviolable, his influence was important but limited—and, as it worked out, impermanent. In the steamboat case and in *McCulloch* v. *Maryland,* where he was really deciding between rival property interests, his work was more truly judicial in spirit and far more lasting. In such matters his nationalism enabled him to add form and substance to Hamilton's vision of the economic future of the United States.

Marshall and his colleagues firmly established the principle of judicial limitation on the power of legislatures and made the Supreme Court a vital part of the American system of government. In an age plagued by narrow sectional jealousies, Marshall's contribution was of immense influence and significance, and upon it rests his claim to greatness.

John Marshall died in 1835. Two years later, in the Charles River Bridge case, the court handed down another decision that aided economic development. The state of Massachusetts had built a bridge across the Charles River between Boston and Cambridge that drew traffic from an older, privately owned toll bridge nearby. Since no tolls were collected from users of the state bridge after construction costs were recovered, owners of the older bridge sued for damages on the ground that the free bridge made the stock in their company worthless. They argued that in building the bridge, Massachusetts had violated the contract clause of the Constitution.

The Court, however, now speaking through the new Chief Justice, Roger B. Taney, decided otherwise. The state had a right to place "the comfort and convenience" of the whole community over that of a particular company, Taney declared. "Improvements" that add to public "wealth and property" take precedence. How John Marshall would have voted in this case, in which he would have had to choose between his Dartmouth College and steamboat case arguments, will never be known. But like most of the decisions of the Court that were made while Marshall was chief justice, the Charles River Bridge case advanced the interests of those who favored economic development. Whether they were pursuing political advantage or economic, the Americans of the early 19th century seemed committed to a policy of compromise and accommodation.

Milestones

1790	Samuel Slater sets up first American factory			(*Dartmouth College* v. *Woodward*)
1793	Eli Whitney invents cotton gin			Bank case (*McCulloch* v. *Maryland*)
1807	Robert Fulton's *North River Steam Boat*		**1819–1822**	Depression of 1819
1813	Boston Manufacturing Company opens in Waltham, Massachusetts		**1820–1821**	Missouri Compromise
			1824	Steamboat case (*Gibbons* v. *Ogden*)
1816	Second Bank of the United States		**1825**	J. Q. Adams's presumed "corrupt bargain" with Henry Clay
	James Monroe elected president			Erie Canal completed
1817	American Colonization Society founded		**1837**	*Charles River Bridge* v. *Warren Bridge*
1819	Dartmouth College case			

SUPPLEMENTARY READING

Titles marked with an asterisk have been published in paperback.

On the forces changing the American economy and stimulating the development of industry, see Stuart Bruchey, **The Roots of American Economic Growth*** (1965), and D. C. North, **The Economic Growth of the United States*** (1961). G. R. Taylor, **The Transportation Revolution*** (1951), a book far broader in scope than its title indicates, also discusses this subject intelligently. F. J. Turner, **Rise of the New West*** (1906), is still useful on the expansion of the West during the Era of Good Feelings, but see also the appropriate chapters of R. A. Billington, **Westward Expansion** (1967).

On the industrial revolution in America, see A. D. Chandler, Jr., **The Visible Hand: The Managerial Revolution in American Business** (1977), and B. M. Tucker, **Samuel Slater and the Origins of the American Textile Industry** (1984).

On the spread of cotton cultivation in the South, see C. M. Green, **Eli Whitney and the Birth of American Technology*** (1956), and P. W. Gates, **The Farmer's Age** (1960). On the colonization movement, see P. J. Staudenraus, **The African Colonization Movement** (1961).

Taylor's **Transportation Revolution** is the best introduction to the changes in transportation that took place. P. D. Jordan, **The National Road** (1948), is useful, as is George Dangerfield, **Chancellor Robert R. Livingston of New York** (1960), which contains an excellent account of the planning and operation of the *Clermont*.

On the Erie Canal, see R. E. Shaw, **Erie Water West** (1966), Nathan Miller, **The Enterprise of a Free People** (1962), and R. G. Albion, **The Rise of New York Port** (1939). Two works edited by Carter Goodrich, **Government Promotion of American Canals and Railroads,** (1960) and **Canals and American Economic Development** (1961), describe authoritatively the role of government aid in canal construction.

On Marshall, see F. N. Stites, **John Marshall: Defender of the Constitution** (1981). The most important decisions of the Marshall court in this period are discussed in J. A. Garraty (ed.), **Quarrels That Have Shaped the Constitution*** (1987), and R. K. Newmyer, **The Supreme Court Under Marshall and Taney*** (1968).

X

Jacksonian Democracy

The best government rests on the [whole] people and not on the few, on persons and not on property, on the free development of public opinion and not on authority, . . . the munificent Author of our being has conferred the gifts of mind upon every member of the human race without distinction of outward circumstance.

GEORGE BANCROFT, The Office of the People, *1842*

A t 11 A.M. on March 4, 1829, a bright sunny day, Andrew Jackson, hatless and dressed severely in black, left his quarters at Gadsby's Hotel. Accompanied by a few close associates, he walked up Pennsylvania Avenue to the Capitol. At a few minutes after noon he emerged on the East Portico with the justices of the Supreme Court and other dignitaries. Before a throng of more than 15,000 people he delivered an almost inaudible and thoroughly commonplace inaugural address and then took the presidential oath. The first man to congratulate him was Chief Justice Marshall, who had administered the oath. The second was "Honest George" Kremer, a Pennsylvania congressman best known for the leopardskin coat that he affected, who led the cheering crowd that brushed past the barricade and scrambled up the Capitol steps to wring the new president's hand.

Jackson shouldered his way through the crush, mounted a splendid white horse, and rode off to the White House. A reception had been announced, to which "the officially and socially eligible as defined by precedent" had been invited. The day was unseasonably warm after a hard winter, and the streets of Washington were muddy. As Jackson rode down Pennsylvania Avenue, the crowds that had turned out to see the Hero of New Orleans followed—on horseback, in rickety wagons, and on foot. Nothing could keep them out of the executive mansion, and the result was chaos. Long tables laden with cakes, ice cream, and orange punch had been set up in the East Room, but these scarcely deflected the well-wishers. Jackson was pressed back helplessly as men tracked mud across valuable rugs and clambered up on delicate chairs to catch a glimpse of him. The White House shook with their shouts. Glassware splintered, furniture was overturned, women fainted.

Jackson was a thin old man despite his toughness, and soon he was in danger. Fortunately, friends formed a cordon and managed to extricate him through a rear door. The new president spent his first night in office at Gadsby's.

Only a generation earlier Jefferson had felt obliged to introduce pell-mell to encourage informality in the White House. Now a man whom John Quincy Adams called "a barbarian" held Jefferson's office, and, as one Supreme Court justice complained, "The reign of King 'Mob' seemed triumphant."

"Democratizing" Politics

Jackson's inauguration, and especially this celebration in the White House, symbolized the triumph of "democracy," the achievement of place and station by "the common man." Having been taught by Jefferson that all men are created equal, the Americans of Jackson's day (conveniently ignoring males with black skins, to say nothing of women, regardless of color) found it easy to believe that every person was as competent and as politically important as his neighbor.

The difference between Jeffersonian democracy and the Jackson variety was more one of attitude than of practice. Jefferson had believed that ordinary citizens could be educated to determine right. Jackson insisted that they knew what was right by instinct. Jefferson's pell-mell encouraged the average citizen to hold up his head; by the time of Jackson, the "common man" gloried in ordinariness and made mediocrity a virtue. The slightest hint of distinctiveness or servility became suspect. That President Washington required his footmen to wear uniforms was taken as a matter of course in the 1790s, but the British minister in Jackson's day found it next to impossible to find Americans willing to don his splendid livery. While most middle-class families could still hire people to do their cooking and housework, the word *servant* itself fell out of fashion, replaced by the egalitarian *help*.

The Founding Fathers had not foreseen all the implications of political democracy for a society like the one that existed in the United States. They believed that the ordinary man should have political power in order to protect himself against the superior man, but they assumed that the latter would always lead. The people would naturally choose the best men to manage public affairs. In Washington's day and even in Jefferson's this was generally the case, but the inexorable logic of democracy gradually produced a change. The new western states, unfettered by systems created in a less democratic age, drew up constitutions that eliminated property qualifications for voting and holding office. Many more public offices were made elective rather than appointive. The eastern states revised their own frames of government to accomplish the same purposes.

Even the presidency, designed to be removed from direct public control by the electoral college, felt the impact of the new thinking. By Jackson's time only two states, Delaware and South Carolina, still provided for the choice of presidential electors by the legislature; in all others they were selected by popular vote. The system of permitting the congressional caucus to name the candidates for the presidency came to an end before 1828. Jackson and Adams were put forward by state legislatures, and soon thereafter the still more democratic system of nomination by national party conventions was adopted.

Certain social changes reflected a new way of looking at political affairs. The final disestablishment of churches reveals a dislike of special privilege. The beginnings of the free-school movement, the earliest glimmerings of interest in adult education, and the slow spread of secondary education all bespeak a concern for improving the knowledge and judgment of the ordinary citizen. The rapid increase in the number of newspapers, their declining prices, and their ever-greater concentration on political affairs indicate that an effort was being made to bring political news to the common man's attention.

All these changes emphasized the idea that every citizen was equally important and the conviction that all should participate actively in government. Officeholders began to stress the fact that they were *representatives* as well as leaders and to appeal more openly and much more intensively for votes. The public responded. At each succeeding presidential election, a larger percentage of the population went to the polls. Roughly 300,000 ballots were cast in 1824, 1.1 million four years later, and 2.4 million in 1840.

As voting became more important, so did competition between the candidates, and this led to changes in the role and structure of political parties. It took money, people, and organized effort to run the campaigns and get out the vote. Parties became powerful institutions; as a result, they attracted voters' loyalties powerfully. This development took place first at the state level and at different times in different states. According to Richard P. McCormick, whose book *The Second American Party System* describes the process, the 1828 election stimulated party formation because instead of several sectional candidates, each dominant in his own region, competing for the presidency, it pitted two nationally known men against each other. This compelled local leaders to make a choice and then to organize their forces in order to convince local voters to accept their judgment. This was especially true in states where neither Adams nor Jackson had a preponderance of backers. Thus the new system established itself much faster in New York and Pennsylvania than in New England, where Adams was strong, or Tennessee, where the native son Jackson had overwhelming support.

Like most institutions, the new parties created bureaucracies to keep them running smoothly. Devoted party workers were rewarded with political office when their efforts were successful. "To the victors belong the spoils," said the New York politician William L. Marcy, and the image, drawn from war and piracy, was appropriate. Although the vigorous wooing of voters constituted a recognition of their importance and commitment to keeping them informed, campaigning—another military term— frequently degenerated into demagoguery. The most effective way to attract the average voter, politicians soon decided, was by flattery.

1828: *The New Party System in Embryo*

The new system could scarcely have been imagined in 1825 while John Quincy Adams ruled over the White House; Adams was not well equipped either to lead King Mob or to hold it in check. Indeed, it was the battle to succeed Adams that caused the system to develop. The campaign began almost on the day of his selection by the House of Representatives. Jackson felt that he, the man with the largest vote, had been cheated of the presidency in 1824 by "the corrupt bargain" that he believed Adams had made with Henry Clay, and he sought vindication.

Relying heavily on his military reputation and

on Adams's talent for making enemies, Jackson avoided taking a stand on issues and on questions where his views might displease one or another faction. The political situation thus became monumentally confused, one side unable to marshal support for its policies, the other unwilling to adopt policies for fear of losing support.

The campaign was disgraced by character assassination and lies of the worst sort. Administration supporters denounced Jackson as a bloodthirsty military tyrant, a drunkard, and a gambler. His wife Rachel, ailing and shy, was dragged into the campaign, her good name heartlessly besmirched. Previously married to a cruel, unbalanced man named Lewis Robards, she had begun living with Jackson before her divorce from Robards had been legally completed. When this fact came to light, she and Jackson had to remarry. Seizing on this incident, an Adams pamphleteer wrote: "Ought a convicted adulteress and her paramour husband be placed in the highest offices of this free and christian land?"

Furious, the Jacksonians (now calling themselves Democrats) replied in kind. They charged that while American minister to Russia, Adams had supplied

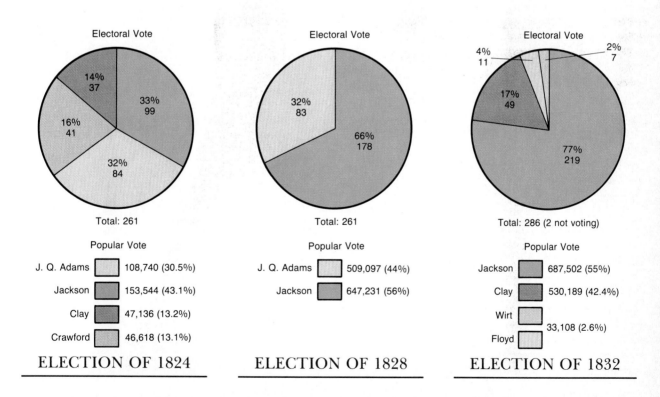

ELECTION OF 1824

Electoral Vote

14%
37

33%
99

16%
41

32%
84

Total: 261

Popular Vote

J. Q. Adams — 108,740 (30.5%)
Jackson — 153,544 (43.1%)
Clay — 47,136 (13.2%)
Crawford — 46,618 (13.1%)

ELECTION OF 1828

Electoral Vote

32%
83

66%
178

Total: 261

Popular Vote

J. Q. Adams — 509,097 (44%)
Jackson — 647,231 (56%)

ELECTION OF 1832

Electoral Vote

4%
11

2%
7

17%
49

77%
219

Total: 286 (2 not voting)

Popular Vote

Jackson — 687,502 (55%)
Clay — 530,189 (42.4%)
Wirt
Floyd — 33,108 (2.6%)

a beautiful American virgin for the delectation of the czar. Discovering that the president had purchased a chess set and a billiard table for the White House, they accused him of squandering public money on gambling devices. They translated his long and distinguished public service into the statistic that he had received over the years a sum equal to $16 for every day of his life in government pay. The great questions of the day were largely ignored.

All this was inexcusable, and both sides must share the blame. But as the politicians noticed when the votes were counted, their efforts had certainly brought out the electorate. *Each* candidate received far more votes than all four candidates had received in the preceding presidential election.

When inauguration day arrived, Adams refused to attend the ceremonies because Jackson had failed to pay the traditional preinaugural courtesy call on him at the White House, but the Old Puritan may have been equally, if unconsciously, motivated by shame at tactics he had countenanced during the campaign. Jackson felt vindication, not shame, but in any case, deep personal feelings were uppermost in everyone's mind at the formal changing of the guard. The real issues, however, remained. Andrew Jackson would now have to deal with them.

The Jacksonian Appeal

Some historians claim that despite his supposed fondness for the common man, Andrew Jackson was not a democrat at all and anything but a consistent friend of the weak and underprivileged. They point out that he was a wealthy land speculator and the owner of a fine Tennessee plantation, the Hermitage, and of many slaves. Before becoming president he had opposed cheap-money schemes and pressed lawsuits against more than 100 individuals who owed him money. Although his supporters liked to cast him as the political heir of Jefferson, he was in many ways like the conservative Washington: a soldier first, an inveterate speculator in western lands, a man with few intellectual interests and only sketchily educated.

Nor was Jackson quite the rough-hewn frontier character he sometimes seemed. True, he could not spell (again, like Washington), he possessed the unsavory habits of the tobacco chewer, and he had a

violent temper, but his manners and life-style were those of a southern planter. His judgment was intuitive yet usually sound; his frequent rages were often feigned, designed to accomplish some carefully thought-out purpose. "He would sometimes extemporize a fit of passion in order to overwhelm an adversary," one contemporary noted, "but his self-command was always perfect." Once, after scattering a delegation of protesters with an exhibition of Jovian wrath, he turned to an observer and said impishly: "They thought I was mad."

It is of small importance to anyone interested in Jacksonian democracy to know exactly how "democratic" Jackson was or how sincere was his interest

A figurehead of Andrew Jackson carved by Laban S. Beecher for the frigate Constitution. *Soon after it was mounted on the ship, an anti-Jackson agitator sawed off the head just below the nose! (It was later neatly mended.) The figurehead is almost 12 feet tall.*

in the welfare of the common man. Whatever his personal convictions, he stood as the symbol for a movement supported by a new, democratically oriented generation. That he was both a great hero and in many ways a most extraordinary person helps explain his mass appeal. He had defeated a mighty British army and killed hosts of Indians, but he acted on hunches and not always consistently, shouted and pounded his fist when angry, put loyalty to old comrades above efficiency when making appointments, distrusted "aristocrats" and all special privilege. Perhaps he was rich, perhaps conservative, but he was a man of the people, born in a frontier cabin, familiar with the problems of the average citizen.

Jackson epitomized many American ideals. He was intensely patriotic, generous to a fault, natural and democratic in manner (at home alike in the forest and in the ballroom of a fine mansion). He admired good horseflesh and beautiful women, yet no sterner moralist ever lived; he was a fighter, a relentless foe, but a gentleman in the best American sense. That some special providence watched over him (as over the United States) appeared beyond argument to those who had followed his career. He seemed, in short, both an average and an ideal American, one the people could identify with and still revere.

For these reasons Jackson drew support from every section and every social class: western farmers and southern planters, urban workers, and bankers and merchants. In this sense he was profoundly democratic—and in the sense, too, that whatever his position on public issues, he believed in equality of opportunity, distrusted entrenched status of every sort, and rejected no free American because of humble origins or inadequate education.

The Spoils System

Jackson took office with the firm intention of punishing the "vile wretches" who had attacked him so viciously during the campaign. (Rachel Jackson died shortly after the election, and her devoted husband was convinced that the indignities heaped on her by Adams partisans had speeded her decline.) The new concept of political office as a reward for victory seemed to justify a housecleaning in Washington. Henry Clay captured the fears of anti-Jackson government workers. "Among the official corps here there is the greatest solicitude and apprehension," he said. "The members of it feel something like the inhabitants of Cairo when the plague breaks out; no one knows who is next to encounter the stroke of death."

Eager for the "spoils," an army of politicians invaded Washington. There was nothing especially innovative about this invasion, for the principle of filling offices with one's partisans was almost as old as the republic. However, the long lapse of time since the last real political shift, and the recent untypical example of John Quincy Adams, who rarely removed or appointed anyone for political reasons, made Jackson's policy appear revolutionary. His removals were not entirely unjustified, for many government workers had grown senile and others corrupt. A number of officials were found to be short in their accounts; a few were hopeless drunks. Jackson was determined to root out the thieves. Even Adams admitted that some of those Jackson dismissed deserved their fate.

Aside from going along with the spoils system and eliminating crooks and incompetents, Jackson advanced another reason for turning experienced government employees out of their jobs: the principle of rotation. "No man has any more intrinsic right to official station than another," he said. Those who hold government jobs for a long time "are apt to acquire a habit of looking with indifference upon the public interests and of tolerating conduct from which an unpracticed man would revolt." By "rotating" jobholders periodically, more citizens could participate in the tasks of government, and the danger of creating an entrenched bureaucracy would be eliminated. The problem was that the constant replacing of trained workers by novices was not likely to increase the efficiency of the government. Jackson's response to this argument was typical: "The duties of all public officers are . . . so plain and simple that men of intelligence may readily qualify themselves for their performance.

Contempt for expert knowledge and the belief that ordinary Americans can do anything they set their minds to became fundamental tenets of Jacksonian democracy. To apply them to present-day government would be to court disaster, but in the early 19th century it was not so preposterous, because the role that government played in American life was simple and nontechnical.

Furthermore, Jackson did not practice what he preached. By and large his appointees were anything but common men. A majority came from the same social and intellectual elite as those they replaced. As the historian Sidney H. Aronson pointed out, "Circumstances made it difficult for him to locate such common men in the crowd." He did not try to rotate civil servants in the War and Navy departments, where to do so might have been harmful. In general, he left pretty much alone what a modern administrator would call middle management, the backbone of every organization.

Nevertheless, the spoilsmen roamed the capital

in force during the spring of 1829, seeking, as the forthright Jackson said, "a tit to suck the treasury pap." Their philosophy was well summarized by a New Yorker: "No d——d rascal who made use of his office . . . for the purpose of keeping Mr. Adams in, and Genl. Jackson out of power is entitled to the least lenity or mercy. . . . Whether or not I shall get anything in the general scramble for plunder, remains to be proven, but I rather guess I shall."

President of All the People

President Jackson was not cynical about the spoils system. As a strong man who intuitively sought to

Jackson's spoils-system policies were repeatedly attacked by opposition cartoonists. "Office Hunters for the Year 1834," for example, portrays the president as a demon dangling the spoils of his office, including banquets, money, weapons, appointments, and—for some obscure reason—millinery, above his greedy supporters.

increase his authority, the idea of making government workers dependent on him made excellent sense. His opponents had pictured him as a simple soldier fronting for a rapacious band of politicians, but he soon proved he would exercise his authority directly. Except for Martin Van Buren, the secretary of state, his Cabinet was not distinguished, and he did not rely on it for advice. He turned instead to an informal "Kitchen Cabinet," which consisted of the influential Van Buren and a few close friends. But these men were advisers, not directors; Jackson was clearly master of his own administration.

More than any earlier president, he conceived of himself as the direct representative of all the people and therefore the embodiment of national power. From Washington to John Quincy Adams, his predecessors together had vetoed only nine bills, always on the ground that they believed the measures unconstitutional. Jackson vetoed 12, some simply because he thought the legislation inexpedient. Yet he had no ambition to expand the scope of federal authority at the expense of the states. Basically he was a Jeffersonian; he favored a "frugal," constitutionally limited national government. Furthermore, he was a poor administrator, given to penny-pinching and lacking in imagination. His strong prejudices and his contempt for expert advice, even in fields such as banking where his ignorance was almost total, did him no credit and the country considerable harm.

Jackson's great success (not merely his popularity) was primarily the result of his personality. A shrewd French observer, Michel Chevalier, after commenting on "his chivalric character, his lofty integrity, and his ardent patriotism," pointed out what was probably the central element in Jackson's appeal. "His tactic in politics, as well as in war," Chevalier wrote in 1824, "is to throw himself forward with the cry of *Comrades, follow me!*" Sometimes he might be wrong, but always he was a leader.

Sectional Tensions Revived

In office Jackson had to say something about western lands, the tariff, and other issues. He tried to steer a moderate course, urging a slight reduction of the tariff and "constitutional" internal improvements. He suggested that once the rapidly disap-

pearing federal debt had been paid off, the surplus revenues of the government might be "distributed" among the states.

Even these cautious proposals caused conflict, so complex were the interrelations of sectional disputes. If the federal government turned its expected surplus over to the states, it could not afford to reduce the price of public land without going into the red. This disturbed westerners, notably Senator Thomas Hart Benton of Missouri, and western concern suggested to southern opponents of the protective tariff an alliance of South and West. The southerners argued that a tariff levied only to raise revenue would increase foreign imports, bring more money into the treasury, and thus make it possible to reduce the price of public land.

The question came up in the Senate in December 1829, when an obscure Connecticut senator, Samuel A. Foot, suggested restricting the sale of government land. Benton promptly denounced the proposal. On January 19, 1830, Senator Robert Y. Hayne of South Carolina, a spokesman for Vice-President Calhoun, supported Benton vigorously, suggesting an alliance of South and West based on cheap land and low tariffs. Daniel Webster then rose to the defense of northeastern interests, cleverly goading Hayne by accusing South Carolina of advocating disunionist policies. Responding to this attack, the South Carolinian, a glib speaker but a rather imprecise thinker, launched into an impassioned exposition of the states' rights doctrine.

Webster then took the floor again and for two days, before galleries packed with the elite of Washington society, cut Hayne's argument to shreds. The Constitution was a compact of the American people, not merely of the states, he insisted, the Union perpetual and indissoluble. Webster made the states' rights position appear close to treason; his "second reply to Hayne" effectively prevented the formation of a West-South alliance.

Jackson Versus Calhoun

The Webster-Hayne debate revived discussion of the idea of nullification. Although southern-born, Jackson had devoted too much of his life to fighting for the entire United States to countenance disunion. Therefore, when the states' rights faction invited him to a dinner to celebrate the anniversary of Jefferson's birth, he came prepared. The evening reverberated with speeches and toasts of a states' rights tenor, but when the president was called on to volunteer a toast, he raised his glass, fixed his eyes on John C. Calhoun, and said: "Our *Federal* Union: It must be preserved!" Calhoun took up the challenge at once. "The Union," he retorted, "next to our liberty, most dear!"

It is difficult to measure the importance of the animosity between Jackson and Calhoun in the crisis to which this clash was a prelude. Calhoun wanted very much to be president. He had failed to inherit the office from John Quincy Adams and had accepted the vice-presidency again under Jackson in the hope of succeeding him at the end of one term, if not sooner, for Jackson's health was known to be frail. Yet Old Hickory showed no sign of passing on or retiring. Jackson also seemed to place special confidence in the shrewd Van Buren, who, as secretary of state, also had claim to the succession.

A silly social fracas in which Calhoun's wife appeared to take the lead in the systematic snubbing of Peggy Eaton, wife of the secretary of war, had estranged Jackson and Calhoun. (Peggy was supposed to have had an affair with Eaton while she was still married to another man, and Jackson, undoubtedly sympathetic because of the attacks he and Rachel had endured, stoutly defended her good name.) Then, shortly after the Jefferson Day dinner, Jackson discovered that in 1818, when he had invaded Florida, Calhoun, then secretary of war, had recommended to President Monroe that Jackson be summoned before a court of inquiry and charged with disobeying orders. Since Calhoun had repeatedly led Jackson to believe that he had supported him at the time, the revelation convinced the president that Calhoun was not a man of honor.

The personal difficulties are worth stressing because Jackson and Calhoun were not far apart ideologically except on the ultimate issue of the right of a state to overrule federal authority. Jackson was a strong president, but he did not believe that the area of national power was large or that it should be expanded. His interests in government economy, in the distribution of federal surpluses to the states, and in interpreting the powers of Congress narrowly were all similar to Calhoun's. Like most westerners, he favored internal improvements, but he preferred that local projects be left to the states. In 1830 he vetoed a bill providing aid for the construction of the Maysville Road because the route was wholly within Kentucky. There were political reasons for this veto, which was a slap at Kentucky's hero, Henry Clay, but it could not fail to please Calhoun.

Indian Removals

The president also took a states' rights position in the controversy that arose between the Cherokee Indians and Georgia. Jackson subscribed to the theory, advanced by Jefferson, that Indians were "savage" because they roamed wild in a trackless wilderness. The "original inhabitants of our forests" were "incapable of self-government," Jackson claimed, ignoring the fact that they had governed themselves without trouble before the whites arrived. If they settled on small farms, they would become "civilized," and all would be well between them and the whites.

Most Indians preferred to maintain their tribal ways, so Jackson pursued a policy of removing them from the path of western settlement. This policy seems heartless to modern critics, but since few Indians were willing to adopt the white way of life, most contemporary whites considered removal the only humane solution if the nation was to continue to expand. Jackson insisted that the Indians receive fair prices for their lands and that the government bear the expense of resettling them. He believed that moving them beyond the Mississippi would protect them from the "degradation and destruction to which they were rapidly hastening . . . in the States."

Many tribes resigned themselves to removal without argument. Between 1831 and 1833 some 15,000 Choctaws migrated from their lands in Mississippi to the region west of Arkansas Territory.

In *Democracy in America*, the Frenchman Alexis de Tocqueville described "the frightful sufferings that attend these forced migrations," and he added sadly that the migrants "have no longer a country, and soon will not be a people." He vividly described a group of Choctaws crossing the Mississippi River at Memphis in the dead of winter.

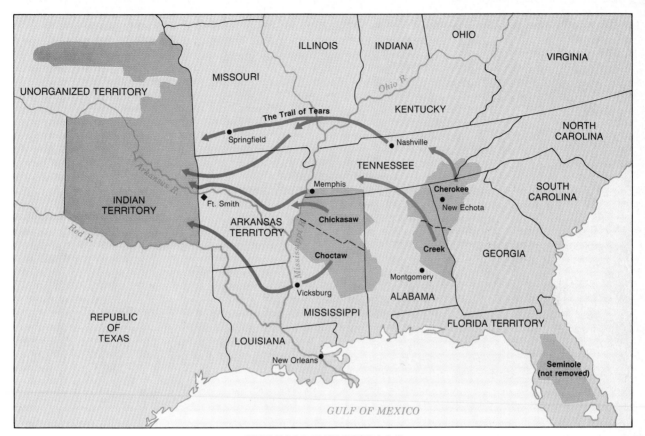

INDIAN REMOVALS

The cold was unusually severe; the snow had frozen hard upon the ground, and the river was drifting huge masses of ice. The Indians had their families with them, and they brought in their train the wounded and the sick, with children newly born and old men upon the verge of death. They possessed neither tents nor wagons, but only their arms and some provisions. I saw them embark to pass the mighty river, and never will that solemn spectacle fade from my remembrance. No cry, no sob, was heard among the assembled crowd; all were silent.

Tocqueville was particularly moved by the sight of an old woman whom he described in a letter to his mother. She was "naked save for a covering which left visible, at a thousand places, the most emaciated figure imaginable. . . . To leave one's country at that age to seek one's fortune in a foreign land, what misery!" "In the whole scene," he went on, "there was an air of ruin and destruction, something which betrayed a final and irrevocable adieu; one couldn't watch without feeling one's heart wrung."

A few tribes, such as Black Hawk's Sac and Fox in Illinois and Osceola's Seminoles in Florida, resisted removal and were subdued by troops. One Indian nation, the Cherokee, sought to hold on to its lands by adjusting to white ways. They took up farming and cattle raising, developed a written language, drafted a constitution, and tried to establish a state within a state in northwestern Georgia. Several treaties with the United States seemed to establish the legality of their government. But Georgia would not recognize the Cherokee Nation. It passed a law in 1828 declaring all Cherokee laws void and the region part of Georgia.

Several hundred Seminole Indians in Florida refused to abandon their tribal lands and move west. Although their leader, Osceola, was treacherously captured in 1837 and soon died in prison, other Seminoles fought on until forced to surrender in 1842; the warriors in this picture are attacking a federal fort. Some Seminoles hid out in the swamps and never gave themselves up.

The Indians challenged this law in the Supreme Court. In *Cherokee Nation* v. *Georgia* (1831) Chief Justice John Marshall had ruled that the Cherokees were "not a foreign state, in the sense of the Constitution" and therefore could not sue in a United States court. However, in *Worcester* v. *Georgia* (1832), a case involving two missionaries to the Cherokees who had not procured licenses required by Georgia law, he ruled that the state could not control the Cherokees or their territory. Later, when a Cherokee named Corn Tassel, convicted in a Georgia court of the murder of another Indian, appealed on the ground that the crime had taken place in Cherokee territory, Marshall declared the Georgia action unconstitutional on the same grounds.

Jackson backed Georgia's position. No inde-pendent nation could exist within the United States, he insisted. Georgia thereupon hanged poor Corn Tassel. In 1838, after Jackson had left the White House, the United States forced 15,000 Cherokees to leave Georgia for Oklahoma. About 4,000 of them died on the way; the route has been named the Trail of Tears.

Jackson's willingness to allow Georgia to ignore decisions of the Supreme Court persuaded extreme southern states' righters that he would not oppose the doctrine of nullification should it be formally applied to a law of Congress. They deceived themselves egregiously. Jackson did not challenge Georgia because he approved of the state's position. He spoke of "the poor deluded . . . Cherokees" and called William Wirt, the distinguished lawyer who defended their cause, a "truly wicked" man. Jackson was not one to worry about being inconsistent. When South Carolina revived the talk of nullification in 1832, he acted in quite a different manner.

The Nullification Crisis

The proposed alliance of South and West to reduce the tariff and the price of land had not materialized, partly because Webster had discredited the South in the eyes of western patriots and partly because the planters of South Carolina and Georgia, fearing the competition of fertile new cotton lands in Alabama and Mississippi, opposed the rapid exploitation of the West almost as vociferously as northern manufacturers did. When a new tariff law was passed in 1832, it lowered duties much less than the southerners desired. At once talk of nullifying it began to be heard in South Carolina.

In addition to the economic woes of the up-country cotton planters, the great planter-aristocrats of the rice-growing Tidewater, though relatively prosperous, were troubled by northern criticisms of slavery. In the rice region, blacks outnumbered whites two to one; it was the densest concentration of blacks in the United States. Thousands of these slaves were African-born, brought in during the burst of importations before Congress outlawed the trade in 1808. Controlled usually by overseers of the worst sort, the slaves seemed to their masters like savage beasts straining to rise up against their oppressors. In 1822 the exposure in Charleston of a planned revolt organized by Denmark Vesey, who had bought his freedom with money won in a lottery, had alarmed many whites. News of a far more serious uprising in Virginia led by the slave Nat Turner in 1831, just as the tariff controversy was coming to a head, added to popular concern. Radical South Carolinians saw protective tariffs and agitation against slavery as the two sides of one coin; against both aspects of what appeared to them the tyranny of the majority, nullification seemed the logical defense. Yield on the tariff, editor Henry L. Pinckney of the influential *Charleston Mercury* warned, and "abolition will become the order of the day."

Endless discussions of Calhoun's doctrine after the publication of his "Exposition and Protest" in 1828 had produced much interesting theorizing without clarifying the issue. William H. Freehling, a modern student of the controversy, sums it up aptly: "The theory of nullification was a veritable snarl of contradictions." Admirers of Calhoun praised his "power of analysis & profound philosophical reasonings," but his idea was ingenious rather than profound. Plausible at first glance, it was based on false assumptions: that the Constitution was subject to definitive interpretation; that one party could be permitted to interpret a compact unilaterally without destroying it; that a minority of the nation could reassume its sovereign independence but that a minority of a state could not.

President Jackson was in this respect Calhoun's exact opposite. The South Carolinian's mental gymnastics he brushed aside; intuitively he realized the central reality: If a state could nullify a law of Congress, the Union could not exist. "Tell . . . the Nullifiers from me that they can talk and write resolutions and print threats to their hearts' content," he warned a South Carolina representative when Congress adjourned in July 1832. "But if one drop of blood be shed there in defiance of the laws of the United States, I will hang the first man of them I can get my hands on to the first tree I can find."

The warning was not taken seriously in South Carolina. In October the state legislature provided for the election of a special convention, which, when it met, contained a solid majority of nullifiers. On November 24, 1832, the convention passed an ordinance of nullification prohibiting the collection of tariff duties in the state after February 1, 1833. The legislature then authorized the raising of an army and appropriated money to supply it with weapons.

Jackson quickly began military preparations of his own, telling friends that he would have 50,000 men ready to move in a little over a month. He also made a statesmanlike effort to end the crisis peaceably. First he suggested to Congress that it lower the tariff further. On December 10 he delivered a "Proclamation to the People of South Carolina." Nullification could only lead to the destruction of the Union, he said. "The laws of the United States must be executed. I have no discretionary power on the subject. . . . Those who told you that you might peaceably prevent their execution deceived you." Old Hickory added sternly: "Disunion by armed force is *treason*. Are you really ready to incur its guilt?"

This line of reasoning profoundly shocked even opponents of nullification for two quite different reasons. First of all, it undermined the very basis of states' rights, the belief that sovereignty in the United States had been divided between local and national governments so that local interests could not be dominated by a national majority. Beyond this, Jackson's threat to use force would mean civil war if South Carolina did not back down and possibly the destruction of the Union the president claimed to be defending. Large numbers of people who admired Jackson nonetheless, as Van Buren later wrote, "distrusted his prudence," fearing that he would "commit some rash act." They believed in dealing with the controversy by discussion and compromise.

As a result, in Congress pressure for compromise was tremendous. Administration leaders introduced both a new tariff bill and a Force Bill granting the president additional authority to execute the revenue laws. Calhoun, having resigned as vice-president to accept appointment as senator from South Carolina, led the fight against the Force Bill. Jackson was perfectly willing to see the tariff reduced but insisted that he was determined to enforce the law. As the February 1 deadline approached, he claimed that he could raise 200,000 men if needed to suppress resistance. "Union men, fear not," he said. *"The Union will be preserved."*

Jackson's determination sobered the South Carolina radicals. Their appeal for the support of other southern states fell on deaf ears: All rejected the idea of nullification. The unionist minority in South Carolina added to the radicals' difficulties by threatening civil war if federal authority were defied. Calhoun, though a brave man, was alarmed for his own safety, for Jackson had threatened to "hang him as high as Haman" if nullification were attempted. Observers described him as "excessively uneasy." He was suddenly eager to avoid a showdown.

Ten days before the deadline, South Carolina postponed nullification pending the outcome of the tariff debate. Then Calhoun joined forces with Henry Clay to push a compromise tariff through

As a contemporary observer pictured it, nullification could end only in despotism. Calhoun reaches for a crown as the Constitution and the Union lie dead beneath him. Jackson, at right, restrains one of Calhoun's followers and threatens him and all his ilk with hanging.

Congress. As part of the agreement Congress also passed the Force Bill, mostly as a face-saving device for the president. The compromise reflected the willingness of the North and West to make concessions in the interest of national harmony. Senator Silas Wright of New York, closely affiliated with Van Buren, explained the situation: "People will neither cut throats nor dismember the Union for protection. There is more patriotism and love of country than that left yet. The People will never balance this happy government against ten cents a pound upon a pound of wool."

And so the Union weathered the storm. Having stepped to the brink of civil war, the nation had drawn hastily back. The South Carolina legislature professed to be satisfied with the new tariff (in fact it made few immediate reductions, providing for a gradual lowering of rates over a ten-year period) and repealed the Nullification Ordinance, saving face by nullifying the Force Act, which was now a dead letter. But the radical South Carolina planters were becoming convinced that only secession would protect slavery. The nullification fiasco had proved that they could not succeed without the support of other slave states. Thereafter they devoted themselves ceaselessly to obtaining it.

"The Bank . . . I Will Kill It!"

Jackson's strong stand against South Carolina was the more effective because in the fall of 1832 he had been reelected president. The main issue in this election, aside from Jackson's personal popularity, was the president's determination to destroy the second Bank of the United States. In the "Bank war," Jackson won as complete a victory as in his battle with the nullifiers, yet the effects of his triumph were anything but beneficial to the country.

After *McCulloch* v. *Maryland* had presumably established its legality and the conservative Langdon Cheves had gotten it on a sound footing, the Bank of the United States had flourished. In 1823 Cheves was replaced as president by Nicholas Biddle, who managed it brilliantly. A talented Philadelphian, only 37 when he took over the Bank, Biddle was experienced in literature, the law, and diplomacy as well as in finance. Almost alone in the United States, Biddle realized that his institution could act as a rudimentary central bank, regulating the availability of credit throughout the nation by controlling the lending policies of the state banks. Small banks, possessing limited amounts of gold and silver, sometimes overextended themselves in making large amounts of bank notes available to borrowers in order to earn interest. All this paper money was legally convertible into hard cash on demand, but in the ordinary run of business, people seldom bothered to convert their notes so long as they thought the issuing bank was sound.

Bank notes passed freely from hand to hand and from bank to bank in every section of the country. Eventually much of the paper money of the local banks came across the counter of one or another of the 22 branches of the Bank of the United States. By collecting these notes and presenting them for conversion into specie, Biddle could compel the local banks to maintain adequate reserves of gold and silver—in other words, make them hold their lending policies within bounds. "The Bank of the United States," he explained, "has succeeded in keeping in check many institutions which might otherwise have been tempted into extravagant and ruinous excesses."

Biddle's policies in the 1820s were good for his own institution, which earned substantial profits, for the state banks, and probably for the country. Pressures on local bankers to make loans were enormous. The nation had an insatiable need for capital, and the general mood of the people was optimistic. Everyone wanted to borrow, and everyone expected values to rise, as in general they did. But by making liberal loans to produce merchants, for example, rural bankers indirectly stimulated farmers to expand their output beyond current demand, which eventually led to a decline in prices and an agricultural depression. In every field of economic activity, reckless lending caused inflation and greatly exaggerated the ups and downs of the business cycle. It can be argued, however, that by restricting the lending of state banks, Biddle was slowing the rate of economic growth and that in a predominantly agricultural society an occasional slump was not a large price to pay for rapid economic development.

Biddle's policies acted to stabilize the economy, and many interests, including a substantial percentage of state bankers, supported them. They also provoked a great deal of opposition. In part the opposition originated in pure ignorance: Distrust of paper money did not disappear, and people who disliked all paper saw the Bank as merely the largest (and thus the worst) of many bad institutions. At the other extreme, some bankers chafed under Biddle's restraints because by discouraging them from lending freely, he was limiting their profits. Few financiers realized what Biddle was trying to accomplish. The historian Bray Hammond estimated that in this period no more than one banker in four understood what was happening when he made a loan. What was "sound" banking practice? Honest people disagreed, and many turned against the ideas of Nicholas Biddle.

Bankers who did understand what Biddle was doing also resisted him. New York bankers resented the fact that a Philadelphia institution could wield so much power over their affairs. New York was the nation's largest importing center; huge amounts of tariff revenue were collected there. Yet since this money was deposited to the credit of the Bank of the United States, Biddle controlled it from Philadelphia. Finally, some people objected to the Bank because it was a monopoly. Distrust of chartered corporations as agents of special privilege tended to focus on the Bank, which had a monopoly of public funds but was managed by a private citizen and controlled by a handful of rich men. Biddle's wealth and social position intensified this feeling. Like many brilliant people, he sometimes appeared arrogant. He was unused to criticism and disdainful of ignorant and stupid attacks, failing to see that they were sometimes the most dangerous.

Jackson's Bank Veto

This formidable opposition to the Bank was diffuse and unorganized until Andrew Jackson brought it together. When he did, the Bank was quickly destroyed. Jackson belonged among the ignorant enemies of the institution, a hard-money man suspicious of all commercial banking. "I think it right to be perfectly frank with you," he told Biddle in 1829. "I do not dislike your Bank any more than all banks. But ever since I read the history of the South Sea Bubble I have been afraid of banks."

Jackson's attitude dismayed Biddle. It also mystified him, since the Bank was the country's best defense against a speculative mania like the 18th-century South Sea Bubble, in which hundreds of naive British investors had been fleeced. Almost against his will, Biddle found himself gravitating toward Clay and the new National Republican party, offering advantageous loans and retainers to politicians and newspaper editors in order to build up a following. Thereafter, events moved inevitably toward a showdown, for the president's combative instincts were easily aroused. "The Bank," he told Van Buren, "is trying to kill me, *but I will kill it!*"

Henry Clay, Daniel Webster, and other prominent National Republicans hoped to use the Bank controversy against Jackson. They reasoned that the institution was so important to the country that Jackson's opposition to it would undermine his popularity. They therefore urged Biddle to ask Congress to renew the Bank's charter. The charter would not expire until 1836, but by pressing the issue before the 1832 presidential election, they could force Jackson either to approve the recharter bill or to veto it (which would give candidate Clay a lively issue in the campaign). The banker yielded to this strategy reluctantly, for he would have preferred to postpone the showdown, and a recharter bill passed Congress early in July 1832. Jackson promptly vetoed it.

Jackson's message explaining why he had rejected the bill was immensely popular, but it adds nothing to his reputation as a statesman. Being a good Jeffersonian—and no friend of John Marshall—he insisted that the Bank was unconstitutional. (*McCulloch* v. *Maryland* he brushed aside, saying that as president he had sworn to uphold the Constitution as *he* understood it.) The Bank was inexpedient, he argued. Being a dangerous private monopoly that allowed a handful of rich men to accumulate "many millions" of dollars, the Bank was making "the rich richer and the potent more powerful." Furthermore, many of its stockholders were foreigners: "If we must have a bank . . . it should be *purely American.*" Little that he said made any more sense than this absurdity.*

---

* The country needed all the foreign capital it could attract. Foreigners owned only $8 million of the $35 million stock, and in any case they could not vote their shares.

The "Set To Between Old Hickory and Bully Nick" is pictured in this cartoon of 1834–1835. Jackson seconds are "Little Van" Martin Van Buren and Major Jack Downing; Biddle is seconded by "Long Harry" (Henry Clay) and "Black Dan" Webster.

The most unfortunate aspect of Jackson's veto was that he could have reformed the Bank instead of destroying it. The central banking function was too important to be left in private hands. Biddle once boasted that he could put nearly any bank in the United States out of business simply by forcing it to exchange specie for its bank notes; he thought he was demonstrating his forbearance, but in fact he was revealing a dangerous flaw in the system. When the Jacksonians called him Czar Nicholas, they were not far from the mark. Moreover, private bankers were making profits that in justice belonged to the people, for the government received no interest from the large sums it kept on deposit in the Bank. Jackson would not consider reforms. He set out to smash the Bank of the United States without any real idea of what might be put in its place—a foolhardy act.

Biddle considered Jackson's veto "a manifesto of anarchy," its tone like "the fury of a chained panther biting the bars of his cage." A large majority of the voters, however, approved of Jackson's hard-hitting attack. He was easily reelected president, defeating Clay 219 to 49 in the electoral college.

Buttressed by his election triumph, Jackson acted swiftly. "Until I can strangle this hydra of corruption, the Bank, I will not shrink from my duty," he said. Shortly after the start of his second term, he decided to withdraw the government funds deposited in its vaults. Under the law only the secretary of the treasury could remove the deposits. When Secretary Louis McLane refused to do so, believing that the alternative depositories, the state banks, were less safe, Jackson promptly "promoted" him to secretary of state and appointed William J. Duane, a Pennsylvania lawyer, to the treasury post. Foolishly, he failed to ask Duane his views on the issue before appointing him. Too late he discovered that the new secretary agreed with McLane! It would not be "prudent" to entrust the government's money to "local and irresponsible" banks, Duane said.

Believing that Cabinet officers should obey the president as automatically as a colonel obeys a general, Jackson dismissed Duane, replacing him with Attorney General Roger B. Taney, who had been advising him closely on Bank affairs. Taney carried out the order by depositing new federal receipts in seven state banks in eastern cities while continuing to meet government expenses with drafts on the Bank of the United States.

The situation was confused and slightly unethical. Set on winning the Bank war, Jackson lost sight of his fear of unsound paper money. Taney, however, knew exactly what he was doing. One of the state banks receiving federal funds was the Union Bank of Baltimore. Taney owned stock in this institution, and its president was his close friend. Little wonder that Jackson's enemies were soon calling the favored state banks "pet" banks. This charge was not entirely fair because Taney took pains to see that the deposits were placed in financially sound institutions. Furthermore, by 1836 the government's funds had been spread out reasonably equitably in about 90 banks. But neither was the charge entirely unfair; the administration certainly favored institutions whose directors were politically sympathetic to it.

When Taney began to remove the deposits, the government had $9,868,000 to its credit in the Bank of the United States; within three months the figure fell to about $4 million. Faced with the withdrawal of so much cash, Biddle had to contract his operations. He decided to exaggerate the contraction, pressing the state banks hard by presenting all their notes and checks that came across his counter for conversion into specie and drastically limiting his own bank's business loans. He hoped that the resulting shortage of credit would be blamed on Jackson and that it would force the president to return the deposits. "Nothing but the evidence of suffering . . . will produce any effect," he reasoned.

For a time the strategy appeared to be working. Paper money became scarce, specie almost unobtainable. A serious panic threatened. New York banks were soon refusing to make any loans at all. "Nobody buys; nobody can sell," a French visitor to the city observed. Memorials and petitions poured in on Congress. Worried and indignant delegations of businessmen began trooping to Washington seeking "relief." Clay, Webster, and Calhoun thundered against Jackson in the Senate.

The president would not budge. "I am fixed in my course as firm as the Rockey Mountain," he wrote Vice-President Van Buren. No "frail mortals" who worshiped "the golden calf" could change his mind. To others he swore he would sooner cut off his right arm and "undergo the torture of ten Span-

ish inquisitions" than restore the deposits. When delegations came to him, he roared at them harshly: "Go to Nicholas Biddle. . . . Biddle has all the money!" And in the end—because he was right— business leaders began to take the old general's advice. Pressure on Biddle mounted swiftly, and in July 1834 he suddenly reversed his policy and began to lend money freely. The artificial crisis ended.

Boom and Bust

While the government insisted that its pet banks maintain large reserves, other state banks began to offer credit on easy terms, aided by a large increase in their reserves of gold and silver resulting from causes unconnected with the policies of either the government or Biddle's Bank. A decline in the Chinese demand for Mexican silver led to increased exports of the metal to the United States, and the rise of American interest rates attracted English capital into the country. Heavy English purchases of American cotton at high prices also increased the flow of specie into American banks. These developments caused bank notes in circulation to jump from $82 million in January 1835 to $120 million in December 1836. Bank deposits rose even more rapidly.

Much of the new money flowed into speculation in land; a mania to invest in property swept the country. The increased volume of currency caused prices to soar 15 percent in six months, buoying investors' spirits and making them ever more optimistic about the future. By the summer of 1835 one observer estimated that in New York City, which had about 250,000 residents, enough house lots had been laid out and sold to support a population of 2 million. Chicago at this time had only 2,000 to 3,000 inhabitants, yet most of the land for 25 miles around had been sold and resold in small lots by speculators anticipating the growth of the area. Throughout the West farmers borrowed money from local banks by mortgaging their land, used the money to buy more land from the government, and then borrowed still more money from the banks on the strength of their new deeds.

So long as prices rose, the process could be repeated endlessly. In 1832, while the Bank of the United States still regulated the money supply, federal income from the sale of land was $2.6 million.

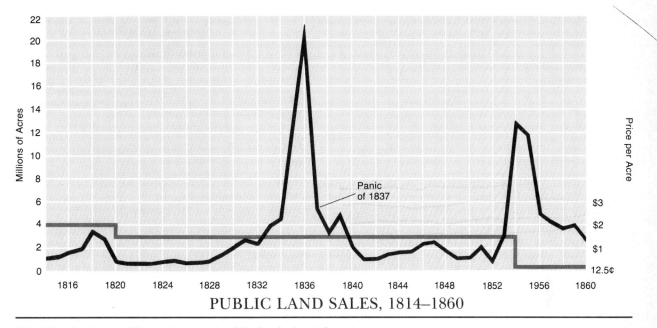

PUBLIC LAND SALES, 1814–1860

The left axis shows millions of acres of public land; the right axis price per acre. The speculative peak of 1836 burst with the Panic of 1837. The size of land parcels offered varied from 160 acres in 1830 to 40 or more acres in 1832 and at later times. Starting in 1830, squatters on public land were allowed to buy it at the minimum price. The 12.5¢ price per acre in 1854 applied to land on the market for 30 years or more.

In 1834 it was $4.9 million; in 1835, $14.8 million. In 1836 it rose to $24.9 million, and the government found itself totally free of debt and with a surplus of $20 million!

Finally Jackson became alarmed by the speculative mania. In the summer of 1836 he issued the Specie Circular, which provided that purchasers must henceforth pay for public land in gold or silver. At once the rush to buy land came to a halt. As demand slackened, prices sagged. Speculators, unable to dispose of lands mortgaged to the banks, had to abandon them to the banks, but the banks could not realize enough on the foreclosed property to recover their loans. Suddenly the public mood changed. Commodity prices tumbled 30 percent between February and May. Hordes of depositors sought to withdraw their money in the form of specie, and soon the banks exhausted their supplies. Panic swept the country in the spring of 1837 as every bank in the nation was forced to suspend specie payments. The boom was over.

Major swings in the business cycle can never be attributed to the actions of a single person, however powerful, but there is no doubt that Jackson's war against the Bank exaggerated the swings of the economic pendulum, not so much by its direct effects as by the impact of the president's ill-considered policies on popular thinking. His Specie Circular did not prevent speculators from buying land—at most it caused purchasers to pay a premium for gold or silver. But it convinced potential buyers that the boom was going to end and led them to make decisions that in fact ended it. Old Hickory's combination of impetuousness, combativeness, arrogance, and ignorance rendered the nation he loved so dearly a serious disservice. He lacked, as Glyndon Van Deusen wrote in *The Jacksonian Era*, "the capacity for that slow and often painful balancing of opposite viewpoints, the fruit of philosophic reflection, which is the characteristic of the man of culture." This was his greatest failing, as a president and as a man.

Jacksonianism Abroad

Jackson's emotional and dogmatic side also influenced his handling of foreign affairs. His patriotism was often so extravagant as to be ludicrous; in less peaceful times he might well have embroiled the country in far bloodier battles than his war with Nicholas Biddle produced. By pushing relentlessly for the solution of minor problems, he won a number of diplomatic successes. Several advantageous reciprocal trade agreements were negotiated, including one with Great Britain that finally opened British West Indian ports to American ships. American claims dating from the Napoleonic wars were pressed vigorously. The most important result of this policy came in 1831, when France agreed to pay about $5 million to compensate for damages to American property during that long conflict.

This settlement, however, led to trouble because the French Chamber of Deputies refused to appropriate the necessary funds. When the United States submitted a bill for the first installment in 1833, it was unable to collect. Jackson at once adopted a belligerent stance, his ire further aroused by a bill for $170,041.18 submitted by Nicholas Biddle for the services of the Bank of the United States in attempting to collect the money. When France ignored the second installment, Jackson sent a blistering message to Congress, full of such phrases as "not to be tolerated" and "take redress into our own hands." He asked for a law "authorizing reprisals upon French property" if the money was not paid.

Jackson's case was ironclad, yet the matter did not merit such vigorous prosecution. Congress wisely took no action. Jackson suspended diplomatic relations with France and ordered the navy readied. The French—in part, no doubt, because they were clearly in the wrong—were insulted by Jackson's manner. Irresponsible talk of war was heard in both countries. Fortunately, the French Chamber finally appropriated the money, Jackson moderated his public pronouncements, and the issue subsided.

Similarly, when a snag delayed the negotiation of the West Indian treaty, Jackson had suggested forcing Great Britain to make concessions by imposing a boycott on trade with Canada. In both cases he showed poor judgment, being ready to take monumental risks to win petty victories. His behavior reinforced the impression held by foreigners that the United States was a rash young country with a chip on its shoulder, pathologically mistrustful of the good faith of European powers.

The Jacksonians

Jackson's personality had a large impact on the shape and tone of American politics and thus with the development of the second party system. When he came to office, nearly everyone professed to be a follower of Jefferson. By 1836 being a Jeffersonian no longer meant much; what mattered was how one felt about Andrew Jackson. He had ridden to power at the head of a diverse political army, but he left behind him an organization with a fairly cohesive, if not necessarily consistent, body of ideas. This Democratic party contained rich citizens and poor, easterners and westerners, abolitionists as well as slaveholders. It was not yet a close-knit national organization, but—always allowing for individual exceptions—the Jacksonians agreed on certain underlying principles. These included suspicion of special privilege and large business corporations, both typified by the Bank of the United States; freedom of economic opportunity, unfettered by private or governmental restrictions; absolute political freedom, at least for white males; and the conviction that any ordinary man is capable of performing the duties of most public offices.

Jackson's ability to reconcile his belief in the supremacy of the Union with his conviction that the area of national authority should be held within narrow limits tended to make the Democrats the party of those who believed that the powers of the states should not be diminished. Tocqueville caught this aspect of Jackson's philosophy perfectly: "Far from wishing to extend Federal power," he wrote, "the president belongs to the party that wishes to limit that power."

Although the radical Locofoco* wing of the party championed the idea, nearly all Jacksonians, like their leader, favored giving the small man his chance—by supporting public education, for example, and by refusing to place much weight on a person's origin, dress, or manners. "One individual is as good as another" (for accuracy we must insert the adjective *white*) was their axiom. This attitude helps explain why immigrants, Catholics, and other minority groups usually voted Democratic. How-

---

* A locofoco was a type of friction match. The name was first applied in politics when a group of New York Jacksonians used these matches to light candles when a conservative faction tried to break up their meeting by turning off the gaslights.

ever, the Jacksonians showed no tendency either to penalize the wealthy or to intervene in economic affairs to aid the underprivileged. The motto "That government is best which governs least" graced the masthead of the chief Jacksonian newspaper, the *Washington Globe*, throughout the era.

Rise of the Whigs

The opposition to Jackson was far less cohesive. Henry Clay's National Republican party provided a nucleus, but Clay never dominated that party as Jackson dominated the Democrats. Its orientation was basically anti-Jackson. It was as though the American people were a great block of granite from which some sculptor had just fashioned a statue of Jackson, the chips scattered about the floor of the studio representing the opposition.

While Jackson was president, the impact of his personality delayed the formation of a true two-party system, but as soon as he surrendered power,

the opposition, taking heart, began to coalesce. Many Democrats could not accept the odd logic of Jacksonian finance. As early as 1834 they, together with the Clay element, the extreme states' righters who followed Calhoun, and other dissident groups, were calling themselves Whigs, the name (harking back to the Revolution) implying patriotic resistance to the tyranny of "King Andrew." This coalition possessed great resources of wealth and talent. Anyone who understood banking was almost obliged to become a Whig unless he was connected with one of Jackson's "pets." Those spiritual descendants of Hamilton who rejected the administration's refusal to approach economic problems from a broadly national perspective also joined in large numbers. Those who found the coarseness and "pushiness" of the Jacksonians offensive were another element in the new party. The anti-intellectual and antiscientific bias of the administration (Jackson rejected proposals for a national university, an observatory, and a scientific and literary institute) drove many well-educated people

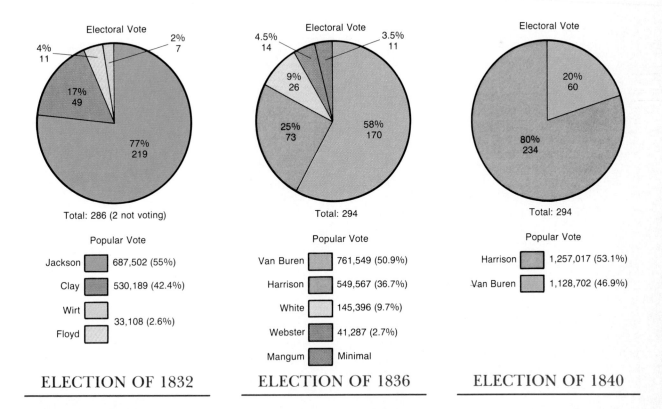

Electoral Vote

4% 11 — 17% 49 — 77% 219 — 2% 7

Total: 286 (2 not voting)

Popular Vote

Jackson	687,502 (55%)
Clay	530,189 (42.4%)
Wirt	33,108 (2.6%)
Floyd	

ELECTION OF 1832

Electoral Vote

4.5% 14 — 9% 26 — 25% 73 — 58% 170 — 3.5% 11

Total: 294

Popular Vote

Van Buren	761,549 (50.9%)
Harrison	549,567 (36.7%)
White	145,396 (9.7%)
Webster	41,287 (2.7%)
Mangum	Minimal

ELECTION OF 1836

Electoral Vote

20% 60 — 80% 234

Total: 294

Popular Vote

| Harrison | 1,257,017 (53.1%) |
| Van Buren | 1,128,702 (46.9%) |

ELECTION OF 1840

into the Whig fold. Whig arguments also appealed to ordinary voters who were predisposed to favor strong governments that would check the "excesses" of unrestricted individualism.

The Whigs were slow to develop an effective party organization. They had too many generals and not enough troops. It was hard for them to agree on any issue more complicated than opposition to Jackson. Furthermore, they stood in conflict with the major trend of their age: the glorification of the common man.

Lacking a dominant leader in 1836, the Whigs relied on "favorite sons," hoping to throw the presidential election into the House of Representatives. Daniel Webster ran in New England. For the West and South, Hugh Lawson White of Tennessee, a former friend who had broken with Jackson, was counted on to carry the fight. General William Henry Harrison was supposed to win in the Northwest and to draw support everywhere from those who liked to vote for military heroes. This sorry strategy failed; Jackson's handpicked candidate, Martin Van Buren, won a majority of both the popular and the electoral votes.

An extensive unpaid bill alarms a debtor, one of many who suffered from the tightening of credit that followed the Panic of 1837.

WHO'LL HAVE THE SPECIE?—

Like the United States, Europe experienced a depression and specie shortage in the late 1830s. France and England, symbolized here by a rooster and bulldog, respectively, asked for American debt payments in hard currency. They were rebuffed by Van Buren, the wily monkey at left.

Martin Van Buren: Jacksonianism Without Jackson

The Red Fox, the Little Magician—Van Buren's brilliance as a political manipulator has tended to obscure his statesmanlike qualities and his engaging personality. High office sobered Van Buren and improved his judgment. He fought the Bank of the United States as a monopoly, but he also opposed irresponsible state banks. New York's Safety Fund System, requiring all banks to contribute to a fund, supervised by the state, to be used to redeem the notes of any member bank that failed, was established largely through his efforts. Van Buren believed in public construction of internal improvements, but he favored state rather than national programs, and he urged a rational approach: Each project must stand on its own as a useful and profitable public utility.

He continued to equivocate spectacularly on the tariff—in his *Autobiography* he described two of his supporters walking home after listening to him talk on the tariff, each convinced that it had been a brilliant speech, but neither having obtained the slightest idea as to where Van Buren stood on the subject—but he was never in the pocket of any special interest group or tariff lobbyist. He accounted himself a good Jeffersonian, tending to prefer state action to federal, but he was by no means doctrinaire. Basically he approached most questions rationally and pragmatically.

Van Buren had outmaneuvered Calhoun easily in the struggle to succeed Jackson, winning the old hero's confidence and serving him well. In 1832 he was elected vice-president and thereafter was conceded to be the "heir apparent." In 1835 the Democratic National Convention nominated him for president unanimously.

Van Buren took office just as the Panic of 1837 struck the country. Its effects were frightening but short-lived. When the banks stopped converting paper money into gold and silver, they outraged conservatives but in effect eased the pressure on the money market: Interest rates declined, and business loans again became relatively easy to obtain. In 1836, at the height of the boom in land sales, Congress had voted to "distribute" the new treasury surplus to the states, and this flow of money, which the states promptly spent, also stimulated the revival. Late in 1838 the banks resumed specie payments.

But in 1839 a bumper crop caused a sharp decline in the price of cotton. Then a number of state governments that had overextended themselves in road- and canal-building projects were forced to default on their debts. This discouraged investors, particularly foreigners. A general economic depression ensued that lasted until 1843.

Van Buren was not responsible for the panic or the depression, but his manner of dealing with economic issues was scarcely helpful. He saw his role as being concerned only with problems plaguing the government, ignoring the economy as a whole. "The less government interferes with private pursuits the better for the general prosperity," he pontificated. As Daniel Webster scornfully pointed out, Van Buren was following a policy of "leaving the people to shift for themselves," one that many Whigs rejected.

Such a hands-off approach to the depression seems foolish by modern standards. Van Buren's refusal to assume any responsibility for the general welfare appears to explode the theory that the Jacksonians were deeply concerned with the fate of ordinary citizens. In *The Concept of Jacksonian Democracy,* Lee Benson argues that the Whigs, rather than the Democrats, were the "positive liberals" of the era. Benson cites many statements by Whigs about applying "the means of the state boldly and liberally to aid . . . public works."

This approach helps correct past oversimplifications, but it judges the period by the standards of a later age. The country in the 1830s was still mainly agricultural, and for most farmers the depression, though serious, did not spell disaster. Moreover, many Jacksonians were perfectly willing to see the states act to stimulate economic growth in bad times—as indeed most states did.

Van Buren's chief goal was finding a substitute for the state banks as a place to keep federal funds. The depression and the suspension of specie payments embarrassed the government along with private depositors. He soon settled on the idea of "divorcing" the government from all banking activities. His independent treasury bill called for the construction of government-owned vaults where federal revenues could be stored until needed. To en-

sure absolute safety, all payments to the government were to be made in hard cash. After a battle that lasted until the summer of 1840, the Independent Treasury Act passed both the House and the Senate.

Opposition to the Independent Treasury Act had been bitter, and not all of it was partisan. Bankers and businessmen objected to the government's withholding so much specie from the banks, which needed all the hard money they could get to support loans that were the lifeblood of economic growth. It seemed irresponsible for the federal government to turn its back on the banks, which so obviously performed a semipublic function. These criticisms made good sense, but through a lucky combination of circumstances, the system worked reasonably well for many years. By creating suspicion in the public mind, officially stated distrust of banks acted as a damper on their tendency to overexpand. No acute shortage of specie developed because heavy agricultural exports and the investment of much European capital in American railroads beginning in the mid-1840s brought in large amounts of new gold and silver. After 1849 the discovery of gold in California added another important source of specie. The supply of money and bank credit kept pace roughly with the growth of the economy, but through no fault of the government. "Wildcat" banks proliferated. Fraud and counterfeiting were common, and the operation of everyday business affairs was inconvenienced in countless ways. The disordered state of the currency remained a grave problem until corrected by Civil War banking legislation.

The Log Cabin Campaign

It was not his financial policy that led to Van Buren's defeat in 1840. The depression naturally hurt the Democrats, and the Whigs were far better organized than in 1836. The Whigs also adopted a different strategy, cynical but effective. The Jacksonians had come to power on the coattails of a popular general whose views on public questions they concealed or ignored. They had maintained themselves by shouting the praises of the common man. Now the Whigs seized on these techniques and carried them to their logical—or illogical—conclusion. Not even bothering to draft a program, and passing over Clay

The 1840 presidential campaign was the first to use circus hoopla and the techniques of mass appeal that came to characterize political contests in the United States. This fanciful drawing adorned the sheet music for "General Harrison's Log Cabin March."

and Webster, whose views were known and therefore controversial, they nominated General William Henry Harrison for president. The Hero of Tippecanoe was counted on to conquer the party created in the image of the Hero of New Orleans. To "balance" the ticket, the Whigs chose a former Democrat, John Tyler of Virginia, an ardent supporter of states' rights, as their vice-presidential candidate.

The Whig argument was specious but effective: General Harrison is a plain man of the people who lives in a log cabin (where the latchstring is always out). Contrast him with the suave Van Buren, luxuriating amid "the Regal Splendor of the President's Palace." Harrison drinks ordinary hard cider and eats hog meat and grits, while Van Buren drinks expensive foreign wines and fattens on fancy concoctions prepared by a French chef. The general's furniture is plain and sturdy; the president dines off gold plates and treads on Royal Wilton carpets that cost the people $5 a yard. In a country where all are equal, the people will reject an aristocrat like "Martin Van Ruin" and put their trust in General Harrison, a simple, brave, honest, public-spirited common man.

Harrison came from a distinguished family, being the son of Benjamin Harrison, a signer of the Declaration of Independence and a former governor of Virginia. He was well educated and in at least comfortable financial circumstances, and he certainly did not live in a log cabin. The Whigs ignored these facts. The log cabin and the cider barrel became their symbols, which every political meeting saw reproduced in a dozen forms. The leading Whig campaign newspaper, edited by a vigorous New Englander named Horace Greeley, was called the *Log Cabin*. Cartoons, doggerel, slogans, and souvenirs were everywhere substituted for argument.

The Democrats used the same methods as the Whigs and were equally well organized, but they had little heart for the fight. The best they could come up with was the fact that their vice-presidential candidate, Richard Mentor Johnson, had killed Tecumseh, not merely defeated him. Van Buren tried to focus public attention on issues, but his voice could not be heard above the huzzahs of the Whigs. When the Whigs chanted "Tippecanoe and Tyler too!" and "Van, Van, is a used-up man" and rolled out another barrel of hard cider, the best the Democrats could come up with was:

Rumpsey, Dumpsey,
Colonel Johnson
Killed Tecumseh.

A huge turnout (four-fifths of the eligible voters) carried Harrison to victory by a margin of almost 150,000. The electoral vote was 234 to 60.

The Democrats had been blown up by their own bomb. In 1828 they had portrayed John Quincy Adams as a bloated aristocrat and Jackson as a simple farmer. The lurid talk of Van Buren dining off golden plates was no different from the stories that made Adams out to be a passionate gambler. If Van Buren was a lesser man than Adams, Harrison was a pale imitation indeed of Andrew Jackson.

The Whigs continued to repeat history by rushing to gather the spoils of victory. Washington was again flooded by office seekers, the political confusion monumental. Harrison had no ambition to be an aggressive leader. He believed that Jackson had misused the veto and professed to put as much emphasis as Washington did on the principle of the separation of legislative and executive powers. This delighted the Whig leaders in Congress, who had had their fill of the "executive usurpation" of Jackson. Either Clay or Webster seemed destined to be the real ruler of the new administration, and soon the two were squabbling over their old general like sparrows over a crust.

At the height of their squabble, less than a month after his inauguration, Harrison fell gravely ill. Pneumonia developed, and on April 4 he died. John Tyler of Virginia, honest and conscientious but doctrinaire, became president of the United States. The political climate of the country changed dramatically. Events began to march in a new direction, one that led ultimately to Bull Run, to Gettysburg, and to Appomattox.

Milestones

1828	Tariff of Abominations
1829–1837	Andrew Jackson's "Kitchen Cabinet"
1830	Daniel Webster's "Second Reply to Hayne"
	Jackson vetoes the Maysville road bill
1831–1838	Removal of southern Indians to Oklahoma
1832	South Carolina Ordinance of Nullification
	Force Act
	Jackson vetoes the Bank recharter bill
1833	Removal of U.S. Treasury funds from the Bank of the United States
	Compromise Tariff Act
1836	Specie Circular
1837–1838	Panic of 1837
1840	Independent Treasury Act
	"Log Cabin" campaign

SUPPLEMENTARY READING

Titles marked with an asterisk have been published in paperback.

On Jackson's presidency, see R. V. Remini, **Andrew Jackson and the Course of American Freedom** (1981) and **Andrew Jackson and the Course of American Democracy** (1984). Alexis de Tocqueville analyzed brilliantly the nature of Jacksonian democracy in **Democracy in America*** (1835–1840). A. M. Schlesinger, Jr., **The Age of Jackson*** (1945), stresses the democratic character of Jacksonianism. D. T. Miller, **Jacksonian Aristocracy** (1967), and two works by Edward Pessen, **Riches, Class and Power Before the Civil War** (1973) and **Jacksonian America*** (1969), describe the growth and extent of economic and class distinctions.

A number of contemporary commentaries by foreigners throw much light on Jacksonian democracy. See especially, in addition to Tocqueville, Frances Trollope, **Domestic Manners of the Americans*** (1832), Michel Chevalier, **Society, Manners and Politics in the United States*** (1961), Harriet Martineau, **Retrospect of Western Travel** (1838) and **Society in America*** (1837), and F. J. Grund, **Aristocracy in America*** (1959). On Jackson's administration of the government and the development of the spoils system, see L. D. White, **The Jacksonians*** (1954), and S. H. Aronson, **Status and Kinship in the Higher Civil Service** (1964); on the development of parties, consult R. P. McCormick, **The Second American Party System*** (1966). On Jackson's Indian policy, refer to F. P. Prucha, **American Indian Policies in the Formative Years*** (1962), B. W. Sheehan, **Seeds of Extinction*** (1973), and R. N. Satz, **American Indian Policy in the Jacksonian Era** (1975).

On the nullification controversy, see R. E. Ellis, **The Union at Risk** (1987), and W. W. Freehling, **Prelude to Civil War: The Nullification Controversy in South Carolina*** (1966), which shows the close relationship between the nullifiers and the slavery issue. The struggle with the Bank is discussed in Bray Hammond, **Banks and Politics in America from the Revolution to the Civil War*** (1957), and J. M. McFaul, **The Politics of Jacksonian Finance** (1972). Peter Temin, **The Jacksonian Economy*** (1969), minimizes the effects of Jackson's policies on economic conditions. Temin also provides an interesting analysis of economic trends throughout the period. T. P. Govan's **Nicholas Biddle*** (1959) is excellent on Biddle's view of banking but too apologetic.

The political and economic ideas of Whigs and Democrats are discussed in Lee Benson, **The Concept of Jacksonian Democracy*** (1961), R. P. Formisano, **The Transformation of Political Culture** (1983), and D. W. Howe, **The Political Culture of the American Whigs** (1980). On the development of the Whig party, in addition to the biographies of leading Whigs, see McCormick's **Second American Party System.** On the Van Buren administration, see John Niven, **Martin Van Buren** (1983), and M. L. Wilson, **The Presidency of Martin Van Buren** (1984). The election of 1840 is treated in R. G. Gunderson, **The Log-Cabin Campaign** (1957), J. A. Garraty, **Silas Wright** (1949), and the biographies of Clay and Webster.

XI

The Making of Middle-Class America

A great democratic revolution is taking place in our midst; everybody sees it, but by no means everybody judges it in the same way. . . . No man on earth can affirm, absolutely and generally, that the new state of societies is better than the old, but it is already easy to see that it is different.

ALEXIS DE TOCQUEVILLE, *1836*

O n May 12, 1831, two French aristocrats, Alexis de Tocqueville and Gustave de Beaumont, arrived in New York City from Le Havre on the packet *President*. Their official purpose was to make a study of American prisons for the French government. But they really came, as Tocqueville explained, "to see what a great republic is like."

Tocqueville and Beaumont were only the most insightful of dozens of Europeans who visited the United States during the first half of the 19th century in order to study the "natives." Their visit, for example, overlapped with that of Frances Trollope, whose *Domestic Manners of Americans* (1834) advised English readers that Americans were just as uncouth as they had imagined. A decade later, the English novelist Charles Dickens made what by then had become an almost obligatory pass through this crude outpost of civilization before publishing his report on his "sharp dealing" cousins in *American Notes* (1842). A little later, in a novel, Dickens described the United States as a "Republic . . . full of sores and ulcers."

Tocqueville and Beaumont in America

Unlike Trollope, Dickens, and other uncharitable foreign visitors, Tocqueville and Beaumont did not come to America chock-full of preconceived notions. Both believed that Europe was passing from its aristocratic past into a democratic future. How better to prepare for the change, they believed, than by studying the United States, where democracy was already the "enduring and normal state" of the land. In the nine months they spent in America, they traveled from New York to Boston, then back through New York in order to inspect the state prison at Auburn, then on to Ohio. ("No one has been born there; no one wants to stay there," Tocqueville later said of Ohio.) They examined conditions on the frontier in Michigan Territory, then sailed down the Mississippi River to New Orleans, where they heard an opera good enough to make them imagine they were back in France. They also attended a "Quadroon ball," where, according to Tocqueville, "all the men [were] white, all the women coloured."

From New Orleans they went on to "semi-barbarous" Alabama before turning north to Washington, a city that Beaumont declared to be "very ugly." Finally back to New York, whence they sailed for France on February 20, 1832. All told, they had met and interviewed some 250 individuals, ranking from President Jackson—Beaumont insisted on referring to Old Hickory as "Monsieur"—to a number of Chippewa Indians.

It had indeed been a "useful" trip for the two Frenchmen. It resulted in their prison report and in *Marie, ou l'Esclavage aux États Unis* (1835), Beaumont's account of American race problems, cast in the form of a novel. But above all else, the visit provided the material for Tocqueville's classic *De la Démocratie en Amérique*, published in France in 1835 and a year later in an English translation. *Democracy in America* has been the starting point for virtually all subsequent writers who have tried to describe what Tocqueville called "the creative elements" of American institutions.

Tocqueville in Judgment

The gist of *Democracy in America* is contained in the book's first sentence: "No novelty in the United

Among the scores of noted Europeans who visited the United States in its first fifty years, Alexis de Tocqueville is perhaps the best remembered, thanks to his exhaustive and insightful published account of his travels. This lithograph portrait is by Leon Noël.

half the city's wealth in 1828, about two-thirds in 1845. The number of New Yorkers worth $100,000 or more tripled in that period. A similar concentration of wealth was occurring in Philadelphia and Boston.

Moreover, there was substantial poverty in Jacksonian America that Tocqueville did not recognize. Particularly in the cities, bad times forced many unskilled laborers and their families into dire poverty. Tocqueville took little notice of such inequalities, in part because he was so captivated by the theme of American equality. He also had little interest in how industrialization and urbanization were affecting society. When he did take notice of working conditions, he remarked that wages were higher in America than in Europe and the cost of living was lower, facts obvious to the most obtuse European visitor. Furthermore, as with most foreign visitors, nearly all his contacts were with members of the upper crust. "We hardly see anyone," he acknowledged, "except people of distinction."

Despite his blind spots, Tocqueville realized that America was undergoing some fundamental social changes. These changes, he wrote, were being made by "an innumerable crowd who are . . . not exactly rich nor yet quite poor [and who] have enough property to want order and not enough to excite envy." In his notes he put it even more succinctly: "The whole society seems to have turned into one middle class."

States struck me more vividly during my stay there than the equality of conditions." Tocqueville meant not that Americans lived in a state of total equality, but that the inequalities that did exist among white Americans were not enforced by institutions or supported by public opinion. Moreover, the inequalities paled when compared with those of Europe. "In America," he concluded, "men are nearer equality than in any other country in the world." The circumstances of one's birth meant little, one's education less, and one's intelligence scarcely anything. Economic differences, while real and certainly "paraded" by those who enjoyed "a pre-eminence of wealth," were transitory. "Such wealth," Tocqueville assured his readers, "is within reach of all."

These sweeping generalizations, however comforting to Americans then and since, are simplifications. Few modern students of Jacksonian America would accept them without qualification. The historian Edward Pessen has pointed out that in the 1830s and 1840s a wide and growing gap existed between the rich and poor in the larger eastern cities. According to Pessen, the wealthiest 4 percent of the population of New York controlled about

A Restless People

"In America, men never stay still," Tocqueville noted. "Something is almost always provisional about their lives." Other European observers came away equally struck by the restlessness of Americans, without necessarily agreeing that democratic institutions made them so. Frances Trollope thought their "incessant bustling" of a piece with their eating too fast and spitting too often. It stemmed from their "universal pursuit of money," she claimed.

One reason Americans seemed continually on the move was that every year there were more of them. The first federal census in 1790 recorded that there were 3.9 million people in the country. In 1850 there were more than 23 million. The population was doubling every 22 years, just about what Franklin had predicted in 1751! The growth can be

The Dinner Party *was painted around 1825 by Boston artist Henry Sargent. Alexis de Tocqueville tolerated but rarely praised American haute cuisine. After one banquet, he recorded that the dinner represented the infancy of the art: "The vegetables and fish before the meat, the oysters for dessert. In a word, complete barbarism."*

measured geographically by the admission of new states in the 1830s and 1840s: Arkansas in 1836, Michigan in 1837, Florida in 1845, Texas in 1846, and Wisconsin in 1848.

Yet by contemporary European standards, even the settled parts of the United States were sparsely populated in the 1830s and 1840s. But for people accustomed to wide-open spaces, the presence of more than a handful of neighbors was reason enough for moving on. Abraham Lincoln's father Thomas (1778–1851) was typical. He grew up in Kentucky, pioneered in Indiana, and died in Illinois.

The Move to Town

The urge to move had an urban dimension as well. For every "young man" who took the advice of the New York newspaperman Horace Greeley to "go west," several young men and women went instead to town. By the tens of thousands they exchanged the rigors of farming for the uncertain risks and rewards of city life. Boston, New York, and Philadelphia had a combined population of 50,000 at the time of the Revolution. Each expanded rapidly during the first half of the next century. Boston had 40,000 residents in 1820, nearly 140,000 in 1850. Philadelphia grew even more rapidly, from just under 100,000 in 1820 to almost 400,000 in 1850. New York, which had forged ahead of Philadelphia around 1810, grew from 125,000 in 1820 to more than 500,000 in 1850.

However spectacular the growth of the largest cities, the emergence of new towns was more significant. In 1820 the Northeast contained 5 cities with populations above 25,000 and 13 with popu-

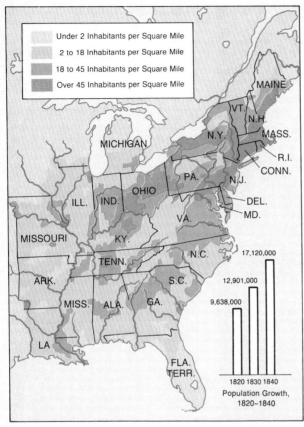

POPULATION DENSITY, 1840

The accelerating westward movement is evident in this map. Arkansas entered the Union in 1836, Michigan in 1837. During the 1830s the population of the nation as a whole increased by nearly one-third. Of the 4.2 million increase, a little over 10 percent were immigrants.

lations above 10,000. Thirty years later, 26 cities had more than 25,000 residents and 62 had more than 10,000.

Even though the <u>Old Northwest remained primarily agricultural</u>, its towns grew as fast as its farms. Pittsburgh, St. Louis, Cincinnati, Louisville, and Lexington attracted settlers in such numbers that by 1850 all but Lexington had populations of over 35,000. Cincinnati, "the Emporium of the West," with a population of 100,000, ranked seventh in the country.

The trek to town that was transforming the

Northeast did not occur in the South. There were four cities of respectable size in the region—Mobile, Savannah, Charleston, and Baltimore—and one large city, New Orleans, which had a population of 120,000 in 1850. Yet all were located on the region's perimeter. Neither Virginia nor North Carolina had an urban center of even modest dimensions. Charleston, the oldest and most typically southern city, scarcely grew at all after 1830.

Strangers at the Door

Between 1790 and 1820 the population of the United States more than doubled to 9.6 million. The most remarkable feature of this growth was that it

As the balance of rural and urban population began to shift during the years from 1820 to 1860, the number of cities with populations over 100,000 grew from one in 1820—New York—to nine in 1870, including southern and western cities like New Orleans and San Francisco.

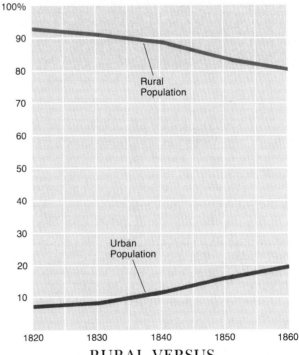

RURAL VERSUS URBAN POPULATION, 1820–1860

resulted almost entirely from natural increase. The birthrate in the early 19th century exceeded 50 per 1,000 population, a rate substantially higher than that of any country in the world today. Fewer than 250,000 immigrants entered the United States between 1790 and 1820. European wars, the ending of the slave trade, and doubts about the viability of the new republic slowed the flow of humanity across the Atlantic to a trickle.

But soon after the final defeat of Napoleon in 1815, immigration began to pick up. In the 1820s some 150,000 European immigrants arrived; in the 1830s, 600,000; in the 1840s, l.7 million. The 1850 census, the first to make the distinction, estimated that of the nation's population of 23 million, more than 10 percent were foreign-born. In the Northeast the proportion exceeded 15 percent.

Most of this human tide came from Germany and Ireland, but substantial numbers also came from Great Britain and the Scandinavian countries. As with earlier immigrants, many were drawn to America by the prospect of abundant land, high wages, and economic opportunity generally. Some too were attracted by the promise of political and religious freedom. But many came simply because to stay where they were meant to face starvation. This was particularly true of those from Ireland, where a potato blight triggered the flight of tens of thousands. This exodus continued throughout the century, by which time there were more people of Irish origin in America than in Ireland.

Once ashore in New York, Boston, or Philadelphia, most relatively prosperous immigrants pushed directly westward. Others found work in the new factory towns along the route of the Erie Canal, in the lower Delaware Valley southeast of Philadelphia, or along the Merrimack River north of Boston. But most of the Irish immigrants, "the poorest and most wretched population that can be found in the world," one of their priests called them, lacked the means to go west. Aside from the cost of transportation, starting a farm required far more capital than they could raise. Like it or not, they had to settle in the eastern cities.

Viewed in historical perspective, this massive wave of immigration stimulated the American econ-

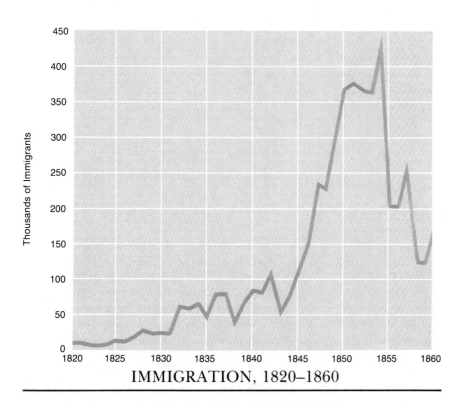

IMMIGRATION, 1820–1860

Immigration before the Civil War was primarily from the northern European countries of Britain, Ireland, and Germany. Between 1820 and 1860, about 800,000 immigrants came from Britain, 3.5 million from Ireland, and 1.5 million from Germany. Famine in Ireland and political upheavals and economic hard times in Germany during the 1840s and 1850s accounted for much of the flow.

Between 1830 and 1850, some 2.5 million immigrants fled hardship and op-pression in Europe to settle in the United States. They were packed into the filthy, airless holds of ships for the transatlantic crossing. Many died of disease. If they were lucky, passengers such as these aboard the Cornelius Grinnell *were allowed a few hours on deck.*

omy. In the short run, the influx of the 1830s and 1840s depressed living standards and strained the social fabric. For the first time the nation had ac-quired a culturally distinctive, citybound, and prop-ertyless class. The poor Irish immigrants had to accept whatever wages employers offered them. By doing so they caused resentment among native workers, resentment exacerbated by the unfamili-arity of the Irish with city ways and by their Roman Catholic faith, which the Protestant majority asso-ciated with European authoritarianism and corruption.

Off to Work

"It is as if all America were but one gigantic work-shop," the Austrian Francis Grund remarked in 1838. However enlightening to European readers, the fact that practically all Americans worked for their livings must have struck Americans as a blind-ing glimpse of the obvious. Ever since John Smith's assurances to the Jamestown settlers that if they did not work they would not eat, they had always done the one to assure themselves of the other. What was changing in the 1830s was that they worked outside their homes, if not exactly in "gigantic workshops."

In 1820, despite the growth of cities, three out of every four Americans were still engaged in agriculture. An efficient farming family used the labor of all its members, with chores assigned according to age, strength, and experience. Parents, children, and sometimes grandparents lived in the same house, or in adjoining houses, together with unrelated hired hands, when such existed. Except on large southern plantations run by overseers, farming remained a family enterprise.

By 1850, however, fewer than two out of three workers were farmers, in Massachusetts one of three. Outside the South, the way people earned a living had been transformed.

Until the 1820s and 1830s, the household was also the focus of most nonagricultural pursuits. The typical urban worker was a self-employed artisan. Whether a tailor, shoemaker, printer, baker, or carpenter, he had been apprenticed to a master while still a lad. After five to seven years of training, he became a journeyman and began to earn wages. Eventually, if he was reasonably talented, frugal, and industrious, he could open a shop of his own, take on apprentices, and thus perpetuate the system.

Since an apprentice lived and worked under the same roof as his master and his family, it was natural for the master to have familial as well as occupational authority over him. So intertwined did the life of an apprentice and his master become that the words *employee* and *employer* do not describe the relationship accurately. The historian Sean Wilentz has characterized the preindustrial workshop as "a benevolent hierarchy of skill." Apprentices were sometimes exploited and even physically abused, but just as often strong, personal bonds developed. Some apprentices married one of the master's daughters, thus helping to keep the trade in the family.

Forced reliance on domestically manufactured goods during the embargo and the War of 1812 and the improvements in transportation that were taking place steadily in the 1820s and 1830s prompted many master craftsmen and artisans to expand production. They took on more workers, in some cases as apprentices, more often as relatively unskilled wage earners. Work was broken down into separate simple tasks that the unskilled help could learn easily and repeat endlessly. As a business grew bigger and the division of labor became more complex, the master-turned-businessman spent less time working with his employees and more marketing the product. Elaborate rules evolved regu-

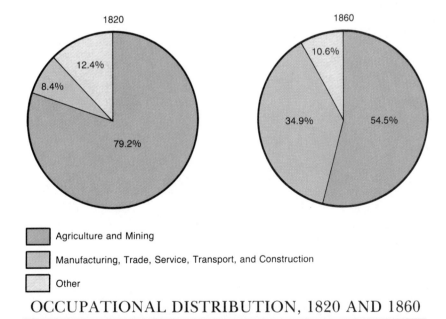

Agriculture and Mining

Manufacturing, Trade, Service, Transport, and Construction

Other

OCCUPATIONAL DISTRIBUTION, 1820 AND 1860

lating the hours of labor and the on-the-job behavior of workers. Drinking on the job, which in an earlier day had been considered normal and even desirable, was by 1850 almost universally forbidden.

Larger operations required more work space, and the need to locate near suppliers, customers, or a source of waterpower meant that the owner's home could no longer serve as a workplace. During the second quarter of the 19th century, Boston, New York, Philadelphia, and other cities sorted themselves into commercial and residential districts; the residential districts further separated into working-class and employer-class neighborhoods.

Even before the widespread use of machinery, large economies of scale were possible. Until the introduction of sewing machines in the 1850s, shoes were made entirely by hand, yet by the 1830s the shoe manufacturers of Lynn, Massachusetts, had shifted from making finely finished shoes for individual customers to mass-producing the rough brogans worn by slaves and other farmers. Custom-fitted shoes required the attention of a skilled craftsman, but brogans were made by several unskilled laborers, each performing a different function. Only the last handled the finished product.

An Industrial Proletariat?

As the importance of skilled labor declined, so did the ability of workers to influence working conditions. Skilled workers either became employers and

The first mill operations performed only the task of spinning wool, cotton, and other fibers into thread; soon weaving was also mechanized, so that fabric ready to be cut and sewn was manufactured. Note the child at left, working under the spindles where an adult could not stand.

developed entrepreneurial and managerial skills or descended into the mass of wage earners. Simultaneously, the changing structure of work widened the gap between owners and workers and blurred the distinction between skilled and unskilled workers.

These trends might have been expected to generate hostility between workers and employers. To some extent they did. There were strikes for higher wages and to protest work speedups throughout the 1830s and again in the 1850s. Efforts to found unions and to create political organizations dedicated to advancing the interests of workers were also undertaken.

But well into the 1850s Americans displayed few signs of the class solidarity common among European workers. Why America did not produce a self-conscious working class is a question that has long intrigued historians. As with most such large questions, no single answer has been forthcoming. Some historians argue that the existence of the frontier siphoned off displaced and dissatisfied workers. Others believe that ethnic and racial differences kept workers from seeing themselves as a distinct class with common needs and common enemies. Still others have suggested that the influx of needy immigrants willing to accept any job available at almost any wage undercut the organizational efforts of the native-born workers. The fact that the expanding economy created many opportunities for laborers to rise out of the working class was another reason why so few of them developed strong class feelings.

These answers help explain the relative absence of class conflict during the early stages of the industrial revolution in America, but so does the fact that conditions in the early shops and factories represented an improvement for the people who worked in them.

Most factory workers, especially in the textile industry, were drawn from outside the regular labor market. Relatively few hand spinners and weavers became factory workers; indeed, some of them continued to work as they had, for it was many years before the factories could even begin to satisfy the ever-increasing demand for cloth. Nor did immigrants attend the new machines. Instead, the mill owners relied chiefly on women and children. They did so because machines lessened the need for skill

and strength and because the labor shortage made it necessary to tap unexploited sources. By the early 1820s about half the cotton textile workers in the factories were under 16 years of age.

Most people of that generation considered this a good thing. They reasoned that the work was easy and that it kept youngsters busy at useful tasks while providing their families with extra income. Roxanna Foote, whose daughter Harriet Beecher Stowe wrote *Uncle Tom's Cabin*, came from a solid middle-class family in Guilford, Connecticut. Nevertheless, she worked full time before her marriage in her grandfather's small spinning mill. "This spinning-mill was a favorite spot," a relative recalled many years later. "Here the girls often received visitors, or read or chatted while they spun." Roxanna explained her daily regimen as a mill girl matter-of-factly: "I generally rise with the sun, and, after breakfast, take my wheel, which is my daily companion, and the evening is generally devoted to reading, writing, and knitting."

This seems a somewhat idealized picture, or perhaps working for one's grandfather made a difference. Another young girl, Emily Chubbock, later a well-known writer, had a less pleasant recollection of her experience as an 11-year-old factory hand earning $1.25 a week. "My principal recollections . . . are of noise and filth, bleeding hands and aching feet, and a very sad heart." In any case, a society accustomed to seeing the children of fairly well-to-do farmers working full time in the fields was not shocked by the sight of children working all day in mills. In some factories laborers were hired in family units. No member earned very much, but with a couple of adolescent daughters and perhaps a son of 9 or 10 helping out, a family could take home enough to live decently. For most working Americans, then as now, that was success enough.

Instead of hiring children, the Boston Associates developed the Waltham System of employing young, unmarried women in their new textile mills. The young women were lodged in company boardinghouses, which, like college dormitories, became centers of social life and not merely places to eat and sleep. Unlike college dormitories, the boardinghouses were strictly supervised; straitlaced New Englanders did not hesitate to permit their daughters to live in them. The regulations laid down by one company, for example, required that all employees "show that they are penetrated by a laudable love of temperance and virtue." "Ardent spirits" were banished from company property, "games of hazard and cards" prohibited. A 10 P.M. curfew was strictly enforced.

For a generation after the opening of the Merrimack Manufacturing Company in 1823, the thriving factory towns of Lowell, Chicopee, and Manchester provided the background for a remarkable industrial idyll. Young women came from farms all over New England to work for a year or two in the mills. They earned between $2.50 and $3.25 a week, about half of which went for room and board. Some of the remainder they sent home, the rest (what there was of it) they could spend as they wished.

Most of these young women did not have to support themselves. They worked to save for a trousseau, to help educate a younger brother, or simply for the experience and excitement of meeting new people and escaping the confining environment of the farm. "The feeling that at this new work the few hours they had of every-day leisure was entirely their own was a satisfaction to them," one Lowell worker recalled. Anything but an industrial proletariat, they filled the windows of the factories with flowering plants, organized sewing circles, edited their own literary periodicals, and attended lectures on edifying subjects. That such activity was possible on top of a 70-hour workweek is a commentary on both the resiliency of youth and the leisurely pace of these early factories. Dickens, though scarcely enchanted by other American ways, was impressed by his visit to Lowell, which he compared most favorably to "those great haunts of misery," the English manufacturing towns. "They were all well dressed," he wrote of the workers. "They were healthy in appearance, many of them remarkably so, and had the manners and deportment of young women. . . . The rooms in which they worked were as well ordered as themselves."

Life in the mills was not all it might have been. Though they made up 85 percent of the work force, women were kept out of supervisory positions. In 1834 workers in several mills "turned out" to protest cuts in their wages and a hike in board. This work stoppage did not force a reversal of management policy. Another strike two years later in response to a work speedup was somewhat more successful. But when a drop in prices in the 1840s led the owners to introduce new rules designed to increase

production, workers lacked the organizational strength to block them. By then young women of the kind that had flocked to the mills in the 1820s and 1830s were able to find work as schoolteachers or clerks. Mill owners turned increasingly to Irish immigrants to operate their machines.

The Family Recast

The factory system and the growth of cities undermined the importance of home and family as the unit of economic production. This happened first in the cities of the Northeast, then in the West, and eventually wherever nonagricultural jobs occupied a substantial percentage of the work force. More and more people did their work in shops, in offices, or on factory floors. Whether a job was skilled or unskilled, white-collar or blue-collar, or strictly professional, it took the family breadwinner out of the house during working hours six days a week. This did not mean that the family necessarily ceased to be an economic unit. But the labor of the father and any children with jobs came home in the form of cash, thus at least initially in the custody of the individual earners. The social consequences of this change were enormous for the traditional "head of the family" and for his wife and children.

Because he was away so much, the husband had to surrender to his wife some of the power in the family that he had formerly exercised, if for no other reason than that she was always there. The situation bore a superficial resemblance to the relationship of the king of England to the colonies in the 17th century: Whatever the king's power under the law, his authority was limited by his lack of close contact with his colonial "offspring." Perhaps this is what Noah Webster had in mind when he used a similar comparison in describing the ideal father's authority as "like the mild dominion of a limited monarch, and not the iron rule of an austere tyrant." It certainly explains why Tocqueville concluded that "a sort of equality reigns around the domestic hearth" in America. It also explains why American men began to place women on a pedestal, presuming them to be by nature almost saintly, pure of mind and body, selflessly devoted to the care of others.

The new power and prestige that wives and mothers enjoyed was not obtained without cost. Since they were exercising day-to-day control over

Family structure changed as a result of the industrial revolution. Not only did couples have fewer children, but husbands were expected to earn the family's living and concern themselves with worldly business while wives assumed all domestic duties.

household affairs, they were expected to tend only to those affairs. Anything that might take them away from the family hearth was frowned on. Where the typical wife had formerly been a partner in a family enterprise, she now left earning a living entirely to her husband. Time spent away from home or devoted to matters unrelated to the care of husband and family was, according to the new doctrine of "separate spheres," time misappropriated.

This trend widened the gap between the middle and lower classes. For a middle-class wife and mother to take a job or, still worse, to devote herself to any "frivolous" activity outside the home was considered a dereliction of duty. Such an attitude could not possibly develop in families where everyone had to work simply to keep food on the table.

Some women objected to the discrimination implicit in what the historian Barbara Welter has called "the cult of true womanhood." Others escaped its more suffocating aspects by forming close friendships with other women. But most women, including such forceful proponents of women's rights as the educator Catharine Beecher and Sarah Hale, the editor of *Godey's Ladies Book,* subscribed in their writing to the view that a woman's place was in the home. "The formation of the moral and intellectual character of the young is committed mainly to the female hand," Beecher wrote in *A Treatise on Domestic Economy for the Use of Young Ladies.* "The mother forms the character of the future man."

Another reason for the switch in power and influence from husbands to wives was that women began to have fewer children. Here again, the change happened earliest and was most pronounced among families in the rapidly urbanizing Northeast. But the birthrate gradually declined all over the country. People married later than in earlier periods. Long courtships and broken engagements were common, probably because prospective marriage partners were becoming more choosy. On average, women began having their children two or three years later than their mothers had, and they stopped two or three years sooner. Apparently many middle-class couples made a conscious effort to limit family size, even when doing so required sexual abstinence.

Having fewer children led parents to value children more highly, or so it would seem from the additional time and affection they lavished on them. Here again, the mother provided most of both. Child rearing fell within her "sphere" and occupied the time that earlier generations of mothers had devoted to such tasks as weaving, sewing, and farm chores. Not least of these new responsibilities was overseeing the children's education, both secular and religious.

As families became smaller, relations within them became more caring. Parents ceased to think of their children mostly as future workers. The earlier tendency even among loving parents to keep their children at arm's length, yet within reach of the strap, gave way to more intimate relationships. Gone was the Puritan notion that children possessed "a perverse will, a love of what's forbid," and with it the belief that parents were responsible for crushing all juvenile resistance to their authority. In its place arose the view described by Lydia Maria Child in *The Mother's Book* (1831) that children "come to us from heaven, with their little souls full of innocence and peace." Mothers "should not interfere with the influence of angels," Child advised her readers.

Bronson Alcott, another proponent of gentle child-rearing practices, went still further. Children, he insisted, were the moral superiors of their parents. Alcott banished "the rod and all its append-

ages" from his own household, wherein four daughters (one, Louisa May, later the author of *Little Women* and other novels) were raised, and urged other parents to follow his example. "Childhood hath saved me!" he wrote. The English poet William Wordsworth's "Ode on Intimations of Immortality," in which babies entered the world "trailing clouds of glory," served some American parents as a child-rearing manual.

The Second Great Awakening

Belief in the innate goodness of children was of course in direct conflict with the Calvinist doctrine of infant damnation, to which most American Prot-

During the Second Great Awakening, Americans flocked in vast numbers to hear evangelists such as Charles Grandison Finney preach. At huge outdoor camp meetings, which sometimes lasted three or four days and offered a change from the loneliness of frontier life, men and women enthusiastically embraced salvation. "Its sincerity could not be doubted," wrote an English observer after witnessing an emotional conversion at a camp meeting, "but it was the effect of over-excitement, not of sober reasoning."

estant churches formally subscribed. "Of all the impious doctrines which the dark imagination of man ever conceived," Bronson Alcott wrote in his journal, "the worst [is] the belief in original and certain depravity of infant nature." Alcott was far from alone in thinking infant damnation a "debased doctrine," despite its standing as one of the central tenets of orthodox Calvinism.

The inclination to set aside other Calvinist tenets, such as predestination, became more pronounced as a new wave of revivalism took shape in the 1790s. This Second Great Awakening began as a counteroffensive to the deistic thinking and other forms of "infidelity" that New England Congregationalists and southern Methodists alike identified with the French Revolution. Prominent New England ministers, who considered themselves traditionalists but also revivalists, men such as Yale's president, Timothy Dwight, and Dwight's student, the Reverend Lyman Beecher, placed less stress in their sermons on God's arbitrary power over mortals, more on His mercy, love, and "disinterested benevolence." When another of Dwight's students, Horace Bushnell, declared in a sermon on "Christian nurture" in 1844 that Christian parents should prepare their children "for the skies," he meant that parents could contribute to their children's salvation.

Calvinism came under more direct assault from Charles Grandison Finney, probably the most effective of a number of charismatic evangelists who brought the Second Great Awakening to its crest. In 1821 Finney abandoned a promising career as a lawyer and became an itinerant preacher. His most spectacular successes occurred during a series of revivals conducted in towns along the Erie Canal, a region Finney called "the burned-over district" because it had been the site of so many revivals before his own. From Utica, where his revival began in 1826, to Rochester, where it climaxed in 1831, he exhorted his listeners to take their salvation into their own hands. He insisted that people could control their own fate. He dismissed Calvinism as a "theological fiction." Salvation was available to anyone. But the day of judgment was just around the corner; there was little time to waste.

During and after Finney's efforts in Utica, declared conversions increased sharply. In Rochester, church membership doubled in six months. Elsewhere in the country, churches capitalized on the efforts of other evangelists to fill their pews. In 1831 alone, church membership grew by 100,000, an increase according to a New England minister, "unparalleled in the history of the church." The success of the evangelists of the Second Great Awakening stemmed from the timeliness of their assault on Calvinist doctrines, which were ripe for discrediting, and even more from their methods. Finney, for example, consciously set out to be entertaining as well as edifying. The singing of hymns and the solicitation of personal testimonies provided his meetings with emotional release and human interest. Prominent among his innovations was the "anxious bench," where leading members of the community awaited the final prompting from within before coming forward to declare themselves saved.

But the economic changes of the times and the impact of these changes on family life had as important effects on the Second Awakening as even the most accomplished of the evangelists. The growth of industry and commerce that followed the completion of the Erie Canal in 1825, along with the disappearance of undeveloped farmland, led hundreds of young men to leave family farms to seek their fortunes in Utica and other towns along the canal. There, uprooted, uncertain, buffeted between ambition, hope, and anxiety, they found it hard to resist the comfort promised by the revivalists to those who were saved.

But women, and especially the wives of the business leaders of the community, were, as Mary P. Ryan writes, the people "most receptive to the admonitions of the evangelical clergy." Aside from concern for their own salvation, they felt particularly responsible for the Christian education of their children, which fell within their separate sphere. Most of these upper-middle-class women had servants to handle household chores so that they had time and energy to devote to their own and their offsprings' salvation.

Paradoxically, this caused many of them to venture out of that sphere and in doing so they moved further out of the shadow of their husbands. They founded the Oneida County Female Missionary Society, an association that did most of the organizing and a good deal of the financing of the climactic years of the Second Awakening. The Female Missionary Society raised more than $1,000 a year (no small sum at that time) to support the revival in Utica, in its environs, and throughout the burned-over district. "These women," Professor Ryan explains, "orchestrated the revival and devised a sphere for women that had not been anticipated." Apparently without consciously intending to do so, they challenged the authority of the paternalistic, authoritarian churches they so fervently embraced. Then, by mixtures of exhortation, example, and affection, they set out to save the souls of their loved ones, first their children and ultimately their husbands too.

The Era of Associations

Alongside the recast family and the "almost revolutionized" church, a third pillar of the emerging American middle class was the voluntary association. Unlike the other two, it had neither colonial precedents nor contemporary European equivalents. The voluntary association of early 19th-century America was unique. "In France," Tocqueville wrote of this phenomenon, "if you want to proclaim a truth or propagate some feeling . . . you would find the government or in England some territorial magnate." In America, however, "you are sure to find an association."

The leaders of these associations tended to be ministers, lawyers, or merchants, but the rank and file consisted of tradesmen, foremen, clerks, and their wives. Some of these associations were formed around a local cause that some townspeople wished to advance, such as the provision of religious instruction for orphaned children; others were affiliated with associations elsewhere for the purposes of combating some national evil, such as drunkenness. Some, such as the American Board of Commissioners of Foreign Missions, founded in Boston in 1810, quickly became large and complex enterprises. (By 1860 the board had sent 1,250 missionaries into the "heathen world" and raised $8 million to support them.) Others lasted only as long as it took to accomplish a specific good work, such as the construction of a school or a library.

In a sense the associations were assuming functions previously performed in the family, such as caring for old people and providing moral guidance to the young, but without the paternalistic discipline of the old way. They constituted a "benevolent empire," eager to make society over into their members' idea of how God wanted it to be.

Backwoods Utopias

Americans frequently belonged to several associations at the same time, and more than a few made

The simplicity of Shaker life is apparent in this spartan bedroom, with its plain, narrow bed, its washstand, and the hanging pegs which are a practical way of storing articles such as hats, towels, and even a looking glass.

reform their life's work. The most adventuresome tested their reform theories by withdrawing from workaday American society and establishing experimental communities. The communitarian point of view aimed at "commencing a wholesale social reorganization by first establishing and demonstrating its principles completely on a small scale." The first communitarians were religious reformers. In a sense the Pilgrims fall into this category, along with a number of other groups in colonial times, but only in the 19th century did the idea flourish.

One of the earliest significant groups was founded by George Rapp, who brought some 600 Germans to western Pennsylvania in 1804. Rappites renounced marriage and sex and took every word in the Bible literally. They believed that the millennium was at hand; people must have their affairs constantly in order so as to be ready to meet their Maker on short notice. Industrious, pious, and isolated from other Americans by their language and beliefs, the Rappites prospered but had little influence on their neighbors.

More influential were the Shaker communities founded by an Englishwoman, Ann Lee, who came to America in 1774. Mother Ann, as she was called, saw visions that convinced her that Christ would come to earth again as a woman and that she was that woman. With a handful of followers she founded a community near Albany, New York. The group grew rapidly, and after her death in 1784 her movement continued to expand. By the 1830s her followers had established about 20 successful communities.

Like the Rappites, the Shakers practiced celibacy; believing that the millennium was imminent, they saw no reason for perpetuating the human race. Each group lived in a large Family House, the sexes strictly segregated. Property was held in common but controlled by a ruling hierarchy. So much stress was placed on equality of labor and reward and on voluntary acceptance of the rules, however, that the system does not seem to have been oppressive.

The Shaker religion, joyful and fervent, was marked by much group singing and dancing, which provided the members with emotional release from their tightly controlled regimen. An industrious, skillful people, they made a special virtue of simplicity; some of their designs for buildings and, especially, furniture achieved a classic beauty seldom equaled among untutored artisans. Despite their odd customs, the Shakers were universally tolerated and even admired.

There were many other religious colonies, such as the Amana Community, which flourished in New York and Iowa in the 1840s and 1850s, and John Humphrey Noyes's Oneida Community, where the members practiced "complex" marriage—a form of promiscuity based on the principle that every man in the group was married to every woman. They prospered by developing a number of manufacturing skills.

The most important of the religious communitarians was the Mormons. A remarkable Vermont farm boy, Joseph Smith, founded the religion in western New York in the 1820s. Smith saw visions; he claimed to have discovered and translated an ancient text, the Book of Mormon, written in hieroglyphics on plates of gold, which described the adventures of a tribe of Israelites that had populated America from biblical times until their destruction in a great war in A.D. 400. With a small band of followers, Smith established a community in Ohio in 1831. The Mormons' dedication and economic efficiency attracted large numbers of converts, but their unorthodox religious views and their exclusivism, product of their sense of being a chosen people, caused resentment among unbelievers. The Mormons were forced to move first to Missouri and then back to Illinois, where in 1839 they founded the town of Nauvoo.

Nauvoo flourished—by 1844 it was the largest city in the state, with a population of 15,000—but once again the Mormons ran into local trouble. They quarreled among themselves, especially after Smith secretly authorized polygamy (he called it "celestial marriage") and a number of other unusual rites for members of the "Holy Order," the top leaders of the church.* They created a paramilitary organization, the Nauvoo Legion, headed by Smith, envisaging themselves as a semi-independent state within the Union. Smith announced that he was a candidate for president of the United States. Rumors circulated that the Mormons intended to take over the entire Northwest for their "empire." Once

---

* The justification of polygamy, paradoxically, was that marriage was a sacred, eternal state. If a man remarried after his wife's death, eventually he would have two wives in Heaven. Therefore why not on earth?

Persecution forced the Mormons to move from New York to Ohio to Missouri, before settling for a time in Nauvoo, Illinois. In 1830, Mormon leaders were tarred and feathered, as this print shows. Fourteen years later, founder Joseph Smith and his brother Hyrum were arrested by local authorities and murdered in their jail cell by a hostile mob.

again local "gentiles" rose against them; Smith was arrested, then murdered by a mob.

Under a new leader, Brigham Young, the Mormons sought a haven beyond the frontier. In 1847 they marched westward, pressing through the mountains until they reached the desolate wilderness on the shores of Great Salt Lake. There, at last, they established their Zion and began to make their truly significant impact on American history. Irrigation made the desert flourish, precious water wisely being treated as a community asset. Hard, cooperative, intelligently directed effort spelled growth and prosperity; more than 11,000 people were living in the area when it became part of Utah Territory as a result of the Compromise of 1850. In time the communal Mormon settlement broke down, but the religion has remained, along with a distinctive Mormon culture that has been a major force in the shaping of the West. The Mormon church is still by far the most powerful single influence in Utah and is a thriving organization in many other parts of the United States and in Europe.

Despite their many common characteristics, the religious communities varied enormously; subordination of the individual to the group did not destroy group individualism. Their sexual practices, for example, ranged from the "complex marriage" of the Oneidans through Mormon polygamy and ordinary monogamy to the reluctant acceptance of sexual intercourse by the Amana Community and the absolute celibacy of the Rappites and Shakers. The communities are more significant as reflections of the urgent reform spirit of the age than they are for their accomplishments.

The communities had some influence on reformers who wished to experiment with social organization. When Robert Owen, a British utopian socialist who believed in economic as well as political equality and who considered competition debasing, decided to create an ideal community in America, he purchased the Rappite settlement at New Harmony, Indiana. Owen's advocacy of free love and "enlightened atheism" did not add to the stability of his group or to its popularity among outsiders. The colony was a costly failure.

The American followers of Charles Fourier, a French utopian socialist who proposed that society should be organized in cooperative units called phalanxes, fared better. Fourierism did not seek to tamper with sexual and religious mores. Its advocates included important journalists, such as Horace Greeley of the *New York Tribune* and Parke Godwin of the *New York Evening Post.* In the 1840s several dozen Fourierist colonies were established in the northern and western states. Members worked at whatever tasks they wished and only as much as they wished. Wages were paid according to the "repulsiveness" of the tasks performed; the person who "chose" to clean out a cesspool would receive more than someone hoeing corn or mending a fence or engaging in some task requiring complex skills. As might be expected, none of the communities lasted very long.

The Age of Reform

The communitarians were the most colorful of the reformers, their proposals the most spectacular. More effective, however, were the many individuals who took upon themselves responsibility for caring for the physically and mentally disabled and for the rehabilitation of criminals. The work of Thomas Gallaudet in developing methods for educating deaf people reflects the spirit of the times. Gallaudet's school in Hartford, Connecticut, opened its doors in 1817; by 1851 similar schools for the deaf had been established in 14 states.

Dr. Samuel Gridley Howe did similar work with the blind, devising means for making books with raised letters (Louis Braille's system of raised dots was not introduced until later in the century) that the blind could "read" with their fingers. Howe headed a school for the blind in Boston, the pioneering Perkins Institution, which opened in 1832. Of all that Charles Dickens observed in America, nothing so favorably impressed him as Howe's success in educating 12-year-old Laura Bridgman, who was deaf, mute, and blind. Howe was also interested

in trying to educate the mentally defective, and in other causes, including antislavery. "Every creature in human shape should command our respect," he insisted. "The strong should help the weak, so that the whole should advance as a band of brethren."

One of the most striking aspects of the reform movement was the emphasis reformers placed on establishing special institutions for dealing with social problems. In the colonial period, orphans, indigent persons, the insane, and the feebleminded were usually cared for by members of their own families or boarded in a neighboring household. They remained part of the community. Even criminals were seldom "locked away" for extended jail terms; punishment commonly consisted of whipping, being placed in stocks in the town square, or (for serious crimes) execution. But once persuaded that people were primarily shaped by their surroundings, reformers demanded that deviant and dependent members of the community be taken from their present corrupting circumstances and placed in specialized institutions where they could be trained or rehabilitated. The result, according to the historian David J. Rothman, was "the discovery of the asylum." Almshouses, orphanages, reformatories, prisons, and lunatic asylums sprang up throughout the United States like mushrooms in a forest after a summer rain.

The rationale for this movement was scientific; elaborate statistical reports attested to the benefits that such institutions would bring to both inmates and society as a whole. The motivating spirit of the founders of these asylums was humane, though many of the institutions seem anything but humane to the modern eye. The highly regarded Philadelphia prison system was based on strict solitary confinement, which was supposed to lead culprits to reflect on their sins and then reform their ways. The prison was literally a penitentiary, a place to repent. In fact, the system drove some inmates mad, and soon a rival Auburn system was introduced in New York State that allowed for some social contact among prisoners and for work in shops and stone quarries. Absolute silence was required at all times. The prisoners were herded about in lockstep and punished by flogging for the slightest infraction of the rules. Regular "moral and religious instruction" was provided, which the authorities believed would lead inmates to reform their lives. Tocqueville and Beaumont, in their report on American prisons,

A daguerreotype of Dorothea Lynde Dix, the pioneer reformer who worked to improve the lot of the insane in the United States. She also traveled to Europe, where she urged Queen Victoria and Pope Pius IX to support her efforts.

concluded that the Philadelphia system produced "the deepest impression on the soul of the convict," while the Auburn system made the convict "more conformable to the habits of man in society."

The hospitals for mental patients were intended to cure inmates, not merely to confine them. The emphasis was on isolating them from the pressures of society; on order, quiet, routine; on control but not on punishment. The unfortunates were seen as *de*ranged; the task was to *ar*range their lives in a rational manner. In practice, shortages of trained personnel, niggardly legislative appropriations, and the inherent difficulty of managing violent and irrational patients often produced deplorable conditions in the asylums.

This situation led Dorothea Dix, a woman of almost saintlike selflessness, to devote 30 years of her life to a campaign to improve the care of the insane. She traveled to every state in the Union and as far afield as Turkey and Japan, inspecting asylums and poorhouses. Insane persons in Massachusetts, she wrote in a memorial intended to shock state legislators into action, were being kept in cages

and closets, *"chained, naked, beaten with rods, and lashed into obedience!"* Her reports led to some improvement in conditions in Massachusetts and other states, but in the long run the bright hopes of the reformers were never realized. Institutions founded to uplift the deviant and dependent all too soon lost their reformist intentions and became instead places where society's "misfits" might safely be kept out of sight.

"Demon Rum"

Reformers must of necessity interfere with the affairs of others; thus there is often something of the busybody and the arrogant meddler about them. How they are regarded usually turns on the observer's own attitude toward their objectives. What is to some an unjustified infringement on a person's private affairs is to others a necessary intervention for that person's own good and for the good of society. Consider the temperance movement, the most widely supported and successful reform of the age of reform.

Americans in the 1820s consumed prodigious amounts of alcohol, more than ever before or since. Not that the colonists had been teetotalers. Liquor, mostly in the form of rum or hard apple cider, was cheap and everywhere available; taverns were an integral part of colonial society. There were alcoholics in colonial America, but because neither political nor religious leaders considered drinking dangerous, there was no alcohol "problem." Most doctors recommended the regular consumption of alcohol as healthy. John Adams, certainly the soul of propriety, drank a tankard of hard cider every day for breakfast. Dr. Benjamin Rush's *Inquiry into the Effects of Ardent Spirits* (1784), which questioned the medicinal benefits of alcohol, fell on deaf ears. However, alcohol consumption increased markedly in the early years of the new republic, thanks primarily to the availability of cheap corn and rye whiskey distilled in the new states of Kentucky and Tennessee. In the 1820s the per capita consumption of hard liquor reached 5 gallons, well over twice what it is today. Since small children and many grown people did not drink that much, others obviously drank a great deal more. Many women drank, if mostly at home; and reports of carousing among

14-year-old college freshmen show that youngsters did too. But the bulk of the heavy drinking occurred when men got together, at taverns or grogshops and at work.

Artisans and common laborers regarded their twice-daily "dram" of whiskey as part of their wages. In workshops, masters were expected to halt production periodically to drink with their apprentices and journeymen. Trips to the neighborhood grogshop also figured into the workaday routine. In 1829 Secretary of War John Eaton estimated that three-quarters of the nation's laborers drank at least 4 ounces of distilled spirits a day.

The foundation of the American Temperance Union in 1826 signaled the start of a national crusade against drunkenness. Employing lectures, pamphlets, rallies, essay contests, and other techniques, the union set out to persuade people to "sign the pledge" not to drink liquor. Primitive sociological studies of the effects of drunkenness (reformers were able to show a high statistical correlation between alcohol consumption and crime) added to the effectiveness of the campaign.

In 1840 an organization of reformed drunkards, the Washingtonians, set out to reclaim alcoholics. One of the most effective Washingtonians was John B. Gough, rescued by the organization after seven years in the gutter. "Crawl from the slimy ooze, ye drowned drunkards," Gough would shout, "and with suffocation's blue and livid lips speak out against the drink!"

Revivalist ministers like Charles Grandison Finney argued that alcohol was one of the great barriers to conversion, which helps explain why Utica, a town of fewer than 13,000 residents in 1840, supported four separate temperance societies in that year. Employers all over the country also signed on, declaring their businesses henceforward to be "cold-water" enterprises. Soon the temperance movement claimed a million members.

The temperance people aroused bitter opposition, particularly after they moved beyond calls for restraint to demands for prohibition of all alcohol. German and Irish immigrants, for the most part Catholic, objected to being told by reformers, for the most part Protestant, that their drinking would have to stop. But by the early 1840s the reformers had secured legislation in many states that imposed strict licensing systems and heavy liquor taxes. Local option laws permitted towns and counties to ban the sale of alcohol altogether.

In 1851 Maine passed the first effective law prohibiting the manufacture and sale of alcoholic beverages. The leader of the campaign was Mayor Neal Dow of Portland, a businessman who became a prohibitionist after seeing the damage done by drunkenness among workers in his tannery. By 1855 a dozen other states had passed laws based on the Maine statute, and the nation's per capita consumption of alcohol had plummeted to 2 gallons a year.

The Abolitionist Crusade

No reform movement of this era was more significant, more ambiguous, or more provocative of later historical investigation than the drive to abolish slavery. That slavery should have been a cause of indignation to reform-minded Americans was inevitable. Humanitarians were outraged by the master's whip and by the practice of disrupting families. Democrats protested the denial of political and civil rights to slaves. Perfectionists of all stripes deplored the fact that slaves had no chance to improve themselves. However, well into the 1820s, the abolitionist cause attracted few followers because there seemed to be no way of getting rid of slavery short of revolution. While a few theorists argued that the Fifth Amendment, which provides that no one may be "deprived of life, liberty, or property, without due process of law," could be interpreted to mean that the Constitution outlawed slavery, the great majority believed that the institution was not subject to federal control.

Particularly in the wake of the Missouri Compromise, antislavery northerners neatly compartmentalized their thinking. Slavery was wrong; they would not tolerate it in their own communities. But since the Constitution obliged them to tolerate it in states where it existed, they felt no responsibility to fight it. The issue was explosive enough even when limited to the question of the expansion of slavery into the territories. People who advocated any kind of forced abolition in states where it was legal were judged irresponsible in the extreme. In 1820 presidential hopeful John Quincy Adams called slavery "the great and foul stain upon the North American

Union." "If the Union must be dissolved," he added, "slavery is precisely the question upon which it ought to break." But Adams expressed these opinions in the privacy of his diary, not in a public speech. Most critics of slavery therefore confined themselves to urging "colonization" or persuading slave owners to treat their property humanely.

One of the few Americans in the 1820s to go further was the Quaker Benjamin Lundy, editor of the Baltimore-based newspaper *The Genius of Universal Emancipation.* Lundy was no fanatic; he urged the use of persuasion in the South rather than interference by the federal government. He also explored the possibility of colonizing free blacks and slaves in Haiti and Canada. But he refused to mince words, and consequently he was subject to frequent harassment.

Even more provocative and less accommodating to local sensibilities was Lundy's youthful assistant, William Lloyd Garrison of Massachusetts. Garrison pronounced himself for "immediate" abolition. When his absolutely unyielding position made continued residence in Baltimore impossible, he returned to Boston, where in 1831 he established his own newspaper, *The Liberator.* "I am in earnest," he announced in the first issue. "I will not equivocate—

Former slave Frederick Douglass was one of the most effective spokesmen of the Massachusetts Anti-Slavery Society in the 1840s.

William Lloyd Garrison founded The Liberator *and edited it for 35 years; the newspaper was one of the nation's leading antislavery publications.*

I will not excuse—I will not retreat a single inch—and I will be heard."

Garrison's position, and that espoused by the New England Anti-Slavery Society, which he organized in 1831, was absolutely unyielding: Slaves must be freed immediately and treated as equals; compensated emancipation was unacceptable, colonization unthinkable. Because the United States government countenanced slavery, Garrison refused to engage in political activity to achieve his ends. Burning a copy of the Constitution—that "agreement with hell"—became a regular feature at Society-sponsored public lectures.

Few white Americans found Garrison's line of argument convincing, and many were outraged by his confrontational tactics. Whenever he spoke in public, he risked being mobbed by what newspaper accounts approvingly described as "gentlemen of property and standing." In 1833 a Garrison meeting in New York City was broken up by colonizationists. Two years later a mob dragged Garrison through the streets of his own Boston. That same day a mob broke up the convention of the New York Anti-Slavery Society in Utica. In 1837 Elijah Lovejoy, a

Garrisonian newspaper editor in Alton, Illinois, first saw his press destroyed by fire and then was himself murdered by a mob. When the proprietors of Philadelphia's Pennsylvania Hall booked an abolitionist meeting in 1838, a mob burned the hall to the ground to prevent the meeting from taking place. The historian Leonard L. Richard has documented more than 100 attacks on abolitionists in the North between 1833 and 1838.

In the wake of this violence some of Garrison's backers had second thoughts about his strategy of immediatism. The wealthy New York businessmen Arthur and Lewis Tappan, who had subsidized *The Liberator,* turned instead to Theodore Dwight Weld, a young minister who was part of Charles Grandison Finney's "holy band" of revivalists. Weld and his followers spoke of "immediate" emancipation "gradually" achieved, and they were willing to engage in political activity to achieve that goal.

In 1840 the Tappans and Weld openly broke with Garrison over the issue of involvement in politics and the participation of female abolitionists as public lecturers. Garrison, ever the radical, supported the women; Weld thought they would needlessly antagonize would-be supporters. The Tappans then organized the Liberty party, which nominated as its presidential candidate James G. Birney, a Kentucky slaveholder who had been converted to evangelical Christianity and abolitionism by Weld. Running on a platform of universal emancipation to be gradually brought about through legislation, Birney received only 7,000 votes.

Many blacks were abolitionists long before the white movement began to attract attention. In 1830 some 50 black antislavery societies existed, and thereafter these groups grew in size and importance, being generally associated with the Garrisonian wing. White abolitionists eagerly sought out black speakers, especially runaway slaves, whose heartrending accounts of their experiences aroused sympathies and who, merely by speaking clearly and with conviction, stood as living proof that blacks were neither animals nor fools.

Frederick Douglass, a former slave who had escaped from Maryland, was one of the most remarkable Americans of his generation. While a bondsman he had received a full portion of beatings and other indignities; but he had been allowed to learn to read and write and to master a trade, opportunities denied the vast majority of slaves. Settling in Boston, he became an agent of the Massachusetts Anti-Slavery Society and a featured speaker at its public meetings.

Douglass was a tall, majestically handsome man who radiated determination and indignation. Slavery, he told white audiences, "brands your republicanism as a sham, your humanity as a base pretense, your Christianity as a lie." In 1845 he published his *Narrative of the Life of Frederick Douglass,* one of the most gripping autobiographical accounts of a slave's life ever written. Douglass insisted that freedom for blacks required not merely emancipation but full equality, social and economic as well as political. Not many white northerners accepted his reasoning, but few who heard him or read his works could afterward maintain the illusion that all blacks were dull-witted or resigned to inferior status.

At first Douglass was, in his own words, "a faithful disciple" of Garrison, prepared to tear up the Constitution and destroy the Union to gain his ends. In the late 1840s, however, he changed his mind, deciding that the Constitution, created to "establish Justice, insure domestic Tranquility . . . and secure the Blessings of Liberty," as its preamble states, "could not well have been designed at the same time to maintain and perpetuate a system of rapine and murder like slavery." Thereafter he fought slavery and race prejudice from within the system, something Garrison was never willing to do.

Garrison's importance cannot be measured by the number of his followers, which was never large. Unlike more moderately inclined enemies of slavery, he recognized that abolitionism was a revolutionary movement, not merely one more middle-class reform. He also understood that achieving racial equality, not merely "freeing" the slaves, was the only way to reach the abolitionists' professed objective: full justice for blacks. And he saw clearly that few whites, even among abolitionists, believed that blacks were their equals.

At the same time, Garrison seemed utterly indifferent to what effect the "immediate" freeing of the slaves would have on the South. He and his followers came close to claiming that all southern whites were villains, all blacks saints. Garrison said he would rather be governed by "the inmates of our penitentiaries" than by southern congressmen, whom he characterized as "desperadoes." The life of the slave owner, he wrote, is "one of unbridled lust, of filthy amalgamation, of swaggering brag-

gadocio, of haughty domination, of cowardly ruf-
fianism, of boundless dissipation, of matchless in-
solence, of infinite self-conceit, of unequaled
oppression, of more than savage cruelty." His followers were no less fanatical in their judgments.
"Slavery and cruelty cannot be disjoined," one
wrote. "Consequently every slaveholder must be in-
human."

Both Garrison's insights into the limits of northern racial egalitarianism and his blind contempt for
southern whites led him to the conclusion that
American society was rotten to the core. Hence his
refusal to make any concession to the existing establishment, religious or secular. He was hated in
the North as much for his explicit denial of the idea
that a constitution that supported slavery merited
respect as for his implicit denial of the idea that a
professed Christian who tolerated slavery for even
an instant could hope for salvation. He was, in short,
a perfectionist, a trafficker in moral absolutes who
wanted his Kingdom of Heaven in the here and
now. By contrast, most other American reformers
were willing to settle for perfection on the installment plan.

Women's Rights

The question of slavery was related to another major
reform movement of the era, the crusade for wom-
en's rights. The relationship was personal and ideological, direct and indirect, simple and profound.
Superficially, the connection can be explained in
this way: Women were as likely as men to find slavery
offensive and to protest against it. When they did
so, they ran into even more adamant resistance, the
prejudices of those who objected to abolitionists being reinforced by their feelings that women should
not speak in public or participate in political affairs.
Thus female abolitionists, driven by the urgencies
of conscience, were almost forced to become advocates of women's rights. "We have good cause to
be grateful to the slave," the feminist Abby Kelley
wrote. "In striving to strike his irons off, we found
most surely, that we were manacled ourselves."

At a more profound level, the reference that
abolitionists made to the Declaration of Independence to justify their attack on slavery radicalized
women with regard to their own place in society.
Were only all men created equal and endowed by

*Elizabeth Cady Stanton at the age of 41 with her
youngest daughter. In 1848 she helped draft the Declaration Principles, spelling out the injustices of man to
woman. The conclusion: "He has endeavored, in every
way he could, to destroy her confidence in her own powers, to lessen her self-respect, and to make her willing to
lead a dependent and abject life."*

God with unalienable rights? For many women the
question was a consciousness-raising experience;
they began to believe that, like blacks, they were
imprisoned from birth in a caste system, legally subordinated and assigned menial social and economic
roles that prevented them from developing their
full potentialities. Such women considered themselves in a sense worse off than blacks, who had at
least the psychological advantage of confronting an
openly hostile and repressive society rather than one
concealed behind the cloying rhetoric of romantic
love.

With the major exception of Margaret Fuller,
whose book *Women in the Nineteenth Century* (1844)
made a frontal assault on all forms of sexual discrimination, the leading advocates of equal rights

for women began their public careers in the abolitionist movement. Among the first were Sarah and Angelina Grimké, South Carolinians who abandoned their native state and the domestic sphere to devote themselves to speaking out against slavery. (In 1841 Angelina married Theodore Dwight Weld.) Male objections to the Grimkés' activities soon made them advocates of women's rights. Similarly, the refusal of delegates to the World Anti-Slavery Convention held in London in 1840 to let women participate in their debates precipitated the decision of two American abolitionists, Lucretia Mott and Elizabeth Cady Stanton, to turn their attention to the women's rights movement.

Slavery aside, there were other aspects of feminist consciousness-raising. Some women rejected the idea that they should confine themselves to a sphere of activity consisting mostly of child rearing and housekeeping. As the historian Nancy Cott has shown, the very effort to enforce this kind of specialization made women aware of their second-class citizenship and thus more likely to be dissatisfied. They lacked not merely the right to vote, of which they did not make a major issue, but if married, the right to own property or to make a will. Lydia Maria Child, a popular novelist, found this last restriction particularly offensive. It excited her "towering indignation" that her husband had to sign her will. David Child was not what today would be called a chauvinist, but, as she explained, "I was indignant for womankind made chattels personal from the beginning of time."

As Lydia Child noted, the subordination of women was as old as civilization. The attack on it came not because of any new discrimination but for the same reasons that motivated reformers against other forms of injustice: belief in progress, a sense of personal responsibility, the conviction that institutions could be changed and that the time for changing them was limited.

When women sought to involve themselves in reform, they became aware of perhaps the most serious handicap that society imposed on them— the conflict between their roles as wives and mothers and their urge to participate in the affairs of the larger world. Elizabeth Cady Stanton has left a striking description of this dilemma. She lived in the 1840s in Seneca Falls, a small town in central New York. Her husband was frequently away on business; she had a brood of growing children and little

domestic help. When, stimulated by her interest in abolition and women's rights, she sought to become active in the movements, her family responsibilities made it almost impossible even to read about them.

"I now fully understood the practical difficulties most women had to contend with," she recalled in her autobiography, *Eighty Years and More* (1898). "The general discontent I felt with woman's portion as wife, mother, housekeeper, physician, and spiritual guide, the chaotic condition into which everything fell without her constant supervision, and the wearied, anxious look of the majority of women, impressed me with the strong feeling that some active measures should be taken." Active measures she took. Together with Lucretia Mott and a few others of like mind, she organized a meeting, the Seneca Falls Convention (July 1848), and drafted the Declaration of Principles, patterned on the Declaration of Independence. "We hold these truths to be self-evident: that all men and women are created equal," it stated, and it went on to list the "injuries and usurpations" of men, just as Jefferson had outlined those of George III.

From this seed the movement grew. During the 1850s a series of national conventions was held, and more and more reformers, including William Lloyd Garrison, joined the cause. Of the recruits, Susan B. Anthony was the most influential, for she was the first to see the need for thorough organization if effective pressure was to be brought to bear on male-dominated society. Her first campaign, mounted in 1854 and 1855 in behalf of a petition to the New York legislature calling for reform of the property and divorce laws, accumulated 6,000 signatures. But the petition did not persuade the legislature to act. Indeed, the feminists achieved very few practical results during the age of reform. Their leaders, however, were persevering types, most of them extraordinarily long-lived. Their major efforts lay in the future.

Despite the aggressiveness of many reformers and the extremity of some of their proposals, little social conflict blighted these years. Most citizens readily accepted the need for improving society and showed a healthy tolerance for even the most harebrained schemes for doing so. When Sylvester Graham, inventor of the graham cracker, traveled up and down the land praising the virtues of hard mattresses, cold showers, and homemade bread, he was mobbed by professional bakers, but otherwise, as his biographer says, "he was the subject of jokes, lampoons, and caustic editorials" rather than violence. Americans argued about everything from prison reform to vegetarianism, from women's rights to phrenology (a pseudoscience much occupied with developing the diagnostic possibilities of measuring the bumps on people's heads). But

they seldom came to blows. Even the abolitionist movement might not have caused serious social strife if the territorial expansion of the late 1840s had not dragged the slavery issue back into politics. When that happened, politics again assumed center stage, public discourse grew embittered, and the first great age of reform came to an end.

Milestones

1774	Ann Lee founds the first Shaker community
1817	Thomas Gallaudet's school for the deaf founded
1820–1850	Rapid increase in European immigration Rapid growth of cities Rapid growth of manufacturing
1823	Merrimack Manufacturing Company opens in Lowell, Massachusetts
1826	American Temperance Union founded
1830	Joseph Smith, *The Book of Mormon*
1830s	Second Great Awakening
1830–1850	Utopian communities flourish
1831	William Lloyd Garrison founds *The Liberator*
1831–1832	Alexis de Tocqueville and William Beaumont tour America
1832	Perkins Institution for the Blind founded
1837	The abolitionist Elijah Lovejoy murdered
1843	Dorothea Dix, *Memorial to the Legislature of Massachusetts*
1844	Joseph Smith lynched
1845	Frederick Douglass, *Narrative of the Life of Frederick Douglass*
1847	Mormon migration to the Great Salt Lake
1848	Seneca Falls Convention Declaration of Principles
1851	Maine bans alcoholic beverages

SUPPLEMENTARY READING

Titles marked with an asterisk have been published in paperback.

On Tocqueville and his views of America, Alexis de Tocqueville, **Democracy in America,*** (ed.) J. P. Mayer, 1966, "Tocqueville's Travel Notes" in J. P. Mayer (ed.), **Journey to America** (1960), and G. W. Pierson, **Tocqueville and Beaumont in America** (1938). For other visitors' accounts, see Frances Trollope, **Domestic Manners of the Americans** (1832), F. J. Grund, **Aristocracy in America*** (1839), Charles Dickens, **American Notes** (1847), and Harriet Martineau, **Retrospect of Western Travel** (1838). Edward Pessen, **Riches, Class and Power Before the Civil War*** (1973), and Rowland Berthoff, **An Unsettled People*** (1971), offer views different from Tocqueville's.

The growth of cities in the Jacksonian era can be traced in R. C. Wade, **The Urban Frontier*** (1957) and **Slavery in the Cities*** (1964), and in Howard Chudacoff, **The Evolution of American Urban Society*** (1981). A. F. Davis and Mark Halle (eds.), **The Peoples of Philadelphia*** (1973), S. B. Warner, Jr., **The Private City: Philadelphia in Three Periods of Its Growth*** (1968), Oscar Handlin, **Boston's Immigrants*** (1968), and P. R. Knights, **The Plain People of Boston*** (1971), deal with individual cities.

On immigration and ethnicity, see P. T. Knoble, **Paddy and the Republic** (1986), J. P. Dolan, **Immigrant Church: New York's Irish and German Catholics*** (1982), and, generally, Philip Taylor, **The Distant Mirror: European Migration to the United States** (1971), and Stephan Thernstrom (ed.), **Harvard Encyclopedia of American Ethnic Groups** (1980).

On changes in the nature of work in America, consult

A. F. C. Wallace, **Rockdale*** (1978), Alan Dawley, **Class and Community*** (1976), Thomas Dublin, **Women at Work** (1979), and Sean Wilencz, **Chants Democratic** (1984). On the changing place of the family and the changes within it, see M. P. Ryan, **Cradle of the Middle Class: The Family in Oneida, New York*** (1981), Nancy Cott, **The Bonds of Womanhood*** (1977), and Philip Greven, **The Protestant Temperament: Patterns of Child-Rearing, Religious Experience, and the Self in Early America** (1980). On demographic developments, see Walter Nugent, **Structures in American Social History** (1981), and M. A. Vinovskis, **Fertility in Massachusetts from the Revolution to the Civil War** (1981).

The Second Great Awakening has been examined both as a religious phenomenon and as a social one. Still useful are Whitney Cross, **The Burned-over District*** (1950), and Bernard Weisberger, **They Gathered at the River** (1958), but see also William McLoughlin, **Modern Revivalism: Finney to Graham** (1959), Timothy Smith, **Revivalism and Reform** (1965), and P. E. Johnson, **A Shopkeeper's Millennium*** (1978).

On utopianism generally, see Arthur Bestor, **Backwoods Utopias** (1950). N. G. Bringhurst, **Brigham Young and the Expanding American Frontier*** (1985), is informative on the Mormons. R. G. Walters, **American Reformers, 1815–1860*** (1978), is useful. On the social-control implications of reform, see C. S. Griffin, **Their Brothers' Keepers*** (1960), and D. J. Rothman, **Age of the Asylum: Social Order and Disorder in the New Republic*** (1971). Accounts of the temperance movement include Ian Tyrrell, **Sobering Up: From Temperance to Prohibition in Ante-Bellum America** (1979), and W. J. Rorabaugh, **The Alcoholic Republic*** (1979).

For sharply contrasting views of the abolitionist movement, see Stanley Elkins, **Slavery*** (1975), Aileen Kraditor, **Means and Ends in American Abolitionism*** (1967), and Lewis Perry and Michael Fellman (eds.), **Anti-Slavery Reconsidered*** (1979). Biographical accounts include J. L. Thomas, **The Liberator: William Lloyd Garrison*** (1963), Gerda Lerner, **The Grimké Sisters from South Carolina*** (1967), and Nathan Huggins, **Slave and Citizen: The Life of Frederick Douglass*** (1980). On antiabolitionists, see L. L. Richards, **"Gentlemen of Property and Standing"*** (1970).

Two recent interpretive accounts of the history of women and women's rights are Carl Degler, **At Odds: Women and Family in America from the Revolution to the Present*** (1980), and Nancy Woloch, **Women and the American Experience*** (1984). Elizabeth Griffith, **In Her Own Rights: The Life of Elizabeth Cady Stanton** (1984), and K. K. Sklar, **Catharine Beecher** (1973), are solid biographies of important women in the Jacksonian era.

PORTFOLIO THREE
The Way West

In the years after 1815, the lure of cheap land drew hundreds of thousands of pioneers west over the Appalachian mountains. The earliest settlers hauled their possessions along primitive, rutted roads. Once settled, however, the newcomers were not content to live in isolated self-sufficiency. They clamored for better ways to get their produce to markets in the East.

Private entrepreneurs and state governments responded by building roads, canals, and rail-roads. These "internal improvements" made possible commercial agriculture and spurred the growth of cities in the West. "The spectacle of a young people," marveled a French visitor in 1835, "executing in the short space of fifteen years, a series of works, which the most powerful States of Europe . . . would have shrunk from undertaking, is in truth a noble sight. The advantages which result from these enterprises to the public prosperity are incalculable."

Conestoga wagons, often associated with pioneers on the Oregon Trail, were used by earlier pioneers as well. Left, wagons and cattle jam the Frederick Road leading west from Baltimore. Rapid settlement of the Maryland and Pennsylvania hinterland helped make Baltimore one of the nation's largest cities in the mid-1800s.

The Appalachian mountains presented a daunting barrier to westward travelers. Above, a family on the way to Pittsburgh takes a needed rest and waters its horses. Even with the coming of canals and railroads, crossing the mountains was not easy. In 1837, the Pioneer Fast Line could boast of making the 300-mile trip from Philadelphia to Pittsburgh in "only" 3½ days.

River crossings could be painless or perilous, depending on circumstances. By 1860, Harper's Ferry in the Shenandoah Valley was a well-settled community. Travelers on the Baltimore & Ohio Railroad crossed the Potomac River comfortably over a sturdy covered bridge. (The smokestack on the far side of the river [upper illustration] is the armory made notorious by John Brown's 1859 raid.) Less fortunate travelers are rowed across the Susquehanna River in a flat-bottomed scow (lower illustration).

Starting in 1811, steamboats revolutionized river transportation in the West. Paddlewheelers slashed the cost of shipping goods upstream, thus making the Mississippi and Ohio rivers into two-way thoroughfares. "Steam is crowding our eastern cities with western flour . . . and lading the western steamboats with eastern emigrants and eastern merchandise," wrote an observer in 1841. In the decade after 1840, this busy Mississippi trade transformed St. Louis from a town of 16,000 to a city of 77,000 inhabitants (below). Although the steamboat dominated upriver travel, rafts were still used to ship farm products and bulky goods such as timber and coal downstream (above).

As in colonial times, frontier settlers lived in close contact with Indians. Conflict often resulted. In the West, the Army built forts to protect settlers and maintain order. These outposts were also trading centers where Indians exchanged their furs for manufactured goods of all kinds. Indians camp beside Fort Snelling in Wisconsin in the 1850s.

Emigrants to the Far West had to set out from Missouri in early spring in order to cross the Rockies and Sierras before the first snows of winter. These travelers on the Oregon Trail are fording Medicine Bow Creek in present-day Wyoming. The painting is by Samuel Colman.

Mormons followed the Oregon Trail in the 1840s on their way to the Great Salt Lake. By the 1850s, the Mormons could no longer afford draft animals to pull their wagons, but nevertheless thousands crossed the prairies and the Rockies drawing two-wheeled hand-carts similar to rickshaws (above). Other pioneers, seeking gold, not God, made their way by boat to San Francisco. Below, prospectors in a hurry to reach the diggings squatted in tents on San Francisco's Telegraph Hill.

A Democratic Culture

We have listened too long to the courtly muses of Europe.

RALPH WALDO EMERSON, *1837*

It's good to be shifty in a new country.

J. J. HOOPER, The Adventures of Simon Suggs, *1846*

As the United States grew larger, richer, and more centralized, it began to evolve a more distinctive culture. Still the child of Europe, by mid-century it was clearly the offspring rather than an imitation of the parent society. Jefferson had drawn most of his ideas from classical authors and 17th-century English thinkers. He gave to these doctrines an American cast, as when he stressed the separation of church and state or the pursuit of happiness instead of property in describing the "unalienable rights" of men. But Ralph Waldo Emerson, whose views were roughly similar to Jefferson's and who was also influenced by European thinkers, was an American philosopher. He and his generation drew quite self-consciously on native sources and inspirations. In doing so they described convincingly the emergence of a distinctly democratic culture.

In Search of Native Grounds

Early 19th-century literary groups such as Boston's Anthology Club and the Friendly Club in New York consciously set out to "foster American genius" and to encourage the production of a distinctively Amer-

ican literature. According to the historian Russel B. Nye, in the period between the Revolution and 1830 "every author of note made at least one effort to use American history in a major literary work."

Yet Nye admitted that in nearly every case "nothing of consequence appeared." Of the novelists before 1830, only James Fenimore Cooper made successful use of the national heritage. Beginning with *The Spy* (1821), *The Pioneers* (1823), and *The Last of the Mohicans* (1826), he wrote a long series of tales of Indians and settlers that presented a vivid, if romanticized, picture of frontier life. (Cooper's Indians, Mark Twain quipped, belonged to "an extinct tribe that never existed.") Cooper's work marked a shift from the classicism of the 18th century, which emphasized reason and orderliness in writing, to the romanticism of the early 19th century, with its stress on highly subjective emotional values and its concern for the beauties of nature and the freedom of the individual.

Most novelists of the period slavishly imitated British writers. Some looked to the sentimental novels of Samuel Richardson for a model; others aped satirical writers like Daniel Defoe and Tobias Smollett. Most popular were historical romances done in the manner of the Waverley novels of Sir Walter Scott. None approached the level of the best British writers, and as a result American novelists were badly outdistanced in their own country by the British, both in prestige and popularity. Since foreign copyrights were not recognized in the United States, British books were shamelessly pirated and sold cheaply. Half a million volumes of Scott were sold in America before 1823. American readers benefited but not American writers.

New York City was the literary capital of the country. Its leading light was Washington Irving, whose comical *Diedrich Knickerbocker's History of New York* (1809) made its young author famous on both sides of the Atlantic. Yet Irving soon abandoned the United States for Europe. *The Sketch Book* (1819), which included "Rip Van Winkle" and other well-known tales and legends of the Dutch in the Hudson Valley, was written while the author was residing in Birmingham and London. Outside New York there was much less literary activity. New England was only on the verge of its great literary flowering.

American painting in this period reached a level comparable to that of contemporary European work, but the best received most of their training

In paintings such as Kaaterskill Falls, *artist Thomas Cole captured the splendor of the American landscape. As founder of the Hudson River School, Cole developed a distinctly American style of painting. Like other romantics, he used nature to explore human emotions. But he was also a careful observer of nature, accurately capturing details of tangled underbrush, cascading waters, and individual trees.*

in Europe. Benjamin West, the first and in his day the most highly regarded, went to Europe before the Revolution and never returned; he can scarcely be considered an American. John Singleton Copley, whose stern, straightforward portraits display a more distinctly American character than the work of any of his contemporaries, was a Bostonian. No one so well captured the vigor and integrity of the Revolutionary generation. Charles Willson Peale, after studying under West in London, settled in Philadelphia, where he established a museum containing fossils, stuffed animals, and various natural curiosities as well as paintings. Peale helped found the Pennsylvania Academy of the Fine Arts, and he did much to encourage American painting. Not the

least of his achievements was the production of a large brood of artistic children to whom he gave such names as Rembrandt, Titian, and Rubens. The most talented of Peale's children was (appropriately) Rembrandt, whose portrait of Jefferson, executed in 1800, is one of the finest likenesses of the Sage of Monticello.

Another outstanding artist of this generation was Gilbert Stuart, who is best known for his many studies of George Washington. Stuart studied in England with Benjamin West, and his brush was much in demand in London. He was probably the most technically accomplished of the early American portrait painters. He was fond of painting his subjects with ruddy complexions (produced by means of a judicious mixture of vermilion, purple, and white pigment), which made many of his elderly sitters appear positively cherubic. He once remarked that the pallid flesh tones used by a rival looked "like putrid veal a little blown with green flies."

In general, the painting of the period was less obviously imitative of European models than the national literature. Wealthy merchants, manufacturers, and planters wished their likenesses preserved, and the demand for portraits of the nation's Revolutionary heroes seemed insatiable. Since paintings could not be reproduced as books could be, American artists did a flourishing business. And they remained unmistakably in the European tradition.

Exceptions to this generalization can be found in the work of a number of self-trained artists like Jonathan Fisher, Charles Octavius Cole, and J. William Jennys. These primitive painters supplied rural and middle-class patrons in the same way that Copley and Stuart catered to the tastes of the rich and prominent. Jennys, for example, received $24 in 1801 for portraits of Dr. William Stoddard Williams of Deerfield, Massachusetts, and his wife. Cole specialized in New England sea captains, whom he often painted holding brassbound spyglasses. One historian has discovered traces of more than 20 artisan-painters within the single state of Maine in the 1830s and 1840s. Some of these primitive canvases have great charm and distinction.

The Romantic View of Life

In the western world the romantic movement was a revolt against the bloodless logic of the Age of Reason. It was a noticeable if unnamed point of view in Germany, France, and England as early as the 1780s and in America a generation later; by the second quarter of the 19th century, few intellectuals were unmarked by it. "Romantics" believed that change and growth were the essence of life, for individuals and for institutions. They valued feeling and intuition over pure thought, and they stressed the differences between individuals and societies rather than the similarities. Ardent love of country characterized the movement; individualism, optimism, ingenuousness, and emotion were its bywords. Whereas the Puritans, believing that nearly

everyone was destined to endure the tortures of Hell for all eternity, contemplated death with dread, romantics, assuming that good people would go to Heaven, professed to look forward to death.

Romanticism perfectly fitted the mood of 19th-century America. Interest in raw nature and in primitive peoples, worship of the individual, praise of folk culture, the subordination of intellect to feeling—were these primarily romantic ideas or American ideas? Jacksonian democracy with its self-confidence, careless prodigality, contempt for learning, glorification of the ordinary—was it a product of the American experience or a reflection of a wider world view?

The romantic way of thinking found its fullest American expression in the transcendentalist movement. Transcendentalism, a New England creation, is difficult to describe because it emphasized the indefinable and the unknowable. It was a mystical, intuitive way of looking at life that subordinated facts to feelings. Its literal meaning was "to go beyond the world of the senses," by which the transcendentalists meant the material and observable world. To the transcendentalists, human beings were truly divine because they were part of nature, itself the essence of divinity. Their intellectual capacities did not define their capabilities, for they could "transcend" reason by having faith in themselves and in the fundamental benevolence of the universe. Transcendentalists were complete individualists, seeing the social whole as no more than the sum of its parts. Organized religion, indeed all institutions were unimportant if not counterproductive; what mattered was the single person and that people aspire, stretch *beyond* their known capabilities. Failure resulted only from lack of effort. The expression "Hitch your wagon to a star" is of transcendentalist origin.

Emerson and Thoreau

The leading transcendentalist thinker was Ralph Waldo Emerson. Born in 1803 and educated at Harvard, Emerson became a minister, but in 1832 he gave up his pulpit, deciding that "the profession is antiquated." After traveling in Europe, where he met many romantic writers, including Samuel Taylor Coleridge, William Wordsworth, and (especially important) Thomas Carlyle, he settled in Concord,

Ralph Waldo Emerson was largely responsible for generating the transcendentalist movement, and in a broader sense for fostering romantic thought in the United States.

Massachusetts, to a long career as essayist, lecturer, and sage.

Emerson managed to restore to what he called "corpse-cold" Unitarianism the fervor and purposefulness characteristic of 17th-century Puritanism. His philosophy was at once buoyantly optimistic and rigorously intellectual, self-confident and conscientious. In a notable address at Harvard in 1837, "The American Scholar," he urged Americans to put aside their devotion to things European and seek inspiration in their immediate surroundings. He saw himself as pitting "spiritual powers" against "the mechanical powers and the mechanical philosophy of this time." The new industrial society of New England disturbed him profoundly.

Emerson favored change and believed in progress. It was America's destiny to fulfill "the postponed expectations of the world." Temperamentally, however, he was too serene and too much his own man to fight for the causes other reformers espoused, and he was too idealistic to accept the compromises that most reformers make to achieve their ends. To abolitionist friends who sought his aid he said: "God must govern his own world. . . . I have quite other slaves to face than those Negroes, to wit, imprisoned thoughts . . . which have no watchman or lover or defender but me."

Because he put so much emphasis on self-reliance, Emerson disliked powerful governments. "The less government we have the better," he said. In a sense he was the prototype of some modern alienated intellectuals, so repelled by the world as it was that he would not actively try to change it. Nevertheless, he thought strong leadership essential, perhaps being influenced in this direction by his friend Carlyle's glorification of the role of great men in history. Emerson also had a strong practical streak. He made his living by lecturing, tracking tirelessly across the country, talking before every type of audience for fees ranging from $50 to several hundreds.

Closely identified with Emerson was his Concord neighbor Henry David Thoreau. After graduating from Harvard in 1837, Thoreau taught school for a time and helped out in a small pencil-making business run by his family. He was a strange man, gentle, a dreamer, content to absorb the beauties of nature almost intuitively, yet stubborn and individualistic to the point of selfishness. "He is the most unmalleable fellow alive," one acquaintance wrote. The hectic scramble for wealth that Thoreau saw all about him he found disgusting—and alarming, for he believed it was destroying both the natural and the human resources of the country.

Like Emerson, Thoreau objected to many of society's restrictions on the individual. "That government is best which governs not at all," he said, going both Emerson and the Jeffersonians one better. He was perfectly prepared to see himself as a majority of one. Emerson reduced him to a phrase when he called him "a born protestant." "When were the good and the brave ever in a majority?" Thoreau asked. "If a man does not keep pace with his companions," he wrote on another occasion, "perhaps it is because he hears a different drummer."

In 1845 Thoreau decided to put to the test his theory that a person need not depend on society for a satisfying existence. He built a cabin at Walden Pond on some property owned by Emerson and lived there alone for two years. He did not try to

WALDEN;

OR,

LIFE IN THE WOODS.

BY HENRY D. THOREAU,

AUTHOR OF "A WEEK ON THE CONCORD AND MERRIMACK RIVERS."

I do not propose to write an ode to dejection, but to brag as lustily as chanticleer in **the** morning, standing on his roost, if only to wake my neighbors up. — Page 92.

BOSTON:
TICKNOR AND FIELDS.
M DCCC LIV.

"I went to the woods," wrote Henry David Thoreau about his purpose in going to Walden Pond, "because I wished to live deliberately, to front only the essential facts of life, and see if I could not learn what it had to teach, and not, when I came to die, to discover that I had not lived." The title page of Walden *shows the cabin that Thoreau built on Emerson's land.*

be entirely self-sufficient: He was not above returning to his family or to Emerson's for a square meal on occasion, and he generally purchased the building materials and other manufactured articles that he needed. Instead he set out, by experimenting, to prove that *if necessary,* an individual could get along without the products of civilization. He used manufactured plaster in building his Walden cabin, but he also gathered a bushel of clamshells and made a small quantity of lime himself, to prove that it could be done.

At Walden, Thoreau wrote *A Week on the Concord and Merrimack Rivers* (1849), which used an account of a trip he had taken with his brother as a vehicle for a discussion of his ideas about life and literature. He spent much time observing the quiet world around the pond, thinking, and writing in his journal. The best fruit of this period was that extraordinary book *Walden* (1854). Superficially, *Walden* is the story of Thoreau's experiment, moving and beautifully written. It is also an acid indictment of the social behavior of the average American, an attack on unthinking conformity, on subordinating one's own judgment to that of the herd.

The most graphic illustration of Thoreau's confidence in his own values occurred while he was living at Walden. At that time the Mexican War was raging. Thoreau considered the war immoral because it advanced the cause of slavery. To protest, he refused to pay his Massachusetts poll tax. For this he was arrested and lodged in jail, although only for one night because an aunt promptly paid the tax for him. His essay "Civil Disobedience," explaining his view of the proper relation between the individual and the state, resulted from this experience. Like Emerson, however, Thoreau refused to participate in practical reform movements. "I love Henry," one of his friends said, "but I cannot like him; and as for taking his arm, I should as soon think of taking the arm of an elm tree."

Edgar Allan Poe

The work of all the imaginative writers of the period reveals romantic influences, and it is possibly an indication of the affinity of the romantic approach to American conditions that a number of excellent writers of poetry and fiction first appeared in the 1830s and 1840s. Edgar Allan Poe, one of the most remarkable, seems almost a caricature of the romantic image of the tortured genius. Poe was born in Boston in 1809, the son of poor actors who died before he was 3. He was raised by a wealthy Virginian, John Allan.

Edgar Allan Poe, widely appreciated in his lifetime, inspired generations of later writers with his detective stories and horror tales.

Few persons as neurotic as Poe have been able to produce first-rate work. In college he ran up debts of $2,500 in less than a year and had to withdraw. He won an appointment to West Point but was discharged after a few months for disobedience and "gross neglect of duty." He was a lifelong alcoholic and an occasional taker of drugs. He married a child of 13. Once he attempted to poison himself; repeatedly he was down and out even to the verge of starvation. He was haunted by melancholia and hallucinations. Yet he was an excellent magazine editor, a penetrating critic, a poet of unique if somewhat narrow talents, and a fine short story writer. Although he died at 40, he turned out a large volume of serious, highly original work.

Poe responded strongly to the lure of romanticism. His works abound with examples of wild imagination and fascination with mystery, fright, and the occult. If he did not invent the detective story, he perfected it; his tales "The Murders in the Rue Morgue" and "The Purloined Letter" stressed the thought processes of a clever detective in solving a mystery by reasoning from evidence. Poe was also one of the earliest writers to deal with what are today called science fiction themes, and "The Pit and the Pendulum" and "The Cask of Amontillado" show that he was a master of the horror tale.

Although dissolute in his personal life, when Poe touched pen to paper, he became a disciplined craftsman. The most fantastic passages in his works are the result of careful, reasoned selection; not a word, he believed, could be removed without damage to the whole. And despite his rejection of most of the values prized by middle-class America, Poe was widely read in his own day. His poem "The Raven" won instantaneous popularity when it was published in 1845. Had he been a little more stable, he might have made a good living with his pen—but in that case he might not have written as he did.

Nathaniel Hawthorne

Another product of the prevailing romanticism was Nathaniel Hawthorne of Salem, Massachusetts. Hawthorne was born in 1804. When he was a small child, his father died and his grief-stricken mother became a recluse. Left largely to his own devices, he grew to be a lonely, introspective person. Wandering about New England by himself in summertime, he soaked up local lore, which he drew upon in writing short stories. For a time he lived in Concord, where he came to know most of the leading transcendentalists. However, he disliked the egoism of the transcendental point of view and rejected its bland optimism outright. He called Emerson an "everlasting rejector of all that is," a "seeker for he knows not what."

Hawthorne was fascinated by the past, particularly by the Puritan heritage of New England and its continuing influence on his own generation. He scorned "minute fidelity" to the real world in his fiction, seeking "a severer truth . . . the truth of the human heart." But he was active in politics and an admirer of Andrew Jackson. Three Democratic presidents—Martin Van Buren, James K. Polk, and Franklin Pierce—appointed him to minor political offices.

Hawthorne's early stories, originally published in magazines, were brought together in *Twice-told Tales* (1837). They made excellent use of New England culture and history for background but were concerned chiefly with the struggles of individuals with sin, guilt, and especially the pride and isolation that often afflict those who place too much reliance

Like his contemporaries Emerson and Thoreau, Nathaniel Hawthorne settled in Concord, Massachusetts. As a young man, Hawthorne had isolated himself in order to write. A severe critic of his own work, Hawthorne burned many of his early stories. This portrait of Hawthorne was painted a few years after the publication of Twice-Told Tales, *when he began to emerge from his self-imposed seclusion.*

his success in creating word pictures of a somber, mysterious world, he considered America too prosaic a country to inspire good literature. "There is no shadow, no antiquity, no mystery, no picturesque and gloomy wrong, nor anything but a commonplace prosperity," he complained.

Herman Melville

In 1850, while writing *The House of the Seven Gables,* Hawthorne was introduced by his publisher to another writer in the midst of a novel. This was Herman Melville, the book *Moby Dick.* The two became good friends at once, for despite their dissimilar backgrounds, they had a great deal in common. Melville was a New Yorker, born in 1819, one of eight children of a merchant of distinguished lineage. His father, however, lost all his money and died when the boy was 12. Herman left school at 15, worked briefly as a bank clerk, and in 1837 went to sea. For 18 months, in 1841 and 1842, he was crewman on the whaler *Acushnet.* Then he jumped ship in the South Seas. For a time he lived among a tribe of cannibals in the Marquesas; later he made his way to Tahiti, where he idled away nearly a year. After another year at sea he returned to America in the fall of 1844.

Although he had never before attempted serious writing, in 1846 he published *Typee,* an account of his life in the Marquesas. The book was a great success, for Melville had visited a part of the world almost unknown to Americans, and his descriptions of his bizarre experiences suited the taste of a romantic age. Success inspired him to write a sequel, *Omoo* (1847); other books followed quickly.

As he wrote Melville became conscious of deeper powers. In 1849 he began a systematic study of Shakespeare, pondering the bard's intuitive grasp of human nature. Like Hawthorne, Melville could not accept the prevailing optimism of his generation. Unlike his friend, he admired Emerson, seconding the Emersonian demand that Americans reject European ties and develop their own literature. "Believe me," he wrote, "men not very much inferior to Shakespeare are this day being born on the banks of the Ohio." Yet he considered Emerson's vague talk about striving and the inherent goodness of mankind complacent nonsense.

Experience made Melville too aware of the evil

on their own judgment. His greatest works were two novels written after the Whigs turned him out of his government job in 1849. *The Scarlet Letter* (1850), a grim yet sympathetic analysis of adultery, condemned not the woman, Hester Prynne, but the people who presumed to judge her. *The House of the Seven Gables* (1851) was a gripping account of the decay of an old New England family brought on by the guilt feelings of the current owners of the house, caused by the way their ancestors had cheated the original owners of the property.

Like Poe, Hawthorne was appreciated in his own day and widely read; unlike Poe, he made a modest amount of money from his work. Yet he was never very comfortable in the society he inhabited. He had no patience with the second-rate. And despite

in the world to be a transcendentalist. His novel *Redburn* (1849), based on his adventures on a Liverpool packet, was, as the critic F. O. Matthiessen put it, "a study in disillusion, of innocence confronted with the world, of ideals shattered by facts." Yet Melville was no cynic; he expressed deep sympathy for the Indians and for immigrants, crowded like animals into the holds of transatlantic vessels. He denounced the brutality of discipline in the United States Navy in *White-Jacket* (1850). His essay "The Tartarus of Maids," a moving if somewhat overdrawn description of young women working in a paper factory, protested the subordination of human beings to machines.

Hawthorne, whose dark view of human nature coincided with Melville's, encouraged him to press ahead with *Moby Dick* (1851). This book, Melville said, was "broiled in hellfire." Against the background of a whaling voyage (no better account of whaling has ever been written), he dealt subtly and symbolically with the problems of good and evil, of courage and cowardice, of faith, stubbornness, pride. In Captain Ahab, driven relentlessly to hunt down the huge white whale Moby Dick, which had destroyed his leg, Melville created one of the great figures of literature; in the book as a whole, he produced one of the finest novels written by an American, comparable to the best in any language.

As Melville's work became more profound, it lost its appeal to the average reader, and its originality and symbolic meaning escaped most of the critics. *Moby Dick*, his masterpiece, received little attention, and most of that was unfavorable. He kept on writing until his death in 1891 but was virtually ignored. Only in the 1920s did the critics rediscover him and give him his merited place in the history of American literature. His "Billy Budd, Foretopman," now considered one of his best stories, was not published until 1924.

Walt Whitman

Walt Whitman, whose *Leaves of Grass* (1855) was the last of the great literary works of this brief outpouring of genius, was the most romantic and by far the most distinctly American writer of his age. He was born on Long Island, outside New York City, in 1819. At 13 he left school and became a printer's devil; thereafter he held a succession of newspaper jobs in the metropolitan area. He was an ardent Jacksonian and later a Free Soiler, which got him into hot water with a number of the publishers for whom he worked.

Although genuinely a "common man," thoroughly at home among tradesmen and laborers, he was surely not an ordinary man. Deeply introspective, he read omnivorously, if in a rather disorganized fashion while working out a new, intensely personal mode of expression. During the early 1850s, while employed as a carpenter and composing the poems that made up *Leaves of Grass*, he regularly carried a book of Emerson in his lunch box. "I was simmering, simmering, simmering," he later recalled. "Emerson brought me to a boil." The transcendental idea that inspiration and aspiration are at the heart of all achievement captivated him. A poet could best express himself, he believed, by relying uncritically on his natural inclinations without regard for rigid metrical forms.

Leaves of Grass consisted of a preface, in which Whitman made the extraordinary statement that Americans had "probably the fullest poetical na-

Criticized as undisciplined and pretentious, Walt Whitman expressed a fresh viewpoint on commonplace subjects.

ture" of any people in history, and 12 poems in free verse: rambling, uneven, appearing to most readers shocking both in the commonplace nature of the subject matter and the coarseness of the language. Emerson, Thoreau, and a few others saw a fresh talent in these poems, but most readers and reviewers found them offensive. Indeed, the work was so undisciplined and so much of it had no obvious meaning that it was easy to miss the many passages of great beauty and originality that were scattered throughout.

Part of Whitman's difficulty arose because there was much of the charlatan in his makeup; often his writing did not ring true. He loved to use foreign words and phrases, and since he had no more than a smattering of any foreign language, he frequently sounded pretentious and sometimes downright foolish when he did so. In reality a sensitive, effeminate person, he tried to pose as a great, rough character. (Later in his career he bragged of fathering no less than six illegitimate children, which was assuredly untrue.) He never married, and his work suggests that his strongest emotional ties were with men. Thomas Carlyle once remarked shrewdly that Whitman thought he was a big man because he lived in a big country.

Whitman's work was more authentically American than that of any contemporary. His egoism—he titled one of his finest poems "Song of Myself"—was tempered by his belief that he was typical of all humanity.

> I celebrate myself and sing myself
> And what I assume you shall assume,
> For every atom belonging to me as good belongs to
>   you.

He had a remarkable ear for rendering common speech poetically, for employing slang, for catching the breezy informality of Americans and their faith in themselves.

> Earth! you seem to look for something at my hands,
> Say, old top-knot, what do you want?
> I bequeath myself to the dirt to grow from the grass
>   I love,
> If you want me again look for me under your boot-
>   soles.

Because of these qualities and because in his later work, especially during the Civil War, he occasionally struck a popular chord, Whitman was never as neglected as Melville. When he died in 1892, he was, if not entirely understood, at least widely appreciated.

The Wider Literary Renaissance

Emerson, Thoreau, Poe, Hawthorne, Melville, and Whitman were the great figures of American literature before the Civil War. A number of others, if they lacked genius, were leading literary lights in their day and are still worth reading. One was Henry Wadsworth Longfellow. In 1835, while still in his twenties, Longfellow became professor of modern languages at Harvard. Although he published a fine translation of Dante's *Divine Comedy* and was expert in many languages, his fame came from his poems: "The Village Blacksmith"; "Paul Revere's Ride"; *The Courtship of Miles Standish*, a sentimental tale of Pilgrim days; and *The Song of Hiawatha*, the romantic retelling of an Indian legend. These brought him excellent critical notices and considerable fortune; his work was widely translated and reprinted.

Though musical, polished, and full of vivid images, Longfellow's poetry, like the man, lacked profundity, originality, and force. But it was neither cheap nor trivial. When Longfellow wrote "Life is real! life is earnest! / And the grave is not its goal," he expressed the heartfelt belief of most of his generation. In this sense he captured the spirit of his times better than any of his great contemporaries, better even than Whitman.

Longfellow was the most talented of a group of minor New England writers who collectively gave that region great intellectual vitality. John Greenleaf Whittier, a poet nearly as popular as Longfellow, believed ardently in the abolition of slavery. A few of his poems can still be read with pleasure, among them "The Barefoot Boy," dealing with his rural childhood. Somewhat more weighty was the achievement of James Russell Lowell, the first editor of the *Atlantic Monthly*, founded in Boston in 1857. Lowell's humorous stories written in the New England dialect made an original and influential contribution to the national literature. Dr. Oliver Wendell Holmes, professor of medicine at Harvard, was widely known as a poet and essayist. A few of his poems, such as "The Chambered Nautilus" and "Old Ironsides," are interesting examples of American romantic verse.

So did the important historians of the period, all of them New Englanders. George Bancroft, one of the first Americans to study in Germany, began in 1834 to publish a ten-volume *History of the United States,* based on thorough research. William Hickling Prescott, though nearly blind, wrote extensively on the history of Spain and Spain's American empire, his *Conquest of Mexico* (1843) and *Conquest of Peru* (1847) being his most important works. John Lothrop Motley, another German-trained historian, published his *Rise of the Dutch Republic* in 1856, and Francis Parkman began his great account of the struggle between France and Great Britain for the control of North America with *Conspiracy of Pontiac* in 1851.

The public read these histories avidly. They suited the taste of the times, they were written with a mass audience in mind, and they were thoroughly in the romantic tradition. As David Levin said in his important study *History as Romantic Art,* "They all shared an 'enthusiastic' attitude toward the Past, an affection for grand heroes, an affection for Nature and the 'natural.' "

Southern literature was even more markedly romantic than that of New England. John Pendleton Kennedy of Baltimore wrote several novels with regional historical themes, much in the manner of Sir Walter Scott. Kennedy was also a Whig politician of some importance who served several terms in Congress; in 1852 he became secretary of the navy in the Fillmore Cabinet. The more versatile and influential William Gilmore Simms of South Carolina wrote nearly two dozen novels, several volumes of poetry, and a number of biographies. At his peak in the 1830s he earned as much as $6,000 a year with his pen. *The Partisan* (1835), one of a series of novels dealing with the Revolution, and *The Yemassee* (1835), the story of an early-18th-century Indian war, seem too melodramatic for modern tastes. His portraits of the planter class are too bloodless and reverential to be convincing. His female characters are nearly all pallid and fragile. Only when Simms wrote of frontier life and people did his work possess much power.

Domestic Tastes

Architecture flourished in the northern cities chiefly as a result of the work of Charles Bulfinch and some of his disciples. Bulfinch was influenced by British

The Smithsonian Institution Building, made of red sandstone, is popularly know as "The Castle" because of its eight crenelated towers. Its architect, James Renwick, Jr., also designed New York's Grace Church and Saint Patrick's Cathedral in the popular Gothic Revival style.

architects, but he developed a manner all his own. His "Federal" style gave parts of Boston a dignity and charm equal to the finest sections of London. The State House, numerous other public buildings, and, best of all, many of Bulfinch's private houses—austere yet elegant, solid yet airy and graceful—gave the town a distinction it had lacked before the Revolution.

In the 1830s and 1840s new techniques made it possible to weave colored patterns into cloth by machine, to manufacture wallpaper printed with complicated designs, and to produce rugs and hangings that looked like tapestries. Combined with the use of machine methods in the furniture business, these inventions had a powerful impact on public taste. That impact, at least in the short run, was aesthetically unfortunate. As Russell Lynes writes in his entertaining study *The Tastemakers,* "Styles ran riot. . . . The new chairs and sofas, bedecked with fruit, flowers, and beasties and standing on twisted spindles, crowded into living rooms and parlors."

Wood-turning machinery added to the popularity of the elaborately decorated "Gothic" style of architecture. The irregularity and uniqueness of Gothic buildings suited the prevailing romanticism; their aspiring towers, steeples, and arches and their flexibility (a new wing or extension could always be added without spoiling the effect) made them especially attractive to a people enamored of progress.

A lifelong resident of rural Long Island, William Sidney Mount took everyday life of that corner of America as his inspiration. Eel Spearing at Setauket, *1845, is one of his most characteristic canvases. Mount's subject matter had universal appeal; engravings of his work sold widely in Europe.*

The huge pile of pink masonry of the Smithsonian Institution in Washington, with its nine distinct types of towers, represents American Gothic at its most giddy and lugubrious stage. The building, which was designed in 1846 by James Renwick, confounded generations of architects, but with the passage of time it came to seem the perfect setting for the vast collection of mementos that fill "the nation's attic." "Greek" and "Italian" styles also flourished in this period, the former particularly in the South; elsewhere the Gothic was by all odds the most popular.

Increasingly, Americans of the period were purchasing native art. George Catlin, who painted hundreds of pictures of Indians and their surroundings, all rich in authentic detail, displayed his work before admiring crowds in many cities. Genre painters (artists whose canvases told stories, usually drawn from everyday life), were wildly popular. The best were William Sidney Mount of New York and George Caleb Bingham of Missouri. Rumor had it that Mount received $1,000 for his first important canvas; Bingham's paintings commanded excellent prices; and the public bought engravings of the work of both men in enormous numbers.

The more academic artists of the period were popular as well. The "luminists" and members of the romantic Hudson River school specialized in

Miniature copies of Hiram Powers's The Greek Slave, *Henry James said, stood "exposed under little glass covers" in parlors from Boston to San Francisco.*

grandiose pictures of wild landscapes. In the 1840s Thomas Doughty regularly collected $500 each for his paintings. The works of Asher B. Durand, John Kensett, and Thomas Cole were in demand. The collector Luman Reed commissioned five large Cole canvases for an allegorical series, *The Course of Empire,* and crowds flocked to see another of Cole's series, *The Voyage of Life,* when it was exhibited in New York.

In 1839 the American Art-Union was formed in New York to encourage native art. The Art-Union hit on the ingenious device of selling what were in effect lottery tickets and using the proceeds to purchase paintings, which became the prizes in the lottery. Annual "memberships" sold for $5; 814 people subscribed in 1839, nearly 19,000 ten years later. Soon the Art-Union was giving every member an engraving of one of its principal prizes. The organization had to disband after a New York court outlawed the lottery in 1851, but in 1854 a new Cosmopolitan Art-Union was established in Ohio. In the years before the Civil War it boomed, reaching a peak of 38,000 members and paying as much as $6,000 for an individual work—the sculptor Hiram Powers's boneless female nude, *The Greek Slave.* It also distributed an art magazine and each year gave a young artist a gold medal and $2,000 for foreign study.

The art unions made little effort to encourage innovators, but they were a boon to many artists. The American Art-Union paid out as much as $40,000 for its prizes in a single year. By distributing thousands of engravings and colored prints, they introduced competent American works of art into middle-class homes.

Beginning in the late 1850s, the prints of the firm of Currier and Ives brought a crude but charming kind of art to a still wider audience. Currier and Ives lithographs portrayed horse racing, trains, rural landscapes, and "every tender domestic moment, every sign of national progress, every regional oddity, every private or public disaster from a cut finger to a forest fire." They were issued in very large editions and sold for as little as 15 cents.

Education for Democracy

Except on the edge of the frontier and in the South, most youngsters between the ages of 5 and 10 attended a school for at least a couple of months of the year. These schools, however, were privately run and charged fees. Attendance was not required and fell off sharply once children learned to read and do their sums well enough to get along in day-to-day life. The teachers were usually young men waiting for something better to turn up.

All this changed with the rise of the common school movement. At the heart of the movement was the belief, widely expressed in the first days of the Republic, that a government based on democratic rule must provide the means, as Jefferson put it, to "diffuse knowledge throughout the mass of the people." This meant free tax-supported schools, which all children were expected to attend. It also came to mean that such an educational system should be administered on a statewide basis and that teaching should become a profession that required formal training.

The two most effective leaders of the common school movement were Henry Barnard and Horace Mann. Both were New Englanders, Whigs, trained in the law, and in other ways conservative types. They shared an unquenchable faith in the improvability of the human race through education. Barnard served in educational posts in Connecticut, Rhode Island, and New York in the 1840s and 1850s and as editor of the *American Journal of Education* from 1855 until 1882. Mann drafted the 1837 Massachusetts law creating a state school board, and then became its first secretary. Over the next decade Mann's annual reports carried the case for common schools to every corner of the land. Seldom given to understatement, Mann called common schools "the greatest discovery ever made by man." In his reports he criticized wealthy parents who sent their children to private academies rather than bring them into contact with their poorer neighbors in the local school. He encouraged young women to become teachers while commending them to school boards by claiming that they could get along on lower salaries than men.

By the 1850s every state outside the South provided free elementary schools and supported institutions for training teachers. Many extended the concept of publicly financed education to include high schools, and Michigan and Iowa even established publicly supported colleges.

Historians differ in explaining the success of the common school movement. Some stress the argu-

*The typical one-room schoolhouse could hold up to 80 students. The schoolyard
was a clearing nearby, as artist Henry Inman shows in* Dismissal of School
on an October Afternoon. *Inspired by Horace Mann, the great educational
awakening of the mid-1800s led to such improvements as the first normal
schools to train teachers.*

ments Mann used to win support from employers
by appealing to their need for trained and well-
disciplined workers. Others see the schools as designed to "Americanize" the increasing numbers of
non-English and non-Protestant immigrants who
were flooding into the country. (Force is lent to this
argument by the fact that Catholic bishops in New
York and elsewhere opposed laws requiring Catholic children to attend these "Protestant" schools
and set up their own parochial schools.)

Still other scholars argue that middle-class reformers favored public elementary school on the
theory that they would instill the values of hard
work, punctuality, and submissiveness to authority

in children of the laboring classes. According to this
argument, the reformers favored the new public
high schools mainly because they provided free education for their own children. In truth, almost no
working-class children attended high school, public
or private, until late in the 19th century.

All these reasons played a part in advancing the
cause of the common schools. Yet it remains the
case, as the historians Carl F. Kaestle and Maris
Vinovskis have shown, that the most compelling
argument for common schools was cultural; more
effectively than any other institution, they brought
Americans of different economic circumstances and
ethnic backgrounds into early and mutually bene-

ficial contact with one another. They served the two roles that Mann assigned to them: "the balance wheel of the social machinery" and "the great equalizer."

Engines of Culture

As the population grew and became more concentrated, and as society, especially in the North, was permeated by a middle-class point of view, popular concern for "culture" in the formal sense increased. A largely literate people, committed to the idea of education but not generally well educated, set their hearts on being "refined" and "cultivated." Industrialization made it easier to satisfy this new demand for culture, though the new machines also tended to make the artifacts of culture more stereotyped.

Improved printing techniques reduced the cost of books, magazines, and newspapers. In the 1850s one publisher sold a 50-volume set of Sir Walter Scott for $37.50. The first penny newspaper was the *New York Sun* (1833), but James Gordon Bennett's *New York Herald,* founded in 1835, brought the cheap new journalism to perfection. The *Boston Daily Times* and the *Philadelphia Public Ledger* soon followed. The penny newspapers depended on sensation, crime stories, and society gossip to attract readers, but they covered important national and international news too.

In the 1850s the moralistic and sentimental "domestic" novel entered its prime. The most successful writers in this genre were women, which prompted Hawthorne to complain bitterly that "a d——d mob of scribbling women" was taking over American literature. Typical were Susan Warner's book *The Wide, Wide World* (1850), a sad tale about a pious, submissive girl who cried "more readily and more steadily than any other tormented child in a novel at the time," and Maria Cummins's book *The Lamplighter* (1854), the story of little Gerty, an orphan rescued by a kindly lamplighter, appropriately named Trueman Flint. *The Lamplighter* sold 70,000 copies within a year of publication. The historian Ann Douglas claims in *The Feminization of American Culture* that such novels provided readers (most of whom were women) with the consumer pleasures that today are provided by television soap operas.

Besides reading countless volumes of sentimental nonsense (the books of another novelist, Mary Jane Holmes, sold over a million copies in these years), Americans consumed reams of religious literature. In 1840 the American Tract Society distributed 3 million copies of its publications; in 1855, more than 12 million. The society had hundreds of missionary-salesmen, called colporteurs, who

The Lyceum movement sponsored lectures on every imaginable subject in hundreds of towns. In this lively 1841 caricature, meteorologist James Pollard Espy holds forth to a mixed audience at Clinton Hall in New York City.

fanned out across the country preaching the gospel and selling or giving away religious pamphlets and books. These publications played down denominational differences in favor of a generalized brand of evangelical Christianity. They bore titles such as *Quench Not the Spirit* (over 900,000 copies distributed by 1850) and *The Way to Heaven*. The American Bible Society issued hundreds of thousands of copies of the Old and New Testaments each year. Americans also devoured books on self-improvement, some aimed at uplifting the reader's character, others, which would today be called "how-to-do-it" books, at teaching everything from raising chickens to carving tombstones.

Philanthropists contributed large sums to charity and other good causes; Stephen Girard left $6 million for "educating poor white orphan boys" in his adopted Philadelphia; John Jacob Astor of New York and George Peabody of Massachusetts endowed libraries; John Lowell, son of the pioneer cotton manufacturer, left $500,000 to establish the Lowell Institute in Boston to sponsor free public lectures. In the late 1850s the industrialist Peter Cooper founded the Cooper Institute in New York City, where workers could take free courses in practical subjects. Mechanics' libraries sprang up in every industrial center and attracted so many readers that pressure was soon applied to grant them state funds. In 1848 Massachusetts led the way by authorizing the use of public money to back the Boston Public Library, and soon several states were encouraging local communities to fund tax-supported libraries.

The desire for knowledge and culture in America is well illustrated by the success of the mutual improvement societies known as lyceums. The movement began in Great Britain; in the United States its prime mover was Josiah Holbrook, an itinerant lecturer and sometime schoolmaster from Connecticut. Holbrook founded the first lyceum in 1826 at Millbury, Massachusetts; within five years there were over 1,000 scattered across the country. The lyceums conducted discussions, established libraries, and lobbied for better schools. Soon they began to sponsor lecture series on topics of every sort. Many of the nation's political and intellectual leaders, such as Webster, Emerson, Melville, and Lowell, regularly graced their platforms. So did other, less famous lecturers who in the name of culture pronounced on subjects ranging from

"Chemistry Applied to the Mechanic Arts" to a description of the tombs of the Egyptian pharaohs.

The State of the Colleges

Unlike common schools, with their democratic overtones, private colleges had at best a precarious place in Jacksonian America. For one thing, there were too many of them. Any town with pretensions of becoming a regional center felt it had to have a college. Ohio had 25 in the 1850s, Tennessee 16. Many of these institutions were short-lived. Of the 14 colleges founded in Kentucky between 1800 and 1850, only half were still operating in 1860.

The problem of supply was compounded by a demand problem—too few students. Enrollment at the largest, Yale, never topped 400 until the mid-1840s. Higher education was beyond the means of the average family. Although most colleges charged less than half the $55 tuition required by Harvard, that still represented a substantial outlay for most families, wages being what they were. So desperate was the shortage that colleges accepted applicants as young as 11 and 12 and as old as 30.

Once enrolled, students had little worry about making the grade, not least because grades were not given. Since students were hard to come by and classwork was relatively unimportant, discipline was lax. Official authority was frequently challenged, and rioting was known to break out over such weighty matters as the quality of meals. A father who visited his son's college dormitory in 1818 found it inhabited by "half a dozen loungers in a state of oriental lethargy, each stretched out upon two or three chairs, with scarce any indication of life in them [other] than the feeble effort to keep up the fire of their cigarrs."

The typical college curriculum, dominated by the study of Latin and Greek, had almost no practical relevance except for future clergymen. The Yale faculty, most of them ministers, defended the classics as admirably providing for both "the discipline and the furniture of the mind," but these subjects commended themselves to college officials chiefly because they did not require costly equipment or a faculty that knew anything else. Professors spent most of their time in and out of the classroom trying to maintain a semblance of order, "to the exclusion of any great literary undertakings to which their choice might lead them," one explained. "Our country is yet too young for old professors," a Bostonian informed a foreign visitor in the 1830s, "and, besides, they are too poorly paid to induce first rate men to devote themselves to the business of lecturing. . . . We consider professors as secondary men."

Fortunately for the future of higher education, some college officials recognized the need for a drastic overhaul of their institutions. President Francis Wayland of Brown University used his 1842 address, "On the Present Collegiate System," to call for a thorough revamping of the curriculum to make it responsive to the economic realities of American society. This meant more courses in science, economics (where Wayland's own *Elements of Political Economy* might be used), modern history, and applied mathematics; fewer in Hebrew, biblical studies, Greek, and ancient history.

Yale established a separate school of science in 1847, which it hoped would attract serious-minded students and research-minded professors. At Harvard, which also opened a scientific school, students were allowed to choose some of their courses and were compelled to earn grades as a stimulus to study. Colleges in the West and the South began to offer mechanical and agricultural subjects relevant to their regional economies. Oberlin enrolled four female students in 1837, and the first women's college, the Georgia Female College, opened its doors in 1839.

These reforms slowed the downward spiral of colleges; they did not restore them to the honored place they had enjoyed in the Revolutionary era. Of the first six presidents of the United States, only Washington did not graduate from college. Beginning in 1829, seven of the next eleven did not. In this Presidents Jackson, Van Buren, Harrison, Taylor, Fillmore, Lincoln, and Johnson were like 98 of every 100 white males, all blacks and Indians, and all but a handful of white women in mid-19th-century America. Going to college had yet, in Wayland's words, to "commend itself to the good sense and patriotism of the American people."

Civic Cultures

Unlike the capitals of Europe, which were centers of art and culture, Washington was a cultural backwater, and the politicians seemed content to keep it that way. Whether the United States had *any* cul-

By mid-century, immigrants from Europe and displaced farmers were flooding into American cities, causing tremendous growth. In the Midwest, the rapid expansion of Cincinnati was due in part to its strategic location. This painting, Fourth Street, Cincinnati, *shows the principal downtown artery. The elegant façades attest to the city's prosperity.*

tural center, and if so, where it was, is another matter. Boston, Philadelphia, and New York vied for primacy, but many smaller cities, such as Lexington, Kentucky, the self-proclaimed "Athens of the West," set the tone for the surrounding hinterland.

In the cities members of the "learned professions," especially lawyers, were generally accepted as the arbiters of taste in literature and art. "At the bar or the bench the American aristocracy is found," and there too resides "the most intellectual section of society," the ever-insightful Tocqueville reported. Lawyers came mostly from the upper reaches of the city's economic order, usually from families long in residence.

Emerson only half mockingly called Boston "the hub of the universe," but this was a case when local pride triumphed over his usual good judgment. Boston was indeed the home of the country's leading literary magazine, the *North American Review,* founded in 1815, but Philadelphia had *Graham's,* the country's first illustrated magazine, and *Godey's Ladies Book,* which reached 150,000 subscribers in the 1850s, an enormous number for that date. By 1825 New York's House of Harper, organized in 1817, was the largest book publisher in the nation. Boston was the home of the nation's leading historians, and Philadelphia, with the Pennsylvania Academy of Fine Arts (1815) and the Philadelphia Academy of Music (1857), was conceded by all but blind Bostonians and tin-eared New Yorkers to predominate in artistic and musical matters.

In the West, Cincinnati could point to its seven weekly and two daily newspapers, a literary monthly, a medical journal, and a magazine for teenagers. The first Beethoven symphony ever heard in America was performed in Cincinnati in 1817. By the 1830s such coups had enabled the "Queen City" to replace the "Athens of the West" as the center of trans-Allegheny culture. Having quickly accomplished so much, its boosters reasoned, Cincinnati would soon assume national leadership in cultural matters, as it already had in the processing of pork bellies.

Even smaller cities like Portland, Providence, Hartford, Albany, and Pittsburgh had literary and natural history societies and were regular stops on the lyceum circuit. All in all, American cities had a vitality and diversity that foreign visitors both celebrated and decried. Life in the towns was by some standards crude; many of the people were pushy, crass, and dedicated to the accumulation of wealth. But on this last count, the English novelist Charles Dickens offered some international perspective. "The golden calf they worship," he wrote of Americans in 1841, "is a pigmy compared with the giant effigies set up in other parts of that vast counting-house which lies beyond the Atlantic; and the almighty dollar sinks into something comparatively insignificant amidst a whole Pantheon of better gods."

Scientific Stirrings

Some historians have suggested that American interest in science—and contributions to its advancement—had declined in the early 19th century from the levels achieved during the Revolutionary era. Despite Jefferson's assurances in the 1780s that the United States would soon "produce her full quota of genius," a half century had gone by without a single American scientist even approaching the international recognition accorded Benjamin Franklin.

Tocqueville attributed Americans' indifference to science to their distrust of theory and abstract knowledge. "The purely practical side," he conceded, "is cultivated admirably." Contemporaries cited more pressing needs. "We are a new country," a Boston doctor reminded his son, who wished to pursue a scientific career. "We have, as it were, just landed on these shores; there is a vast deal to be done; and he who will not be doing, must be set down as a drone."

There was progress. State-sponsored geological surveys provided at least temporary livings for the European-trained geologist James Hall and the botanist Asa Gray. (Later, as a Harvard professor, Gray was the leading American advocate of his friend Charles Darwin's theory of natural selection.) Additional jobs opened up with the expansion of the United States Coastal Survey, directed by Benjamin Franklin's great-grandson, Alexander Dallas Bache, in 1843. The opening in 1846 of the Smithsonian Institution in Washington, to which the physicist Joseph Henry was appointed first secretary, helped too. Henry's researches in electromagnetism in the 1830s led to Samuel F. B. Morse's invention of the telegraph, and Bache's lobbying resulted in the founding of the American Association for the Advancement of Science in 1848.

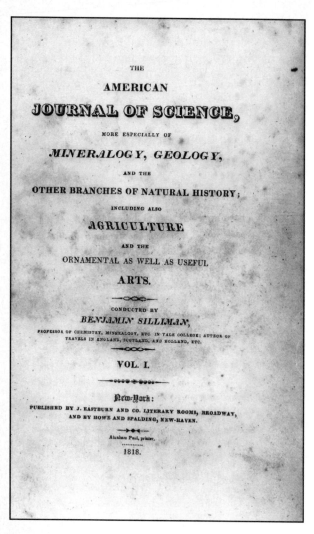

THE

AMERICAN

JOURNAL OF SCIENCE,

MORE ESPECIALLY OF

MINERALOGY, GEOLOGY,

AND THE

OTHER BRANCHES OF NATURAL HISTORY;

INCLUDING ALSO

AGRICULTURE

AND THE

ORNAMENTAL AS WELL AS USEFUL

ARTS.

CONDUCTED BY
BENJAMIN SILLIMAN,
PROFESSOR OF CHEMISTRY, MINERALOGY, ETC. IN YALE COLLEGE; AUTHOR OF
TRAVELS IN ENGLAND, SCOTLAND, AND HOLLAND, ETC.

VOL. I.

New-York:
PUBLISHED BY J. EASTBURN AND CO. LITERARY ROOMS, BROADWAY,
AND BY HOWE AND SPALDING, NEW-HAVEN.

Abraham Paul, printer.

1818.

Benjamin Silliman, a Yale scholar, was the country's leading geologist and the moving force behind the American Journal of Science and Arts. *Through such scientific journals, scholars exchanged ideas and knowledge that contributed to scientific advances.*

Yet few Americans pursued science except on a part-time basis. The star sightings and tidal measurements that went into Nathaniel Bowditch's internationally recognized manual, *The New American Practical Navigator,* had to be made in his spare time. He made his living as an actuary in an insurance company. Maria Mitchell, America's best-known 19th-century woman scientist, won international celebrity and a gold medal from the king of Denmark for calculating the position of a new comet in 1847. She was employed as a librarian in Nantucket when she made the calculations.

For all the practical obstacles in the way of doing serious science in Jacksonian America, its near-wilderness circumstances sometimes provided those on the lookout with unexpected targets of opportunity. An almost literal case in point is that of Dr. William Beaumont. In 1822, while serving as an army surgeon in upstate New York, Beaumont was called to attend to Alexis St. Martin, a 19-year-old Canadian woodsman who had been shot by accident. The shell, fired from no more than 3 feet away, had blasted a hole in his chest the size of a grapefruit; it had blown away the sixth rib, fractured the fifth, and left protruding a portion of his lung "as large as a turkey's egg." There was also something else sticking out. "What at first view I could not believe possible," Beaumont recorded in his diary, "on closer observation, I found to be actually the stomach with a puncture in the protruding portion large enough to receive my forefinger, and through which a portion of the food he had taken for breakfast had come out and lodged in his clothing."

Believing the patient to be a goner, Dr. Beaumont did what he could to administer relief and dress the wound. But the young man survived, exposed stomach and all. Eventually a flap formed over the opening in the stomach, but it could be pushed back, exposing the inner workings of the organ. After St. Martin recovered, Beaumont took him into his household and began studying how he digested food.

Over the next decade Beaumont performed hundreds of experiments testing the relative digestibility of foods and analyzing the chemical properties of gastric juices. His *Experiments and Observations on the Gastric Juices and the Physiology of Digestion* (1833), though largely ignored in the United States, won him a reputation among European physiologists as the world's leading expert on the human gastric system. His fame, however, did not prevent his army superiors, perhaps resenting the time he was diverting from his official duties, from forcing him to resign in 1840. St. Martin then returned to Canada, where he married, fathered four children, and died at the ripe age of 83.

American Humor

The clash between the desire of a few for a "high" culture and the simpler tastes of the majority led

James Fenimore Cooper to conclude that Americans would be forever "wanting in most of the high tastes, and consequently in the high enjoyments." But other writers were not so sure, and some, rather than despair over the cultural incongruities, found in them a rich source of humor.

They were hardly the first to do so. The comic potential in juxtaposing high ideals and low reality had been exploited by the Greek playwright Aristophanes; by Rabelais, the creator of *Gargantua;* and by Cervantes in *The Adventures of Don Quixote*—all, incidentally, works available in mid-century America. William Byrd and Benjamin Franklin had both used the differences between the pretensions of colonial sophisticates and the ways of common folk to good comic effect. But the possibilities of this kind of humor were greatly enlarged in the Jacksonian era. Where else was there a country theoretically based on equality whose inhabitants were so strikingly varied?

One of the first writers to exploit the comic aspects of Jacksonian democracy was Seba Smith, a newspaperman from Portland, Maine. Smith's fictional creation, Major Jack Downing, was a Jackson man from a part of the country suspicious of both the general's politics and his intelligence. Smith had Major Downing accompany the president on his 1833 tour of New England, which included, among other adventures, an appearance at Harvard to receive an honorary degree. In the presence of so many learned gentlemen with political views contrary to his own, Downing advised the president "jest to say nothing, but look as knowing as any of them." Which was exactly what Jackson did, even when faced by snickering "sassy students." "The General stood it out like a hero," the major assured his readers, "and got through very well."

A writer who turned the possibilities of "Down East" humor to more telling satirical effect was James Russell Lowell, author of the *Bigelow Papers*, which began appearing in 1847. Lowell juxtaposed Hosea Biglow, a Yankee farmer of "homely common-sense heated up by conscience," and Birdofredum Sawin, a scoundrel hoping to turn a profit on his patriotism. When approached by a recruiting officer, Hosea Biglow set his opposition to the Mexican War (actually Lowell's) to verse:

> They may talk o' Freedom's airy
> Till they're pupple in the face,—
> It's a grand gret cemetary

> For the barthrights of our race;
> They jest want this Californy
> So's to lug new slave-states in
> To abuse ye, an' to scorn ye,
> An' to plunder ye like sin.

Birdofredum, in contrast, signed up to fight in Mexico, where he lost an eye, a leg, and his left arm. When he returned home he ran for political office. As to his platform:

> Ef, wile you're 'lectioneerin round, some curus
>   chaps should beg
> To know my views o' state affairs, jest answer
>   WOODEN LEG!
> Ef they aint settisfied with thet, an' kin o' pry an'
>   doubt
> An' ax fer sutthin' deffynit, jest say ONE EYE
>   PUT OUT!

The Old Southwest provided another locale for juxtaposing the genteel and the vulgar. Life in the region provided chroniclers with more than enough violence to capture the attention of their "gentle readers." Violence figures prominently in Augustus Baldwin Longstreet's story "The Fight," in which one Ransy Sniffle, "who, in his earlier days, had fed copiously upon red clay and blackberries," promoted a wrestling match between two toughs, Bill and Bob. After provoking both to do battle, Ransy sat back to enjoy the slaughter. And slaughter it was. Bob, the victor, "entirely lost his left ear and a large piece of his left cheek." As for Bill, he

> presented a hideous spectacle. About a third of his nose, at the lower extremity, was bit off, and his face so swelled and bruised that it was difficult to discover anything of the human visage, much more the fine features which he carried into the fight.

Johnson J. Hooper's creation Simon Suggs was the ultimate frontier rogue as confidence man. Whether engaged in horse swapping or faking a conversion experience at a camp meeting in order to steal the collection basket, Suggs lived by the maxim "It is good to be shifty in a new country." He was not alone in this opinion. In a new country, it made sense not to take oneself too seriously. While the outcome of the nation's experiment in combining democracy and cultural aspiration remained in doubt, most Americans took their laughs where they could find them.

Milestones

1827–1838	John Audubon, *Birds of America*	**1845**	Edgar Allan Poe, "The Raven"
1834	George Bancroft, *History of the United States*	**1845–1846**	Henry David Thoreau lives at Walden Pond
1835	James Gordon Bennett's *New York Herald* founded	**1846**	Smithsonian Institution opens
1836	John Lowell endows Lowell Institute public lectures	**1847**	James Russell Lowell, *Bigelow Papers*
1837	Ralph Waldo Emerson's Harvard lecture, "The American Scholar"	**1848**	American Association for the Advancement of Science founded
	Oberlin College enrolls the first women students	**1850**	Nathaniel Hawthorne, *The Scarlet Letter*
1837–1848	Horace Mann serves as secretary of the Massachusetts Board of Education	**1851**	Herman Melville, *Moby Dick*
			Francis Parkman, *The Conspiracy of Pontiac*
1839	Establishment of the American Art Union	**1854**	Thoreau, *Walden*
1842–1843	Herman Melville lives in the South Pacific	**1855–1892**	Walt Whitman, *Leaves of Grass* (various editions)
1843	Hiram Powers, *The Greek Slave* (sculpture)	**1857**	*Atlantic Monthly* first published
		1859	Peter Cooper founds Cooper Institute

SUPPLEMENTARY READING

Titles marked with an asterisk have been published in paperback.

Useful surveys of cultural and intellectual currents in this period are Merle Curti, **The Growth of American Thought** (1951), R. B. Nye, **Society and Culture in America*** (1974), and Rush Welter, **The Mind of America, 1820–1860*** (1975). See also Richard Hofstadter, **Anti-intellectualism in American Life*** (1963), and Stow Persons, **The Decline of American Gentility** (1975), for a more critical assessment. F. O. Mattheissen, **American Renaissance** (1941), remains valuable.

On transcendentalism, see Perry Miller (ed.), **The American Transcendentalists** (1957). Two books by Joel Porte, **Emerson and Thoreau: Transcendentalists in Conflict** (1966) and **Representative Man: Ralph Waldo Emerson in His Time*** (1979), cover the transcendentalist "community." For a critical appraisal, see Quentin Anderson, **The Imperial Self** (1971).

On American literature, Van Wyck Brooks, **The Flowering of New England*** (1936), remains a readable survey. Alfred Kazin, **On Native Grounds*** (1942), is more critically disposed. David Levin, **History as Romantic Art**

(1959), is excellent on the era's historians and their approaches to their craft.

On the cultural life of the South, see Clement Eaton, **The Mind of the Old South*** (1964), and Drew Faust, **A Sacred Circle** (1977). On education, see L. A. Cremin, **American Education: The National Experience*** (1980), and C. F. Kaestle, **Pillars of the Republic** (1983); see also Jonathan Messerli, **Horace Mann** (1972). M. B. Katz, in **The Irony of Early School Reform*** (1968), questions the motives of the reformers; Diane Ravitch, in **The Revisionists Revised*** (1978), challenges Katz. C. F. Kaestle and Maris Vinovskis, **Education and Social Change** (1980), is excellent.

Popular culture is discussed in Carl Bode, **The American Lyceum*** (1956) and **The Anatomy of Popular Culture** (1959), and Russell Lynes, **The Tastemakers*** (1954). Ann Douglas, **The Feminization of American Culture** (1977), is excellent on the pervasiveness and impact of sentimental literature. Neil Harris, **The Artist in American Society*** (1966), puts art in its social setting. See also

Barbara Novak, **Nature and Culture: American Landscape Painting** (1980).

The standard sources for the history of American colleges remain Richard Hofstadter, **Academic Freedom in the Age of the College** (1955), and Fred Rudolph, **The American College and University** (1961). But see also David Allmendinger, **Paupers and Scholars** (1975), R. A. McCaughey, "The Transformation of American Academic Life," in **Perspectives in American History** (1975), Ronald Story, **The Forging of an Aristocracy** (1980), and

Colin Burke, **American Collegiate Populations** (1982).

Scientific activities are examined in G. H. Daniels, **American Science in the Age of Jackson** (1968), W. H. Goetzmann, **Exploration and Empire*** (1967), William Stanton, **The Great United States Exploring Expedition** (1975), and A. H. Dupree, **Science in the Federal Government** (1957).

On American humor before the Civil War, see K. S. Lynn (ed.), **The Comic Tradition in America*** (1958), and Constance Rourke, **American Humor** (1931).

XIII

Expansion and Slavery

Were other reasoning wanting in favor of now elevating this question . . . it is surely to be found, found abundantly, in . . . the fulfilment of our manifest destiny to overspread the continent allotted by Providence for the free development of our yearly multiplying millions.

JOHN L. O'SULLIVAN, *1845*

President John Tyler was a thin, rather delicate-appearing man with pale blue eyes and a long nose. Courteous, tactful, soft-spoken, he gave the impression of being weak, an impression reinforced by his professed belief that the president should defer to Congress in the formulation of policy. This was a false impression; John Tyler was stubborn and proud, and these characteristics combined with an almost total lack of imagination to make him worship consistency, as so many second-raters do. He had turned away from Jackson because of the aggressive way the president had used his powers of appointment and the veto, but he also disagreed with Henry Clay and the northern Whigs about the Bank, protection, and federal internal improvements. Being a states' rights southerner, he considered such measures unconstitutional. Nevertheless, he was prepared to cooperate with Clay as the leader of what he called the "more immediate representatives" of the people, the members of Congress. But he was not prepared to be Clay's puppet. He asked all of Harrison's Cabinet to remain in office.

Tyler's Troubles

Tyler and Clay did not get along, and for this Clay was chiefly to blame. He behaved in an overbearing manner that was out of keeping with his nature, probably because he resented having been passed over by the Whigs in 1840. (When news of Harrison's nomination reached him in Washington, he was half drunk. His face darkened. "I am the most unfortunate man in the history of parties," he said, "always run . . . when sure to be defeated, and now betrayed for a nomination when I, or anyone, would be sure of an election.") He considered himself the real head of the Whig party and intended to exercise his leadership.

In Congress, Clay announced a comprehensive program that ignored Tyler's states' rights view of the Constitution. Most important was his plan to set up a new Bank of the United States. A bill to repeal the Independent Treasury Act caused no difficulty, but when Congress passed a new Bank bill, Tyler vetoed it. The entire Cabinet except Secretary of State Webster thereupon resigned in protest.

Abandoned by the Whigs, Tyler attempted to build a party of his own. He failed to do so, and for the remainder of his term the political squabbling in Washington was continuous. Clay wanted to distribute the proceeds from land sales to the states, presumably to bolster their sagging finances but actually to reduce federal revenues in order to justify raising the tariff. To win western votes for distribution, he agreed to support the Preemption Act of 1841 legalizing the right of squatters to occupy unsurveyed land and to buy it later at $1.25 an acre without bidding for it at auction. However, the southerners insisted on an amendment pledging that distribution would be stopped if the tariff were raised above the 20 percent level, and when the Whigs blithely tried to push a high tariff through Congress without repealing the Distribution Act, Tyler vetoed the bill. Finally, the Distribution Act was repealed and Tyler signed the new Tariff Act of 1842, raising duties to about the levels of 1832.

The Webster-Ashburton Treaty

Webster's decision to remain in the Cabinet was motivated in part by his desire to settle the boundary between Maine and New Brunswick. The intent of

John Tyler posed for a daguerreotypist about 1850, after he had retired from public life. Tyler voted in favor of Virginia's secession ordinance in 1861.

took Valley timber but needed part of the territory to the north to build a military road connecting Halifax and Quebec. Webster, who thought any settlement desirable simply to eliminate a possible cause of war, willingly agreed.

The problem of placating Maine and Massachusetts, which wanted every acre of the land in dispute, Webster solved in an extraordinary manner. It was known that during the peace negotiations ending the Revolution, Franklin had marked the boundary between Maine and Canada on a map with a heavy red line, but no one could find the Franklin map. Webster obtained an old map of the area and had someone mark off in red a line that followed the British version of the boundary. He showed this document to representatives of Maine and Massachusetts, convincing them that they had better agree to his compromise before the British got wind of it and demanded the whole region! It later came out that the British had a true copy of the Franklin map, which showed that the entire area rightfully belonged to the United States.

Webster's generosity made excellent sense. Lord Ashburton, gratified by having obtained the strategic territory, made concessions elsewhere along the Canadian and American border. The Senate ratified the Webster-Ashburton Treaty in August 1842. Its importance, more symbolic than practical, was nonetheless great. British dependence on foreign foodstuffs was increasing; America's need for British capital was rising. War, or even unsettled affairs, would have injured vital business relations and produced no compensating gains.

The Texas Question

The settlement with Great Britain won support in every section of the United States, but the same could not be said for Tyler's attempt to annex the Republic of Texas, for this involved the question of slavery. In the Transcontinental Treaty of 1819 with Spain, the boundary of the United States had been drawn in such a way as to exclude Texas. This seemed unimportant at the time, yet within months of ratification of the treaty in February 1821, Americans led by Stephen F. Austin had begun to settle in the area, by then part of an independent Mexico. Cotton flourished on the fertile Texas plains, and the Mexican authorities offered free land to groups

the peace treaty of 1783 had been to award the United States all land in the area drained by rivers flowing into the Atlantic rather than the St. Lawrence, but the wording was obscure and the old maps conflicting. The issue became critical in 1838 when Canadians began cutting timber in the Aroostook Valley, which was claimed by the United States. When Maine sent an agent to remonstrate with the lumberjacks, he was arrested. Maine and New Brunswick each called up militia and the "Aroostook war" followed. No one was killed, yet the danger of a real war was great. Acting with admirable restraint, Van Buren sent General Winfield Scott to the area, and Scott managed to arrange a truce.

In 1842 the British sent a new minister, Lord Ashburton, to the United States to try to settle all outstanding disputes. Ashburton, head of a London banking house that had large investments in the United States, made an ideal ambassador. He and Webster easily worked out a compromise boundary. The British cared relatively little about the Aroos-

of settlers. By 1830 there were some 20,000 white Americans in Texas, about 2,000 slaves, and only a few thousand Mexicans.

President John Quincy Adams had offered Mexico $1 million for Texas, and Jackson was willing to pay $5 million, but Mexico would not sell. Nevertheless, the flood of American settlers alarmed the Mexican authorities. The immigrants apparently felt no loyalty to Mexico. Most were Protestants, though Mexican law required that all immigrants be Catholics; few attempted to learn more than a few words of Spanish. When Mexico outlawed slavery, they evaded the law by "freeing" their slaves and then signing them to lifetime contracts as indentured servants. In 1830 Mexico prohibited further immigration of Americans into Texas, though again the law proved impossible to enforce.

As soon as the Mexican government began to restrict them, the Texans began to seek independence. In 1835 a series of skirmishes escalated into a full-scale rebellion. The Mexican president, Antonio López de Santa Anna, marched north with 6,000 soldiers to subdue the rebels. Late in February 1836 he reached San Antonio.

A force of 187 men under Colonel William B. Travis held the city. They took refuge behind the stout walls of a former mission called the Alamo. For ten days they beat off Santa Anna's assaults, inflicting terrible casualties on the attackers. Finally, on March 6, the Mexicans breeched and scaled the walls. Once inside they killed everyone, even the wounded, then soaked the corpses in oil and burned them. Among the dead were the legendary Davy Crockett and Jim Bowie, inventor of the Bowie knife.

After the Alamo and a similar slaughter at another garrison at Goliad, southeast of San Antonio, peaceful settlement of the dispute between Texas and Mexico was impossible. Meanwhile, on March 2, 1836, Texas had declared its independence. Sam Houston, a former congressman and governor of Tennessee and an experienced Indian fighter, was placed in charge of the rebel army. For a time Houston retreated before Santa Anna's troops, who greatly outnumbered his own. At the San Jacinto River he took a stand. On April 21, 1836, shouting "Forward! Charge! Remember the Alamo! Remember Goliad!" his troops routed the Mexican army, which soon retreated across the Rio Grande. In October, Houston was elected president of the Republic of Texas, and a month later a plebiscite revealed that an overwhelming majority favored annexation by the United States.

President Jackson hesitated. To take Texas might lead to war with Mexico. Assuredly it would stir up the slavery controversy. On his last day in office he recognized the republic, but he made no move to accept it into the Union, nor did his successor, Van Buren. Texas thereupon went its own way, which involved developing friendly ties with Great Britain. An independent Texas suited British tastes perfectly, for it could provide an alternative

By 1834, "Anglos," or immigrants from the United States, greatly outnumbered Spanish-speaking settlers in Texas. When the demands of Texans for a separate state within Mexico were rejected, tensions with the Mexican government increased. Soon after hostilities erupted in 1835, this rebel force led by Stephen Austin captured Fort San Antonio de Bexar.

"I am determined to sustain myself as long as possible," wrote 27-year-old Colonel William B. Travis, in a message from the besieged Alamo, *"and die like a soldier, who never forgets what is due to his honor and that of his country. Victory or Death!"* Like frontiersman Davy Crockett, shown in this woodcut, Travis died at the hands of the Mexican army that captured the Alamo.

supply of raw cotton and a market for manufactures unfettered by tariffs.

These events caused alarm in the United States, especially among southerners, who dreaded the possibility that a Texas dominated by Great Britain might abolish slavery. As a southerner, Tyler shared these feelings; as a beleaguered politician, spurned by the Whigs and held in contempt by most Democrats, he saw in annexation a chance to revive his fortunes. When Webster resigned as secretary of state in 1843, Tyler replaced him with a fellow Virginian, Abel P. Upshur, whom he ordered to seek a treaty of annexation. The South was eager to take Texas, and in the West and even the Northeast the patriotic urge to add such a magnificent new territory to the national domain was great. Counting noses, Upshur convinced himself that the Senate would approve annexation by the necessary two-thirds majority. He negotiated a treaty in February 1844, but before he could sign it he was killed by the accidental explosion of a cannon on U.S.S. *Princeton* during a weapons demonstration.

To ensure the winning of Texas, Tyler appointed John C. Calhoun secretary of state. This was a blunder; by then Calhoun was so closely associated with the South and with slavery that his appointment alienated thousands of northerners who might otherwise have welcomed annexation. Suddenly Texas became a hot political issue. Clay and Van Buren, who seemed assured of the 1844 Whig and Democratic presidential nominations, promptly announced that they opposed annexation, chiefly on the grounds that it would probably

lead to war with Mexico. With a national election in the offing, northern and western senators refused to vote for annexation, and in June the Senate rejected the treaty, 35 to 16. The Texans were angry and embarrassed, the British eager again to take advantage of the situation.

Manifest Destiny

The Senate, Clay, and Van Buren had all misinterpreted public opinion. John C. Calhoun, whose world was so far removed from that of the average citizen, in this case came much closer to comprehending the mood of the country than any of its other leaders.

For two centuries Americans had been gradually conquering a continent. The first colonists had envisaged a domain extending from the Atlantic to the Pacific, though they had not realized the immensity of the New World. By the time their descendants came to appreciate its size, they had been chastened by the experience of battling the Indians for possession of the land and then laboriously developing it. The Revolution and its aftermath of nationalism greatly stimulated expansion, and then, before the riches of trans-Appalachia had even been inventoried, Jefferson had stunned the country with Louisiana, an area so big that the mere thought of it left Americans giddy.

The westward march from the 17th century to the 1840s had seemed fraught with peril, the prize golden but attainable only through patient labor and fearful hardships. Wild animals and wild men, mighty forests and mighty foreign powers beset the path. John Adams wrote of "conquering" the West "from the trees and rocks and wild beasts." He was "enflamed" by the possibilities of "that vast scene which is opening in the West," but to win it the United States would have to "march *intrepidly* on."

Quite rapidly (as historians measure time) the atmosphere changed. Each year of national growth increased the power and confidence of the people, and every forward step revealed a wider horizon. Now the West seemed a ripe apple, to be picked almost casually. Where pioneers had once stood in awe before the majesty of the Blue Ridge, then hesitated to venture from the protective shadows of the forest into the open prairies of Illinois, they now shrugged their shoulders at great deserts and began to talk of the Rocky Mountains as "mere molehills" along the road to the Pacific. After 200 years of westward expansion had brought them as far as Missouri and Iowa, Americans perceived their destined goal. *The whole continent was to be theirs!* Theirs to exploit, and theirs to make into one mighty nation, a land of opportunity, a showcase to display the virtues of democratic institutions, living proof that Americans were indeed God's chosen people. A New York journalist, John L. O'Sullivan, captured the new mood in a sentence. Nothing must interfere, he wrote in 1845, with "the fulfillment of our *manifest destiny* to overspread the continent allotted by Providence for the free development of our yearly multiplying millions."

The politicians did not sense the new mood in 1844; even Calhoun, who saw the acquisition of Texas as part of a broader program, was thinking of balancing sectional interests rather than of national expansion. In fact, the expansion, stimulated by the natural growth of the population and by a revived flood of immigration, was going on in every section and with little regard for political boundaries. New settlers rolled westward in hordes. Between 1830 and 1835 some 10,000 entered "foreign" Texas, and this was a trickle compared to what the early 1840s were to bring.

Life on the Trail

The romantic myths attached by later generations to this mighty human tide have obscured the ad-justments forced on the pioneers and focused attention on the least significant of the dangers they faced and the hardships they endured. For example, Indians could, of course, be deadly enemies, but pioneers were more likely to complain that the Indians they encountered were dirty, lazy, and thieving than to worry about the danger of Indian attack. Women tended to fear their strangeness, not their actual behavior. Far more dangerous was the possibility of accidents on the trail, particularly to children, and also unsanitary conditions and exposure to the elements.

"Going west" had always been laborious, but in the 1840s the distances covered were longer by far and the comforts and conveniences of "civilization" that had to be left behind, being more extensive than those available to earlier generations, tended to be more painful to surrender. Moving west disrupted the new pattern of family life; there were few, if any, "separate spheres" on the trail and relatively few in frontier settlements, at least in the first years. "Far from city marketplaces and factories," the historian Julie Roy Jeffries writes, "the pioneer family had to become self-sufficient. Much of the model of appropriate female behavior had to be disregarded." Women learned to load wagons, pitch tents, chase stray cattle. Men, for their part, had to keep an eye on children and help with tasks like cooking and washing.

Travel on the plains west of the Mississippi was especially taxing for women. Guidebooks promised them that "regular exercise, in the open air . . . gives additional vigor and strength." But the books did not prepare them for having to collect dried buffalo dung for fuel, for the heat and choking dust of summer, for enduring a week of steady rain, for the monotony, the dirt, the cramped quarters. Caring for an infant or a 2-year-old in a wagon could be torture week after week on the trail, for there were limits to what the average husband could or would do on the way west. In their letters and journals pioneer women mostly complained of being bone weary and about the difficulties of day to-day existence. "It is impossible to keep anything clean," one recorded, and it is not hard to envisage the difficulty of doing so while living for weeks on end on the trail. "Oh dear," another wrote in her journal, "I do so want to get there it is now almost four months since we have slept in a house." What sort of a house a pioneer family would actually sleep in when they reached their destination is a question this woman did not record, which was probably fortunate for her peace of mind.

California and Oregon

By 1840 many Americans had settled far to the west in California, which was unmistakably Mexican territory, and in the Oregon country, jointly claimed by the United States and Great Britain, and it was to these distant regions that the pioneers were going in increasing numbers as the decade progressed. California was a sparsely settled land of some 7,000 Spanish-speaking ranchers and a handful of "Anglo" settlers from the United States. Until the 1830s, when their estates were broken up by the anticlerical Mexican government, 21 Catholic missions, stretching north from San Diego to San Francisco, controlled more than 30,000 Indian converts, who were little better off than slaves. Richard Henry Dana, a Harvard College student, sailed around South America to California as an ordinary seaman on the brig *Pilgrim* in 1834. His account of that voyage in *Two Years Before the Mast* (1840) contains a fine description of what life was like in the region: "There is no working class (the Indians being practically serfs and doing all the hard work) and every rich man looks like a grandee, and every poor scamp like a broken-down gentleman."

Oregon, a vaguely defined area between California and Russian Alaska, proved still more alluring to Americans. Captain Robert Gray had sailed up the Columbia River in 1792, and Lewis and Clark had visited the region on their great expedition. In 1811 John Jacob Astor's Pacific Fur Company had established trading posts on the Columbia. Two decades later Methodist, Presbyterian, and Catholic missionaries began to find their way into the Willamette Valley, a green land of rich soil, mild climate, and tall forests teeming with game. Gradually a small number of settlers followed, until by 1840 there were about 500 Americans in the Willamette area.

In the early 1840s, fired by the spirit of manifest destiny, the country suddenly burned with "Oregon fever." In dozens upon dozens of towns, societies were founded to collect information and organize groups to make the march to the Pacific. Land hunger (stimulated by glowing reports from the scene) drew the new migrants most powerfully, but the patriotic concept of manifest destiny gave the trek across the 2,000 miles of wilderness separating Oregon from the western edge of American settlement in Missouri the character of a crusade. In 1843 nearly 1,000 pioneers made the long trip.

The Oregon Trail began at the western border of Missouri and followed the Kansas River and the perverse, muddy Platte ("a mile wide and six inches deep") past Fort Laramie to the Rockies. It crossed the Continental Divide by the relatively easy South Pass, veered south to Fort Bridger, on Mexican soil, and then ran north and west through the valley of the Snake River and eventually, by way of the Columbia, to Fort Vancouver, a British post guarding the entrance to the Willamette Valley.

"Oregon Fever" swept the country in the mid-1840s, setting thousands of emigrants on the Oregon Trail. People full of hope assembled in wagon trains at jumping-off places along the Missouri River. Their optimism often turned to despair as they faced the hardships of the journey, from fording rivers to hauling wagons by ropes, chains, and pulleys over steep rocky ridges.

Over this tortuous path wound the canvas-covered caravans with their scouts and their accompanying herds. Each group became a self-governing community on the march, with regulations democratically agreed on "for the purpose of keeping good order and promoting civil and military discipline." Most of the travelers consisted of young families, some from as far away as the East Coast cities, more from towns and farms in the Ohio Valley. Few could be classified as poor because the cost of the trip for a family of four was about $600, no small sum at that time. (The faster and less fatiguing trip by ship around South America cost about $600 per person.)

For large groups Indians posed no great threat (though constant vigilance was necessary), but the

The Old Spanish Trail was the earliest of the trails west. Part of it was mapped in 1776 by a Franciscan missionary. The Santa Fe Trail came into wide use after 1823. The Oregon Trail was pioneered by trappers and missionaries. The Mormon Trail was first traversed in 1847, while the Oxbow Route, developed under a federal mail contract, was used from 1858 to 1861.

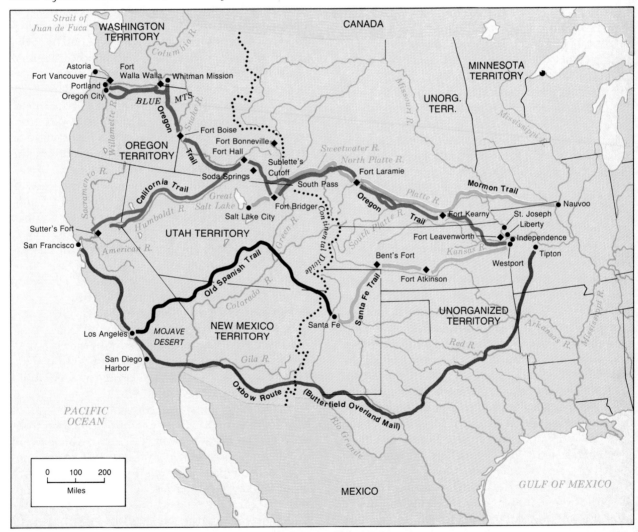

TRAILS WEST

five-month trip was full of labor, discomfort, and uncertainty; in the words of the historian David Lavender, a "remorseless, unending, weather scoured, nerve-rasping plod on and on and on and on, foot by aching foot." And at the end lay the regular tasks of pioneering. The spirit of the trailblazers is caught in an entry from the diary of James Nesmith:

> Friday, October 27.—Arrived at Oregon City at the falls of the Willamette.

> Saturday, October 28.—Went to work.

Behind the dreams of the Far West as an American Eden lay the commercial importance of the three major West Coast harbors: San Diego, San Francisco, and the Strait of Juan de Fuca leading into Puget Sound. Eastern merchants considered these harbors the keys to the trade of the Orient. That San Diego and San Francisco were Mexican and the Puget Sound district was claimed by Great Britain only heightened their desire to possess them. As early as 1835, Jackson tried to buy the San Francisco region. Even Calhoun called San Francisco the future New York of the Pacific and proposed buying all of California from Mexico.

The Election of 1844

In the spring of 1844 expansion did not seem likely to affect the presidential election. The Whigs nominated Clay unanimously and ignored Texas in their party platform. When the Democrats gathered in convention at Baltimore in May, Van Buren appeared to have the nomination in his pocket. He too wanted to keep Texas out of the campaign. That a politician of Van Buren's caliber, controlling the party machinery, could be upset at a national convention seemed unthinkable. But upset he was, for the southern delegates rallied round the Calhoun policy of taking Texas to save it for slavery. "I can beat Clay and Van Buren put together on this issue," Calhoun boasted. "They are behind the age." With the aid of a few northern expansionists the southerners forced through a rule requiring that the choice be by a two-thirds majority. This Van Buren could not muster. After a brief deadlock, a "dark horse," James K. Polk of Tennessee, swept the convention.

Polk was a good Jacksonian; his supporters called him "Young Hickory." He opposed high tariffs and was dead set against establishing another national bank. But he believed in taking Texas, and he favored expansion generally. To mollify the Van Burenites, the convention nominated Senator Silas Wright of New York for vice-president, but Wright was Van Buren's friend and equally opposed to annexation. When the word was flashed to him in Washington over the new "magnetic telegraph" that Samuel F. B. Morse had just installed between the convention hall in Baltimore and the Capitol, he refused to run. The delegates then picked an annexationist, George M. Dallas of Pennsylvania. The Democratic platform demanded that Texas be "reannexed" (implying that it had been part of the Louisiana Purchase) and that all of Oregon be "reoccupied" (suggesting that the joint occupation of the region with Great Britain, which had been agreed to in the Convention of 1818, be abrogated).

Texas was now in the campaign. When Clay sensed the new expansionist sentiment of the voters, he tried to hedge on his opposition to annexation, but by doing so he probably lost as many votes as he gained. The election was extremely close. The campaign followed the pattern established in 1840, with stress on parades, mass meetings, and slogans. Polk carried the country by only 38,000 of 2.7 million votes. In the electoral college the vote was 170 to 105.

The decisive factor in the contest was the Liberty party, an antislavery splinter group organized in 1840. Only 62,000 voters supported candidate James G. Birney, a "reformed" Kentucky slaveholder, but nearly 16,000 of them lived in New York, most in the western part of the state, a Whig stronghold. Since Polk carried New York by barely 5,000, the votes for Birney probably cost Clay the state. Had he won New York's 36 electoral votes, he would have been elected, 141 to 134.

Polk's victory was nevertheless taken as a mandate for expansion. Tyler promptly called on Congress to take Texas by joint resolution, which would avoid the necessity of obtaining a two-thirds majority in the Senate. This was done a few days before Tyler left the White House. Under the resolution, if the new state agreed, as many as four new states might be carved from its territory. Polk accepted this arrangement, and in December 1845 Texas became a state.

Polk as President

President Polk, a slightly built, erect man with grave, steel-gray eyes, was approaching 50. His mind was not of the first order, for he was too tense and calculating to allow his intellect free rein, but he was an efficient, hard worker with a strong will and a tough skin, qualities that stood him in good stead in the White House, and he made politics his whole life. It was typical of the man that he developed a special technique of handshaking in order better to cope with the interminable reception lines that every leader has to endure. "When I observed a strong man approaching," he once explained, "I generally took advantage of him by . . . seizing him

"This is the House That Polk Built" is the title of this 1846 cartoon directed against the president. Polk hatches his eggs and schemes for territorial expansion, reducing the tariff, and gaining fame that make up a house of cards. Contrary to the cartoonist's view, Polk succeeded in his expansionist goals, presiding over the triumph of Manifest Destiny.

by the tip of his fingers, giving him a hearty shake, and thus preventing him from getting a full grip upon me." In four years in office he was away from his desk in Washington for a total of only six weeks.

Polk was uncommonly successful in doing what he set out to do as president. He persuaded Congress to lower the tariff of 1842 and to restore the independent treasury. He opposed federal internal improvements and managed to have his way. He made himself the spokesman of American expansion by committing himself to obtaining, in addition to Texas, both Oregon and the great Southwest. Here again, he succeeded.

Oregon was the first order of business. In his inaugural address Polk stated the American claim to the entire region in the plainest terms, but he informed the British minister in Washington, Richard Pakenham, that he would accept a boundary following the 49th parallel to the Pacific. Pakenham rejected this proposal without submitting it to London, and Polk thereupon decided to insist again on the whole area. When Congress met in December 1845, he asked for authority to give the necessary one year's notice for abrogating the 1818 treaty of joint occupation. "The only way to treat John Bull," he told one congressman, "was to look him straight in the eye." Following considerable discussion, Congress complied, and in May 1846 Polk notified Great Britain that he intended to terminate the joint occupation.

The British then decided to compromise. Officials of the Hudson's Bay Company had become alarmed by the rapid growth of the American settlement in the Willamette Valley. By 1845 there were some 5,000 people there, whereas the country north of the Columbia contained no more than 750 British subjects. A clash between the groups could have but one result. The company decided to shift its base from the Columbia to Vancouver Island. And British experts outside the company reported that the Oregon country could not possibly be defended in case of war. Thus when Polk accompanied the one-year notice with a hint that he would again consider a compromise, the British foreign secretary, Lord Aberdeen, hastily suggested Polk's earlier proposal, dividing the Oregon territory along the 49th parallel. Polk, abandoning his belligerent attitude, agreed. The treaty followed that line from the Rockies to Puget Sound, but Vancouver Island, which extends below the line, was left entirely to the British, so that both nations retained free use of the Strait of Juan de Fuca. Although some northern Democrats accused Polk of treachery because he had failed to fight for all of Oregon, the treaty so obviously accorded with the national interest that the Senate approved it by a large majority in June 1846. Polk was then free to take up the Texas question in earnest.

War with Mexico

One reason for the popularity of the Oregon compromise was that the country was already at war with Mexico and wanted no trouble with Great Britain. The war had broken out in large measure because of the expansionist spirit, and the confidence born of its overwhelming advantages of size and wealth, which certainly encouraged the United States to bully Mexico. Mexican pride was also involved. Texas had been independent for the better part of a decade, and Mexico had made no serious effort to reconquer it; nevertheless, Mexico promptly broke off diplomatic relations when the United States annexed the republic.

Polk, who was ready to fight if he could not obtain what he wanted by negotiation, ordered General Zachary Taylor into Texas to defend the border. However, the location of that border was in dispute. Texas claimed the Rio Grande; Mexico insisted that the boundary was the Nueces River, which emptied into the Gulf about 150 miles to the north. Taylor reached the Nueces in July 1845 with about 1,500 troops and crossed into the disputed territory. He stopped on the southern bank at Corpus Christi, not wishing to provoke the Mexicans by marching to the Rio Grande.

In November, Polk sent an envoy, John Slidell,

The general public obtained glimpses of the war through popular lithographs like this by Currier & Ives. The Mexican soldiers (in green) seem to be powerless, despite their cannons, against the onslaught of "Gringos" in blue.

on a secret mission to Mexico to try to obtain the disputed territory by negotiation. Mexico was in default on some $2 million owed American citizens for losses suffered during political upheavals in the country. Polk authorized Slidell to cancel this debt in return for recognition of the annexation of Texas and acceptance of the Rio Grande boundary. The president also empowered him to offer as much as $30 million if Mexico would sell the United States all or part of New Mexico and California.

It would have been to Mexico's long-range advantage to have made a deal with Slidell. The area Polk wanted, lying in the path of American expansion, was likely to be engulfed as Texas had been, without regard for the actions of the American or Mexican governments. Polk assumed that his tough stance would compel the Mexicans to give in. But the Mexican government refused to receive Slidell. The president, General Mariano Paredes, promptly reaffirmed his country's claim to all of Texas. In March 1846 Slidell returned to Washington convinced that the Mexicans would not negotiate until they had been "chastised."

Polk had already ordered Taylor to advance to the Rio Grande. By March 28 the army, swelled to about 4,000, was drawn up on the north bank of the river, across from the Mexican town of Matamoros. When a Mexican force crossed the river on April 25 and attacked an American mounted patrol, Polk had his pretext. His message to Congress treated the matter as a fait accompli: "War exists," he stated flatly. He asked for authority not merely to drive the Mexicans back but to prosecute the war to "a speedy and successful termination." Congress accepted this reasoning and without actually declaring war voted to raise and supply an additional 50,000 troops.

From the first battle, the outcome of the Mexican War was never in doubt. At Palo Alto, north of the Rio Grande, 2,300 Americans scattered a Mexican force more than twice their number. Then, hotly pursuing, 1,700 Americans routed 7,500 Mexicans at Resaca de la Palma. Fewer than 50 United States soldiers lost their lives in these engagements, while Mexican losses in killed, wounded, and captured exceeded 1,000. Within a week of the outbreak of hostilities, the Mexicans had been driven across the Rio Grande and General Taylor had his troops firmly established on the southern bank.

The Mexican army was poorly equipped and, despite a surfeit of high-ranking officers, poorly led. The well-supplied American forces had a hard core of youthful West Pointers eager to make their reputations and regulars trained in Indian warfare to provide the leadership needed to turn volunteer soldiers into first-rate fighting men. Yet Mexico was a large, rugged country with few decent roads; conquering it proved to be a formidable task.

To the Halls of Montezuma

President Polk insisted not only on directing grand strategy (he displayed real ability as a military planner) but on supervising hundreds of petty details, down to the purchase of mules and the promotion of enlisted men. But he allowed party considerations to control his choice of generals. This partisanship caused unnecessary turmoil in army ranks. He wanted, as Thomas Hart Benton said, "a small war, just large enough to require a treaty of peace, and not large enough to make military reputations dangerous for the presidency."

Unfortunately for Polk, both Taylor and Winfield Scott, the commanding general in Washington, were Whigs. Polk, who tended to suspect the motives of anyone who disagreed with him, feared that one or the other would make political capital of his popularity as a military leader. The examples of his hero, Jackson, and of General Harrison loomed large in Polk's thinking.

Polk's attitude was narrow, almost unpatriotic, but not unrealistic. Zachary Taylor was not a brilliant soldier. He had joined the army in 1808 and made it his whole life. He cared so little for politics that he had never bothered to cast a ballot in an election. Polk believed that he lacked the "grasp of mind" necessary for high command, and General Scott complained of his "comfortable, laborsaving contempt for learning of every kind." But Taylor commanded the love and respect of his men (they called him Old Rough and Ready and even Zack), and he knew how to deploy them in the field. He had won another victory against a Mexican force three times larger than his own at Buena Vista in February 1847.

The dust had barely settled on the field of Buena Vista when Whig politicians began to pay Taylor court. "Great expectations and great consequences rest upon you," a Kentucky politician explained to him. "People everywhere begin to talk of converting you into a political leader, when the War is done."

Polk's concern was heightened because domestic opposition to the war was growing. Many northerners feared that the war would lead to the expansion of slavery. Others—among them an obscure Illinois congressman named Abraham Lincoln—felt that Polk had misled Congress about the original outbreak of fighting and that the United States was the aggressor. The farther from the Rio Grande one went in the United States, the less popular "Mr. Polk's war" became; in New England opposition was almost as widespread as it had been to "Mr. Madison's war" in 1812.

Polk's design for prosecuting the war consisted of three parts. First, he would clear the Mexicans

American naval power proved a decisive factor in the Mexican War. The Pacific Squadron, under John D. Sloat and Robert F. Stockton, secured California, and a 200-vessel fleet conveyed Winfield Scott's army to Veracruz. The light salmon-colored area was later ceded to the United States by Texas.

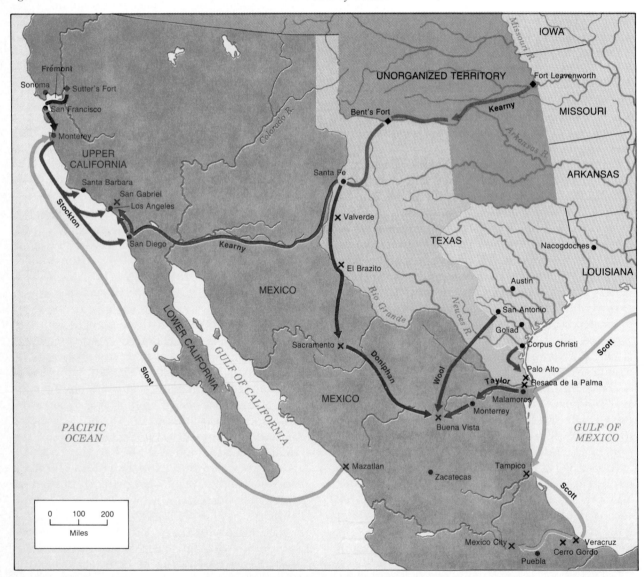

THE MEXICAN WAR, 1846–1848

THE TREATY OF GUADALUPE HIDALGO

from Texas and occupy the northern provinces of Mexico. Second, he would take possession of California and New Mexico. Finally, he would march on Mexico City. Proceeding west from the Rio Grande, Taylor swiftly overran Mexico's northern provinces. In June 1846, American settlers in the Sacramento Valley seized Sonoma and raised the Bear Flag of the Republic of California. Another group, headed by Captain John C. Frémont, leader of an American exploring party that happened to be in the area, clashed with the Mexican authorities around Monterey, California, and then joined with the Sonoma rebels. A naval squadron under Commodore John D. Sloat captured Monterey and San Francisco in July 1846, and a squadron of cavalry joined the other American units in mopping-up operations around San Diego and Los Angeles. By February 1847 the United States had won control of nearly all of Mexico north of the capital city.

The campaign against Mexico City was the most difficult of the war. Fearful of Taylor's growing popularity and entertaining certain honest misgivings about his ability to oversee a complicated campaign, Polk put Winfield Scott in charge of the offensive. He tried to persuade Congress to make Thomas Hart Benton a lieutenant general so as to have a Democrat in nominal control, but the Senate had the good sense to vote down this absurd proposal.

About Scott's competence no one entertained a doubt. But he seemed even more of a threat to the Democrats than Taylor, because he had political ambitions as well as military ability. In 1840 the Whigs had considered running him for president. Scion of an old Virginia family, Scott stood nearly $6\frac{1}{2}$ feet tall; in uniform his presence was commanding. He was intelligent, even-tempered, and cultivated, if somewhat pompous. After a sound but not spectacular record in the War of 1812, he had added to his reputation by helping to modernize military administration and strengthen the professional training of officers. The vast difference between the army of 1812 and that of 1846 was chiefly his doing. On the record, and despite the politics of the situation, Polk had little choice but to give him this command.

Scott landed his army south of Veracruz, Mexico, on March 9, 1847, laid siege to the city, and obtained its surrender in less than three weeks with the loss of only a handful of his 10,000 men. Marching westward through hostile country, he maintained effective discipline, avoiding atrocities that might

have inflamed the countryside against him. Finding his way blocked by well-placed artillery and a large army at Cerro Gordo, where the national road rose steeply toward the central highlands, Scott outflanked the Mexican position and then carried it by storm, capturing more than 3,000 prisoners and much equipment. By mid-May he had advanced to Puebla, only 80 miles southeast of Mexico City.

After delaying until August for the arrival of reinforcements, he pressed on, won two hard-fought victories at the outskirts of the capital, and on September 14 hammered his way into the city. In every engagement the American troops had been outnumbered, yet they always exacted a far heavier toll from the defenders than they themselves were forced to pay. In the fighting on the edge of Mexico City, for example, Scott's army sustained about 1,000 casualties, for the Mexicans defended their capital bravely. But 4,000 Mexicans were killed or wounded in the engagements, and 3,000 (including eight generals, two of them former presidents of the republic) were taken prisoner. No less an authority than the duke of Wellington, the conqueror of Napoleon, called Scott's campaign the most brilliant of modern times.

The Treaty of Guadalupe Hidalgo

The Mexicans were thoroughly beaten, but they refused to accept the situation. As soon as the news of the capture of Veracruz reached Washington, Polk sent Nicholas P. Trist, chief clerk of the State Department, to accompany Scott's army and to act as peace commissioner after the fall of Mexico City. Trist possessed impeccable credentials as a Democrat, for he had married a granddaughter of Thomas Jefferson and had served for a time as secretary to Andrew Jackson. Long residence as United States consul at Havana had given him an excellent command of Spanish.

Trist joined Scott at Veracruz in May. The two men took an instant dislike to each other. Scott considered it a "personal dishonor" to be asked to defer to what he considered a State Department flunky, and his feelings were not salved when Trist sent him an officious 30-page letter discoursing on the nature of his assignment. However, Scott was eager to end the war and realized that a petty quarrel with the president's emissary would not advance that objec-

This 1846 daguerreotype is the earliest known American war photograph. U.S. General John E. Wool poses with his staff in Saltillo, Mexico.

tive. Trist fell ill, and Scott sent him a jar of guava marmalade; after that they became good friends.

Because of the confused state of affairs following the fall of Mexico City, Trist was unable to open negotiations with Mexican peace commissioners until January 1848. Polk, unable to understand the delay, became impatient. Originally he had authorized Trist to pay $30 million for New Mexico, Upper and Lower California, and the right of transit across Mexico's narrow isthmus of Tehuantepec. Now, observing the disorganized state of Mexican affairs, he began to consider demanding more territory and paying less for it. He summoned Trist home.

Trist, with Scott's backing, ignored the order. He realized that unless a treaty was arranged soon, the Mexican government might disintegrate, leaving no one in authority to sign a treaty. He dashed off a 65-page letter to the president, in effect refusing to be recalled, and proceeded to negotiate. Early in February the Treaty of Guadalupe Hidalgo was completed. By its terms Mexico accepted the Rio Grande as the boundary of Texas and ceded New Mexico and Upper California to the United States. In return the United States agreed to pay Mexico $15 million and to take on the claims of American citizens against Mexico, which by that time amounted to another $3.25 million.

When he learned that Trist had ignored his orders, the president seethed. Trist was "contemptibly base," he thought, an "impudent and unqualified scoundrel." He ordered Trist placed under arrest and fired from his State Department job.* Yet Polk had no choice but to submit the treaty to the Senate, for to have insisted on more territory would have meant more fighting, and the war had become increasingly unpopular. The relatively easy military victory made some people ashamed that their country was crushing a weaker neighbor. Abolitionists, led by William Lloyd Garrison, called it an "invasion . . . waged solely for the detestable and horrible purpose of extending and perpetuating American slavery." The Senate, subject to the same pressures as the president, ratified the agreement by a vote of 38 to 14.

The Fruits of Victory

The Mexican War, won quickly and at relatively small cost in lives and money, brought huge ter-

---

* Trist was retired to private life without being paid for his time in Mexico. In 1870, when he was on his deathbed, Congress finally awarded him $14,299.20.

ritorial gains. The Pacific Coast from south of San Diego to the 49th parallel and all the land between the coast and the Continental Divide had become the property of the American people. Immense amounts of labor and capital would have to be invested before this new territory could be made to yield its bounty, but the country clearly had the capacity to accomplish the job.

In this atmosphere came what seemed a sign from the heavens. In January 1848, while Scott's veterans rested on their victorious arms in Mexico City, a mechanic named James W. Marshall was building a sawmill on the American River in the Sacramento Valley east of San Francisco. One day, while supervising the deepening of the millrace, he noticed a few flecks of yellow in the bed of the stream. These he gathered up and tested. They were pure gold.

Other strikes had been made in California and been treated skeptically or as matters of local curiosity; since the days of Jamestown, too many pioneers had run fruitlessly in search of El Dorado, and too much fool's gold had been passed off as the real thing. Yet this discovery produced an international sensation. The gold was real and plentiful—$200 million of it was extracted in four years—but equally important was the fact that everyone was ready to believe the news. The gold rush reflected the heady confidence inspired by Guadalupe Hidalgo; it seemed the ultimate justification of manifest destiny. Surely an era of continental prosperity and harmony had dawned.

Slavery: The Fire Bell in the Night Rings Again

Prosperity came in full measure but harmony did not, for once again expansion brought the nation face to face with the divisive question of slavery. This giant chunk of North America, most of it vacant, its future soon to be determined—should it be slave or free? The question, in one sense, seems hardly worth the national crisis it provoked. Slavery appeared to have little future in New Mexico, less in California and Oregon. Why did the South fight so hard for the right to bring slaves into a region so poorly suited to their exploitation?

Narrow partisanship provides part of the explanation. In districts where slavery was entrenched, a congressman who watched over the institution with the eyes of Argus, ever ready to defend it against the most trivial slight, usually found himself a popular hero. In the northern states, the representatives who were vigilant in what they might describe as "freedom's cause" seldom regretted it on election day. But slavery raised a moral question. Most Americans tried to avoid confronting this truth; as patriots they assumed that any sectional issue could be solved by compromise. However, while the majority of whites had little respect for blacks, slave or free, few persons, northern or southern, could look upon the ownership of one human being by another as simply an alternative form of economic organization and argue its merits as they would those of the protective tariff or a national bank. Twist the facts as they might, slavery was either right or it was wrong; being on the whole honest and moral, they could not, having faced that truth, stand by unconcerned while the question was debated.

The question could come up in Congress only indirectly, for the Constitution did not give the federal government any control over slavery in the states. But Congress had complete control in the territories. Therefore, the fact that slavery had no future in the Mexican cession was unimportant—in fact, for the foes of slavery it was an advantage. By attacking slavery where it did not and probably never could exist, they could conceal from the slaveholders—and perhaps even from themselves—their hope ultimately to extinguish the institution.

Slavery had complicated the Texas problem from the start, and it beclouded the future of the Southwest even before the Mexican flag had been stripped from the staffs at Santa Fe and Los Angeles. The northern, Van Burenite wing of the Democratic party had become increasingly uneasy about the proslavery cast of Polk's policies, which were unpopular in their part of the country. Once it became likely that the war would bring new territory into the Union, these northerners felt compelled to try to check the president and to assure their constituents that they would resist the admission of further slave territory. On August 8, 1846, during the debate on a bill appropriating money for the conduct of the war, Democratic Congressman David Wilmot of Pennsylvania introduced an amendment that provided "as an express and fundamental condition to the acquisition of any territory from the Republic of Mexico" that "neither slavery nor involuntary servitude shall ever exist in any part of said territory, except for crime, whereof the party shall first be duly convicted."

The Wilmot Proviso passed the House, where northern congressmen outnumbered southern, but lost in the Senate, where southerners held the balance. To counter it, Calhoun, again senator from South Carolina, introduced resolutions in February 1846 that argued that Congress had no right to bar slavery from any territory; since territories belonged to all the states, slave and free, all should have equal rights in them. From this position it was only a step (soon taken) to demanding that Congress guarantee the right of slave owners to bring slaves into the territories and establish federal slave codes in the territories. Most northerners considered this proposal as repulsive as southerners found the Wilmot Proviso.

Calhoun's resolutions could never pass the House of Representatives, and Wilmot's proviso had no chance in the Senate. Yet their very existence threatened the Union; as Senator Benton remarked, they were like the blades of a pair of scissors, ineffective separately, an efficient cutting tool taken together.

To resolve the territorial problem, two compromises were offered. One, eventually backed by President Polk, would extend the Missouri Compromise line to the Pacific. The majority of southerners were willing to go along with this scheme, but most northerners would no longer agree to the reservation of *any* new territory for slavery. The other possibility, advocated by Senator Lewis Cass of Michigan, called for organizing new territories without mention of slavery, thus leaving it to local settlers, through their territorial legislatures, to determine their own institutions. Cass's "popular sovereignty," known more vulgarly as "squatter sovereignty," had the superficial merit of appearing to be democratic. Its virtue for the members of Congress, however, was that it allowed them to escape the responsibility of deciding the question themselves.

The Election of 1848

One test of strength occurred in August, before the 1848 presidential election. After six months of acrimonious debate, Congress passed a bill barring slavery from Oregon. The test, however, proved little. If it required half a year to settle the question for Oregon, how could an answer ever be found for California and New Mexico? Plainly the time had come, in a democracy, to go to the people. The coming presidential election seemed to provide an ideal opportunity.

The opportunity was missed. The politicians of parties hedged, fearful of losing votes in one section or another. With the issues blurred, the electorate had no real choice. That the Whigs should behave in such a manner was perhaps to be expected of the party of "Tippecanoe and Tyler too," but in 1848 they outdid even their 1840 performance, nominating Zachary Taylor for president. They chose the general despite his lack of political sophistication and after he had flatly refused to state his opinion on any current subject. The party offered no platform. Taylor was a brave man and a fine general; the Democrats had mistreated him; he was a common, ordinary fellow, unpretentious and warmhearted. Such was the Whig "argument." Taylor's contribution to the campaign was so naive as to be pathetic. "I am a Whig, *but not an ultra Whig*. . . . If elected . . . I should feel bound to administer the government untrammeled by party schemes."

The Democratic party had little better to offer. All the drive and zeal characteristic of it in the Jackson period had gradually seeped away. Polk's espousal of Texas's annexation had driven many northerners from its ranks. Individuals like James Buchanan of Pennsylvania, Polk's secretary of state, and William L. Marcy of New York, his secretary of war—cautious, cynical politicians interested chiefly in getting and holding office—now came to the fore in northern Democratic politics.

The Democratic nominee was Lewis Cass, the father of popular sovereignty, but the party did not endorse that or any other solution to the territorial question. Cass was at least an experienced politician, having been governor of Michigan Territory, secretary of war, minister to France, and senator. Nevertheless, his approach to life was exemplified by an annoying habit he displayed at Washington social functions: A teetotaler, he would circulate among the guests with a glass in hand, raising it to his lips repeatedly but never swallowing a drop.

The Van Buren wing of the Democratic party was known as the Barnburners to call attention to their radicalism—supposedly they would burn down the barn to get rid of the rats. The Barnburners could not stomach Cass, in part because he was willing to countenance the extension of slavery into new territories, in part because he had led the swing to Polk in the 1844 Democratic convention. Combining with the antislavery Liberty party, they formed the Free Soil party and nominated Van Buren.

Van Buren knew he could not be elected, but he believed the time had come to take a stand. "The minds of nearly all mankind have been penetrated by a conviction of the evils of slavery," the onetime "Fox" and "Magician" declared. The Free Soil party polled nearly 300,000 votes, about 10 percent of the total, in a very dull campaign. Offered a choice between the honest ignorance of Taylor and the cynical opportunism of Cass, the voters—by a narrow margin—chose the former, Taylor receiving 1.36 million votes to Cass's 1.22 million. Taylor carried 8 of the 15 slave states and 7 of the 15 free states, proof that the sectional issue had been avoided.

The Gold Rush

It was now clear that the question of slavery in the territories had to be faced. The discovery of gold had brought an army of prospectors into California. By the summer of 1848 San Francisco had become almost a ghost town, and an estimated two-thirds

The hard road to El Dorado was sketched by J. Goldsborough Bruff, a Washington, D.C., draftsman who led a company "to see the elephant" (in the phrase of the day) in 1849. Two self-portraits from Bruff's diary neatly sum up the journey, with pencil notes reading as follows. Leaving Home (No. 1): "D——n your $3, when one can make $100 a day easy." Arrival in California (No. 5): "The mule understands breaking better than being broke . . . 40 miles more without fodder! rather tight, but then the jig's up and I'll soon have my pile! so I'll drive on." The sign on the tree reads "Only 40 mi. to the Settlements. Flour $2.25 lb."

of the adult males of Oregon had hastened south to the gold fields. After President Polk confirmed the "extraordinary character" of the strike in his annual message of December 1848, there was no containing the gold seekers. During 1849 some 25,000 Americans made their way to California from the East by ship; more than 55,000 others crossed the continent by overland routes. About 8,000 Mexicans, 5,000 South Americans, and numbers of Europeans joined the rush.

The rough limits of the gold country had been quickly marked out. For 150 miles and more along the western slope of the Sierra stretched the great mother lode. Along the expanse any stream or canyon, any ancient gravel bed might conceal a treasure in nuggets, flakes, or dust. Armed with pickaxes and shovels, with washing pans, even with knives and spoons, the eager prospectors hacked and dug and sifted, each accumulating a horde, some great, some small, of gleaming yellow metal.

The impact on the region was enormous. Between 1849 and 1860 about 200,000 people, nearly all of them males, crossed the Rockies to California and thousands more reached California by ship. Almost overnight the Spanish-American population was reduced to the status of a minority. Disregarding justice and reason alike, the newcomers from the East, as one observer noted, "regarded every man but a native [North] American as an interloper." They referred to people of Latin American origin as "greasers" and sought by law and by violence to keep them from mining for gold. Even the local Californians (now American citizens) were discriminated against. The few free blacks in California and the several thousand more who came in search of gold were treated no better. As for the far larger Indian population, it was almost wiped out. There were about 150,000 Indians in California in the mid-1840s but only 35,000 in 1860.

The ethnic conflict was only part of the problem. Rough, hard men, separated from women, lusting for gold in a strange wild country where fortunes could be made in a day, gambled away in an hour, or stolen in an instant—the situation demanded the establishment of a territorial government. President Taylor appreciated this, and in his gruff, simple-hearted way he suggested an uncomplicated answer: Admit California directly as a state, letting the Californians decide for themselves about slavery. The rest of the Mexican Cession could be formed into another state. No need for Congress, with its angry rivalries, to meddle at all, he believed. In this way the nation could avoid the divisive effects of sectional debate.

The Californians reacted favorably to Taylor's proposal. They were overwhelmingly opposed to slavery, though not for humanitarian reasons. On the contrary, they tended to look upon blacks as they did Mexicans and feared that if slavery were permitted, white gold seekers would be disadvantaged. "They would be unable," one delegate to the California constitutional convention predicted, "to compete with the bands of negroes who would be set to work under the direction of capitalists. It would become a monopoly." By October 1849 they had drawn up a constitution that outlawed slavery, and by December the new state government was functioning.

At this the South stood aghast. Taylor was the owner of a large plantation and many slaves; southerners had assumed (without bothering to ask) that he would fight to keep the territories open to slavery. To admit California would destroy the balance between free and slave states in the Senate; to allow all the new land to become free would doom the South to wither in a corner of the country, surrounded by hostile free states. Should that happen, how long could slavery sustain itself even in South Carolina? Radicals were already saying that the South would have to choose between secession and surrender. Taylor's plan played into the hands of extremists.

The Compromise of 1850

This was no longer a squabble over territorial governments. With the Union itself at stake, Henry Clay rose to save the day. He had been as angry and frustrated when the Whigs nominated Taylor as he was when they passed him over for Harrison. Now, well beyond 70 and in ill health, he put away his ambition and his resentment and for the last time concentrated his remarkable vision on a great, multifaceted national problem. California must be free and soon admitted to the Union, but the South must have some compensation. For that matter, why not seize the opportunity to settle every outstanding sectional conflict related to slavery? Clay wondered long and hard, drew up a plan, then consulted his

Two leading lights of the day, Clay and Webster, as they looked at about the time they played major roles in the Compromise of 1850. The daguerreotype of Clay dates from the late 1840s; that of Webster from 1851, a year before his death. Both are by the noted Boston firm of Southworth and Hawes.

old Whig rival Webster and obtained his general approval. On January 29, 1850, he laid his proposal, "founded upon mutual forbearance," before the Senate. A few days later he defended it on the floor of the Senate in the last great speech of his life.

California should be brought directly into the Union as a free state, he argued. The rest of the Southwest should be organized as a territory without mention of slavery: The southerners would retain the right to bring slaves there, while in fact none would do so. "You have got what is worth more than a thousand Wilmot Provisos," Clay pointed out to his northern colleagues. "You have nature on your side." Empty lands in dispute along the Texas border should be assigned to New Mexico Territory, Clay continued, but in exchange the United States should take over Texas's preannexation debts. The slave trade should be abolished in the District of Columbia (but not slavery itself), and a more effective federal fugitive slave law should be enacted and strictly enforced in the North.

Clay's proposals occasioned one of the most magnificent debates in the history of the Senate.

Every important member had his say. Calhoun, perhaps even more than Clay, realized that the future of the nation was at stake and that his own days were numbered (he died four weeks later). Too feeble to deliver his speech himself, he sat impassive, wrapped in a great cloak, while Senator James M. Mason of Virginia read it to the crowded Senate. Calhoun thought his plan would save the Union, but his speech was an argument for secession; he demanded that the North yield completely on every point, ceasing even to discuss the question of slavery. Clay's compromise was unsatisfactory; he himself had no other to offer. If you will not yield, he said to the northern senators, "let the States . . . agree to separate and part in peace. If you are unwilling we should part in peace, tell us so, and we shall know what to do."

Three days later, on March 7, Daniel Webster took the floor. He too had begun to fail; the brilliant volubility and the thunder were gone, and when he spoke his face was bathed in sweat and there were strange pauses in his delivery. But his argument was lucid. Clay's proposals should be adopted. Since the

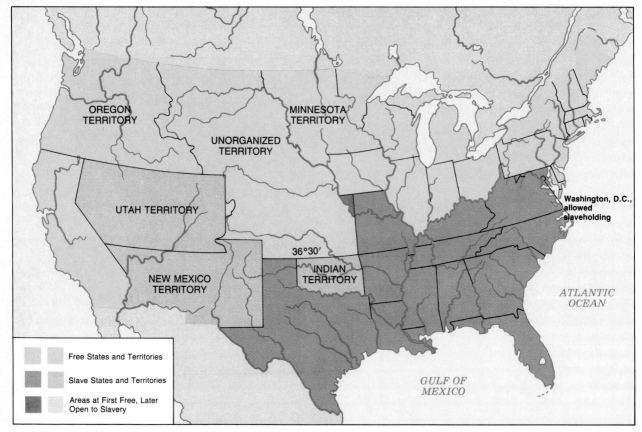

FREE AND SLAVE AREAS, 1850

This map and the map on the facing page show different aspects of the Compromise of 1850. Here, the two shades of salmon and the two shades of green show clearly the distribution of slave and free areas. The Utah and New Mexico territories were allowed to choose to be either free or slave, as their own constitutions determined.

future of all the territories had already been fixed by geographic and economic factors, the Wilmot Proviso was unnecessary. The North's constitutional obligation to yield fugitive slaves, he said, braving the wrath of New England abolitionists, was "binding in honor and conscience." (A cynic might say that once again Webster was placing property rights above human rights.) The Union, he continued, could not be sundered without bloodshed. At the thought of the dread possibility, the old fire flared: "Peaceable secession!" Webster exclaimed, "Heaven forbid! Where is the flag of the republic to remain? Where is the eagle still to tower?"

The debate did not end with the aging giants.

Every possible viewpoint was presented, argued, rebutted, rehashed. Senator William H. Seward of New York, a new Whig leader, close to Taylor's ear, caused a stir while arguing against concessions to the slave interests by saying that despite the constitutional obligation to return fugitive slaves, a "higher law" than the Constitution, the law of God, forbade anything that countenanced the evil of slavery.

The majority clearly favored some compromise, but nothing could have been accomplished without the death of President Taylor on July 9. Obstinate, probably resentful because few people paid him half the heed they paid Clay and other prominent mem-

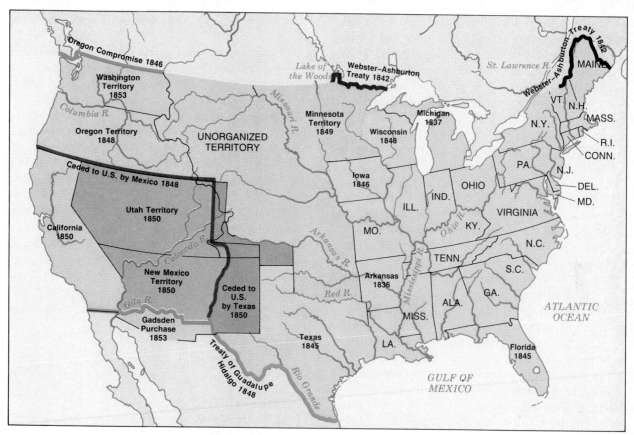

THE UNITED STATES AT MID-CENTURY

This map indicates the provisions of the Compromise of 1850 that applied to the Mexican Cession. Beginning with the annexation of Texas in 1845 and ending with the Gadsden Purchase in 1853 (to furnish a route for a southern transcontinental railroad), the United States acquired more than 869 million acres of territory. With the Gadsden Purchase, the geographical expansion of the continental United States was completed.

bers of Congress, he had insisted on his own plan to bring both California and New Mexico directly into the Union. When Vice-President Millard Fillmore succeeded him, the deadlock between the White House and Capitol Hill was broken. Even so, each part of the compromise had to be voted on separately, for too many stubborn congressmen were willing to overturn the whole plan because they objected to specific parts of it. Senator Benton, for example, announced against Clay's omnibus bill because he objected to the fugitive slave provision and the Texas boundary settlement.

The final congressional maneuvering was man-

aged by another relative newcomer, Senator Stephen A. Douglas of Illinois, who took over when Washington's summer heat prostrated the exhausted Clay. Partisanship and economic interests complicated Douglas's problem. According to rumor, Clay had persuaded an important Virginia newspaper editor to back the compromise by promising him a $100,000 government printing contract. This inflamed many southerners. New York merchants, fearful of the disruption of their southern business, submitted a petition bearing 25,000 names in favor of compromise, a document that had a favorable effect in the South. The prospect of the federal government's paying the debt of Texas made ardent compromisers of a horde of speculators. Between February and September, Texas bonds rose erratically from 29 to over 60, while men like W. W. Corcoran, whose Washington bank held more than $400,000 of these securities, entertained legislators and supplied lobbyists with large amounts of cash.

In the Senate and then in the House, tangled combinations pushed through the separate measures, one by one. California became the thirty-first state. The rest of the Mexican Cession was divided into two territories, New Mexico and Utah, each to be admitted to the Union when qualified, "with or without slavery as [its] constitution may prescribe." Texas received $10 million to pay off its debt in return for accepting a narrower western boundary. The slave trade in the District of Columbia was abolished as of January 1, 1851. The Fugitive Slave Act of 1793 was amended to provide for the appointment of federal commissioners with authority to issue warrants, summon posses, and compel citizens under pain of fine or imprisonment to assist in the capture of fugitives. Accused fugitives could not testify in their own defense. They were to be returned to the South without jury trial merely upon the submission of an affidavit by their "owner."

Only 4 senators and 28 representatives voted for all these bills. The two sides did not meet somewhere in the middle as is the case with most compromises. Each bill passed because those who preferred it outnumbered those opposed. In general, the Democrats gave more support to the compromise than the Whigs, but party lines never held firmly. In the Senate, for example, 17 Democrats and 15 Whigs voted to admit California as a free state. A large number of congressmen absented themselves when parts of the settlement unpopular in their home districts came to a vote; 21 senators and 36 representatives failed to commit themselves on the new fugitive slave bill. Senator Jefferson Davis of Mississippi voted for the fugitive slave measure and the bill creating Utah Territory, remained silent on the New Mexico bill, and opposed the other measures. Senator Salmon P. Chase of Ohio, an abolitionist, supported only the admission of California and the abolition of the slave trade.

In this piecemeal fashion the Union was preserved. The credit belongs mostly to Clay, whose original conceptualization of the compromise enabled lesser minds to understand what they must do.

Everywhere sober and conservative citizens sighed with relief. Mass meetings throughout the country "ratified" the result. Hundreds of newspapers gave the compromise editorial approval. In Washington patriotic harmony reigned. "You would suppose that nobody had ever thought of disunion," Webster wrote. "All say they always meant to stand by the Union to the last." When Congress met again in December, it seemed that party asperities had been buried forever. "I have determined never to make another speech on the slavery question," Senator Douglas told his colleagues. "Let us cease agitating, stop the debate, and drop the subject." If this were done, he predicted, the compromise would be accepted as a "final settlement." With this bit of wishful thinking the year 1850 passed into history.

Milestones

1835 Fall of the Alamo mission

1837 United States recognizes the Republic of Texas

1840 Richard Henry Dana, *Two Years Before the Mast*

1841 Vice-President John Tyler becomes president

Preemption Act grants "squatters' rights"

1842 Webster-Ashburton Treaty determines Maine boundary

1843 Oregon Trail opens

1845 Texas annexed

John L. O'Sullivan coins the expression *manifest destiny*

1846 Oregon boundary dispute settled

War with Mexico

House of Representatives adopts the Wilmot Proviso

1847 General Winfield Scott captures Mexico City

1848 Discovery of gold at Sutter's Mill, California

Treaty of Guadalupe Hidalgo

1850 Compromise of 1850

SUPPLEMENTARY READING

Titles marked with an asterisk have been published in paperback.

G. G. Van Deusen, **The Jacksonian Era*** (1959), provides a convenient summary of the period. On the Tyler administration, see R. J. Morgan, **A Whig Embattled: The Presidency Under John Tyler** (1954).

On diplomatic affairs, see P. A. Varg, **United States Foreign Relations, 1820–1860** (1979), and D. M. Pletcher, **The Diplomacy of Annexation: Texas, Oregon, and the Mexican War** (1973).

The new expansionism is discussed in A. K. Weinberg, **Manifest Destiny*** (1935), and in two works by Frederick Merk, **Manifest Destiny and Mission in American History*** (1963) and **The Monroe Doctrine and American Expansionism** (1966). H. N. Smith, **Virgin Land*** (1950), is also important for an understanding of this subject. The course of western development is treated in R. A. Billington, and Martin Ridge, **The Far Western Frontier*** (1982). On Oregon, see David Lavender, **Westward Vision*** (1963), J. R. Jeffrey, **Frontier Women** (1979), J. D. Unruh, **The Plains Across** (1979), Sandra Myres (ed.), **Ho for California! Women's Overland Diaries** (1980), and Francis Parkman's classic account, **The Oregon Trail*** (1849).

On the election of 1844, see J. C. N. Paul, **Rift in the Democracy*** (1961). The standard biography of Polk is C. G. Sellers, **James K. Polk** (1957–1966), but see also P. H. Bergeron, **The Presidency of James K. Polk** (1987). N. A. Graebner, **Empire on the Pacific** (1955), is the fullest analysis of the factors influencing the Oregon boundary compromise.

There are a number of good brief accounts of the Mexican War, including R. W. Johannsen, **To the Halls of Montezuma** (1987), and O. A. Singletary, **The Mexican War*** (1960). J. H. Schroeder, **Mr. Polk's War** (1973), discusses American opposition to the conflict. For details on the discovery of gold in California, in addition to the works by Billington and Ridge already mentioned, see R. W. Paul, **California Gold: The Beginning of Mining in the Far West*** (1947). On the treatment of Mexicans and blacks, see R. F. Heize and A. J. Almquist, **The Other Californians*** (1971), and R. M. Lapp, **Blacks in Gold Rush California** (1977).

The fullest study of the Compromise of 1850 is Holman Hamilton, **Prologue to Conflict*** (1964). See also the biographies of Clay, Calhoun, and Webster cited in earlier chapters, R. W. Johannsen, **Stephen A. Douglas** (1973), Holman Hamilton, **Zachary Taylor** (1951), and A. O. Craven, **The Growth of Southern Nationalism** (1953).

The Sections Go Their Ways

It is a great mistake to suppose that disunion can be effected by a single blow. The cords which bind these states together in one common Union are far too numerous and powerful for that. Disunion must be the work of time.

JOHN C. CALHOUN, *March 4, 1850*

A nation growing as rapidly as the United States in the middle decades of the 19th century changed continually in hundreds of ways. It was developing a national economy marked by the dependence of each area on all the others, the production of goods in one region for sale in all, the increased specialization of agricultural and industrial producers, and the growth in size of units of production.

Cotton remained the most important southern crop and the major American export. However, manufacturing in the Northeast and the railroads, which revolutionized transportation and communication, became the mainsprings of economic growth. The continuing westward movement of agriculture had significant new effects. American foreign commerce changed radically, and the flood of European immigration had an impact on manufacturing, town life, and farming.

The South

The South was less affected than the other sections by urbanization, European immigration, the transportation revolution, and industrialization. The region remained predominantly agricultural; cotton was still king, slavery the most distinctive southern institution. But important changes were occurring. Cotton continued to march westward until by 1859 fully 1.3 million of the 4.3 million bales grown in the United States came from beyond the Mississippi. In the Upper South, Virginia held its place as the leading tobacco producer, but states beyond the Appalachians were raising more than half the crop. The introduction of Bright Yellow, a mild variety of tobacco that (miraculously) grew best in poor soil, gave a great stimulus to production. The older sections of Maryland, Virginia, and North Carolina shifted to the kind of diversified farming usually associated with the Northeast. By 1849 the wheat crop of Virginia was worth twice as much as the tobacco crop.

In the time of Washington and Jefferson, progressive Virginia planters had experimented with crop rotation and fertilizers. In the mid-19th century, Edmund Ruffin introduced the use of marl, an earth rich in calcium, to counteract the acidity of worn-out tobacco fields. Ruffin discovered that dressings of marl, combined with the use of fertilizers and with proper drainage and plowing methods, doubled and even tripled the yield of corn and wheat. In the 1840s some southerners began to import Peruvian guano, a high-nitrogen fertilizer of bird droppings, which increased yields. Others experimented with contour plowing to control erosion and with improved breeds of livestock, new types of plows, and agricultural machinery.

The Economics of Slavery

The increased importance of cotton in the South strengthened the hold of slavery on the region. The price of slaves rose until by the 1850s a prime field hand was worth as much as $1,800, roughly three times the cost in the 1820s. While the prestige value of owning this kind of property affected prices, the rise chiefly reflected the increasing value of the South's agricultural output. "Crop value per slave" jumped from less than $15 early in the century to more than $125 in 1859.

In the cotton fields of the Deep South, slaves brought several hundred dollars per head more than in the older regions; thus the tendency to sell them "down the river" continued. Mississippi took in some 10,000 slaves a year throughout the period; by 1830 the black population of the state exceeded the white. Slave trading became a big business. There were about 50 dealers in Charleston in the 1850s and 200 in New Orleans. The largest traders were Isaac Franklin and John Armfield, who collected slaves from Virginia and Maryland at their "model jail" in Alexandria and shipped them by land

and sea to a depot near Natchez. Each of the partners cleared half a million dollars before retiring, and some smaller operators did proportionately well.

The impact of the trade on the slaves was frequently disastrous. Husbands were often separated from wives, parents from children. This was somewhat less likely to happen on large, well-managed plantations than on small farms, but it was common enough everywhere. Because the business was so profitable, the prejudice against slave traders abated as the price of slaves rose. Men of high social status became traders, and persons of humble origin who had prospered in the trade had little difficulty in

Not surprisingly, the areas of greatest cotton production were also the areas of the highest proportion of slaves in the population. Note the concentrations of both in the Piedmont, the Alabama Black Belt, and the lower Mississippi Valley, and the relative absence of both in the Appalachian Mountains.

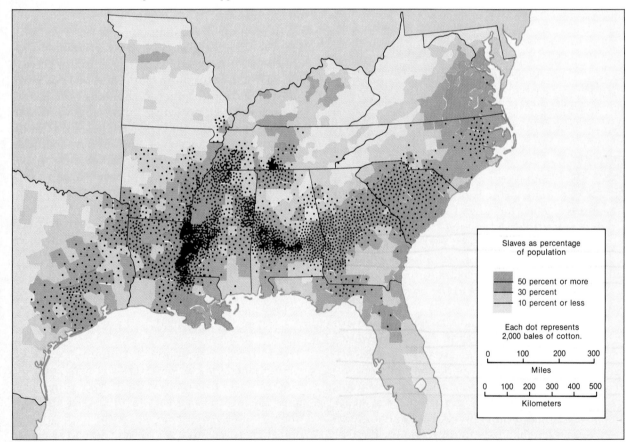

COTTON AND SLAVES IN THE SOUTH, 1860

buying land and setting up as respectable planters.

As blacks became more expensive, the ownership of slaves became more concentrated. In 1860 only about 46,000 of the 8 million white residents of the slave states had as many as 20. When one calculates the cost of 20 slaves and the land to keep them profitably occupied, it is easy to understand why this figure is so small. The most efficient size of a plantation worked by gangs of slaves ranged between 1,000 and 2,000 acres. In every part of the South the majority of farmers cultivated no more than 200 acres, in many sections less than 100 acres. On the eve of the Civil War only one white family in four owned any slaves at all. A few large plantations and many small farms—this was the pattern.

There were few genuine economies of scale in

These reportorial views of slavery were sketched by a young Austrian, Franz Hölzlhuber, who toured the South between 1856 and 1860. Above is a rice plantation on the Arkansas River. The slaves at right, harvesting sugar cane in Louisiana, are dressed in striped garb to discourage attempts at escape.

southern agriculture. Small farmers grew the staple crops, and many of them owned a few slaves, often working beside them in the fields. These yeomen farmers were hardworking, self-reliant, and moderately prosperous, quite unlike the "poor white trash" of the pine barrens and the remote valleys of the Appalachians who scratched a meager subsistence from substandard soils and lived in ignorance and squalor.

Well-managed plantations yielded annual profits of 10 percent and more, and in general, money invested in southern agriculture earned at least a modest return. Considering the way the work force was exploited, this is hardly surprising. Recent estimates indicate that after allowing for the cost of land and capital, the average plantation slave "earned" cotton worth $78.78 in 1859. It cost masters about $32 a year to feed, clothe, and house a slave. In other words, almost 60 percent of the product of slave labor was expropriated by the masters.

The South failed to develop locally owned marketing and transportation facilities, and for this slavery was at least partly responsible. In 1840 *Hunt's Merchant Magazine* estimated that it cost $2.85 to move a bale of cotton from the farm to a seaport and that additional charges for storage, insurance, port fees, and freight to a European port exceeded $15. Middlemen from outside the South commonly earned most of this money. New York capitalists gradually came to control much of the South's cotton from the moment it was picked, and a large percentage of the crop found its way into New York warehouses before being sold to manufacturers. The same middlemen supplied most of the foreign goods that the planters purchased with their cotton earnings.

Southerners complained about this state of affairs but did little to correct it. Capital tied up in the ownership of labor could not be invested in anything else, and social pressures in the South militated against investment in trade and commerce. Ownership of land and slaves yielded a kind of psychic income not available to any middleman. As one British visitor pointed out, the southern blacks were "a nonconsuming class." Still more depressing, under slavery the enormous reservoir of intelligence and skill that the blacks represented was almost entirely wasted. Many slave artisans worked on the plantations, and a few free blacks made their way in the South remarkably well, but the amount of talent unused, energy misdirected, and imagination smothered can only be guessed.

Foreign observers in New England frequently noted the alertness and industriousness of ordinary laborers and attributed this, justifiably, to the high level of literacy. Nearly everyone in New England could read and write. Correspondingly, the stagnation and inefficiency of southern labor could be attributed in part to the high degree of illiteracy, for over 20 percent of *white* southerners could not read or write, another tragic squandering of human resources.

Antebellum Plantation Life

There was never any such thing as a "typical" plantation, but it is possible to describe, in a general way, what a medium-to-large operation employing 20 or more slaves was like in the two decades preceding the Civil War. Such a plantation was more like a small village than a northern-type agricultural unit, and in another way more like a self-sufficient colonial farm than a 19th-century commercial operation, although its major activity involved producing cotton or some other cash crop.

In addition to the master's house with its complement of barns and stables, there would usually be a kitchen, a smoke house, a wash house, a home for the overseer should one be employed, perhaps a schoolhouse, a gristmill, a forge, and of course the slave quarters, off at a distance (but not too far) from the center.

Slaveholding families were also quite different from northern families of similar status, in part because they were engaged in agriculture and in part because of their so-called peculiar institution. Husbands and wives did not function in separate spheres to nearly the same extent, though their individual functions were different and gender-related.

Although planter families purchased their fine clothes, furniture, and china, as well as other manufactured products such as sewing machines, cooking utensils, books, and musical instruments, plantations were busy centers of household manufacture, turning out most of the clothing of slaves except for shoes and the everyday clothing of their own children, along with bedding and other textiles. Spinning, weaving, and sewing were women's work, both for whites and blacks. Nearly all the food con-

Profits from cash crops allowed successful planters to build graceful homes like this one on the Mississippi River. The "Big House," in which the master and his family lived, might be a splendid mansion that offered imported luxuries, or a much simpler, plain wooden dwelling.

sumed was raised on the land; only tea and coffee and a few other food items were commonly purchased.

The master was in general charge and his word was law—the system was literally paternalistic. But his wife nearly always had immense responsibilities. Running the household meant supervising the servants (and punishing them when necessary, which often meant wielding a lash), nursing the sick, taking care of the vegetable and flower gardens, planning meals, and seeing to the education of her own children and the training of young slaves. It could also involve running the entire plantation on the frequent occasions when her husband was away on business. At the same time, her role entailed being a "southern lady," refined, graceful, supposedly untroubled by worldly affairs.

Most slaveholding women had to learn all these things by doing; in general, southern women mar-

ried while still in their teens and had been given little or no training in the household arts. Unmarried "young ladies" had few responsibilities beyond caring for their own rooms and persons and perhaps such "ladylike" tasks as arranging flowers.

The majority of the slaves of both sexes were field hands who labored on the land from dawn to dusk. Household servants and artisans, indeed any slave other than small children and the aged and infirm, might be called on for such labor when needed. Slave women were expected to cook for their own families and do other chores after working in the fields.

Children, free and slave, were cared for by slaves, the former by household servants, the latter usually by an elderly woman, perhaps with the help of a girl only a little older than the children. Infants were brought to their mothers in the fields for nursing several times a day, for after a month or two at most, slave mothers were required to go back to work. Slave children were not put to work until they were 6 or 7 and until they were about 10 were given only small tasks such as feeding the chickens or minding a smaller child. Black and white youngsters played together and were often cared for by the same nursemaid.

Slave cabins were simple and crude; most consisted of a single room, dark, with a fireplace for cooking and heat. Usually the flooring was raised above ground level, though some were set on the bare earth. Though certainly Spartan, these quarters compared favorably with those of European peasants of the time and the poorest white American farmers. And as Elizabeth Fox-Genovese explains in *Within the Plantation Household,* they were "primarily places to sleep, take shelter, and eat the last meal of the day," and "did not harbor the real life of slave families, much less the slave community."

The Sociology of Slavery

It is difficult to generalize about the peculiar institution because so much depended on the individual master's behavior. Owners exercised power over their human possessions "as absolute . . . as the Khan of Tartary." Asked about how slave "criminals" were dealt with, an ex-slave reported: "I ain't heard nothin' 'bout no jails. . . . What they done was 'most beat de life out of de niggers to make 'em behave." Yet most owners provided adequate clothing, housing, and food for their slaves. Only a fool or a sadist would fail to take care of such valuable property. However, vital statistics indicate that infant mortality among slaves was twice the white rate, life expectancy at least five years less. One student of this subject, Richard Sutch, concludes: "The returns from slavery were maximized by using force to extract the maximum amount of work from the slaves while providing them only with sufficient food, shelter, clothing, and health care to keep them healthy and hard working."

On balance, it is significant that the United States was the only nation in the Western Hemisphere where the slave population grew by natural increase. After the ending of the slave trade in 1808, the black population increased at nearly the same rate as the white. Put differently, during the entire period from

the founding of Jamestown to the Civil War, only a little more than half a million slaves were imported into the country, about 5 percent of the number of Africans carried by slavers to the New World. Yet in 1860 there were about 4 million blacks in the United States.

Most owners felt responsibilities toward their slaves, and slaves were dependent on and in some ways imitative of white values. However, powerful fears and resentments, not always recognized, existed on both sides. The plantation environment forced the two races to live in close proximity. From this circumstance could arise every sort of human relationship. One planter, using the appropriate pseudonym Clod Thumper, could write: "Africans are nothing but brutes, and they will love you better for whipping, whether they deserve it or not." Another, describing a slave named Bug, could say: "No one knows but myself what feeling I have for him. Black as he is we were raised together." One southern white woman tended a dying servant with "the kindest & most unremitting attention." Another, discovered crying after the death of a slave she had repeatedly abused, is said to have explained her grief by complaining that she "didn't have nobody to whip no more."

Such diametrically conflicting sentiments often existed within the same person. And almost no white southerners had any difficulty exploiting the labor of slaves for whom they felt genuine affection.

Slaves were without rights; they developed a distinctive way of life by attempting to resist oppression and injustice while accommodating themselves to the system. Their marriages had no legal status, but their partnerships seem to have been as loving and stable as those of their masters. Certainly they were acutely conscious of family relationships and responsibilities.

Slave religion, on the surface an untutored form of Christianity tinctured with some African survivals, seemed to most slave owners a useful instrument for teaching meekness and resignation and for providing harmless emotional release, which it sometimes was and did. However, religious meetings, secret and open, provided slaves with the opportunity to organize, which led at times to rebellions and more often to less drastic ways of resisting white domination. Religion also sustained the slaves' sense of their own worth as beings made in the image of

God, and it taught them, therefore, that while human beings can be enslaved in body, their spirits cannot be enslaved without their consent.

Nearly every white observer claimed that slaves were congenitally lazy; George Washington, for example, wrote that "when an overlooker's back is turned, the most of them will slight their work, or be idle altogether." Sarah Gayle, an admirable woman capable of showing real concern for her servants, could convince herself that her "indulgence" had made them all "idle and full of complaints," a charge that her journal, in which she described the activities of her household, totally disproves. If the typical slave was indeed lazy, it can be explained as a rational response to forced, uncompensated labor. As one planter confessed, slaves "are not stimulated to care and industry as white people are, who labor for themselves." "Laziness" was also a reflection of a peasantlike view of the world, one that was a product of their surroundings, not of their servile status. The historian Eugene D. Genovese says that owners might have liked their slaves to behave like clock-punching factory workers, but plantations were not factories, and no one, least of all the masters, punched a clock. "Do as I say, not as I do," is not an effective way of teaching anything. Moreover, it must be remembered that under slavery the "overlooker's back" was rarely turned. Slaves worked long and hard, whatever their innate tendencies might have been.

Observing that slaves often seemed happy and were only rarely overtly rebellious, whites persuaded themselves that most blacks accepted the system without resentment and indeed preferred slavery to the uncertainties of freedom. There was much talk about "loyal and faithful servants." The Civil War, when slaves flocked to the Union lines once assured of freedom and fair treatment, would disabuse them of this illusion.

As slaves rose in price and as northern opposition to the institution grew more vocal, the system hardened perceptibly. Southerners made much of the danger of insurrection. When a plot was uncovered or a revolt took place, instant and savage reprisals resulted. In 1822, after the conspiracy of Denmark Vesey was exposed by informers, 37 slaves were executed and another 30-odd deported, although no overt act of rebellion had occurred. After an uprising in Louisiana, 16 blacks were decapitated, their heads left to rot on poles along the Mississippi as a grim warning.

The Nat Turner revolt in Virginia in 1831 was the most sensational of the slave uprisings; 57 whites lost their lives before it was suppressed. Southerners treated runaways almost as brutally as rebels, though they posed no real threat to whites. The authorities tracked down fugitives with bloodhounds and subjected captives to merciless lashings.

After the Nat Turner revolt, interest in doing away with slavery vanished in the white South. The southern states made it increasingly difficult for masters to free their slaves; during 1859 only about 3,000 in a slave population of nearly 4 million were given their freedom.

Slavery did not flourish in urban settings, and cities did not flourish in societies where slavery was important. Most southern cities were small, and within them, slaves made up a small fraction of the labor force. The existence of slavery goes a long way toward explaining why the South was so rural and why it had so little industry. Blacks were much harder to supervise and control in urban settings. More important, as the historian Barbara Jeanne Fields has explained, there was a "profound basis for antagonism between slavery and urban development." Individual slaves were successfully employed in southern manufacturing plants, but they made up only an insignificant fraction of the South's small industrial labor supply. Wherever there was industrial development, the proportion of slaves in the population was declining.

Southern whites considered the existence of free blacks undesirable, no matter where they lived. The mere fact that they could support themselves disproved the notion that blacks were by nature childlike and shiftless, unable to work efficiently without white guidance. From the whites' point of view, free blacks set a bad example for slaves. At a minimum, the sight of "a vile and lazy free negro lolling in the sun-shine" might make slaves envious. Still worse, it might encourage them to try to escape, and worst of all, the free blacks might help them do so.

Many southern states passed laws aimed at forcing free blacks to emigrate, but these laws were not well enforced. There is ample evidence that the white people of, say, Maryland would have liked to get rid of the state's large free-black population. Free blacks were barred from occupations in which

Slave traders continued to smuggle their cargoes to America long after importation was outlawed. This engraving of the deck of the Wildfire *upon the ship's capture at Key West was published in* Harper's Weekly *in June 1860.*

they might cause trouble—no free black could be the captain of a ship, for example—and they were required by law to find a "respectable" white person who would testify as to their "good conduct and character." But whites did not try very hard to expel them, as Professor Fields has shown, because they needed their labor.

Some unscrupulous southerners engaged in smuggling blacks from Africa. About 54,000 slaves were brought to America illegally after the trade was outlawed in 1808, not a very large number relative to the slave population. British, French, Portuguese, and American naval vessels patrolled the African coast continuously. The American navy alone seized more than 50 suspected slavers in the two decades before 1860. However, the fast, sharklike pirate cruisers were hard to catch, and the anti-slave-trade laws were imperfectly worded and unevenly enforced. Many accounts tell of slaves in America long after 1808 with filed teeth, tattoos, and other signs of African origin, yet no one owning

such a person was ever charged with the possession of contraband goods.

Psychological Effects of Slavery

The injustice of slavery needs no proof; less obvious is the fact that it had a corrosive effect on the personalities of southerners, slave and free alike. By "the making of a human being an animal without hope," the system bore heavily on all slaves' sense of their own worth. Some found the condition absolutely unbearable. They became the habitual runaways who collected whip scars like medals, the "loyal" servants who struck out in rage against a master knowing that the result would be certain death, and the leaders of slave revolts.

Denmark Vesey of South Carolina, even after buying his freedom, could not stomach the subservience demanded of slaves by the system. When he saw Charleston slaves step into the gutter to make way for whites, he taunted them: "You deserve to remain slaves!" For years he preached resistance to his fellows, drawing his texts from the Declaration of Independence and the Bible and promising help from black Haiti. So vehemently did he argue that some of his followers claimed they feared Vesey more than their masters, even more than God. He planned his uprising for five years, patiently working out the details, only to see it aborted at the last moment when a few of his recruits lost their nerve and betrayed him. For Denmark Vesey, death was probably preferable to living with such rage as his soul contained.

Yet Veseys were rare. Most slaves appeared, if not contented, at least resigned to their fate. Many seemed even to accept the whites' evaluation of their inherent abilities and place in society. Of course, in most instances it is impossible to know whether or not this apparent subservience was feigned in order to avoid trouble.

Slaves had strong family and group attachments and a complex culture of their own, maintained, so to speak, under the noses of their masters. By a mixture of subterfuge, accommodation, and passive resistance, they erected subtle defenses against exploitation, achieving a sense of community that helped sustain the psychic integrity of individuals. But slavery discouraged, if it did not extinguish, independent judgment and self-reliance. These

In the 1800s, a few artists recorded scenes of slave life. Benjamin Latrobe called this watercolor "Preparation for the enjoyment of a fine Sunday." In their limited free time, slaves attended religious services, sang, danced, and relaxed with friends and family.

qualities are difficult enough to develop in human beings under the best circumstances; when every element in white society encouraged slaves to let others do their thinking for them, to avoid questioning the status quo, to lead a simple, animal existence, many did so willingly enough. Was this not slavery's greatest shame?

Slavery also warped the whites. Professor Fox-Genovese has shown how slaveholders developed contradictory stereotypes of slave nature. They described black men either as "Sambos" (lazy and subservient) or "Bucks" (superpotent and aggressive), females either as "Mammys" (nurturing and faithful) or "Jezebels" (wanton and seductive). The Sambo image enabled idle slave owners to exact labor from their slaves by brute force and justify their cruel whips by arguing that *black* men were

inherently lazy. Buck, Fox-Genovese argues, was a reversal of the white ideal of a southern cavalier, morally inferior, thus properly kept in bondage. And by picturing black men as sexual threats to white women, slaveholders could avoid facing the fact that they could and often did take advantage of their power to avail themselves of black women. (Estimates of the proportion of the slave population fathered by whites range from 4 to 8 percent.) As for Jezebel, that stereotype "legitimated the wanton behavior of white men by proclaiming black women to be lusty wenches in whom sexual impulse overwhelmed all restraint." By contrast, Mammy was a way that whites "displaced [black women's normal] sexuality into nurture" and "potential hostility into sustenance and love."

The harm done to the slaves by such mental

distortions is obvious. More obscure is the effect on the masters: Self-indulgence is perhaps only contemptible; self-delusion is pitiable and ultimately destructive.

Probably the large majority of owners respected the most fundamental personal rights of their slaves. Indeed, so far as sexual behavior is concerned, there are countless known cases of lasting relationships based on love and mutual respect between owners and what law and the community defined as their property. But the psychological injury inflicted on whites by slavery can be demonstrated without resort to Freudian insights. By associating working for others with servility, it discouraged many poor southerners from hiring out to earn a stake. It provided the weak, the shiftless, and the unsuccessful with a scapegoat that made their own miserable state easier to bear but harder to escape.

More subtly, the patriarchal nature of the slave system reinforced the already existing tendency toward male dominance over wives and children typical of the larger society. For men of exceptional character, the responsibilties of ownership could be ennobling, but for hotheads, alcoholics, or others with psychological problems, the power could be brutalizing, with terrible effects on the whole plantation community, whites and blacks alike.

Aside from its fundamental immorality, slavery caused basically decent people to commit countless petty cruelties. "I feel badly, got very angry and whipped Lavinia," one Louisiana woman wrote in her diary. "O! for government over my temper." But for slavery, she would surely have had better self-control. Similar, though again more subtle, was the interaction of the institution with the American tendency to brag and bluster. "You can manage ordinary niggers by lickin' 'em and by givin' 'em a taste of hot iron once in a while when they're extra ugly," one uncouth Georgian was heard to say at a slave auction shortly before the Civil War. "But if a nigger ever sets himself up against me, I can't never have any patience with him. I just get my pistol and shoot him right down; and that's the best way." With the price of slaves as high as it was, this was probably just talk, but bad talk, harmful to speaker and listener alike. Northern braggarts, perforce, were less objectionable.

Still, braggarts are inconsequential in most social situations; historians need seldom pay them much

heed. However, the finest white southerners were often warped by the institution. Even those who abhorred slavery sometimes let it corrupt their thinking: "I consider the labor of a breeding woman as no object, and that a child raised every 2 years is of more profit than the crop of the best laboring man." This cold calculation came from the pen of the author of the Declaration of Independence.

Manufacturing in the South

Although the temper of southern society discouraged business and commercial activities, considerable manufacturing developed. Small flour and lumber mills flourished. Iron and coal were mined in Virginia, Kentucky, and Tennessee. In the 1850s the Tredegar Iron Works in Richmond did an annual business of about $1 million.

The availability of the raw material and the abundance of waterpower along the Appalachian slopes made it possible to manufacture textiles profitably in the South. By 1825 a thriving factory was functioning at Fayetteville, North Carolina, and soon others sprang up elsewhere in North Carolina and in adjoining states. William Gregg's factory, at Graniteville, South Carolina, established in 1846, was a constant moneymaker. An able propagandist as well as a good businessman, Gregg saw the textile business not only as a source of profit but also as a device for improving the lot of the South's poor whites. He worked hard to weaken the southern prejudice against manufacturing and made his plant a model of benevolent paternalism similar to that of the early mills of Lowell. As with every other industry, however, southern textile manufacturing amounted to very little when compared with that of the North. Gregg employed only about 300 textile workers in 1850, the whole state of South Carolina fewer than 900. Lowell, Massachusetts, had more spindles turning in 1860 than the entire South.

Less than 15 percent of all the goods manufactured in the United States in 1860 came from the South; the region did not really develop an industrial society. Its textile manufacturers depended on the North for machinery, for skilled workers and technicians, for financing, and for insurance. When the English geologist Charles Lyell visited New Orleans in 1846, he was astounded to discover that the thriving city supported not a single book publisher.

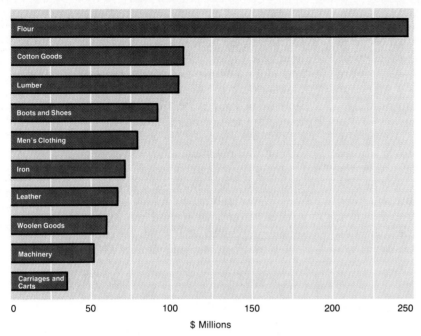

The leading American industries as listed in the 1860 census of manufacturers are ranked here by value of product. The boot and shoe industry employed the most workers—123,000. Next were cotton goods and men's clothing, each with just under 115,000 workers.

TEN LEADING MANUFACTURED PRODUCTS, 1860

Even a local guidebook that he purchased bore a New York imprint.

The Northern Industrial Juggernaut

The most obvious change in the North in the decades before the Civil War was the rapid growth of industry. The best estimates suggest that immediately after the War of 1812, the United States was manufacturing annually less than $200 million worth of goods. In 1859 the northeastern states alone produced $1.27 billion of the national total of almost $2 billion.

Manufacturing expanded in so many directions that it is difficult to portray or to summarize its evolution. The factory system made great strides. The development of rich anthracite coal fields in Pennsylvania was particularly important in this connection. The coal could be floated cheaply on canals to convenient sites and used to produce both heat for smelting and metalworking and steam power to drive machinery. Steam permitted greater flexibility in locating factories and in organizing work within them, and since waterpower was already being used to capacity, steam was essential for the expansion of output.

American industry displayed a remarkable receptivity to technological change. In *March of the Iron Men*, Roger Burlingame provides a long list of inventions and processes developed between 1825 and 1850, including—besides such obviously important items as the sewing machine, the vulcanization of rubber, and the cylinder press—the screw-making machine, the friction match, the lead pencil, and an apparatus for making soda water. A society in flux put a premium on resourcefulness; an environment that offered so much freedom to the individual encouraged experimentation. The expanding market inspired businessmen to use new techniques. With skilled labor always in short supply, the pressure to substitute machines for trained hands was great.

In the 1820s a foreign visitor noted: "Everything new is quickly introduced here, and all the latest inventions. . . . The moment an American hears the word *invention* he pricks up his ears." Twenty years later a Frenchman wrote: "If they continue to work with the same ardor, they will soon have nothing more to desire or to do. All the mountains will be flattened, the valleys filled, all matter rendered productive." By 1850 the United States led the world in the manufacture of goods that required the use of precision instruments, and in certain industries the country was well on the way toward modern mass production methods. American clocks, pistols, rifles, and locks were outstanding.

The American exhibits at the London Crystal Palace Exhibition of 1851 so impressed the British that they sent two special commissions to the United States to study manufacturing practices. After visiting the Springfield Arsenal, where a worker took apart ten muskets, each made in a different year, mixed up the parts, and then reassembled the guns, each in perfect working order, the British investigators placed a large order for gunmaking machinery. They also hired a number of American technicians to help organize what became the Enfield rifle factory. They were amazed by the lock and clock factories of New England and by the plants where screws, files, and similar metal objects were turned out in volume by automatic machinery. Instead of resisting new laborsaving machines, the investigators noted, "the workingmen hail with satisfaction all mechanical improvements."

Invention alone does not account for the industrial advance. Every year new natural resources were discovered and made available by the westward march of settlement, and the expansion of agriculture produced an ever-larger supply of raw materials for the mills and factories. Of the ten leading

The 1853 New York Crystal Palace Exhibition celebrated American ingenuity in manufacturing and agriculture. The huge glass and iron building shown in this color lithograph was modeled on London's Crystal Palace. The exhibits displayed impressive examples of American inventions and industrial progress. The building was gutted by fire in 1856.

industries in 1860, eight (flour milling, cotton textiles, lumber, shoes, men's clothing, leather, woolen goods, and liquor) relied on farm products for their raw materials.

In the 1850s the earlier prejudice against the corporation began to break down; by the end of the decade the northern and northwestern states had all passed general incorporation laws. Of course, the corporate device made possible larger accumulations of capital. While the federal government did not charter business corporations, two actions of Congress illustrate the shift in public attitudes. In 1840 a group of scientists sought a federal charter for a National Institution for the Promotion of Science. They were turned down on constitutional grounds; if Congress "went on erecting corporations in this way," one legislator said, "they would come, at last, to have corporations for everything." In 1863, however, the bill creating the National Academy of Science went through both houses without debate.

Industrial growth led to a great increase in the demand for labor. The effects, however, were mixed. Skilled artisans, technicians, and toolmakers earned good wages and found it relatively easy to set themselves up first as independent craftsmen, later as small manufacturers. The expanding frontier drained off much agricultural labor that might otherwise have been attracted to industry, and the thriving new towns of the West absorbed large numbers of eastern artisans of every kind. At the same time, the pay of an unskilled worker was never enough to support a family decently, and the new machines weakened the bargaining power of artisans by making skill less important.

Many other forces acted to stimulate manufacturing. As discussed earlier, immigration increased rapidly in the 1830s and 1840s. An avalanche of strong backs, willing hands, and keen minds descended on the country from Europe. European investors poured large sums into the booming American economy, and the savings of millions of Americans and the great hoard of new California gold added to the supply of capital. Improvements in transportation, the growth of the population, the absence of internal tariff barriers, and the relatively high per capita wealth of the people all meant an ever-expanding market for manufactured goods.

Self-generated Expansion

The pace of the advance is best explained by the many interactions that industrial activity produced. The cotton textile business was clearly the most important example. Samuel Slater built his first machines in his own little plant, but soon the industry spawned dozens of companies devoted to the manufacture of looms, spinning frames, and other machines. They in turn stimulated the growth of machine-tool production, metalworking companies, and eventually the mining and refining of iron. "For a considerable . . . period," George S. Gibb wrote in *Textile Machinery Building in New England, 1813–1849,* "the manufacture of textile machinery appears to have been America's greatest heavy goods industry. . . . From the textile mills and the textile machine shops came the men who supplied most of the tools for the American Industrial Revolution."

Other examples abound. The invention of the sewing machine in 1846 by Elias Howe (who got his early training in a Lowell cotton-machine factory) resulted in the creation of the ready-made clothing industry. The sewing machine also revolutionized the shoe industry, speeding the trend toward factory production and triggering the same kind of secondary growth that occurred in the textile business. The new agricultural machinery business, besides stimulating other industries, made possible a huge expansion of farm production, which stimulated economic growth still more.

A Nation of Immigrants

Rapid industrialization influenced American life in countless ways, none more significant than its effect on the character of the work force and consequently on the structure of society. The jobs created by industrial expansion attracted European immigrants by the tens of thousands. It is a truism that America is a nation of immigrants—even the ancestors of the Indians came to the New World from Asia. But only with the development of nationalism, that is, with the establishment of the independent United States, did the word *immigrant,* meaning a foreign-born resident, come into existence.

The "native" population (native in this case

BOOM AND BUST IN THE EARLY REPUBLIC, 1790–1860

The price scale on the left axis applies to the blue line and shows changes in wholesale commodity prices as they rise above and fall below the base line of 100. During most of this era, wholesale prices were depressed. The base line of 100 is also the long-term trend line for the United States economy as a whole. The peaks and valleys above and below the long-term trend line give a general sense of boom and bust periods. The right axis and green line show, for comparison, the price of a year's tuition at Harvard College. In 1790 it was $24, but by 1860 it had risen to $104.

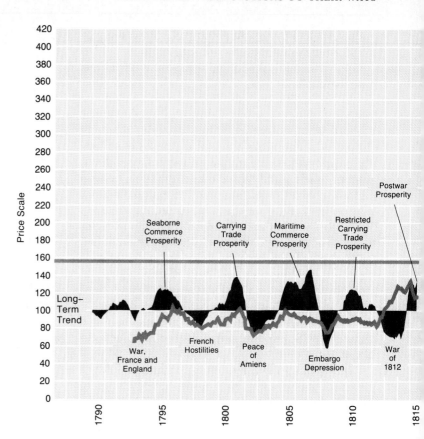

meaning those whose ancestors had come from Europe rather than the only true native Americans, the Indians) tended to look down on immigrants, and many of the immigrants, in turn, developed prejudices of their own. The Irish, for example, disliked the blacks, with whom they often competed for work. One Irish leader in the old country, Daniel O'Connell, admitted that the American Irish were "among the worst enemies of the colored race." And of course blacks responded with equal bitterness. "Every hour sees us elbowed out of some employment to make room for some newly arrived emigrant from the Emerald Isle, whose hunger and color entitle him to special favor," one of them complained. Antiblack prejudice was less noticeable among other immigrant groups but by no means absent; most immigrants adopted the views of the local majority, which was in every area unfriendly to blacks.

Social and racial rivalries aside, unskilled immigrants caused serious disruptions of economic patterns wherever they appeared. Their absorption into the factories of New England speeded the disintegration of the system of hiring young farm women. Already competition and technical advances in the textile industry were increasing the pace of the machines and reducing the number of skilled workers needed to run them. Fewer young farm women were willing to work under these conditions. Recent immigrants, who required less "coddling" and who seemed to provide the mills with a "permanent" working force, replaced the women in large numbers. By 1860 Irish immigrants alone made up more than 50 percent of the labor force in the New England mills.

How Wage Earners Lived

The influx of immigrants does not entirely explain the low standard of living of industrial workers during this period. Low wages and the crowding that resulted from the swift expansion of city populations produced slums that would make the most

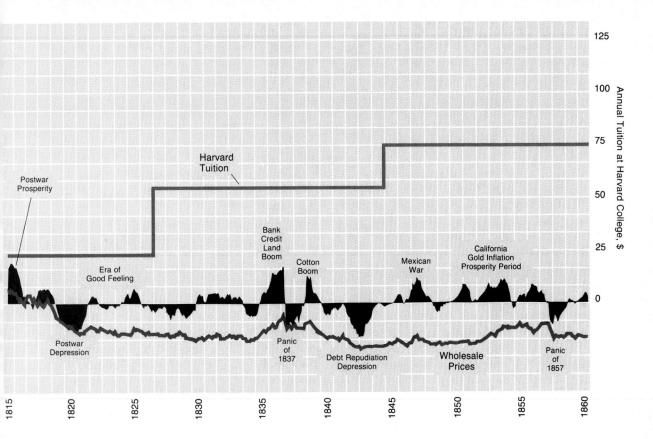

noisome modern ghetto seem a paradise. A Boston investigation in the late 1840s described one district as "a perfect hive of human beings . . . huddled together like brutes." In New York tens of thousands of the poor lived in dark, rank cellars, those in the waterfront districts often invaded by high tides. Tenement houses like great gloomy prisons rose back to back, each with many windowless rooms and often without heat or running water.

Out of doors, city life for the poor was almost equally squalid. Slum streets were littered with garbage and trash. Recreational facilities were almost nonexistent; work on Central Park in New York City, the first important urban park in the country, was not begun until the mid-1850s. Police and fire protection in the cities were pitifully inadequate. "Urban problems" were less critical than a century later only because they affected a smaller part of the population; for those who experienced them, they were, all too often, crushing. In the mid-1850s large numbers of children in New York scrounged a bare existence by begging and scavenging. They took shelter at night in coal bins and empty barrels.

In the early factory towns, most working families maintained small vegetable gardens and a few chickens; low wage rates did not necessarily reflect a low standard of living. But in the new industrial slums even a blade of grass was unusual. In 1851 the editor Horace Greeley's *New York Tribune* published a minimum weekly budget for a family of five. The budget, which allowed nothing for savings, medical bills, recreation, or other amenities (Greeley did include 12 cents a week for newspapers), came to $10.37. Since the weekly pay of a factory hand seldom reached $5, the wives and children of most male factory workers also had to labor in the factories merely to survive. And child labor in the 1850s differed fundamentally from child labor in the 1820s. The pace of the machines had become much faster by then, and the working environment more depressing.

Relatively few workers belonged to unions, but federations of craft unions sprang up in some cities, and during the boom that preceded the Panic of

1837, a National Trades Union representing a few northeastern cities managed to hold conventions. Early in the Jackson era, "workingmen's" political parties enjoyed a brief popularity, occasionally electing a few local officials. These organizations were made up mostly of skilled craftsmen, professional reformers, and even businessmen. They soon expired, destroyed by internal bickering over questions that had little or nothing to do with working conditions.

The depression of the late 1830s led to the demise of most trade unions. Nevertheless, skilled workers improved their lot somewhat in the 1840s and 1850s. The working day declined gradually from about 12½ hours to 10 or 11 hours. Many states passed 10-hour laws and laws regulating child labor, but they were poorly enforced. Most states, however, enacted effective mechanic's lien laws, giving workers first call on the assets of bankrupt and defaulting employers, and the Massachusetts court's decision in the case of *Commonwealth* v. *Hunt* (1842), establishing the legality of labor unions, became a judicial landmark when other state courts followed the precedent.

The flush times of the early 1850s caused the union movement to revive. Many strikes occurred, and a few new national organizations appeared. However, most unions were local institutions, weak and with little control over their membership. The Panic of 1857 dealt the labor movement another body blow. Thus there was no trend toward the general unionization of labor between 1820 and the Civil War.

For this the workers themselves were partly responsible: Craftsmen took little interest in unskilled workers except to keep them down. Few common laborers considered themselves part of a permanent working class with different objectives from those of their employers. Although hired labor had existed throughout the colonial period, it was only with the growth of factories and other large enterprises that significant numbers of people worked for wages. To many, wage labor seemed almost unAmerican, a violation of the republican values of freedom and independence that had triumphed in the Revolution. Jefferson's professed dislike of urban life was based in part on his fear that people who worked for wages would be so beholden to their employers that they could not act independently.

This republican value system, along with the fluidity of society, the influx of job-hungry immigrants, and the widespread employment of women and children in unskilled jobs, made labor organization difficult. The assumption was that nearly anyone who was willing to work could eventually escape from the wage-earning class. "If any continue through life in the condition of the hired laborer," Abraham Lincoln declared in 1859, "it is . . . because of either a dependent nature which prefers it, or improvidence, folly, or singular misfortune."

Progress and Poverty

Any investigation of American society before the Civil War reveals a paradox that is obvious but difficult to resolve. The United States was a land of opportunity, a democratic society with a prosperous, expanding economy and few class distinctions. Its people had a high standard of living in comparison with the citizens of European countries. Yet within this rich, confident nation there existed a class of miserably underpaid and depressed unskilled workers, mostly immigrants, who were worse off materially than nearly any southern slave. The literature is full of descriptions of needleworkers earning 12 cents a day, of women driven to prostitution because they could not earn a living decently, of hunger marches and soup kitchens, of disease and crime and people sunk into apathy by hopeless poverty. In 1848 more than 56,000 New Yorkers, about a quarter of the population, were receiving some form of public relief. A police drive in that city in 1860 brought in nearly 500 beggars.

The middle-class majority seemed indifferent to or at best unaware of these conditions. Reformers conducted investigations, published exposés, and labored to help the victims of urbanization and industrialization. They achieved little. Great fires burned in these decades to release the incredible energies of America. The poor were the ashes, sifting down silent and unnoticed beneath the dazzle and the smoke. While the industrial revolution was making the United States the most prosperous nation in the world, it was also creating, as the historian Robert H. Bremner has said, "a poverty problem, novel in kind and alarming in size." Industrialization produced poverty and riches (in Marxist terminology, a proletarian class and an aristocracy of capitalists). Tenements sprang up cheek by jowl with the urban palaces of the new rich and the tree-lined streets of the prosperous middle class.

Economic opportunities were great, and taxation was minimal. Little wonder that as the generations passed, the rich got richer. Industrialization accelerated the process and by stimulating the immigration of masses of poor workers skewed the social balance still further. Society became more stratified, and differences in wealth and status among citizens grew greater. But the ideology of egalitarian democracy held its own. By the mid-19th century, Americans were convinced that all men were equal, and indeed all *white* men had equal political rights. Socially and economically, however, the distances between top and bottom were widening. This situation endured for the rest of the century, and in some respects it still endures.

Foreign Commerce

Changes in the pattern of foreign commerce were less noticeable than those in manufacturing but were nevertheless significant. After increasing erratically during the 1820s and 1830s, both imports and exports leapt forward in the next 20 years. The nation remained primarily an exporter of raw materials and an importer of manufactured goods, and in most years it imported more than it exported. Cotton continued to be the most valuable export, in 1860 accounting for a record $191 million of total exports of $333 million. Despite America's own thriving industry, textiles still held the lead among imports, with iron products second. As in earlier days, Great Britain was both the best customer of the United States and its leading supplier.

The success of sailing packets, those "square-riggers on schedule," greatly facilitated the move-

Whaling voyages could last for three years as ships scoured the oceans for sperm whales. Once whales were sighted, crews in whaleboats chased and killed their prey. Here, a carcass has been towed back to the whaler to be stripped of blubber and other valuable parts. The blubber was boiled down into oil. The oil from one sperm whale could fill 45 barrels.

ment of passengers and freight. Fifty-two packets were operating between New York and Europe by 1845, and many more plied between New York and other American ports. The packets accelerated the tendency for trade to concentrate in New York and to a lesser extent in Philadelphia, Baltimore, and New Orleans. The commerce of Boston and smaller New England towns like Providence and New Haven, which had flourished in earlier days, now languished.

New Bedford and a few other southern New England towns shrewdly saved their prosperity by concentrating on whaling, which boomed between 1830 and 1860. The supply of whales seemed unlimited—as indeed it was, given the primitive hunting techniques of the age of sail. By the mid-1850s, with sperm oil selling at more than $1.75 a gallon and the country exporting an average of $2.7 million worth of whale oil and whalebone a year, New Bedford boasted a whaling fleet of well over 300 vessels and a population approaching 25,000.

The whalers ranged the oceans of the world; they lived a hard, lonely life punctuated by moments of exhilaration when they sighted the great mammoths of the deep and drove the harpoon home. They also made magnificent profits. To clear 100 percent in a single voyage was merely routine.

The increase in the volume and value of trade and its concentration at larger ports had a marked effect on the construction of ships. By the 1850s the average vessel was three times the size of those built 30 years earlier. Startling improvements in design, culminating in the long, sleek, white-winged clipper ships, made possible speeds previously undreamed of. Appearing just in time to supply the need for fast transportation to the California gold fields, the clippers cut sailing time around Cape Horn to San Francisco from five or six months to three, the record of 89 days being held jointly by the *Andrew Jackson* and Donald McKay's famous *Flying Cloud.* Another McKay-designed clipper, *Champion of the Seas,* once logged 465 nautical miles in 24 hours, far in excess of the best efforts of modern yachts. To achieve such speeds, cargo capacity had to be sacrificed, making clippers uneconomical for carrying the bulky produce that was the mainstay of commerce. But for specialty goods, in their brief heyday the clippers were unsurpassed. Hong Kong merchants, never known for extravagance, willingly

paid 75 cents a cubic foot to ship tea by clipper to London even though slower vessels charged only 28 cents. In the early 1850s clippers sold for as much as $150,000; with decent luck a ship might earn its full cost in a voyage or two.

Steam Conquers the Atlantic

The reign of the clipper ship was short. Like so many other things, ocean commerce was being mechanized. Steamships conquered the high seas more slowly than the rivers because early models were unsafe in rough waters and uneconomical. A riverboat could take on fuel along its route, whereas an Atlantic steamer had to carry tons of coal across the ocean, thereby reducing its capacity for cargo. However, by the late 1840s, steamships were capturing most of the passenger traffic, mail contracts, and first-class freight. These vessels could not keep up with the clippers in a heavy breeze, but their average speed was far greater, especially on the westward voyage against the prevailing winds. Steamers were soon crossing the Atlantic in less than ten days. Nevertheless, for very long voyages, such as the 15,000-mile haul around South America to California, fast-sailing ships held their own for many years.

The steamship, and especially the iron ship, which had greater cargo-carrying capacity and was stronger and less costly to maintain, took away the advantages that American shipbuilders had held since colonial times. American lumber was cheap, but the British excelled in iron technology. Although the United States invested about $14.5 million in subsidies for the shipping industry, the funds were not employed intelligently and did little good. In 1858 government efforts to aid shipping were abandoned.

The combination of competition, government subsidy, and technological advance drove down shipping rates. Between the mid-1820s and the mid-1850s the cost of moving a pound of cotton from New York to Liverpool fell from 1 cent to about a third of a cent. Transatlantic passengers could obtain the best accommodations on the fastest ships for under $200, good accommodations on slower packets for as little as $75.

Rates were especially low for European emi-

Commerce on the lower Mississippi depended heavily on steamboats, because railroads were far less extensive in the South than in the North.

grants willing to travel to America on cargo vessels. By the 1840s at least 4,000 ships were engaged in carrying bulky American cotton and Canadian lumber to Europe. On their return trips with manufactured goods they had much unoccupied space, which they converted into rough quarters for passengers. Conditions on these ships were crowded, gloomy, and foul. Frequently, epidemics took a fearful toll among steerage passengers. On one crossing of the ship *Lark,* 158 of 440 passengers died of typhus.

Yet without this cheap means of transportation, thousands of poor immigrants would simply have remained at home. Bargain freight rates also help explain the clamor of American manufacturers for high tariffs, for transportation costs added relatively little to the price of European goods.

Canals and Railroads

Another dramatic change was the shift in the direction of the nation's internal commerce and its immense increase. From the time of the first settlers in the Mississippi Valley, the Great River had controlled the flow of goods from farm to market. The completion of the Erie Canal in 1825 heralded a shift, speeded by the feverish canal construction of the following decade. In 1830 there were 1,277 miles of canal in the United States; by 1840 there were 3,326 miles.

Each year saw more western produce moving to market through the canals. In 1845 the Erie was still drawing over two-thirds of its west-east traffic from within New York, but by 1847, despite the fact that this local business held steady, more than half of its traffic came from west of Buffalo, and by 1851 more than two-thirds. The volume of western commerce over the Erie in 1851 amounted to more than 20 times what it had been in 1836, while the value of western goods reaching New Orleans in this period increased only $2\frac{1}{2}$ times.

The expanding traffic and New York's enormous share of it caused businessmen in other eastern cities whose canal projects had been unsuccessful to respond promptly when a new means of transport, the railroad, became available. The first railroads were built in England in the 1820s. In 1830 the first American line, the ambitiously named Baltimore and Ohio Railroad, carried 80,000 passengers over a 13-mile stretch of track. By 1833 Charleston, South Carolina, had a line reaching 136 miles to Hamburg, on the Savannah River. Two years later the cars began rolling on the Boston and

Worcester Railroad. The Panic of 1837 slowed construction, but by 1840 the United States had 3,328 miles of track, equal to the canal mileage and nearly double the railroad mileage of all Europe.

The first railroads did not compete with the canals for intersectional traffic. The through connections needed to move goods economically over great distances materialized slowly. Of the 6,000 miles of track operating in 1848, nearly all lay east of the Appalachians, and little of it had been coordinated into railroad systems. The intention of most early builders had been to monopolize the trade of surrounding districts, not to establish connections with competing centers. Frequently, railroads used tracks of different widths deliberately to prevent other lines from tying into their tracks.

Engineering problems held back growth. Steep grades and sharp curves—unavoidable in many parts of the country if the cost of the roads was not to be prohibitive—required more powerful and flexible engines than yet existed. Sparks from wood-burning locomotives caused fires. Wooden rails topped with strap iron wore out quickly and broke loose under the weight and vibration of heavy cars. In time the iron T rail and the use of crossties set in loose gravel to reduce vibration increased the durability of the tracks and made possible heavier, more efficient equipment. Modifications in the design of locomotives enabled the trains to negotiate sharp curves. Engines that could burn hard coal appeared, thereby eliminating the danger of starting fires along the right-of-way and reducing fuel costs.

Between 1848 and 1852 railroad mileage nearly doubled. Three years later it had doubled again, and by 1860 the nation had 30,636 miles of track. During this extraordinary burst of activity, four companies drove lines of gleaming iron from the Atlantic seaboard to the great interior valley. In 1851 the Erie, longest road in the world with 537 miles of track, linked the Hudson River north of New York City with Dunkirk on Lake Erie. Late the next year the Baltimore and Ohio reached the Ohio River at Wheeling, and in 1853 a banker named Erastus Corning consolidated eight short lines connecting Albany and Buffalo to form the New York Central. Finally, in 1858 the Pennsylvania Railroad completed a line across the mountains from Philadelphia to Pittsburgh.

In the states beyond the Appalachians, building went on at an even more feverish pace. In the 1850s builders in Ohio laid more than 2,300 miles of track, in Illinois more than 2,600, in Wisconsin nearly 900. By 1855 passengers could travel from Chicago or St. Louis to the East Coast at a cost of $20 to $30, the trip taking, with luck, less than 48 hours. A generation earlier such a trip required two to three weeks. Construction was slower in the South: Mississippi laid about 800 miles, Alabama 600.

Financing the Railroads

Railroad building required immense amounts of labor and capital at a time when many other demands for these resources existed. Immigrants or (in the South) slaves did most of the heavy work. Raising the necessary money proved a more complex task.

Private investors supplied about three-quarters of the money invested in railroads before 1860, more than $800 million in the 1850s alone. Much of this capital came from local merchants and businessmen and from farmers along the proposed rights-of-way. Funds were easy to raise because subscribers seldom had to lay out the full price of their stock at one time; instead they were subject to periodic "calls" for a percentage of their commitment as construction progressed. If the road made money, much of the additional mileage could be paid for out of earnings from the first sections built. The Utica and Schenectady Railroad, one of the lines that became part of the New York Central, was capitalized in 1833 at $2 million (20,000 shares at $100). Only $75 per share was ever called; in 1844 the road had been completed, shares were selling at $129, and shareholders were receiving handsome cash dividends.

The Utica and Schenectady was a short road in a rich territory; for less favorably situated lines, stocks were hard to sell. Of the lines connecting the seaboard with the Middle West, the New York Central alone needed no public aid, chiefly because it ran through prosperous, well-populated country and across level terrain. The others were all "mixed enterprises," drawing about half their capital from state and local governments.

Public aid took many forms. Towns, counties, and the states themselves lent money to railroads and invested in their stock. Special privileges, such as exemption from taxation and the right to condemn property, were often granted, and in a few cases states built and operated roads as public corporations.

As with earlier internal improvement proposals, federal financial aid to railroads was usually blocked in Congress by a combination of eastern and southern votes. But in 1850 a scheme for granting federal lands to the states to build a line from Lake Michigan to the Gulf of Mexico passed both houses. The main beneficiary was the Illinois Central Railroad, which received a 200-foot right-of-way and alternate strips of land along the track 1 mile wide and 6 miles deep, a total of almost 2.6 million acres. By mortgaging this land and by selling portions of it to farmers, the Illinois Central raised nearly all the $23.4 million it spent on construction. The success of this operation led to additional grants of almost 20 million acres in the 1850s, benefiting more than 40 railroads. Far larger federal grants were made after the Civil War, when the transcontinental lines were built.

Frequently, the capitalists who promoted railroads were more concerned with making money out of the construction of the lines than with operating them. The banker Erastus Corning was a good railroad man; his lines were well maintained and efficiently run. Yet he was also mayor of Albany, an important figure in state and national politics, and a manufacturer of iron. He accepted no salary as president of the Utica and Schenectady, "asking only that he have the privilege of supplying all the rails, running gear, tools and other iron and steel articles used." When he could not himself produce rails of the proper quality, he purchased them in England, charging the railroad a commission for his services. Corning's actions led to stockholder complaints, and a committee was appointed to investigate. He managed to control this group easily enough, but it did report that "the practice of buying articles for the use of the Railroad Company from its own officers might in time come to lead to abuses of great magnitude." The prediction proved all too accurate in the generation following the Civil War.

Corning, it must be emphasized, was honest enough; his mistake, if mistake it was, lay in overestimating his own impartiality a little. Others in the business were unashamedly crooked and avidly took advantage of the public passion for railroads.

This Illinois Central advertisement offers land for sale along its right of way. By encouraging settlement, railroads helped develop the lands beyond the Appalachians. By mid-century, a network of rail lines crisscrossed the Northeast and Midwest, hauling freight and passengers between rural and urban areas.

ILLINOIS CENTRAL RAILROAD COMPANY
OFFER FOR SALE
ONE MILLION ACRES OF SUPERIOR FARMING LANDS,
IN FARMS OF
40, 80 & 160 acres and upwards at from $8 to $12 per acre.
THESE LANDS ARE
NOT SURPASSED BY ANY IN THE WORLD.
THEY LIE ALONG
THE WHOLE LINE OF THE CENTRAL ILLINOIS RAILROAD.
For Sale on LONG CREDIT, SHORT CREDIT and for CASH, they are situated near TOWNS, VILLAGES, SCHOOLS and CHURCHES.

Some officials issued stock to themselves without paying for it and then sold the shares to gullible investors. Others manipulated the books of their corporations and set up special construction companies and paid them exorbitant returns out of railroad assets. These practices did not become widespread until after the Civil War, but all of them first sprang up in the period now under discussion. At the same time that the country was first developing a truly national economy, it was also producing its first really big-time crooks.

Railroads and the Economy

The effects of so much railroad construction were profound. Though the main reason that farmers put more land under the plow was an increase in the price of agricultural products, the railroad helped determine just what land was used and how profitably it could be farmed. Much of the fertile prairie through which the Illinois Central ran had been available for settlement for many years before 1850, but development had been slow because it was remote from navigable waters and had no timber. In 1840 the three counties immediately northeast of Springfield had a population of about 8,500. They produced about 59,000 bushels of wheat and 690,000 bushels of corn. In the next decade the region grew slowly by the standards of that day: The three counties had about 14,000 people in 1850 and produced 71,000 bushels of wheat and 2.2 million bushels of corn. Then came the railroad and with it an agricultural revolution. By 1860 the population of the three counties had soared to over 38,000, wheat production had topped 550,000 bushels, and corn 5.7 million bushels. "Land-grant" railroads such as the Illinois Central stimulated agricultural expansion by advertising their lands widely and selling farm sites at low rates on liberal terms.

Access to world markets gave the farmers of the upper Mississippi Valley an incentive to increase output. Land was plentiful and cheap, but farm labor was scarce; consequently, agricultural wages rose sharply, especially after 1850. New tools and machines appeared in time to ease the labor shortage. First came the steel plowshare, invented by John Deere, a Vermont-born blacksmith who had

moved to Illinois in 1837. The prairie sod was tough and sticky, but Deere's smooth metal plows cut through it easily. In 1839 Deere turned out ten such plows in his little shop in Moline, Illinois. By 1857 he was selling 10,000 a year.

Still more important was the perfection of the mechanical reaper, for wheat production was limited more by the amount that farmers could handle during the brief harvest season than by the acreage they could plant and cultivate. The major figure in the development of the reaper was Cyrus Hall McCormick. McCormick's horse-drawn reaper bent the grain against the cutting knife and then deposited it neatly on a platform, whence it could easily be raked into windrows. With this machine, two workers could cut 14 times as much wheat as with scythes.

McCormick prospered, but despite his patents, he could not keep other manufacturers out of the business. Competition led to continual improvement of the machines and kept prices within the reach of most farmers. Installment selling added to demand. By 1860 nearly 80,000 reapers had been sold; their efficiency helps explain why wheat output rose by nearly 75 percent in the 1850s.

The railroad had an equally powerful impact on American cities. The eastern seaports benefited, and so did countless intermediate centers, such as Buffalo and Cincinnati. But no city was affected more profoundly by railroads than Chicago. In 1850 not a single line had reached there; five years later it was terminal for 2,200 miles of track and controlled the commerce of an imperial domain. By extending half a dozen lines west to the Mississippi, it drained off nearly all the river traffic north of St. Louis. The Illinois Central sucked the expanding output of the prairies into Chicago as well. Most of this freight went eastward over the new railroads or on the Great Lakes and the Erie Canal. Nearly 350,000 tons of shipping plied the lakes by 1855.

The railroads, like the textile industry, stimulated other kinds of economic activity. They transformed agriculture, as we have seen; both real estate values and buying and selling of land increased whenever the iron horse puffed into a new district. The railroads spurred regional concentration of industry and an increase in the size of business units. Their insatiable need for capital stimulated the growth of investment banking. The complexity of their operations made them, as the historian Alfred

Cyrus McCormick invented his mechanical reaper on his father's farm in Virginia. However, he built his first factory in Chicago in 1847 and was soon supplying reapers to the rapidly expanding farms of the Midwest. The McCormick Reaper Factory, above, helped make Chicago the capital of the farm-machinery industry.

D. Chandler, Jr., writes, "the first modern business enterprises," the first to employ large numbers of salaried managers and to develop "a large internal organizational structure with carefully defined lines of responsibility."

Although they apparently did not have much effect on general manufacturing before the Civil War, the roads consumed nearly half the nation's output of bar and sheet iron in 1860. Probably more labor and more capital were occupied in economic activities resulting from the development of railroads than in the roads themselves—another way of saying that the railroads were immensely valuable internal improvements.

The proliferation of trunk lines and the competition of the canal system (for many products the slowness of canal transportation was not a serious handicap) led to a sharp decline in freight and passenger rates. Periodically, railroads engaged in "wars" to capture business. At times a person could travel from New York to Buffalo for as little as

$4; anthracite was being shipped from the Pennsylvania mines to the coast for $1.50 a ton. The Erie Canal reduced its toll charges by more than two-thirds in the face of railroad competition, and the roads in turn cut rates drastically until, on the eve of the Civil War, it cost less than 1 cent per ton-mile to send produce through the canal and only slightly more than 2 cents a mile on the railroads. By that time one could ship a bushel of wheat from Chicago to New York by railroad for less than 35 cents.

Cheap transportation had a revolutionary effect on western agriculture. Farmers in Iowa could now raise grain to feed the factory workers of Lowell and even of Manchester, England. Two-thirds of the meat consumed in New York City was soon arriving by rail from beyond the Appalachians. The center of American wheat production shifted westward to Illinois, Wisconsin, and Indiana. When the Crimean War (1853–1856) and European crop failures increased foreign demand, these regions boomed. Success bred success for farmers and for the railroads. Profits earned carrying wheat enabled the roads to build feeder lines that opened up still wider areas to commercial agriculture and made it easy to bring in lumber, farm machinery, household furnishings, and the settlers themselves at low cost.

Railroads and the Sectional Conflict

Increased production and cheap transportation boosted the western farmer's income and standard of living. The days of isolation and self-sufficiency, even for the family on the edge of the frontier, rapidly disappeared. Pioneers quickly became operators of businesses and, to a far greater extent than their forbears, consumers, buying all sorts of manufactured articles that their ancestors had made for themselves or done without. This had its cost. Like southern planters, they now became dependent on middlemen and lost some of their feeling of self-reliance. Overproduction became a problem. It began to take more capital to buy a farm, for as profits increased, so did the price of land. Machinery was an additional expense. The proportion of farm laborers and tenants increased.

The linking of East and West had fateful effects on politics. The increased ease of movement from section to section and the ever-more-complex social and economic integration of East and West stimulated nationalism and thus became a force for the preservation of the Union. Without the railroads and canals, Illinois and Iowa would scarcely have dared to side against the South in 1861. When the Mississippi ceased to be essential to them, citizens of the upper valley could afford to be more hostile to slavery and especially to its westward extension. Economic ties with the Northeast reinforced cultural connections.

The South might have preserved its influence in the Northwest if it had pressed forward its own railroad-building program. It failed to do so. There were many southern lines but nothing like a southern system. As late as 1856 one could get from Memphis to Richmond or Charleston only by very indirect routes. As late as 1859 the land-grant road extending the Illinois Central to Mobile, Alabama,

was not complete, nor did any economical connection exist between Chicago and New Orleans.

This state of affairs could be accounted for in part by the scattered population of the South, the paucity of passenger traffic, the seasonal nature of much of the freight business, and the absence of large cities. Southerners placed too much reliance on the Mississippi: The fact that traffic on the river continued heavy throughout the 1850s blinded them to the precipitous rate at which their relative share of the nation's trade was declining. But the fundamental cause of the South's backwardness in railroad construction was the attitude of its leaders. Southerners of means were no more interested in commerce than in industry; their capital found other outlets.

The Economy on the Eve of the Civil War

Between the mid-1840s and the mid-1850s the United States experienced one of the most remarkable periods of growth in the history of the world. Every economic indicator surged forward: manufacturing, grain and cotton production, population, railroad mileage, gold production, sales of public land. The building of the railroads stimulated business, and by making transportation cheaper, the completed lines energized the nation's economy. The American System that Henry Clay had dreamed of arrived with a rush just as Clay was passing from the scene.

Inevitably, this growth caused dislocations that were aggravated by the boom psychology that once again infected the popular mind. In 1857 there was a serious collapse. The return of Russian wheat to the world market after the Crimean War caused grain prices to fall. This checked agricultural expansion, which hurt the railroads and cut down on the demand for manufactures. Unemployment increased. Frightened depositors started runs on banks, most of which had to suspend specie payments.

People called this abrupt downturn the Panic of 1857. Yet the vigor of the economy was such that the bad times did not last long. The upper Mississippi Valley suffered most, for so much new land

PRIMARY RAILROADS, 1860

*This map shows trunk lines (lines carrying through traffic) in operation in
1860. Certain towns and cities owed their spectacularly rapid growth to the railroad, Chicago being an outstanding example. The map suggests the strong influence of the railroads on the expansion and economic prosperity of smaller cities
such as Fort Wayne, Milwaukee, and Nashville. At the outbreak of the Civil
War in 1861, the relative lack of railroads in the South was a bad omen for the
Confederacy. Note especially the gap at Chattanooga.*

383

had been opened up that supplies of farm produce greatly exceeded demand. Elsewhere conditions improved rapidly.

The South, somewhat out of the hectic rush to begin with, was affected very little by the collapse of 1857, for cotton prices continued high. This gave planters the false impression that their economy was immune to such violent downturns. Some began to argue that the South would be better off out of the Union.

Before a new national upward swing could become well established, however, the sectional crisis between North and South shook people's confidence in the future. Then the war came, and a new set of forces shaped economic development.

Milestones

1808	Congress bans further importation of slaves	**1842**	*Commonwealth* v. *Hunt* establishes the legality of unions
1822	"Conspiracy" of Denmark Vesey		
1825	Erie Canal completed	**1846**	Elias Howe invents the sewing machine
1830	Baltimore and Ohio Railroad begins operation	**1850**	Congress grants land to aid construction of the Illinois Central Railroad
1831	Nat Turner's slave uprising		
1837	Cyrus Hall McCormick opens reaper factory in Chicago	**1854**	Clipper ship *Flying Cloud* sails from New York to San Francisco in 89 days
1839	John Deere begins manufacturing steel plows		
1840–1857	Boom in manufacturing, railroad construction, and foreign commerce	**1857**	Brief economic depression (Panic of 1857)

SUPPLEMENTARY READING

Titles marked with an asterisk have been published in paperback.

Most of the volumes dealing with economic developments mentioned in Chapter 8 continue to be useful for this period. See especially G. R. Taylor, **The Transportation Revolution*** (1951), P. W. Gates, **The Farmer's Age*** (1960), D. C. North, **The Economic Growth of the United States*** (1961), and Stuart Bruchey, **The Roots of American Economic Growth*** (1965). On the Panic of 1857, see J. L. Huston, **The Panic of 1857 and the Coming of the Civil War** (1987).

An excellent survey of the antebellum South is Clement Eaton, **The Growth of Southern Civilization*** (1961). For more detailed coverage, see Gavin Wright, **The Political Economy of the Cotton South** (1978).

The literature on slavery is extensive and of high quality. See especially K. M. Stampp, **The Peculiar Institution*** (1956), E. D. Genovese, **Roll, Jordan, Roll*** (1975), Elizabeth Fox-Genovese, **Within the Plantation House-** hold* (1988), J. W. Blassingame, **The Slave Community*** (1972), L. W. Levine, **Black Culture and Black Consciousness** (1977), H. G. Gutman, **The Black Family in Slavery and Freedom** (1976), and Catharine Clinton, **Plantation Mistress** (1984). Among specialized volumes, Bertram Wyatt-Brown, **Southern Honor** (1982), and Ira Berlin, **Slaves Without Masters** (1975), provide important information about free blacks. On slave insurrections, E. D. Genovese, **From Rebellion to Revolution** (1979), and S. B. Oates, **The Fires of Jubilee: Nat Turner's Fierce Rebellion** (1975), are excellent. R. C. Wade, **Slavery in the Cities*** (1964), contains much interesting material, as does W. K. Scarborough, **The Overseer** (1966).

On industrial developments, in addition to the books mentioned in Chapter 9, see H. J. Habbakuk, **American and British Technology in the Nineteenth Century*** (1962), and Nathan Rosenberg, **Technology and Amer-**

ican Economic Growth (1972). On labor history, see Thomas Dublin, Women at Work (1977), R. A. Mohl, Poverty in New York (1971), and B. M. Wertheimer, We Were There (1977). For detals on workingmen's political activities, see Edward Pessen, Most Uncommon Jacksonians* (1967).

Immigration is dealt with in M. A. Jones, American Immigration* (1960), poverty in R. H. Bremner, From the Depths* (1956), and in Mohl's Poverty in New York. Taylor's Transportation Revolution is outstanding on de-

velopments in commerce and communication. J. F. Stover, Iron Road to the West (1978), provides a good survey of railroad building in the 1850s. Among the specialized studies of railroad development are T. C. Cochran, Railroad Leaders (1953), P. W. Gates, The Illinois Central Railroad and its Colonization Work (1934), E. C. Kirkland, Men, Cities, and Transportation (1948), and Albert Fishlow, American Railroads and the Transformation of the Ante-Bellum Economy (1965).

XV

The Coming of the Civil War

"*A house divided against itself cannot stand.*" I believe this government cannot endure permanently half slave and half free. I do not expect the Union to be dissolved; I do not expect the house to fall; but I do expect it will cease to be divided. It will become all one thing, or all the other.

ABRAHAM LINCOLN, *June 17, 1858*

The political settlement between North and South that Henry Clay designed in 1850 lasted only four years. One specific event wrecked it, but it was probably doomed in any case. Americans continued to migrate westward by the thousands, and as long as slaveholders could carry their human property into federally controlled territories, northern resentment would smolder. Slaves continued to seek freedom in the North, and the stronger federal Fugitive Slave Act did not guarantee their capture and return. Abolitionists intensified their propaganda.

The Slave Power Comes North

The new fugitive slave law encouraged more southerners to try to recover escaped slaves. Something approaching panic reigned in the black communities of northern cities after its passage. Thousands of blacks, not all of them former slaves, fled to Canada, but many remained. A few were arrested, generally without incident. However, not all the captives were in fact runaways, and northerners frequently refused to stand aside while these people were dragged off in chains.

Shortly after the passage of the act, a New Yorker, James Hamlet, was seized, convicted, and rushed off to slavery in Maryland without even being allowed to communicate with his wife and children. The New York black community was outraged, and with help from white neighbors it swiftly raised $800 to buy his freedom. In 1851 Euphemia Williams, who had lived for years as a free woman in Pennsylvania, was seized, her presumed owner claiming also her six children, all Pennsylvania-born. A federal judge released the Williamses, but the case caused alarm in the North.

Abolitionists often interfered with the enforcement of the law. When two Georgians came to Boston to reclaim William and Ellen Craft, admitted fugitives, a "vigilance committee" forced them to return home empty-handed. The Crafts prudently—or perhaps in disgust—decided to leave the United States for England. Early in 1851 a Virginia agent captured Frederick "Shadrach" Wilkins, a waiter in a Boston coffeehouse. While Wilkins was being held for deportation, a mob of blacks broke into the courthouse and freed him. That October a slave named Jerry, who had escaped from Missouri, was arrested in Syracuse, New York. Within minutes the whole town had the news. Crowds surged through the streets, and when night fell, a mob smashed into the building where Jerry was being held and spirited him away to safety in Canada.

Such incidents exacerbated sectional feelings. Southerners accused the North of reneging on one of the main promises made in the Compromise of 1850, while the sight of harmless human beings being hustled off to a life of slavery disturbed many northerners who were not abolitionists. Although most white northerners were probably not prepared to break it, in some states the Fugitive Slave Act became virtually unenforceable. Massachusetts passed a strong personal liberty law. When a newspaperman in Wisconsin was convicted of raising a mob to free a captured runaway, the state supreme court declared the Fugitive Slave Act unconstitutional and released him. After long delays the United States Supreme Court overruled this decision (*Ableman* v. *Booth*, 1859), but in the meantime the act was a dead letter in Wisconsin and in other states as well. In all, in the decade of the act's existence, about 300 fugitives were returned to their owners. In the process far larger numbers of white northerners got an eyewitness view of the heartlessness of slavery.

"Uncle Tom's Cabin"

Tremendously important in increasing sectional tensions and bringing home the evils of slavery to still more people in the North was Harriet Beecher Stowe's novel *Uncle Tom's Cabin* (1852). Stowe was neither a professional writer nor an abolitionist, and she had almost no firsthand knowledge of slavery. But her conscience had been roused by the Fugitive Slave Act. In gathering material for the book, she depended heavily on abolitionist writers, many of whom she knew. She dashed it off quickly; as she later recalled, it seemed to write itself. Nevertheless, *Uncle Tom's Cabin* was an enormous success: 10,000

copies were sold in a week, 300,000 in a year. It was translated into dozens of languages. Dramatized versions were staged in countries throughout the world.

Harriet Beecher Stowe was hardly a distinguished writer; it was her approach to the subject that explains the book's success. Her tale of the pious, patient slave Uncle Tom, the saintly white child Eva, and the callous slave driver Simon Legree appealed to an audience far wider than that reached by the abolitionists. She avoided the self-righteous, accusatory tone of most abolitionist tracts and did not seek to convert readers to belief in racial equality. Many of her southern white characters were fine, sensitive people, while the cruel Simon Legree was a transplanted Connecticut Yankee. There were many heartrending scenes of pain, self-sacrifice, and heroism. The story proved especially effective on the stage: The slave Eliza crossing the frozen Ohio River to freedom, the death of Little Eva, Eva and Tom ascending to Heaven—these scenes left audiences in tears.

Southern critics pointed out, correctly enough, that Stowe's picture of plantation life was distorted, her slaves atypical. They called her a "coarse, ugly, long-tongued woman" and accused her of trying to "awaken rancorous hatred and malignant jealousies" that would undermine national unity. Most northerners, having little basis on which to judge the accuracy of the book, tended to discount southern criticism as biased. In any case, *Uncle Tom's Cabin* raised questions that transcended the issue of accuracy. Did it matter if every slave was not as kindly as Uncle Tom, as determined as George Harris? What if only one white master was as evil as Simon Legree? No earlier white American writer had looked at slaves as people.

Uncle Tom's Cabin touched the hearts of millions. Some became abolitionists; others, still hesitating to step forward, asked themselves as they put the book down: Is slavery just?

A poster advertising Uncle Tom's Cabin *in 1852, the year of its publication. The following year, Stowe published* A Key to Uncle Tom's Cabin, *intended to provide documentary evidence in support of disputed details of her indictment of slavery.*

"Young America"

Clearly, a distraction was needed to help keep the lid on sectional troubles. Some people hoped to find one in foreign affairs. The spirit of manifest destiny explains this in large part; once the United States had reached the Pacific, expansionists began to think of transmitting the dynamic, democratic spirit of the United States to other countries by aiding local revolutionaries, opening up new markets, perhaps even annexing foreign lands.

This "Young America" spirit was partly emotional, a mindless confidence that democracy would triumph everywhere, that public opinion was "stronger than the Bayonet." At the time of the European revolutions of 1848, Americans talked freely about helping the liberals in their struggles against autocratic governments. Horace Greeley's *New York Tribune* predicted that Europe would soon become "one great and splendid Republic . . . and we shall all be citizens of the world." When the Austrians crushed a rebellion in Hungary, Secretary of State Daniel Webster addressed an insulting note full of vague threats to the Austrian chargé d'affaires in Washington. Hungarian revolutionary hero Louis Kossuth visited the United States in search of aid in 1851 and 1852; President Fillmore put U.S.S. *Mississippi* at his disposal, and great crowds turned out to cheer him.

The United States had no intention of going to war to win independence for the Hungarians, as Kossuth soon learned to his sorrow. However, the same democratic-expansionist sentiment led to dreams of conquests in the Caribbean area. In 1855 a freebooter named William Walker, backed by an American company engaged in transporting migrants to California across Central America, seized control of Nicaragua and elected himself president. He was ousted two years later but made repeated attempts to regain control until, in 1860, he died before a Honduran firing squad. Another would-be dictator, "General" George W. L. Bickley, claiming that he was disturbed by that "crookedest of all boundary lines, the Rio Grande," tried to organize an expedition to conquer Mexico.

Though many northerners suspected them of engaging in plots to obtain more territory for slavery, Walker and Bickley were primarily adventurers trying to use the prevailing mood of buoyant expansionism for selfish ends. But there were reasons unrelated to slavery why Central America suddenly seemed important. The rapid development of California created a need for improved communication with the West Coast. A canal across Central America would cut weeks from the sailing time between New York and San Francisco. In 1850 Secretary of State John M. Clayton and the British minister to the United States, Henry Lytton Bulwer, negotiated a treaty providing for the demilitarization and joint Anglo-American control of any canal across the isthmus.

As this area assumed strategic importance to the

MASTER JONATHAN TRIES TO SMOKE A CUBA, BUT IT DOESN'T AGREE WITH HIM!!

Despite opposition from European nations, expansionists in the United States believed Cuba should become an American possession. In 1850, a small private army left New Orleans for Cuba. The invaders were soon forced to flee. In this Punch *cartoon, the British delight in the failure of Master Jonathan—the United States—to seize Cuba.*

United States, the desire to obtain Cuba grew stronger. In 1854 President Franklin Pierce instructed his minister to Spain, Pierre Soulé of Louisiana, to offer $130 million for the island. Since Soulé was a hotheaded bungler, the administration arranged for him first to confer in Belgium with the American ministers to Great Britain and France, James Buchanan and John Y. Mason, to work out a plan for persuading Spain to sell. Out of this meeting came the Ostend Manifesto, a confidential dispatch to the State Department suggesting that if Spain refused to sell Cuba, "the great law of self-preservation" might justify "wresting" it from Spain by force.

News of the manifesto leaked out, and it had to be published. Northern opinion was outraged by this "slaveholders' plot." Europeans claimed to be shocked by such "dishonorable" and "clandestine" diplomacy. The government had to disavow the manifesto, and any hope of obtaining Cuba or any other territory in the Caribbean vanished.

The expansionist mood of the moment also explains President Fillmore's dispatching an expedition under Commodore Matthew C. Perry to try for commercial concessions in the isolated kingdom of Japan in 1852. Perry's expedition was a great success. The Japanese, impressed by American naval power, agreed to establish diplomatic relations. In 1858 an American envoy, Townsend Harris, negotiated a commercial treaty that opened to American ships six Japanese ports heretofore closed to foreigners. President Pierce's negotiation of a Canadian reciprocity treaty with Great Britain in 1854 and an unsuccessful attempt, also made under

Japanese artist Gessan Ogata painted this watercolor of Commodore Perry's "First landing at Kurihama, July 14, 1853." The "black ships" of Perry's squadron are in the background.

Pierce, to annex the Hawaiian Islands are further demonstrations of the assertive foreign policy of the period.

The Little Giant

The most prominent spokesman of the Young America movement was Stephen A. Douglas. The senator from Illinois was the Henry Clay of his generation. Like Clay at his best, Douglas was able to see the needs of the nation in the broadest perspective. He held a succession of state offices before being elected to Congress in 1842 at the age of 29. After only two terms in the House, he was chosen United States senator.

Douglas succeeded at almost everything he attempted. His law practice was large and prosperous. He dabbled in Chicago real estate and made a fortune. Politics suited him to perfection. Rarely has a man seemed so closely attuned to his time and place in history. Although very short, he had powerful shoulders, a large head, strong features, and deep-set, piercing eyes. His high forehead was made to appear even bolder by the way he wore his hair, swept back in a pompadour and draped over his collar. His appearance was so imposing that friends called him "the Little Giant." "I live with my con-

stituents," he once boasted, "drink with them, lodge with them, pray with them, laugh, hunt, dance, and work with them. I eat their corn dodgers and fried bacon and sleep two in a bed with them." Yet he was no mere backslapper. He read widely, wrote poetry, financed a number of young American artists, served as a regent of the Smithsonian Institution, and was interested in scientific farming.

The foundations of Douglas's politics were expansion and popular sovereignty. He had been willing to fight for all of Oregon in 1846, and he supported the Mexican War to the hilt, in sharp contrast to his one-term Illinois colleague in Congress, Abraham Lincoln. That local settlers should determine their own institutions was, to his way of thinking, axiomatic. Arguments over the future of slavery in the territories he believed a foolish waste of energy and time since he was convinced that natural conditions would keep the institution out of the West.

The main thing, he insisted, was to get on with the development of the United States. Let the nation build railroads, acquire new territory, expand its trade. He believed slavery "a curse beyond computation" for both blacks and whites, but he refused to admit that any moral issue was involved. He cared not, he boasted, whether slavery was voted up or voted down. This was not really true, but the question was interfering with the rapid exploitation of

"By God, sir, I made James Buchanan, and by God, sir, I will unmake him!" Stephen A. Douglas remarked with characteristic exaggeration during the debate over Kansas.

the continent. Douglas wanted it settled so that the country could concentrate on more important matters.

Douglas's success in steering the Compromise of 1850 through Congress added to his reputation. In 1851, he set out to win the Democratic presidential nomination, reasoning that since he was the brightest, most imaginative, and hardest-working Democrat around, he had every right to press his claim.

This brash aggressiveness proved his undoing. He expressed open contempt for James Buchanan and said of his other chief rival, Lewis Cass, who had won considerable fame while serving as minister to France, that his "reputation was beyond the C."

At the 1852 Democratic convention Douglas had no chance. Cass and Buchanan killed each other off, and the delegates finally chose a dark horse, Franklin Pierce of New Hampshire. The Whigs, rejecting the colorless Fillmore, nominated General Winfield Scott, who was known as Old Fuss and Feathers "because of his punctiliousness in dress and decorum." In the campaign both sides supported the Compromise of 1850. The Democrats won an easy victory, 254 electoral votes to 42.

So handsome a triumph seemed to ensure stability, but in fact it was a prelude to political chaos. The Whig party was crumbling fast. The "Cotton" Whigs of the South, alienated by the antislavery sentiments of their northern brethren, were flocking into the Democratic fold. In the North the radical "Conscience" Whigs and the "Silver Gray" faction that was undisturbed by slavery found themselves more and more at odds with each other. Congress fell overwhelmingly into the hands of proslavery southern Democrats, a development profoundly disturbing to northern Democrats as well as to Whigs.

The Kansas-Nebraska Act

Franklin Pierce was a youthful-appearing 48 when he took office. He was generally well liked by politicians. His career had included service in both houses of Congress. Alcohol had become a problem for him in Washington, however, and in 1842 he had resigned from the Senate and returned home to try to best the bottle, a struggle in which he was

successful. His law practice boomed, and he added to his reputation by serving as a brigadier general during the Mexican War. Though his nomination for president came as a surprise, once made, it had appeared perfectly reasonable. Great things were expected of his administration, especially after he surrounded himself with men of all factions: To balance his appointment of a radical states' rights Mississippian, Jefferson Davis, as secretary of war, for example, he named a conservative northerner, William L. Marcy of New York, as secretary of state.

Only a strong leader, however, can manage a ministry of all talents, and that President Pierce was not. He followed, as the historian Allan Nevins put it, a "policy of smiling on everybody but specially favoring both ends against the middle." The ship of state was soon drifting; Pierce seemed incapable of holding firm the helm.

This was the situation in January 1854 when Senator Douglas, chairman of the Committee on Territories, introduced what looked like a routine bill organizing the land west of Missouri and Iowa as Nebraska Territory. Since settlers were beginning to trickle into the area, the time had arrived to set up a civil administration. But Douglas also acted because a territorial government was essential to railroad development. As a director of the Illinois Central line and as a land speculator, he hoped to make Chicago the terminus of a transcontinental railroad, but construction could not begin until the route was cleared of Indians and brought under some kind of civil control.

Southerners, wishing to bring the transcontinental line to Memphis or New Orleans, pointed out that a right-of-way through organized territory already existed across Texas and New Mexico Territory. In 1853 the United States minister to Mexico, James Gadsden, a prominent southern railroad executive, had engineered the purchase of more than 29,000 square miles of Mexican territory south of the Gila River, which provided an easy route through the mountains for such a railroad. Douglas, whose vision of the economic potentialities of the nation was Hamiltonian, would have been willing to support the construction of two or even three transcontinental railroads, but he knew that Congress would not go that far. In any case, he believed that the Nebraska region must be organized promptly.

The Gadsden Purchase was signed on July 4, 1854, at Mesilla, New Mexico
Territory, in a formal ceremony attended by local residents. This painting was
executed by a Mesilla native to commemorate the event on its 75th anniversary.

The powerful southern faction in Congress would not go along with Douglas's proposal as it stood. The railroad question aside, Nebraska would presumably become a free state, for it lay north of latitude 36°30′ in a district from which slavery had been excluded by the Missouri Compromise. Under pressure from the southerners, led by Senator David R. Atchison of Missouri, Douglas agreed first to divide the region into two territories, Kansas and Nebraska, and then—a fateful concession—to repeal the part of the Missouri Compromise that excluded slavery from land north of 36°30′. Whether the new territories should become slave or free, he argued, should be left to the decision of the settlers in accordance with the democratic principle of popular sovereignty. The fact that he might advance his presidential ambitions by making concessions to the South must have influenced Douglas too, as must the local political situation in Missouri, where slaveholders feared being "surrounded" on three sides by free states.

Douglas's miscalculation of northern sentiment was monumental. It was one thing to apply popular sovereignty to the new territories in the Southwest, quite another to apply it to a region that had been part of the United States for half a century and free soil for 34 years. Word that the area was to be opened to slavery caused an indignant outcry; many moderate opponents of slavery were radicalized. A group of abolitionist congressmen issued what they called their "Appeal of the Independent Democrats" (actually, all were Free Soilers and Whigs) denouncing the Kansas-Nebraska bill as "a gross violation of a sacred pledge" and calling for a campaign of letter writing, petitions, and public meetings to prevent its passage. The unanimity and force of the northern public's reaction was like nothing in America since the days of the Stamp Act and the Intolerable Acts.

But protests could not defeat the bill. Southerners in both houses backed it regardless of party. Douglas, at his best when under attack, pushed it with all his power. The authors of the "Appeal," he charged, were "the pure unadulterated representatives of Abolitionism, Free Soilism, [and] Niggerism." President Pierce added whatever force the administration could muster. As a result, the northern Democrats split, and the bill became law late in May 1854. In this manner the nation took the greatest single step in its march toward the abyss of secession and civil war.

The repeal of the Missouri Compromise struck the North like a slap in the face—at once shameful and challenging. Presumably the question of slavery in the territories had been settled forever; now, seemingly without justification, it had been reopened. Two days after the Kansas-Nebraska bill passed the House of Representatives, Anthony Burns, a slave who had escaped from Virginia by stowing away on a ship, was arrested in Boston. A mob tried to free him but was thrown back by federal agents. President Pierce ordered the Boston district attorney to "incur any expense" to enforce the law, and he sent a revenue cutter to Boston to carry Burns back to Virginia. Troops were rushed to the scene to restrain the swelling crowds.

Burns was returned to his master, but it required two companies of artillery and 1,000 police and marines to get him aboard ship. As the grim parade marched past buildings festooned with black crepe, the crowd screamed, "Kidnappers! Kidnappers!" at the soldiers. Estimates of the cost of returning this single slave to his owner ran as high as $100,000. In previous cases Boston's conservative leaders,

Whig to a man, had tended to hold back; after the Burns incident, they were thoroughly radicalized. "We went to bed one night old fashioned . . . Whigs," one of them explained, "and waked up stark mad Abolitionists."

Know-Nothings and Republicans

There were 91 free-state Democrats in the House of Representatives when the Kansas-Nebraska Act was passed, only 25 after the next election. With the Whig party already moribund, dissidents flocked to two new parties.

One was the American, or "Know-Nothing," party, so called because it grew out of a secret society whose members used the password "I don't know." The Know-Nothings were primarily nativists—immigration was soaring in the early 1850s, and the influx of poor foreigners was causing genuine social problems. Crime was on the rise in the cities along with drunkenness and other "diseases of poverty."

Several emotion-charged issues related to the fact that a large percentage of the immigrants were Irish and German Catholics also troubled the Know-Nothings. Questions such as public financing of parochial schools, lay control of church policies, the prohibition of alcoholic beverages, and increasing the time before an immigrant could apply for citizenship (the Know-Nothings favored 21 years) were matters of major importance to them. Since these were divisive issues, the established political parties tried to avoid them; hence the development of the new party.

The American party was important in the South as well as in the North, and while most Know-Nothings disliked blacks and considered them inherently inferior beings, they tended to adopt the dominant view of slavery in whichever section they were located. In the North most opposed the Kansas-Nebraska Act.

Operating often in tacit alliance with the antislavery forces (dislike of slavery did not prevent many abolitionists from being prejudiced against Catholics and immigrants), the northern Know-Nothings won a string of local victories in 1854 and elected more than 40 congressmen.

Far more significant in the long run was the

KIDNAPPING
AGAIN!!
A MAN WAS STOLEN LAST NIGHT BY THE
Fugitive Slave Bill COMMISSIONER!
HE WILL HAVE HIS
MOCK TRIAL
ON SATURDAY, MAY 27, AT 9 O'CLOCK,
In the Kidnapper's 'Court,' before the Hon. Slave Bill Commissioner,
AT THE COURT HOUSE, IN COURT SQUARE.
SHALL BOSTON STEAL ANOTHER MAN?
Thursday, May 25, 1854.

Anthony Burns, the subject of this Boston poster, was the third runaway slave to be seized and returned to the South under the hated Fugitive Slave Act of 1850. The Burns case galvanized public opinion just when Congress was debating the Kansas-Nebraska Act. The passage of that bill further outraged northerners.

formation of the Republican party, which was made up of former Free Soilers, Conscience Whigs, and "Anti-Nebraska" Democrats. The American party was a national organization, but the Republican party was purely sectional. It sprang up spontaneously throughout the Old Northwest and caught on with a rush in New England.

Republicans presented themselves as the party of freedom. They were not abolitionists (though most abolitionists were soon voting Republican), but they insisted that slavery be kept out of the territories. They believed that if America was to remain a land of opportunity, free white labor must have exclusive access to the West. Thus the party appealed not only to voters who disapproved of slavery, but also to those who wished to keep blacks—free or slave—out of their states. In 1854 the Republicans won over 100 seats in the House of Representatives and control of many state governments.

The Whig party had almost disappeared in the northern states and the Democratic party had been gravely weakened, but it was unclear how these two new parties would fare. The Know-Nothing party had the superficial advantage of being a nationwide organization, but where slavery was concerned, this was anything but advantageous. And many northerners who disliked slavery were troubled by the harsh Know-Nothing policies toward immigrants and Catholics. If the Know-Nothings were in control, said former Whig congressman Abraham Lincoln in 1855, the Declaration of Independence would read "all men are created equal, except negroes, *and foreigners, and catholics.*"

"Bleeding Kansas"

Still the furor might have died down if settlement of the new territories had proceeded in an orderly manner. Almost none of the settlers who flocked to Kansas owned slaves, and relatively few of them were primarily interested in the slavery question. Most had a low opinion of blacks. ("I kem to Kansas to live in a free state," one northerner explained. "I don't want niggers a-trampin' over my grave.") Like nearly all frontier settlers, they wanted land and local political office, lucrative government contracts, and other business opportunities.

The Cavalry Engagement.
Battle of Hickory Point K.T. Sept 13, 1856.

By 1855, civil war had erupted in Kansas as bands of proslavery settlers fought free staters. Northerners and southerners contributed to the agony of "Bleeding Kansas" by sending money and arms to those who supported their views. In this sketch, free staters fire on the proslavery settlement of Hickory Point near Leavenworth.

When Congress opened the gates to settlement in May 1854, none of the land in the territory was available for sale. Treaties extinguishing Indian titles had yet to be ratified, and public lands had not been surveyed. In July, Congress authorized squatters to occupy unsurveyed federal lands, but much of this property was far to the west of the frontier and practically inaccessible. The situation led to confusion over property boundaries, to graft and speculation, and to general uncertainty, thereby exacerbating the difficulty of establishing an orderly government.

The legal status of slavery in Kansas became the focus of all these conflicts. Both northern abolitionists and southern defenders of slavery were determined to have Kansas. They made of the territory first a testing ground and then a battlefield, thus exposing the fatal flaw in the Kansas-Nebraska Act and the idea of popular sovereignty. The law said that the people of Kansas were "perfectly free" to decide the slavery question. But the citizens of territories were not entirely free because territories were not sovereign political units. The act had created a political vacuum, which its vague statement that the settlers must establish their domestic institutions "subject . . . to the Constitution" did not begin to fill. When should the institutions be established? Was it democratic to let a handful of first

comers make decisions that would affect the lives of the thousands soon to follow? The virtues of the time-tested system of congressional control established by the Northwest Ordinance became fully apparent only when the system was discarded.

More serious was the fact that outsiders, North and South, refused to permit Kansans to work out their own destiny. The contest for control began at once. The New England Emigrant Aid Society was formed, with grandiose plans for transporting antislavery settlers to the area. The society transported only a handful of New Englanders to Kansas. Yet the New Englanders were very conspicuous, and the society helped many middle western antislavery settlers to make the move.

In doing so, it stirred southerners to action. The proslavery forces enjoyed several advantages in this struggle. The first inhabitants in frontier regions nearly always came from lands immediately to the east. In this case they were proslavery Missourians. When word spread that "foreigners" from New England were seeking to "steal" Kansas, many Missourians rushed to protect their "rights." "If we win we carry slavery to the Pacific Ocean," Senator Atchison boasted.

In November 1854 an election was held in Kansas to pick a territorial delegate to Congress. A large band of Missourians crossed over specifically to vote

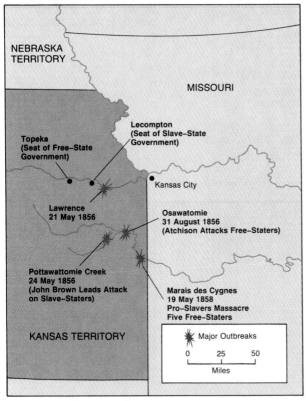

"BLEEDING KANSAS"

night. They dragged five unsuspecting men from their rude cabins and murdered them. This slaughter brought men on both sides to arms by the hundreds. As Brown's biographer, Stephen B. Oates, has written, "Kansas was in complete chaos." Armed bands, one led by Brown himself, "prowled the countryside, shooting at one another and looting."

Brown and his followers escaped capture and were never indicted for the murders, but pressure from federal troops eventually forced him to go into hiding. He finally left Kansas in October 1856. By that time some 200 persons had lost their lives.

A certain amount of violence was normal in any frontier community, but it suited the political interests of the Republicans to make the situation in Kansas seem worse than it was. Exaggerated accounts of "bleeding Kansas" filled the pages of northern newspapers. The Democrats were also partly to blame, for although residents of nearby states often tried to influence elections in new territories, the actions of the border ruffians made a mockery of the democratic process.

However, the main responsibility for the Kansas tragedy must be borne by the Pierce administration. Under popular sovereignty, the national government was supposed to see that elections were orderly and honest. Instead, the president acted as a partisan. When the first governor of the territory objected to the manner in which the proslavery legislature had been elected, Pierce replaced him with a man who backed the southern group without question.

for a proslavery candidate and elected him easily. In March 1855 some 5,000 "border ruffians" again descended on Kansas and elected a territorial legislature. A census had recorded 2,905 elegible voters, but 6,307 votes were cast. The legislature promptly enacted a slave code and laws prohibiting abolitionist agitation. Antislavery settlers refused to recognize this regime and held elections of their own. By January 1856 two governments existed in Kansas, one based on fraud, the other extralegal.

By denouncing the free-state government located at Topeka, President Pierce encouraged the proslavery settlers to assume the offensive. In May, 800 of them sacked the antislavery town of Lawrence. An extremist named John Brown then took the law into his own hands in retaliation. By his reckoning, five Free Soilers had been killed by proslavery forces. In May 1856, together with six companions (four of them his sons), Brown stole into a settlement on Pottawatomie Creek in the dead of

Making a Senator a Martyr

As counterpoint to the fighting in Kansas there arose an almost continuous cacophony in the halls of Congress. Red-faced legislators traded insults and threats. Epithets like "liar" were freely tossed about. Prominent in these angry outbursts was a new senator, Charles Sumner of Massachusetts. Brilliant, learned, and articulate, Sumner had made a name for himself in New England as a reformer interested in the peace movement, prison reform, and the abolition of slavery. He possessed great magnetism and was, according to the tastes of the day, an accomplished orator, but he suffered inner torments of a complex nature that warped his personality. He was egotistical and humorless. His un-

A well-known contemporary drawing gives a dramatic view of Brooks caning Sumner. Beneath Sumner's left hand is a scroll inscribed "Kansas." The cartoon's title is "Southern Chivalry—Argument versus Clubs."

yielding devotion to his principles was less praise-worthy than it seemed on casual examination, for it resulted from his complete lack of respect for the principles of others. Reform movements evidently provided him with a kind of emotional release; he became combative and totally lacking in objectivity when espousing a cause.

In the Kansas debates Sumner displayed an icy disdain for his foes. Colleagues threatened him with assassination, called him a "filthy reptile" and a "leper." He was impervious to such hostility. In the spring of 1856 he loosed a dreadful blast titled "The Crime Against Kansas." Characterizing administration policy as tyrannical, imbecilic, absurd, and infamous, he demanded that Kansas be admitted to the Union at once as a free state. Then he began a long and intemperate attack on both Douglas and the elderly Senator Andrew P. Butler of South Carolina, who was not present to defend himself.

Sumner described Butler as a "Don Quixote" who had taken "the harlot, slavery" as his mistress, and he spoke scornfully of "the loose expectoration" of Butler's speech. This was an inexcusable reference to the uncontrollable drooling to which the elderly senator was subject. While he was still talking, Douglas, who shrugged off most political name-calling as part of the game, was heard to mutter, "That damn fool will get himself killed by some other damn fool."

Such a "fool" quickly materialized in the person of Congressman Preston S. Brooks of South Carolina, a nephew of Senator Butler. Since Butler was absent from Washington, Brooks, who was probably as mentally unbalanced as Sumner, assumed the responsibility of defending his kinsman's honor. A southern romantic par excellence, he decided that caning Sumner would reflect his contempt more effectively than challenging him to a duel. Two days after the speech, Brooks entered the Senate as it adjourned. Sumner remained at his desk writing. After waiting with exquisite punctilio until a talkative woman in the lobby had left so that she would be spared the sight of violence, Brooks walked up to Sumner and rained blows on his head with a gutta-percha cane until he fell, unconscious and bloody, to the floor. "I . . . gave him about 30 first-rate stripes," Brooks later boasted. "Towards the last he bellowed like a calf. I wore my cane out completely but saved the head which is gold." The physical damage suffered by Sumner was relatively superficial, but the incident so affected him psychologically that he was unable to return to his seat in Congress until 1859.

Both sides made much of this disgraceful incident. When the House censured him, Brooks resigned, returned to his home district, and was triumphantly reelected. A number of well-wishers sent him souvenir canes. Northerners viewed the affair as illustrating the brutalizing effect of slavery on southern whites and made a hero of Sumner.

Buchanan Tries His Hand

Such was the atmosphere surrounding the 1856 presidential election. The Republican party now dominated much of the North. It nominated John C. Frémont, "the Pathfinder," one of the heroes of the conquest of California during the Mexican War. Frémont fitted the Whig tradition of presidential candidates: a popular military man with almost no political experience. Unlike Taylor and Scott, however, he was sound and articulate on the issue of slavery in the territories. Although citizens of diverse interests had joined the party, Republicans expressed their objectives in one simple slogan: "Free soil, free speech, and Frémont."

The Democrats cast aside the ineffectual Pierce, but they did not dare nominate Douglas because he had raised such a storm in the North. They settled on James Buchanan, chiefly because he had been out of the country serving as minister to Great Britain during the long debate over Kansas! The American party nominated ex-president Fillmore, a choice the remnants of the Whigs endorsed. Walt Whitman had been an ardent Democrat. But the party's stand on slavery in the territories disgusted him. In 1856 he wrote a poem, "The 18th Presidency," denouncing both Buchanan and Fillmore:

> *Two galvanized old men, close on*
> *the summons to depart this life*
> *. . . relics and proofs of the little*
> *political bargains . . .*

In the campaign, the Democrats concentrated on denouncing the Republicans as a sectional party that threatened to destroy the Union. On this issue they carried the day. Buchanan won only a minority of the popular vote, but he had strength in every section. He got 174 electoral votes to Frémont's 114 and Fillmore's 8. The significant contest took place in the populous states just north of slave territory—Pennsylvania, Ohio, Indiana, and Illinois. Buchanan carried all but Ohio, though by narrow margins.

James Buchanan "never made a witty remark, never wrote a memorable sentence, and never showed a touch of distinction," according to historian Allan Nevins.

No one could say that James Buchanan lacked political experience. He had been elected to the Pennsylvania legislature in 1815 when only 24. He served for well over 20 years in Congress and had been minister to Russia, then Polk's secretary of state, then minister to Great Britain under Pierce.

Personally, Buchanan was a bundle of contradictions. Dignified in bearing and by nature cautious, he could consume enormous amounts of liquor without showing the slightest sign of inebriation. A big, heavy man, he was nonetheless remarkably graceful and light on his tiny feet, of which he was inordinately proud. He wore a very high collar to conceal a scarred neck, and because of an eye defect he habitually carried his head to one side and slightly forward, which gave him, as his biographer says, "a perpetual attitude of courteous deference and attentive interest" that sometimes led individuals to believe they had won a greater share of his attention and support than was actually the case. In fact he was extremely stubborn and sometimes vindictive.

Buchanan was popular with women and attracted to them as well, but although he contemplated marriage on more than one occasion, he never took the final step. Over the years many strong men in politics had, like Walt Whitman, held him in contempt. Yet he was patriotic, conscientious, and moderate. While Republican extremists called him a "Doughface"—they believed he lacked the force of character to stand up against southern extremists—many voters in 1856 thought he had the qualities necessary to steer the nation to calmer waters.

The Court's Turn

Before Buchanan could fairly take the Kansas problem in hand, an event occurred that drove another deep wedge between North and South. Back in 1834 Dr. John Emerson of St. Louis joined the army as a surgeon and was assigned to duty at Rock Island, Illinois. Later he was transferred to Fort Snelling, in Wisconsin Territory. In 1838 he returned to Missouri. Accompanying him on these travels was his body servant, Dred Scott, a slave. In 1846, after Emerson's death, Scott and his wife Harriet, whom he had married while in Wisconsin, with the help of a friendly lawyer brought suit in the Missouri courts for their liberty, arguing that residence in Illinois, where slavery was barred under the Northwest Ordinance, and in Wisconsin Territory, where the Missouri Compromise outlawed it, had made them free.

The future of Dred and Harriet Scott mattered not at all to the country or the courts; at issue was the question of whether Congress or the local legislatures had the power to outlaw slavery in the territories. After many years of litigation, the case reached the Supreme Court. On March 6, 1857, two days after Buchanan's inauguration, the high tribunal acted. Free or slave, the Court declared, blacks were not citizens; therefore, Scott could not sue in a federal court. This was dubious legal logic because many blacks were accepted as citizens in some states when the Constitution was drafted and ratified, and Article 4, Section 2, says that "the citizens of each state shall be entitled to all privileges and immunities of citizens in the several states." But it settled Scott's fate.

However, the Court went further. Since the plaintiff had returned to Missouri, the laws of Illinois no longer applied to him. His residence in Wisconsin Territory—this was the most controversial part of the decision—did not make him free because the Missouri Compromise was unconstitutional. According to the Bill of Rights (the Fifth Amendment), the federal government cannot deprive any person of life, liberty, or property without due process of law.* Therefore, Chief Justice Roger B. Taney reasoned, "An Act of Congress which deprives a person . . . of his liberty or property merely because he came himself or brought his property into a particular Territory . . . could hardly be dignified with the name of due process of law."

The Dred Scott decision has been widely criticized on legal grounds. Each justice filed his own opinion, and in several important particulars there was no line of argument that any five of the nine agreed on. Some critics have reasoned that the justices should not have gone beyond the minimum of argument necessary to settle the case, and many have made much of the fact that a majority of the justices were southerners. It would be going too far, however, to accuse them of plotting to extend slavery. They were trying to settle the vexing question of slavery in the territories once and for all. If this objective could only be accomplished by fuzzy reasoning, it would not be the first or the last time in the history of jurisprudence that an important result rested on shaky logic.

In addition to invalidating the already repealed Missouri Compromise, the decision threatened Douglas's principle of popular sovereignty, for if Congress could not exclude slaves from a territory, how could a mere territorial legislature do so? Until statehood was granted, slavery seemed as inviolate as freedom of religion or speech or any other civil liberty guaranteed by the Constitution. Where formerly freedom (as guaranteed in the Bill of Rights) was a national institution and slavery a local one, now, according to the Court, slavery was nationwide, excluded only where states had specifically abolished it.

The irony of employing the Bill of Rights to keep blacks in chains did not escape northern critics. Now

---

* Some state constitutions had similar provisions, but the slave states obviously did not.

slaves could be brought into Minnesota Territory, even into Oregon. In his inaugural address Buchanan had sanctimoniously urged the people to accept the forthcoming ruling, "whatever this may be," as a final settlement. Many assumed (indeed, it was true) that he had put pressure on the Court to act as it did and that he knew in advance of his speech what the decision would be. If this "greatest crime in the judicial annals of the Republic" was allowed to stand, northerners argued, the Republican party would have no reason to exist: Its program had been declared unconstitutional! The Dred Scott decision convinced thousands that the South was engaged in an aggressive attempt to extend the peculiar institution so far that it could no longer be considered peculiar.

The Lecompton Constitution

Kansas soon provided a test for northern suspicions. Initially Buchanan handled the problem of Kansas well by appointing Robert J. Walker as governor. Although he was from Mississippi, Walker had no desire to foist slavery on the territory against the will of its inhabitants. He was a small man but a courageous one, patriotic, vigorous, tough-minded, much like Douglas in temper and belief. A former senator and Cabinet member, he had more political stature by far than any previous governor of the territory.

The proslavery leaders in Kansas had managed to convene a constitutional convention at Lecompton, but the Free Soil forces had refused to participate in the election of delegates. When this rump body drafted a proslavery constitution and then refused to submit it to a fair vote of all the settlers, Walker denounced its work and hurried back to Washington to explain the situation to Buchanan.

The president refused to face reality. His prosouthern advisers were clamoring for him to "save" Kansas. Instead of rejecting the Lecompton constitution, he asked Congress to admit Kansas to the Union with this document as its frame of government.

Buchanan's decision brought him head-on against Stephen A. Douglas, and the repercussions of their clash shattered the Democratic party. Principle and self-interest (an irresistible combination)

forced Douglas to oppose the leader of his party. If he stood aside while Congress admitted Kansas, not only would he be abandoning popular sovereignty, but he would be committing political suicide as well. He was up for reelection to the Senate in 1858. All but one of the 56 newspapers in Illinois had declared editorially against the Lecompton constitution; if he supported it, defeat was certain. In a dramatic confrontation at the White House, he and Buchanan argued the question at length, tempers rising. Finally, the president tried to force him into line. "Mr. Douglas," he said, "I desire you to remember that no Democrat ever yet differed from an Administration of his own choice without being crushed." "Mr. President," Douglas replied contemptuously, "I wish you to remember that General Jackson is dead!" And he stalked out of the room.

Buchanan then compounded his error by putting tremendous political pressure on Douglas, cutting off his Illinois patronage on the eve of his reelection campaign. Of course Douglas persisted, openly joining the Republicans in the fight. Congress rejected the Lecompton bill.

Meanwhile, the extent of the fraud perpetrated at Lecompton became clear. In October 1857 a new legislature had been chosen in Kansas, antislavery voters participating in the balloting. It ordered a referendum on the Lecompton constitution in January 1858. The constitution was overwhelmingly rejected; this time the proslavery settlers boycotted the test. When Buchanan persisted in pressing Congress to admit Kansas under the Lecompton constitution, Congress ordered another referendum. To slant the case in favor of approval, the legislators stipulated that if the constitution was voted down, Kansas could not be admitted into the Union until it had a population of 90,000. Nevertheless, the Kansans rejected it by a ratio of six to one.

More than opposition to slavery influenced this vote, for by 1858 most Kansans were totally alienated from the Democratic administration in Washington because of its bungling and corrupt management of the public lands. After delaying sales unconscionably, Buchanan suddenly put 8 million acres up for auction in 1858. Squatters on this land were faced, in the midst of a depression, with finding $200 in cash to cover the minimum price of their quarter sections or losing their improvements. Local protests forced a delay of the sales, but Kansans by the thousands were convinced that Buchanan had thrown the land on the market out of pique at their rejection of the Lecompton constitution.

The Emergence of Lincoln

These were dark days. During the Panic of 1857 northerners put the blame for the hard times on the southern-dominated Congress, which had just reduced tariff duties to the lowest levels in nearly half a century. As prices plummeted and unemployment rose, they attributed the collapse to foreign competition and accused the South of having sacrificed the prosperity of the rest of the nation for its selfish advantage. The South in turn read in its relative immunity from the depression proof of the superiority of the slave system, which further stimulated the running sectional debate about the relative merits of free and slave labor.

Dissolution threatened the Union. To many Americans, Stephen A. Douglas seemed to offer the best hope of preserving it. For this reason unusual attention was focused on his campaign for reelection to the Senate in 1858. The importance of the contest and Douglas's national prestige put great pressure on the Republicans of Illinois to nominate someone who would make a good showing against him. The man they chose was Abraham Lincoln.

After a towering figure has passed from the stage, it is always difficult to discover what he was like before his rise to prominence. This is especially true of Lincoln, who changed greatly when power, responsibility, and fame came to him. Lincoln was not unknown in 1858, but his public career had not been distinguished. He was born in Kentucky in 1809, and the story of his early life can be condensed, as he once said himself, into a single line from Gray's *Elegy:* "The short and simple annals of the poor." His illiterate father, Thomas Lincoln, was a typical frontier wanderer. When Abraham was 7 the family moved to Indiana. In 1830 they pushed west again into southern Illinois. The boy received almost no formal schooling.

However, Lincoln had a good mind, and he was extremely ambitious. He cut loose from his family, made a trip to New Orleans, and for a time managed a general store in New Salem, Illinois. In 1834, when barely 25, he won a seat in the Illinois legislature

as a Whig. Meanwhile, he studied law and was admitted to the bar in 1836.

Lincoln remained in the legislature until 1842, displaying a perfect willingness to adopt the Whig position on all issues. In 1846 he was elected to Congress. While not engaged in politics he worked at the law, maintaining an office in Springfield and following the circuit, taking a variety of cases, few of much importance. He earned a decent but by no means sumptuous living. After one term in Congress, marked by his partisan opposition to Polk's Mexican policy, his political career petered out. He seemed fated to pass his remaining years as a small-town lawyer.

Even during this period Lincoln's personality was extraordinarily complex. His bawdy sense of humor and his endless fund of stories and tall tales made him a legend first in Illinois and then in Washington. He was admired in Illinois as an expert axman and a champion wrestler. He was thoroughly at home with toughs like the "Clary's Grove Boys" of New Salem and in the convivial atmosphere of a party caucus. But in a society where most men drank heavily, he never touched liquor. And he was subject to periods of melancholy so profound as to appear almost psychopathic. Friends spoke of him as having "cat fits," and he wrote of himself in the early 1840s: "I am now the most miserable man living. If what I felt were equally distributed to the whole human family, there would not be one cheerful face on earth."

In a region swept by repeated waves of religious revivalism, Lincoln managed to be at once a man of calm spirituality and a skeptic without appearing offensive to conventional believers. He was a party wheelhorse, a corporation lawyer, even a railroad lobbyist, yet his reputation for integrity was stainless.

The revival of the slavery controversy in 1854 stirred Lincoln deeply. No abolitionist, he had tried to take a "realistic" view of the problem. The Kansas-Nebraska bill led him to see the moral issue more clearly. "If slavery is not wrong, nothing is wrong," he stated with the directness and simplicity of expression for which he later became famous. Compromises made in the past for the sake of sectional harmony had always sought to preserve as much territory as possible for freedom. Yet unlike most Free Soilers, he did not blame the southerners for

How Lincoln aged during his term of office is evident when one compares Alexander Hesler's portrait, taken on June 3, 1860, with one by an unnamed photographer taken on April 10, 1865.

slavery. "They are just what we would be in their situation," he confessed.

The moderation of his position combined with its moral force won Lincoln many admirers in the great body of citizens who were trying to reconcile their low opinion of blacks and their patriotic desire to avoid an issue that threatened the Union with their growing conviction that slavery was sinful. Anything that aided slavery was wrong, Lincoln argued. But before casting the first stone, northerners should look into their own hearts: "If there be a man amongst us who is so impatient of [slavery] as a wrong as to disregard its actual presence among us and the difficulty of getting rid of it suddenly in a satisfactory way . . . that man is misplaced if he is on our platform." And Lincoln confessed:

> If all earthly power were given to me, I should not know what to do as to the existing institution. But . . . [this] furnishes no more excuse for permitting slavery to go into our free territory than it would for reviving the African slave trade.

Thus Lincoln was at once compassionate toward the slave owner and stern toward the institution. "A house divided against itself cannot stand," he warned. "I believe this government cannot endure permanently half slave and half free." Without minimizing the difficulties or urging a hasty or ill-considered solution, Lincoln demanded that the people look toward a day, however remote, when not only Kansas but the entire country would be free.

The Lincoln-Douglas Debates

As Lincoln developed these ideas, his reputation grew. In 1855 he almost won the Whig nomination for senator. He became a Republican shortly thereafter, and in June 1856, at the first Republican National Convention, he received 110 votes for the vice-presidential nomination. He seemed the logical man to pit against Douglas in 1858.

In July, Lincoln challenged Douglas to a series

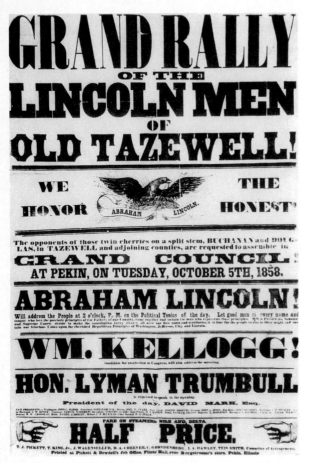

The Lincoln-Douglas debates began in June 1858 with Lincoln's "House Divided" speech and lasted until October. At rallies such as the one announced in this poster, the tall, awkward "Rail Splitter" challenged the "Little Giant" to thoroughly examine the slavery question.

of seven debates. The senator accepted. The debates were well attended and widely reported, for the idea of a direct confrontation between candidates for an important office captured the popular imagination.

The choice of the next senator lay, of course, in the hands of the Illinois legislature. Technically, Douglas and Lincoln were campaigning for candidates for the legislature who were pledged to support them for the Senate seat. They presented a sharp physical contrast that must have helped voters sort out their differing points of view. Douglas was short and stocky, Lincoln long and lean. Douglas gave the impression of irrepressible energy. While speaking, he roamed the platform; he used broad

gestures and bold, exaggerated arguments. He did not hesitate to call "Honest Abe" a liar. Lincoln, on his part, was slow and deliberate of speech, his voice curiously high-pitched. He seldom used gestures or oratorical tricks, trying rather to create an impression of utter sincerity to add force to his remarks.

The two employed different political styles each calculated to project a particular image. Douglas epitomized efficiency and success. He dressed in the latest fashion, favoring flashy vests and the finest broadcloth. He was a glad-hander and a heavy drinker—apparently he died of cirrhosis of the liver. Ordinarily he arrived in town in a private railroad car, to be met by a brass band, then to ride at the head of a parade to the appointed place.

Lincoln appeared before the voters as a man of the people. He wore ill-fitting black suits and a stove-pipe hat—repository for letters, bills, scribbled notes, and other scraps—that exaggerated his great height. He presented a worn and rumpled appearance, partly because he traveled from place to place on day coaches, accompanied by only a few advisers. When local supporters came to meet him at the station, he preferred to walk with them through the streets to the scene of the debate.

Lincoln and Douglas maintained a high intellectual level in their speeches, but these were political debates. They were seeking not to influence future historians (who have nonetheless pondered their words endlessly) but to win votes. They tended to exaggerate their differences, which were not in fact enormous. Neither wanted to see slavery in the territories or thought it economically efficient, and neither sought to abolish it by political action or by force. Both believed blacks congenitally inferior to whites, though Douglas took more pleasure in expounding on supposed racial differences than Lincoln did.

Douglas's strategy was to make Lincoln look like an abolitionist. He accused the Republicans of favoring racial equality and refusing to abide by the decision of the Supreme Court in the Dred Scott case. Himself he pictured as a heroic champion of democracy, attacked on one side by the "black" Republicans and on the other by the Buchananites, yet ready to fight to his last breath for popular sovereignty.

Lincoln tried to picture Douglas as proslavery and a defender of the Dred Scott decision. "Slavery is an unqualified evil to the negro, to the white man, to the soil, and to the State," he said. "Judge Douglas," he also said, "is blowing out the moral lights around us, when he contends that whoever wants slaves has a right to hold them."

However, Lincoln often weakened the impact of his arguments, being perhaps too eager to demonstrate his conservatism. The historian David M. Potter drew a nice distinction in Lincoln's position between "what he would do for the slave" and "what he would do for the Negro." "All men are created equal," he would say on the authority of the Declaration of Independence, only to add: "I am not, nor ever have been, in favor of bringing about in any way the social and political equality of the white and black races." He opposed allowing blacks to vote, to sit on juries, to marry whites, even to be citizens. He predicted the "ultimate extinction" of slavery, but when pressed he predicted that it would not occur "in less than a hundred years at the least." He took a fence-sitting position on the question of abolition in the District of Columbia and stated flatly that he did not favor repeal of the Fugitive Slave Act.

In the debate at Freeport, a town northwest of Chicago near the Wisconsin line, Lincoln asked Douglas if, considering the Dred Scott decision, the people of a territory could exclude slavery before the territory became a state. Unhesitatingly Douglas replied that they could, simply by not passing the local laws essential for holding blacks in bondage. "It matters not what way the Supreme Court may hereafter decide as to the abstract question," he said. "The people have the lawful means to introduce or exclude it as they please, for the reason that slavery cannot exist . . . unless it is supported by local police regulations."

This argument saved Douglas in Illinois. The Democrats carried the legislature by a narrow margin, whereas it is almost certain that if Douglas had accepted the Dred Scott decision outright, the balance would have swung to the Republicans. But the so-called Freeport Doctrine cost him heavily two years later when he made his bid for the Democratic presidential nomination. "It matters not what way the Supreme Court may hereafter decide"—southern extremists would not accept a man who suggested that the Dred Scott decision could be circumvented, though in fact Douglas had only stated the obvious.

Probably Lincoln had not thought beyond the senatorial election when he asked the question; he was merely hoping to keep Douglas on the defensive and perhaps injure him in southern Illinois, where considerable proslavery sentiment existed. In any case, defeat did Lincoln no harm politically. He had more than held his own against one of the most formidable debaters in politics, and his distinctive personality and point of view had impressed themselves on thousands of minds. Indeed, the defeat revitalized his political career.

The campaign of 1858 marked Douglas's last triumph, Lincoln's last defeat. Elsewhere the elections in the North went heavily to the Republicans. When the old Congress reconvened in December, northern-sponsored economic measures (a higher tariff, the transcontinental railroad, river and harbor improvements, a free homestead bill) were all blocked by southern votes.

Whether the South could continue to prevent the passage of this legislation in the new Congress was problematical. In early 1859 even many moderate southerners were uneasy about the future. The radicals, made panicky by Republican victories and their own failure to win in Kansas, spoke openly of secession if a Republican was elected president in 1860. Lincoln's "house divided" speech was quoted out of context, while Douglas's Freeport Doctrine added to southern woes. When Senator William H. Seward of New York spoke of an "irrepressible conflict" between freedom and slavery, southerners became still more alarmed.

Naturally they struck back. Led by such self-described "fire-eaters" as William L. Yancey of Alabama and Senators Jefferson Davis of Mississippi, John Slidell of Louisiana, and James H. Hammond of South Carolina, they demanded a federal slave code for the territories and talked of annexing Cuba and reviving the African slave trade.

John Brown's Raid

In October 1859 John Brown, the scourge of Kansas, made his second contribution to the unfolding sectional drama. Gathering a group of 18 followers, white and black, he staged an attack on Harpers Ferry, Virginia, a town on the Potomac River upstream from Washington. Having boned up on guerrilla tactics, he planned to seize the federal arsenal there; arm the slaves, whom he thought would

The image of John Brown as martyr was memorialized in art as well as in song and story. Here is a senti-mental interpretation, The Last Moments of John Brown, *painted in 1884 by American genre artist Thomas Hovenden.*

flock to his side; and then establish a black republic in the mountains of Virginia.

Simply by overpowering a few night watchmen, Brown and his men occupied the arsenal and a nearby rifle factory. They captured several hostages, one of them Colonel Lewis Washington, a great-grandnephew of George Washington. But no slaves came forward to join them. Federal troops commanded by Robert E. Lee soon trapped Brown's men in an engine house of the Baltimore and Ohio Railroad. After a two-day siege in which the attackers picked off ten of his men, Brown was captured.

No incident so well illustrates the role of emotion and irrationality in the sectional crisis as John Brown's raid. Over the years before his Kansas escapade, Brown had been a drifter, horse thief, and swindler, several times a bankrupt—a failure in everything he attempted. His maternal grandmother, his mother, and five aunts and uncles were certifiably insane, as were 2 of his 20 children and many collateral relatives. After his ghastly Pottawatomie murders it should have been obvious to anyone that he was both fanatical and mentally unstable: Some of the victims were hacked to bits. Yet numbers of high-minded northerners, including Emerson and Thoreau, had supported him and his antislavery "work" after 1856. Some—among them Franklin B. Sanborn, a teacher; Thomas Wentworth Higginson, a clergyman; and the merchant George

L. Stearns—contributed knowingly to his Harpers Ferry enterprise. After Brown's capture, Emerson, in an essay called "Courage," called him "a martyr" who would "make the gallows as glorious as the cross."

Southerners reacted to Harpers Ferry with equal irrationality, some with a rage similar to Brown's. Dozens of hapless northerners in the southern states were arrested, beaten, or driven off. One, falsely suspected of being an accomplice of Brown, was lynched.

Brown's fate lay in the hands of the Virginia authorities. Ignoring his obvious derangement, they charged him with treason, conspiracy, and murder. He was speedily convicted and sentenced to death by hanging.

Yet "Old Brown" had still one more contribution to make to the developing sectional tragedy. Despite the furor he had created, cool heads everywhere called for calm and denounced his attack. Most Republican politicians repudiated him. Even execution would probably not have made a martyr of Brown had he behaved like a madman after his capture. Instead, an enormous dignity descended on him as he lay in his Virginia jail awaiting death. Whatever his faults, he truly believed in racial equality. He addressed blacks who worked for him as "Mister" and arranged for them to eat at his table and sit with his family in church. This conviction served him well in his last days. "If it is deemed necessary that I should forfeit my life for the furtherance of the ends of justice, and mingle my blood further with the blood of . . . millions in this slave country whose rights are disregarded by wicked, cruel, and unjust enactments," he said before the judge pronounced sentence, "I say, let it be done."

This John Brown, with his patriarchal beard and sad eyes, so apparently incompatible with the bloody terrorist of Pottawatomie and Harpers Ferry, led thousands in the North to ignore his past and treat him almost as a saint.

And so Brown became to the North a hero and to the South a symbol of northern ruthlessness. The historian C. Vann Woodward put it this way: "Paranoia continued to induce counterparanoia, each antagonist infecting the other reciprocally, until the vicious spiral ended in war." Soon, as the popular song had it, Brown's body lay "a-mould-ering in the grave," and the memory of his bloody act did indeed go "marching on."

The Election of 1860

By 1860 the nation was teetering on the brink of disunion. Radicals North and South were heedlessly provoking one another. When a disgruntled North Carolinian, Hinton Rowan Helper, published *The Impending Crisis of the South* (1857), an attempt to demonstrate statistically that slavery was ruining the South's economy and corrupting its social structure, the Republicans flooded the country with an abridged edition, though they knew that southerners considered the book an appeal for social revolution. "I have always been a fervid Union man," one southerner wrote in 1859, "but I confess the [northern] endorsement of the Harpers Ferry outrage and Helper's infernal doctrine has shaken my fidelity."

Extremism was more evident in the South, and to any casual observer that section must have seemed the aggressor in the crisis. Yet even in demanding the reopening of the African slave trade, southern radicals believed that they were defending themselves against attack. They felt surrounded by hostility. The North was growing at a much faster rate; if nothing was done, they feared, a flood of new free states would soon be able to amend the Constitution and emancipate the slaves. John Brown's raid, with its threat of an insurrection like Nat Turner's, reduced them to a state of panic.

When legislatures in state after state in the South cracked down on freedom of expression, made the manumission of slaves illegal, banished free blacks, and took other steps that northerners considered blatantly provocative, the advocates of these policies believed that they were only defending the status quo. Perhaps, by seceding from the Union, the South could raise a dike against the tide of abolitionism. Secession also provided an emotional release, a way of dissipating tension by striking back at criticism.

Stephen A. Douglas was probably the last hope of avoiding a rupture between North and South. But when the Democrats met at Charleston, South Carolina, in April 1860 to choose a presidential candidate, the southern delegates would not support him unless he promised not to disturb slavery in the territories. Indeed, they went further in their demands. The North, William L. Yancey of Alabama insisted, must accept the proposition that slavery was not merely tolerable but right. Of course, the northerners would not go so far. "Gentlemen of the South," said Senator George E. Pugh of Ohio in replying to Yancey, "you mistake us—you mistake us! We will not do it!" When southern proposals were voted down, most of the delegates from the Deep South walked out and the convention adjourned without naming a candidate.

In June the Democrats reconvened at Baltimore. Again they failed to reach agreement. The two wings then met separately, the northerners nominating Douglas, the southerners John C. Breckinridge of Kentucky, Buchanan's vice-president. On the question of slavery in the territories, the northerners promised to "abide by the decision of the Supreme Court," which meant, in effect, that they stood for Douglas's Freeport Doctrine. The southerners announced their belief that neither Congress nor any territorial government could prevent citizens from settling "with their property" in any territory.

Meanwhile, the Republicans, who met in Chicago in mid-May, had drafted a platform attractive to all classes and all sections of the northern and western states. For manufacturers they proposed a high tariff, for farmers a homestead law providing free land for settlers. Internal improvements "of a National character," notably a railroad to the Pacific, should receive federal aid. No restrictions should be placed on immigration. As to slavery in the territories, the Republicans did not equivocate: "The normal condition of all the territory of the United States is that of freedom." Neither Congress nor a local legislature could "give legal existence to Slavery in any Territory."

In choosing a presidential candidate the Republicans displayed equally shrewd political judgment. Senator Seward was the front-runner, but he had taken too extreme a stand and appeared unlikely to carry the crucial states of Pennsylvania, Indiana, and Illinois. He led on the first ballot but could not get a majority. Then the delegates began to look closely at Abraham Lincoln. His thoughtful and moderate views on the main issue of the times and his formidable debating skills attracted many, and so did his political personality. "Honest Abe,"

the "Railsplitter," a man of humble origins (born in a log cabin), self-educated, self-made, a common man but by no means an ordinary man—the combination seemed unbeatable.

It also helped that Lincoln was from a crucial state and had an excellent team of convention managers. Taking advantage of the fact that the convention was meeting in Lincoln's home state, they packed the gallery with leather-lunged Chicago ward heelers assigned the task of shouting for their man. They also made a series of deals with the leaders of other state delegations to win additional votes. "I authorize no bargains and will be bound by none," Lincoln telegraphed the convention. "Lincoln ain't here and don't know what we have to meet," one of his managers remarked—and proceeded to trade off two Cabinet posts for the votes of key states.

On the second ballot Lincoln drew shoulder to shoulder with Seward; on the third he was within two votes of victory. Before the roll could be called again, delegates began to switch their votes, and in a landslide, soon made unanimous, Lincoln was nominated.

A few days earlier the remnants of the American and Whig parties had formed the Constitutional Union party and nominated John Bell of Tennessee for president. "It is both the part of patriotism and of duty," they resolved, "to recognize no political principle other than the Constitution of the country, the union of the states, and the enforcement of the laws." Ostrichlike, the Constitutional Unionists ignored the conflicts rending the nation. Only in the border states, where the consequences of disunion were sure to be most tragic, did they have any following.

With four candidates in the field, no one could win a popular majority, but it soon became clear that Lincoln was going to be elected. Breckinridge had most of the slave states in his pocket and Bell would run strong in the border regions, but the populous northern and western states had a majority of the electoral vote, and there the choice lay between the Republicans and the Douglas Democrats. In such a contest the Republicans, with their attractive economic program and their strong stand against slavery in the territories, were sure to come out on top.

Lincoln avoided campaigning and made no public statements. Douglas, recognizing the certainty of Lincoln's victory, accepted his fate and for the first

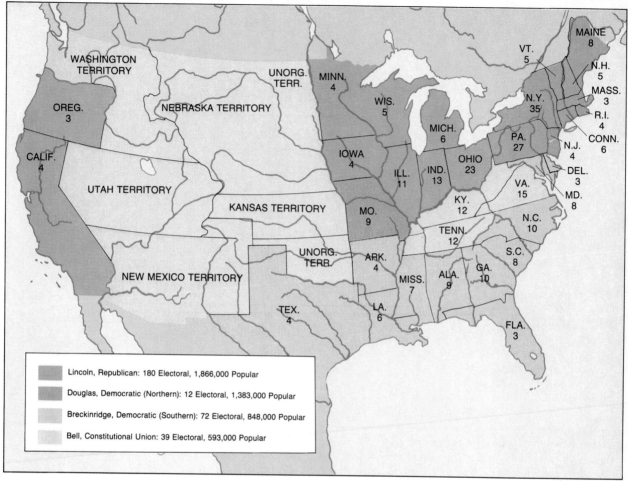

THE ELECTION OF 1860

time in his career rose above ambition. "We must try to save the Union," he said. "I will go South." In the heart of the Cotton Kingdom, he appealed to the voters to stand by the Union whoever was elected. He was the only candidate to do so; the others refused to remind the people that their election might result in secession and civil war.

When the votes were counted, Lincoln had 1,866,000, almost a million fewer than the combined total of his three opponents, but he swept the North and West, which gave him 180 electoral votes and the presidency. Douglas received 1,383,000 votes, so distributed that he carried only Missouri and part of New Jersey. Breckinridge, with 848,000 popular votes, won most of the South; Bell, with 593,000, carried Virginia, Tennessee, and Kentucky. Lincoln was thus a minority president, but his title to the office was unquestionable. Even if his opponents could have combined their popular votes in each state, Lincoln would have won.

The Secession Crisis

Only days after Lincoln's victory, the South Carolina legislature ordered an election of delegates to a convention to decide the state's future course. On December 20 the convention voted unanimously to secede, basing its action on the logic of Calhoun. "The State of South Carolina has resumed her position among the nations of the world," the delegates announced.

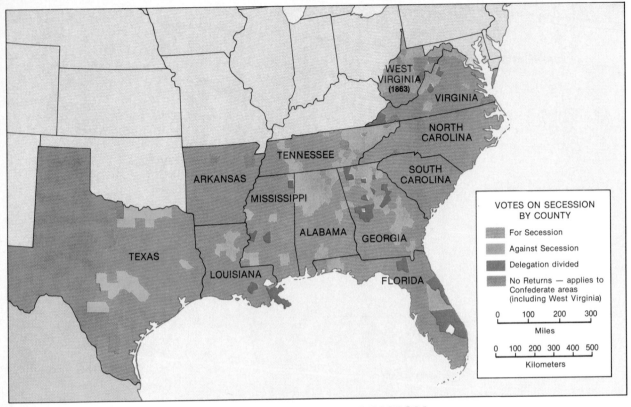

THE VOTE FOR SECESSION

A comparison of this map with the one on page 360 shows the minimal support for secession in the mainly nonslave mountain areas of the Appalachians. The strong antisecession sentiment in mountainous areas of Virginia eventually led several counties there to break from Virginia in 1863 and form the new state of West Virginia.

By February 1, 1861, the six other states of the Lower South had followed suit. A week later, at Montgomery, Alabama, a provisional government of the Confederate States of America was established. Virginia, Tennessee, North Carolina, and Arkansas did not leave the Union but announced that if the federal government attempted to use force against the Confederacy, they too would secede.

Why were southerners willing to wreck the Union their grandfathers had put together with so much love and labor? No simple explanation is possible. The danger that the expanding North would overwhelm them was for neither today nor tomorrow. Lincoln had assured them that he would re-

spect slavery where it existed. The Democrats had retained control of Congress in the election; the Supreme Court was firmly in their hands as well. If the North did try to destroy slavery, secession would perhaps be a logical tactic, but why not wait until the threat materialized? To leave the Union meant abandoning the very objectives for which the South had been contending for over a decade: a share of the federal territories and an enforceable fugitive slave law.

One reason why the South rejected this line of thinking was the tremendous economic energy generated in the North, which seemed to threaten the South's independence. As one southerner complained at a commercial convention in 1855:

From the rattle with which the nurse tickles the ear of the child born in the South to the shroud which covers the cold form of the dead, everything comes from the North. We rise from between sheets made in Northern looms, and pillow's of Northern feathers, to wash in basins made in the North. . . . We eat from Northern plates and dishes; our rooms are swept with Northern brooms, our gardens dug with Northern spades . . . and the very wood which feeds our fires is cut with Northern axes, helved with hickory brought from Connecticut and New York.

Secession, southerners argued, would "liberate" the South and produce the kind of balanced economy that was proving so successful in the North. Moreover, the mere possibility of emancipation was a powerful force for secession. "We must either submit to degradation, and to the loss of property worth four billions," the Mississippi convention declared, "or we must secede."

The years of sectional conflict, the growing northern criticism of slavery, perhaps even an unconscious awareness that this criticism was well founded, had undermined and in many cases destroyed the patriotic feelings of southerners. Because of the constant clamor set up by New England antislavery groups, the South tended to identify all northerners as "Yankee abolitionists" and to resent them with increasing passion. "I look upon the whole New England race as a troublesome unquiet set of meddlers," one Georgian wrote. In addition, a Republican president would not need the consent of Congress to flood the South with unfriendly federal officials—abolitionists and perhaps even blacks. Such a possibility most southerners found unsupportable. Fear approaching panic swept the region.

Although states' rights provided the rationale for leaving the Union, and southerners expounded the strict constructionist interpretation of the Constitution with great ingenuity, the economic and emotional factors were far more basic. The Lower South decided to go ahead with secession regardless of the cost. "Let the consequences be what they may," an Atlanta newspaper proclaimed. "Whether the Potomac is crimsoned in human gore, and Pennsylvania Avenue is paved ten fathoms in depth with mangled bodies . . . the South will never submit."

Not every slave owner could contemplate secession with such bloodthirsty equanimity. Some believed that the risks of war and slave insurrection were too great. Others retained a profound loyalty

to the United States. Many accepted secession only after the deepest examination of conscience. Lieutenant Colonel Robert E. Lee of Virginia was typical of thousands. "I see only that a fearful calamity is upon us," he wrote during the secession crisis. "There is no sacrifice I am not ready to make for the preservation of the Union save that of honour. If a disruption takes place, I shall go back in sorrow to my people & share the misery of my native state."

In the North there was a foolish but understandable reluctance to believe that the South really intended to break away. President-elect Lincoln was inclined to write off secession as a bluff designed to win concessions he was determined not to make. He also showed lamentable political caution in refusing to announce his plans or to cooperate with the outgoing Democratic administration before his inauguration.

In the South there was an equally unrealistic expectation that the North would not resist secession forcibly. The "Yankees" were timid materialists who would neither bear the cost nor risk their lives to prevent secession. It was commonly believed that "a lady's thimble will hold all the blood that will be shed."

President Buchanan recognized the seriousness of the situation but professed himself powerless. Secession, he said, was illegal, but the federal government had no legal way to prevent it. (This was the same dilemma that had surfaced during the nullification crisis but as Senator Douglas had reminded him, Buchanan was no Andrew Jackson.) He urged making concessions to the South yet lacked the forcefulness to take the situation in hand. Of course, he faced unprecedented difficulties. His term was about to run out, and since he could not commit his successor, his influence was minuscule. Yet a bolder president would have denounced secession in uncompromising terms. Instead Buchanan vacillated between compromise and aimless drift.

Appeasers, well-meaning believers in compromise, and those prepared to fight to preserve the Union were alike incapable of effective action. A group of moderates headed by Henry Clay's disciple, Senator John J. Crittenden of Kentucky, proposed a constitutional amendment in which slavery would be "recognized as existing" in all territories south of latitude 36°30′. The amendment also promised that no future amendment would tamper with the institution in the slave states and offered other guarantees to the South. But Lincoln refused to consider any arrangement that would open new territory to slavery. "On the territorial question," he wrote, "I am inflexible." The Crittenden Compromise got nowhere.

The new southern Confederacy set vigorously to work drafting a constitution, choosing Jefferson Davis as provisional president, seizing arsenals and other federal property within its boundaries, and preparing to dispatch diplomatic representatives to enlist the support of foreign powers. Buchanan bumbled helplessly in Washington. And out in Illinois, Abraham Lincoln juggled Cabinet posts and grew a beard.

Milestones

1850	Compromise of 1850
	Clayton-Bulwer Treaty with Great Britain
1851–1860	Northern resistance to enforcement of the Fugitive Slave Act
1852	Harriet Beecher Stowe, *Uncle Tom's Cabin*
	Commodore Matthew Perry opens Japan to U.S. trade
1853	Gadsden Purchase
1854	Ostend Manifesto
	Kansas-Nebrasaka Act repeals Missouri Compromise
1855	William Walker seizes power in Nicaragua
1856	Caning of Senator Charles Sumner in the Senate
	Pottawatomie Massacre
1856–1858	Unrest in Kansas Territory ("bleeding Kansas")
1857	Dred Scott case (*Dred Scott* v. *Sandford*)
	Panic of 1857
1858	Lincoln-Douglas debates
1859	John Brown's raid on Harpers Ferry
1860	South Carolina secedes from the Union
1861	Confederate States of America established
	Lincoln rejects the Crittenden Compromise

SUPPLEMENTARY READING

Titles marked with an asterisk have been published in paperback.

The events leading to the Civil War have been analyzed by dozens of historians. Allan Nevins provides the fullest and most magisterial treatment in **The Ordeal of the Union** (1947) and **The Emergence of Lincoln*** (1950). An excellent briefer summary is D. M. Potter, **The Impending Crisis*** (1976). See also W. J. Cooper, Jr., **Liberty and Slavery: Southern Politics to 1860** (1983), Michael Holt, **The Political Crisis of the 1850s** (1978), and R. H. Sewell, **Ballots for Freedom: Antislavery Politics** (1976). Eric Foner, **Free Soil, Free Labor, Free Men*** (1970), is an excellent analysis of Republican ideas and policies.

On the enforcement of the Fugitive Slave Act, see S. W. Campbell, **The Slave Catchers** (1970), and T. D. Morris, **Free Men All: The Personal Liberty Laws** (1974). Everyone should read Harriet Beecher Stowe's **Uncle Tom's Cabin.*** R. F. Wilson, **Crusader in Crinoline** (1941), is a satisfactory biography of Stowe, and E. L. McKitrick (ed.), **Slavery Defended*** (1963), contains a typical southern review of **Uncle Tom's Cabin.** Two studies stress the antiblack feelings of whites in the western states and their relation to the sectional crisis: E. H. Berwanger, **The Frontier Against Slavery*** (1967), and V. J. Voegeli, **Free But Not Equal*** (1967).

For details on foreign policy in the 1850s, see C. H. Brown, **Agents of Manifest Destiny** (1980), R. E. May, **The Southern Dream of a Caribbean Empire** (1974), and P. S. Klein, **President James Buchanan** (1962). D. S. Spencer, **Louis Kossuth and Young America** (1977), is also worth reading.

On Stephen A. Douglas, see R. W. Johannsen, **Stephen**

A. **Douglas** (1973). Nevins is particularly good on the Kansas controversy, but see also J. A. Rawley, **Race and Politics: "Bleeding Kansas"** (1969), and P. W. Gates, **Fifty Million Acres: Conflicts over Kansas Land Policy*** (1954).

Sumner's role in the deepening crisis is brilliantly discussed in David Donald, **Charles Sumner and the Coming of the Civil War** (1960). Klein's life of Buchanan is careful and judicious. On the Dred Scott case, see D. E. Fehrenbacher, **The *Dred Scott* Case** (1978).

The best modern biographies of Lincoln are B. P Thomas, **Abraham Lincoln** (1952), and S. B. Oates, **With Malice Toward None*** (1977). On his early career, see D. E. Fehrenbacher, **Prelude to Greatness*** (1962). W. E. Gienapp, **The Origins of the Republican Party** (1987), is a good recent study. S. B. Oates, **To Purge This Land with Blood** (1970), is a good biography of John Brown, but Nevins's **Ordeal of the Union** provides the finest account of the raid on Harpers Ferry. R. F. Nichols, **The Disruption of American Democracy*** (1948), describes the breakup of the Democratic party and the election of 1860. On the secession crisis and the outbreak of the Civil War, consult S. A. Channing, **Crisis of Fear*** (1970), and J. L. Roark, **Masters Without Slaves*** (1977).

XVI

The War to Save the Union

If the thing is pressed I think Lee will surrender.

> GENERAL PHILIP SHERIDAN *to General Ulysses S. Grant,*
> *April 6, 1865*

Let the thing be pressed.

> PRESIDENT ABRAHAM LINCOLN *to Generals Grant and*
> *Sheridan, April 7, 1865*

The nomination of Lincoln had succeeded brilliantly for the Republicans, but was his election a good thing for the country? As the inauguration approached, many Americans had their doubts. Honest Abe was a clever politician who had spoken well about the central issue of the times, but would he act decisively in this crisis? His behavior as president-elect was not reassuring. He spent much time closeted with politicians. Was he too obtuse to understand the grave threat to the Union posed by secession? People remembered uneasily that he had never held executive office, that his congressional career had been short and undistinguished. When he finally uprooted himself from Springfield in February 1861, his occasional speeches en route to Washington were vague, almost flippant. He kissed babies, shook hands, mouthed platitudes. Some people thought it downright cowardly that he let himself be spirited in the dead of night through Baltimore, where feeling against him ran high.

Cabinet Making

Everyone waited tensely to see whether Lincoln would oppose secession with force, but Lincoln seemed concerned only with organizing his Cabinet. The final slate was not ready until the morning of inauguration day, and shrewd observers found it alarming, for the new president had chosen to construct a "balanced" Cabinet representing a wide range of opinion instead of putting together a group of harmonious advisers who could help him face the crisis.

William H. Seward, the secretary of state, was the ablest and best known of the appointees. Despite his reputation for radicalism, the hawk-nosed, chinless, tousle-haired Seward hoped to conciliate the South and was thus in bad odor with the radical wing of the Republican party. In time Seward proved himself Lincoln's strong right arm, but at the start he badly underestimated the president and expected to dominate him. Senator Salmon P. Chase, a bald, square jawed antislavery leader from Ohio, whom Lincoln named secretary of the treasury, represented the radicals. Chase was humorless and vain but able; he detested Seward, agreeing with him only in thinking Lincoln a weakling. Many of the president's other selections worried thoughtful people.

Lincoln's inaugural address was conciliatory but firm. Southern institutions were in no danger from his administration. Secession, however, was illegal, the Union "perpetual." "A husband and wife may be divorced," Lincoln said, employing one of his homely and, by the Victorian standards of the day, slightly risque metaphors, "but the different parts of our country cannot. . . . Intercourse, either amicable or hostile, must continue between them." His tone was calm and warm. His concluding words catch the spirit of the inaugural perfectly:

> I am loath to close. We are not enemies, but friends. We must not be enemies. Though passion may have strained, it must not break, our bonds of affection. The mystic chords of memory, stretching from every battlefield and patriot grave to every living heart . . .

will yet swell the chorus of the Union when again touched, as surely they will be, by the better angels of our nature.

Fort Sumter: The First Shot

While denying the legality of secession, Lincoln had taken a temporizing position. The Confederates had seized most federal property in the Deep South. Lincoln admitted frankly that he would not attempt to reclaim this property. However, two strongholds, Fort Sumter, on an island in Charleston harbor, and Fort Pickens, at Pensacola, Florida, were still in loyal hands. Most Republicans did not want to surrender them without a show of resistance. To do so, one wrote, would be to convert the American eagle into a "debilitated chicken."

Yet to reinforce the forts might mean bloodshed that would make reconciliation impossible. After weeks of indecision, Lincoln took the moderate step of sending a naval expedition to supply the beleaguered Sumter garrison with food. Unwilling to permit this, the Confederates opened fire on the fort on April 12 before the supply ships arrived. After holding out for 34 hours, Major Robert Anderson and his men surrendered.

The attack precipitated an outburst of patriotic indignation in the North. Lincoln issued a call for 75,000 volunteers, and this caused Virginia, North Carolina, Arkansas, and Tennessee to secede. After years of crises and compromises, the nation chose to settle the great quarrel between the sections by force of arms.

Southerners considered Lincoln's call for troops an act of naked aggression. When the first Union regiment tried to pass through Baltimore in mid-April, it was attacked by a mob. The prosouthern chief of police telegraphed the Maryland state's attorney: "Streets red with blood. Send . . . for the riflemen to come, without delay. Fresh hordes will be down on us to-morrow." The chief and the mayor of Baltimore then ordered the railroad bridges connecting Baltimore with the northern states destroyed. Order was not restored until Union troops occupied key points in the city.

The southerners were seeking to exercise what a later generation would call the right of self-determination. How, they asked, could the North square its professed belief in democracy with its refusal to permit the southern states to leave the Union when a majority of their citizens wished to do so?

Lincoln took the position that secession was a rejection of democracy. If the South could refuse to abide by the result of an election in which it had freely participated, then everything that monarchists and other conservatives had said about the instability of republican governments would be proved true. "The central idea of secession is the essence of anarchy," he said. The United States must "demonstrate to the world" that "when ballots have been fairly and constitutionally decided, there can be no successful appeal except to ballots themselves, at succeeding elections."

This was the proper ground to take, both morally and politically. A war against slavery would not have been supported by a majority of northerners. Slavery was the root cause of secession but not of the North's determination to resist secession, which resulted from the people's commitment to the Union. Although abolition was to be one of the major results of the Civil War, the war was fought for nationalistic reasons, not to destroy slavery. Lincoln made this plain when he wrote in response to an editorial by Horace Greeley urging immediate emancipation: "I would save the Union. . . . If I could save the Union without freeing any slave, I would do it; and if I could save it by freeing all the slaves, I would do it; and if I could do it by freeing some and leaving others alone, I would also do that." He added, however, "I intend no modification of my oft-expressed personal wish that all men, everywhere, could be free."

The Blue and the Gray

In any test between the United States and the Confederacy, the former possessed tremendous advantages. There were more than 20 million people in the northern states (excluding Kentucky and Missouri, where opinion was divided) but only 9 million in the South, of whom about 3.5 million were slaves the whites hesitated to trust with arms. The North's economic capacity to wage war was even more preponderant. It was manufacturing nine times as much as the Confederacy (including 97 percent of the nation's firearms) and had a far larger and more efficient railroad system than the South. Northern control of the merchant marine and the navy made possible a blockade of the Confederacy, a particularly potent threat to a region so dependent on foreign markets.

The Confederates discounted these advantages. Many doubted that public opinion in the North would sustain Lincoln if he attempted to meet secession with force. Northern manufacturers needed southern markets, and merchants depended heavily on southern business. Many western farmers were still sending their produce down the Mississippi. War would threaten the prosperity of all these groups, southerners maintained. Should the North try to cut Europe off from southern cotton, the powers, particularly Great Britain, would descend on the land in their might, force open southern ports, and provide the Confederacy with the means of defending itself forever. "You do not dare to make war on cotton," Senator Hammond of South Carolina had taunted his northern colleagues in 1858. "No power on earth dares to make war upon it. Cotton is king."

The Confederacy also counted on certain military advantages. The new nation need only hold what it had; it could fight a defensive war, less costly in men and material and of great importance in maintaining morale and winning outside sympathy. Southerners would be defending not only their social institutions but also their homes and families.

To some extent the South benefited from superior military leadership. Both armies relied on West Pointers for their top commanders. Since most professionals followed the decisions of their home states when the war broke out, about 300 West Pointers became northern officers, about 180 southern. Among officers of lesser rank, the southerners probably excelled in the first years of the struggle, for the military tradition was strong in the South, and many young men had attended military academies, which were far more numerous in the South than in the North. Luck played a part too; the Confederacy quickly found a great commander, while the highest-ranking northern generals in the early stages of the war proved either bungling or indecisive. In battle after battle Union armies were defeated by forces of equal or smaller size.

There was little to distinguish the enlisted men of the two sides. After reading thousands of letters written by Union and Confederate soldiers, the historian Bell I. Wiley concluded that if they were all tossed in the air and identifying marks removed, "it would be impossible to know which were written by Rebs, which by Yanks." Since northern and southern common soldiers were so much alike, superior generalship clearly made some difference.

Both sides faced massive difficulties in organizing for a war long feared but never properly anticipated. After southern defections, the regular army consisted of only 13,000 officers and enlisted men, far too few to absorb the 186,000 who had joined the colors by early summer. Recruiting was left to the states, each being assigned a quota; there was little central organization. Natty companies of "Fire Zouaves" and "Garibaldi Guards" in gorgeous uniforms rubbed shoulders with slovenly units composed of toughs and criminals and with regiments of farm boys from Iowa, Illinois, and Michigan. Unlike later conflicts in which men from all parts of the country were mixed in each regiment, Civil War units were recruited locally. Men in each company tended to have known one another or had friends in common in civilian life. But few knew even the rudiments of soldiering. The hastily composed high command, headed by the elderly Winfield Scott, debated grand strategy endlessly while regimental commanders lacked decent maps of Virginia.

The Whig prejudice against powerful presidents was part of Lincoln's political heritage; conse-

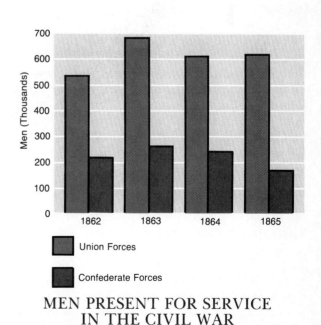

MEN PRESENT FOR SERVICE IN THE CIVIL WAR

quently at the start he did not display the firmness of Jackson or Polk in his dealings with Congress and his Cabinet. But his strength lay in his ability to think problems through, accept their implications, and then to act unflinchingly. Anything but a tyrant by nature, he boldly exceeded the conventional limits of presidential power in the emergency, expanding the army without congressional authorization, suspending the writ of habeas corpus, even emancipating the slaves when he thought military necessity demanded that action. Yet he also displayed remarkable patience and depth of character: He would willingly accept snubs and insults in order to advance the cause. He kept a close check on every aspect of the war effort, but found time for thought too. His young secretary John Nicolay reported seeing him sit sometimes for a whole hour like "a petrified image," lost in contemplation.

Gradually Lincoln's stock rose—first with men like Seward, who saw him close up and experienced both his steel and his gentleness, then with the people at large, who sensed his compassion, his humility, his wisdom. He was only 52 when he became president, and already people were calling him Old Abe. Before long they would call him Father Abraham.

The Confederacy faced far greater problems than the North, for it had to create an entire administration under pressure of war, with the additional handicap of the states' rights philosophy to which it was committed. The Confederate constitution explicitly recognized the sovereignty of the states and contained no broad authorization for laws designed to advance the general welfare. State governments repeatedly defied the central administration, located at Richmond after Virginia seceded, even with regard to military affairs.

Of course, the Confederacy made heavy use of the precedents and administrative machinery taken over from the United States. The government quickly decided that all federal laws would remain in force until specifically repealed, and many former federal officials continued to perform their duties under the new auspices.

The call to arms produced a turnout in the Confederacy perhaps even more impressive than that in the North; by July 1861 about 112,000 men were under arms. As in the North, men of every type enlisted, and morale was high. Some wealthy recruits brought slave servants with them to care for their needs in camp, cavalrymen supplied their own horses, and many men arrived with their own shotguns and hunting rifles. Ordinary militia companies sporting names like Tallapoosa Thrashers, Cherokee Lincoln Killers, and Chickasaw Desperadoes marched in step with troops of "character, blood, and social position" bearing names like Richmond Howitzers and Louisiana Zouaves. ("Zouave" mania swept both North and South, prospective soldiers evidently considering broad sashes and baggy breeches the embodiment of military splendor.)

President Jefferson Davis represented the best type of southern planter, noted for his humane treatment of his slaves. In politics he had pursued a somewhat unusual course. While senator from Mississippi, he opposed the Compromise of 1850 and became a leader of the southern radicals. After Pierce made him secretary of war, however, he took a more nationalistic position, one close to that of Douglas. Davis supported the transcontinental railroad idea and spoke in favor of the annexation of Cuba and other Caribbean areas. He rejected Doug-

Jefferson Davis sat for this portrait in 1863 in his mansion in Richmond. It is the only wartime portrait from life of the Confederate president.

las's position during the Kansas controversy but tried to close the breach that Kansas had opened in Democratic ranks. After the 1860 election he supported secession only reluctantly, preferring to give Lincoln a chance to prove that he meant the South no harm.

Davis was courageous, industrious, and intelligent, but he was rather too reserved and opinionated to make either a good politician or a popular leader. As president he devoted too much time to details, failed to delegate authority, and (unlike Lincoln) was impatient with garrulous and dull-witted people, types political leaders frequently have to deal with. Being a graduate of West Point, he fancied himself a military expert, but he was a mediocre military thinker. Unlike Lincoln, he quarreled frequently with his subordinates, held grudges, and allowed personal feelings to distort his judgment. "If anyone disagrees with Mr. Davis," his wife Varina Davis admitted, "he resents it and ascribes the difference to the perversity of his opponent."

The Test of Battle: Bull Run

"Forward to Richmond!" "On to Washington!" Such shouts propelled the opposing armies into battle long before they were properly trained. On July 21 at Manassas Junction, Virginia, some 20 miles below Washington, on a branch of the Potomac called Bull Run, 30,000 men under General Irvin McDowell attacked a roughly equal force of Confederates commanded by the "Napoleon of the South," Pierre G. T. Beauregard. McDowell swept back the Confederate left flank. Victory seemed sure. Then a Virginia brigade under Thomas J. Jackson rushed to the field by rail from the Shenandoah Valley in the nick of time, held doggedly to a key hill, and checked the advance. (A South Carolina general, seeking to rally his own men, pointed to the hill and shouted: "Look, there is Jackson with his Virginians, standing like a stone wall against the enemy." Thus "Stonewall" Jackson received his nickname.)

The southerners then counterattacked, driving the Union soldiers back. As often happens with green troops, retreat quickly turned to rout. McDowell's men fled toward the defenses of Washington, abandoning their weapons, stumbling through lines of supply wagons, trampling foolish

sightseers who had come out to watch the battle. Panic engulfed Washington. Richmond exulted. Both sides expected the northern capital to fall within hours.

The inexperienced southern troops were too disorganized to follow up their victory. Casualties on both sides were light, and the battle had little direct effect on anything but morale. Southern confidence soared, while the North began to realize how immense the task of subduing the Confederacy would be.

After Bull Run, Lincoln devised a broader, more systematic strategy for winning the war. The navy would clamp a tight blockade on all southern ports. In the West operations designed to gain control of the Mississippi would be undertaken. (This was part of General Scott's "Anaconda Plan," designed to starve the South into submission.) More important, a new army would be mustered at Washington to invade Virginia. Congress promptly authorized the enlistment of 500,000 three-year volunteers. To lead this army and—after General Scott's retirement in November—to command the Union forces, Lincoln appointed a 34-year-old major general, George B. McClellan.

McClellan was the North's first military hero. Units under his command had driven the Confederates from the pro-Union western counties of Virginia, clearing the way for the admission of West Virginia as a separate state in 1863. The fighting had been on a small scale, but McClellan, an incurable romanticizer and something of an egomaniac, managed to inflate its importance. "You have annihilated two armies," he proclaimed in a widely publicized message to his troops. Few northerners noticed that they had "annihilated" only about 250 Confederates.

Despite his penchant for self-glorification, McClellan possessed solid qualifications for command. One was experience. After graduation from West Point in 1846, he had served in the Mexican War. During the Crimean War he spent a year in the field, talking with British officers and studying fortifications. McClellan had a fine military bearing, a flair for the dramatic, and the ability to inspire troops. He was a talented administrator and organizer. He liked to concoct bold plans and dreamed of striking swiftly at the heart of the Confederacy to capture Richmond, Nashville, even New Orleans.

A hasty pencil sketch by an unknown artist captures the panic that swept the Union ranks after the defeat at Bull Run. The scene is the main road leading through Centerville to Washington.

Yet he was sensible enough to insist on massive logistic support, thorough training for the troops, iron discipline, and meticulous staff work before making a move.

Paying for the War

After Bull Run, this policy was exactly right. By the fall of the year a real army was taking shape along the Potomac: disciplined, confident, adequately supplied. Northern shops and factories were producing guns, ammunition, wagons, uniforms, shoes, and the countless other supplies needed to fight a great war. Most manufacturers operated on a small scale, but with the armed forces soon wearing out 3 million pairs of shoes and 1.5 million uniforms a year and with men leaving their jobs by the hundreds of thousands to fight, the tendency of industry to mechanize and to increase the size of the average manufacturing unit became ever more pronounced.

At the beginning of the war Secretary of the Treasury Salmon P. Chase underestimated how much the war would cost. He learned quickly. In August 1861 Congress passed an income tax law (3 percent on incomes over $800, which effectively exempted ordinary wage earners) and assessed a direct tax on the states. Loans amounting to $140 million were authorized. As the war dragged on and expenses mounted, new excise taxes on every imaginable product and service were passed, and still further borrowing was necessary. In 1863 the banking system was overhauled.

During the war the federal government borrowed a total of $2.2 billion and collected $667 million in taxes, slightly over 20 percent of its total expenditures. These unprecedentedly large sums proved inadequate. Some obligations were met by printing paper money unredeemable in coin. About $431 million in "greenbacks"—the term distinguished this fiat money from the redeemable yellowback bills—were issued during the course of the war.

Public confidence in all paper money vacillated with each change in the fortunes of the Union armies.

On balance, the heavy emphasis on borrowing and currency inflation was expensive but not irresponsible. In a country still chiefly agricultural, people had relatively low cash incomes and therefore could not easily bear a heavy tax load. Many Americans considered it reasonable to expect future generations to pay part of the dollar cost of saving the Union when theirs was contributing so heavily in labor and blood.

Politics as Usual

Partisan politics was altered by the war but not suspended. The secession of the southern states left the Republicans with large majorities in both houses of Congress. Most Democrats supported measures necessary for the conduct of the war but objected to the way the Lincoln administration was conducting it. The sharpest conflicts came when slavery and race relations were under discussion, the Democrats adopting a conservative stance and the Republicans dividing into Moderate and Radical wings. Political divisions on economic issues such as

This painting by David G. Blythe shows Lincoln chained by political enemies to strict constitutionality while he fights the dragon of rebellion. Tammany Democrats, led by New York's Mayor Fernando Wood, were among the Northerners who opposed the war and called for peace at any price.

tariffs and land policy tended to cut across party lines and, so far as the Republicans were concerned, to bear little relation to slavery and race.

As the war progressed, the Radical faction became increasingly influential. In 1861 the most prominent Radical senator was Charles Sumner, finally recovered from his caning by Preston Brooks and brimful of hatred for slaveholders. In the House, Thaddeus Stevens of Pennsylvania was the rising power. Sumner and Stevens were uncompromising on all questions relating to slaves; they insisted not merely on abolition but on granting full political and civil rights to blacks. Moderate Republicans objected vehemently to treating blacks as equals and opposed making abolition a war aim, and even many of the so-called Radicals disagreed with Sumner and Stevens on race relations. Senator Benjamin Wade of Ohio, for example, was a lifelong opponent of slavery, yet he had convinced himself that blacks (he habitually called them "niggers") had a distinctive and unpleasant smell. He considered the common white prejudice against blacks perfectly understandable. But prejudice, he maintained, gave no one the right "to do injustice to anybody"; he insisted that blacks were at least as intelligent as whites and were entitled not merely to freedom but to full political equality.

At the other end of the political spectrum stood the so-called Peace Democrats. These "Copperheads" (apparently the reference was not to the poisonous snake but to an earlier time when some hard-money Democrats wore copper pennies around their necks) opposed all measures in support of the war. They hoped to win control of Congress and force a negotiated peace. Few were actually disloyal, but their activities at a time when thousands of men were risking their lives in battle infuriated many northerners.

Lincoln treated dissenters with a curious mixture of repression and tolerance. He suspended the writ of habeas corpus in critical areas and applied martial law freely. Over 13,000 persons were arrested and held without trial, many, as it later turned out, unjustly. The president argued that the government dared not stand on ceremony in a national emergency. His object, he insisted, was not to punish but to prevent. Arbitrary arrests were rarely, if ever, made for purely political purposes, and free elections were held as scheduled throughout the war.

The federal courts compiled an admirable record in defending civil liberties, though when in conflict with the military, they could not enforce their decrees. In *Ex parte Merryman* (1861), Chief Justice Taney held General George Cadwalader in contempt for failing to produce a prisoner for trial when ordered to do so, but Cadwalader went unpunished and the prisoner continued to languish behind bars. After the war, in *Ex parte Milligan* (1866), the Supreme Court declared illegal the military trials of civilians in areas where the regular courts were functioning, but by that time the question was of only academic interest.

The most notorious domestic foe of the administration was the Peace Democrat Congressman Clement L. Vallandigham of Ohio. There were two rebellions in progress, Vallandigham claimed, "the Secessionist Rebellion" and "the Abolitionist Rebellion." "I am against both," he added. In 1863, after he had made a speech urging that the war be ended by negotiation, Vallandigham was seized by the military and thrown into jail. But Lincoln ordered him released and banished to the Confederacy. Once at liberty, Vallandigham moved to Canada, from which refuge he ran unsuccessfully for governor of Ohio.

Vallandigham was a zealot who "chose to ignore expediency," as his biographer put it. "Perish offices," he once said, "perish life itself, but do the thing that is right." In 1864 he returned to Ohio. Although he campaigned against Lincoln in the presidential election, he was not molested. As the historian David Herbert Donald has written, Lincoln was not a dictator. Throughout the conflict, "the harshness of war regulations was often tempered by leniency."

Behind Confederate Lines

The South also revised its strategy after Bull Run. Though it might have been wiser to risk everything on a bold invasion of the North, President Davis relied primarily on a strong defense to wear down the Union's will to fight. In 1862 the Confederate Congress passed a conscription act that permitted the hiring of substitutes and exempted many classes of people (including college professors, druggists, and mail carriers) whose work could hardly have been deemed essential. A provision deferring one slave owner or overseer for every plantation of 20 or more slaves led many to grumble about "a rich man's war and a poor man's fight."

Although the Confederacy did not develop a two-party system, there was plenty of internal political strife. Southern devotion to states' rights and individual liberty (for white men) caused endless trouble. Conflicts were continually erupting between Davis and southern governors jealous of their prerogatives as heads of "sovereign" states.

Finance was the Confederacy's most vexing problem. The blockade made it impossible to raise much money through tariffs. The Confederate Congress passed an income tax together with many excise taxes but all told covered only 2 percent of its needs by taxation. The most effective levy was a tax in kind, amounting to one-tenth of each farmer's production. The South borrowed as much as it could ($712 million), even mortgaging cotton undeliverable because of the blockade, in order to gain European credits. But it relied mainly on printing paper currency; over $1.5 billion poured from the presses during the war. Considering the amount issued, this currency held its value well until late in the war, when the military fortunes of the Confederacy began to decline. Then the bottom fell out, and by early 1865 the Confederate dollar was worth less than 2 cents in gold.

Outfitting the army strained southern resources to the limit. Large supplies of small arms (some 600,000 weapons during the entire war) came from Europe through the blockade, along with other valuable matériel. As the blockade became more efficient, however, it became increasingly difficult to obtain European goods. The Confederates did manage to build a number of munitions plants, and they captured huge amounts of northern arms. No battle was lost because of a lack of guns or other military equipment, though shortages of shoes and uniforms handicapped the Confederate forces on some occasions.

Foreign policy loomed large in Confederate thinking, for the "cotton is king" theory presupposed that the great powers would break any northern blockade to get cotton for their textile mills. Southern expectations were not realized, however. The European nations would have been delighted to see the United States broken up, but none was prepared to support the Confederacy directly. The attitude of Great Britain was decisive. The cutting off of cotton did not hit the British as hard as the South had hoped. They had a large supply on hand when the war broke out, and when that was exhausted, alternative sources in India and Egypt took up part of the slack. Furthermore, British crop failures necessitated the importation of large amounts of northern wheat, providing a powerful reason for not antagonizing the United States. The fact that most ordinary people in Great Britain favored the North also influenced British policy.

Several times the two nations came to the brink of war. In November 1861 U.S.S. *San Jacinto* stopped a British vessel, the *Trent,* on the high seas and forcibly arrested two Confederate envoys, James M. Mason and John Slidell, who were en route to London. This violation of international law would probably have led to war had not Lincoln decided to turn the southerners loose. In 1862 two powerful cruisers, the *Florida* and the *Alabama,* were built for the Confederates in English shipyards under the most transparent of subterfuges. Despite American protests, they were permitted to put to sea and were soon wreaking havoc among northern merchant ships. When two ironclad "rams" were also built in Britain for the Confederates, the United States made it clear that it would declare war if the ships were delivered. The British government then confiscated the vessels, avoiding a showdown.

Charles Francis Adams, the American minister in London, ably handled the many vexing problems that arose. However, the military situation determined British policy; once the North obtained a clear superiority on the battlefield, the possibility of intervention vanished.

War in the West: Shiloh

After Bull Run no heavy fighting took place until early 1862. Then, while McClellan continued his deliberate preparations to attack Richmond, Union forces in the West, led by a shabby, cigar-smoking West Pointer named Ulysses S. Grant, invaded Tennessee from a base at Cairo, Illinois. Making effective use of armored gunboats, Grant captured Forts Henry and Donelson, strongholds on the Tennessee and Cumberland rivers in northern Tennessee, taking 14,000 prisoners. Next he marched toward Corinth, Mississippi, an important railroad junction.

To check Grant's advance, the Confederates

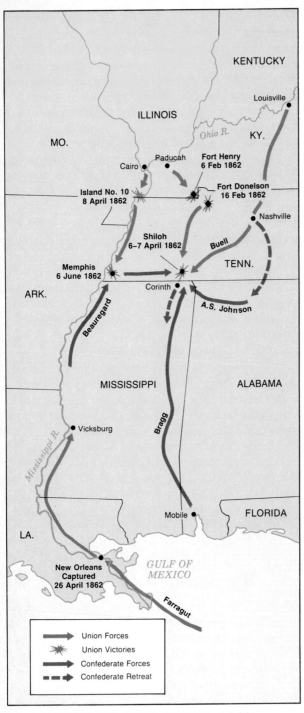

WAR IN THE WEST, 1862

The bloody battle at Shiloh in April of 1862 left Vicksburg, and thus control of the Mississippi, in Southern hands.

massed 40,000 men under Albert Sidney Johnston. On April 6, while Grant slowly concentrated his forces, Johnston struck suddenly at Shiloh, 20 miles north of Corinth. Some Union soldiers were caught half-dressed, others in the midst of brewing their morning coffee. A few died in their blankets. "We were more than surprised," one Illinois officer later admitted. "We were astonished." However, Grant's men stood their ground. At the end of a day of ghastly carnage, the Confederates held the advantage, but fresh Union troops poured in during the night, and on the second day of battle the tide turned. The Confederates fell back toward Corinth, exhausted and demoralized.

Grant was so shaken by the unexpected attack and appalled by his losses that he allowed the enemy to escape. This cost him the fine reputation he had won in capturing Fort Henry and Fort Donelson. He was relieved of his command. Although Corinth eventually fell and New Orleans was captured by a naval force under the command of Captain David Farragut, Vicksburg, key to control of the Mississippi, remained firmly in Confederate hands. A great opportunity had been lost.

Shiloh had other results. The staggering casualties shook the confidence of both belligerents. More Americans fell there in two days than in all the battles of the Revolution, the War of 1812, and the Mexican War combined. Union losses exceeded 13,000 out of 63,000 engaged; the Confederates lost 10,699, including General Johnston. Technology in the shape of more accurate guns that could be fired far more rapidly than the muskets of earlier times and more powerful artillery were responsible for the carnage. Gradually the generals began to reconsider their tactics and to experiment with field fortifications and other defensive measures. And the people, North and South, stopped thinking of the war as a romantic test of courage and military guile.

McClellan, the Reluctant Warrior

In Virginia, General McClellan, after unaccountable delays, was finally moving against Richmond. Instead of trying to advance across the difficult terrain of northern Virginia, he transported his army by water to the tip of the peninsula formed by the York and James rivers in order to attack Richmond from the southeast. After the famous battle (March 9, 1862) between U.S.S. *Monitor* and the Confederate *Merrimack,* the first fight in history between armored warships, control of these waters was securely in northern hands.

While McClellan's plan alarmed many congressmen because it seemed to leave Washington relatively unprotected, it simplified the problem of keeping the army supplied in hostile country. But McClellan now displayed the weaknesses that even-

tually ruined his career. His problems were both intellectual and psychological. Basically, he approached tactical questions in the manner of a typical 18th-century general. He considered war a kind of gentlemanly contest (similar to chess with its castles and knights) in which maneuver, guile, and position determined victory. He saw the Civil War not as a mighty struggle over fundamental beliefs but as a sort of complex game that commanders played at a leisurely pace and for limited stakes. He believed it more important to capture Richmond than to destroy the army protecting it. With their capital in

After the first battle at Bull Run, in July of 1861, there was little action until the following spring, when McClellan launched his Peninsula campaign. The battle of Antietam was the culmination of the fighting in the summer of 1862.

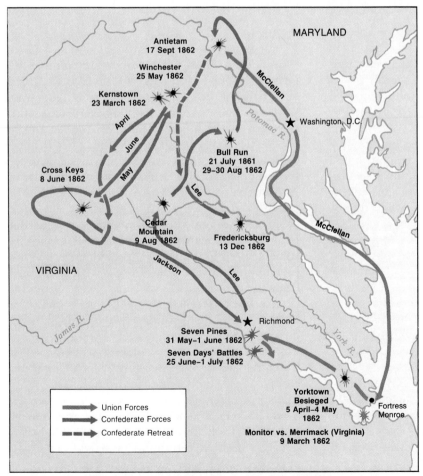

WAR IN THE EAST, 1861–1862

In the Peninsula campaign, the cautious McClellan faced the South's most brilliant generals, Robert E. Lee and Thomas J. "Stonewall" Jackson. During the Seven Days Battle as McClellan moved on Richmond, Lee attacked Union supply lines. This sketch by Alfred Waud shows McClellan's retreat after the failed attempt to take Richmond.

northern hands, surely the southerners (outwitted and outmaneuvered by a brilliant general) would acknowledge defeat and agree to return to the Union. The idea of crushing the South seemed to him wrongheaded and uncivilized.

Beyond this, McClellan was temperamentally unsuited for a position of so much responsibility. Beneath the swagger he was profoundly insecure. He talked like Napoleon, but he did not like to fight. He called repeatedly for more men; when he got them, he demanded still more. He knew how to get ready, but he was never ready in his own mind. What was said of another Union general would have been better said of McClellan: He was "watching the enemy as fast as he can."

McClellan began the Peninsula campaign in mid-March. Proceeding deliberately, he floated an army of 112,000 men down the Potomac and by May 14 had established a base at White House Landing, less than 25 miles from Richmond. A swift thrust might have ended the war quickly, but McClellan delayed, despite the fact that he had 80,000 men in striking position and large reserves. As he pushed forward slowly, the Confederates caught part of his force separated from the main body by the rain-swollen Chickahominy River and attacked. The Battle of Seven Pines was indecisive yet resulted in more than 10,000 casualties.

At Seven Pines the Confederate commander, General Joseph E. Johnston, was severely wounded; leadership of the Army of Northern Virginia then passed to Robert E. Lee. Although a reluctant supporter of secession, Lee was a superb soldier. During the Mexican War his gallantry under fire inspired General Scott to call him the bravest man in the army; another officer rhapsodized over his "daring reconnaissances pushed up to the cannon's mouth." He also had displayed an almost instinctive mastery of tactics. Admiral Raphael Semmes, who accompanied Scott's army on the march to Mexico City, recalled in 1851 that Lee "seemed to receive impressions intuitively, which it cost other men much labor to acquire."

Lee was McClellan's antithesis. McClellan seemed almost deliberately to avoid understanding his foes, acting as though every southern general was an Alexander. Lee, a master psychologist on the battlefield, took the measure of each Union general and devised his tactics accordingly. Where McClellan was complex, egotistical, perhaps even unbalanced, Lee was courtly, tactful, and entirely without McClellan's vainglorious belief that he was a man of destiny. Yet on the battlefield Lee's boldness skirted the edge of foolhardiness.

To relieve the pressure on Richmond, Lee sent General "Stonewall" Jackson, soon to be his most trusted lieutenant, on a diversionary raid in the Shenandoah Valley, west of Richmond and Washington. Jackson struck hard and swiftly at scattered Union forces in the region, winning a number of battles and capturing vast stores of equipment. Lincoln dispatched 20,000 reserves to the Shenandoah to check him—to the dismay of McClellan, who wanted the troops to attack Richmond from the north. But after Seven Pines, Lee ordered Jackson back to Richmond. While Union armies streamed toward the valley, Jackson slipped stealthily between them. On June 25 he reached Ashland, directly north of the Confederate capital.

Before that date McClellan had possessed clear numerical superiority yet had only inched ahead; now the advantage lay with Lee and the very next day he attacked. For seven days the battle raged. Lee's plan was brilliant but too complicated for an army yet untested: the full weight of his force never hit the northern army at any one time. Nevertheless, the shock was formidable. McClellan, who excelled in defense, fell back, his lines intact, exacting a fearful toll. Under difficult conditions he managed to transfer his troops to a new base on the James River at Harrison's Landing, where the guns of the navy could shield his position. Again the loss of life was terrible: Northern casualties totaled 15,800, those of the South nearly 20,000.

Lee Counterattacks: Antietam

McClellan was still within striking distance of Richmond, in an impregnable position with secure supply lines and 86,000 soldiers ready to resume battle. Lee had absorbed heavy losses without winning any significant advantage. Yet Lincoln was exasperated with McClellan for having surrendered the initiative and, after much deliberation, reduced his authority by placing him under General Henry W. Halleck. Halleck called off the Peninsula campaign and ordered McClellan to move his army from the James to the Potomac, near Washington. He was to join General John Pope, who was gathering a new army between Washington and Richmond.

It is possible, as James McPherson suggests in his gripping account of the war, *Battle Cry of Freedom*, that if McClellan had persisted and captured Richmond, the war might have ended and the Union been restored without the abolition of slavery, since

Lee in 1863, by Julian Vannerson. "So great is my confidence in General Lee," Stonewall Jackson remarked, "that I am willing to follow him blind-folded."

at that point the North was still fighting for union, not for freedom for the slaves. Ironically, as McPherson puts it, "by defeating McClellan, Lee assured a prolongation of the war until it destroyed slavery." Of course, no one expressed this idea at the time.

For the president to have lost confidence in McClellan was understandable. Nevertheless, to allow Halleck to pull back the troops was a bad mistake. When they withdrew, Lee seized the initiative. With typical decisiveness and daring, he marched rapidly north. Late in August his Confederates drove General Pope's confused troops from the same ground, Bull Run, where the first major engagement of the war had been fought.

Thirteen months had passed since the first failure at Bull Run, and despite the expenditure of thousands of lives, the Union army stood as far from Richmond as ever. Dismayed by Pope's incompetence, Lincoln turned in desperation back to McClellan. When his secretary protested that McClellan had expressed contempt for the president, Lincoln replied gently: "We must use what tools we have."

While McClellan was regrouping the shaken Union Army, Lee once again took the offensive. He realized that no number of individual southern triumphs could destroy the enormous material advantages of the North. Unless some dramatic blow, delivered on northern soil, persuaded the people of the United States that military victory was impossible, the South would surely be crushed in the long run by the weight of superior resources. Lee therefore marched rapidly northwest around the defenses of Washington.

Acting with even more than his usual boldness, Lee divided his army of 60,000 into a number of units. One, under Stonewall Jackson, descended on weakly defended Harpers Ferry, capturing more than 11,000 prisoners. Another pressed as far north as Hagerstown, Maryland, nearly to the Pennsylvania line. McClellan pursued with his usual deliberation until a captured dispatch revealed to him Lee's dispositions. Then he moved a bit more swiftly, forcing Lee to stand and fight on September 17 at Sharpsburg, Maryland, between the Potomac and Antietam Creek.* On a field that offered Lee

---

* Southerners tended to identify battles by nearby towns, northerners by bodies of water. Thus Manassas and Bull Run, Sharpsburg and Antietam, Murfreesboro and Stone's River, and so on.

no room to maneuver, 70,000 Union soldiers clashed with 40,000 Confederates. When darkness fell, more than 22,000 lay dead or wounded on the bloody field.

Although casualties were evenly divided and the Confederate lines remained intact, Lee's position was perilous. His men were exhausted. McClellan had not yet thrown in his reserves, and new federal units were arriving hourly. A bold northern general would have continued the fight without respite through the night. One of ordinary aggressiveness would have waited for first light and then struck with every soldier who could hold a rifle, for with the Potomac at his back, Lee could not retreat under fire without inviting disaster. McClellan, however, did nothing. For an entire day, while Lee scanned the field in futile search of some weakness in the Union lines, he held his fire. That night the Confederates slipped back across the Potomac into Virginia.

Lee's invasion had failed; his army had been badly mauled; the gravest threat to the Union in the war had been checked. But McClellan had let victory slip through his fingers. Soon Lee was back behind the defenses of Richmond, rebuilding his army.

Once again, this time finally, Lincoln dismissed McClellan from his command.

The Emancipation Proclamation

Antietam, though hardly the victory he had hoped for, gave Lincoln the excuse he needed to take a step that changed the character of the war decisively. When the fighting started, fear of alienating the border states was reason enough for not making emancipation a war aim. However, pressures to act against the South's peculiar institution mounted steadily. Slavery had divided the nation; now it was driving northerners to war within themselves. Love of country led them to fight to save the Union, but fighting aroused hatreds and caused many to desire to smash the enemy. Sacrifice, pain, and grief made abolitionists of many who had no love for blacks—they sought to free the slave only to injure the master.

To make abolition an object of the war might encourage the slaves to revolt, but Lincoln disclaimed this objective. Nevertheless, the possibility existed. Already the slaves seemed to be looking to the North for freedom: Whenever Union troops invaded Confederate territory, slaves flocked into their lines.

As the war progressed, the Radical faction in Congress gradually chipped away at slavery. In April 1862 the Radicals pushed through a bill abolishing slavery in the District of Columbia; two months later another measure outlawed it in the territories; in July the Confiscation Act "freed" all slaves owned by persons in rebellion against the

The genesis of the Emancipation Proclamation seen from diametrically opposed viewpoints. The drawing at left is by Adalbert Johann Volck, a Baltimore dentist and vitriolic propagandist for the Confederate cause. A satanic Lincoln, one foot on the Constitution, is inspired by a portrait of John Brown with a halo and a depiction of the alleged excesses of the Saint Domingue slave revolt of the 1790s. David Gilmour Blythe, a staunch administration supporter, left no doubt in his painting (below) that the sources of Lincoln's inspiration were of a much higher order.

United States. In fighting for these measures and in urging general emancipation, some Radicals made statements harshly critical of Lincoln; but while he carefully avoided being identified with them or with any other faction, the president was never very far from their position. He resisted emancipation because he feared it would divide the country and injure the war effort, not because he personally disapproved. Indeed, he frequently offered Radical pressure as an excuse for doing what he wished to do on his own.

Lincoln would have preferred to see slavery done away with by state law, with compensation for slave owners and federal aid for former slaves willing to leave the United States. He tried repeatedly to persuade the loyal slave states to adopt this policy, but without success. By the summer of 1862 he was convinced that for military reasons and to win the support of liberal opinion in Europe, the government should make abolition a war aim. "We must free the slaves or be ourselves subdued," he explained to a member of his Cabinet. He delayed temporarily, fearing that a statement in the face of military reverses would be taken as a sign of weakness. The "victory" at Antietam Creek gave him his opportunity, and on September 22 he made public the Emancipation Proclamation. After January 1, 1863, it said, all slaves in areas in rebellion against the United States "shall be then, thenceforward, and forever free."

No single slave was freed directly by Lincoln's announcement, which did not apply to the border states or to those sections of the Confederacy, like New Orleans and Norfolk, Virginia, already controlled by federal troops. The proclamation differed in philosophy, however, from the Confiscation Act in striking at the institution, not at the property of rebels. Henceforth every Union victory would speed the destruction of slavery without regard for the attitudes of individual masters.

Some of the president's advisers thought the proclamation inexpedient, and others considered it illegal. Lincoln justified it as a way to weaken the enemy. The proclamation is full of phrases like "as a fit and necessary war measure" and "warranted by the Constitution upon military necessity."

Southerners considered the Emancipation Proclamation an incitement to slave rebellion—as one of them put it, an "infamous attempt to . . . convert the quiet, ignorant, and dependent black son of toil into a savage incendiary and brutal murderer." Most antislavery groups thought it did not go far enough. Lincoln "is only stopping on the edge of Niagara, to pick up a few chips," one abolitionist declared. "He and they will go over together." Foreign opinion was mixed: Liberals tended to applaud, conservatives to react with alarm or contempt.

As Lincoln anticipated, the proclamation had a subtle but continuing impact in the North. Its immediate effect was to aggravate racial prejudices. Millions of whites disapproved of slavery yet abhorred the idea of equality for blacks. David Wilmot, for example, insisted that his famous proviso was designed to preserve the territories for whites rather than to weaken slavery, and as late as 1857 the people of Iowa rejected black suffrage by a vote of 49,000 to 8,000. To some, emancipation seemed to herald an invasion of the North by blacks who would compete for jobs, drive down wages, commit crimes, spread diseases, and eventually destroy the "purity" of the white race. The word *miscegenation* was coined in 1863 by David G. Croly, an editor of the *New York World*, directly as a result of the Emancipation Proclamation. Its original meaning was "the mingling of the white and black races on the continent *as a consequence of the freedom of the latter*." Of course, the fact of miscegenation in its current, more general meaning long antedated the freeing of any slave.

The Democrats spared no effort to make political capital of these fears and prejudices even before Lincoln's Emancipation Proclamation, and they made large gains in the 1862 election, especially in the Northwest. So strong was antiblack feeling that most of the Republican politicians who defended emancipation did so with racist arguments. Far from encouraging southern blacks to move north, they claimed, the ending of slavery would lead to a mass migration of northern blacks to the South.

When the Emancipation Proclamation began actually to free slaves, the government pursued a policy of "containment," that is, of keeping the ex-slaves in the South. Panicky fears of an inundation of blacks subsided in the North. Nevertheless, emancipation remained a cause of social discontent. In March 1863, volunteering having fallen off, Congress passed a conscription act. The law applied to all men between 20 and 45, but it allowed draftees to hire substitutes and even to buy exemption for $300, provisions that were patently unfair to the poor. During the remainder of the war 46,000 men were actually drafted, whereas 118,000 hired substitutes, and another 161,000 "failed to report." Conscription represented an enormous expansion of national authority, since in effect it gave the government the power of life and death over individual citizens.

Negrophobia and the Draft Riots

After the passage of the Conscription Act, draft riots erupted in a number of cities. By far the most serious disturbance occurred in New York City in July 1863. Many workers resented conscription in principle and were embittered by the $300 exemption fee (which represented a year's wages). The idea of being forced to risk their lives to free slaves who would then, they believed, compete with them for jobs infuriated them. On July 13 a mob attacked the office where the names of conscripts were being drawn. Most of the rioters were poor Irish Catholic laborers who resented both the blacks and the middle-class Protestant whites who seemed to them responsible for the special attention blacks were suddenly receiving. For four days the city was an inferno. Public buildings, shops, and private residences were put to the torch. What began as a protest against the draft became an assault on blacks and the well-to-do. It took federal troops and the temporary suspension of the draft in the city to put an end to the rioting. By the time order was restored over 100 people (most of them rioters) had lost their lives.

The Emancipation Proclamation does not entirely account for the draft riots. The new policy neither reflected nor triggered a revolution in white thinking about the race question. Its significance was subtle but real; both the naive view that Lincoln freed the slaves on January 1, 1863, and the cynical one that his action was a mere propaganda trick are incorrect. Northern hostility to emancipation arose from fear of change more than from hatred of blacks, while liberal disavowals of any intention to treat blacks as equals were in large measure designed to quiet this fear. To a degree the racial backlash that the proclamation inspired reflected the public's awareness that a change, frightening but irreversible, *had occurred.*

Most white northerners did not surrender their comforting belief in black inferiority, and Lincoln was no exception. Yet Lincoln was evolving. He talked about deporting ex-slaves to the tropics, but he did not send any there. And he began to receive black leaders in the White House and to allow black groups to hold meetings on the grounds.

Many other Americans were changing too. The brutality of the New York riots horrified many white citizens. Over $40,000 was swiftly raised to aid the victims, and some conservatives were so appalled by the Irish rioters that they began to talk of giving blacks the vote. The influential *Atlantic Monthly* commented: "It is impossible to name any standard . . . that will give a vote to the Celt and exclude the negro."

The Emancipated People

To blacks, both slave and free, the Emancipation Proclamation served as a beacon. Even if it failed immediately to liberate one slave or to lift the burdens of prejudice from one black back, it stood as a promise of future improvement. "I took the proclamation for a little more than it purported," Frederick Douglass recalled in his autobiography, "and saw in its spirit a life and power far beyond its letter." Lincoln was by modern standards a racist, but his most militant black contemporaries respected him deeply. The *Anglo-African,* an uncompromising black newspaper (the position of which is revealed in an 1862 editorial that asked: "Poor, chicken-hearted, semi-barbarous Caucasians, when will you learn that "the earth was made for MAN?"), referred in 1864 to Lincoln's "many noble acts" and urged his reelection. Douglass said of him: "Lincoln was not . . . either our man or our model. In his interests, in his association, in his habits of thought and in his prejudices, he was a white man." Nevertheless, Douglass described Lincoln as "one whom I could love, honor, and trust without reserve or doubt."

As for the slaves of the South, after January 1, 1863, whenever the "Army of Freedom" approached, they laid down their plows and hoes and flocked to the Union lines in droves. "We-all knows about it," one black confided to a northern clergyman early in 1863. "Only we darsen't let on. We *pretends* not to know." Such behavior came as a shock to the owners. "[The slaves] who loved us best—as we thought—were the first to leave us," one planter mourned. Talk of slave "ingratitude" increased. Instead of referring to their workers as "servants" or "my black family," many owners began to describe them as "slaves" or "niggers."

Black Soldiers

A revolutionary shift occurred in white thinking about using black men as soldiers. Although they had fought in the Revolution and in the Battle of New Orleans during the War of 1812, a law of 1792 barred blacks from the army. During the early stages of the rebellion, despite the eagerness of thousands of free blacks to enlist, the prohibition remained in force. By 1862, however, the need for manpower was creating pressure for change. In August Secretary of War Edwin M. Stanton authorized the military government of the captured South Carolina sea islands to enlist slaves in the area. After the Emancipation Proclamation specifically authorized the enlistment of blacks, the governor of Massa-

chusetts moved to organize a black regiment, the famous Massachusetts 54th. Swiftly thereafter, other states began to recruit black soldiers, and in May 1863 the federal government established a Bureau of Colored Troops to supervise their enlistment. By the end of the war one soldier in eight in the Union army was black.

Enlisting large numbers of black soldiers changed the war from a struggle to save the Union to a kind of revolution. "Let the black man . . . get an eagle on his button and a musket on his shoulder," wrote Frederick Douglass, "and there is no power on earth which can deny that he has earned the right to citizenship."

Black soldiers were segregated and commanded by white officers. For example, the Massachusetts 54th regiment was commanded by Colonel Robert Gould Shaw of Boston, called by one admirer "the very type and flower of the Anglo-Saxon race." At first black soldiers received only $7 a month, about half what white soldiers were paid. But they soon proved themselves in battle; of the 180,000 who served in the Union army, 37,000 were killed, a rate of loss about 40 percent higher than that among

The Emancipation Proclamation allowed free blacks to enlist in the Union army. By late 1863, the Union had 58 black regiments. The skepticism of white commanders soon faded as black troops proved their bravery under fire. Here, soldiers from the 22nd U.S. Colored Troops charge an enemy position outside Petersburg in June 1864.

white troops. Their bravery under fire convinced thousands of northern white soldiers that blacks were not by nature childish or cowardly.

Southerners were another matter. There is no doubt that black soldiers were cruelly mistreated in Confederate prison camps. Still worse, many black captives were killed on the spot. After overrunnng the garrison of Fort Pillow on the Mississippi River, the Confederates massacred several dozen black soldiers, along with their white commander. Lincoln was tempted to order reprisals, but he and his advisers realized that this would have been both morally wrong (two wrongs never make a right) and likely to lead to still more atrocities. "Blood can not restore blood," Lincoln said in his usual direct way.

Antietam to Gettysburg

It was well that Lincoln seized on Antietam to release his proclamation; had he waited for a more impressive victory, he would have waited nearly a year. To replace McClellan, he chose General Ambrose E. Burnside, best known to history for his magnificent side-whiskers (originally called burnsides, later, at first jokingly, sideburns). Burnside was a corps commander, but he lacked the self-confidence essential to anyone who takes responsibility for major decisions. He knew his limitations and tried to avoid high command, but patriotism and his sense of duty compelled him, when pressed, to accept leadership of the Army of the Potomac. He prepared to march on Richmond.

Unlike McClellan, Burnside was aggressive—too aggressive. He planned to ford the Rappahannock River at Fredericksburg. Supply problems and bad weather delayed him until mid-December, giving Lee time to concentrate his army in impregnable positions behind the town. Although he had more than 120,000 men against Lee's 75,000, Burnside should have called off the attack when he saw Lee's advantage; instead he ordered the troops forward. Crossing the river over pontoon bridges, his divisions occupied Fredericksburg. Then, in wave after wave, they charged the Confederate defense line while Lee's artillery riddled them from nearby Marye's Heights. Watching the battle from his command post on the heights, General Lee was deeply moved. Turning to General James Longstreet, he

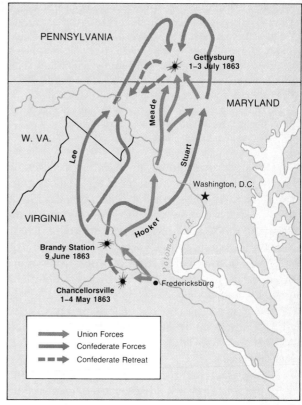

GETTYSBURG CAMPAIGN, 1863

Gettysburg, in July of 1863, marked the turning point of the war; after it the South never again tried to invade the North.

said: "It is well that war is so terrible—we should grow too fond of it!"

On December 14, the day following this futile assault, General Burnside, tears streaming down his cheeks, ordered the evacuation of Fredericksburg. Shortly thereafter, General Joseph Hooker replaced him.

Unlike Burnside, "Fighting Joe" Hooker was ill-tempered, vindictive, and devious. In naming him to command the Army of the Potomac, Lincoln sent him a letter that was a measure of his desperation but is now famous for what it reveals of the president's character:

I think that during Gen. Burnside's command of the Army, you have taken counsel of your ambition, and thwarted him as much as you could, in which you did a great wrong to the country. . . . I have heard, in such a way as to believe it, of you, recently saying that both the Army and the Government need a Dictator. Of course it is not *for* this, but in spite of it, that I have given you the command. Only those generals who gain successes, can set up dictators. What I now ask of you is military success, and I will risk the dictatorship. . . . Beware of rashness, but with energy and sleepless vigilance, go forward, and give us victories.

Hooker proved no better than his predecessor, but his failings were more like McClellan's than Burnside's. By the spring of 1863 he had 125,000 men ready for action. Late in April he forded the Rappahannock and quickly concentrated at Chancellorsville, about 10 miles west of Fredericksburg. His army outnumbered the Confederates by more than two to one; he should have forced a battle at once. Instead he delayed, and while he did, Lee sent Stonewall Jackson's corps of 28,000 men across tangled countryside to a position directly athwart Hooker's unsuspecting flank. At 6 P.M. on May 2, Jackson attacked.

Completely surprised, the Union right crumbled, brigade after brigade overrun before it could wheel to meet Jackson's charge. At the first sound of firing, Lee had struck along the entire front to impede Union troop movements. If the battle had begun earlier in the day, the Confederates might have won a decisive victory; as it happened, nightfall brought a lull, and the next day the Union troops rallied and held their ground. Heavy fighting continued until May 5, when Hooker abandoned the field and retreated in good order behind the Rappahannock.

Chancellorsville cost the Confederates dearly, for their losses, in excess of 12,000, were almost as heavy as the North's and harder to replace. They also lost Stonewall Jackson, struck down by the bullets of his own men while returning from a reconnaissance. Nevertheless, the Union army had suffered another fearful blow to its morale.

Lee knew that time was still on the side of the North; to defend Richmond was not enough. Already federal troops in the West were closing in on Vicksburg, threatening to cut Confederate communications with Arkansas and Texas. Now was the time to strike, while the morale of the northern people was at low ebb. With 75,000 soldiers he crossed the Potomac again, a larger Union force

dogging his right flank. By late June his army had fanned out across southern Pennsylvania in a 50-mile arc from Chambersburg to the Susquehanna. Gray-clad soldiers ranged 50 miles northwest of Baltimore, within 10 miles of Harrisburg.

As Union soldiers had been doing in Virginia, Lee's men destroyed property and commandeered food, horses, and clothing wherever they could find them. They even seized a number of blacks and sent them south to be sold as slaves. On July 1 a Confederate division looking for shoes in the town of Gettysburg clashed with two brigades of Union cavalry northwest of the town. Both sides sent out calls for reinforcements. Like iron filings drawn to a magnet, the two armies converged. The Confederates won control of the town, but the Union army, now commanded by General George G. Meade, took a strong position on Cemetery Ridge, a hook-shaped stretch of high ground just to the south. Lee's men occupied Seminary Ridge, a parallel position. On this field the fate of the Union was probably decided. For two days the Confederates attacked Cemetery Ridge, pounding it with the heaviest artillery barrage ever seen in America and sweeping bravely up its flanks in repeated assaults. During General George E. Pickett's famous charge, a handful of his men actually reached the Union lines, but reserves drove them back. By nightfall on July 3 the Confederate army was spent and bleeding, the Union lines unbroken.

The following day was the Fourth of July. The two weary forces rested on their arms. Had the Union army attacked in force, the Confederates might have been crushed, but just as McClellan had hesitated after Antietam, Meade let opportunity pass. On July 5 Lee retreated to safety. For the first time he had been clearly bested on the field of battle.

Lincoln Finds His General: Vicksburg

On that same Independence Day, far to the west, federal troops won another great victory. When General Halleck was called east in July 1862, Ulysses S. Grant reassumed command of the Union troops. Grant was one of the most controversial officers in the army. At West Point he had compiled an indifferent record, ranking 21st in a class of 39. During the Mexican War he served well, but when he was later assigned to a lonely post in Oregon, he took to drink and was forced to resign his commission. Thereafter he was by turns a farmer, a real estate agent, and a clerk in a leather goods store. In 1861, approaching 40, he seemed well into a life of frustration and mediocrity.

The war gave him a second chance. Back in service, however, his reputation as a ne'er-do-well and his unmilitary bearing worked against him, as did the heavy casualties suffered by his troops at Shiloh. Yet the fact that he knew how to manage a large army and win battles did not escape Lincoln. According to tradition, when a gossip tried to poison the president against Grant by referring to his drinking, Lincoln retorted that if he knew what brand Grant favored, he would send a barrel of it to some of his other generals.* Grant never used alcohol as a substitute for courage. "Old Ulysses," one of his soldiers said, "he don't scare worth a damn."

Grant's major aim was to capture Vicksburg, a city of tremendous strategic importance. Together with Port Hudson, a bastion north of Baton Rouge, Louisiana, it guarded a 150-mile stretch of the Mississippi. The river between these points was inaccessible to federal gunboats. So long as Vicksburg remained in southern hands, the trans-Mississippi region could send men and supplies to the rest of the Confederacy.

Vicksburg sits on a high bluff overlooking a sharp bend in the river. When it proved unapproachable from either the west or the north, Grant devised an audacious scheme for getting at it from the east. He descended the Mississippi from Memphis to a point a few miles north of the city. Then, leaving part of his force behind to create the impression that he planned to attack from the north, he crossed the west bank and slipped quickly southward. Recrossing the river below Vicksburg, he abandoned his communications and supply lines and struck at Jackson, the capital of Mississippi. In a series of swift engagements his troops captured Jackson, cutting off the army of General John C. Pemberton, defending Vicksburg, from other Con-

In outward appearance, Ulysses S. Grant was an unlikely leader. Despite his neatness in the formal portrait, Grant usually wore a sloppy, tobacco-stained uniform, and he had a reputation as a drunkard. During the war, critics pressed Lincoln to replace Grant, but the president replied, "I can't spare this man. He fights!"

federate units. Turning next on Pemberton, Grant defeated him in two decisive battles, Champion's Hill and Big Black River, and drove him inside the Vicksburg fortifications. By mid-May the city was under siege. Grant applied relentless pressure, and on July 4 Pemberton surrendered. With Vicksburg in Union hands, federal gunboats could range the entire length of the Mississippi.* Texas and Arkansas were for all practical purposes lost to the Confederacy.

---

* Lincoln denied having said this, pointing out that it was a version of a remark about General James Wolfe attributed to King George II. When a critic claimed that Wolfe was a madman, the King is said to have replied: "I wish he would bite some of the others."

---

* Port Hudson, isolated by Vicksburg's fall, surrendered on July 9.

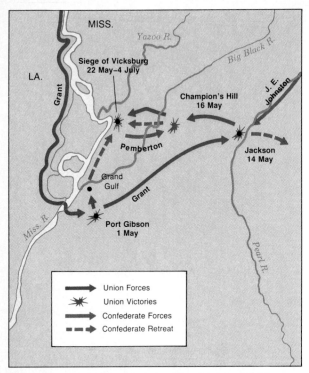

VICKSBURG CAMPAIGN, 1863

When Vicksburg fell to the Union troops on July 4, 1863, the Mississippi River was reopened to the free passage of Federal forces.

Lincoln had disliked Grant's plan for capturing Vicksburg. Now he generously confessed his error and placed Grant in command of all federal troops west of the Appalachians. Grant promptly took charge of the fighting around Chattanooga, where Confederate advances, beginning with the Battle of Chickamauga (September 19–20), were threatening to develop into a major disaster for the North. Shifting corps commanders and bringing up fresh units, he won another decisive victory at Chattanooga in a series of battles ending on November 25, 1863. This cleared the way for an invasion of Georgia. Suddenly this unkempt, stubby little man, who looked more like a tramp than a general, emerged as the military leader the North had been so desperately seeking. In March 1864 Lincoln summoned him to Washington, named him lieutenant general, and gave him supreme command of the armies of the United States.

Economic and Social Effects, North and South

Though much blood would yet be spilled, by the end of 1863 the Confederacy was on the road to defeat. Northern military pressure, gradually increasing, was eroding the South's most precious resource: manpower. An ever-tightening naval blockade was reducing its economic strength. Shortages developed that, combined with the flood of currency pouring from the presses, led to drastic inflation. By 1864 an officer's coat cost $2,000 in Confederate money, cigars sold for $10 each, butter was $25 a pound, and flour went for $275 a barrel. Wages rose too, but not nearly as rapidly.

The southern railroad network was gradually wearing out, the major lines maintaining operations only by cannibalizing less vital roads. Imported products such as coffee disappeared; even salt became scarce. Efforts to increase manufacturing were only moderately successful because of the shortage of labor, capital, and technical knowledge. In general, southern prejudice against centralized authority prevented the Confederacy from making effective use of its scarce resources. Even blockade running was left in private hands until 1864. Precious cargo space that should have been reserved for medical supplies and arms was often devoted to high-priced luxuries.

In the North, after a brief depression in 1861 caused by the uncertainties of the situation and the loss of southern business, the economy flourished. Government purchases greatly stimulated certain lines of manufacturing, the railroads operated at close to capacity and with increasing efficiency, the farm machinery business boomed because so many farmers left their fields to serve in the army, and bad harvests in Europe boosted agricultural prices.

Congress passed a number of economic measures long desired but held up in the past by southern opposition. The Homestead Act (1862) gave 160 acres to any settler who would farm the land for five years. The Morrill Land Grant Act of the same year provided the states with land at the rate of 30,000 acres for each member of Congress to support state agricultural colleges. Various tariff acts raised the duties on manufactured goods to an average rate of 47 percent in order to protect domestic manufacturers from foreign competition. The Pacific Railway Act (1862) authorized subsidies

in land and money for the construction of a transcontinental railroad. And the National Banking Act
of 1863 gave the country, at last, a uniform currency. Under this act, banks could obtain federal
charters by investing at least one-third of their capital in United States bonds. They might then issue
currency up to 90 percent of the value of those
bonds. A 10 percent tax on the issues of state banks
drove state bank notes out of circulation.

All these laws stimulated the economy. Whether
the overall economic effect of the Civil War on the
Union was beneficial is less clear. Since it was fought
mostly with rifles, light cannon, horses, and wagons,
it had much less effect on heavy industry than later
wars would have. Although the economy grew, it
did so more slowly during the 1860s than in the
decades preceding and following. Prices soared beginning in 1862, averaging about 80 percent over
the 1860 level by the end of the war. As in the South,
wages did not keep pace. This did not make for a
healthy economy; nor did the fact that there were
chronic shortages of labor in many fields, shortages
aggravated by a sharp drop in the number of immigrants entering the country.

As the war dragged on and the continuing inflation eroded purchasing power, resentment on the
part of workers deepened. During the 1850s iron
moulders, cigarmakers, and some other crafts had
formed national unions. This trend continued
through the war years. There were many strikes.
Inflation and shortages encouraged speculation and
fostered a selfish, materialistic attitude toward life.
Many contractors took advantage of wartime confusion to sell the government shoddy goods. By
1864 cotton was worth $1.90 a pound in New En-
gland. It could be had for 20 cents a pound in the
South. Though it was illegal to traffic in the staple
across the lines, unscrupulous operators did so and
made huge profits. "Cotton was the great corrupter
of the Civil War," the historian James McPherson
has written.

Yet the war undoubtedly hastened industrialization and laid the basis for many other aspects of
modern civilization. It posed problems of organization and planning, both military and civilian, that
challenged the talents of creative persons and thus
led to a more complex and efficient economy. The
mechanization of production, the growth of large
corporations, the creation of a better banking system, and the emergence of business leaders attuned

to these conditions would surely have occurred in
any case, for industrialization was under way long
before the South seceded. Nevertheless, the war
greatly speeded all these changes.

Women in Wartime

Many southern women took over the management
of farms and small plantations when their menfolk
went off to war. Others became volunteer nurses,
and after an initial period of resistance, the Confederate army began to enlist women in the medical
corps. At least two female nurses, Captain Sally
Tompkins and Kate Cumming, left records of their
experiences that throw much light on how the
wounded were treated during the war. Other southern women worked as clerks in newly organized
government departments.

Large numbers of women also contributed to
the northern war effort. As in the South, farm
women went out into fields to plant and harvest
crops, aided in many instances by new farm machinery. Many others took jobs in textile factories;
in establishments making shoes, uniforms, and
other supplies for the army; and in government
agencies. But as was usually the case, the low wages
traditionally paid women acted as a brake on wage
increases for their male colleagues.

Besides working in factories and shops and on
farms, northern women, again like their southern
counterparts, aided the war effort more directly.
Elizabeth Blackwell, the first American woman doctor of medicine, had already founded the New York
Infirmary for Women and Children. After war
broke out she helped set up what became the United
States Sanitary Commission, an organization of
women dedicated to improving sanitary conditions
at army camps, supplying hospitals with volunteer
nurses, and raising money for medical supplies.
Many thousands of women volunteers took part in
Sanitary Commission, YMCA, and similar programs.

An additional 3,000-odd women served as regular army nurses during the conflict. At the start
the high command of both armies resisted the efforts of women to help, but necessity and a grudging
recognition of the competence of these women
gradually brought the generals around. The
"proper sphere" of American women was expand-

Despite enormous difficulties, Elizabeth Blackwell managed to complete medical school and become the first woman doctor in the United States. During the Civil War, she organized the Women's Central Association of Relief, which trained nurses for war work. Women such as Dorothea Dix and Clara Barton in the North and Sally Tompkins in the South nursed sick and wounded soldiers.

ing, another illustration of the modernizing effect of the war.

Grant in the Wilderness

Grant's strategy as supreme commander was simple, logical, and ruthless. He would attack Lee and try to capture Richmond. General William Tecumseh Sherman would drive from Chattanooga toward Atlanta, Georgia. Like a lobster's claw, the two armies could then close to crush all resistance. Early in May 1864 Grant and Sherman commenced operations, each with more than 100,000 men.

Grant marched the Army of the Potomac directly into the tangled wilderness area south of the Rappahannock, where Hooker had been routed a year earlier. Lee, having only 60,000 men, forced the battle in the roughest possible country, where Grant found it difficult to make efficient use of his larger force. For two days (May 5–6) the Battle of the Wilderness raged. When it was over, the North had sustained another 18,000 casualties, far more than the Confederates. But unlike his predecessor, Grant did not fall back after being checked, nor did he expose his army to the kind of devastating counterattack at which Lee was so expert. Instead he shifted his troops to the southeast, attempting to outflank the Confederates. Divining his intent, Lee rushed his divisions southeastward and disposed them behind hastily erected earthworks in well-placed positions around Spotsylvania Court House. Grant attacked. After five more days, at a cost to the Union army of another 12,000 men, the Confederate lines were still intact.

Grant had grasped the fundamental truth that the war could be won only by grinding the South down beneath the weight of numbers. His own losses of men and equipment could be replaced; Lee's could not. When critics complained of the cost, he replied doggedly that he intended to fight on in the same manner if it took all summer. Once more he pressed southeastward in an effort to outflank the enemy. At Cold Harbor, 9 miles from Richmond, he found the Confederates once more in strong defenses. He attacked. It was a battle as foolish and nearly as one-sided as General Pakenham's assault on Jackson's line outside New Orleans in 1815. "At Cold Harbor," the forthright Grant confessed in his memoirs, "no advantage whatever was gained to compensate for the heavy losses we sustained."

Sixty thousand casualties in less than a month! The news sent a wave of dismay through the North. There were demands that "Butcher" Grant be removed from command. Lincoln, however, stood firm. Although the price was fearfully high, Grant was gaining his objective. At Cold Harbor, Lee had to fight without a single regiment in general reserve while Grant's army was larger than at the start of the offensive. When Grant next swung around his flank, striking south of the James River toward Petersburg, Lee had to rush his troops to that city to hold him.

As Grant pushed southward, both Union and Confederate armies took heavy casualties. At Cold Harbor, Grant lost 12,000 men. This photograph, taken from a church steeple, shows Union commanders planning the attack on Cold Harbor. Grant, standing at left, leans over the back of a wooden pew to study the map held by another officer.

As the Confederates dug in, Grant put Petersburg under siege. Soon both armies had constructed complicated lines of breastworks and trenches, running for miles in a great arc south of Petersburg, much like the fortifications that would be used in France in World War I. Methodically the Union forces extended their lines, seeking to weaken the Confederates and cut the rail connections supplying Lee's troops and the city of Richmond. Grant could not overwhelm him, but by late June, Lee was

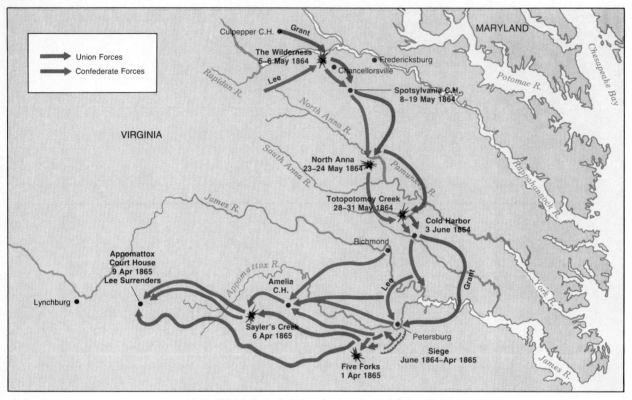

WAR ENDS IN VIRGINIA, 1864–1865

Grant's repeated and costly attempts (60,000 casualties the first month) to out-flank Lee are detailed here. At Five Forks the long seige of Petersburg was bro-ken; Richmond was evacuated. A week later, Lee surrendered.

pinned to earth. Moving again would mean having to abandon Richmond—tantamount, in southern eyes, to surrender.

Sherman in Georgia

The summer of 1864 saw the North submerged in pessimism. The Army of the Potomac held Lee at bay but appeared powerless to defeat him. In Georgia, General Sherman inched forward methodically against the wily Joseph E. Johnston, but when he tried a direct assault at Kennesaw Mountain on June 27, he was thrown back with heavy casualties. In July Confederate raiders under General Jubal Early dashed suddenly across the Potomac from the Shenandoah Valley to within 5 miles of Washington before being turned back. A draft call for 500,000 additional men did not improve the public temper. Huge losses and the absence of a decisive victory

were taxing the northern will to continue the fight.

In June, Lincoln had been renominated on a National Union ticket, with the Tennessee Unionist Andrew Johnson, a former Democrat, as his running mate. He was under attack not only from the Democrats, who nominated General McClellan and came out for a policy that might almost be characterized as peace at any price, but also from the Radical Republicans, many of whom had wished to dump him in favor of Secretary of the Treasury Chase.

Then, almost overnight, the atmosphere changed. On September 2 General Sherman's army fought its way into Atlanta. When the Confederates countered with an offensive northward toward Tennessee,* Sherman did not follow. Instead he aban-

---

* This force was crushed before Nashville in December by a Union army under General George Thomas.

Union Troops

Total: 1,566,678

Wounded: 275,175

Died of Wounds: 110,070

Died of Disease: 249,458

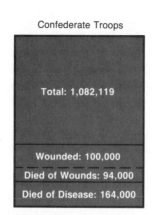

Confederate Troops

Total: 1,082,119

Wounded: 100,000

Died of Wounds: 94,000

Died of Disease: 164,000

CASUALTIES OF THE CIVIL WAR

The Union death rate was 23 percent, the Confederate rate 24 percent. In general, twice as many soldiers were killed by disease as were killed by bullets.

doned his communications with Chattanooga and marched unopposed through Georgia, "from Atlanta to the sea."

Far more completely than most military men of his generation, Sherman believed in total war—in appropriating or destroying everything that might help the enemy continue the fight. The march through Georgia had many objectives besides conquering territory. One obvious one was economic, the destruction of southern resources. "[We] must make old and young, rich and poor feel the hard hand of war," Sherman said. Before taking Atlanta he wrote his wife: "We have devoured the land. . . . All the people retire before us and desolation is behind. To realize what war is one should follow our tracks."

Another object of Sherman's march was psychological. "If the North can march an army right through the South," he told General Grant, southerners will take it "as proof positive that the North can prevail." This was certainly true of Georgia's blacks, who flocked to the invaders by the thousands, women and children as well as men, all cheering mightily when the soldiers put their former masters' homes to the torch. "They pray and shout and mix up my name with Moses," Sherman explained.

Sherman's victories staggered the Confederacy and the anti-Lincoln forces in the North. In November the president was easily reelected, 212 electoral votes to 21. The country was determined to carry on the struggle.

At last the South's will to resist began to crack. Sherman entered Savannah on December 22, having denuded a strip of Georgia 60 miles wide. Early in January 1865 he marched northward, leaving behind "a broad black streak of ruin and desolation—the fences all gone; lonesome smoke-stacks, surrounded by dark heaps of ashes and cinders, marking the spots where human habitations had stood." In February his troops captured Columbia, South Carolina. Soon they were in North Carolina, advancing relentlessly. In Virginia, Grant's vise grew daily tighter, the Confederate lines thinner and more ragged.

To Appomattox Court House

On March 4 Lincoln took the presidential oath and delivered his second inaugural address. Photographs taken at about this time show how four years of war had marked him. Somehow he had become both gentle and steel-tough, both haggard and inwardly calm. With victory sure, he spoke for tolerance, mercy, and reconstruction. "Let us judge not," he said after stating again his personal dislike of slavery, "that we be not judged." He urged all Americans to turn without malice to the task of mending the damage and to make a just and lasting peace between the sections.

Now the Confederate troops around Petersburg could no longer withstand the federal pressure. Desperately Lee tried to pull his forces back to the Richmond and Danville Railroad at Lynchburg, but the swift wings of Grant's army enveloped them. Richmond fell on April 3. With fewer than 30,000 effectives to oppose Grant's 115,000, Lee recognized the futility of further resistance. On April 9 he and Grant met by prearrangement at Appomattox Court House.

It was a scene at once pathetic and inspiring. Lee was noble in defeat, Grant, despite his rough-hewn exterior, sensitive and magnanimous in victory. "I met you once before, General Lee, while we were serving in Mexico," Grant said after they had shaken hands. "I have always remembered your appearance, and I think I should have recognized you anywhere." They talked briefly of that earlier war, and then, acting on Lincoln's instructions, with which he was in full accord, Grant outlined his terms. All that would be required was that the Confederate soldiers lay down their arms. They could return to their homes in peace. When Lee hinted (he was too proud to ask outright for the concession) that his men would profit greatly if allowed to retain possession of their horses, Grant agreed to let them do so.

Costs and Prospects

And so the war ended. It had cost the nation more than 600,000 lives, nearly as many as in all other American wars combined. The story of one of the

The war was a private as well as a public agony. Countless families lost fathers, brothers, husbands, and sons who fell in battle or died of wounds and disease. Before leaving home, men sat for formal photographs, leaving these bittersweet reminders for their families. This Union private poses with his Colt revolver and saber.

lost thousands must stand for all, Union and Confederate. Jones Budbury, a tall, 19-year-old redhead, was working in a Pennsylvania textile mill when the war broke out, and he enlisted at once. His regiment first saw action at Bull Run. He took part in McClellan's Peninsula campaign. He fought at Second Bull Run, at Chancellorsville, and at Gettysburg. A few months after Gettysburg he was wounded in the foot and spent some time in an army hospital. By the spring of 1864 he had risen through the ranks to first sergeant and his hair had turned gray. In June he was captured and sent to Andersonville military prison, but he fell ill and the Confederates released him. In March 1865 he was back with his regiment in the lines besieging Richmond. On April 6, three days before Lee's surrender, Jones Budbury was killed while pursuing Confederate units near Sailor's Creek, Virginia.

The war also caused enormous property losses, especially in the Confederacy. All the human and material destruction explains the eroding hatred and bitterness that the war implanted in millions of hearts. The corruption, the gross materialism, and the selfishness generated by wartime conditions were other disagreeable by-products of the conflict. Such sores fester in any society, but the Civil War bred conditions that inflamed and multiplied them. The war produced many examples of charity, self-sacrifice, and devotion to duty as well, yet if the general moral atmosphere of the postwar generation can be said to have resulted from the experiences of 1861–1865, the effect overall was bad.

What had been obtained at this price? Slavery was dead. Paradoxically, while the war had been fought to preserve the Union, after 1865 the people tended to see the United States not as a union of states but as a nation. After Appomattox, secession was almost literally inconceivable. In a strictly political sense, as Lincoln had predicted from the start, the northern victory heartened friends of republican government and democracy throughout the world. A better-integrated society and a more technically advanced and productive economic system also resulted from the war.

The Americans of 1865 estimated the balance between cost and profit according to their individual fortunes and prejudices. Only the wisest realized that no final accounting could be made until the people had decided what to do with the fruits of victory. That the physical damage would be repaired no one could reasonably doubt; that even the loss

THE WAR MOVES SOUTH, 1863–1865

Confederate John B. Hood's "forlorn hope" offensive toward Nashville failed to deter Sherman from marching through Georgia. Joseph E. Johnston could offer little resistance to Sherman's drive through the Carolinas.

of human resources would be restored in short order was equally apparent. But would the nation make good use of the opportunities the war had made available? What would the ex-slaves do with freedom? How would whites, northern and southern, react to emancipation? To what end would the new technology and social efficiency be directed? Would the people be able to forget the recent past and fulfill the hopes for which so many brave soldiers had given their "last full measure of devotion"?

The cost of total war was evident throughout the South after Sherman's armies moved through Georgia and the Carolinas. Photographs documented stark scenes of destruction like this one taken by George W. Barnard showing the ruined railroad depot at Charleston, South Carolina.

Milestones

1861	Confederates attack Fort Sumter; Lincoln calls for 75,000 volunteers
	First Battle of Bull Run
	Lincoln appoints George B. McCllelan commander of the Union army
	Ex parte Merryman
	Trent Affair
1862	Confederate Congress passes Conscription Act
	Battle of Shiloh
	Robert E. Lee named commander of the Army of Northern Virginia
	Seven Days' Battle for Richmond
	Second Battle of Bull Run
	Battle of Antietam; McClellan relieved of his command
	Lincoln issues the Emancipation Proclamation

	Congress passes the Homestead, Morrill Land Grant, and Pacific Railway acts
	Battle of Fredericksburg
1863	Congress passes the Conscription and National Banking acts
	Draft riots in New York City
	Battle of Chancellorsville
	Battle of Gettysburg
	Siege and capture of Vicksburg
1864	Battle of the Wilderness
	Battle of Spottsylvania Court House
	Battle of Cold Harbor
	Capture of Atlanta
	Sherman's March through Georgia; capture of Savannah
1864–1865	Siege of Petersburg
1865	Capture of Columbia, South Carolina
	Lee surrenders to Grant at Appomattox Court House

SUPPLEMENTARY READING

Titles marked with an asterisk have been published in paperback.

The best recent survey of the Civil War period is J. M. McPherson, **Battle Cry of Freedom** (1988), but Allan Nevins's eight-volume **Ordeal of the Union** (1947–1971), continues to be valuable, both as an account of the fighting and as an analysis of political, social, and economic developments. J. G. Randall, **Lincoln, the President*** (1945–1955), is an excellent scholarly study (the last volume of this work was completed after Randall's death by R. N. Current). Political and constitutional problems are dealt with in H. M. Hyman, **A More Perfect Union** (1973). Lincoln's dealings with the Radicals have been extensively investigated. H. L. Trefousse, **The Radical Republicans: Lincoln's Vanguard for Racial Justice*** (1969), which praises Lincoln's management of the Radicals and minimizes his differences with them, is a good summary, but see also A. G. Bogue, **The Earnest Men: Republicans in the Civil War Senate** (1981), F. L. Klement, **The Cop-**

perheads in the Middle West (1960), and J. H. Silbey, **A Respectable Minority: The Democratic Party in the Civil War Era*** (1977).

For the movement to make abolition a war aim and the reaction to it, see J. M. McPherson, **The Struggle for Equality*** (1964), G. M. Frederickson, **The Inner Civil War*** (1965), and V. J. Voegeli, **Free but Not Equal: The Midwest and the Negro During the Civil War*** (1967).

The activities and attitudes of blacks during the war are summarized in D. T. Cornish, **The Sable Arm: Negro Troops in the Union Army*** (1956), L. F. Litwak, **Been in the Storm So Long** (1979), B. J. Fields, **Slavery and Freeedom on the Middle Ground** (1985), C. L. Mohr, **On the Threshold of Freedom** (1986), and Benjamin Quarles, **The Negro in the Civil War*** (1969). On the New York draft riots, see Adrian Cook, **The Armies of the Streets** (1974).

For aspects of economic and social history, see P. W. Gates, **Agriculture and the Civil War** (1965), M. E. Massey, **Bonnet Brigades: American Women and the Civil War** (1966), and R. P. Sharkey, **Money, Class, and Party.**

E. M. Thomas, **The Confederate Nation** (1979), is a good survey. The fullest biography of Jefferson Davis is Hudson Strode, **Jefferson Davis** (1955–1965).

The voluminous literature on the military history of the Civil War can only be sampled. K. P. Williams, **Lincoln Finds a General** (1949–1952), is exhaustive and judicious. T. H. Williams, **Lincoln and His Generals*** (1952), is briefer and more lively. See also three books by Bruce Catton: **Mr. Lincoln's Army*** (1951), **Glory Road*** (1952), and **A Stillness at Appomattox*** (1953). The famous **Battles and Leaders of the Civil War,** written during the 1880s by participants, is available in condensed form edited by Ned Bradford (1956). B. I. Wiley, in both

The Life of Billy Yank* (1952) and **The Life of Johnny Reb** (1943), discusses the role of the common soldier. For the naval side of the conflict, see R. S. West, Jr., **Mr. Lincoln's Navy** (1957).

Among the biographies of Civil War generals the following are especially noteworthy: W. S. McFeely, **Grant** (1981), S. W. Sears, **George B. McClellan** (1988), Lloyd Lewis, **Sherman, Fighting Prophet** (1932), D. S. Freeman, **R. E. Lee** (1934–1935), and Frank Vandiver, **Mighty Stonewall** (1957). U. S. Grant's, **Personal Memoirs*** (1885) should not be missed.

The diplomacy of the Civil War period is covered in D. P. Crook, **The North, the South, and the Powers** (1974), M. B. Duberman, **Charles Francis Adams*** (1961), and F. L. Owsley and H. C. Owsley, **King Cotton Diplomacy** (1959).

American Lives:
Three Families in the Post–Civil War South

The Village Post Office

William La Fayette Black, a Confederate veteran, was a citizen of Harlan, a small community in a remote section of northern Alabama. He farmed a considerable acreage, but his main business was running the Harlan general store. His wife Martha was the village postmistress.

In his store Black sold farm tools, seed, coffee, tobacco, cloth, and all sorts of other goods. Most of his customers were white farmers; slightly more than 10 percent were black. Some owned their own land, and some were tenants or sharecroppers. (Unlike many southern merchants, Black made a point of treating black customers fairly.)

Local farmers had to buy things on credit because they had many expenses and little money during the planting and growing seasons. They gave Black a lien on their fall crops as security for what they needed during the spring and summer.

Black was therefore an important person in the community. People gathered in his store to talk about politics and crop prospects, to gossip, and perhaps to play a game of checkers. Farmers could scarcely exist without the credit he advanced them, and in hard times he readily carried them as long as possible. It was in his interest to do so, because it was always possible that low prices or a crop failure would hurt him almost as much as the debtors. Still, he also had to borrow to run his business; over the years he accumulated a great deal of land when people who owed him money went bankrupt.

However, the Blacks' life-style was far from easy. Their home was originally a one-room log cabin. As the family grew Black added to it until by 1889 there were four bedrooms and a kitchen as well as the original building. But the house had no cellar. It stood a foot or so above the ground resting on stone pillars. Hogs, chickens, dogs, and cats took shelter beneath it. The house was drafty, heated only by a single stone fireplace. There was no running water.

Black sometimes worked in the fields along with his sons and his tenants. They grew corn, wheat, oats, and of course cotton, which was their cash crop. They worked hard. During the winter they cleared woodland, uprooted stumps, and mended fences and equipment. After plowing and planting, there were the usual tasks of hoeing out weeds and ultimately harvesting the grain. Then in the fall they picked and ginned the cotton. Besides doing the cooking and other household tasks, Martha Black and her daughters milked the family cows, spun cotton, and wove cotton and wool into cloth for the family's use.

In 1889 the Blacks moved to Ashland, a larger town. Black purchased a more substantial house and a part interest in another general store. His partner was a power in the local Democratic party. Black himself was what he called "a Grover Cleveland Democrat." He would have nothing to do with the Populists, who were strong in many sections of Alabama.

When he died in 1900, Black left an estate valued at $25,000. One of his sons, Hugo, became a justice of the United States Supreme Court.

Samuel and Patsy McLeod owned a small cotton farm near Mayesville, South Carolina. The McLeods had been born slaves. Some of their 17 children had been sold away from them. After the war Patsy McLeod continued to work as a cook for her former master. Her wages, carefully saved, had helped make it possible for the family to buy five acres of cotton land.

The McLeod's "Homestead"

McLeod and his sons had then built a log house on the property, which the McLeods proudly christened "The Homestead." It was very small (especially for such a large family) and lacking in conveniences. The floor was of dirt and the two windows had shutters, but no glass panes. The children slept in bunk beds built against the walls. A solid brick fireplace supplied heat. A kitchen with its own chimney was later attached to the cabin.

Gradually the McLeods improved the property, building a barn and other outbuildings. Each fall they took their cotton to the farm of a white neighbor, where it was ginned and baled. Patsy McLeod spun some of this cotton and wove the thread to make shirts and underwear for the family. Shoes and most of their other clothes had to be purchased in the town of Sumter, which was 12 miles from the farm. Shopping in Sumter was an all-day trip by horse and wagon, but exciting for the children whose turn it was to accompany Samuel McLeod on such an expedition.

The McLeods were industrious and thrifty. Everyone worked on the farm. The youngest children gathered fruits and vegetables and fed and tended the animals. Others fished and hunted in the steams and woods of the area. The oldest boys worked for wages on nearby farms and what they earned helped pay for more land. Some of this land was too swampy for growing cotton, so the McLeods began to grow rice also.

Most of the McLeod children had little formal education, but Mary, the fifteenth child, born in 1875, was sent to a school for blacks operated by the Presbyterian Church near Mayesville, where the pupils learned to read by studying the Bible. Mary went into teaching and eventually founded a school of her own in Florida. She gradually elevated what began as an elementary school first to high school, then to junior college status. It finally became Bethune-Cookman College, a four-year liberal arts institution.

Simon Baruch emigrated to the United States from East Prussia in 1855, when he was 15. He came to Camden, South Carolina, because two friends from his hometown had started a business there. With their help he was able to go to medical school and become a doctor. He served in the Confederate army during the Civil War, then married Isabelle Wolfe. Isabelle's parents had been wealthy, but their home and property (along with nearly everything in the Camden area) had been destroyed by General Sherman's army during the late stages of the war.

Dr. Baruch was a tall, dignified man, very formal. His son Bernard claimed that despite the heat of South Carolina summers, he had never seen his father in shirtsleeves. But Baruch was a typical country doctor. He made his rounds in the countryside, treating both white and black patients. Times were hard in South Carolina during Reconstruction. Since money was scarce, Baruch often had to accept payment in goods—a cord of wood, perhaps, or some cotton or corn. Isabelle Baruch helped out by giving piano lessons for 25 cents an hour.

Gradually things improved. There was never a great deal of money but the Baruchs lived well. They had a large house, servants, and three acres of land on which Baruch ran a genuine farm in miniature. He raised cotton, corn, vegetables, and even sugarcane, which his servants refined into brown sugar for the family's use.

Although he was less prejudiced than most white southerners, Baruch detested the "Black Republican" government that controlled South Carolina in the 1870s. He joined the Ku Klux Klan. His children went to a small private school, but in their free time they mingled freely with black children. Many years later Bernard Baruch wrote: "What a cruel thing it was when I grew old enough to appreciate the gulf that separated the white and black races!" He did not add that it must have seemed much more cruel to the black children than to him.

In 1880 Dr. Baruch gave up his practice in South Carolina and moved the family to New York City.

XVII

Reconstruction and the South

No great social revolution ever took place without causing great temporary loss and inconvenience.

THE NATION, *1867*

The experiment has totally failed.

THE NATION, *1871*

This is socialism.

THE NATION, *1874*

O n April 5, 1865, Abraham Lincoln visited Richmond. The fallen capital lay in ruins, sections blackened by fire, but the president was able to walk the streets unmolested and almost unattended. Everywhere black people crowded around him worshipfully; some fell to their knees as he passed, crying "Glory, Hallelujah," hailing him as a messiah. But even white townspeople seemed to have accepted defeat without resentment.

A few days later, in Washington, Lincoln delivered an important speech on Reconstruction, urging compassion and open-mindedness. On April 14 he held a Cabinet meeting at which postwar readjustment was considered at length. That evening, while Lincoln was watching a performance of the play *Our American Cousin* at Ford's Theater, a half-mad actor, John Wilkes Booth, slipped into his box and shot him in the back of the head with a small pistol. Early the next morning, without having regained consciousness, Lincoln died.

The murder was part of a complicated plot organized by die-hard prosoutherners. Seldom have fanatics displayed so little understanding of their own interests, for with Lincoln perished the South's best hope for a mild peace. After his body had been taken home to Illinois, the national mood hardened; apparently the awesome drama was still unfolding; retribution and a final humbling of the South were inevitable.

Presidential Reconstruction

Despite its bloodiness, the Civil War had caused less intersectional hatred than might have been expected. Although civilian property was often seized or destroyed, the invading armies treated the southern population with remarkable forbearance, both during the war and after Appomattox. While he was ensconced in Richmond behind Lee's army, northerners boasted that they would "hang Jeff Davis to a sour apple tree," and when he was captured in Georgia in May 1865, he was at once clapped into irons preparatory to being tried for treason and murder. But feeling against Davis subsided quickly. In 1867 the military turned him over to the civil courts, which released him on bail. He was never brought to trial. A few other Confederate officials spent short periods behind bars, but the only southerner executed for war crimes was Major Henry Wirz, the commandant of Andersonville military prison.

The legal questions related to bringing the defeated states back into the Union were extremely complex. Since southerners believed that secession was legal, logic should have compelled them to argue that they were out of the Union and would thus have to be formally readmitted. Northerners should have taken the contrary position, for they had fought to prove that secession was illegal. Yet the people of both sections did just the opposite. Senator Charles Sumner and Congressman Thaddeus Stevens, in 1861 uncompromising expounders of the theory that the Union was indissoluble, now insisted that the Confederate states had "committed suicide" and should be treated like "conquered provinces." Lincoln believed the issue a "pernicious abstraction" and tried to ignore it.

The process of readmission began in 1862, when Lincoln reappointed provisional governors for those parts of the South that had been occupied by federal troops. On December 8, 1863, he issued a proclamation setting forth a general policy. With the exception of high Confederate officials and a few other special groups, all southerners could reinstate themselves as United States citizens by taking a simple loyalty oath. When, in any state, a number equal to ten percent of those voting in the 1860 election had taken this oath, they could set up a state government. Such governments had to be republican in form, must recognize the "permanent freedom" of the slaves, and must provide for black education. The plan, however, did not require that blacks be given the right to vote.

The "ten percent plan" reflected Lincoln's lack of vindictiveness and his political wisdom. He realized that any government based on such a small minority of the population would be, as he put it, merely "a tangible nucleus which the remainder . . . may rally around as fast as it can," a sort of puppet regime, like the paper government established in those sections of Virginia under federal control.* The regimes established under this plan in Tennessee, Louisiana, and Arkansas bore, in the president's mind, the same relation to finally reconstructed states that an egg bears to a chicken. "We shall sooner have the fowl by hatching it than by smashing it," he remarked. He knew that eventually representatives of the Southern states would again be sitting in Congress, and he wished to lay the groundwork for a strong Republican party in the section. Yet he realized that Congress had no intention of seating representatives from the "ten percent" states at once.

The Radicals in Congress disliked the ten percent plan, partly because of its moderation and partly because it enabled Lincoln to determine Union policy toward the recaptured regions. In July 1864 they passed the Wade-Davis bill, which provided for constitutional conventions only after a *majority* of the voters in a Southern state had taken a loyalty oath. Confederate officials and anyone who had "voluntarily borne arms against the United States" were barred from voting in the election or serving at the convention. Besides prohibiting slavery, the new state constitutions would have to repudiate Confederate debts. Lincoln disposed of the Wade-Davis bill with a pocket veto, and there matters stood when Andrew Johnson became president following the assassination.

Andrew Johnson, as recorded by Matthew Brady's camera in 1865. Johnson, Charles Dickens reported, radiated purposefulness but no "genial sunlight."

Lincoln had picked Johnson for a running mate in 1864 because he was a border-state Unionist Democrat and something of a hero as a result of his courageous service as military governor of Tennessee. From origins even more lowly than Lincoln's, Johnson had risen to be congressman, governor of Tennessee, and United States senator. He was able and ambitious but fundamentally unsure of himself, as could be seen in his boastfulness and stubbornness. His political strength came from the poor whites and yeomen farmers of eastern Tennessee, and he was fond of extolling the common man and attacking "stuck-up aristocrats."

Thaddeus Stevens called Johnson a "rank demagogue" and a "damned scoundrel," and it is true that he was a masterful rabble-rouser. But few politicians of his generation labored so consistently in behalf of small farmers. Free homesteads, public education, absolute social equality—such were his objectives. The father of communism, Karl Marx, a close observer of American affairs at this time, wrote approvingly of Johnson's "deadly hatred of the oligarchy."

---

* By approving the separation of the western counties that had refused to secede, this government provided a legal pretext for the creation of West Virginia.

Johnson was a Democrat, but because of his record and his reassuring penchant for excoriating southern aristocrats, the Republicans in Congress were ready to cooperate with him. "Johnson, we have faith in you," said Senator Ben Wade, author of the Wade-Davis bill, the day after Lincoln's death. "By the gods, there will be no trouble now in running the government!"

Johnson's reply, "Treason must be made infamous," delighted the Radicals, but the president proved temperamentally unable to work with them. As Eric L. McKitrick has shown in *Andrew Johnson and Reconstruction,* Johnson was an "outsider," a "lone wolf" in every way. Like Randolph of Roanoke, his antithesis intellectually and socially, opposition was his specialty; he soon alienated every powerful Republican in Washington.

Radical Republicans listened to Johnson's diatribes against secessionists and the great planters and assumed that he was antisouthern. Nothing could have been further from the truth. He had great respect for states' rights and he shared most of his poor white Tennessee constituents' contempt of blacks. "Damn the negroes, I am fighting these traitorous aristocrats, their masters," he told a friend during the war. "I wish to God," he said on another occasion, "every head of a family in the United States had one slave to take the drudgery and menial service off his family."

The new president did not want to injure or humiliate all southerners. He issued an amnesty proclamation only slightly more rigorous than Lincoln's. It assumed, correctly enough, that with the war over most southern voters would freely take the loyalty oath; thus it contained no ten percent clause. More classes of Confederates, including those who owned taxable property in excess of $20,000, were excluded from the general pardon. By the time Congress convened in December 1865, all of the southern states had organized governments, ratified the Thirteenth Amendment abolishing slavery, and elected senators and representatives. Johnson promptly recommended these new governments to the attention of Congress.

Republican Radicals

Peace found the Republicans in Congress no more united than they had been during the war. A small

Matthew Brady's photograph of the stalwart radical Republican, Thaddeus Stevens. Stevens served in the House from 1859 until his death in 1868.

group of "ultra" Radicals were demanding immediate and absolute civil and political equality for blacks; they should be given, for example, the vote, a plot of land, and access to a decent education. Senator Sumner led this faction. A second group of Radicals, headed by Thaddeus Stevens in the House and Ben Wade in the Senate, agreed with the ultras' objectives but were prepared to accept half a loaf if necessary to win the support of less radical colleagues.

Nearly all Radicals distinguished between the "natural" God-given rights described in the Declaration of Independence, and social equality. "Equality," said Stevens, "does not mean that a negro shall sit in the same seat or eat at the same table with a white man. That is a matter of taste which every man must decide for himself." This did not reflect personal prejudice in Stevens's case. When he died, he was buried in a black cemetery. Here is his epitaph, written by himself: "I repose in this quiet and secluded spot, not from any natural preference for solitude, but finding other cemeteries limited as to race, by charter rules, I have chosen this that I might illustrate in my death the principles which I advocated through a long life, equality of man before his Creator."

The moderate Republicans wanted to protect ex-slaves from exploitation and guarantee their basic rights but were unprepared to push for full political equality. A handful of Republicans sided with the Democrats in support of Johnson's approach, but all the rest insisted at least on the minimum demands of the moderates. Thus Johnsonian Reconstruction was doomed.

Johnson's proposal had no chance in Congress for reasons having little to do with black rights. The Thirteenth Amendment had the effect of increasing the representation of the southern states in Congress because it made the Three-fifths Compromise meaningless. Henceforth those who had been slaves would be counted as whole persons in apportioning seats in the House of Representatives. If Congress seated the southerners, the balance of power might swing to the Democrats. To expect the Republicans to surrender power in such a fashion was unrealistic. Former Copperheads gushing with extravagant praise for Johnson put them instantly on guard.

In addition, the ex-Confederates were not overflowing with goodwill toward their conquerors. A minority would have nothing to do with amnesties and pardons:

Oh, I'm a good old rebel,
Now that's just what I am;
For the "fair land of freedom,"
I do not care a dam.
I'm glad I fit against it—
I only wish we'd won
And I don't want no pardon
For anything I done.

Southern voters had further provoked northern resentment by their choice of congressmen. Georgia elected Alexander H. Stephens, vice-president of the Confederacy, to the Senate, although he was still in a federal prison awaiting trial for treason! Several dozen men who had served in the Confederate Congress had been elected to either the House or the Senate, together with four generals and many other high officials. It was understandable that southern people would select locally respected and experienced leaders, but it was equally reasonable that these choices would sit poorly with northerners.

Finally, the so-called Black Codes enacted by southern governments to control former slaves alarmed the North. These varied in severity from state to state. When seen in historical perspective, even the strictest codes represented a considerable improvement over slavery. Most permitted blacks to sue and to testify in court, at least in cases involving members of their own race. Blacks were allowed to own certain kinds of property; marriages were made legal; other rights were guaranteed. However, blacks could not bear arms, be employed in occupations other than farming and domestic service, or leave their jobs without forfeiting back pay. The Louisiana code required them to sign labor contracts for the year during the first ten days of January. A similar rule was put into effect in Mississippi, where, in addition, drunkards, vagrants, beggars, "common night-walkers," and even persons who "misspend what they earn" and who could not pay the stiff fines assessed for such misbehavior were to be "hired out . . . at public outcry" to the white persons who would take them for the shortest period in return for paying the fines. Such laws, apparently designed to get around the Thirteenth Amendment, outraged northerners.

For all these reasons the Republicans in Congress rejected Johnsonian Reconstruction. Quickly they created a joint committee on Reconstruction, headed by Senator William P. Fessenden of Maine, a moderate, to study the question of readmitting the southern states.

The committee held public hearings that produced much evidence of the mistreatment of blacks. Colonel George A. Custer, stationed in Texas, testified: "It is of weekly, if not of daily occurrence that Freedmen are murdered." The nurse Clara Barton told a gruesome tale about a pregnant woman who had been brutally whipped. Others described the intimidation of blacks by poor whites. The hearings strengthened the hands of the Radicals, who had been claiming all along that the South was perpetuating slavery under another name.

President Johnson's attitude speeded the swing toward the Radical position. While the hearings were in progress, Congress passed a bill expanding and extending the Freedmen's Bureau, which had

Agents of the Freedmen's Bureau helped defend former slaves against white attacks and provided them with food, clothing, and medical care. They also set up schools. However, hostility toward the activities of the Freedmen's Bureau was widespread. In 1866, during a race riot in Memphis, mobs killed 46 blacks and burned this Freedmen's schoolhouse.

been established in March 1865 to care for refugees. The bureau, a branch of the War Department, was already exercising considerable coercive and supervisory power in the South. Now Congress sought to add to its authority in order to protect the black population. Although the bill had wide support, Johnson vetoed it, arguing that it was an unconstitutional extension of military authority in peacetime. Congress then passed a Civil Rights Act that, besides declaring specifically that blacks were citizens of the United States, denied the states the power to restrict their rights to testify in court, to make contracts for their labor, and to hold property. In other words, it put teeth in the Thirteenth Amendment.

Once again the president refused to go along, although his veto was sure to drive more moderates into the arms of the Radicals. On April 9, 1866, Congress repassed the Civil Rights Act by a two-thirds majority, the first time in American history that a major piece of legislation became law over the veto of a president. This event marked a revolution in the history of Reconstruction, indeed, in federal-state relations, north as well as south. Thereafter Congress, not President Johnson, had the upper hand.

In the clash between the president and Congress, Johnson was his own worst enemy. His language was often intemperate, his handling of opponents inept, his analysis of southern conditions incorrect. He had assumed that the small southern farmers who made up the majority in the Confederacy shared his prejudices against the planter class. They did not, as their choices in the postwar elections demonstrated. In fact, Johnson's hatred of the southern aristocracy may have been based more on jealousy than on principle. Under the Reconstruction plan, persons excluded from the blanket amnesty could apply individually for the restoration of their rights. When wealthy and socially prominent southerners flocked to Washington, hat in hand, he found their flattery and humility exhilarating. He issued pardons wholesale. "I did not expect to keep out all who were excluded from the amnesty," he explained. "I intended they should sue for pardon, and so realize the enormity of their crime."

The president misread northern opinion. He believed that Congress had no right to pass laws affecting the South before southern representatives had been readmitted to Congress. However, in the light of the refusal of most southern whites to grant any real power or responsibility to the freedmen (an attitude that Johnson did not condemn), the public would not accept this point of view. Johnson placed his own judgment over that of the overwhelming majority of northern voters, and this was a great error, morally and tactically. By encouraging southerners to resist efforts to improve the lot of blacks, Johnson played into the hands of northern extremists.

The Radicals encountered grave problems in fighting for their program. Northerners might object to the Black Codes and to seating "rebels" in Congress, but few believed in racial equality. Between 1865 and 1868 Wisconsin, Minnesota, Connecticut, Nebraska, New Jersey, Ohio, Michigan, and Pennsylvania all rejected bills granting blacks the vote.

The Radicals were in effect demanding not merely equal rights for freedmen but extra rights; not merely the vote but special protection of that right against the pressure that southern whites would surely apply to undermine it. This idea flew in the face of conventional American beliefs in equality before the law and individual self-reliance. Such protection would involve interference by the federal government in local affairs, a concept at variance with American practice. Events were to show that the Radicals were correct—that what amounted to a political revolution in state-federal relations was essential if blacks were to achieve real equality. But in the climate of that day their proposals encountered bitter resistance, and not only from southerners.

Thus, while the Radicals sought partisan advantage in their battle with Johnson and sometimes played on war-bred passions in achieving their ends, they were taking large political risks in defense of genuinely held principles. One historian has aptly called them the "moral trustees" of the Civil War.

The Fourteenth Amendment

In June 1866 Congress submitted to the states a new amendment to the Constitution. The Fourteenth Amendment was, in the context of the times, a truly radical measure. Never before had newly freed slaves been granted significant political rights. For example, in the British Caribbean sugar islands, where slavery had been abolished in the 1830s, stiff property qualifications and poll taxes kept freedmen from voting. The Fourteenth Amendment was also a milestone along the road to the centralization of political power in the United States because it

reduced the power of all the states. In this sense it confirmed the great change wrought by the Civil War: the growth of a more complex, more closely integrated social and economic structure requiring closer national supervision. Few people understood this aspect of the amendment at the time.

First the amendment supplied a broad definition of American citizenship: "All persons born or naturalized in the United States, and subject to the jurisdiction thereof, are citizens of the United States and of the State wherein they reside." Obviously this included blacks. Then it struck at discriminatory legislation like the Black Codes: "No State shall make or enforce any law which shall abridge the privileges or immunities of citizens of the United States; nor shall any State deprive any person of life, liberty, or property, without due process of law." The next section attempted to force the southern states to permit blacks to vote. If a state denied the vote to any class of its adult male citizens, its representation was to be reduced proportionately. Under another clause, former federal officials who had served the Confederacy were barred from holding either state or federal office unless specifically pardoned by a two-thirds vote of Congress. Finally, the Confederate debt was repudiated.

While the amendment did not specifically outlaw segregation or prevent a state from disfranchising blacks, the southern states would have none of it. Without them the necessary three-fourths majority of the states could not be obtained.

President Johnson vowed to make the choice between the Fourteenth Amendment and his own policy the main issue of the 1866 congressional elections. He embarked on "a swing around the circle" to rally the public to his cause. He failed dismally. Northern women objected to the implication in the amendment that black men were more fitted to vote than white women, but a large majority of northern voters was determined that blacks must have at least formal legal equality. The Republicans won better than two-thirds of the seats in both houses, together with control of all of the northern state governments. Johnson emerged from the campaign discredited, the Radicals stronger and determined to have their way. The southern states, Congressman James A. Garfield of Ohio said in February 1867, have "flung back into our teeth the magnanimous offer of a generous nation. It is now our turn to act."

The Reconstruction Acts

Had the southern states been willing to accept the Fourteenth Amendment, coercive measures might have been avoided. Their recalcitrance and continuing indications that local authorities were persecuting blacks finally led to the passage, on March 2, 1867, of the First Reconstruction Act. This law divided the former Confederacy—exclusive of Tennessee, which had ratified the Fourteenth Amendment—into five military districts, each controlled by

Johnson tried to turn public opinion against the Radicals' plan for Reconstruction. He toured the country, stumping for the Constitution with the same speech at every stop. His efforts failed as mobs greeted him with the cry. "Shut up, Johnson." This Harper's Weekly *cartoon reflects public criticism of Johnson as a parrot repeating a single word.*

a major general. It gave these officers almost dictatorial power to protect the civil rights of "all persons," maintain order, and supervise the administration of justice. To rid themselves of military rule, the former states were required to adopt constitutions guaranteeing blacks the right to vote and disfranchising broad classes of ex-Confederates. If the new constitutions proved satisfactory to Congress, and if the new governments ratified the Fourteenth Amendment, their representatives would be admitted to Congress and military rule ended. Johnson's veto of the act was easily overridden.

Although drastic, the Reconstruction Act was so vague that it proved unworkable. Military control was easily established. But in deference to moderate Republican views, the law had not spelled out the process by which the new constitutions were to be drawn up. Southern whites preferred the status quo, even under army control, to enfranchising blacks and retiring their own respected leaders. They made no effort to follow the steps laid down in the law. Congress therefore passed a second act requiring the military authorities to register voters and supervise the election of delegates to constitutional conventions. A third act further clarified procedures.

Still white southerners resisted. The laws required that the constitutions be approved by a majority of the registered voters. Simply by staying away from the polls, whites prevented ratification in state after state. At last, in March 1868, a full year after the First Reconstruction Act, Congress changed the rules again. The constitutions were to be ratified by a majority of the voters. In June 1868, Arkansas, having fulfilled the requirements, was readmitted to the Union, and by July a sufficient number of states had ratified the Fourteenth Amendment to make it part of the Constitution. But it was not until July 1870 that the last southern state, Georgia, qualified to the satisfaction of Congress.

Congress Takes Charge

To carry out this program in the face of determined southern resistance required singlemindedness over a long period to an extent seldom demonstrated by an American legislature. The persistence resulted in part from the suffering and frustrations of the war years. The refusal of the South to accept the spirit of even the mild reconstruction designed by Johnson goaded the North to ever more overbearing efforts to bring the ex-Confederates to heel. President Johnson's stubbornness also influenced the Republicans. They became obsessed with the need to defeat him. The unsettled times and the large Republican majorities, always threatened by the possibility of a Democratic resurgence if "unreconstructed" southern congressmen were readmitted, sustained their determination.

These considerations led Republicans to attempt a kind of grand revision of the federal government, one that almost destroyed the balance between judicial, executive, and legislative power established in 1789. A series of measures passed between 1866 and 1868 increased the authority of Congress over the army, over the process of amending the Constitution, and over Cabinet members and lesser appointive officers. Even the Supreme Court was affected. Its size was reduced and its jurisdiction over civil rights cases limited. Finally, in a showdown caused by emotion more than by practical considerations, the Republicans attempted to remove President Johnson from office.

Johnson was a poor president and out of touch with public opinion, but he had done nothing to merit ejection from office. While he had a low opinion of blacks, his opinion was so widely shared by whites that it is unhistorical to condemn him as a reactionary on this ground. Johnson believed that he was fighting to preserve constitutional government. He was honest and devoted to duty, and his record easily withstood the most searching examination. When Congress passed laws taking away powers granted him by the Constitution, he refused to submit.

The chief issue was the Tenure of Office Act of 1867, which prohibited the president from removing officials who had been appointed with the consent of the Senate without first obtaining Senate approval. In February 1868 Johnson "violated" this act by dismissing Secretary of War Edwin M. Stanton, who had been openly in sympathy with the Radicals for some time. The House, acting under the procedure set up in the Constitution for removing the president, promptly impeached him before the bar of the Senate, Chief Justice Salmon P. Chase presiding.

The trial was conducted in a partisan and vindictive manner. Johnson's lawyers easily established that he had removed Stanton only in an effort to prove the Tenure of Office Act unconstitutional. They demonstrated that the act did not protect Stanton to begin with, since it gave Cabinet members tenure "during the term of the President by whom they may have been appointed," and Stanton had been appointed in 1862, during Lincoln's first term!

Nevertheless the Radicals pressed the charges (11 separate articles) relentlessly. To the argument that Johnson had committed no crime, the learned Senator Sumner retorted that the proceedings were "political in character" rather than judicial. Thaddeus Stevens, directing the attack on behalf of the House, warned the senators that although "no corrupt or wicked motive" could be attributed to Johnson, they would "be tortured on the gibbet of everlasting obloquy" if they did not convict him. Tremendous pressure was applied to the handful of Republican senators who were unwilling to disregard the evidence.

Seven of them resisted to the end, and the Senate failed by a single vote to convict Johnson. This was probably fortunate. Had he been forced from office on such flimsy grounds, the independence of the executive might have been permanently weakened. Then the legislative branch would have become supreme.

The Fifteenth Amendment

The failure of the impeachment did not affect the course of Reconstruction. The president was acquitted on May 16, 1868. A few days later, the Republican National Convention nominated General Ulysses S. Grant for the presidency. At the Democratic convention Johnson had considerable support, but the delegates nominated Horatio Seymour, a former governor of New York. In November Grant won an easy victory in the electoral college, 214 to 80, but the popular vote was close: 3 million to 2.7 million. Although he would probably have carried the electoral college in any case, Grant's margin in the popular vote was supplied by southern blacks enfranchised under the Reconstruction Acts, about 450,000 of whom supported him. A majority of white voters probably preferred Sey-

The black vote helped Grant win five former Confederate states in the election of 1868. Although Republicans had avoided supporting suffrage for blacks during the campaign, they changed course after their victory and proposed the Fifteenth Amendment. In this cartoon, Grant, standing on shore, advises white Southerners to accept black suffrage.

mour. Since many citizens undoubtedly voted Republican because of personal admiration for General Grant, the election statistics suggest that a substantial white majority opposed the policies of the Radicals.

The Reconstruction Acts and the ratification of the Fourteenth Amendment achieved the purpose of enabling black southerners to vote. The Radicals, however, were not satisfied; despite the unpopularity of the idea in the North, they wished to guarantee the right of blacks to vote in every state. Another amendment seemed the only way to accomplish this objective, but passage of such an amendment appeared impossible. The Republican platform in the 1868 election had smugly distinguished between blacks voting in the South ("demanded by every consideration of public safety, of gratitude, and of justice") and in the North (where the question "properly belongs to the people").

However, after the election had demonstrated how important the black vote could be, Republican strategy shifted. Grant had carried Indiana by less than 10,000 votes and lost New York by a similar number. If blacks in these and other closely divided states had voted, Republican strength would have been greatly enhanced.

Suddenly Congress blossomed with suffrage amendments. After considerable bickering over details, the Fifteenth Amendment was sent to the states for ratification in February 1869. It forbade all the states to deny the vote to anyone "on account of race, color, or previous condition of servitude." Once again nothing was said about denial of the vote on the basis of sex, which caused feminists such as Elizabeth Cady Stanton to be even more outraged than they had been by the Fourteenth Amendment.

Most southern states, still under federal pressure, ratified the amendment swiftly. The same was true in most of New England and in some western states. Bitter battles were waged in Connecticut, New York, Pennsylvania, and the states immediately north of the Ohio River, but by March 1870 most of them had ratified the amendment and it became part of the Constitution.

The debates occasioned by these contests show that partisan advantage was not the only reason why voters approved black suffrage at last. The unfairness of a double standard of voting, North and South, the contribution of black soldiers during the war, and the hope that by passing the amendment the strife of Reconstruction could finally be ended all played a part.

When the Fifteenth Amendment went into effect, President Grant called it "the greatest civil change and . . . the most important event that has occurred since the nation came to life." The American Anti-Slavery Society formally dissolved itself, its work apparently completed. "The Fifteenth Amendment confers upon the African race the care of its own destiny," Radical Congressman James A.

Garfield wrote proudly after the amendment was ratified. "It places their fortunes in their own hands."

Many of the celebrants lived to see the amendment subverted in the South. That it could be evaded by literacy tests and other restrictions was apparent at the time and may even have influenced some persons who voted for it. But a stronger amendment—one, for instance, that positively granted the right to vote to all men and put the supervision of elections under national control—could not have been ratified.

"Black Republican" Reconstruction: Scalawags and Carpetbaggers

The Radicals had at last succeeded in imposing their will upon the South. Throughout the region former slaves had real political influence; they voted, held office, and exercised the "privileges" and enjoyed the "immunities" guaranteed them by the Fourteenth Amendment. Almost to a man they voted Republican.

The spectacle of blacks not five years removed from slavery in positions of power and responsibility attracted much attention at the time and has since been examined exhaustively by historians. The subject is controversial, but certain facts are beyond argument. Black officeholders were neither numerous nor inordinately influential. None was ever elected governor of a state; fewer than a dozen and a half during the entire period served in Congress. Blacks held many minor offices and were influential in southern legislatures, although (except in South Carolina) they never made up the majority. Certainly they did not share the spoils of office in proportion to their numbers.

The real rulers of the "black Republican" governments were white, the "scalawags"—southerners willing to cooperate with the Republicans because they accepted the results of the war and to advance their own interests—and the "carpetbaggers"—northerners who went to the South as idealists to help the freed slaves, as employees of the federal government, or more commonly as settlers hoping to improve themselves.

The scalawags were by far the more numerous. A few were prewar politicians or well-to-do planters, men such as the Mississippi planter John L. Alcorn and Joseph E. Brown, the Confederate governor of Georgia. General James Longstreet, one of Lee's most important lieutenants, was another prominent southerner who cooperated with the Republicans. But most were people who had supported the Whig party before the secession crisis and who saw the

During Reconstruction, fourteen blacks won election to the House of Representatives and two, Hiram Revels and Blanche K. Bruce, served in the Senate. Revels, at far left, won the Mississippi Senate seat that Jefferson Davis had once held. He later became president of Alcorn University. Congressman R. Brown Elliot, at far right, had been educated at Eton in England.

Republicans as the logical successors of the Whigs.

The carpetbaggers were a particularly varied lot. Most had mixed motives for coming south and personal gain was certainly among them. But so were opposition to slavery and the belief that blacks deserved to be treated decently and given a chance to get ahead in the world. Among the most admirable of the carpetbaggers was Adelbert Ames of Maine, who was governor of Mississippi in 1874–1875. Ames was, in the words of historian Richard N. Current, "about as pure and incorruptible a governor as Mississippi or any other state is likely ever to have."

Many northern blacks became carpetbaggers: former Union soldiers, missionaries from northern black churches, and also teachers, lawyers, and other members of the small northern black professional class. Many of these became officeholders, but like southern black politicans their influence was limited.

That blacks should fail to dominate southern governments is certainly understandable. They lacked experience in politics and were mostly poor and uneducated. They were nearly everywhere a minority. Those blacks who held office during Reconstruction tended to be better educated and more prosperous than most southern blacks. In his interesting analysis of black South Carolina politicians, Thomas Holt shows that a disproportionate number of them had been free before the war. Of those freed by the Thirteenth Amendment, a large percentage had been house servants or artisans, not field hands. Mulatto politicians were also disproportionately numerous and (as a group) more conservative and economically better off than other black leaders.

In South Carolina and elsewhere, blacks proved in the main able and conscientious public servants, able because the best tended to rise to the top in such a fluid situation, and conscientious because most of those who achieved importance sought eagerly to demonstrate the capacity of their race for self-government. Even at the local level, where the quality of officials was usually poor, there was little difference in the degree of competence displayed by white and black officeholders. In power, the blacks were not vindictive; by and large they did not seek to restrict the rights of ex-Confederates.

Not all black legislators and administrators were paragons of virtue. In South Carolina, despite their control of the legislature, they broke up into factions repeatedly and failed to press for laws that would improve the lot of poor black farm workers. In *The Prostrate South* (1874), James S. Pike, a northern newspaperman, wrote: "The rule of South Carolina should not be dignified with the name of government. It is the installation of a huge system of brigandage." Like many northern commentators, Pike exaggerated the immorality and incompetence of the blacks, but waste and corruption were common in Reconstruction governments. Half the budget of Louisiana in some years went for salaries and "mileage" for representatives and their staffs. One Arkansas black took $9,000 from the state for repairing a bridge that had cost only $500 to build. A South Carolina legislator was voted an additional $1,000 in salary after he lost that sum betting on a horse race.

However, the corruption must be seen in perspective. The big thieves were nearly always white; blacks got mostly crumbs. Furthermore, graft and callous disregard of the public interest characterized government in every section and at every level during the decade after Appomattox. Big-city bosses in the North embezzled sums that dwarfed the most brazen southern frauds. The New York City Tweed Ring probably made off with more money than all the southern thieves, black and white, combined. While the evidence does not justify the southern corruption, it suggests that the unique features of Reconstruction politics—black suffrage, military supervision, carpetbagger and scalawag influence—do not explain it.

The "black Republican" governments displayed qualities that grew directly from the ignorance and political inexperience of the former slaves. There was a tragicomic aspect to the South Carolina legislature during these years, its many black members—some dressed in old frock coats, others in rude farm clothes—rising to points of order and personal privilege without reason, discoursing ponderously on subjects they did not understand. But those who complained about the ignorance and irresponsibility of blacks conveniently forgot that the tendency of 19th-century American democracy was away from educational, financial, or any other restrictions on the franchise. Thousands of white southerners were as illiterate and uncultured as the freedmen, yet no one suggested depriving them of the ballot.

In fact, the Radical southern governments ac-

The Freedmen's Bureau established 4,329 schools, attended by some 250,000 ex-slaves, in the postwar South. Harper's Weekly *artist Alfred Waud sketched a Freedmen's Bureau school in Vicksburg, Mississippi, in 1866. Many of the teachers were white women from the North.*

complished a great deal. They spent money freely but not entirely wastefully. Tax rates zoomed, but the money financed the repair and expansion of the South's dilapidated railroad network, rebuilt crumbling levees, and expanded social services. Before the Civil War, as Eric Foner points out in *Reconstruction: America's Unfinished Revolution,* "slavery had sharply curtailed the scope of public authority" because the slaves were governed by private individuals (their owners) far more than by the state. The planters possessed a disproportionate share of political as well as economic power, and they spent relatively little public money on education and public services of all kinds. During Reconstruction an enormous gap had to be filled, and it took money to fill it. The Freedmen's Bureau made a start, and northern religious and philanthropic organizations did important work. Eventually, however, the state governments established and supported hospitals, asylums, and systems of free public education that, while segregated, greatly benefited everyone, whites as well as blacks. Much state money was also spent on economic development: land reclamation, repairing and expanding the war-ravaged railroads, maintaining levees.

The former slaves grasped eagerly at the opportunities to learn. Nearly all appreciated the immense importance of knowing how to read and write; the sight of elderly men and women poring laboriously over elementary texts beside their grandchildren was common everywhere. Schools and other institutions were supported chiefly by property taxes, and these, of course, hit well-to-do white farmers hard. Hence much of the complaining about the "extravagance" of Reconstruction governments concealed selfish objections to paying for public projects. Eventually the benefits of expanded government services to the entire population became clear, and when white supremacy was reestablished, most of the new services remained in force, and the corruption and inefficiency inherited from the carpetbagger governments continued.

The Ravaged Land

The South's grave economic problems complicated the rebuilding of its political system. The section had never been as prosperous as the North, and wartime destruction left it desperately poor by any standard. In the long run the abolition of slavery released immeasurable quantities of human energy previously stifled, but the immediate effect was to create confusion. Freedom to move without a pass, to "see the world," was one of the ex-slaves' most cherished benefits of emancipation. Understandably, many at first equated legal freedom with freedom from having to earn a living, a tendency reinforced for a time by the willingness of the Freedmen's Bureau to provide rations and other forms of relief in war-devastated areas. Most, however, soon accepted the fact that they must earn a living; a small plot of land of their own ("40 acres and a mule") would complete their independence.

This objective was forcefully supported by the relentless Congressman Thaddeus Stevens, whose hatred of the planter class was pathological. "The property of the chief rebels should be seized," he stated. If the lands of the richest "70,000 proud, bloated and defiant rebels" were confiscated, the federal government would obtain 394 million acres. Every adult male ex-slave could easily be supplied with 40 acres. The beauty of his scheme, Stevens insisted, was that "nine-tenths of the (southern) people would remain untouched." Dispossessing the great planters would make the South "a safe republic," its lands cultivated by "the free labor of intelligent citizens." If the plan drove the planters into exile, "all the better."

Although Stevens's figures were faulty, many Radicals agreed with him. "We must see that the freedmen are established on the soil," Senator Sumner declared. "The great plantations, which have been so many nurseries of the rebellion, must be broken up, and the freedmen must have the pieces." Stevens, Sumner, and others who wanted to give land to the freedmen weakened their case by associating it with the idea of punishing the former rebels; the average American had too much respect for property rights to support a policy of confiscation.

Aside from its vindictiveness, the extremists' view was simplistic. Land without tools, seed, and other necessities would have done the freedmen little good. Congress did throw open 46 million acres of poor-quality federal land in the South to blacks under the Homestead Act, but few settled upon it. Establishing former slaves on small farms with adequate financial aid would have been of incalculable benefit to them and to the nation. This would have been practicable, but it was not done.

The former slaves therefore had to work out their destiny within the established framework of southern agriculture. White planters, influenced by the precipitous decline of sugar production in Jamaica and other Caribbean islands that had followed the abolition of slavery there, expected them to be incapable of self-directed effort. If allowed to become independent farmers, they would either starve to death or descend into barbarism. Of course the blacks did neither. True, the output of cotton and other southern staples declined precipitously after slavery was abolished. Observers soon came to the conclusion that a free black produced much less than a slave had produced. "You can't get only about two-thirds as much out of 'em now as you could when they were slaves," an Arkansas planter complained.

However, the decline in productivity was not caused by the *inability* of free blacks to work independently. What happened was that since they now held, in the pithy phrase of the economist Robert Higgs, "property rights over their own bodies," they chose no longer to work like slaves. They let their children play instead of forcing them into the fields. Mothers devoted more time to child care and housework, less to farm labor. Elderly blacks worked less.

Noting these changes, white critics spoke scornfully of black laziness and shiftlessness. "You cannot make the negro work without physical compulsion," was the common view. As the economic historians Roger Ransom and Richard Sutch have said, the perfectly reasonable desire of ex-slaves to devote more time to leisure was "taken as 'evidence' to support racist characterizations of blacks as lazy, incompetent, and unwilling to work." A leading southern magazine complained in 1866 that black women now expected their husbands "to support them in idleness." It would never have made such a comment about white housewives. Ransom and Sutch also point out that, while working less, emancipated blacks were far better off materially than under slavery. Their earnings brought them almost 30 percent more than the value of the subsistence provided by their former masters.

The family life of ex–slaves was changed in other ways. Male authority increased when husbands became true heads of families. (Under slavery the ultimate responsibility for providing for women and children was the master's.) When blacks became citizens, the men acquired rights and powers denied to all women, such as the right to hold public office and serve on juries. Similarly, black women became more like white women, devoting themselves to separate "spheres" where their lives revolved around housekeeping and child rearing.

Sharecropping and the Crop Lien System

Before the passage of the Reconstruction Acts, plantation owners tried to farm their land with gang labor, the same system as before, only now paying wages to the ex-slaves. This method did not work well for two entirely different reasons. Money was scarce, and capital, never adequate even before the collapse of the Confederacy, accumulated slowly. Interest rates were extremely high. This situation made it difficult for landowners to pay their laborers in cash. More important, blacks did not like working for wages because it kept them under the direction of whites and thus reminded them of slavery. They wanted to be independent, to manage not merely their free time but their entire lives for themselves. Since the voluntary withdrawal of so much black labor from the work force had produced a shortage, the blacks had their way. "I had to yield," one planter admitted, "or lose my labor."

Quite swiftly, a new agricultural system known as sharecropping emerged. Instead of cultivating the land by gang labor as in antebellum times, plant-

ers broke up their estates into small units and established on each a black family. The planter provided housing, agricultural implements, draft animals, seed, and other supplies, and the family provided labor. The crop was divided between them, usually on a fifty-fifty basis. If the landlord supplied only land and housing, the laborer got a larger share. This was called share tenancy.

Sharecropping gave blacks the day-to-day control of their lives that they craved and the hope of earning enough to buy a small farm. But few achieved this ambition because whites resisted their efforts adamantly. As late as 1880 blacks owned less than 10 percent of the agricultural land in the South, although they made up more than half of the region's farm population. Mississippi actually prohibited the purchase of farmland by blacks.

Many white farmers in the South were also trapped by the sharecropping system and by white efforts to keep blacks in a subordinate position. New fencing laws kept them from grazing livestock on undeveloped land, a practice common before the Civil War. But the main cause of southern rural poverty for whites as well as blacks was the lack of enough capital to finance the sharecropping system. Like their colonial ancestors, the landowners had to borrow against October's harvest to pay for April's seed. Thus the crop-lien system developed,

After the Civil War, most blacks worked as sharecroppers on land owned by whites. In this photograph, black sharecroppers pick cotton, a major cash crop of the South. Because the price for cotton remained low, sharecroppers often fell into debt and were tied to the land almost as tightly as under slavery.

and to protect their investments, lenders insisted that the grower concentrate on readily marketable cash crops: tobacco, sugar, and especially cotton.

The system injured everyone. Diversified farming would have reduced the farmers' need for cash, preserved the fertility of the soil, and, by placing a premium on imagination and shrewdness, aided the best of them to rise in the world. Under the crop-lien system, both landowner and sharecropper depended on credit supplied by local bankers, merchants, and storekeepers for everything from seed, tools, and fertilizer to overalls, coffee, and salt. Crossroads stores proliferated, and a new class of small merchants appeared. The prices of goods sold on credit were high, adding to the burden borne by the rural population. The small southern merchants were almost equally victimized by the system, for they also lacked capital, bought goods on credit, and had to pay high interest rates.

Seen in broad perspective, the situation is not difficult to understand. The South, drained of every resource by the war, was competing for funds with the North and West, both vigorous and expanding and therefore voracious consumers of capital. Reconstruction, in the literal sense of the word, was accomplished chiefly at the expense of the standard of living of the producing classes. The crop-lien system and the small storekeeper were only agents of an economic process dictated by national, perhaps even worldwide, conditions.

This does not mean that the South's economy was paralyzed by the shortage of capital or that recovery and growth did not take place. But compared with the rest of the country, progress was slow. Just before the Civil War cotton harvests averaged about 4 million bales. During the conflict, output fell to about half a million, and the former Confederate states did not enjoy a 4-million-bale year again until 1870. Only after 1874 did the crop begin to top that figure consistently. In contrast, national wheat production in 1859 was 175 million bushels and in 1878, 449 million. About 7,000 miles of railroad were built in the South between 1865 and 1879; in the rest of the nation nearly 45,000 miles of track were laid.

In manufacturing the South made important gains after the war. The tobacco industry, stimulated by the sudden popularity of the cigarette, expanded rapidly. Virginia and North Carolina tobacco towns like Richmond, Lynchburg, and

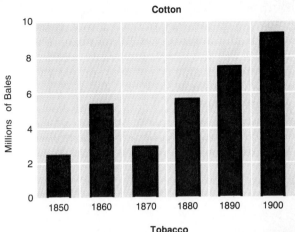

Cotton

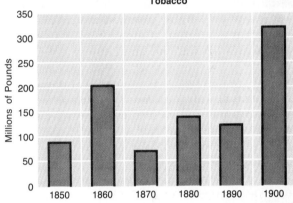

Tobacco

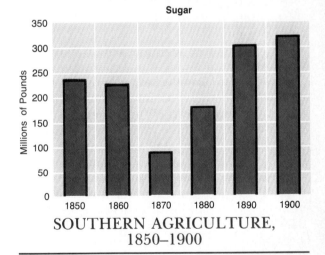

Sugar

SOUTHERN AGRICULTURE,
1850–1900

Cotton production recovered to its prewar level by 1880, but tobacco and sugar production lagged. Not until 1900 did tobacco growers have a better year than they had in 1860. The years following 1870 saw a general downward trend in wholesale prices for farm commodities. (Statistics are for the 11 states of the Confederacy.)

Durham flourished. The exploitation of the coal and iron deposits of northeastern Alabama in the early 1870s made a boom town of Birmingham. The manufacture of cotton cloth increased, productive capacity nearly doubling between 1865 and 1880. Yet the mills of Massachusetts alone had eight times the capacity of the entire South in 1880. Despite the increases, the South's share of the national output of manufactured goods declined sharply during the Reconstruction era.

The White Counterrevolution

Radical southern governments could sustain themselves only so long as they had the support of a significant proportion of the white population, for except in South Carolina and Louisiana, the blacks were not numerous enough to win elections alone. The key to survival lay in the hands of the wealthy merchants and planters, mostly former Whigs. People of this sort had nothing to fear from black economic competition. Taking a broad view, they could see that improving the lot of the former slaves would benefit all classes.

Southern white Republicans used the Union League of America, a patriotic club founded during the war, to control the black vote. Employing secret rituals, exotic symbols, and other paraphernalia calculated to impress unsophisticated people, they enrolled the freedmen in droves and marched them to the polls en masse.

Powerless to check the League by open methods, dissident southerners established a number of secret terrorist societies, bearing such names as the Ku Klux Klan, the Knights of the White Camelia, and the Pale Faces. The most notorious of these organizations was the Klan, which was organized in Tennessee in 1866. At first it was purely a social club, but by 1868 it had been taken over by vigilante types dedicated to driving blacks out of politics, and it was spreading rapidly across the South. Sheet-clad night riders roamed the countryside, frightening the impressionable and chastising the defiant. Klansmen, using a weird mumbo jumbo and claiming to be the ghosts of Confederate soldiers, spread horrendous rumors and published broadsides designed to persuade the freedmen that it was unhealthy for them to participate in politics:

Niggers and Leaguers, get out of the way,
We're born of the night and we vanish by day.
No rations have we, but the flesh of man—
And love niggers best—the Ku Klux Klan;
We catch 'em alive and roast 'em whole,
Then hand 'em around with a sharpened pole.
Whole Leagues have been eaten, not leaving a man,
And went away hungry—the Ku Klux Klan. . . .

When intimidation failed, the Klansmen resorted to force. After being whipped by one group in Tennessee, a recently elected justice of the peace reported: "They said they had nothing particular against me . . . but they did not intend any nigger to hold office." In hundreds of cases the KKK murdered their opponents, often in the most gruesome manner.

Congress struck at the Klan with three Force Acts (1870–1871), which placed elections under federal jurisdiction and imposed fines and prison sentences on persons convicted of interfering with any citizen's exercise of the franchise. Troops were dispatched to areas where the Klan was strong, and by 1872 the federal authorities had arrested enough Klansmen to break up the organization.

Nevertheless the Klan contributed substantially to the destruction of Radical regimes in the South. Its depredations weakened the will of white Republicans (few of whom really believed in racial equality), and it intimidated many blacks, who gave up trying to exercise their rights. The fact that the army had to be called in to suppress it was a glaring illustration of the weakness of the Reconstruction governments.

Gradually it became respectable to intimidate black voters. Beginning in Mississippi in 1874, terrorism spread through the South. Instead of hiding behind masks and operating in the dark, these terrorists donned red shirts, organized into military companies, and paraded openly. Mississippi red-shirts seized militant blacks and whipped them publicly. Killings were frequent. When blacks dared to fight back, heavily armed whites easily put them to rout. In other states similar results followed.

Terrorism fed on fear, fear on terrorism. White violence led to fear of black retaliation and thus to even more brutal attacks. The slightest sign of resistance came to be seen as the beginning of race war, and when the blacks suffered indignities and

A graphic warning by the Alabama Klan "of the fate in store for" scalawags and carpetbaggers, "those great pests of Southern society," from the Tuscaloosa Independent Monitor, *September 1, 1868.*

persecutions in silence, the awareness of how much they must resent the mistreatment made them appear more dangerous still. Thus self-hatred was displaced, guilt suppressed, aggression justified as self-defense, individual conscience submerged in the animality of the mob.

Before long the blacks learned to stay home on election day. One by one, "Conservative" parties—Democratic in national affairs—took over southern state governments. Intimidation was only a partial explanation of this development. The increasing solidarity of whites, northern and southern, was equally significant.

The North had subjected the South to control from Washington while preserving state sovereignty in the North itself. In the long run this discrimination proved unworkable. Many northerners had supported the Radical policy only out of irritation with President Johnson. After his retirement their enthusiasm waned. The war was fading into the past and with it the worst of the anger it had generated.

Northern voters could still be stirred by references to the sacrifices Republicans had made to save the Union and by reminders that the Democratic party was the organization of rebels, Copperheads, and the Ku Klux Klan. "If the Devil himself were at the helm of the ship of state," wrote the novelist

Lydia Maria Child in 1872, "my conscience would not allow me to aid in removing him to make room for the Democratic party." Yet emotional appeals could not convince northerners that it was still necessary to maintain a large army in the South. In 1869 the occupying forces were down to 11,000 men. After Klan disruption and intimidation had made a farce of the 1874 elections in Mississippi, Governor Ames appealed to Washington for help. President Grant's attorney general, Edwards Pierrepont, refused to act. "The whole public are tired out with these autumnal outbreaks in the South," he told Ames. "Preserve the peace by the forces of your own state."

Nationalism was reasserting itself. Had not Washington and Jefferson been Virginians? Was not Andrew Jackson Carolina-born? Since most northerners had little real love or respect for blacks, their interest in racial equality flagged once they felt reasonably certain that blacks would not be reenslaved if left to their own devices in the South.

Another, much subtler force was also at work. The prewar Republican party had stressed the common interest of workers, manufacturers, and farmers in a free and mobile society, a land of equal opportunity where all could work in harmony. Southern whites had insisted that laborers must be disciplined if large enterprises were to be run efficiently. By the 1870s, as large industrial enterprises developed in the northern states, the thinking of business leaders changed—the southern argument began to make sense to them, and they became more sympathetic to the southern demand for more control over "their" labor force.

Grant as President

Other matters occupied the attention of northern voters. The expansion of industry and the rapid development of the West, stimulated by a new wave of railroad building, loomed more important to many than the fortunes of ex-slaves. Beginning in 1873, when a stock market panic struck at public confidence, economic difficulties plagued the country for nearly a decade. Heated controversies arose over tariff policy, with western agricultural interests seeking to force reductions from the high levels established during the war, and over the handling of the wartime greenback paper money, with debtor groups and many manufacturers favoring further expansion of the supply of dollars and conservative merchants and bankers arguing for retiring the greenbacks in order to return to a "sound" currency.

More damaging to the Republicans was the failure of Ulysses S. Grant to live up to expectations as president. Qualities that had made Grant a fine military leader for a democracy—his dislike of political maneuvering and his simple belief that the popular will could best be observed in the actions of Congress—made him a poor chief executive. When Congress failed to act on his suggestion that the quality of the civil service needed improvement, he announced meekly that if Congress did nothing, he would assume the country did not want anything done. Grant was honest, but his honesty was of the naive type that made him the dupe of unscrupulous friends and schemers.

His most serious weakness as president was his failure to deal effectively with economic and social problems, but the one that injured him and the Republicans most was his inability to cope with government corruption. Grant did not cause the corruption, nor did he participate in the remotest way in the rush to "fatten at the public trough," as the reformers of the day might have put it. But he did nothing to prevent the scandals that disgraced his administration. Out of a misplaced belief in the sanctity of friendship, he protected some of the worst culprits and allowed calculating tricksters to use his good name and the prestige of his office to advance their own interests at the country's expense.

The worst of the scandals—such as the Whiskey Ring affair, which implicated Grant's private secretary, Orville E. Babcock, and cost the government millions in tax revenue, and the defalcations of Secretary of War William W. Belknap in the management of Indian affairs—did not become public knowledge during Grant's first term. However, in 1872 Republican reformers, alarmed by rumors of corruption and disappointed by Grant's failure to press for civil service reform, organized the Liberal Republican party and nominated Horace Greeley, the able but eccentric editor of the *New York Tribune*, for president.

The Liberal Republicans were mostly well educated, socially prominent types—editors, college presidents, and economists, along with a sprinkling of businessmen and politicians. Their liberalism was of the *laissez faire* variety; they were for low tariffs and sound money, and against what they called "class legislation," meaning measures benefiting particular groups, whether labor unions or railroad companies or farm organizations. Nearly all had supported Reconstruction at the start, but by the early 1870s most were including southern blacks among the special interests that ought to be left to their own devices. Their observation of urban corruption and of unrestricted immigration led them to disparage universal suffrage, which, one of them said, "can only mean in plain English the government of ignorance and vice."

The Democrats also nominated Greeley in 1872, although he had devoted his political life to flailing the Democratic party in the *Tribune*. That surrender to expediency, together with Greeley's temperamental unsuitability for the presidency, made the campaign a fiasco for the reformers. Grant triumphed easily, with a popular majority of nearly 800,000.

Nevertheless, the defection of the Liberal Republicans hurt the Republican party in Congress. In the 1874 elections, no longer hampered as in the presidential contest by Greeley's notoriety and Grant's fame, the Democrats carried the House of Representatives. It was clear that the days of military rule in the South were ending. By the end of 1875 only three southern states—South Carolina, Flor-

In 1872, Republicans who opposed Grant's renomination bolted the party and nominated Horace Greeley. These Liberal Republicans—some of them former Radicals—sought to conciliate the South. In this cartoon, Thomas Nast, a Grant supporter, condemns the actions of Greeley and Charles Sumner as they push a black man to shake hands with a Klan member and a Copperhead.

ida, and Louisiana—were still under Republican control.

The Republican party in the South was "dead as a doornail," a reporter noted. He reflected the opinion of thousands when he added: "We ought to have a sound sensible republican . . . for the next President as a measure of safety; but only on the condition of absolute noninterference in Southern local affairs, for which there is no further need or excuse."

The Disputed Election of 1876

Against this background the presidential election of 1876 took place. Since corruption in government was the most widely discussed issue, the Republicans passed over their most attractive political personality, the dynamic James G. Blaine, Speaker of the House of Representatives, who had been connected with some chicanery involving railroad securities. Instead they nominated Governor Rutherford B. Hayes of Ohio, a former general with an unsmirched reputation. The Democrats picked Governor Samuel J. Tilden of New York, a wealthy lawyer who had attracted national attention for his part in breaking up the Tweed Ring in New York City.

In November early returns indicated that Tilden had carried New York, New Jersey, Connecticut, Indiana, and all the southern states, including Louisiana, South Carolina, and Florida, where Republican regimes were still in control. This seemed to give him 203 electoral votes to Hayes's 165, and a popular plurality in the neighborhood of 250,000 out of more than 8 million votes cast. However, Republican leaders had anticipated the possible loss of Florida, South Carolina, and Louisiana and were prepared to use their control of the election machinery in those states to throw out sufficient Democratic ballots to alter the results if doing so would change the national outcome. Realizing that the electoral votes of those states were exactly enough to elect their man, they telegraphed their henchmen on the scene, ordering them to go into action. The local Republicans then invalidated Democratic ballots in wholesale lots and filed returns showing Hayes the winner. Naturally the local Democrats protested vigorously and filed their own returns.

The Constitution provides (Article II, section 1) that presidential electors must meet in their respective states to vote and forward the results to "the Seat of the Government." There, it adds, "the President of the Senate shall, in the Presence of the Senate and House of Representatives, open all the Certificates, and the Votes shall then be counted." But who was to do the counting? The House was Democratic, the Senate Republican; neither would agree to allow the other to do the job. On January 29, 1877, scarcely a month before inauguration day, Congress created an electoral commission to decide the disputed cases. The commission consisted of five senators (three Republicans and two Democrats), five representatives (three Democrats and two Republicans), and five justices of the Supreme Court (two Democrats, two Republicans, and one "independent" judge, David Davis). Since it was a foregone conclusion that the others would vote for their party no matter what the evidence, Davis would presumably swing the balance in the interest of fairness.

But before the commission met, the Illinois legislature elected Davis senator! He had to resign from the Court and the commission. Since independents were rare even on the Supreme Court, no neutral was available to replace him. The vacancy went to Associate Justice Joseph P. Bradley of New Jersey, a Republican.

Evidence presented before the commission revealed a disgraceful picture of election shenanigans. On the one hand, in all three disputed states Dem-

ocrats had clearly cast a majority of the votes; on the other, it was unquestionable that many blacks had been forcibly prevented from voting.

In truth, both sides were shamefully corrupt. Lew Wallace, a northern politician later famous as the author of the novel *Ben Hur*, visited Louisiana and Florida shortly after the election. "It is terrible to see the extent to which all classes go in their determination to win," he wrote his wife from Florida. "Money and intimidation can obtain the oath of white men as well as black to any required statement. . . . If we win, our methods are subject to impeachment for possible fraud. If the enemy win, it is the same thing." The governor of Louisiana was reportedly willing to sell his state's electoral votes for $200,000. The Florida election board was supposed to have offered itself to Tilden for the same price. "That seems to be the standard figure," Tilden remarked ruefully.

Most modern authorities take the view that in a fair election the Republicans would have carried South Carolina and Louisiana but that Florida would have gone to Tilden, giving him the election, 188 electoral votes to 181. In the last analysis, this opinion has been arrived at simply by counting white and black noses: blacks were in the majority in South Carolina and Louisiana. Amid the tension and confusion of early 1877, however, even a Solomon would have been hard pressed to judge rightly amid the rumors, lies, and contradictory statements, and the electoral commission was not composed of Solomons. The Democrats had some hopes that Justice Bradley would be sympathetic to their case, for he was known to be opposed to harsh Reconstruction policies. On the eve of the commission's decision in the Florida controversy, he was apparently ready to vote in favor of Tilden. But the Republicans subjected him to tremendous political pressure. When he read his opinion on February 8, it was for Hayes. Thus, by a vote of 8 to 7, the commission awarded Florida's electoral votes to the Republicans.

The rest of the proceedings were routine. The commission assigned all the disputed electoral votes (including one in Oregon where the Democratic governor had seized on a technicality to replace a single Republican elector with a Democrat) to Hayes.

With the spitefulness common to rejected suitors, the Democrats assailed Bradley until, as *The New York Times* put it, he seemed like "a middle-aged St. Sebastian, stuck full of Democratic darts." Unlike Sebastian, however, Bradley was protected from the arrows by the armor of his Republican faith.

To such a level had the republic of Jefferson and John Adams descended. Democratic institutions, shaken by the South's refusal to go along with the majority in 1860 and by the suppression of civil rights during the rebellion, and further weakened by military intervention and the intimidation of blacks in the South during Reconstruction, now seemed a farce. According to Tilden's campaign manager, angry Democrats in 15 states, chiefly war veterans, were readying themselves to march on Washington to force the inauguration of Tilden. Tempers flared in Congress, where some spoke om-

inously of a filibuster that would prevent the recording of the electoral vote and leave the country, on March 4, with no president at all.

The Compromise of 1877

Fortunately, forces for compromise had been at work behind the scenes in Washington for some time. Although northern Democrats threatened to fight to the last ditch, many southern Democrats were willing to accept Hayes if he would promise to remove the troops and allow the southern states to manage their internal affairs by themselves. Ex-Whig planters and merchants who had reluctantly abandoned the carpetbag governments and who sympathized with Republican economic policies hoped that by supporting Hayes they might con-

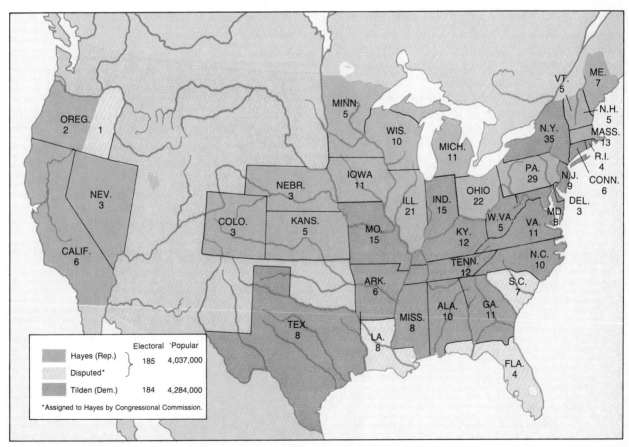

THE COMPROMISE OF 1877

tribute to the restoration of the two-party system that had been destroyed in the South during the 1850s. Ohio Congressman James A. Garfield urged Hayes to find "some discreet way" of showing these southerners that he favored "internal improvements." Hayes replied: "Your views are so nearly the same as mine that I need not say a word."

Tradition has it that a great compromise between the sections was worked out during a dramatic meeting at the Wormley Hotel* in Washington on February 26. Actually, as C. Vann Woodward has demonstrated in his important book *Reunion and Reaction,* the negotiations were long-drawn-out and informal, and the Wormley conference was but one of many. With the tacit support of many Democrats, the electoral vote was counted by the president of the Senate on March 2, and Hayes was declared elected, 185 votes to 184.

Like all compromises, this agreement was not entirely satisfactory; like most, it was not honored in every detail. Hayes recalled the last troops from South Carolina and Louisiana in April. He appointed a former Confederate general, David M. Key of Tennessee, postmaster general and delegated to him the congenial task of finding southerners willing to serve their country as officials of a Republican administration. But the alliance of ex-Whigs and northern Republicans did not flourish; the South remained solidly Democratic. The major significance of the compromise, one of the great intersectional political accommodations of American history, has been well summarized by Professor Woodward:

> The Compromise of 1877 marked the abandonment of principles and force and a return to the traditional ways of expediency and concession. It wrote an end to Reconstruction and recognized a new regime in the South. More profoundly than Constitutional amendments and wordy statutes it shaped the future of four million freedmen and their progeny for generations to come.

For most of the former slaves, this future was to be bleak. Forgotten in the North, manipulated and then callously rejected by the South, rebuffed by the Supreme Court, voiceless in national affairs,

they and their descendants were condemned in the interests of sectional harmony to lives of poverty, indignity, and little hope. Meanwhile, the rest of the United States continued its golden march toward wealth and power.

Milestones

1863	Lincoln announces "Ten Percent Plan" for Reconstruction
Mar. 1865	Establishment of the Freedmen's Bureau
Apr. 1865	General Lee surrenders at Appomattox Court House
Apr. 1865	Assassination of Abraham Lincoln, Andrew Johnson becomes President
May 1865	Johnson's Amnesty plan
Dec. 1865	Thirteenth Amendment ratified
1865–1866	Enactment of Black Codes by southern states
Apr. 1866	Civil Rights Act passed over Johnson's veto
Sept. 1866	Johnson campaigns for his Reconstruction policy
Mar. 1867	First Reconstruction Act
Feb. 1868	House of Representatives impeaches Johnson
Mar. 1868	Fourth Reconstruction Act
May 1868	Senate acquits Johnson
July 1868	Fourteenth Amendment ratified
Nov. 1868	Ulysses S. Grant elected President
1868–1872	Ku Klux Klan in action
Mar. 1870	Fifteenth Amendment ratified
1870–1871	Force (Ku Klux Klan) Acts destroys Klan
1872	Liberal Republican party nominates Horace Greeley for President
Nov. 1872	Grant reelected President
1876	Disputed presidential election
Feb. 1877	Electoral Commission awards disputed votes to Rutherford B. Hayes
	Hayes agrees to Compromise of 1877

---

* Ironically, the hotel was owned by James Wormley, reputedly the wealthiest black in Washington.

SUPPLEMENTARY READING

Titles marked with an asterisk have been published in paperback.

The finest of many excellent overviews of the Reconstruction Era is Eric Foner's **Reconstruction: America's Unfinished Revolution*** (1988). The older approach to the period, stressing the excesses of black-influenced governments and criticizing the Radicals, derives from the seminal work of W. A. Dunning, **Reconstruction, Political and Economic*** (1907). W. E. B. Du Bois, **Black Reconstruction in America*** (1935) was the pioneering counterattack against the Dunning view. See also Eric Foner, **Politics and Ideology in the Age of the Civil War** (1980), and Foner's **Nothing But Freedom*** (1984).

Lincoln's ideas about Reconstruction are analyzed in W. B. Hesseltine, **Lincoln's plan of Reconstruction*** (1960), and in many of the Lincoln volumes mentioned in earlier chapters. Albert Castel, **The Presidency of Andrew Johnson** (1979), is a balanced recent account. On Johnson's battle with the congressional Radicals, see H. L. Trefousse, **The Radical Republicans: Lincoln's Vanguard for Racial Justice*** (1969), E. L. McKitrick, **Andrew Johnson and Reconstruction*** (1960), and M. L. Benedict, **The Impeachment and Trial of Andrew Johnson** (1973). A number of biographies provide information helpful in understanding the Radicals. These include David Donald, **Charles Sumner and the Rights of Man** (1970), B. P. Thomas and H. M. Hyman, **Stanton** (1962), R. N. Current, **Old Thad Stevens** (1942), and H. L. Trefousse, **Benjamin Franklin Wade** (1963). J. M. McPherson, **The Struggle for Equality: Abolitionists and the Negro in the Civil War and Reconstruction*** (1964), is also valuable. On the Fourteenth Amendment, see Joseph James, **The Framing of the Fourteenth Amendment*** (1956); on the Fifteenth Amendment, see William Gillette, **The Right to Vote: Politics and the Passage of the Fifteenth Amendment*** (1965).

Conditions in the South during Reconstruction are discussed in R. H. Abbott, **The Republican Party and the South** (1986), Michael Perman, **Reunion Without Compromise** (1973), H. N. Rabinowitz, **Race Relations in the Urban South** (1978), J. L. Roark, **Masters Without Slaves** (1977), and Leon Litwack, **Been in the Storm Too Long** (1979).

For state studies, see W. L. Rose, **Rehearsal for Re-construction: The Port Royal Experiment*** (1964), Thomas Holt, **Black over White: Negro Political Leadership in South Carolina** (1977), W. C. Harris, **The Day of the Carpetbagger: Republican Reconstruction in Mississippi** (1979) and Joel Williamson, **After Slavery: The Negro in South Carolina During Reconstruction*** (1965). See also Joel Williamson, **The Crucible of Race: Black-White Relations in the American South Since Emancipation** (1984), a psychoanalytical interpretation of racism. G. R. Bentley, **A History of the Freedmen's Bureau** (1955), discusses the work of that important organization, but see also W. S. McFeely, **Yankee Stepfather: General O. O. Howard and the Freedmen*** (1968). On the Ku Klux Klan, see G. C. Rable, **But There Was No Peace*** (1984), and A. W. Trelease, **White Terror: The Ku Klux Klan Conspiracy and Southern Reconstruction** (1971).

On the economic and social effects of Reconstruction, see G. D. Jaynes, **Branches Without Roots: Genesis of the Black Working Class** (1986), R. L. Ransom and Richard Sutch, **One Kind of Freedom: The Economic Consequences of Emancipation*** (1977), Robert Higgs, **Competition and Coercion: Blacks in the American Economy, 1865–1914** (1977), and C. F. Oubre, **Forty Acres and a Mule** (1978). F. A. Shannon, **The Farmer's Last Frontier*** (1945), is also a useful text on southern agriculture. For the growth of industry, see J. F. Stover, **The Railroads of the South** (1955).

On Grant's presidency, see W. S. McFeely, **Grant** (1981); Allan Nevins, **Hamilton Fish: The Inner History of the Grant Administration** (1936), and Matthew Josephson, **The Politicos*** (1938), contain much additional information. On the Republican reform movement, see J. G. Sproat, **"The Best Men": Liberal Reformers in the Gilded Age*** (1968), and M. B. Duberman, **Charles Francis Adams*** (1961). For the disputed election of 1876 and the compromise following it, consult C. V. Woodward, **Reunion and Reaction*** (1951), and K. I. Polakoff, **The Politics of Inertia: The Election of 1876 and the End of Reconstruction** (1973). William Gillette, **Retreat from Reconstruction** (1980), is also an important study.

Blacks in Slavery and Freedom

It is much easier to generalize about what life was like for American blacks under slavery than for free people of that time. Indeed, the fact that the restrictions imposed upon slaves reduced drastically their possibilities for individual development and self-expression was the basic injustice of the slave system. Nevertheless, as these illustrations show, the institution affected its victims in many different ways. Seen from this perspective, the ending of slavery expanded the ability of individual blacks to "be themselves." Even after more than a century, however, the possibilities open to the average black are still more limited than those available to the average white. Finally ending this discrimination is one of the major tasks our society faces today.

The three views of slave life on this page throw different lights on "the peculiar institution." Edwin White, an academic painter, titled his carefully humble yet dignified portrayal of a quite moment Thoughts of Liberia. Actually, few blacks ever returned to Africa in spite of colonization efforts by well-meaning groups.

In 1862, T. H. O'Sullivan made this extraordinary photograph of five generations of a slave family. All were born on the plantation of J. J. Smith in Beaufort, South Carolina.

A Northern visitor, George Fuller, traveled through Alabama in 1858 to observe the conditions under which slaves lived. He sketched this woman, her skirts hitched up and the reins of a plantation mule looped around her neck, plowing a field. In the background are a cotton gin (the building on stilts) and a cotton press, which was used to compress the ginned cotton into bales for shipping.

Before 1860, many of the free blacks of the northern states lived in cities and towns. For most, the church was the center of community life. This 1853 scene from Frank Leslie's Illustrated Newspaper *shows a prayer meeting in the African Church of Cincinnati, Ohio.*

Thomas "Daddy" Rice was a popular vaudeville star in the pre–Civil War years. He introduced the character "Jim Crow" in a song-and-dance blackface act ("Wheel a-bout and turn a-bout/And jump . . . Jim Crow") based on the antics of a black stable boy he claimed to have seen. His "Jump Jim Crow" act helped launch the popular minstrel shows of the 19th century. Unfortunately, they also promoted the stereotype of the shiftless black man. The term **Jim Crow** later came to be applied to the system of Southern segregation laws and customs in the late 19th century.

Slaves, of course, could be bought and sold at their owners' discretion, like any piece of property. Edwin Taylor's 1852 painting **American Slave Market** catches a sense of the mundane way that most owners viewed the trade in human beings. With the slave went a bill of sale. Below is a receipt covering the sale of "a Negro man by the name of Ned about 38 or 40 years of age which negro I warrant to be a slave for life" for $800. The note in the upper right corner, added by the buyer's great-grandson, comments that Ned was reputed to be a good cabinet maker.

My Great Grand Father Jas. Benson Zachry Old Henry County Present Newton County This slave was reputed to be a good cabin maker.

Columbus 95th May 1842

Received of James B Zachry by the hands of John Morton Eight Hundred dollars in full consideration for a Negro Man by the name of Ned about 38 or 40 years of age which negro I warrant to be a slave for life & to be sound & well both in body & mind & I also warrant him against the claims of Myself my heirs or against the Claim of any other person or persons whomsoever given under my hand and seal this day and year above written

Henry Morton

Jois Boswell

Stephen Neal

Reconstruction meant a new set of accommodations to freedom within an older social order. Winslow Homer's tense painting, A Visit from the Old Mistress, *conveys a feeling of the complex relationships that developed between newly freed blacks and their former owners.*

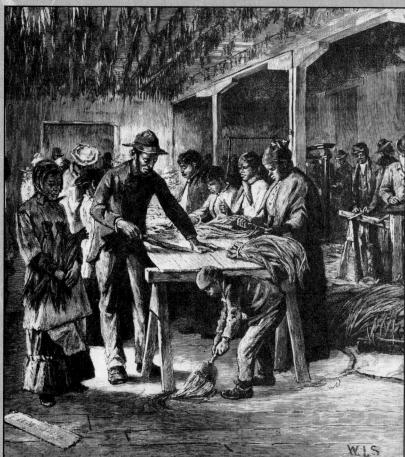

For most former slaves, day-to-day activity in the rural South remained a round of planting, cultivating, and harvesting. For example, the way that hogs were slaughtered and the meat cured or made into sausage did not change. Some blacks, however, did not stay on the land, but instead worked in individual settings, such as this tobacco-processing plant in Danville, Virginia, where men, women, and children were employed stripping tobacco.

The Declaration of Independence

When in the Course of human events, it becomes necessary for one people to dissolve the political bands which have connected them with another, and to assume among the Powers of the earth, the separate and equal station to which the Laws of Nature and of Nature's God entitle them, a decent respect to the opinions of mankind requires that they should declare the causes which impel them to the separation.

We hold these truths to be self-evident, that all men are created equal, that they are endowed by their Creator with certain unalienable Rights, that among these are Life, Liberty and the pursuit of Happiness. That to secure these rights, Governments are instituted among Men, deriving their just powers from the consent of the governed, That whenever any Form of Government becomes destructive of these ends, it is the Right of the People to alter or to abolish it, and to institute new Government, laying its foundation on such principles and organizing its powers in such form, as to them shall seem most likely to effect their Safety and Happiness. Prudence, indeed, will dictate that Governments long established should not be changed for light and transient causes; and accordingly all experience hath shown, that mankind are more disposed to suffer, while evils are sufferable, than to right themselves by abolishing the forms to which they are accustomed. But when a long train of abuses and usurpations, pursuing invariably the same Object evinces a design to reduce them under absolute Despotism, it is their right, it is their duty, to throw off such Government, and to provide new Guards for their future security.—Such has been the patient sufferance of these Colonies; and such is now the necessity which constrains them to alter their former Systems of Government. The history of the present King of Great Britain is a history of repeated injuries and usurpations, all having in direct object the establishment of an absolute Tyranny over these States. To prove this, let Facts be submitted to a candid world.

He has refused his Assent to Laws, the most wholesome and necessary for the public good.

He has forbidden his Governors to pass Laws of immediate and pressing importance, unless suspended in their operation till his Assent should be obtained; and when so suspended, he has utterly neglected to attend to them.

He has refused to pass other Laws for the accommodation of large districts of people, unless those people would relinquish the right of Representation in the Legislature, a right inestimable to them and formidable to tyrants only.

He has called together legislative bodies at places unusual, uncomfortable, and distant from the depository of their Public Records, for the sole purpose of fatiguing them into compliance with his measures.

He has dissolved Representative Houses repeatedly, for opposing with manly firmness his invasions on the rights of the people.

He has refused for a long time, after such dissolutions, to cause others to be elected; whereby the Legislative Powers, incapable of Annihilation, have returned to the People at large for their exercise; the State remaining in the mean time exposed to all the dangers of invasion from without, and convulsions within.

He has endeavoured to prevent the population of these States; for that purpose obstructing the Laws of Naturalization of Foreigners; refusing to pass others to encourage their migration hither, and raising the conditions of new Appropriations of Lands.

He has obstructed the Administration of Justice, by refusing his Assent to Laws for establishing Judiciary Powers.

He has made Judges dependent on his Will alone, for the tenure of their offices, and the amount and payment of their salaries.

He has erected a multitude of New Offices, and sent hither swarms of Officers to harass our People, and eat out their substance.

He has kept among us, in times of peace, Standing Armies without the Consent of our legislature.

He has affected to render the Military independent of and superior to the Civil Power.

He has combined with others to subject us to a jurisdiction foreign to our constitution, and unacknowledged by our laws; giving his Assent to their acts of pretended legislation:

For quartering large bodies of armed troops among us:

For protecting them, by a mock Trial, from Punishment for any Murders which they should commit on the Inhabitants of these States:

For cutting off our Trade with all parts of the world:

For imposing taxes on us without our Consent:

For depriving us in many cases, of the benefits of Trial by Jury:

For transporting us beyond Seas to be tried for pretended offences:

For abolishing the free System of English Laws in a neighbouring Province, establishing therein an Arbitrary government, and enlarging its Boundaries so as to render it at once an example and fit instrument for introducing the same absolute rule into these Colonies:

For taking away our Charters, abolishing our most valuable Laws, and altering fundamentally the Forms of our Governments:

For suspending our own Legislature, and declaring themselves invested with Power to legislate for us in all cases whatsoever.

He has abdicated Government here, by declaring us out of his Protection and waging War against us.

He has plundered our seas, ravaged our Coasts, burnt our towns, and destroyed the lives of our people.

He is at this time transporting large armies of foreign mercenaries to compleat the works of death, desolation and tyranny, already begun with circumstances of Cruelty & perfidy scarcely paralleled in the most barbarous ages, and totally unworthy the Head of a civilized nation.

He has constrained our fellow Citizens taken Captive on the high Seas to bear Arms against their Country, to become the executioners of their friends and Brethren, or to fall themselves by their Hands.

He has excited domestic insurrections amongst us, and has endeavoured to bring on the inhabitants of our frontiers, the merciless Indian Savages, whose known rule of warfare, is an undistinguished destruction of all ages, sexes and conditions.

In every stage of these Oppressions We have Petitioned for Redress in the most humble terms: Our repeated Petitions have been answered only by repeated injury. A Prince, whose character is thus marked by every act which may define a Tyrant, is unfit to be the ruler of a free People.

Nor have We been wanting in attention to our British brethren. We have warned them from time to time of attempts by their legislature to extend an unwarrantable jurisdiction over us. We have reminded them of the circumstances of our emigration and settlement here. We have appealed to their native justice and magnanimity, and we have conjured them by the ties of our common kindred to disavow these usurpations, which, would inevitably interrupt our connections and correspondence. They too have been deaf to the voice of justice and of consanguinity. We must, therefore, acquiesce in the necessity, which denounces our Separation, and hold them, as we hold the rest of mankind, Enemies in War, in Peace Friends.

We, therefore, the Representatives of the united States of America, in General Congress, Assembled, appealing to the Supreme Judge of the world for the rectitude of our intentions, do, in the Name, and by Authority of the good People of these Colonies, solemnly publish and declare, That these United Colonies are, and of Right ought to be Free and Independent States; that they are Absolved from all Allegiance to the British Crown, and that all political connection between them and the State of Great Britain, is and ought to be totally dissolved; and that as Free and Independent States, they have full Power to levy War, conclude Peace, contract Alliances, establish Commerce, and to do all other Acts and Things which Independent States may of right do. And for the support of this Declaration, with a firm reliance on the Protection of Divine Providence, we mutually pledge to each other our Lives, our Fortunes and our sacred Honor.

John Hancock,

Josiah Bartlett, Wm Whipple, Saml Adams, John Adams, Robt Treat Paine, Elbridge Gerry, Steph. Hopkins, William Ellery, Roger Sherman, Samel Huntington, Wm Williams, Oliver Wolcott, Matthew Thornton, Wm Floyd, Phil Livingston, Frans Lewis, Lewis Morris, Richd Stockton, Jno Witherspoon, Fras Hopkinson, John Hart, Abra Clark, Robt Morris, Benjamin Rush, Benja Franklin, John Morton, Geo Clymer, Jas Smith, Geo. Taylor, James Wilson, Geo. Ross, Caesar Rodney, Geo Read, Thos M:Kean, Samuel Chase, Wm Paca, Thos Stone, Charles Carroll of Carrollton, George Wythe, Richard Henry Lee, Th. Jefferson, Benja Harrison, Thos Nelson, Jr., Francis Lightfoot Lee, Carter Braxton, Wm Hooper, Joseph Hewes, John Penn, Edward Rutledge, Thos Heyward, Junr., Thomas Lynch, Junor., Arthur Middleton, Button Gwinnett, Lyman Hall, Geo Walton.

The Constitution
of the United States

We the people of the United States, in Order to form a more perfect Union, establish Justice, insure domestic Tranquility, provide for the common defence, promote the general Welfare, and secure the Blessings of Liberty to ourselves and our Posterity, do ordain and establish this CONSTITUTION for the United States of America.

ARTICLE I

Section 1. All legislative Powers herein granted shall be vested in a Congress of the United States, which shall consist of a Senate and House of Representatives.

Section 2. The House of Representatives shall be composed of Members chosen every second Year by the People of the several States, and the Electors in each State shall have the Qualifications requisite for Electors of the most numerous Branch of the State Legislature.

No Person shall be a Representative who shall not have attained to the Age of twenty-five Years, and been seven Years a Citizen of the United States, and who shall not, when elected, be an Inhabitant of that State in which he shall be chosen.

Representatives and direct Taxes shall be apportioned among the several States which may be included within this Union, according to their respective Numbers, which shall be determined by adding to the whole Number of free Persons, including those bound to Service for a Term of Years, and excluding Indians not taxed, three fifths of all other Persons. The actual Enumeration shall be made within three Years after the first Meeting of the Congress of the United States, and within every subsequent Term of ten Years, in such Manner as they shall by Law direct. The Number of Representatives shall not exceed one for every thirty Thousand, but each State shall have at Least one Representative; and until such enumeration shall be made, the State of New Hampshire shall be entitled to chuse three, Massachusetts eight, Rhode-Island and Providence Plantations one, Connecticut five, New-York six, New Jersey four, Pennsylvania eight, Delaware one, Maryland six, Virginia ten, North Carolina five, South Carolina five, and Georgia three.

When vacancies happen in the Representation from any State, the Executive Authority thereof shall issue Writs of Election to fill such Vacancies.

The House of Representatives shall chuse their Speaker and other Officers; and shall have the sole Power of Impeachment.

Section 3. The Senate of the United States shall be composed of two Senators from each State, chosen by the Legislature thereof, for six Years; and each Senator shall have one Vote.

Immediately after they shall be assembled in Consequence of the first Election, they shall be divided as equally as may be into three Classes. The Seats of the Senators of the first Class shall be vacated at the Expiration of the second Year, of the second Class at the Expiration of the fourth Year, and of the third Class at the Expiration of the sixth Year, so that one-third may be chosen every second Year; and if Vacancies happen by Resignation, or otherwise, during the Recess of the Legislature of any State, the Executive thereof may make temporary Appointments until the next Meeting of the Legislature, which shall then fill such Vacancies.

No Person shall be a Senator who shall not have attained to the Age of thirty Years, and been nine Years a Citizen of the United States, and who shall not, when elected, be an Inhabitant of that State in which he shall be chosen.

The Vice President of the United States shall be President of the Senate, but shall have no vote, unless they be equally divided.

The Senate shall chuse their other Officers, and also a President pro tempore, in the absence of the Vice President, or when he shall exercise the Office of the President of the United States.

The Senate shall have the sole Power to try all Impeachments. When sitting for that purpose, they shall be on Oath or Affirmation. When the President of the United States is tried, the Chief Justice shall preside: And no person shall be convicted without the Concurrence of two thirds of the Members present.

Judgment in Cases of Impeachment shall not extend further than to removal from Office, and disqualification to hold and enjoy any Office of honor, Trust, or Profit under the United States: but the Party convicted shall nevertheless be liable and subject to Indictment, Trial, Judgment, and Punishment, according to Law.

Section 4. The Times, Places and Manner of holding

Elections for Senators and Representatives, shall be prescribed in each state by the Legislature thereof; but the Congress may at any time by Law make or alter such Regulations, except as to the Places of Chusing Senators.

The Congress shall assemble at least once in every Year, and such Meeting shall be on the first Monday in December, unless they shall by Law appoint a different Day.

Section 5. Each House shall be the Judge of the Elections, Returns and Qualifications of its own Members, and a Majority of each shall constitute a Quorum to do Business; but a smaller number may adjourn from day to day, and may be authorized to compel the Attendance of absent Members, in such Manner, and under such Penalties, as each House may provide.

Each House may determine the Rules of its Proceedings, punish its Members for disorderly Behavior, and, with the Concurrence of two thirds, expel a Member.

Each House shall keep a Journal of its Proceedings, and from time to time publish the same, excepting such Parts as may in their Judgment require Secrecy; and the Yeas and Nays of the Members of either House on any question shall, at the Desire of one fifth of those Present, be entered on the Journal.

Neither House, during the Session of Congress, shall, without the Consent of the other, adjourn for more than three days, nor to any other Place than that in which the two Houses shall be sitting.

Section 6. The Senators and Representatives shall receive a Compensation for their Services, to be ascertained by Law, and paid out of the Treasury of the United States. They shall in all Cases, except Treason, Felony, and Breach of the Peace, be privileged from arrest during their Attendance at the Session of their respective Houses, and in going to and returning from the same; and for any Speech or Debate in either House, they shall not be questioned in any other Place.

No Senator or Representative shall, during the Time for which he was elected, be appointed to any civil Office under the Authority of the United States, which shall have been created, or the Emoluments whereof shall have been increased, during such time; and no Person holding any Office under the United States shall be a Member of either House during his continuance in Office.

Section 7. All Bills for raising Revenue shall originate in the House of Representatives; but the Senate may propose or concur with Amendments as on other bills.

Every Bill which shall have passed the House of Representatives and the Senate, shall, before it become a Law, be presented to the President of the United States; If he approve he shall sign it, but if not he shall return it, with his Objections, to that House in which it shall have originated, who shall enter the Objections at large on their Journal, and proceed to reconsider it. If after such Reconsideration two thirds of that House shall agree to pass the bill, it shall be sent, together with the objections, to the other House, by which it shall likewise be reconsidered, and if approved by two thirds of that House, it shall become a Law. But in all such Cases the Votes of both Houses shall be determined by Yeas and Nays, and the Names of the Persons voting for and against the Bill shall be entered on the Journal of each House respectively. If any Bill shall not be returned by the President within ten Days (Sundays excepted) after it shall have been presented to him, the Same shall be a Law, in like Manner as if he had signed it, unless the Congress by their Adjournment prevent its Return, in which Case it shall not be a Law.

Every Order, Resolution, or Vote to which the Concurrence of the Senate and House of Representatives may be necessary (except on a question of Adjournment) shall be presented to the President of the United States; and before the Same shall take Effect, shall be approved by him, or being disapproved by him, shall be repassed by two thirds of the Senate and House of Representatives, according to the Rules and Limitations prescribed in the Case of a Bill.

Section 8. The Congress shall have Power To lay and collect Taxes, Duties, Imposts and Excises, to pay the Debts and provide for the common Defence and general Welfare of the United States; but all Duties, Imposts and Excises shall be uniform throughout the United States;

To borrow money on the credit of the United States;

To regulate Commerce with foreign Nations, and among the several States, and with the Indian Tribes;

To establish an uniform Rule of Naturalization, and uniform Laws on the subject of Bankruptcies throughout the United States;

To coin Money, regulate the Value thereof, and of foreign Coin, and fix the Standard of Weights and Measures;

To provide for the Punishment of counterfeiting the Securities and current Coin of the United States;

To establish Post Offices and post Roads;

To promote the Progress of Science and useful Arts, by securing for limited Times to Authors and Inventors the exclusive Right to their respective Writings and Discoveries;

To constitute Tribunals inferior to the Supreme Court;

To define and punish Piracies and Felonies committed on the high Seas, and Offences against the Law of Nations;

To declare War, grant Letters of Marque and Reprisal, and make Rules concerning Captures on Land and Water;

To raise and support Armies, but no Appropriation of Money to that Use shall be for a longer Term than two Years;

To provide and maintain a Navy;

To make Rules for the Government and Regulation of the land and naval forces;

To provide for calling forth the Militia to execute the Laws of the Union, suppress Insurrections and repel Invasions;

To provide for organizing, arming, and disciplining the Militia, and for governing such Part of them as may be employed in the Service of the United States, reserving to the States respectively, the Appointment of the Officers, and the Authority of training the Militia according to the discipline prescribed by Congress;

To exercise exclusive Legislation in all Cases whatsoever, over such District (not exceeding ten Miles square) as may, by Cession of particular States, and the acceptance of Congress, become the Seat of Government of the United States, and to exercise like Authority over all Places purchased by the Consent of the Legislature of the State in which the Same shall be, for the Erection of Forts, Magazines, Arsenals, dock-Yards, and other needful Buildings;—And

To make all Laws which shall be necessary and proper for carrying into Execution the foregoing Powers, and all other Powers vested by this Constitution in the government of the United States, or in any Department or Officer thereof.

Section 9. The Migration or Importation of such Persons as any of the States now existing shall think proper to admit, shall not be prohibited by the Congress prior to the Year one thousand eight hundred and eight, but a tax or duty may be imposed on such Importation, not exceeding ten dollars for each Person.

The privilege of the Writ of Habeas Corpus shall not be suspended, unless when in Cases of Rebellion or Invasion the public Safety may require it.

No Bill of Attainder or ex post facto Law shall be passed.

No capitation, or other direct, Tax shall be laid unless in Proportion to the Census or Enumeration herein before directed to be taken.

No Tax or Duty shall be laid on Articles exported from any State.

No Preference shall be given by any Regulation of Revenue to the Ports of one State over those of another: nor shall Vessels bound to, or from, one State, be obliged to enter, clear, or pay Duties in another.

No Money shall be drawn from the Treasury, but in Consequence of Appropriations made by Law; and a regular Statement and Account of the Receipts and Expenditures of all public Money shall be published from time to time.

No Title of Nobility shall be granted by the United States: And no Person holding any Office of Profit or Trust under them, shall, without the Consent of the Congress, accept of any present, Emolument, Office, or Title, of any kind whatever, from any King, Prince, or foreign State.

Section 10. No State shall enter into any Treaty, Alliance, or Confederation; grant Letters of Marque and Reprisal; coin Money; emit Bills of Credit; make any Thing but gold and silver Coin a Tender in Payment of Debts; pass any Bill of Attainder, ex post facto Law, or Law impairing the Obligation of Contracts, or grant any Title of Nobility.

No State shall, without the Consent of the Congress, lay any Imposts or Duties on Imports or Exports, except what may be absolutely necessary for executing its inspection Laws: and the net Produce of all Duties and Imposts, laid by any State on Imports or Exports, shall be for the Use of the Treasury of the United States; and all such Laws shall be subject to the Revision and Control of the Congress.

No State shall, without the Consent of Congress, lay any duty of Tonnage, keep Troops, or Ships of War in time of Peace, enter into any Agreement or Compact with another State, or with a foreign Power, or engage in War, unless actually invaded, or in such imminent Danger as will not admit of delay.

ARTICLE II

Section 1. The executive Power shall be vested in a President of the United States of America. He shall hold his Office during the Term of four years, and, together with the Vice President, chosen for the same Term, be elected, as follows:

Each State shall appoint, in such Manner as the Legislature thereof may direct, a Number of Electors, equal to the whole Number of Senators and Representatives to which the State may be entitled in the Congress; but no Senator or Representative, or Person holding an Office of Trust or Profit under the United States, shall be appointed an Elector.

The Electors shall meet in their respective States, and vote by Ballot for two persons, of whom one at least shall not be an Inhabitant of the same State with themselves. And they shall make a List of all the Persons voted for, and of the Number of Votes for each; which List they shall sign and certify, and transmit sealed to the Seat of the Government of the United States, directed to the President of the Senate. The President of the Senate shall, in the Presence of the Senate and House of Representatives, open all the Certificates, and the Votes shall then be counted. The Person having the greatest Number of Votes shall be the President, if such Number be a Majority of the whole Number of Electors appointed; and if there be more than one who have such Majority, and have an equal Number of Votes, then the House of Representatives shall immediately chuse by Ballot one of them for President; and if no Person have a Majority, then from the five highest on the List the said House shall in like Manner chuse the President. But in chusing the President, the votes shall be taken by States, the Representation from each State having one Vote; a quorum for this Purpose shall consist of a Member or Members from two-thirds of the States, and a Majority of all the States shall be necessary to a Choice. In every Case, after the Choice of the President, the Person having the greatest Number of Votes of the Electors shall be the Vice President. But if there should remain two or more who have equal votes, the Senate shall chuse from them by Ballot the Vice President.

The Congress may determine the time of chusing the Electors, and the Day on which they shall give their Votes; which Day shall be the same throughout the United States.

No person except a natural-born Citizen, or a Citizen of the United States, at the time of the Adoption of this Constitution, shall be eligible to the Office of President; neither shall any Person be eligible to that Office who shall not have attained to the Age of thirty-five years, and been fourteen Years a Resident within the United States.

In Case of the Removal of the President from Office, or of his Death, Resignation, or Inability to discharge the Powers and Duties of the said Office, the same shall devolve on the Vice President, and the Congress may by Law provide for the Case of Removal, Death, Resignation, or Inability, both of the President and Vice President, declaring what Officer shall then act as President, and such Officer shall act accordingly, until the disability be removed, or a President shall be elected.

The President shall, at stated Times, receive for his Services a Compensation, which shall neither be increased nor diminished during the Period for which he shall have been elected, and he shall not receive within that Period any other Emolument from the United States, or any of them.

Before he enter on the execution of his Office, he shall take the following Oath or Affirmation:—"I do solemnly swear (or affirm) that I will faithfully execute the Office of President of the United States, and will, to the best of my Ability, preserve, protect, and defend the Constitution of the United States."

Section 2. The President shall be Commander in Chief of the Army and Navy of the United States, and of the Militia of the several States, when called into the actual Service of the United States; he may require the Opinion, in writing, of the principal Officer in each of the executive Departments, upon any subject relating to the Duties of their respective Offices, and he shall have Power to Grant Reprieves and Pardons for Offences against the United States, except in Cases of Impeachment.

He shall have Power, by and with the Advice and Consent of the Senate, to make Treaties, provided two thirds of the Senators present concur; and he shall nominate, and by and with the Advice and Consent of the Senate, shall appoint Ambassadors, other public Ministers and Consuls, Judges of the supreme Court, and all other Officers of the United States, whose Appointments are not herein otherwise provided for, and which shall be established by Law: but the Congress may by Law vest the Appointment of such inferior Officers, as they think proper, in the President alone, in the Courts of Law, or in the Heads of Departments.

The President shall have Power to fill up all Vacancies that may happen during the Recess of the Senate, by granting Commissions which shall expire at the End of their next Session.

Section 3. He shall from time to time give to the Congress Information of the State of the Union, and recommend to their Consideration such Measures as he shall judge necessary and expedient; he may, on extraordinary occasions, convene both Houses, or either of them, and in Case of Disagreement between them, with respect to the Time of Adjournment, he may adjourn them to such Time as he shall think proper; he shall receive Ambassadors and other public Ministers; he shall take Care that the Laws be faithfully executed, and shall Commission all the Officers of the United States.

Section 4. The President, Vice President and all civil Officers of the United States, shall be removed from Office on Impeachment for, and Conviction of, Treason, Bribery, or other high Crimes and Misdemeanors.

ARTICLE III

Section 1. The judicial Power of the United States, shall be vested in one supreme Court, and in such inferior Courts as the Congress may from time to time ordain and establish. The Judges, both of the supreme and inferior Courts, shall hold their Offices during good Behaviour, and shall, at stated Times, receive for their Services, a Compensation, which shall not be diminished during their Continuance in Office.

Section 2. The judicial Power shall extend to all Cases, in Law and Equity, arising under this Constitution, the Laws of the United States, and treaties made, or which shall be made, under their Authority;—to all Cases affecting ambassadors, other public ministers and consuls;—to all cases of admiralty and maritime Jurisdiction;—to Controversies to which the United States shall be a Party;—to Controversies between two or more States;—between a State and Citizens of another State;—between

Citizens of different States,—between Citizens of the same State claiming Lands under Grants of different States, and between a State, or the Citizens thereof, and foreign States, Citizens or Subjects.

In all Cases affecting Ambassadors, other public Ministers and Consuls, and those in which a State shall be Party, the supreme Court shall have original Jurisdiction. In all the other Cases before mentioned, the supreme Court shall have appellate Jurisdiction, both as to Law and Fact, with such Exceptions, and under such Regulations as the Congress shall make.

The trial of all Crimes, except in Cases of Impeachment, shall be by Jury; and such Trial shall be held in the State where the said Crimes shall have been committed; but when not committed within any State, the Trial shall be at such Place or Places as the Congress may by Law have directed.

Section 3. Treason against the United States, shall consist only in levying War against them, or in adhering to their Enemies, giving them Aid and Comfort. No Person shall be convicted of Treason unless on the testimony of two Witnesses to the same overt Act, or on Confession in open Court.

The Congress shall have power to declare the Punishment of Treason, but no Attainder of Treason shall work Corruption of Blood, or Forfeiture except during the Life of the Person attained.

ARTICLE IV

Section 1. Full Faith and Credit shall be given in each State to the public Acts, Records, and judicial Proceedings of every other State. And the Congress may by general Laws prescribe the Manner in which such Acts, Records and Proceedings shall be proved, and the Effect thereof.

Section 2. The Citizens of each State shall be entitled to all Privileges and Immunities of Citizens in the several States.

A Person charged in any State with Treason, Felony, or other Crime, who shall flee from Justice, and be found in another State, shall on demand of the executive Authority of the State from which he fled, be delivered up, to be removed to the State having Jurisdiction of the crime.

No Person held to Service or Labour in one State, under the Laws thereof, escaping into another, shall, in Consequence of any Law or Regulation therein, be discharged from such Service or Labour, but shall be delivered up on Claim of the Party to whom such Service or Labour may be due.

Section 3. New States may be admitted by the Congress into this Union; but no new State shall be formed or erected within the Jurisdiction of any other State; nor any State be formed by the Junction of two or more States, or parts of States, without the Consent of the Legislatures of the States concerned as well as of the Congress.

The Congress shall have Power to dispose of and make all needful Rules and Regulations respecting the Territory or other Property belonging to the United States; and nothing in this Constitution shall be so construed as to Prejudice any Claims of the United States, or of any particular State.

Section 4. The United States shall guarantee to every State in this Union a Republican Form of Government, and shall protect each of them against Invasion; and on Application of the Legislature, or the Executive (when the Legislature cannot be convened) against domestic Violence.

ARTICLE V

The Congress, whenever two-thirds of both Houses shall deem it necessary, shall propose Amendments to this Constitution, or, on the Application of the Legislatures of two-thirds of the several States, shall call a Convention for proposing Amendments, which, in either Case, shall be valid to all Intents and Purposes, as part of this Constitution, when ratified by the Legislatures of three-fourths of the several States, or by Conventions in three-fourths thereof, as the one or the other Mode of Ratification may be proposed by the Congress; Provided that no Amendment which may be made prior to the Year One thousand eight hundred and eight shall in any Manner affect the first and fourth Clauses in the Ninth Section of the first Article; and that no State, without its Consent, shall be deprived of its equal Suffrage in the Senate.

ARTICLE VI

All Debts contracted and Engagements entered into, before the Adoption of this Constitution, shall be as valid against the United States under this Constitution, as under the Confederation.

This Constitution, and the Laws of the United States which shall be made in Pursuance thereof; and all Treaties made, or which shall be made, under the Authority of the United States, shall be the supreme Law of the Land; and the Judges in every State shall be bound thereby, any Thing in the Constitution or Laws of any State to the Contrary notwithstanding.

The Senators and Representatives before mentioned, and the Members of the several State Legislatures, and all executive and judicial Officers, both of the United States and of the several States, shall be bound by Oath or Affirmation to support this Constitution; but no religious Test shall ever be required as a qualification to any Office or public Trust under the United States.

ARTICLE VII

The Ratification of the Conventions of nine States shall be sufficient for the Establishment of this Constitution between the States so ratifying the same.

Done in Convention by the Unanimous Consent of the States present the Seventeenth Day of September in the Year of our Lord one thousand seven hundred and Eighty seven, and of the Independence of the United States of America the Twelfth. In Witness whereof We have hereunto subscribed our Names.

Go. Washington, *President and deputy from Virginia; Attest* William Jackson, *Secretary; Delaware:* Geo. Read,* Gunning Bedford, Jr., John Dickinson, Richard Bassett, Jaco. Broom; *Maryland:* James McHenry, Daniel of St. Thomas' Jenifer, Danl. Carroll; *Virginia:* John Blair, James Madison, Jr.; *North Carolina:* Wm. Blount, Richd. Dobbs Spaight, Hu Williamson; *South Carolina:* J. Rutledge, Charles Cotesworth Pinckney, Charles Pinckney, Pierce Butler; *Georgia:* William Few, Abr. Baldwin; *New Hampshire:* John Langdon, Nicholas Gilman; *Massachusetts:* Nathaniel Gorham, Rufus King; *Connecticut:* Wm. Saml. Johnson, Roger Sherman;* *New York:* Alexander Hamilton; *New Jersey:* Wil. Livingston, David Brearley, Wm. Paterson, Jona. Dayton; *Pennsylvania:* B. Franklin,* Thomas Mifflin, Robt. Morris,* Geo. Clymer,* Thos. FitzSimons, Jared Ingersoll, James Wilson, Gouv. Morris.

Articles in Addition to, and Amendment of, the Constitution of the United States of America, Proposed by Congress, and Ratified by the Legislatures of the Several States, Pursuant to the Fifth Article of the Original Constitution.

AMENDMENT I [1791]

Congress shall make no law respecting an establishment of religion, or prohibiting the free exercise thereof; or abridging the freedom of speech, or of the press; or the right of the people peaceably to assemble, and to petition the Government for a redress of grievances.

AMENDMENT II [1791]

A well regulated Militia, being necessary to the security of a free State, the right of the people to keep and bear Arms shall not be infringed.

AMENDMENT III [1791]

No Soldier shall, in time of peace, be quartered in any house, without the consent of the Owner, nor in time of war, but in a manner to be prescribed by law.

---

* Also signed the Declaration of Independence

AMENDMENT IV [1791]

The right of the people to be secure in their persons, houses, papers, and effects, against unreasonable searches and seizures, shall not be violated, and no Warrants shall issue, but upon probable cause, supported by Oath or affirmation, and particularly describing the place to be searched, and the persons or things to be seized.

AMENDMENT V [1791]

No person shall be held to answer for a capital or otherwise infamous crime, unless on a presentment or indictment of a Grand Jury, except in cases arising in the land or naval forces, or in the Militia, when in actual service in time of War or public danger; nor shall any person be subject for the same offence to be twice put in jeopardy of life or limb; nor shall be compelled in any criminal case to be a witness against himself, nor be deprived of life, liberty, or property, without due process of law; nor shall private property be taken for public use, without just compensation.

AMENDMENT VI [1791]

In all criminal prosecutions, the accused shall enjoy the right to a speedy and public trial, by an impartial jury of the State and district wherein the crime shall have been committed, which district shall have been previously ascertained by law, and to be informed of the nature and cause of the accusation; to be confronted with the winesses against him; to have compulsory process for obtaining witnesses in his favor, and to have the Assistance of Counsel for his defence.

AMENDMENT VII [1791]

In suits at common law, where the value in controversy shall exceed twenty dollars, the right of trial by jury shall be preserved, and no fact tried by a jury, shall be otherwise reexamined in any Court of the United States, than according to the rules of the common law.

AMENDMENT VIII [1791]

Excessive bail shall not be required, nor excessive fines imposed, nor cruel and unusual punishments inflicted.

AMENDMENT IX [1791]

The enumeration in the Constitution, of certain rights, shall not be construed to deny or disparage others retained by the people.

AMENDMENT X [1791]

The powers not delegated to the United States by the Constitution, nor prohibited by it to the States, are reserved to the States respectively, or to the people.

AMENDMENT XI [1798]

The Judicial power of the United States shall not be construed to extend to any suit in law or equity, commenced or prosecuted against one of the United States by Citizens of another State, or by Citizens or Subjects of any Foreign State.

AMENDMENT XII [1804]

The Electors shall meet in their respective States and vote by ballot for President and Vice-President, one of whom, at least, shall not be an inhabitant of the same State with themselves; they shall name in their ballots the person voted for as President, and in distinct ballots the person voted for as Vice-President, and they shall make distinct lists of all persons voted for as President, and of all persons voted for as Vice-President, and of the number of votes for each, which lists they shall sign and certify, and transmit sealed to the seat of the government of the United States, directed to the President of the Senate;—The President of the Senate shall, in the presence of the Senate and House of Representatives, open all the certificates and the votes shall then be counted;—The person having the greatest number of votes for President, shall be the President, if such number be a majority of the whole number of Electors appointed; and if no person have such majority, then from the persons having the highest numbers not exceeding three on the list of those voted for as President, the House of Representatives shall choose immediately, by ballot, the President. But in choosing the President, the votes shall be taken by states, the representation from each state having one vote; a quorum for this purpose shall consist of a member or members from two-thirds of the states, and a majority of all the states shall be necessary to a choice. And if the House of Representatives shall not choose a President whenever the right of choice shall devolve upon them, before the fourth day of March next following, then the Vice-President shall act as President, as in the case of the death or other constitutional disability of the President.—The person having the greatest number of votes as Vice-President, shall be the Vice-President, if such number be a majority of the whole number of Electors appointed, and if no person have a majority, then from the two highest numbers on the list, the Senate shall choose the Vice-President; a quorum for the purpose shall consist of two-thirds of the whole number of Senators, and a majority of the whole number shall be necessary to a choice. But no person constitutionally ineligible to the office of President shall be eligible to that of Vice-President of the United States.

AMENDMENT XIII [1865]

Section 1. Neither slavery nor involuntary servitude, except as a punishment for crime whereof the party shall have been duly convicted, shall exist within the United States, or any place subject to their jurisdiction.

Section 2. Congress shall have power to enforce this article by appropriate legislation.

AMENDMENT XIV [1868]

Section 1. All persons born or naturalized in the United States, and subject to the jurisdiction thereof, are citizens of the United States and of the State wherein they reside. No State shall make or enforce any law which shall abridge the privileges or immunities of citizens of the United States; nor shall any State deprive any person of life, liberty, or property, without due process of law; nor deny to any person within its jurisdiction the equal protection of the laws.

Section 2. Representatives shall be apportioned among the several States according to their respective numbers, counting the whole number of persons in each State, excluding Indians not taxed. But when the right to vote at any election for the choice of electors for President and Vice-President of the United States, Representatives in Congress, the Executive and Judicial officers of a State, or the members of the Legislature thereof, is denied to any of the male inhabitants of such State, being twenty-one years of age, and citizens of the United States, or in any way abridged, except for participation in rebellion, or other crime, the basis of representation therein shall be reduced in the proportion which the number of such male citizens shall bear to the whole number of male citizens twenty-one years of age in such State.

Section 3. No person shall be a Senator or Representative in Congress, or elector of President and Vice-President, or hold any office, civil or military, under the United States, or under any State, who, having previously taken an oath, as a member of Congress, or as an officer of the United States, or as a member of any State legislature, or as an executive or judicial officer of any State, to support the Constitution of the United States, shall have engaged in insurrection or rebellion against the same, or given aid or comfort to the enemies thereof. But Congress may by a vote of two-thirds of each House, remove such disability.

Section 4. The validity of the public debt of the United States, authorized by law, including debts incurred for payment of pensions and bounties for services in suppressing insurrection or rebellion, shall not be questioned. But neither the United States nor any State shall assume or pay any debt or obligation incurred in aid of insurrection or rebellion against the United States, or any claim for the loss or emancipation of any slave; but all such debts, obligations, and claims shall be held illegal and void.

Section 5. The Congress shall have the power to enforce, by appropriate legislation, the provisions of this article.

AMENDMENT XV [1870]

Section 1. The right of citizens of the United States to vote shall not be denied or abridged by the United States or by any State on account of race, color, or previous condition of servitude—

Section 2. The Congress shall have power to enforce this article by appropriate legislation.

AMENDMENT XVI [1913]

The Congress shall have power to lay and collect taxes on incomes, from whatever source derived, without apportionment among the several States, and without regard to any census or enumeration.

AMENDMENT XVII [1913]

The Senate of the United States shall be composed of two Senators from each State, elected by the people thereof, for six years; and each Senator shall have one vote. The electors in each State shall have the qualifications requisite for electors of the most numerous branch of the State legislatures.

When vacancies happen in the representation of any State in the Senate, the executive authority of such State shall issue writs of election to fill such vacancies: *Provided,* That the legislature of any State may empower the executive thereof to make temporary appointments until the people fill the vacancies by election as the legislature may direct.

This amendment shall not be so construed as to affect the election or term of any Senator chosen before it becomes valid as part of the Constitution.

AMENDMENT XVIII [1919]

Section 1. After one year from the ratification of this article the manufacture, sale, or transportation of intoxicating liquors within, the importation thereof into, or the exportation thereof from the United States and all territory subject to the jurisdiction thereof for beverage purposes is hereby prohibited.

Section 2. The Congress and the several States shall have concurrent power to enforce this article by appropriate legislation.

Section 3. This article shall be inoperative unless it shall have been ratified as an amendment to the Constitution by the legislatures of the several States, as provided in the Constitution, within seven years from the date of the submission hereof to the States by the Congress.

AMENDMENT XIX [1920]

The right of citizens of the United States to vote shall not be denied or abridged by the United States or by any State on account of sex.

Congress shall have power to enforce this article by appropriate legislation.

AMENDMENT XX [1933]

Section 1. The terms of the President and Vice-President shall end at noon on the 20th day of January, and the terms of Senators and Representatives at noon on the 3d day of January, of the years in which such terms would have ended if this article had not been ratified; and the terms of their successors shall then begin.

Section 2. The Congress shall assemble at least once in every year, and such meeting shall begin at noon on the 3d day of January, unless they shall by law appoint a different day.

Section 3. If, at the time fixed for the beginning of the term of the President, the President elect shall have died, the Vice-President elect shall become President. If a President shall not have been chosen before the time fixed for the beginning of his term, or if the President elect shall have failed to qualify, then the Vice-President elect shall act as President until a President shall have qualified; and the Congress may by law provide for the case wherein neither a President elect nor a Vice-President elect shall have qualified, declaring who shall then act as President, or the manner in which one who is to act shall be selected, and such person shall act accordingly until a President or Vice-President shall have qualified.

Section 4. The Congress may by law provide for the case of the death of any of the persons from whom the House of Representatives may choose a President whenever the right of choice shall have devolved upon them, and for the case of the death of any of the persons from whom the Senate may choose a Vice-President whenever the right of choice shall have devolved upon them.

Section 5. Sections 1 and 2 shall take effect on the 15th day of October following the ratification of this article.

Section 6. This article shall be inoperative unless it

shall have been ratified as an amendment to the Constitution by the legislatures of three-fourths of the several States within seven years from the date of its submission.

AMENDMENT XXI [1933]

Section 1. The eighteenth article of amendment to the Constitution of the United States is hereby repealed.

Section 2. The transportation or importation into any State, Territory, or possession of the United States for delivery or use therein of intoxicating liquors, in violation of the laws thereof, is hereby prohibited.

Section 3. This article shall be inoperative unless it shall have been ratified as an amendment to the Constitution by conventions in the several States, as provided in the Constitution, within seven years from the date of the submission hereof to the States by the Congress.

AMENDMENT XXII [1951]

No person shall be elected to the office of the President more than twice, and no person who has held the office of President, or acted as President, for more than two years of a term to which some other person was elected President shall be elected to the office of the President more than once.

But this Article shall not apply to any person holding the office of President when this Article was proposed by the Congress, and shall not prevent any person who may be holding the office of President, or acting as President, during the term within which this Article becomes operative from holding the office of President or acting as President during the remainder of such term.

AMENDMENT XXIII [1961]

Section 1. The District constituting the seat of Government of the United States shall appoint in such manner as the Congress may direct:

A number of electors of President and Vice President equal to the whole number of Senators and Representatives in Congress to which the District would be entitled if it were a State, but in no event more than the least populous State; they shall be in addition to those appointed by the States, but they shall be considered, for the purposes of the election of President and Vice President, to be electors appointed by a State; and they shall meet in the District and perform such duties as provided by the twelfth article of amendment.

Section 2. The Congress shall have power to enforce this article by appropriate legislation.

AMENDMENT XXIV [1964]

Section 1. The right of citizens of the United States to vote in any primary or other election for President or Vice President, for electors for President or Vice President, or for Senator or Representative in Congress, shall not be denied or abridged by the United States or any State by reason of failure to pay any poll tax or other tax.

Section 2. The Congress shall have the power to enforce this article by appropriate legislation.

AMENDMENT XXV [1967]

Section 1. In case of the removal of the President from office or his death or resignation, the Vice President shall become President.

Section 2. Whenever there is a vacancy in the office of the Vice President, the President shall nominate a Vice President who shall take the office upon confirmation by a majority vote of both houses of Congress.

Section 3. Whenever the President transmits to the President pro tempore of the Senate and the Speaker of the House of Representatives his written declaration that he is unable to discharge the powers and duties of his office, and until he transmits to them a written declaration to the contrary, such powers and duties shall be discharged by the Vice President as Acting President.

Section 4. Whenever the Vice President and a majority of either the principal officers of the executive departments, or of such other body as Congress may by law provide, transmit to the President pro tempore of the Senate and the Speaker of the House of Representatives their written declaration that the President is unable to discharge the powers and duties of his office, the Vice President shall immediately assume the powers and duties of the office as Acting President.

Thereafter, when the President transmits to the President pro tempore of the Senate and the Speaker of the House of Representatives his written declaration that no inability exists, he shall resume the powers and duties of his office unless the Vice President and a majority of either the principal officers of the executive departments, or of such other body as Congress may by law provide, transmit within four days to the President pro tempore of the Senate and the Speaker of the House of Representatives their written declaration that the President is unable to discharge the powers and duties of his office. Thereupon Congress shall decide the issue, assembling within 48 hours for that purpose if not in session. If the Congress, within 21 days after receipt of the latter written declaration, or, if Congress is not in session, within 21 days after Congress is required to assemble, determines by two-thirds vote of both houses that the President is unable to discharge the powers and duties of his office, the Vice President shall continue to discharge the same as Acting President; otherwise, the President shall resume the powers and duties of his office.

AMENDMENT XXVI [1971]

Section 1. The right of citizens of the United States, who are 18 years of age or older, to vote shall not be denied or abridged by the United States or any state on account of age.

Section 2. The Congress shall have the power to enforce this article by appropriate legislation.

Presidential Elections, 1789–1988

Year	Candidates	Party	Popular Vote*	Electoral Vote**
1789	**George Washington**			69
	John Adams			34
	Others			35
1792	**George Washington**			132
	John Adams			77
	George Clinton			50
	Others			5
1796	**John Adams**	Federalist		71
	Thomas Jefferson	Democratic Republican		68
	Thomas Pinckney	Federalist		59
	Aaron Burr	Democratic Republican		30
	Others			48
1800	**Thomas Jefferson**	Democratic Republican		73
	Aaron Burr	Democratic Republican		73
	John Adams	Federalist		65
	Charles C. Pinckney	Federalist		64
1804	**Thomas Jefferson**	Democratic Republican		162
	Charles C. Pinckney	Federalist		14
1808	**James Madison**	Democratic Republican		122
	Charles C. Pinckney	Federalist		47
	George Clinton	Independent Republican		6
1812	**James Madison**	Democratic Republican		128
	DeWitt Clinton	Federalist		89
1816	**James Monroe**	Democratic Republican		183
	Rufus King	Federalist		34
1820	**James Monroe**	Democratic Republican		231
	John Quincy Adams	Independent Republican		1
1824	**John Quincy Adams**	Democratic Republican	108,704 (30.5%)	84
	Andrew Jackson	Democratic Republican	153,544 (43.1%)	99
	Henry Clay	Democratic Republican	47,136 (13.2%)	37
	William H. Crawford	Democratic Republican	46,618 (13.1%)	41
1828	**Andrew Jackson**	Democratic	647,231 (56.0%)	178
	John Quincy Adams	National Republican	509,097 (44.0%)	83

* Because only the leading candidates are listed, popular vote percentages do not always total 100.
** The elections of 1800 and 1824, in which no candidate received an electoral vote majority, were decided in the House of Representatives.

Year	Candidates	Party	Popular Vote*	Electoral Vote**
1832	**Andrew Jackson**	Democratic	687,502 (55.0%)	219
	Henry Clay	National Republican	530,189 (42.4%)	49
	William Wirt	Anti-Masonic	33,108 (2.6%)	7
	John Floyd	National Republican		11
1836	**Martin Van Buren**	Democratic	761,549 (50.9%)	170
	William H. Harrison	Whig	549,567 (36.7%)	73
	Hugh L. White	Whig	145,396 (9.7%)	26
	Daniel Webster	Whig	41,287 (2.7%)	14
1840	**William H. Harrison** (**John Tyler,** 1841)	Whig	1,275,017 (53.1%)	234
	Martin Van Buren	Democratic	1,128,702 (46.9%)	60
1844	**James K. Polk**	Democratic	1,337,243 (49.6%)	170
	Henry Clay	Whig	1,299,068 (48.1%)	105
	James G. Birney	Liberty	62,300 (2.3%)	
1848	**Zachary Taylor** (**Millard Fillmore,** 1850)	Whig	1,360,101 (47.4%)	163
	Lewis Cass	Democratic	1,220,544 (42.5%)	127
	Martin Van Buren	Free Soil	291,263 (10.1%)	
1852	**Franklin Pierce**	Democratic	1,601,474 (50.9%)	254
	Winfield Scott	Whig	1,386,578 (44.1%)	42
1856	**James Buchanan**	Democratic	1,838,169 (45.4%)	174
	John C. Frémont	Republican	1,335,264 (33.0%)	114
	Millard Fillmore	American	874,534 (21.6%)	8
1860	**Abraham Lincoln**	Republican	1,865,593 (39.8%)	180
	Stephen A. Douglas	Democratic	1,382,713 (29.5%)	12
	John C. Breckinridge	Democratic	848,356 (18.1%)	72
	John Bell	Constitutional Union	592,906 (12.6%)	39
1864	**Abraham Lincoln** (**Andrew Johnson,** 1865)	Republican	2,206,938 (55.0%)	212
	George B. McClellan	Democratic	1,803,787 (45.0%)	21
1868	**Ulysses S. Grant**	Republican	3,013,421 (52.7%)	214
	Horatio Seymour	Democratic	2,706,829 (47.3%)	80
1872	**Ulysses S. Grant**	Republican	3,596,745 (55.6%)	286
	Horace Greeley	Democratic	2,843,446 (43.9%)	66
1876	**Rutherford B. Hayes**	Republican	4,036,572 (48.0%)	185
	Samuel J. Tilden	Democratic	4,284,020 (51.0%)	184
1880	**James A. Garfield** (**Chester A. Arthur,** 1881)	Republican	4,449,053 (48.3%)	214
	Winfield S. Hancock	Democratic	4,442,035 (48.2%)	155
	James B. Weaver	Greenback Labor	308,578 (3.4%)	
1884	**Grover Cleveland**	Democratic	4,874,986 (48.5%)	219
	James G. Blaine	Republican	4,851,981 (48.2%)	182
	Benjamin F. Butler	Greenback Labor	175,370 (1.8%)	

Year	Candidates	Party	Popular Vote*	Electoral Vote**
1888	**Benjamin Harrison**	Republican	5,444,337 (47.8%)	233
	Grover Cleveland	Democratic	5,540,050 (48.6%)	168
1892	**Grover Cleveland**	Democratic	5,554,414 (46.0%)	277
	Benjamin Harrison	Republican	5,190,802 (43.0%)	145
	James B. Weaver	People's	1,027,329 (8.5%)	22
1896	**William McKinley**	Republican	7,035,638 (50.8%)	271
	William Jennings Bryan	Democratic; Populist	6,467,946 (46.7%)	176
1900	**William McKinley** **(Theodore Roosevelt,** 1901)	Republican	7,219,530 (51.7%)	292
	William Jennings Bryan	Democratic; Populist	6,356,734 (45.5%)	155
1904	**Theodore Roosevelt**	Republican	7,628,834 (56.4%)	336
	Alton B. Parker	Democratic	5,084,401 (37.6%)	140
	Eugene V. Debs	Socialist	402,460 (3.0%)	
1908	**William H. Taft**	Republican	7,679,006 (51.6%)	321
	William Jennings Bryan	Democratic	6,409,106 (43.1%)	162
	Eugene V. Debs	Socialist	420,820 (2.8%)	
1912	**Woodrow Wilson**	Democratic	6,286,820 (41.8%)	435
	Theodore Roosevelt	Progressive	4,126,020 (27.4%)	88
	William H. Taft	Republican	3,483,922 (23.2%)	8
	Eugene V. Debs	Socialist	897,011 (6.0%)	
1916	**Woodrow Wilson**	Democratic	9,129,606 (49.3%)	277
	Charles E. Hughes	Republican	8,538,221 (46.1%)	254
1920	**Warren G. Harding** **(Calvin Coolidge,** 1923)	Republican	16,152,200 (61.0%)	404
	James M. Cox	Democratic	9,147,353 (34.6%)	127
	Eugene V. Debs	Socialist	919,799 (3.5%)	
1924	**Calvin Coolidge**	Republican	15,725,016 (54.1%)	382
	John W. Davis	Democratic	8,385,586 (28.8%)	136
	Robert M. La Follette	Progressive	4,822,856 (16.6%)	13
1928	**Herbert C. Hoover**	Republican	21,392,190 (58.2%)	444
	Alfred E. Smith	Democratic	15,016,443 (40.8%)	87
1932	**Franklin D. Roosevelt**	Democratic	22,809,638 (57.3%)	472
	Herbert C. Hoover	Republican	15,758,901 (39.6%)	59
	Norman Thomas	Socialist	881,951 (2.2%)	
1936	**Franklin D. Roosevelt**	Democratic	27,751,612 (60.7%)	523
	Alfred M. Landon	Republican	16,681,913 (36.4%)	8
	William Lemke	Union	891,858 (1.9%)	
1940	**Franklin D. Roosevelt**	Democratic	27,243,466 (54.7%)	449
	Wendell L. Willkie	Republican	22,304,755 (44.8%)	82
1944	**Franklin D. Roosevelt** **(Harry S Truman,** 1945)	Democratic	25,602,505 (52.8%)	432
	Thomas E. Dewey	Republican	22,006,278 (44.5%)	99

Year	Candidates	Party	Popular Vote*	Electoral Vote**
1948	**Harry S Truman**	Democratic	24,105,812 (49.5%)	303
	Thomas E. Dewey	Republican	21,970,065 (45.1%)	189
	J. Strom Thurmond	States' Rights	1,169,063 (2.4%)	39
	Henry A. Wallace	Progressive	1,157,172 (2.4%)	
1952	**Dwight D. Eisenhower**	Republican	33,936,234 (55.2%)	442
	Adlai E. Stevenson	Democratic	27,314,992 (44.5%)	89
1956	**Dwight D. Eisenhower**	Republican	35,590,472 (57.4%)	457
	Adlai E. Stevenson	Democratic	26,022,752 (42.0%)	73
1960	**John F. Kennedy** **(Lyndon B. Johnson,** 1963)	Democratic	34,227,096 (49.9%)	303
	Richard M. Nixon	Republican	34,108,546 (49.6%)	219
1964	**Lyndon B. Johnson**	Democratic	43,126,233 (61.1%)	486
	Barry M. Goldwater	Republican	27,174,989 (38.5%)	52
1968	**Richard M. Nixon**	Republican	31,783,783 (43.4%)	301
	Hubert H. Humphrey	Democratic	31,271,839 (42.7%)	191
	George C. Wallace	Amer. Independent	9,899,557 (13.5%)	46
1972	**Richard M. Nixon** **(Gerald R. Ford,** 1974)	Republican	45,767,218 (60.6%)	520
	George S. McGovern	Democratic	28,357,668 (37.5%)	17
1976	**Jimmy Carter**	Democratic	40,828,657 (50.6%)	297
	Gerald R. Ford	Republican	39,145,520 (48.4%)	240
1980	**Ronald Reagan**	Republican	43,899,248 (51%)	489
	Jimmy Carter	Democratic	36,481,435 (41%)	49
	John B. Anderson	Independent	5,719,437 (6%)	
1984	**Ronald Reagan**	Republican	54,455,075 (59%)	525
	Walter F. Mondale	Democratic	37,577,185 (41%)	13
1988	**George Bush**	Republican	48,881,221 (54%)	426
	Michael Dukakis	Democratic	41,805,422 (46%)	111

Vice-Presidents and Cabinet Members, by Administration

Washington, 1789–1797

Vice-President	John Adams	1789–1797
Secretary of State	Thomas Jefferson	1789–1793
	Edmund Randolph	1794–1795
	Timothy Pickering	1795–1797
Secretary of War	Henry Knox	1789–1794
	Timothy Pickering	1795–1796
	James McHenry	1796–1797
Secretary of Treasury	Alexander Hamilton	1789–1795
	Oliver Wolcott, Jr.	1795–1797
Postmaster General	Samuel Osgood	1789–1791
	Timothy Pickering	1791–1794
	Joseph Habersham	1795–1797
Attorney General	Edmund Randolph	1789–1793
	William Bradford	1794–1795
	Charles Lee	1795–1797

John Adams, 1797–1801

Vice-President	Thomas Jefferson	1797–1801
Secretary of State	Timothy Pickering	1797–1800
	John Marshall	1800–1801
Secretary of War	James McHenry	1797–1800
	Samuel Dexter	1800–1801
Secretary of Treasury	Oliver Wolcott, Jr.	1797–1800
	Samuel Dexter	1800–1801
Postmaster General	Joseph Habersham	1797–1801
Attorney General	Charles Lee	1797–1801
Secretary of Navy	Benjamin Stoddert	1798–1801

Jefferson, 1801–1809

Vice-President	Aaron Burr	1801–1805
	George Clinton	1805–1809
Secretary of State	James Madison	1801–1809
Secretary of War	Henry Dearborn	1801–1809
Secretary of Treasury	Samuel Dexter	1801
	Albert Gallatin	1801–1809
Postmaster General	Joseph Habersham	1801
	Gideon Granger	1801–1809
Attorney General	Levi Lincoln	1801–1805
	Robert Smith	1805
	John C. Breckinridge	1805–1806
	Caesar A. Rodney	1807–1809
Secretary of Navy	Robert Smith	1801–1809

Madison, 1809–1817

Vice-President	George Clinton	1809–1813
	Elbridge Gerry	1813–1817
Secretary of State	Robert Smith	1809–1811
	James Monroe	1811–1817
Secretary of War	William Eustis	1809–1812
	John Armstrong	1813–1814
	James Monroe	1814–1815
	William H. Crawford	1815–1817
Secretary of Treasury	Albert Gallatin	1809–1813
	George W. Campbell	1814
	Alexander J. Dallas	1814–1816
	William H. Crawford	1816–1817
Postmaster General	Gideon Granger	1809–1814
	Return J. Meigs, Jr.	1814–1817
Attorney General	Caesar A. Rodney	1809–1811
	William Pinkney	1811–1814
	Richard Rush	1814–1817
Secretary of Navy	Paul Hamilton	1809–1813
	William Jones	1813–1814
	Benjamin W. Crowninshield	1814–1817

Monroe, 1817–1825

Vice-President	Daniel D. Tompkins	1817–1825
Secretary of State	John Quincy Adams	1817–1825
Secretary of War	George Graham	1817
	John C. Calhoun	1817–1825
Secretary of Treasury	William H. Crawford	1817–1825

Monroe, 1817–1825 (continued)

Postmaster General	Return J. Meigs, Jr.	1817–1823
	John McLean	1823–1825
Attorney General	Richard Rush	1817
	William Wirt	1817–1825
Secretary of Navy	Benjamin W. Crowninshield	1817–1818
	Smith Thompson	1818–1823
	Samuel L. Southard	1823–1825

John Quincy Adams, 1825–1829

Vice-President	John C. Calhoun	1825–1829
Secretary of State	Henry Clay	1825–1829
Secretary of War	James Barbour	1825–1828
	Peter B. Porter	1828–1829
Secretary of Treasury	Richard Rush	1825–1829
Postmaster General	John McLean	1825–1829
Attorney General	William Wirt	1825–1829
Secretary of Navy	Samuel L. Southard	1825–1829

Jackson, 1829–1837

Vice-President	John C. Calhoun	1829–1832
	Martin Van Buren	1833–1837
Secretary of State	Martin Van Buren	1829–1831
	Edward Livingston	1831–1833
	Louis McLane	1833–1834
	John Forsyth	1834–1837
Secretary of War	John H. Eaton	1829–1831
	Lewis Cass	1831–1837
	Benjamin Butler	1837
Secretary of Treasury	Samuel D. Ingham	1829–1831
	Louis McLane	1831–1833
	William J. Duane	1833
	Roger B. Taney	1833–1834
	Levi Woodbury	1834–1837
Postmaster General	William T. Barry	1829–1835
	Amos Kendall	1835–1837
Attorney General	John M. Berrien	1829–1831
	Roger B. Taney	1831–1833
	Benjamin F. Butler	1833–1837
Secretary of Navy	John Branch	1829–1831
	Levi Woodbury	1831–1834
	Mahlon Dickerson	1834–1837

Van Buren, 1837–1841

Vice-President	Richard M. Johnson	1837–1841
Secretary of State	John Forsyth	1837–1841
Secretary of War	Joel R. Poinsett	1837–1841
Secretary of Treasury	Levi Woodbury	1837–1841
Postmaster General	Amos Kendall	1837–1840
	John M. Niles	1840–1841
Attorney General	Benjamin F. Butler	1837–1838
	Felix Grundy	1838–1840
	Henry D. Gilpin	1840–1841
Secretary of Navy	Mahlon Dickerson	1837–1838
	James K. Paulding	1838–1841

William Harrison, 1841

Vice-President	John Tyler	1841
Secretary of State	Daniel Webster	1841
Secretary of War	John Bell	1841
Secretary of Treasury	Thomas Ewing	1841
Postmaster General	Francis Granger	1841
Attorney General	John J. Crittenden	1841
Secretary of Navy	George E. Badger	1841

Tyler, 1841–1845

Vice-President	None	
Secretary of State	Daniel Webster	1841–1843
	Hugh S. Legaré	1843
	Abel P. Upshur	1843–1844
	John C. Calhoun	1844–1845
Secretary of War	John Bell	1841
	John C. Spencer	1841–1843
	John M. Porter	1843–1844
	William Wilkins	1844–1845
Secretary of Treasury	Thomas Ewing	1841
	Walter Forward	1841–1843
	John C. Spencer	1843–1844
	George M. Bibb	1844–1845
Postmaster General	Francis Granger	1841
	Charles A. Wickliffe	1841
Attorney General	John J. Crittenden	1841
	Hugh S. Legaré	1841–1843
	John Nelson	1843–1845

Secretary of Navy	George Badger	1841
	Abel P. Upshur	1841
	David Henshaw	1843–1844
	Thomas W. Gilmer	1844
	John Y. Mason	1844–1845

Polk, 1845–1849

Vice-President	George M. Dallas	1845–1849
Secretary of State	James Buchanan	1845–1849
Secretary of War	William L. Marcy	1845–1849
Secretary of Treasury	Robert J. Walker	1845–1849
Postmaster General	Cave Johnson	1845–1849
Attorney General	John Y. Mason	1845–1846
	Nathan Clifford	1846–1848
	Isaac Toucey	1848–1849
Secretary of Navy	George Bancroft	1845–1846
	John Y. Mason	1846–1849

Taylor, 1849–1850

Vice-President	Millard Fillmore	1849–1850
Secretary of State	John M. Clayton	1849–1850
Secretary of War	George W. Crawford	1849–1850
Secretary of Treasury	William M. Meredith	1849–1850
Postmaster General	Jacob Collamer	1849–1850
Attorney General	Reverdy Johnson	1849–1850
Secretary of Navy	William Preston	1849–1850
Secretary of Interior	Thomas Ewing	1849–1850

Fillmore, 1850–1853

Vice-President	None	
Secretary of State	Daniel Webster	1850–1852
	Edward Everett	1852–1853
Secretary of War	Charles M. Conrad	1850–1853
Secretary of Treasury	Thomas Corwin	1850–1853
Postmaster General	Nathan K. Hall	1850–1852
	Sam D. Hubbard	1852–1853

Attorney General	John J. Crittenden	1850–1853
Secretary of Navy	William A. Graham	1850–1852
	John P. Kennedy	1852–1853
Secretary of Interior	Thomas M. T. McKennan	1850
	Alexander H. H. Stuart	1850–1853

Pierce, 1853–1857

Vice-President	William R. King	1853
Secretary of State	William L. Marcy	1853–1857
Secretary of War	Jefferson Davis	1853–1857
Secretary of Treasury	James Guthrie	1853–1857
Postmaster General	James Campbell	1853–1857
Attorney General	Caleb Cushing	1853–1857
Secretary of Navy	James C. Dobbins	1853–1857
Secretary of Interior	Robert McClelland	1853–1857

Buchanan, 1857–1861

Vice-President	John C. Breckinridge	1857–1861
Secretary of State	Lewis Cass	1857–1860
	Jeremiah S. Black	1860–1861
Secretary of War	John B. Floyd	1857–1861
	Joseph Holt	1861
Secretary of Treasury	Howell Cobb	1857–1860
	Philip F. Thomas	1860–1861
	John A. Dix	1861
Postmaster General	Aaron V. Brown	1857–1859
	Joseph Holt	1859–1861
	Horatio King	1861
Attorney General	Jeremiah S. Black	1857–1860
	Edwin M. Stanton	1860–1861
Secretary of Navy	Isaac Toucey	1857–1861
Secretary of Interior	Jacob Thompson	1857–1861

Lincoln, 1861–1865

Vice-President	Hannibal Hamlin	1861–1865
	Andrew Johnson	1865
Secretary of State	William H. Seward	1861–1865

Lincoln, 1861–1865 (continued)

Secretary of War	Simon Cameron	1861–1862
	Edwin M. Stanton	1862–1865
Secretary of Treasury	Samuel P. Chase	1861–1864
	William P. Fessenden	1864–1865
	Hugh McCulloch	1865
Postmaster General	Horatio King	1861
	Montgomery Blair	1861–1864
	William Dennison	1864–1865
Attorney General	Edward Bates	1861–1864
	James Speed	1864–1865
Secretary of Navy	Gideon Welles	1861–1865
Secretary of Interior	Caleb B. Smith	1861–1863
	John P. Usher	1863–1865

Andrew Johnson, 1865–1869

Vice-President	None	
Secretary of State	William H. Seward	1865–1869
Secretary of War	Edwin M. Stanton	1865–1867
	Ulysses S. Grant	1867–1868
	John M. Schofield	1868–1869
Secretary of Treasury	Hugh McCulloch	1865–1869
Postmaster General	William Dennison	1865–1866
	Alexander W. Randall	1866–1869
Attorney General	James Speed	1865–1866
	Henry Stanbery	1866–1868
	William M. Evarts	1868–1869
Secretary of Navy	Gideon Welles	1865–1869
Secretary of Interior	John P. Usher	1865
	James Harlan	1865–1866
	Orville H. Browning	1866–1869

Grant, 1869–1877

Vice-President	Schuyler Colfax	1869–1873
	Henry Wilson	1873–1875
Secretary of State	Elihu B. Washburne	1869
	Hamilton Fish	1869–1877
Secretary of War	John A. Rawlins	1869
	William T. Sherman	1869
	William W. Belknap	1869–1876
	Alphonso Taft	1876
	James D. Cameron	1876–1877
Secretary of Treasury	George S. Boutwell	1869–1873
	William A. Richardson	1873–1874
	Benjamin H. Bristow	1874–1876
	Lot M. Morrill	1876–1877

Postmaster General	John A. J. Creswell	1869–1874
	James W. Marshall	1874
	Marshall Jewell	1874–1876
	James N. Tyner	1876–1877
Attorney General	Ebenezer R. Hoar	1869–1870
	Amos T. Ackerman	1870–1871
	G. H. Williams	1871–1875
	Edwards Pierrepont	1875–1876
	Alphonso Taft	1876–1877
Secretary of Navy	Adolph E. Borie	1869
	George Robeson	1869–1877
Secretary of Interior	Jacob D. Cox	1869–1870
	Columbus Delano	1870–1875
	Zachariah Chandler	1875–1877

Hayes, 1877–1881

Vice-President	William A. Wheeler	1877–1881
Secretary of State	William B. Evarts	1877–1881
Secretary of War	George W. McCrary	1877–1879
	Alexander Ramsey	1879–1881
Secretary of Treasury	John Sherman	1877–1881
Postmaster General	David M. Key	1877–1880
	Horace Maynard	1880–1881
Attorney General	Charles Devens	1877–1881
Secretary of Navy	Richard W. Thompson	1877–1880
	Nathan Goff, Jr.	1881
Secretary of Interior	Carl Schurz	1877–1881

Garfield, 1881

Vice-President	Chester A. Arthur	1881
Secretary of State	James G. Blaine	1881
Secretary of War	Robert T. Lincoln	1881
Secretary of Treasury	William Windom	1881
Postmaster General	Thomas L. James	1881
Attorney General	Wayne MacVeagh	1881
Secretary of Navy	William H. Hunt	1881
Secretary of Interior	Samuel J. Kirkwood	1881

Arthur, 1881–1885

Vice-President	None	
Secretary of State	Frederick T. Frelinghuysen	1881–1885
Secretary of War	Robert T. Lincoln	1881–1885
Secretary of Treasury	Charles J. Folger Walter Q. Gresham Hugh McCulloch	1881–1884 1884 1884–1885
Postmaster General	Timothy O. Howe Walter Q. Gresham Frank Hatton	1881–1883 1883–1884 1884–1885
Attorney General	Benjamin H. Brewster	1881–1885
Secretary of Navy	William H. Hunt William E. Chandler	1881–1882 1882–1885
Secretary of Interior	Samuel J. Kirkwood Henry M. Teller	1881–1882 1882–1885

Cleveland, 1885–1889

Vice-President	Thomas A. Hendricks	1885
Secretary of State	Thomas F. Bayard	1885–1889
Secretary of War	William C. Endicott	1885–1889
Secretary of Treasury	Daniel Manning Charles S. Fairchild	1885–1887 1887–1889
Postmaster General	William F. Vilas Don M. Dickinson	1885–1888 1888–1889
Attorney General	Augustus H. Garland	1885–1889
Secretary of Navy	William C. Whitney	1885–1889
Secretary of Interior	Lucius Q. C. Lamar William F. Vilas	1885–1888 1888–1889
Secretary of Agriculture	Norman J. Colman	1889

Benjamin Harrison, 1889–1893

Vice-President	Levi P. Morton	1889–1893
Secretary of State	James G. Blaine John W. Foster	1889–1892 1892–1893
Secretary of War	Redfield Proctor Stephen B. Elkins	1889–1891 1891–1893
Secretary of Treasury	William Windom Charles Foster	1889–1891 1891–1893
Postmaster General	John Wanamaker	1889–1893
Attorney General	William H. H. Miller	1889–1891
Secretary of Navy	Benjamin F. Tracy	1889–1893
Secretary of Interior	John W. Noble	1889–1893
Secretary of Agriculture	Jeremiah M. Rusk	1889–1893

Cleveland, 1893–1897

Vice-President	Adlai E. Stevenson	1893–1897
Secretary of State	Walter Q. Gresham Richard Olney	1893–1895 1895–1897
Secretary of War	Daniel S. Lamont	1893–1897
Secretary of Treasury	John G. Carlisle	1893–1897
Postmaster General	Wilson S. Bissell William L. Wilson	1893–1895 1895–1897
Attorney General	Richard Olney Judson Harmon	1893–1895 1895–1897
Secretary of Navy	Hilary A. Herbert	1893–1897
Secretary of Interior	Hoke Smith David R. Francis	1893–1896 1896–1897
Secretary of Agriculture	Julius Sterling Morton	1893–1897

McKinley, 1897–1901

Vice-President	Garret Hobart Theodore Roosevelt	1897–1899 1901
Secretary of State	John Sherman William R. Day John M. Hay	1897–1898 1898 1898–1901
Secretary of War	Russell A. Alger Elihu Root	1897–1899 1899–1901
Secretary of Treasury	Lyman J. Gage	1897–1901
Postmaster General	James A. Gary Charles E. Smith	1897–1898 1898–1901
Attorney General	Joseph McKenna John W. Griggs Philander C. Knox	1897–1898 1898–1901 1901
Secretary of Navy	John D. Long	1897–1901
Secretary of Interior	Cornelius N. Bliss Ethan A. Hitchcock	1897–1899 1899–1901
Secretary of Agriculture	James Wilson	1897–1901

Theodore Roosevelt, 1901–1909

Vice-President	Charles Warren Fairbanks	1905–1909
Secretary of State	John M. Hay	1901–1905
	Elihu Root	1905–1909
	Robert Bacon	1909
Secretary of War	Elihu Root	1901–1904
	William Howard Taft	1904–1908
	Luke E. Wright	1908–1909
Secretary of Treasury	Lyman J. Gage	1901–1902
	Leslie M. Shaw	1902–1907
	George B. Cortelyou	1907–1909
Postmaster General	Charles Emory Smith	1901–1902
	Henry C. Payne	1902–1904
	Robert J. Wynne	1904–1905
	George B. Cortelyou	1905–1907
	George von L. Meyer	1907–1909
Attorney General	Philander C. Knox	1901–1904
	William H. Moody	1904–1906
	Charles J. Bonaparte	1906–1909
Secretary of Navy	John D. Long	1901–1902
	William H. Moody	1902–1904
	Paul Morton	1904–1905
	Charles J. Bonaparte	1905–1906
	Victor H. Metcalf	1906–1908
	Truman H. Newberry	1908–1909
Secretary of Interior	Ethan A. Hitchcock	1901–1907
	James R. Garfield	1907–1909
Secretary of Agriculture	James Wilson	1901–1909
Secretary of Labor and Commerce	George B. Cortelyou	1903–1904
	Victor H. Metcalf	1904–1906
	Oscar S. Straus	1906–1909

Taft, 1909–1913

Vice-President	James S. Sherman	1909–1912
Secretary of State	Philander C. Knox	1909–1913
Secretary of War	Jacob M. Dickinson	1909–1911
	Henry L. Stimson	1911–1913
Secretary of Treasury	Franklin MacVeagh	1909–1913
Postmaster General	Frank H. Hitchcock	1909–1913
Attorney General	George W. Wickersham	1909–1913
Secretary of Navy	George von L. Meyer	1909–1913
Secretary of Interior	Richard A. Ballinger	1909–1911
	Walter Lowrie Fisher	1911–1913
Secretary of Agriculture	James Wilson	1909–1913
Secretary of Labor and Commerce	Oscar S. Straus	1909
	Charles Nagel	1909–1913

Wilson, 1913–1921

Vice-President	Thomas R. Marshall	1913–1921
Secretary of State	William Jennings Bryan	1913–1915
	Robert Lansing	1915–1920
	Bainbridge Colby	1920–1921
Secretary of War	Lindley M. Garrison	1913–1916
	Newton D. Baker	1916–1921
Secretary of Treasury	William Gilbert McAdoo	1913–1918
	Carter Glass	1918–1920
	David F. Houston	1920–1921
Postmaster General	Albert Sidney Burleson	1913–1921
Attorney General	James Clark McReynolds	1913–1914
	Thomas Watt Gregory	1914–1919
	A. Mitchell Palmer	1919–1921
Secretary of Navy	Josephus Daniels	1913–1921
Secretary of Interior	Franklin Knight Lane	1913–1920
	John Barton Payne	1920–1921
Secretary of Agriculture	David F. Houston	1913–1920
	Edwin T. Meredith	1920–1921
Secretary of Commerce	William C. Redfield	1913–1919
Secretary of Labor	William Bauchop Wilson	1913–1921

Harding, 1921–1923

Vice-President	Calvin Coolidge	1921–1923
Secretary of State	Charles Evans Hughes	1921–1923
Secretary of War	John W. Weeks	1921–1923
Secretary of Treasury	Andrew W. Mellon	1921–1923
Postmaster General	Will H. Hays	1921–1922
	Hubert Work	1922–1923
	Harry S. New	1923
Attorney General	Harry M. Daugherty	1921–1923
Secretary of Navy	Edwin Denby	1921–1923
Secretary of Interior	Albert B. Fall	1921–1923
	Hubert Work	1923
Secretary of Agriculture	Henry C. Wallace	1921–1923
Secretary of Commerce	Herbert C. Hoover	1921–1923
Secretary of Labor	James J. Davis	1921–1923

Coolidge, 1923–1929

Vice-President	Charles G. Dawes	1925–1929
Secretary of State	Charles Evans Hughes	1923–1925
	Frank B. Kellogg	1925–1929
Secretary of War	John W. Weeks	1923–1925
	Dwight F. Davis	1925–1929
Secretary of Treasury	Andrew W. Mellon	1923–1929
Postmaster General	Harry S. New	1923–1929
Attorney General	Harry M. Daugherty	1923–1924
	Harlan Fiske Stone	1924–1925
	John G. Sargent	1925–1929
Secretary of Navy	Edwin Derby	1923–1924
	Curtis D. Wilbur	1924–1929
Secretary of Interior	Hubert Work	1923–1928
	Roy O. West	1928–1929
Secretary of Agriculture	Henry C. Wallace	1923–1924
	Howard M. Gore	1924–1925
	William M. Jardine	1925–1929
Secretary of Commerce	Herbert C. Hoover	1923–1928
	William F. Whiting	1928–1929
Secretary of Labor	James J. Davis	1923–1929

Hoover, 1929–1933

Vice-President	Charles Curtis	1929–1933
Secretary of State	Henry L. Stimson	1929–1933
Secretary of War	James W. Good	1929
	Patrick J. Hurley	1929–1933
Secretary of Treasury	Andrew W. Mellon	1929–1932
	Ogden L. Mills	1932–1933
Postmaster General	Walter F. Brown	1929–1933
Attorney General	William D. Mitchell	1929–1933
Secretary of Navy	Charles F. Adams	1929–1933
Secretary of Interior	Ray L. Wilbur	1929–1933
Secretary of Agriculture	Arthur M. Hyde	1929–1933
Secretary of Commerce	Robert P. Lamont	1929–1932
	Roy D. Chapin	1932–1933
Secretary of Labor	James J. Davis	1929–1930
	William N. Doak	1930–1933

Franklin D. Roosevelt, 1933–1945

Vice-President	John Nance Garner	1933–1941
	Henry A. Wallace	1941–1945
	Harry S Truman	1945
Secretary of State	Cordell Hull	1933–1944
	Edward R. Stettinius, Jr.	1944–1945
Secretary of War	George H. Dern	1933–1936
	Henry A. Woodring	1936–1940
	Henry L. Stimson	1940–1945
Secretary of Treasury	William H. Woodin	1933–1934
	Henry Morgenthau, Jr.	1934–1945
Postmaster General	James A. Farley	1933–1940
	Frank C. Walker	1940–1945
Attorney General	Homer S. Cummings	1933–1939
	Frank Murphy	1939–1940
	Robert H. Jackson	1940–1941
	Francis Biddle	1941–1945
Secretary of Navy	Claude A. Swanson	1933–1940
	Charles Edison	1940
	Frank Knox	1940–1944
	James V. Forrestal	1944–1945
Secretary of Interior	Harold L. Ickes	1933–1945
Secretary of Agriculture	Henry A. Wallace	1933–1940
	Claude R. Wickard	1940–1945
Secretary of Commerce	Daniel C. Roper	1933–1939
	Harry L. Hopkins	1939–1940
	Jesse H. Jones	1940–1945
	Henry A. Wallace	1945
Secretary of Labor	Frances Perkins	1933–1945

Truman, 1945–1953

Vice-President	Alben W. Barkley	1949–1953
Secretary of State	Edward R. Stettinius, Jr.	1945
	James F. Byrnes	1945–1947
	George C. Marshall	1947–1949
	Dean G. Acheson	1949–1953
Secretary of War	Robert P. Patterson	1945–1947
	Kenneth C. Royall	1947
Secretary of Treasury	Fred M. Vinson	1945–1946
	John W. Snyder	1946–1953
Postmaster General	Frank C. Walker	1945
	Robert E. Hannegan	1945–1947
	Jesse M. Donaldson	1947–1953
Attorney General	Tom C. Clark	1945–1949
	J. Howard McGrath	1949–1952
	James P. McGranery	1952–1953
Secretary of Navy	James V. Forrestal	1945–1947
Secretary of Interior	Harold L. Ickes	1945–1946
	Julius A. Krug	1946–1949
	Oscar L. Chapman	1949–1953

Truman, 1945–1953 (continued)

Secretary of Agriculture	Clinton P. Anderson	1945–1948
	Charles F. Brannan	1948–1953
Secretary of Commerce	Henry A. Wallace	1945–1946
	W. Averell Harriman	1946–1948
	Charles W. Sawyer	1948–1953
Secretary of Labor	Lewis B. Schwellenbach	1945–1948
	Maurice J. Tobin	1948–1953
Secretary of Defense	James V. Forrestal	1947–1949
	Louis A. Johnson	1949–1950
	George C. Marshall	1950–1951
	Robert A. Lovett	1951–1953

Eisenhower, 1953–1961

Vice-President	Richard M. Nixon	1953–1961
Secretary of State	John Foster Dulles	1953–1959
	Christian A. Herter	1959–1961
Secretary of Treasury	George M. Humphrey	1953–1957
	Robert B. Anderson	1957–1961
Postmaster General	Arthur E. Summerfield	1953–1961
Attorney General	Herbert Brownell, Jr.	1953–1958
	William P. Rogers	1958–1961
Secretary of Interior	Douglas McKay	1953–1956
	Fred A. Seaton	1956–1961
Secretary of Agriculture	Ezra Taft Benson	1953–1961
Secretary of Commerce	Sinclair Weeks	1953–1958
	Lewis L. Strauss	1958–1959
	Frederick H. Mueller	1959–1961
Secretary of Labor	Martin P. Durkin	1953
	James P. Mitchell	1953–1961
Secretary of Defense	Charles E. Wilson	1953–1957
	Neil H. McElroy	1957–1959
	Thomas S. Gates, Jr.	1959–1961
Secretary of Health, Education, and Welfare	Oveta Culp Hobby	1953–1955
	Marion B. Folsom	1955–1958
	Arthur S. Flemming	1958–1961

Kennedy, 1961–1963

Vice-President	Lyndon B. Johnson	1961–1963
Secretary of State	Dean Rusk	1961–1963
Secretary of Treasury	C. Douglas Dillon	1961–1963
Postmaster General	J. Edward Day	1961–1963
	John A. Gronouski	1963
Attorney General	Robert F. Kennedy	1961–1963
Secretary of Interior	Stewart L. Udall	1961–1963
Secretary of Agriculture	Orville L. Freeman	1961–1963
Secretary of Commerce	Luther H. Hodges	1961–1963
Secretary of Labor	Arthur J. Goldberg	1961–1962
	W. Willard Wirtz	1962–1963
Secretary of Defense	Robert S. McNamara	1961–1963
Secretary of Health, Education, and Welfare	Abraham A. Ribicoff	1961–1962
	Anthony J. Celebrezze	1962–1963

Lyndon Johnson, 1963–1969

Vice-President	Hubert H. Humphrey	1965–1969
Secretary of State	Dean Rusk	1963–1969
Secretary of Treasury	C. Douglas Dillon	1963–1965
	Henry H. Fowler	1965–1969
Postmaster General	John A. Gronouski	1963–1965
	Lawrence F. O'Brien	1965–1968
	Marvin Watson	1968–1969
Attorney General	Robert F. Kennedy	1963–1964
	Nicholas Katzenbach	1965–1966
	Ramsey Clark	1967–1969
Secretary of Interior	Stewart L. Udall	1963–1969
Secretary of Agriculture	Orville L. Freeman	1963–1969
Secretary of Commerce	Luther H. Hodges	1963–1964
	John T. Connor	1964–1967
	Alexander B. Trowbridge	1967–1968
	Cyrus R. Smith	1968–1969
Secretary of Labor	W. Willard Wirtz	1963–1969
Secretary of Defense	Robert F. McNamara	1963–1968
	Clark Clifford	1968–1969
Secretary of Health, Education, and Welfare	Anthony J. Celebrezze	1963–1965
	John W. Gardner	1965–1968
	Wilbur J. Cohen	1968–1969
Secretary of Housing and Urban Development	Robert C. Weaver	1966–1969
	Robert C. Wood	1969
Secretary of Transportation	Alan S. Boyd	1967–1969

Nixon, 1969–1974

Vice-President	Spiro T. Agnew	1969–1973
	Gerald R. Ford	1973–1974
Secretary of State	William P. Rogers	1969–1973
	Henry A. Kissinger	1973–1974
Secretary of Treasury	David M. Kennedy	1969–1970
	John B. Connally	1971–1972
	George P. Shultz	1972–1974
	William E. Simon	1974
Postmaster General	Winton M. Blount	1969–1971
Attorney General	John N. Mitchell	1969–1972
	Richard G. Kleindienst	1972–1973
	Elliot L. Richardson	1973
	William B. Saxbe	1973–1974
Secretary of Interior	Walter J. Hickel	1969–1970
	Rogers Morton	1971–1974
Secretary of Agriculture	Clifford M. Hardin	1969–1971
	Earl L. Butz	1971–1974
Secretary of Commerce	Maurice H. Stans	1969–1972
	Peter G. Peterson	1972–1973
	Frederick B. Dent	1973–1974
Secretary of Labor	George P. Shultz	1969–1970
	James D. Hodgson	1970–1973
	Peter J. Brennan	1973–1974
Secretary of Defense	Melvin R. Laird	1969–1973
	Elliot L. Richardson	1973
	James R. Schlesinger	1973–1974
Secretary of Health, Education, and Welfare	Robert H. Finch	1969–1970
	Elliot L. Richardson	1970–1973
	Caspar W. Weinberger	1973–1974
Secretary of Housing and Urban Development	George W. Romney	1969–1973
	James T. Lynn	1973–1974
Secretary of Transportation	John A. Volpe	1969–1973
	Claude S. Brinegar	1973–1974

Ford, 1974–1977

Vice-President	Nelson A. Rockefeller	1974–1977
Secretary of State	Henry A. Kissinger	1974–1977
Secretary of Treasury	William E. Simon	1974–1977
Attorney General	William B. Saxbe	1974–1975
	Edward H. Levi	1975–1977
Secretary of Interior	Rogers C. B. Morton	1974–1975
	Stanley K. Hathaway	1975
	Thomas S. Kleppe	1975–1977
Secretary of Agriculture	Earl L. Butz	1974–1976
	John A. Knebel	1976–1977

Secretary of Commerce	Frederick B. Dent	1974–1975
	Rogers C. B. Morton	1975–1976
	Elliot L. Richardson	1976–1977
Secretary of Labor	Peter J. Brennan	1974–1975
	John T. Dunlop	1975–1976
	W. J. Usery, Jr.	1976–1977
Secretary of Defense	James R. Schlesinger	1974–1975
	Donald H. Rumsfeld	1975–1977
Secretary of Health, Education, and Welfare	Caspar W. Weinberger	1974–1975
	F. David Mathews	1975–1977
Secretary of Housing and Urban Development	James T. Lynn	1974–1975
	Carla Anderson Hills	1975–1977
Secretary of Transportation	Claude S. Brinegar	1974–1975
	William T. Coleman, Jr.	1974–1977

Carter, 1977–1981

Vice-President	Walter F. Mondale	1977–1981
Secretary of State	Cyrus R. Vance	1977–1980
	Edmund S. Muskie	1980–1981
Secretary of Treasury	W. Michael Blumenthal	1977–1979
	G. William Miller	1979–1981
Attorney General	Griffin B. Bell	1977–1979
	Benjamin R. Civiletti	1979–1981
Secretary of Interior	Cecil D. Andrus	1977–1981
Secretary of Agriculture	Robert Bergland	1977–1981
Secretary of Commerce	Juanita M. Kreps	1977–1979
	Philip M. Klutznick	1979–1981
Secretary of Labor	F. Ray Marshall	1977–1981
Secretary of Defense	Harold Brown	1977–1981
Secretary of Health, Education, and Welfare	Joseph A. Califano, Jr.	1977–1979
	Patricia Roberts Harris	1979
Secretary of Health and Human Services	Patricia Roberts Harris	1979–1981
Secretary of Housing and Urban Development	Patricia Roberts Harris	1977–1979
	Moon Landrieu	1979–1981
Secretary of Transportation	Brock Adams	1977–1979
	Neil E. Goldschmidt	1979–1981
Secretary of Energy	James R. Schlesinger, Jr.	1977–1979
	Charles W. Duncan, Jr.	1979–1981
Secretary of Education	Shirley M. Hufstedler	1979–1981

Reagan, 1981–1989

Vice-President	George Bush	1981–1989
Secretary of State	Alexander M. Haig, Jr.	1981–1982
	George P. Shultz	1982–1989
Secretary of Treasury	Donald T. Regan	1981–1985
	James A. Baker, III	1985–1988
	Nicholas F. Brady	1988–1989
Attorney General	William French Smith	1981–1985
	Edwin A. Meese, III	1985–1988
	Richard Thornburgh	1988–1989
Secretary of Interior	James C. Watt	1981–1983
	William P. Clarke, Jr.	1983–1985
	Donald P. Hodel	1985–1989
Secretary of Agriculture	John R. Block	1981–1986
	Richard Lyng	1986–1989
Secretary of Commerce	Malcolm Baldrige	1981–1987
	C. William Verity, Jr.	1987–1989
Secretary of Labor	Raymond J. Donovan	1981–1985
	William E. Brock	1985–1987
	Ann D. McLaughlin	1987–1989
Secretary of Defense	Caspar W. Weinberger	1981–1987
	Frank C. Carlucci	1987–1989
Secretary of Health and Human Services	Richard S. Schweiker	1981–1983
	Margaret M. Heckler	1983–1985
	Otis R. Bowen	1985–1989
Secretary of Housing and Urban Development	Samuel R. Pierce, Jr.	1981–1989
Secretary of Transportation	Andrew L. Lewis, Jr.	1981–1983
	Elizabeth Hanford Dole	1983–1987
	James H. Burnley	1987–1989
Secretary of Energy	James B. Edwards	1981–1982
	Donald P. Hodel	1982–1985
	John S. Herrington	1985–1989
Secretary of Education	Terrel H. Bell	1981–1985
	William J. Bennett	1985–1988
	Lauro F. Cavazos	1988–1989

Bush, 1989–

Vice-President	Dan Quayle	1989–
Secretary of State	James A. Baker	1989–
Secretary of Treasury	Nicholas F. Brady	1989–
Attorney General	Richard Thornburgh	1989–
Secretary of Interior	Manuel Lujan, Jr.	1989–
Secretary of Agriculture	Clayton K. Yeutter	1989–
Secretary of Commerce	Robert A. Mosbacher	1989–
Secretary of Labor	Elizabeth Hanford Dole	1989–
Secretary of Defense	Richard Cheney	1989–
Secretary of Health and Human Services	Louis Sullivan	1989–
Secretary of Housing and Urban Development	Jack Kemp	1989–
Secretary of Transportation	Samuel K. Skinner	1989–
Secretary of Energy	James D. Watkins	1989
Secretary of Education	Lauro F. Cavazos	1989–
Secretary of Veterans Affairs	Edward J. Derwinski	1989–

Justices of the Supreme Court

Chief Justices in italics.

	Term of Service	Years of Service		Term of Service	Years of Service
John Jay	1789–1795	5	Ward Hunt	1873–1882	9
John Rutledge	1789–1791	1	*Morrison R. Waite*	1874–1888	14
William Cushing	1789–1810	20	John M. Harlan	1877–1911	34
James Wilson	1789–1798	8	William B. Woods	1880–1887	7
John Blair	1789–1796	6	Stanley Matthews	1881–1889	7
Robert H. Harrison	1789–1790	—	Horace Gray	1882–1902	20
James Iredell	1790–1799	9	Samuel Blatchford	1882–1893	11
Thomas Johnson	1791–1793	1	Lucius Q. C. Lamar	1888–1893	5
William Paterson	1793–1806	13	*Melville W. Fuller*	1888–1910	21
*John Rutledge**	1795	—	David J. Brewer	1890–1910	20
Samuel Chase	1796–1811	15	Henry B. Brown	1890–1906	16
Oliver Ellsworth	1796–1800	4	George Shiras, Jr.	1892–1903	10
Bushrod Washington	1798–1829	31	Howell E. Jackson	1893–1895	2
Alfred Moore	1799–1804	4	Edward D. White	1894–1910	16
John Marshall	1801–1835	34	Rufus W. Peckham	1895–1909	14
William Johnson	1804–1834	30	Joseph McKenna	1898–1925	26
H. Brockholst Livingston	1806–1823	16	Oliver W. Holmes, Jr.	1902–1932	30
Thomas Todd	1807–1826	18	William R. Day	1903–1922	19
Joseph Story	1811–1845	33	William H. Moody	1906–1910	3
Gabriel Duval	1811–1835	24	Horace H. Lurton	1910–1914	4
Smith Thompson	1823–1843	20	Charles E. Hughes	1910–1916	5
Robert Trimble	1826–1828	2	Willis Van Devanter	1911–1937	26
John McLean	1829–1861	32	Joseph R. Lamar	1911–1916	5
Henry Baldwin	1830–1844	14	*Edward D. White*	1910–1921	11
James M. Wayne	1835–1867	32	Mahlon Pitney	1912–1922	10
Roger B. Taney	1836–1864	28	James C. McReynolds	1914–1941	26
Philip P. Barbour	1836–1841	4	Louis D. Brandeis	1916–1939	22
John Catron	1837–1865	28	John H. Clarke	1916–1922	6
John McKinley	1837–1852	15	*William H. Taft*	1921–1930	8
Peter V. Daniel	1841–1860	19	George Sutherland	1922–1938	15
Samuel Nelson	1845–1872	27	Pierce Butler	1922–1939	16
Levi Woodbury	1845–1851	5	Edward T. Sanford	1923–1930	7
Robert C. Grier	1846–1870	23	Harlan F. Stone	1925–1941	16
Benjamin R. Curtis	1851–1857	6	*Charles E. Hughes*	1930–1941	11
John A. Campbell	1853–1861	8	Owen J. Roberts	1930–1945	15
Nathan Clifford	1858–1881	23	Benjamin N. Cardozo	1932–1938	6
Noah H. Swayne	1862–1881	18	Hugo L. Black	1937–1971	34
Samuel F. Miller	1862–1890	28	Stanley F. Reed	1938–1957	19
David Davis	1862–1877	14	Felix Frankfurter	1939–1962	23
Stephen J. Field	1863–1897	34	William O. Douglas	1939–1975	36
Salmon P. Chase	1864–1873	8	Frank Murphy	1940–1949	9
William Strong	1870–1880	10	*Harlan F. Stone*	1941–1946	5
Joseph P. Bradley	1870–1892	22	James F. Byrnes	1941–1942	1
			Robert H. Jackson	1941–1954	13
			Wiley B. Rutledge	1943–1949	6

* Never confirmed as Chief Justice.

	Term of Service	Years of Service
Harold H. Burton	1945–1958	13
Fred M. Vinson	1946–1953	7
Tom C. Clark	1949–1967	18
Sherman Minton	1949–1956	7
Earl Warren	1953–1969	16
John Marshall Harlan	1955–1971	16
William J. Brennan, Jr.	1956–	—
Charles E. Whittaker	1957–1962	5
Potter Stewart	1958–1981	23
Byron R. White	1962–	—
Arthur J. Goldberg	1962–1965	3
Abe Fortas	1965–1969	4
Thurgood Marshall	1967–	—
Warren E. Burger	1969–1986	18
Harry A. Blackmun	1970–	—
Lewis F. Powell, Jr.	1971–1987	15
*William H. Rehnquist***	1971–	—
John P. Stevens III	1975–	—
Sandra Day O'Connor	1981–	—
Antonin Scalia	1986–	—
Anthony M. Kennedy	1988–	—

** Chief Justice from 1986 on.

Territorial Expansion

Louisiana Purchase	1803
Florida	1819
Texas	1845
Oregon	1846
Mexican Cession	1848
Gadsden Purchase	1853
Alaska	1867
Hawaii	1898
Philippines	1898–1946
Puerto Rico	1899
Guam	1899
American Samoa	1900
Canal Zone	1904
U.S. Virgin Islands	1917
Pacific Islands Trust Territory	1947

Population, 1790–1980

1790	3,929,214
1800	5,308,483
1810	7,239,881
1820	9,638,453
1830	12,866,020
1840	17,069,453
1850	23,191,876
1860	31,443,321
1870	39,818,449
1880	50,155,783
1890	62,947,714
1900	75,994,575
1910	91,972,266
1920	105,710,620
1930	122,775,046
1940	131,669,275
1950	151,325,798
1960	179,323,175
1970	204,765,770
1980	226,504,825

Picture Credits

Artist unknown, *Telegraph Hill, San Francisco,* late 1840s: Wells Fargo Bank, San Francisco.

Portfolio Four: **472** "Freedom to Slaves," 1863: Library Company of Philadelphia. **473** Edwin White, *Thoughts of Liberia,* ca. 1830–1840: New-York Historical Society. George Fuller, "Cotton Press and Gin, Feb. 2, 1858": Private Collection. Five generations of a South Carolina slave family, photo by T. H. O'Sullivan, 1862: Library of Congress. **474** "Meeting in the African Church, Cincinnatti, Ohio," *Frank Leslie's Illustrated Newspaper,* April 30, 1853: Library of Congress. Thomas Rice playing "Jump Jim Crow" on the Bowery, 1833: Museum of the City of New York. **475** Edwin Taylor, *American Slave Market,* 1852: Chicago Historical Society. Bill of sale for Ned: The Old Slave Mart Museum, Charleston, S.C. **476** Winslow Homer, *A View from the Old Mistress,* 1876: National Museum of American Art, Smithsonian Institution. **477** Sharecropper cabin with slaughtered hogs: Library of Congress. W. L. Sheppard, "Workers Stripping Tobacco in Danville, Va.," *Harper's Weekly,* Jan. 29, 1887: Virginia State Library.

American Lives *(listed by page number)*

Benjamin Franklin and John Adams: **69** Detail from *A Westerly View of the Colledges in Cambridge, New England.* Engraving by Paul Revere, 1767: Courtesy American Antiquarian Society.

George Washington: **105** Detail from *A View of Mount Vernon,* c. 1790 or later: American National Gallery of Art, Washington; Gift of Edgar William and Bernice Chrysler Garbisch.

Three Families in the Post–Civil War South: **446** Detail from *Village Post Office,* Thomas Waterman Wood, 1873, Oil on Canvas: New York State Historical Association, Cooperstown. **447** *The Homestead:* Courtesy Bethune Cookman College, Daytona Beach, Florida.

Text *(listed by page number)*

Chapter 1: **2** Theodor de Bry, engraving of Columbus departing from Palos, 1590: New York Public Library, Rare Book Collection. **4** Bettmann Archive. **9** Aztec picture writing, in *Codex Porfirio Diaz:* Tozzer Library, Harvard University. **10** John White, Indians "sitting at meat": Courtesy of the Trustees of the British Museum. **13** Sir Francis Drake: Virginia Historical Society. **15** Early map of Virginia: Hariot: *Virginia* (Dover Publications, Inc.). **17** New York Public Library, Picture Collection. **20** New England primer: American Antiquarian Society. **24** Charles Town, South Carolina: Colonial Williamsburg Society. **26** Mary Evans Picture Library/Photo Researchers, Inc. **27** "'t' Fort nieuw Amsterdam op de Manhattans," ca. 1626–1628 (pub. 1651): Museum of the City of New York.

Chapter 2: **34** Indenture agreement, April 29, 1718: Historical Society of Pennsylvania. **37** Announcement of sale of slaves, Charleston, S.C., May 6, 1763: Library of Congress. **39** William Berkeley: Virginia State Library and Archives. **41** Aquatint idealized view of slave life, from J. Ferrario, *Les Costumes des Peuples. . . .* Milan, 1827: Library Company of Philadelphia. **42** Benjamin Latrobe, *Rippon Lodge:* Maryland Historical Society. **44** G. von Redeker, "A View of Salem," 1787: Moravian Archive. **47** The Mason Children: *David, Joanna, and Abigail,* attributed to the Freake-Gibbs Painter, 1670: The Fine Arts Museums of San Francisco; gift of Mr. and Mrs. John D. Rockefeller III. **51** A Full and Plain Evidence Concerning Witches and Apparitions, London, 1726: Granger Collection. **53** Title page of Eliot's Indian Bible: Bettmann Archive. **60** Carington Bowles, "An East Perspective View of the City of Philadelphia," 1731–1736: New York Public Library, Stokes Collection.

Chapter 3: **72** John Watson, *Governor Lewis Morris:* Brooklyn Museum. **74** Engraving of sugar refining, from P. Pomet, *A Compleat History of Drugs. . . .* London, 1712: Library Company of Philadelphia. Phyllis Wheatley, "An Elegiac Poem, on the Death of . . . George Whitefield," Boston, 1770: Library Company of Philadelphia. **81** David Martin, portrait of Benjamin Franklin, 1767: The White House Historical Association: photo by National Geographic Society. **82** David Rittenhouse, orrery, 1950s restoration: Princeton University Observatory. **84** Detail of illustration of Sir William Johnson's Indian Testimonial, wood engraving c. 1770: New-York Historical Society. **87** Thomas Davies, watercolor of seizure of Louisbourg, 1758: Royal Artillery Museum, London. **94** J. W. Barber, wood engraving of New Hampshire stamp master in effigy, from Interesting Events in the History of the U.S., 1829: Metropolitan Museum of Art; bequest of Charles Allen Munn. **95** Cockpit Hill factory, Derby: ceramic teapot, "Stamp Act Repeal'd," ca. 1766: Essex Institute, Salem, Mass. **97** John Singleton Copley, portrait of Samuel Adams, ca. 1771: Museum of Fine Arts, Boston. **98** Paul Revere, engraving of Boston Massacre: American Antiquarian Society. **100** Society of Patriotic Ladies: Library of Congress. **101** John Carter Brown Library, Brown University. **102** Premiere Assembleé Du Congress: Library of Congress.

Chapter 4: **108** Amos Doolittle after Ralph Earle, "Engagement at the North Bridge in Concord," Plate III: Chicago Historical Society. **111** John Trumbull, detail from *Declaration of Independence,* 1786: Yale University Art Gallery. **117** Library of Congress. **121** Hanging of Major André: Library of Congress. **122** "The Times, Anno 1783," 1783: Library Company of Philadelphia. **124** Requisition issued by George Washington, Dec. 20, 1777: Historical Society of Pennsylvania. **126** Anne S. K. Brown Military Collection, Brown University Library. **128** "Portrait Traditionally Said to be of Abigail Adams": New York Historical Association, Cooperstown. **132** Charles Wilson Peale, portrait of George Washington, 1776: Brooklyn Museum.

Chapter 5: **138** Whitehall Plantation on the Mississippi,

after Christophe Colomb: Historic New Orleans Collection.   **139** Chinese export porcelain plate showing the ship *Friendship* of Salem: Peabody Museum of Salem.   **142** Gilbert Stuart, portrait of James Madison, 1805–1807: Bowdoin College Museum of Art, Brunswick, Maine.   **147** Convention room, Independence Hall (restored): Independence National Historic Park, Philadelphia.   **149** "The Federal Edifice," from *The Mass Centinel,* Aug. 2, 1788: New-York Historical Society.   **151** Anonymous tapestry, "Washington's Triumphal Entry into New York," 1783: Abby Aldrich Rockefeller Folk Art Center, Williamsburg, Va.   **153** James Sharples, portrait of Alexander Hamilton, ca. 1796: National Portrait Gallery.   **156** Cartoon: Atwater Kent Museum.   **158** "The Times: A Political Portrait-Triumph Government Perish All Its Enemies," ca. 1790: New-York Historical Society.   **162** Recruiting poster, 1798: Historical Society of Pennsylvania.   **164** John Trumbull, portrait of John Adams, 1793: National Portrait Gallery.
Chapter 6:   **168** Cartoon, "The Providential Detection": Library Company of Philadelphia.   **170** Cartoon, "Venerate the Plough": Library of Congress.   **171** Charles Saint-Mémin, portrait of Thomas Jefferson: Worchester Art Museum.   **173** William Heath, "American Naval Officer Resisting An Attacking Tripolitan": New-York Historical Society.   **176** Portrait of Robert Livingston by Gilbert Stuart c. 1794: New-York Historical Society.   **179** Drawings, Lewis and Clark: Missouri Historical Society.   **181** Gilbert Stuart, portrait of John Randolph, 1805: National Gallery of Art, Washington, D.C., Andrew W. Mellon Collection.   **182** Charles Saint-Mémin, portrait of Aaron Burr, 1805: New-York Historical Society.   **185** Song Text: "The Impressment of an American Sailor Boy," War of 1812–1815: Library of Congress.   **186** Alexander Anderson, embargo cartoon, 1807: New-York Historical Society.
Chapter 7:   **198** Portrait of "The Open Door," younger brother of Tecumseh, in McKennery and Hall, *History of the Indian Tribes,* 1836: Library Company of Philadelphia.   **202** Jacob Maentel, *General Schumacker,* 1812: National Gallery of Art; Gift of Edgar William and Bernice Chrysler Garbisch.   **203** Battle of Lake Erie: Mariners Museum, Newport News, Va.   **204** Battle of Thames: A. K. Brown Military Museum, Brown University Library.   **205** Handkerchief (Battle of New Orleans), 1815: Henry Francis duPont Winterthur Museum, Delaware.
Chapter 8:   **221** Francis Alexander, "Black Dan," portrait of Daniel Webster, 1835: Hood Museum of Art, Dartmouth College.   **222** Martin Van Buren: New York Public Library Picture Collection.   **223** Attributed to Charles Bird King, portrait of John C. Calhoun, ca. 1818–1825: National Portrait Gallery, transfer from the National Gallery of Art, Washington, D.C.; gift of Andrew W. Mellon.   **224** Portrait of Henry Clay, after John Neagle, 1824: Chicago Historical Society.   **227** David Claypoole Johnston, "A Foot-Race," Library Company of Philadelphia.   **229** Asher B. Durand, portrait of John Quincy Adams, 1835: New-York Historical Society.
Chapter 9:   **234** Anonymous, "Pawtucket Bridge and Falls": Rhode Island Historical Society.   **235** Detail of

the pewterer's ship on the silk banner carried by the Society of the Pewters, 1788: New-York Historical Society.   **236** Glass factory: Historical Society of Pennsylvania.   **242** Leon Pomarede, *View of St. Louis:* The St. Louis Art Museum, Collection of Arthur Ziern, Jr.   **245** Original drawing of Fulton's second submarine and original plan for Fulton's first steamboat, 1803: Bettmann Archive.   **249** J. Hill, *Broadway, New York,* 1835: New York Public Library, Stokes Collection.   **251** Chester Harding, portrait of John Marshall, 1828: Boston Atheneum.
Chapter 10:   **258** Laban S. Beecher, figurehead of Andrew Jackson, 1834: Museum of the City of New York.   **260** "Office Hunters for the Year 1834": Library Company of Philadelphia.   **264** Attack of the Seminoles on the Block House: Library of Congress.   **266** Nullification cartoon: New York Public Library, Prints Division; Astor, Lenox and Tilden Foundations.   **269** "Set to Between Old Hickory and Bully Nick," 1834–1835: Library Company of Philadelphia.   **274** Debtor with bills: Cincinnati Art Museum.   **275** Cartoon: "Who'll Have the Specie?": Library of Congress.   **277** 1840 Songsheet for Whig Presidential candidate William Henry Harrison: Library of Congress.
Chapter 11:   **282** Leon Noel, lithograph of Alexis de Tocqueville: Yale University Library, Beinecke Rare Book and Manuscript Collection.   **283** Henry Sargent, *The Dinner Party,* ca. 1825: Museum of Fine Arts, Boston; gift of Mrs. Horatio Lamb.   **286** *Aboard the Cornelius Grinnel,* from Liverpool to New York, 1851: Museum of Fine Arts, Boston.   **288** Barfoot for Darton, "Progress of Cotton," Plate No. 6: Yale University Art Gallery, Mabel Brady Garvan Collection.   **291** John H. Davis, *The Tilton Family,* 1837: Abby Aldrich Rockefeller Center for American Folk Art, Williamsburg, Va.   **292** Methodist camp meeting: Smithsonian Institution.   **294** Hancock Shaker Village, Hancock, Mass.   **296** Tarring and Feathering of Joseph Smith: Brown Bros.   **298** Daguerreotype of Dorothea Linde Dix: The Granger Collection.   **300** Daguerreotype of William Lloyd Garrison by Southworth and Hawes: The Metropolitan Museum of Art; gift of I. N. Phelps Stokes, Edward S. Hawes, Alice Mary Hawes, Marion Augusta Hawes, 1937.   **300** Portrait of Frederick Douglass by Ritchie: New-York Historical Society.   **302** Daguerreotype of Elizabeth Cady Stanton and her daughter Harriet, 1856: Library of Congress.
Chapter 12:   **314** Thomas Cole, *Falls of Kaaterskill,* 1826: New York State Historical Association, Cooperstown, N.Y.   **316** William Furness, portrait of Ralph Waldo Emerson: The Pennsylvania Academy of Fine Arts; gift of Horace Howard Furness.   **317** Thoreau: New York Public Library, Picture Collection.   **318** Samuel S. Osgood, portrait of Edgar Allan Poe, ca. 1845: New-York Historical Society.   **319** Charles Osgood, portrait of Nathaniel Hawthorne, 1840: Essex Institute, Salem, Mass.   **320** Daguerreotype of Walt Whitman: National Archives and Record Service.   **322** Smithsonian Institution: Comstock.   **323** William Sidney Mount, *Eel Spearing at Setauket,* 1845: New York Historical Association, Cooperstown, N.Y. Hiram Powers, *The Greek Slave,* 1847: The Newark Museum; gift of Franklin Murphy, Jr., 1926. Photograph

© The Newark Museum. **325** Henry Inman, *The Dismissal of School on an October Afternoon,* 1845: Museum of Fine Arts, Boston. **326** Anonymous, "A Lecture by James Pollard Espy, Meteorologist, at Clinton Hall . . . ," ca. 1841: Museum of the City of New York. **328** John C. Wild. *Fourth Street Cincinnati:* Cincinnati Historical Society. **330** "American Journal of Science and Arts": Beinecke Rare Book and Manuscript Library, Yale University.
Chapter 13: **336** Daguerreotype of John Tyler, ca. 1850: Chicago Historical Society. **337** Texas insurgents taking Ft. San Antonio: Texas State Archives. **338** Davy Crockett's Death-Battle of the Alamo from *Davy Crockett's Almanack,* 1837: Library of Congress. **340** Oregon trail: Denver Public Library, Western History Dept. **343** Polk cartoon: Bettmann Archive. **344** Currier & Ives, "The Battle of Resaca de la Palma, May 9, 1846": Museum of the City of New York. **348** Daguerreotype of General John E. Wood and Staff, Saltillo, Mexico, 1846: Yale University, Beinecke Library. **351** J. Goldsborough Bruff, "Seeing the Elephant No. 1" and "Seeing the Elephant No. 5," ca. 1850: Yale University, Beinecke Library. **353** Southworth and Hawes, daguerreotype of Henry Clay, ca. 1845–1850: The Metropolitan Museum of Art; gift of I. N. Phelps Stokes, Edward S. Hawes, Alice Mary Hawes, Marion Augusta Hawes, 1937. Southworth and Hawes daguerreotype of Daniel Webster, 1851: The Metropolitan Museum of Art; gift of I. N. Phelps Stokes, Edward S. Hawes, Alice Mary Hawes, Marion Augusta Hawes.
Chapter 14: **361** Fran Hölzlhuber, "Rice Fields in the State of Arkansas," 1856–1860, and "Sugar Harvest in Louisiana and Texas," 1856–1860: Glenbow Foundation, Calgary, Alberta. **363** Plantation in the American South; colored engraving, nineteenth century: The Granger Collection. **366** "Deck of the Bark *Wildfire,*" in *Harper's Weekly,* June 2, 1860: Library of Congress. **367** B. H. Latrobe, "Preparations for the enjoyment of a fine Sunday among the Blacks": Maryland Historical Society. **370** Frontispiece, Carstensen and Gildemeister, *New York Crystal Palace* (New-York 1854): New-York Historical Society. **375** New Bedford Whaling Museum, New Bedford, Mass. **377** Steamer *Princess* at mail line packet landing for Vicksburg, Natchez, and New Orleans, ca. 1850–1860: Courtesy the Historic New Orleans Collection. **379** Advertisement, Illinois Central Railroad: The Newberry Library, Chicago. **381** McCormick Plant: from Mayer and Wade, *Growth of a Metropolis:* University of Chicago, 1969.
Chapter 15: **388** Poster, Uncle Tom's ·Cabin: The Granger Collection. **389** Cartoon: Library of Congress. **390** Gesson Ogata, "First Landing at Kurihama, July 14, 1853": United States Naval Academy Museum. **391** Daguerreotype of Stephen A. Douglas, ca.

1860: Library of Congress. **393** Albert J. Fountain, Jr., *The Signing of the Gadsden Purchase,* 1929: Courtesy of Mary Veitch Alexander, Gadsden Museum, Mesilla, N.M. **395** Poster, Kidnapping Again: The Boston Public Library. **396** Battle of Hickory Point: Kansas Historical Society. **398** "Southern Chivalry-Argument versus Clubs," 1856: Library Company of Philadelphia. **399** G. P. A. Healey, portrait of James Buchanan, 1859: Smithsonian Institution, National Portrait Gallery. **402** Alexander Hesler, daguerreotype of Abraham Lincoln, June 3, 1860: Chicago Historical Society. Daguerreotype of Lincoln, April 10, 1865: Library of Congress. **404** Lincoln-Douglas Debate Poster: Illinois State Historical Society. **406** Thomas Hovenden, *The Last Moments of John Brown,* 1884: The Metropolitan Museum of Art; gift of Mr. and Mrs. Carle Stoeckel, 1987.
Chapter 16 **418** John Robertson, portrait of Jefferson Davis, 1863: Museum of the Confederacy, Richmond, Va. **420** Anonymous, "Panic on the Road between Bull Run and Centerville," 1861: Museum of Fine Arts, Boston. **421** David G. Blythe, Lincoln versus the Copperheads: Museum of Fine Arts, Boston. **426** H. R. Wand, *McClellan's Return From Richmond:* Library of Congress. **427** Julian Vannerson, photo of Robert E. Lee, 1863: Library of Congress. **429** Adalbert Johann Volck, "Lincoln Writing the Emancipation Proclamation": Museum of Fine Arts, Boston; M and M Karolik Collection. David Gilmore Blythe, "Abraham Lincoln Writing the Emancipation Proclamation," 1863: Museum of Art, Carnegie Institute; gift of Mr. and Mrs. John F. Walton. **432** 22nd U.S. Colored Troops, Petersburg, June 1864: West Point Museum, New York. **435** M. Brady, U. S. Grant, Washington, D.C., 1862: Chicago Historical Society. **438** Elizabeth Blackwell: Bettmann Archive. **439** Grant at Cold Harbor: Library of Congress. **442** From "Death in the Trenches," Time-Life, 1986. **443** Library of Congress.
Chapter 17 **450** Matthew Brady, daguerreotype of Andrew Johnson: Library of Congress. **451** Matthew Brady, daguerreotype of Thaddeus Stevens: Library of Congress. **453** Freedman's Bureau: Library Company of Philadelphia. **455** The Bettmann Archive. **457** Cartoon: American Antiquarian Society, Worcester, Mass. **458** The First Colored Senators and Representatives in the 41st and 42nd Congress of the United States, 1842, Lithograph by Currier & Ives: Granger Collection. **460** "Primary School for Freedman, in Charge of Mrs. Green," *Harper's Weekly,* June 23, 1866: New-York Historical Society. **462** Black sharecroppers: Culver Pictures. **465** Carpetbaggers being hanged, *Tuscaloosa Independent Monitor,* September 1, 1868: Alabama Department of Archives and History, Montgomery. **467** Nast cartoon: *Harper's Weekly,* August 24, 1872.

Index

Note: Italicized page numbers refer to maps and graphs.